W9-BYT-178

Papers Relating to the

Foreign Relations

of the

United States

1930

(In Three Volumes)
Volume I

United States
Government Printing Office
Washington : 1945

DEPARTMENT OF STATE

PUBLICATION 2229

For sale by the
Superintendent of Documents, U. S. Government Printing Office
Washington 25, D. C.   Price $1.75   (Buckram)

PREFACE

Foreign Relations of the United States is a series of volumes of diplomatic correspondence published by the Department of State for each year beginning with 1861 (excepting 1869). The regular annual volumes have been supplemented by special volumes on particular subjects. For the period beginning with 1914 these extra volumes have included World War Supplements for the years 1914 to 1918 inclusive; volumes on Russia for the years 1918 and 1919; The Lansing Papers, 1914–1920; Japan: 1931–1941; and the Paris Peace Conference, 1919, these last named volumes being still in the course of publication.

The compiling and editing of the *Foreign Relations* volumes is performed by the Research Section in the Division of Research and Publication in accordance with the principles set forth in an order approved on March 26, 1925, by Mr. Frank B. Kellogg, then Secretary of State. This order, which is still in force, is given here in full:

The publication of diplomatic correspondence relating to matters which are still current often presents an insuperable obstacle to effective negotiation, but it is obvious that after the completion of the business in hand, as much of the correspondence as is practicable ought to be made public. This object is attained by the publication of *Foreign Relations* which presents, in a form economical, compact and easily accessible, the documentary history of the foreign relations of the United States. The editing of *Foreign Relations* must, therefore, be recognized as an important part of the duties of the Department of State.

The Chief of the Division of Publications [Division of Research and Publication] is charged with the preparation for this purpose, as soon as practicable after the close of each year, of the correspondence relating to all major policies and decisions of the Department in the matter of foreign relations, together with the events which contributed to the formulation of each decision or policy, and the facts incident to the application of it. It is expected that the material thus assembled, aside from the omission of trivial and inconsequential details, will be substantially complete as regards the files of the Department.

The development of the science of international law has become a matter of such weight and general concern that it is recommended that the Chief of the Division of Publications [Division of Research and Publication], with the help and counsel of the Solicitor [Legal Adviser], should give special attention to the publication of all important decisions made by the Department relating to international law, with a view to making available for general study and use the annual contributions of the Department to this important branch of jurisprudence. It is likewise believed that the Department may profitably inaugurate the practice of printing a record of treaty negotiations, and it is, therefore, suggested that such material be added, beginning with *Foreign Relations 1918*, which is now in the process of editing.

When the documents on a given subject have been assembled in the Division of Publications [Division of Research and Publication], they should be submitted to the Solicitor [Legal Adviser] or to the Chief of the appropriate division which has had immediate supervision of the topic. The Solicitor [Legal Adviser], or the heads of these divisions, respectively, are charged with the duty of reviewing the material thus assembled and indicating any omissions which appear to be required. Omissions of the following kind are recognized as legitimate and necessary:

> (*a*) Matters which if published at the time would tend to embarrass negotiations or other business;
> (*b*) To condense the record and avoid needless details;
> (*c*) To preserve the confidence reposed in the Department by other governments and by individuals;
> (*d*) To avoid needless offense to other nationalities or individuals by excising invidious comments not relevant or essential to the subject; and,
> (*e*) To suppress personal opinions presented in despatches and not adopted by the Department. To this there is one qualification, namely, that in major decisions it is desirable, where possible, to show the choices presented to the Department when the decision was made.

On the other hand, there must be no alteration of the text, no deletions without indicating the place in the text where the deletion is made, and no omission of facts which were of major importance in reaching a decision. Nothing should be omitted with a view to concealing or glossing over what might be regarded by some as a defect of a policy.

Where a document refers to two or more subjects, provided there are no other objections, it should be printed in its entirety, and not divided for purposes of more exact classification in editing. Great care must be taken to avoid the mutilation of documents. On the other hand, when a foreign government, in giving permission to use a communication, requests the deletion of any part of it, it is usually preferable to publish the document in part rather than to omit it entirely. A similar principle may be applied with reference to documents originating with the American Government.

The Chief of the Division of Publications [Division of Research and Publication] is expected to initiate, through the appropriate channels, the correspondence necessary to secure from a foreign government permission to publish any document received from it and which it is desired to publish as a part of the diplomatic correspondence of the United States. Without such permission, the document in question must not be used. The offices and divisions concerned in this process of editing may be expected to cooperate heartily with a view to the preparation of an adequate and honest record.

CONTENTS

MESSAGE OF THE PRESIDENT OF THE UNITED STATES TO CONGRESS, DECEMBER 2, 1930

To the Senate and House of Representatives:

I have the honor to comply with the requirement of the Constitution that I should lay before the Congress information as to the state of the Union, and recommend consideration of such measures as are necessary and expedient.

Substantial progress has been made during the year in national peace and security; the fundamental strength of the Nation's economic life is unimpaired; education and scientific discovery have made advances; our country is more alive to its problems of moral and spiritual welfare.

ECONOMIC SITUATION

During the past 12 months we have suffered with other Nations from economic depression.

The origins of this depression lie to some extent within our own borders through a speculative period which diverted capital and energy into speculation rather than constructive enterprise. Had overspeculation in securities been the only force operating, we should have seen recovery many months ago, as these particular dislocations have generally readjusted themselves.

Other deep-seated causes have been in action, however, chiefly the world-wide overproduction beyond even the demand of prosperous times for such important basic commodities as wheat, rubber, coffee, sugar, copper, silver, zinc, to some extent cotton, and other raw materials. The cumulative effects of demoralizing price falls of these important commodities in the process of adjustment of production to world consumption have produced financial crises in many countries and have diminished the buying power of these countries for imported goods to a degree which extended the difficulties farther afield by creating unemployment in all the industrial nations. The political agitation in Asia; revolutions in South America and political unrest in some European States; the methods of sale by Russia of her increasing agricultural exports to European markets; and our own drought— have all contributed to prolong and deepen the depression.

In the larger view the major forces of the depression now lie outside of the United States, and our recuperation has been retarded by the unwarranted degree of fear and apprehension created by these outside forces.

The extent of the depression is indicated by the following approximate percentages of activity during the past three months as compared with the highly prosperous year of 1928:

Value of department-store sales	93% of 1928
Volume of manufacturing production	80% of 1928
Volume of mineral production	90% of 1928
Volume of factory employment	84% of 1928
Total of bank deposits	105% of 1928
Wholesale prices—all commodities	83% of 1928
Cost of living	94% of 1928

Various other indexes indicate total decrease of activity from 1928 of from 15 to 20 per cent.

There are many factors which give encouragement for the future. The fact that we are holding from 80 to 85 per cent of our normal activities and incomes; that our major financial and industrial institutions have come through the storm unimpaired; that price levels of major commodities have remained approximately stable for some time; that a number of industries are showing signs of increasing demand; that the world at large is readjusting itself to the situation; all reflect grounds for confidence. We should remember that these occasions have been met many times before, that they are but temporary, that our country is to-day stronger and richer in resources, in equipment, in skill, than ever in its history. We are in an extraordinary degree self-sustaining, we will overcome world influences and will lead the march of prosperity as we have always done hitherto.

Economic depression can not be cured by legislative action or executive pronouncement. Economic wounds must be healed by the action of the cells of the economic body—the producers and consumers themselves. Recovery can be expedited and its effects mitigated by cooperative action. That cooperation requires that every individual should sustain faith and courage; that each should maintain his self-reliance; that each and every one should search for method of improving his business or service; that the vast majority whose income is unimpaired should not hoard out of fear but should pursue their normal living and recreations; that each should seek to assist his neighbors who may be less fortunate; that each industry should assist its own employees; that each community and each State should assume its full responsibilities for organization of employment and relief of distress with that sturdiness and independence which built a great Nation.

Our people are responding to these impulses in remarkable degree.

The best contribution of government lies in encouragement of this voluntary cooperation in the community. The Government, National,

State, and local, can join with the community in such programs and do its part. A year ago I, together with other officers of the Government, initiated extensive cooperative measures throughout the country.

The first of these measures was an agreement of leading employers to maintain the standards of wages and of labor leaders to use their influence against strife. In a large sense these undertakings have been adhered to and we have not witnessed the usual reductions of wages which have always heretofore marked depressions. The index of union wage scales shows them to be to-day fully up to the level of any of the previous three years. In consequence the buying power of the country has been much larger than would otherwise have been the case. Of equal importance the Nation has had unusual peace in industry and freedom from the public disorder which has characterized previous depressions.

The second direction of cooperation has been that our governments, National, State, and local, the industries and business so distribute employment as to give work to the maximum number of employees.

The third direction of cooperation has been to maintain and even extend construction work and betterments in anticipation of the future. It has been the universal experience in previous depressions that public works and private construction have fallen off rapidly with the general tide of depression. On this occasion, however, the increased authorization and generous appropriations by the Congress and the action of States and municipalities have resulted in the expansion of public construction to an amount even above that in the most prosperous years. In addition the cooperation of public utilities, railways, and other large organizations has been generously given in construction and betterment work in anticipation of future need. The Department of Commerce advises me that as a result, the volume of this type of construction work, which amounted to roughly $6,300,000,000 in 1929, instead of decreasing will show a total of about $7,000,000,000 for 1930. There has, of course, been a substantial decrease in the types of construction which could not be undertaken in advance of need.

The fourth direction of cooperation was the organization in such States and municipalities, as was deemed necessary, of committees to organize local employment, to provide for employment agencies, and to effect relief of distress.

The result of magnificent cooperation throughout the country has been that actual suffering has been kept to a minimum during the past 12 months, and our unemployment has been far less in proportion than in other large industrial countries. Some time ago it became evident that unemployment would continue over the winter and would necessarily be added to from seasonal causes and that the savings of workpeople would be more largely depleted. We have as a Nation a definite duty to see that no deserving person in our country suffers from hunger or cold. I therefore set up a more extensive organization to stimulate more intensive cooperation throughout the country. There has been a most gratifying degree of response, from governors, mayors, and other public officials, from welfare organizations, and from employers in concerns both large and small. The local communities through their voluntary agencies have assumed the duty of relieving individual distress and are being generously supported by the public.

The number of those wholly out of employment seeking for work was accurately determined by the census last April as about 2,500,000. The Department of Labor index of employment in the larger trades shows some decrease in employment since that time. The problem from a relief point of view is somewhat less than the published estimates of the number of unemployed would indicate. The intensive community and individual efforts in providing special employment outside the listed industries are not reflected in the statistical indexes and tend to reduce such published figures. Moreover, there is estimated to be a constant figure at all times of nearly 1,000,000 unemployed who are not without annual income but temporarily idle in the shift from one job to another. We have an average of about three breadwinners to each two families, so that every person unemployed does not represent a family without income. The view that the relief problems are less than the gross numbers would indicate is confirmed by the experience of several cities, which shows that the number of families in distress represents from 10 to 20 per cent of the number of the calculated unemployed. This is not said to minimize the very real problem which exists but to weigh its actual proportions.

As a contribution to the situation the Federal Government is engaged upon the greatest program of waterway, harbor, flood control, public building, highway, and airway improvement in all our history. This, together with loans to merchant shipbuilders, improvement of the Navy and in military aviation, and other construction work of the Government will exceed $520,000,000 for this fiscal year. This compares with $253,000,000 in the fiscal year 1928. The construction works already authorized and the continuation of policies in Government aid will require a continual expenditure upwards of half a billion dollars annually.

I favor still further temporary expansion of these activities in aid to unemployment during this winter. The Congress will, however, have presented to it numbers of projects, some of them under the guise of, rather than the reality of, their usefulness in the increase of employment during the depression. There are certain common-sense limitations upon any expansions of construction work. The

Government must not undertake works that are not of sound economic purpose and that have not been subject to searching technical investigation, and which have not been given adequate consideration by the Congress. The volume of construction work in the Government is already at the maximum limit warranted by financial prudence as a continuing policy. To increase taxation for purposes of construction work defeats its own purpose, as such taxes directly diminish employment in private industry. Again any kind of construction requires, after its authorization, a considerable time before labor can be employed in which to make engineering, architectural, and legal preparations. Our immediate problem is the increase of employment for the next six months, and new plans which do not produce such immediate result or which extend commitments beyond this period are not warranted.

The enlarged rivers and harbors, public building, and highway plans authorized by the Congress last session, however, offer an opportunity for assistance by the temporary acceleration of construction of these programs even faster than originally planned, especially if the technical requirements of the laws which entail great delays could be amended in such fashion as to speed up acquirements of land and the letting of contracts.

With view, however, to the possible need for acceleration, we, immediately upon receiving those authorities from the Congress five months ago, began the necessary technical work in preparation for such possible eventuality. I have canvassed the departments of the Government as to the maximum amount that can be properly added to our present expenditure to accelerate all construction during the next six months, and I feel warranted in asking the Congress for an appropriation of from $100,000,000 to $150,000,000 to provide such further employment in this emergency. In connection therewith we need some authority to make enlarged temporary advances of Federal-highway aid to the States.

I recommend that this appropriation be made distributable to the different departments upon recommendation of a committee of the Cabinet and approval by the President. Its application to works already authorized by the Congress assures its use in directions of economic importance and to public welfare. Such action will imply an expenditure upon construction of all kinds of over $650,000,000 during the next twelve months.

AGRICULTURE

The world-wide depression has affected agriculture in common with all other industries. The average price of farm produce has fallen to about 80 per cent of the levels of 1928. This average is, however, greatly affected by wheat and cotton, which have participated in world-wide overproduction and have fallen to about 60 per cent of the average price of the year 1928. Excluding these commodities, the prices of all other agricultural products are about 84 per cent of those of 1928. The average wholesale prices of other primary goods, such as nonferrous metals, have fallen to 76 per cent of 1928.

The price levels of our major agricultural commodities are, in fact, higher than those in other principal producing countries, due to the combined result of the tariff and the operations of the Farm Board. For instance, wheat prices at Minneapolis are about 30 per cent higher than at Winnipeg, and at Chicago they are about 20 per cent higher than at Buenos Aires. Corn prices at Chicago are over twice as high as at Buenos Aires. Wool prices average more than 80 per cent higher in this country than abroad, and butter is 30 per cent higher in New York City than in Copenhagen.

Aside from the misfortune to agriculture of the world-wide depression we have had the most severe drought. It has affected particularly the States bordering on the Potomac, Ohio, and Lower Mississippi Rivers, with some areas in Montana, Kansas, Oklahoma, and Texas. It has found its major expression in the shortage of pasturage and a shrinkage in the corn crop from an average of about 2,800,000,000 bushels to about 2,090,000,000 bushels.

On August 14 I called a conference of the governors of the most acutely affected States, and as a result of its conclusions I appointed a national committee comprising the heads of the important Federal agencies under the chairmanship of the Secretary of Agriculture. The governors in turn have appointed State committees representative of the farmers, bankers, business men, and the Red Cross, and subsidiary committees have been established in most of the acutely affected counties. Railway rates were reduced on feed and livestock in and out of the drought areas, and over 50,000 cars of such products have been transported under these reduced rates. The Red Cross established a preliminary fund of $5,000,000 for distress relief purposes and established agencies for its administration in each county. Of this fund less than $500,000 has been called for up to this time as the need will appear more largely during the winter. The Federal Farm Loan Board has extended its credit facilities, and the Federal Farm Board has given financial assistance to all affected cooperatives.

In order that the Government may meet its full obligation toward our countrymen in distress through no fault of their own, I recommend that an appropriation should be made to the Department of Agriculture to be loaned for the purpose of seed and feed for animals. Its application should as hitherto in such loans be limited to a gross amount to any one individual, and secured upon the crop.

The Red Cross can relieve the cases of individual distress by the sympathetic assistance of our people.

FINANCES OF THE GOVERNMENT

I shall submit the detailed financial position of the Government with recommendations in the usual Budget message. I will at this time, however, mention that the Budget estimates of receipts and expenditures for the current year were formulated by the Treasury and the Budget Bureau at a time when it was impossible to forecast the severity of the business depression and have been most seriously affected by it. At that time a surplus of about $123,000,000 was estimated for this fiscal year and tax reduction which affected the fiscal year to the extent of $75,000,000 was authorized by the Congress, thus reducing the estimated surplus to about $48,000,000. Closely revised estimates now made by the Treasury and the Bureau of the Budget of the tax, postal, and other receipts for the current fiscal year indicate a decrease of about $430,000,000 from the estimate of a year ago, of which about $75,000,000 is due to tax reduction, leaving about $355,000,000 due to the depression. Moreover, legislation enacted by Congress subsequent to the submission of the Budget enlarging Federal construction work to expand employment and for increase in veterans' services and other items, have increased expenditures during the current fiscal year by about $225,000,000.

Thus the decrease of $430,000,000 in revenue and the increase of $225,000,000 in expenditure adversely change the original Budget situation by about $655,000,000. This large sum is offset by the original estimated surplus a year ago of about $123,000,000, by the application of $185,000,000 of interest payments upon the foreign debt to current expenditures, by arrangements of the Farm Board through repayments, etc., in consequence of which they reduced their net cash demands upon the Treasury by $100,000,000 in this period, and by about $67,000,000 economies and deferments brought about in the Government, thus reducing the practical effect of the change in the situation to an estimated deficit of about $180,000,000 for the present fiscal year. I shall make suggestions for handling the present-year deficit in the Budget message, but I do not favor encroachment upon the statutory reduction of the public debt.

While it will be necessary in public interest to further increase expenditures during the current fiscal year in aid to unemployment by speeding up construction work and aid to the farmers affected by the drought, I can not emphasize too strongly the absolute necessity to defer any other plans for increase of Government expenditures. The Budget for 1932 fiscal year indicates estimated expenditure of about $4,054,000,000, including postal deficit. The receipts are estimated at about $4,085,000,000 if the temporary tax reduction of last year be discontinued, leaving a surplus of only about $30,000,000. Most rigid economy is therefore necessary to avoid increase in taxes.

NATIONAL DEFENSE

Our Army and Navy are being maintained at a high state of efficiency, under officers of high training and intelligence, supported by a devoted personnel of the rank and file. The London naval treaty has brought important economies in the conduct of the Navy. The Navy Department will lay before the committees of the Congress recommendations for a program of authorization of new construction which should be initiated in the fiscal year of 1932.

LEGISLATION

This is the last session of the Seventy-first Congress. During its previous sittings it has completed a very large amount of important legislation, notably: The establishment of the Federal Farm Board; fixing congressional reapportionment; revision of the tariff, including the flexible provisions and a reorganization of the Tariff Commission; reorganization of the Radio Commission; reorganization of the Federal Power Commission; expansion of Federal prisons; reorganization of parole and probation system in Federal prisons; expansion of veterans' hospitals; establishment of disability allowances to veterans; consolidation of veteran activities; consolidation and strengthening of prohibition enforcement activities in the Department of Justice; organization of a Narcotics Bureau; large expansion of rivers and harbors improvements; substantial increase in Federal highways; enlargement of public buildings construction program; and the ratification of the London naval treaty.

The Congress has before it legislation partially completed in the last sitting in respect to Muscle Shoals, bus regulation, relief of congestion in the courts, reorganization of border patrol in prevention of smuggling, law enforcement in the District of Columbia, and other subjects.

It is desirable that these measures should be completed.

The short session does not permit of extensive legislative programs, but there are a number of questions which, if time does not permit action, I recommend should be placed in consideration by the Congress, perhaps through committees cooperating in some instances with the Federal departments, with view to preparation for subsequent action. Among them are the following subjects:

Electrical Power

I have in a previous message recommended effective regulation of interstate electrical power. Such regulation should preserve the independence and responsibility of the States.

Railways

We have determined upon a national policy of consolidation of the railways as a necessity of more stable and more economically operated transportation. Further legislation is necessary to facilitate such consolidation. In the public interest we should strengthen the railways that they may meet our future needs.

Antitrust Laws

I recommend that the Congress institute an inquiry into some aspects of the economic working of these laws. I do not favor repeal of the Sherman Act. The prevention of monopolies is of most vital public importance. Competition is not only the basis of protection to the consumer but is the incentive to progress. However, the interpretation of these laws by the courts, the changes in business, especially in the economic effects upon those enterprises closely related to the use of the natural resources of the country, make such an inquiry advisable. The producers of these materials assert that certain unfortunate results of wasteful and destructive use of these natural resources together with a destructive competition which impoverishes both operator and worker can not be remedied because of the prohibitive interpretation of the antitrust laws. The well-known condition of the bituminous coal industry is an illustration. The people have a vital interest in the conservation of their natural resources; in the prevention of wasteful practices; in conditions of destructive competition which may impoverish the producer and the wage earner; and they have an equal interest in maintaining adequate competition. I therefore suggest that an inquiry be directed especially to the effect of the workings of the antitrust laws in these particular fields to determine if these evils can be remedied without sacrifice of the fundamental purpose of these laws.

Capital-Gains Tax

It is urged by many thoughtful citizens that the peculiar economic effect of the income tax on so-called capital gains at the present rate is to enhance speculative inflation and likewise impede business recovery. I believe this to be the case and I recommend that a study be made of the economic effects of this tax and of its relation to the general structure of our income tax law.

IMMIGRATION

There is need for revision of our immigration laws upon a more limited and more selective basis, flexible to the needs of the country.

Under conditions of current unemployment it is obvious that persons coming to the United States seeking work would likely become either a direct or indirect public charge. As a temporary measure the officers issuing visas to immigrants have been, in pursuance of the law, instructed to refuse visas to applicants likely to fall into this class. As a result the visas issued have decreased from an average of about 24,000 per month prior to restrictions to a rate of about 7,000 during the last month. These are largely preferred persons under the law. Visas from Mexico are about 250 per month compared to about 4,000 previous to restrictions. The whole subject requires exhaustive reconsideration.

DEPORTATION OF ALIEN CRIMINALS

I urge the strengthening of our deportation laws so as to more fully rid ourselves of criminal aliens. Furthermore, thousands of persons have entered the country in violation of the immigration laws. The very method of their entry indicates their objectionable character, and our law-abiding foreign-born residents suffer in consequence. I recommend that the Congress provide methods of strengthening the Government to correct this abuse.

POST OFFICE

Due to deferment of Government building over many years, previous administrations had been compelled to enter upon types of leases for secondary facilities in large cities, some of which were objectionable as representing too high a return upon the value of the property. To prevent the occasion for further uneconomic leasing I recommend that the Congress authorize the building by the Government of its own facilities.

VETERANS

The Nation has generously expanded its care for veterans. The consolidation of all veterans' activities into the Veterans' Administration has produced substantial administrative economies. The consolidation also brings emphasis to the inequalities in service and allowances. The whole subject is under study by the administrator, and I recommend it should also be examined by the committees of the Congress.

SOCIAL SERVICE

I urge further consideration by the Congress of the recommendations I made a year ago looking to the development through temporary Federal aid of adequate State and local services for the health of children and the further stamping out of communicable disease, particularly in the rural sections. The advance of scientific discovery, methods, and social thought imposes a new vision in these matters. The drain upon the Federal Treasury is comparatively small. The results both economic and moral are of the utmost importance.

GENERAL

It is my belief that after the passing of this depression, when we can examine it in retrospect, we shall need to consider a number of other questions as to what action may be taken by the Government to remove possible governmental influences which make for instability and to better organize mitigation of the effect of depression. It is as yet too soon to constructively formulate such measures.

There are many administrative subjects, such as departmental reorganization, extension of the civil service, readjustment of the postal rates, etc., which at some appropriate time require the attention of the Congress.

FOREIGN RELATIONS

Our relations with foreign countries have been maintained upon a high basis of cordiality and good will.

During the past year the London naval pact was completed, approved by the Senate, and ratified by the governments concerned. By this treaty we have abolished competition in the building of warships, have established the basis of parity of the United States with the strongest of foreign powers, and have accomplished a substantial reduction in war vessels.

During the year there has been an extended political unrest in the world. Asia continues in disturbed condition, and revolutions have taken place in Brazil, Argentina, Peru, and Bolivia. Despite the jeopardy to our citizens and their property which naturally arises in such circumstances, we have, with the cooperation of the governments concerned, been able to meet all such instances without friction.

We have resumed normal relations with the new Governments of Brazil, Argentina, Peru, and Bolivia immediately upon evidence that they were able to give protection to our citizens and their property, and that they recognized their international obligations.

A commission which was supported by the Congress has completed its investigation and reported upon our future policies in respect to Haiti and proved of high value in securing the acceptance of these policies. An election has been held and a new government established. We have replaced our high commissioner by a minister and have begun the gradual withdrawal of our activities with view to complete retirement at the expiration of the present treaty in 1935.

A number of arbitration and conciliation treaties have been completed or negotiated during the year, and will be presented for approval by the Senate.

I shall, in a special message, lay before the Senate the protocols covering the statutes of the World Court which have been revised to accord with the sense of previous Senate reservations.

HERBERT HOOVER

THE WHITE HOUSE, December 2, 1930.

LIST OF PAPERS

[Unless otherwise specified, the correspondence is *from* or *to* officials in the Department of State.]

GENERAL

THE LONDON NAVAL CONFERENCE, JANUARY 21–APRIL 22, 1930

GENERAL

THE LONDON NAVAL CONFERENCE, JANUARY 21–APRIL 22, 1930—Continued

GENERAL

THE LONDON NAVAL CONFERENCE, JANUARY 21–APRIL 22, 1930—Continued

GENERAL

THE LONDON NAVAL CONFERENCE, JANUARY 21–APRIL 22, 1930—Continued

GENERAL

GENERAL

THE LONDON NAVAL CONFERENCE, JANUARY 21–APRIL 22, 1930—Continued

GENERAL

THE LONDON NAVAL CONFERENCE, JANUARY 21–APRIL 22, 1930—Continued

GENERAL

GENERAL

THE LONDON NAVAL CONFERENCE, JANUARY 21–APRIL 22, 1930—Continued

GENERAL

The London Naval Conference, January 21–April 22, 1930—Continued

GENERAL

THE LONDON NAVAL CONFERENCE, JANUARY 21–APRIL 22, 1930—Continued

GENERAL

NEGOTIATIONS LOOKING TOWARD A SOLUTION OF THE PROBLEM OF FRENCH AND ITALIAN NAVAL CONSTRUCTION—Continued

GENERAL

NEGOTIATIONS LOOKING TOWARD A SOLUTION OF THE PROBLEM OF FRENCH AND ITALIAN NAVAL CONSTRUCTION—Continued

GENERAL

NEGOTIATIONS LOOKING TOWARD A SOLUTION OF THE PROBLEM OF FRENCH
AND ITALIAN NAVAL CONSTRUCTION—Continued

GENERAL

NEGOTIATIONS LOOKING TOWARD A SOLUTION OF THE PROBLEM OF FRENCH
AND ITALIAN NAVAL CONSTRUCTION—Continued

GENERAL

PARTICIPATION OF THE UNITED STATES IN THE WORK OF THE PREPARATORY COMMISSION FOR THE DISARMAMENT CONFERENCE, SIXTH SESSION, SECOND PART, NOVEMBER 6–DECEMBER 9, 1930

GENERAL

PARTICIPATION OF THE UNITED STATES IN THE WORK OF THE PREPARATORY COMMISSION FOR THE DISARMAMENT CONFERENCE, SIXTH SESSION, SECOND PART, NOVEMBER 6–DECEMBER 9, 1930—Continued

GENERAL

GENERAL

CONFERENCE FOR THE CODIFICATION OF INTERNATIONAL LAW, HELD AT THE HAGUE, MARCH 13–APRIL 20, 1930, AND TEXT OF PROTOCOL RELATING TO MILITARY OBLIGATIONS IN CERTAIN CASES OF DOUBLE NATIONALITY—Continued

GENERAL

CONFERENCE FOR THE CODIFICATION OF INTERNATIONAL LAW, HELD AT THE HAGUE, MARCH 13–APRIL 20, 1930, AND TEXT OF PROTOCOL RELATING TO MILITARY OBLIGATIONS IN CERTAIN CASES OF DOUBLE NATIONALITY—Continued

ATTITUDE OF THE UNITED STATES REGARDING A PROPOSED AMENDMENT TO THE COVENANT OF THE LEAGUE OF NATIONS

POLICY OF THE UNITED STATES REGARDING THE BANK FOR INTERNATIONAL SETTLEMENTS

GENERAL

PRESENCE OF AMERICAN UNOFFICIAL OBSERVERS AT GENEVA DURING THE INTERNATIONAL CONFERENCES FOR A TARIFF TRUCE, FEBRUARY–MARCH 1930 AND NOVEMBER 1930

GENERAL

CRITICISM OF CERTAIN PROVISIONS IN AMERICAN TARIFF LEGISLATION

REPRESENTATIONS BY FOREIGN GOVERNMENTS REGARDING SENATE BILLS FOR THE DEPORTATION OF CERTAIN ALIEN SEAMEN

INTERNATIONAL CONFERENCE ON LOAD LINES, HELD AT LONDON, MAY 20–JULY 5, 1930

GENERAL

INTERNATIONAL CONFERENCE ON LOAD LINES HELD AT LONDON, MAY 20–
JULY 5, 1930—Continued

DISINCLINATION OF THE UNITED STATES TO ACT TO SECURE RATIFICATION OF
DRAFT CONVENTION ON OIL POLLUTION OF NAVIGABLE WATERS

GENERAL

Cooperation of the United States With Several Other Governments in Reconnaissance Surveys for an Inter-American Highway

GENERAL

COOPERATION OF THE UNITED STATES WITH SEVERAL OTHER GOVERNMENTS IN
RECONNAISSANCE SURVEYS FOR AN INTER-AMERICAN HIGHWAY—Continued

CONVENTION ON THE REGULATION OF AUTOMOTIVE TRAFFIC, SIGNED AT WASH-
INGTON, OCTOBER 6, 1930

GENERAL

THE CHACO DISPUTE BETWEEN BOLIVIA AND PARAGUAY

ACCEPTANCE BY BOLIVIA AND PARAGUAY OF THE URUGUYAN FORMULA FOR CARRYING OUT THE TERMS OF THE CONCILIATION AGREEMENT OF SEPTEMBER 12, 1929

GENERAL

THE CHACO DISPUTE BETWEEN BOLIVIA AND PARAGUAY—Continued

GENERAL

The Chaco Dispute Between Bolivia and Paraguay—Continued

ACCEPTANCE BY BOLIVIA AND PARAGUAY OF THE PROPOSAL OF THE NEUTRAL NATIONS TO INSTITUTE DIRECT NEGOTIATIONS IN WASHINGTON FOR THE SETTLEMENT OF THE BASIC QUESTION

GENERAL

THE CHACO DISPUTE BETWEEN BOLIVIA AND PARAGUAY—Continued

GENERAL

The Chaco Dispute Between Bolivia and Paraguay—Continued

Boundary Disputes

GUATEMALA AND HONDURAS

GENERAL

BOUNDARY DISPUTES—Continued

GENERAL

BOUNDARY DISPUTES—Continued

HONDURAS AND NICARAGUA

GENERAL

BOUNDARY DISPUTES—Continued

GENERAL

BOUNDARY DISPUTES—Continued

ARGENTINA

REVOLUTION IN ARGENTINA

ARGENTINA
Revolution in Argentina—Continued

ARGENTINA

REVOLUTION IN ARGENTINA—Continued

AUSTRIA

CONSENT TO SUBORDINATION OF THE AUSTRIAN RELIEF LOAN TO A PROPOSED NEW AUSTRIAN LOAN

AUSTRIA

CONSENT TO SUBORDINATION OF THE AUSTRIAN RELIEF LOAN TO A PROPOSED
NEW AUSTRIAN LOAN—Continued

AUSTRIA

CONSENT TO SUBORDINATION OF THE AUSTRIAN RELIEF LOAN TO A PROPOSED
NEW AUSTRIAN LOAN—Continued

AUSTRIA

BOLIVIA
REVOLUTION IN BOLIVIA

BOLIVIA
Revolution in Bolivia—Continued

BOLIVIA
Revolution in Bolivia—Continued

BRAZIL
Revolution in Brazil

BRAZIL

REVOLUTION IN BRAZIL—Continued

BRAZIL

REVOLUTION IN BRAZIL—Continued

BRAZIL
REVOLUTION IN BRAZIL—Continued

BRAZIL
REVOLUTION IN BRAZIL—Continued

TERMINATION OF CONTRACT FOR AMERICAN NAVAL MISSION TO BRAZIL, SIGNED JULY 6, 1926

BRAZIL

TERMINATION OF CONTRACT FOR AMERICAN NAVAL MISSION TO BRAZIL, SIGNED
JULY 6, 1926—Continued

GOOD OFFICES OF THE DEPARTMENT OF STATE ON BEHALF OF THE NATIONAL CITY
BANK IN SECURING REMISSION OF FINE IMPOSED UPON ITS SÃO PAULO BRANCH

BRAZIL

GOOD OFFICES OF THE DEPARTMENT OF STATE ON BEHALF OF THE NATIONAL
CITY BANK IN SECURING REMISSION OF FINE IMPOSED UPON ITS SÃO PAULO
BRANCH—Continued

BRAZIL

GOOD OFFICES OF THE DEPARTMENT OF STATE ON BEHALF OF THE NATIONAL CITY BANK IN SECURING REMISSION OF FINE IMPOSED UPON ITS SÃO PAULO BRANCH—Continued

Date and number	Subject	Page
1930 Apr. 2 (14)	*From the Ambassador in Brazil (tel.)* Assurance that Embassy is supporting the matter actively; opinion that it will be better if Bank does not press for immediate action.	471
Apr. 11 (20)	*To the Ambassador in Brazil (tel.)* Instructions, if no objection is perceived, to assist Bank official in obtaining interview with President.	472
June 3 (39)	*To the Ambassador in Brazil (tel.)* Report from Bank that papers regarding fine have been before the President for a month; authorization to make inquiry desired by Bank.	472
June 11 (33)	*From the Ambassador in Brazil (tel.)* Action taken to promote rapid solution; suggestion that the Secretary discuss matter with Dr. Valle, Foreign Office official visiting in the United States.	472
June 14 (42)	*To the Ambassador in Brazil (tel.)* Intention of Mr. Valle to cable Rio de Janeiro regarding the situation.	473
July 11 (41)	*From the Ambassador in Brazil (tel.)* Advice from the President on July 10 that he had given orders to effect the cancelation of the entire fine.	473
July 24 (44)	*From the Ambassador in Brazil (tel.)* Ministerial order canceling fine (extract printed).	473
July 24 (45)	*From the Ambassador in Brazil (tel.)* Text of further provisions of the Ministerial order to the effect that the Bank shall be fined for an infringement of the stamp tax and that there shall be an investigation of an irregularity of functional procedure on the part of the broker of public funds.	474
July 25	*From the National City Bank of New York (tel.)* Expression of appreciation for cooperation given.	474

ARRANGEMENT BETWEEN THE UNITED STATES AND BRAZIL GRANTING RELIEF FROM DOUBLE INCOME TAX ON SHIPPING PROFITS

Date and number	Subject	Page
1929 Mar. 5 (1419)	*From the American Ambassador in Brazil to the Brazilian Minister for Foreign Affairs* Request that vessels operated by the United States Shipping Board be exempt from payment of Brazilian income tax, since U. S. revenue laws seem to meet the requirements of Brazil's Executive Decree No. 5,623 of December 29, 1928.	475
May 31 (NC/56)	*From the Brazilian Minister for Foreign Affairs to the American Ambassador in Brazil* Letter from the Brazilian Finance Minister, May 29 (text printed), explaining that it will be sufficient for the Foreign Ministry to inform the Finance Ministry that the necessary law exists; information that the required action has been taken.	476

BRAZIL

BRAZIL

BULGARIA

CANADA

CANADA

PROPOSED CONVENTION BETWEEN THE UNITED STATES AND CANADA TO AMEND THE CONVENTION FOR THE SUPPRESSION OF SMUGGLING, SIGNED JUNE 6, 1924—Continued

CONVENTION BETWEEN THE UNITED STATES AND CANADA FOR THE PROTECTION OF THE FRASER RIVER SOCKEYE SALMON FISHERIES, SIGNED MAY 26, 1930

CANADA

CANADA

Project for Improvement of the St. Lawrence Waterway by Joint Action of the United States and Canada—Continued

CANADA

AVIATION RADIO CONFERENCE BETWEEN REPRESENTATIVES OF THE UNITED STATES AND CANADA, HELD AT NEW YORK, APRIL 10–11, 1930

CHILE

CONVENTION BETWEEN THE UNITED STATES AND CHILE FOR PREVENTION OF SMUGGLING OF INTOXICATING LIQUORS, SIGNED MAY 27, 1930

GENERAL

THE LONDON NAVAL CONFERENCE, JANUARY 21–APRIL 22, 1930 [1]

[The Governments represented at the Conference were the United States of America, France, Great Britain and the states of the British Empire which were separate members of the League of Nations (Australia, Canada, India, the Irish Free State, New Zealand, and the Union of South Africa), Italy, and Japan.

Following is the list of the American Delegates and Advisers:

DELEGATES

Henry L. Stimson, Secretary of State.
Charles G. Dawes, Ambassador to Great Britain.
Charles Francis Adams, Secretary of the Navy.
Joseph T. Robinson, United States Senator.
David A. Reed, United States Senator.
Hugh S. Gibson, Ambassador to Belgium.
Dwight W. Morrow, Ambassador to Mexico.

ADVISERS

Admiral William V. Pratt.
Hugh R. Wilson, Minister to Switzerland.
Rear Admiral Hilary P. Jones (retired).
Arthur Wilson Page.
J. Theodore Marriner, Chief of the Division of Western European Affairs, Department of State.
Ray Atherton, Counselor of Embassy in Great Britain.
George A. Gordon, Counselor of Embassy in France.
George Rublee.
Lieut. Col. Charles Burnett.]

---

[1] For the antecedents of the Conference, see *Foreign Relations*, 1929, vol. I, pp. 112 ff.

The acts of the Conference and other relevant data are printed in Department of State Conference Series No. 6, *Proceedings of the London Naval Conference of 1930 and Supplementary Documents* (Washington, Government Printing Office, 1931) ; a similar text, in both English and French, was issued by the British Foreign Office under the title *Documents of the London Naval Conference, 1930* (London, 1930). Further pertinent material is contained in Department of State Conference Series No. 3, *London Naval Conference, Speeches and Press Statements by Members of the American Delegation, January 20–April 29, 1930* (Washington, Government Printing Office, 1930).

500.A15a3/621 : Telegram

The Chairman of the American Delegation (Stimson) to the Acting Secretary of State

[Paraphrase]

LONDON, January 19, 1930—11 a. m.

[Received 3 p. m.[2]]

4. For the President and the Acting Secretary of State. My telegram No. 1, January 18, 1 p. m.[2a] Yesterday afternoon I had a conversation of about three and one-half hours with Prime Minister MacDonald. Of this time we spent two hours quite alone. The Prime Minister's son was present for half an hour and Marriner and Craigie[3] joined us for the last three-quarters of an hour. As a result of the Parliamentary session the Prime Minister appeared tired. He said to me that he had never known any day whether or not before the day's session was over he might not find himself out of office.

He agreed with me that if the heads of the delegations were allowed to constitute a steering committee that would be the best system, but that the fact that Tardieu[4] wanted to bring Briand[5] with him to the first meeting to discuss the subject somewhat complicated this. Furthermore, it appears likely that should Tardieu be wanted back in France, Briand might be agreed upon as the head of the delegation. The matter has been left in abeyance until other delegations are heard from, although I said I would be quite willing to come alone even if France brought two.

The Japanese, the Prime Minister said, had been very stiff in demanding a 10–10–7 ratio. Admiral Takarabe[6] was very firm indeed, although he felt that Wakatsuki[7] appeared somewhat more conciliatory. I told him that if a treaty which started out with a condition precedent of such a ratio for Japan were submitted to the American Senate, I felt that there was no possibility of its being accepted. I pointed out that Japan would be more reluctant to allow any treaty to be made without them which might make it possible for Great Britain and the United States to build against them fully two to one, and I also mentioned the financial difficulties of building in Japan at the present time. The Prime Minister agreed with me absolutely on the necessity for remaining stiff against this preliminary demand by Japan for 10–10–7. After Marriner and Craigie

---

[2] Telegram in three sections.
[2a] Not printed.
[3] R. L. Craigie, head of the American Department of the British Foreign Office.
[4] André Tardieu. President of the French Council of Ministers and chief of the French delegation.
[5] Aristide Briand, French Minister for Foreign Affairs and member of the delegation.
[6] Japanese Minister of Marine and member of the delegation.
[7] Reijiro Wakatsuki, chief of the Japanese delegation.

had joined us, somewhat later, we reverted to the question of possible face-saving clauses for the satisfaction of Japanese public opinion. The question of Japan's financial necessities was again stressed by us, and we agreed that unless the battleship program were coupled with a simultaneous agreement on auxiliary vessels we would not consent to its alteration.

The French, the Prime Minister said, had been acting very badly in the whole matter, but they had become somewhat more conciliatory since his rather stiff answer to their last note. He said that with reference to the proposed Mediterranean Pact [8] what France desired was a guarantee, which he could not give of course, nor would he be willing to enter into a treaty which would not embrace all the powers of the Mediterranean, including Yugoslavia and Spain. The Spanish Ambassador had told him, he said, that after the Conference had got under way, Spain could not be brought into it. I told him that if the French were satisfied with a consultative treaty I had a feeling that they might not stand out for an absolute guarantee. Then the Prime Minister told me that in the strictest confidence he would show me a draft which he had made on this subject and which was precisely in the form of the Pacific treaty between the four powers.[9] I told him that I felt that the first article of that treaty as he adapted it might be just the ladder that the French would need to come down on.

After this we discussed the points causing the irritation of the French against the British: (1) the attitude of Snowden at The Hague;[10] (2) the suspicion resulting from the visit to America of the Prime Minister;[11] and (3) the about-face on the trained reserve question made by Cecil.[12]

Tardieu, I pointed out, had won a victory at The Hague, and as he felt reassured respecting the visit to Washington, the other items would be less troublesome. MacDonald also told me that he was prepared to concede the position on trained reserves, and that, in talking to Marriner, Craigie had supplemented this information by saying that this was a concession which they would not wish to make too early in the proceedings and at any rate certainly not before the Conference had opened.

[8] See the French memorandum of December 20, 1929, *Foreign Relations*, 1929, vol. I, p. 299.

[9] Treaty signed at Washington, December 13, 1921, *ibid.*, 1922, vol. I, p. 33.

[10] Philip Snowden, Chancellor of the Exchequer and head of the British representation at the international conference held at The Hague, August 6 to 31, 1929. See Great Britain, Cmd. 3392, Misc. No. 5, (1929): *Protocol With Annexes Approved at the Plenary Session of the Hague Conference, August 31, 1929;* also Cmd. 3417, Misc. No. 7 (1929): *International Agreement on the Evacuation of the Rhineland Territory.*

[11] See *Foreign Relations*, 1929, vol. III, pp. 1 ff.

[12] Viscount Cecil of Chelwood. See League of Nations, *Official Journal*, Special Supplement No. 78, "Records of the Tenth Ordinary Session of the Assembly, Minutes of the Third Committee (Reduction of Armaments)," p. 72.

His discussion of Italy's position he opened by saying that Italy was worse than France, and, as I expressed some surprise, he depicted Italy's economic restlessness and her strong desire for colonies now in the possession of France. In the matter of French and Italian naval building, I told him that I felt, of course, quite disinterested except insofar as it might have reference to the British.

Before we began discussing the possibility of making economies in battleships, Craigie and Marriner had joined us.

The first economy suggestion was that replacements be postponed.

The second was that the units be reduced in size.

The third was that the number of units be reduced.

MacDonald said that while I was at sea he said almost exactly the same thing in a press statement and that, therefore, my statement of the case was almost telepathic. I had already seen an excerpt from it, I said, which stated that he would consent to a full holiday extending until 1936.

Then I offered him congratulations on the advances in this position from that which he had adopted while in Washington. He said that both politically and financially he regretted to have to do this but that this was a point on which he felt he must yield, although he was really worried by the industrial aspect of the matter. I have told him that I desired to warn him that probably we would not be able to go along with Great Britain regarding the question of reduction in size of ships, particularly during the period of transition, and that it was our opinion that not much economy would result from it. The question of the reduction we felt should be by numbers; he said that the British Admiralty, in his opinion and Craigie's, would agree to a reduction in numbers, and he further pointed out that he had been told by the Japanese that if numbers were reduced they would expect an addition to their ratio. It might be dangerous, I pointed out, to reduce the difference in strength existing between battleship fleets and other war vessels, especially with regard to the three main naval powers, and in this matter he said that he felt that there was a practical identity of interests between the United States and Great Britain.

The conversation was most friendly in its whole tone, and I feel that from the British delegation we will have a full measure of cooperation.

STIMSON

500.A15a3/629 : Telegram

The Chairman of the American Delegation (Stimson) to the Acting Secretary of State

[Paraphrase]

LONDON, January 20, 1930—2 p. m.
[Received 2 : 10 p. m.[13]]

8. The following summarizes the situation up to the present.

The element of the situation which is most important is that on the voyage over and here the American delegation has developed into a loyal, harmonious unit which is working together as one man. MacDonald, on the other hand, has to divide authority with his Dominions who insist upon representation in the meetings of committee chairmen. The Dominion representatives, however, are individually friendly and amenable and the smooth working of the Conference will not, in my opinion, be obstructed by them.

At my country house yesterday I had a very friendly and satisfactory conference with the delegation from Italy, and after that Morrow and I had a satisfactory conference with Tardieu and Briand. Tardieu is apparently sincerely desirous of agreement and has definitely abandoned the position that this Conference cannot be final but must be contingent on general disarmament by the League of Nations. Tardieu at the preliminary meeting for organization of the delegation chairmen proved himself to be practical minded and made suggestions in the direction of informality and simplicity in the future working of the Conference. In comparison with the attitude of the French in previous conferences these suggestions were novel.

I believe that MacDonald will cooperate with me in respect to the Japanese demands, although I have had no further conference with the Japanese. A favorable outlook for an agreement resulting from the Conference has in general been confirmed by events since my arrival in England, as it is evident that MacDonald will remain in office on his opponents' sufferance until the Conference has been concluded. One of the most important factors, in my opinion, at present is to convince the British public and the Conservatives that our parity demand is genuine and that we will insist upon it; in case I find it necessary to make some emphatic statement to this effect I hope you will bear this necessity in mind. I also trust that no public statement will be made by the President bearing on the details of negotiations unless I am given opportunity for comment and ample notice as of course any statement that is made by him must be made good while the Prime Minister can, without being taken too seriously here, give utterance to pious hopes and aspirations. This applies among other things to battleship [*sic*] abolition.

STIMSON

---

[13] Telegram in two sections.

500.A15a3/639 : Telegram

The Chairman of the American Delegation (Stimson) to the Acting Secretary of State

[Paraphrase]

LONDON, January 23, 1930—6 p. m.
[Received 7:20 p. m.[14]]

16. For the President and the Acting Secretary of State. Tardieu, Briand, MacDonald, Henderson,[15] and Morrow dined with me on Tuesday evening. The French had as their interpreter Paul Mantoux.[16] The British Prime Minister said he considered it desirable to know what matters were to be discussed at the plenary session today and in the meantime what progress we could make. He was turning over in his mind whether it would not be desirable that the respective delegations hold separate meetings, as for example, between Japan and the United States, between Japan and Great Britain, between Great Britain and the United States, or between France and Italy.

France, Tardieu stated, favored both reduction and limitation of armament but felt that further limitation was the pathway to reduction. It was felt by Henderson that disappointment would result if reduction could not be achieved and that a bolder policy of reduction should be aimed for by the Conference at the outset. This was agreed to in not quite such strong terms by MacDonald. It was suggested by Tardieu that if we should use the present programs of the various Governments as a basis, making it clear that the Conference would result in a reduction in the programs as distinguished from reduction of existing navies, this would be a beginning of reduction of armament. The question of ratios and its consequent concomitant of prestige arose later in the evening. It appeared, I said, that because minds were fixed on prestige, programs were apt to be large. It was pointed out by me that possibly this desire might be satisfied in either one of two ways, by raising the ratios or by a change in the nature of the contract. The dangers inherent in the first method were then pointed out by me, that is, that reduction on the one hand would be prevented by it and antagonisms on the other aroused by it.

The method which I had discussed with the President was then suggested by me, that is, to avoid all implications of contractual inferiority by merely setting out programs which could not be departed from without a notice say of one year and without giving sufficient reason therefor, thus releasing the other signatories from

---

[14] Telegram in two sections.
[15] Arthur Henderson, British Secretary of State for Foreign Affairs and member of the British delegation.
[16] Former head of the Political Department, Secretariat of the League of Nations.

their corresponding programs. The French seemed to consider this suggestion as helpful and I am informed that Tardieu privately said he considered their difficulties might be solved by my proposed second method. I was informed by Hankey [17] on the following day that he was urging this method upon the Prime Minister as for a long time he had been convinced that it would be the ultimate solution.

I conferred yesterday with the Prime Minister concerning agenda of today's plenary session and informed him that I did not propose to set out a long and detailed argumentation for the maintenance of a large navy and that I hoped that he and the other nations would do likewise as it did not seem wise to me to dig in behind any set statement of needs and the reasons why they should be adopted. This was not agreed to altogether by him as I believe the political effect of some patriotic statement of Britain's dependence on the sea was valued by him at this time. Mr. Wakatsuki, upon whom I subsequently called, agreed to the limitation of his statement to generalities. This was done by him. The statement of the Italians was likewise based on the point of view that no reduction could be too great and that naval needs were relative. It was still apparently considered politically necessary by the French that a detailed statement be made by them.

There was no friction in this morning's plenary session; the election of Sir Maurice Hankey as Secretary General and a decision that in case of absence of the Prime Minister the chair should be taken by the heads of the other delegations in the English alphabetical order completed the organization of the Conference. The policy suggested in the paragraph above was followed in the speeches. A very long exposé of French coast line area and commerce was read by Tardieu, who frequently stressed the point that these items for France were only exceeded by similar statistics for Great Britain, the United States and Japan. During most of Tardieu's speech his manner was restrained and almost perfunctory, giving the impression that the effect at home was the essential object of his speech. He stated, however, in the last paragraph that any idea of absolute needs was necessarily modified by relative considerations such as a condition of naval agreement and security. The speech of the Italian delegate was moderate and conciliatory, only stating in principle that equality with the navy of the largest European continental power was the Italian need.

STIMSON

---

[17] Col. Sir Maurice Hankey, secretary of the British delegation.

500.A15a3/641 : Telegram

The Chairman of the American Delegation (Stimson) to the Acting Secretary of State

[Paraphrase]

LONDON, January 24, 1930—6 p. m.
[Received January 24—4:29 p. m.]

18. For the President and the Acting Secretary of State. At Mac-Donald's invitation we had a two hours' conference on Thursday with the heads of the delegations. The only one of the Dominions represented was Australia, the others having been persuaded by MacDonald to eliminate themselves. Procedure was discussed at length with quite favorable results. Speed in providing methods for sorting out and reporting upon all possible questions before the Conference was particularly urged by MacDonald and Tardieu. An agreement resulted that the heads of delegations should meet every day, beginning Monday, in order that they might discuss the various questions before the Conference and examine how the various questions should preliminarily be disposed of for investigation and report, that is, either by reference to subcommittees of various kinds or by the sessions of the chiefs of delegations themselves. The informal meetings between the separate delegations now in progress will not be interfered with by these meetings. We have received today tentative agenda of subjects to be thus considered and will receive these each day for revision in advance of the following day's meeting and no subject which is objected to by any chief delegate will be taken up. Conferences have been held today between some of us and the Italians and the Japanese. Yesterday and today we have also been in almost continuous session, as a delegation, making good progress on our own positions as regards various questions.

We feel in view of this week's experience that our delegation is absolutely harmonious and particularly well prepared in advance of any other delegation here. Figure studies which have been of much use to us are apparently lacking even to the British.

STIMSON

500.A15a3/644 : Telegram

The Ambassador in Japan (Castle) to the Acting Secretary of State

TOKYO, January 25, 1930—9 a. m.
[Received January 25—6 : 48 a. m.]

11. Repeat to London.[18]

1. The only public explanations of the Japanese position with respect to cruisers are based upon formulae representing the strength of opposing sides in the great sea battles of the past, for example, the comparative strengths of the Japanese-Russian fleets in the battle of the Straits of Tsushima, or, of the British and German fleets at the battle of Jutland, and attempt to adduce from the figures the principle that a superior fleet could not be assured of victory unless it had a preponderant relative strength of 10–7, and, conversely, that fleet weaker than its enemy by any proportion less than 7–10 would be certain to meet defeat. It is the opinion of our own Naval Attaché as well as that of other Naval Attachés in Tokyo that this is rubbish.

2. [Paraphrase.] It is undoubtedly only in connection with war with the United States that the 10–7 ratio is considered. The Japanese naval experts believe that the United States in such an event would not permit the development of a war of exhaustion but as soon as possible would seek a final conclusion. This belief is based on the reason that the United States would have to bring over an effective military force; that the use of the best part of the American merchant marine would be required for the transportation of a large army across the Pacific; that the capture of American carrying trade by British and other foreign merchant marines and the loss of the United States foreign marketing would result from the diversion for a long period of time of a large proportion of American merchant vessels. It is consequently believed that as soon as possible the American Navy would try to come to grips with the Japanese Navy.

3. The great distance between Pearl Harbor and Japan, it is believed, would prevent the American battle fleet from effectively carrying on offensive operations against Japan from Pearl Harbor. The American battle fleet, therefore, would immediately upon the outbreak of war proceed to Manila in order that they might operate against Japan from that base which is close enough to permit the freest use of cruisers and submarines as well as of capital ships. The Caroline and Marshall Islands, through which the American battle fleet would have to pass, are mandates of Japan. Excellent places for concealment of submarines are afforded by these islands. For attacks upon the American battle fleet the Japanese would here undoubtedly exploit

---

[18] Transmitted to the American delegation as Department's telegram No. 19, January 25, 9 a. m.

the use of the large submarine contingent upon which they insist. The Japanese realize only a portion of the battle fleet could be destroyed by their submarines, but they appear to have confidence in their ability to destroy enough ships to reduce the preponderance of the American battle fleet, thus making it possible for the Japanese fleet to meet the American fleet on terms which would be more or less equal.

4. There is naturally no public discussion of the above but undoubtedly the demand for a 10–7 ratio would largely disappear if Japan could be made to understand that we have no plans in regard to China which might conceivably lead to war. [End paraphrase.]

CASTLE

500.A15a3/649 : Telegram

The Chairman of the American Delegation (Stimson) to the Acting Secretary of State

[Paraphrase]

LONDON, January 28, 1930—3 p. m.
[Received January 28—12 : 55 p. m.]

22. Three and a half hours were wasted in yesterday morning's meeting of the heads of the five delegations by debate between the French and Italians concerning whether the items proposed by one or the other should precede each other on the informal agenda concerning the disposal of which a consultation was to be held between the heads of delegations. The alphabet, it was finally agreed, should decide this question and the Italian proposition should be preceded by the French proposition so labeled. In the meanwhile progress in the study and consideration of a more detailed plan is being made by the American delegation.

The heads of delegations at their meeting this morning determined to hold a plenary session of the Conference at 10 o'clock on Thursday, the 30th, in order that they might discuss the appointment of a committee on which should be represented not more than two delegates from each of the five countries. This committee would report to the Conference and its duty would be to consider the methods of limitation, i. e. (1) global, (2) by categories, and (3) by categories with a transfer possibility.

A statement will be made by the Italian delegate to the effect that decisions on any of these methods cannot be accepted by Italy until there is a more exact determination of the question of ratio and tonnage level but that the committee will not be opposed by Italy. The general principle and the parliamentary question involved in the setting up of the committee and its terms of reference as above described will be discussed in the plenary session. The plenary session's real object is to prevent the press from getting too restless over the lack of open meetings and to allow time necessary to continue informal discussions between delegates which are now showing real progress and going at full speed.

Admission will be granted to a limited number of press representatives and the arrangements for this are now being elaborated between the press officers of the various delegations and the British press office.

STIMSON

500.A15a3/661 : Telegram

The Ambassador in Japan (Castle) to the Acting Secretary of State

[Paraphrase]

TOKYO, January 31, 1930—1 p. m.
[Received January 31—9 : 35 a. m.]

14. Telegram to be repeated to London.[19]

Evidently acting under instructions, Hanihara [20] last night spoke to me of the impression which prevails in Japan that the plans of the American Navy are based on the possibility of war with Japan in order to force acceptance of our ideas in regard to China. Japan realized, he said, that a war with the United States would be the worst possible disaster and that therefore Japan even from a selfish point of view could never think of it, but that unfortunately on account of the belief above expressed there was extreme nervousness here.

This fear would never be understood in the United States, I said, and I could conceive of no circumstances in which the United States would go to war with Japan over China, that our aims approximated the Japanese as both countries wanted only a China which was substantially and politically sound. I was assured by him that this impression which he said prevailed was not the belief of his Government but that popular opinion had to be taken into account and that popular opinion felt that this possibility of war over some Chinese question was the basis for our opposition to a slightly larger ratio for Japan. Dooman [21] was told very much the same thing by Vice Minister Yoshida who stated that if I could make some authoritative statement contradicting the idea it might be most helpful. I had already planned to say in my speech at the dinner of the America-Japan Society that we have at present no quarrel on the subject of China and that I foresee none in the future but merely closer cooperation in forwarding our

[19] Transmitted to the American delegation as Department's telegram No. 39, January 31, 9 a. m.
[20] Masanao Hanihara, former Japanese Ambassador in the United States.
[21] Eugene H. Dooman, First Secretary of Embassy in Japan.

common aim to help China to achieve political and economic stability. There has been, as you know, a radical change in the Japanese policy toward China and it is now clearly recognized that friendly assistance must be the basis for their relations. The above suspicion of our purpose, in my mind, is certainly the principal reason that a higher ratio in large cruisers is insisted upon by the Japanese.

CASTLE

500.A15a3/661 : Telegram

The Acting Secretary of State to the Ambassador in Japan (Castle)

[Paraphrase]

WASHINGTON, February 1, 1930—5 p. m.

25. Your No. 14, January 31, 1 p. m.

1. The question you present involves problems both of facilitating the work of the Naval Conference and of the continuous conduct of relations with the Far Eastern countries. Mindful of the difficulties which arose in consequence of statements in the Lansing-Ishii notes [23] and in the Anglo-Japanese Treaties of Alliance [24] the Department feels that utmost care should be taken with regard to both substance and phraseology in any attempt to explain policy of the United States in relations with Japan in terms of American and Japanese policy in relation to China.

Careful consideration should be given to the effect not only in Japan but elsewhere of any statement which may be made. For example, it is likely that the statement "closer cooperation in forwarding our common aim to help China to achieve economic and political stability" would be misunderstood in China and would be susceptible to interpretations disadvantageous to us.

One might safely say, instead, that it is the desire of this Government, and we are assured and confident that it is also the desire of Japan, to see China achieve economic and political stability. In brief, we believe that it is not necessary to characterize or define our policy or aims with regard to China in terms of Japan's policy or aims, and that it is desirable to avoid putting the two in the same brackets. The suggestion is offered that you emphasize the point that the China policy of this Government is completely defined in the Washington treaties of 1922, particularly the Nine-Power Pact relating to prin-

---

[23] For Lansing-Ishii agreement of November 2, 1917, see *Foreign Relations,* 1917, p. 264; for cancelation of the agreement, see *ibid.,* 1922, vol. II, p. 591.

[24] For Anglo-Japanese alliance, see treaty of January 30, 1902, *Foreign Relations,* 1902, p. 514; treaty of August 12, 1905, *ibid.,* 1905, p. 488; and treaty of July 13, 1911, *British and Foreign State Papers,* vol. CIV, p. 173.

ciples, [25] and in the Kellogg Peace Pact,[26] agreements which commit the United States and Japan to each other and to countries which are parties to these agreements and which are regarded in the United States as conclusive evidence that no country signatory to them has any aims regarding China likely to lead to armed conflict with any other.

2. Any statement regarding American naval plans should avoid mention, if possible, of any particular country. It would be safe to state officially at any time or place that the foreign policy of the United States rests on principles which preclude any thought on the part of either the American Government or the people of resorting to war as an instrument of policy.

3. We are repeating this telegram to London today.[27] It is assumed that if the Secretary wishes to alter or to add to the suggestions made herein, you will in due course receive a further instruction.

COTTON

500.A15a3/665 : Telegram

The Chairman of the American Delegation (Stimson) to the Acting Secretary of State

LONDON, February 4, 1930—7 p. m.
[Received 9 : 23 p. m.[27a]]

35. [Paraphrase.] For the President. The American delegation, after prolonged consultation with Japanese and British delegations, unanimously favors submitting to Great Britain and Japan the following tentative suggestions which are to be considered not as a collection of separate offers but as a whole. While Admiral Jones approves the balance of the program, he still is convinced that 21 cruisers are essential. The entire plan is cordially endorsed by Admiral Pratt, and all seven American delegates are now united in believing that the 21 cruiser program could be insisted on only with great danger to the Conference's success.

Your criticisms at the earliest possible moment will be appreciated. We have not submitted these written detailed suggestions either to the British or the Japanese, but we are encouraged by their statements in our conferences to believe that a plan along these general lines may be approved by them. The utmost secrecy should be maintained for the present as to the detailed proposal, of which the following will be the substance: [End paraphrase.]

[25] Treaty signed at Washington, February 6, 1922, *Foreign Relations*, 1922, vol. I, p. 276.
[26] Treaty for the Renunciation of War, signed at Paris, August 27, 1928, *ibid.*, 1928, vol. I, p. 153.
[27] Telegram No. 45, 5 p. m. ; not printed.
[27a] Telegram in five sections.

CRUISERS

FOR UNITED STATES

Total tons		Type
180,000	18	10,000 tons carrying guns of 8-inch caliber
70,500	10	Existing *Omahas*
76,500	..	New cruisers carrying guns not exceeding 6-inch caliber
327,000	..	Total

(*a*) The United States shall have the option of the following:

150,000	15	10,000 ton cruisers carrying guns of 8-inch caliber
70,500	10	Existing *Omahas*
118,500	..	New cruisers carrying guns not exceeding 6-inch caliber
339,000	..	Total

FOR GREAT BRITAIN

110,000	11	10,000 [ton] cruisers now completed carrying 8-inch guns
20,000	2	10,000 ton cruisers now building carrying 8-inch guns
16,800	2	8,400 ton cruisers now building carrying 8-inch guns
91,000	14	New cruisers mounting 6-inch guns
101,200	21	Existing cruisers mounting 6-inch guns
339,000	50	Total

(*a*) Great Britain may retain four cruisers of *Hawkins* class carrying 7.5-inch guns until replacement by 6-inch cruisers. To be replaced by 1934–5.

(*b*) Great Britain shall have the option of the following:

176,800	18	10,000 ton (or smaller) cruisers carrying guns of 8-inch caliber
75,000	..	New cruisers carrying guns of 6-inch caliber
75,200	..	Existing cruisers carrying guns of 6-inch caliber
327,000	..	Total

FOR JAPAN

28,400	4	7,100 ton cruisers carrying 8-inch guns
40,000	4	10,000 ton cruisers now completed carrying 8-inch guns
40,000	4	10,000 ton cruisers now building carrying 8-inch guns
81,455	17	Cruisers carrying guns not exceeding 6-inch caliber
8,800	..	Existing or new cruisers carrying guns not exceeding 6 inches
198,655	..	Total

Replacements

1. No cruiser may be replaced until it shall have reached a life of 20 years from date of completion, unless it shall have been lost through an accident.

2. Tonnages are given in Washington standard tons.

3. Old tonnage may be retained over the age limit if not replaced, but the same right of replacement is not lost by delay in scrapping after reaching the age limit.

DESTROYERS

Total tonnage of destroyers and destroyer leaders shall be:

For United States, 200,000; for Great Britain 200,000; for Japan 120,000.

1. Existing destroyers and leaders may be retained and vessels building may be completed up to the above total allowed tonnages.

2. Existing vessels shall not be scrapped except to comply with the allowed tonnage until the vessel has reached an age limit of 16 years.

3. Old tonnage may be retained over the age limit if not replaced, but the right of replacement is not lost by delay in scrapping after reaching the age limit.

4. No new vessels shall be laid down prior to 31 December, 1936, except to replace vessels reaching the age limit or lost through accident.

5. Maximum unit displacements shall be limited as may be agreed upon in conference. We suggest 1,850 tons for United States, Great Britain, and Japan, and 3,000 tons for France and Italy.

SUBMARINES (If retained)

Total tonnage of submarines shall be:

For the United States	60,000.
For Great Britain	60,000.
For Japan	40,000.

1. Existing submarines may be retained and vessels building may be completed up to the above total allowed tonnages.

2. Existing vessels shall not be scrapped except to comply with the allowed tonnage until the vessel has reached an age limit of 13 years.

3. No new vessels shall be laid down prior to 31st December, 1936, except to replace vessels reaching the age limit or lost through accident.

4. Submarine tonnages are given in Geneva standard tons, surface condition.

5. Maximum unit displacement shall be limited as may be agreed upon in conference.

6. Old tonnage may be retained over the age limit if not replaced but the right of replacement is not lost by delay in scrapping after reaching the age limit.

7. Submarines to be limited to the same rules of international law as surface craft, in operations against merchant ships.

BATTLESHIPS

1. The replacement tables of the Washington Treaty [28] are modified as follows to comply with these principles:

(a) Immediate scrapping of old ships down to a total of 15–15–9.

---

[28] Treaty signed at Washington, February 6, 1922, *Foreign Relations*, 1922, vol. I, p. 247.

(*b*) No new ships to be laid down prior to 31 December, 1936 except as provided below in paragraph 4.

(*c*) Each nation may retain two old battleships for training purposes or for use as targets provided these vessels shall be rendered incapable of further war-like service as prescribed in the Washington Treaty.

2. Tonnages are in Washington standard tons. Three thousand standard tons have been added to each of the *Idaho*, *Mississippi* and *New Mexico* to allow for future modernization.

3. Should any provision be made for replacements of battleships, each nation may retain old tonnage if not replaced, and the right of replacement of that tonnage is not lost by such postponement.

4. In order to realize now the parity of battleship tonnage which was ultimately contemplated by the Washington Treaty by balancing the *Rodney* and *Nelson*, the United States may lay down one 35,000 ton battleship in 1933, complete it in 1936, and on completion scrap the *Wyoming*. If the United States shall exercise this option, then a similar option as to replacing one capital ship shall be granted to Japan.

5. "Modernizing" existing ships includes increase in gun elevation.

6. The foregoing principles will result in a schedule substantially as follows:

FOR UNITED STATES

		Standard
Scrap *Florida*	. . . . .	21,900
Utah	. . . . . .	22,000
Arkansas	. . . . .	26,100
Total	. . . . . .	70,000

2. Total tons now on hand, 532,400.
Scrap in 1930–31, 70,000.
Remaining first of January 1936, 462,400.
Scrap *Wyoming* in 1936, 26,000, leaving 436,400.
One new ship 35,000.   Total 471,400.

FOR GREAT BRITAIN

		Standard
Scrap *Iron Duke*	. . . .	26,250
Marlborough	. . .	26,250
Emperor of India	.	26,250
Benbow	. . . . .	26,250
Tiger	. . . . .	28,900
Total	. . . . .	133,900

Total tons now on hand, 606,450.
Scrap [in] 1930–31, 133,900.
Remaining until 31st December 1936, 472,550.

FOR JAPAN

Standard

1. Scrap *Kongo* 26,330
2. Total tons now on hand, 292,400.
Scrap in 1930–31, 26,330.
Remaining until 31st December 1936, 266,070.

AIRCRAFT CARRIERS

The minimum limitation of 10,000 tons shall be stricken from the definition of aircraft carriers in the Washington Treaty, so that all such vessels shall be charged against the permitted tonnage.

EXEMPT CLASS

(*a*) That all naval surface combatant vessels of less than 500 tons standard displacement be exempt.

(*b*) That all naval surface combatant vessels of 500 to 3,000 tons individual standard displacement should be exempt from limitation, provided they have none of the following characteristics:

(1) Mount a gun greater than 5-inch caliber.
(2) Mount more than two guns above 3-inch caliber.
(3) Are designed or fitted to launch torpedoes.
(4) Are designed for a speed greater than 16.5 knots.

(*c*) That all naval vessels not specifically built as fighting ships nor taken in time of peace under Government control for fighting purposes, which are employed in fleet duties or as troop transports or in some other way other than as fighting ships, should be exempt from limitation provided they have none of the following characteristics:

(1) Mount a gun greater than 6-inch caliber.
(2) Mount more than four guns above 3-inch caliber.
(3) Are designed or fitted to launch torpedoes.
(4) Are designed for a speed greater than 16.5 knots.
(5) Are armored.
(6) Are designed or fitted to launch mines.
(7) Are fitted to receive planes on board from the air.
(8) Mount more than one aeroplane—launching apparatus on the center line; or two, one on each broadside.

(*d*) Certain existing vessels of special type to be exempted by mutual agreement.

STIMSON

500.A15a3/665 : Telegram

The Acting Secretary of State to the Chairman of the American Delegation (Stimson)

[Paraphrase]

WASHINGTON, February 5, 1930—10 a. m.

55. The suggestions contained in your telegram No. 35, February 4, have been considered and are heartily approved by the President.

COTTON

500.A15a3/667 : Telegram

The Chairman of the American Delegation (Stimson) to the Acting Secretary of State

[Paraphrase]

LONDON, February 5, 1930—5 p. m.
[Received February 5—1:55 p. m.]

36. At the request of the Secretary of the Navy, and if the President sees no objection, please communicate to Acting Secretary of the Navy Jahncke, for discussion with the President only, the substance of our telegram No. 35, February 4. Thereupon see Senators Swanson and Hale [29] at the request of Senators Robinson and Reed, and communicate to them the substance of our proposal with messages as follows: [30]

"For Senator Swanson from Robinson:
Please keep this strictly confidential except for Senator Hale. All delegates agree that American proposal best possible, and that insistence on 21 cruisers would make Japanese demands for 8-inch gun vessels so large that Australia and New Zealand would insist on building such vessels independently of British Navy. I am thoroughly satisfied with the methods of working out this proposal with the negotiations incident to it, and of the value of the proposal to the interest of the United States.

For Senator Hale from Reed:
Kindly regard this as strictly confidential except for Senator Swanson.
After conversations with British and Japanese our delegation is unanimous that we have outlined the best proposal that can be made. Japanese insistence of basing their figures on American 8-inch-gun cruiser tonnage will bring about cruiser building by Australia and New Zealand, consequently parity could only be obtained with Great Britain alone and not with British Empire. You will see that in other directions we would receive many compensating advantages."

STIMSON

---

[29] The ranking minority member and the chairman, respectively, of the Naval Affairs Committee of the Senate.
[30] Quoted passage not paraphrased.

500.A15a3/668 : Telegram

The Chairman of the American Delegation (Stimson) to the Acting Secretary of State

LONDON, February 6, 1930—5 p. m.
[Received February 6—1 : 05 p. m.]

39. Delegation's No. 36, February 5, 5 p. m. If you have delivered yesterday's message please communicate the following message from Senator Robinson to Senator Swanson:

You will have noted that the American proposal is based on your suggestion that options be given so that Great Britain and the United States may, if they so desire, exactly duplicate each other's cruiser fleets, ship for ship, ton for ton, and gun for gun. The whole delegation joins me in thanking you for this suggestion which has contributed much to the possibility of solution of this problem.

STIMSON

500.A15a3/670 : Telegram

The Chairman of the American Delegation (Stimson) to the Acting Secretary of State

LONDON, February 6, 1930—7 p. m.
[Received February 6—3 : 20 p. m.[31]]

41. Having learned this afternoon that garbled reports of our plan were in the hands of hostile newspapers, in order to place the advantages of the American proposal in the public eye as soon as possible and to prevent all leaks which would concern themselves only with its alleged disadvantages, I have decided, after consultation with the Prime Minister and Mr. Wakatsuki, to issue the attached statement to the press tonight for release for tomorrow (Friday) morning's papers.

At the opening of the Conference the United States delegation made no statement of its position or the needs of its country beyond the historical fact of the agreement in principle for parity between Great Britain and the United States. We are now in a position where we can go further. Following discussions among ourselves and negotiations with the British and Japanese which have clarified the limits of possible agreement, our delegation has made suggestions as follows:

First, with Great Britain immediate parity in every class of ship in the Navy. The gross tonnage of these two fleets is substantially 1,200,000 tons apiece. The negotiations last summer between President Hoover and Prime Minister MacDonald [32] practically reduced

---

[31] Telegram in five sections.
[32] See *Foreign Relations*, 1929, vol. III, pp. 1 ff.

the discussions of parity between them to the comparatively insignificant difference in their respective cruiser class tonnage of 24,000 tons. We propose to settle this difference as follows: Of the larger cruisers armed with 8-inch guns, Great Britain will have 15 and the United States 18, an advantage to the latter of 30,000 tons. In this case our advantage in large cruisers will be compensated to Great Britain by a lesser tonnage on our side in smaller cruisers of 12,000 tons, but under the arrangements stated below this can be equalized at our option.

Of the smaller cruisers armed with 6-inch guns, Great Britain will have an initial advantage; but, in order to insure exact equality of tonnage, the United States makes the suggestion that each country will have the option of duplicating exactly the cruiser fleet of the other. Thus Great Britain would have the option, by reducing its number of small cruisers, to increase its large cruisers from 15 to 18 so as to give it a total tonnage of 327,000 tons, the exact amount of tonnage which the United States now asks. On the other hand, the United States would have the option, by reducing its large cruisers from 18 to 15, to increase the number of its small cruisers so as to give it a total cruiser tonnage of 339,000 tons, the exact amount of tonnage which the British now ask.

In battleships we suggest by reduction in number on both sides to equalize our two fleets in 1931 instead of in 1942. At present the British battleship fleet contains two more vessels than ours. In destroyers and aircraft carriers we suggest equality in tonnage, and in submarines the lowest tonnage possible.

As is well known we will gladly agree to a total abolition of submarines if it is possible to obtain the consent of all five powers to such a proposition, and in any event we suggest that the operations of submarines be limited to the same rules of international law as surface craft in operation against merchant ships so that they cannot attack without providing for the safety of the passengers and crew.

Second, our suggestion to the Japanese would produce an over-all relation satisfactory to us and, we hope, to them. In conformity with our relations in the past it is not based upon the same ratio in every class of ships.

We have not made proposals to the French and Italians whose problems are not so directly related to ours that we feel it appropriate at this time to make suggestions to them. A settlement of the Italian and French problem is essential, of course, to the agreement contemplated.

The United States delegates do not feel at liberty to discuss any further details in figures, and it is obvious that the announcement of hypothetical figures by others is calculated only to provoke argument.

Our delegation is in agreement on every item of our program and we are in the most hopeful spirit that in cooperation with the other delegations the primary purpose of the Conference, namely, the termination and prevention of competitions in naval armament and such reductions as are found consistent with national security, may be accomplished.

This is all that we deem it helpful to state until our suggestions have been considered by the delegations to whom they have been sent.

STIMSON

500.A15a3/671 : Telegram

The Chairman of the American Delegation (Stimson) to the Acting Secretary of State

[Paraphrase]

LONDON, February 7, 1930—10 a. m.
[Received February 7—7 : 10 a. m.]

42. Except for figures contained in statement transmitted in telegram No. 41, February 6, 7 p. m., none will be given out here. It is desired that none be given out in Washington, as to do so would embarrass Japanese negotiations. The statement was very well received by the British press. What is Senator Swanson's reaction?

STIMSON

500.A15a3/671 : Telegram

The Acting Secretary of State to the Chairman of the American Delegation (Stimson)

[Paraphrase]

WASHINGTON, February 7, 1930—2 p. m.

67. Your No. 42, February 7, 10 a. m. No figures have been given out here; and although it is quite clear that your statement had the President's approval, there has been no specific statement made that he approved it. We do not want to give the impression that you are operating under instructions from here. Your concrete proposal has been sent to Castle. Your statement was widely carried in the press here, but it is too early to appraise reaction. It is favorable, as far as we have it. Swanson was very much pleased, I think, and, while he has made no public statement and says that he is going to withhold judgment, I feel certain that his judgment is favorable. Senator Hale has made no public statement, but he does not like it.

My own personal feeling is that the form and matter of your proposal are going to be approved, and that there is not going to be any opposition except that which comes from a small group who would never agree to anything anyway. What makes the most impression is the unanimity of action of your delegation; I think that there will be a very general impression that you have done a good job, and that if you did not ask for more it was for the reason that you are exercising sound judgment on the spot. There is to a rather remarkable degree a willingness to trust the delegation, as far as I can read the press. A note consistently running through the press is the cool, deliberate manner in which the delegation has gone about ascertaining what was wise before they offered proposals.

COTTON

500.A15a3/684d : Telegram

The Acting Secretary of State to the Chairman of the American Delegation (Stimson)

[Paraphrase]

WASHINGTON, February 8, 1930—4 p. m.

75. . . . It is our conviction that the objections which have so far become articulate in Congress to your plans as announced, come from Hale and Britten [33] and that they voice positions which we believe to be untenable. Some regret still exists that the totals in the cruiser category are still so high and we hark back to the negotiations which took place by cable before MacDonald's visit and to the conversations when he was here at which time he hoped to do something further in the direction of cruiser reduction. It is our hope that at some appropriate time and in the delegation's discretion, you will propose to the British that they consider the old suggestion of police cruisers, at least between you and them. At that time there was in our minds a tentative suggestion that there be substituted a special category of police cruisers of limited speed and armament or alternately of 6-inch gun cruisers over age, but kept in service for police purposes, in lieu of a certain tonnage allocated to the 6-inch gun cruiser category. Of course, you will understand the reasons for this suggestion, how it is made, and that we are not attempting to press an instruction on the delegation. Nevertheless, we cannot abandon the hope that MacDonald will be sympathetic toward this proposal. Perhaps it is the sort of suggestion which should be relegated to a later stage in the discussions.

COTTON

500.A15a3/684c : Telegram

The Acting Secretary of State to the Chairman of the American Delegation (Stimson)

[Paraphrase]

WASHINGTON, February 10, 1930—2 p. m.

84. There was one other matter, in discussing your offer further with the President before his departure for Florida, concerning which you probably understand his wishes; at the risk, however, of repetition we again explain that 200,000 tons for destroyers seems to be a very high figure. Presumably it is now being placed that high by you so that negotiations between Great Britain and France may be left in

[33] Fred A. Britten, chairman of the Naval Affairs Committee of the House of Representatives.

a better position; the President hopes, however, that 150,000 tons will be the limit for the final figure.

In regard to your offer, the above is the last comment. It appears to us here that your general strategy is correct; only those who will oppose whatever you do are opposed to your plan.

COTTON

500.A15a3/688 : Telegram

The Chairman of the American Delegation (Stimson) to the Acting Secretary of State

[Paraphrase]

LONDON, February 12, 1930—7 p. m.

[Received February 12—5: 05 p. m.]

60. A conference, in which all pending propositions between the two countries were discussed, was held yesterday afternoon, those present being the Prime Minister, Henderson, Alexander [34] and Craigie for Great Britain, and Adams, Reed, Marriner and myself for the American delegation. It was shown, as a net result of the conference, that an agreement will probably be easy between Great Britain and ourselves, provided France or Japan does not interpose difficulties. With regard to the cruiser proposition, we are standing firm, while it is understood by Great Britain that, unless serious changes should be made in our proposal in other directions which would make it necessary as a counterpoise, the *Rodney* option [35] will probably not be insisted on.

I have, in the private meetings of the chiefs of delegations, sharply, and thus far successfully, prevented any battleship discussion on the ground that, until we are assured that a general agreement in all the auxiliary categories is possible, the United States will discuss no changes in the Washington Treaty. I am, therefore, refusing to discuss battleship questions in the press and trust that, regardless of criticisms either in the press or in the Senate, the same policy will be followed by you in Washington. It is not my desire that I should be forced into a position where a battleship agreement will seem so easy that, even if in the auxiliary categories Japan or France remains obdurate, it will be difficult to avoid pressure for a separate agreement on the subject of battleships.

Tardieu's first figures were received by the Prime Minister yester-

[34] Albert Victor Alexander, First Lord of the Admiralty and member of the British delegation.
[35] See telegram No. 35, February 4, from the chairman of the American delegation, p. 13.

day immediately after the interview with us, and later in the evening he stated that the high levels which they had suggested had somewhat discouraged him. Judging, however, from a private talk with Tardieu, it remains my own feeling that our cruiser figures will be left unchanged by eventual concessions from Tardieu. Japanese counter figures are expected today; we believe, however, that not until after their elections on February 20, will the Japanese come down to earth.

STIMSON

500.A15a3/688c : Telegram

The Acting Secretary of State to the Ambassador in Japan (Castle)

[Paraphrase]

WASHINGTON, February 13, 1930—5 p. m.

36. The situation at the London Conference is difficult to appraise. With regard to Japan, our delegation appears to be standing firm until after the forthcoming Japanese elections; they seem pretty obdurate against any concession to the Japanese point of view. I think it probable that that position contributed to the unanimity in our delegation. We should like to have your comments.

COTTON

500.A15a3/689 : Telegram

The Ambassador in Japan (Castle) to the Acting Secretary of State

[Paraphrase]

TOKYO, February 14, 1930—9 p. m.
[Received February 14—11:55 a. m.]

27. Your telegram No. 36, February 13, 5 p. m. Please repeat to London.[36]

I think that certain thoughtful Japanese regret that demand for 10–7 ratio in auxiliary ships was made practically a *sine qua non* of the Japanese program. They must now face the fact, however, that a large proportion of their people have been taught to look upon this ratio as essential to national safety; that being so, they feel that they cannot surrender. The ratio has become a political doctrine of major importance. The fact that the United States refused to consider this ratio is taken as an indication that we foresee the possibility of war. I have pointed out repeatedly that Japan having accepted the 10–6 ratio in Washington, the belief is general in the United States that Japan's demands for a higher ratio may equally be taken by the

---

[36] Transmitted to the American delegation as Department's telegram No. 103, February 14, noon.

American people as proof of belligerent intentions on the part of Japan. Baron Shidehara [37] told me this afternoon that the press has just been asking him urgently whether America could possibly think that Japan could attack either the mainland or the Philippine Islands because of this larger ratio. He told them that whatever America might think, an attack was impossible since even if it were immediately successful with regard to the Philippines it would be only the beginning of a war in which Japan would in the long run be completely ruined. I reminded him that it was nevertheless true that the man in the street in America, believing Japan to be already fully protected, would inevitably think some such thing, all the more so as no precise or technical reasons had ever, as far as I knew, been advanced as to why Japan needed this 10–7 ratio for defense. Shidehara said that it would be as difficult to give technical reasons as to give convincing technical reasons why the United States must have parity with Great Britain; that all the Navy would say was that Japan might have a sporting chance with this ratio against the United States, whereas with the 10–6 ratio it would have no chance at all. Shidehara added that even with this chance the final result for Japan must be disastrous.

It is also said in Tokyo that no attempt is being made in the London Conference to maintain the Washington ratio with France or Italy, that this proves that the Washington Conference ratios were not intended to cover smaller craft, and that the American attempt to hold Japan to them is unfair. That we have no particular interest in France and Italy is admitted, but this very fact is noted to prove England's greater generosity, in view of her keen interest in European armament.

I have tried to give you in my cables the exact Japanese point of view in the belief that knowledge of it may assist our delegates to suggest compromises if any are possible along the lines of least resistance. I was told yesterday by the French Chargé that he believed no compromise possible on submarines either with France or with Japan. My thought that he might be urging the Japanese Government to stand firm on this point was confirmed by Shidehara who said that the Chargé had told him that Japan and France should stand unwaveringly together on this issue as their interests with regard to it were identical. Shidehara told him that Japan would not make agreements of this sort with anyone, as it would not do to divide the Conference into opposing groups; that each nation must stand on its own feet. I am sure he was sincere in this and that Japan will not make any private agreement.

CASTLE

---

[37] Japanese Minister for Foreign Affairs.

500.A15a3/691 : Telegram

The Chairman of the American Delegation (Stimson) to the Acting Secretary of State

[Paraphrase]

LONDON, February 16, 1930—5 p. m.
[Received February 16—4:20 p. m.[38]]

67. For the President and the Acting Secretary of State. Your telegrams No. 103, February 14, noon,[38a] and No. 106, February 14, 7 p. m.[38b] At present we are in the center of discussions, and three of us by invitation have been sitting in on the negotiations between France and Great Britain for two days. It is our belief that they intend to agree eventually, although on the cruiser question they are still somewhat apart, have not yet reached submarines, and are making counter declarations as to the impossible positions occupied by each other. Great optimism is felt by Morrow, who is familiar with French methods.

We shall meet the Japanese delegation on Monday to make clear our position (1) against any change of the big cruiser ratio, and (2) that, unless a successful treaty covering all auxiliary vessels is negotiated, the Washington battleship treaty should not be modified. We have reason to believe that it is time to communicate these positions directly, even though it has already been done indirectly. An interlude for the above to sink in over the Japanese election day will then probably occur. The Japanese, we feel, have no case for the modification of the Washington ratio in regard to cruisers and no existing construction or program on which to base it, as opposed to the French who have a pretty good case for modification of the Washington ratio. The situation in regard to Japanese submarines is different, and we would desire a compromise which would reduce both sides by 1936. Negotiations, however, are rendered delicate and difficult by the Japanese political situation.

The position of Italy is one of sitting silent on the sidelines; and keeping on friendly personal terms with her delegation is all that we are doing. My new form of treaty with a speech in support of it is being held in reserve; if the time comes when it seems that it will bridge a final gap it is to be used.

.   .   .   .

It is not believed by any of us that the Conference will fail. Three causes are delaying its progress: first, the inability of MacDonald to delegate and organize his work; second, the enforced absences every week of Tardieu in Paris; and third, the elections in Japan referred

---

[38] Telegram in two sections.
[38a] See footnote 36, p. 24.
[38b] Not printed.

to above. The American delegation is well organized and, whenever it did not seem to cost too much on account of apparent eagerness, has taken the initiative. We are as cordial and united as ever, and more helpful and loyal support has never been given a chairman.

STIMSON

500.A15a3/691 : Telegram

The Acting Secretary of State to the Chairman of the American Delegation (Stimson)

[Paraphrase]

WASHINGTON, February 18, 1930—7 p. m.

121. Your telegram No. 67, February 16, 5 p. m., has been considered. We have no particular suggestions to offer. We do not expect the Japanese position to be changed substantially by the elections on the 20th. If before reaching a final result, and to reach it you decide that concessions are to be made by you in the cruiser class although you do not yourselves believe such concessions to be justified, it seems here to be of importance that the right to build such additional unjustified tonnage should arise only toward the very end of the treaty period for the following reasons: (1) that not until that time will the United States have built up its cruiser category anywhere near to where it should be, and the same is not true with regard to Great Britain or Japan; (2) that right to build additional unjustified tonnage should not arise until after or until time of the conference which will be called toward end of the treaty period; (3) that such right to build shall arise at so late a date that any other nation which feels that it is threatened thereby will very shortly be in a position to be free of the treaty and to build as it chooses; and (4) because if this course is followed it will tend to place a financial burden in certain years which would be likely to be a handicap to actual building.

The foregoing are suggestions only.

COTTON

500.A15a3/697 : Telegram

The Chairman of the American Delegation (Stimson) to the Acting Secretary of State

[Paraphrase]

LONDON, February 19, 1930—5 p. m.
[Received February 19—12:57 p. m.]

73. For the President and the Acting Secretary of State. Since the French delegation cannot participate until a new government has been formed, the Conference has been adjourned until February 26. The performance of important informal work will not be interfered with

by this recess.   The adjournment was recommended by me to the Prime Minister because I felt that otherwise the Conference would have an appearance of futility; it is also our hope that the return of the French delegation will tend to be hastened by the knowledge of the fact that the adjournment was made necessary by their situation.   It is also our hope that the pressure for news on correspondents will be lessened by the fact of adjournment.

STIMSON

500.A15a3/704a : Telegram

The Acting Secretary of State to the Chairman of the American Delegation (Stimson)

[Paraphrase]

WASHINGTON, February 22, 1930—11 a. m.

131.   Being somewhat disturbed, we desire that your feeling about the Conference be made known to us more fully.   There is undoubtedly a waning of public interest here.   While this may be inevitable and perhaps should not bother us, there is a strong feeling here that nothing is being done to keep down the levels which in every category being considered by the Conference are terribly high.   I regret to have to bother you, but more frequent reports are needed.

COTTON

500.A15a3/702 : Telegram

The Chairman of the American Delegation (Stimson) to the Acting Secretary of State

[Paraphrase]

LONDON, February 23, 1930—3 p. m.
[Received February 23—12 noon.[39]]

80. For the President and the Acting Secretary of State.   Your No. 131, February 22.   Following adjournment I pushed forward informal negotiations with the British which resulted in situation where agreement could be reached at once unless it were upset by the French figures.   The only issue remaining is whether the total American cruiser tonnage shall be 320,000 or 327,000.   The remainder follows substantially the lines of the offer sent you, with elimination of the new *Rodney;* modernization of old battleships is legalized, an arrangement supported by both Jones and Pratt as parity.   We have hopes of limiting the Japanese to their present fleet, but we have agreed with the British to delay pressing for final conclusions until after the elections in Japan, as it is believed that a showdown before elections would mean increase in Japanese demands.

---

[39] Telegram in three sections.

The presentation of the high French figures and the fall of the French Government which came immediately afterward caused a wave of pessimism here which is evidently echoed in the press. The French figures were not surprising, however, after the French note of December 20 last,[40] and Tardieu intimated to me privately that these would be reduced. The serious feature of the situation is the intense popular feeling among the British against the French, which will make it impossible for the Prime Minister to keep his figures down unless the French recede very substantially. In addition to the above, I have had personal talks with Baldwin, Lloyd George, Churchill and Grey.[41] They all approve parity with us, but they are disturbed lest MacDonald may not meet the threat from France.

Our first problem is, obviously, to get the French to come down from their original figures, which are all we have at present. Then if they will not come down far enough to permit the British to make a satisfactory agreement with us, we shall have to face the second problem: Whether it will be possible to make a three-power agreement with a withdrawal clause to protect the British against the French.

There is no change in the pact situation. The British have suggested a consultative pact to the French, who are still holding out for a guarantee. At one time Briand suggested to me that he would like to discuss with me later a supplement to the Kellogg Pact, but I took this to mean something quite separate from the Naval Conference. I have not given anyone encouragement as to our entering a Mediterranean Pact, either consultative or of guarantee. If the President has any new ideas on this subject, I should like to be advised.

As far as a waning of public interest is concerned, before I sailed I warned everyone that that was inevitable. This work is a slow, persuasive job, consisting of picking up and binding together the fragments left unfinished from the Washington Conference of 1922. We are doing as well as I expected we should do. Indeed, I think that we can say for this administration that it has clearly accomplished one of our chief purposes, that of healing the serious friction which had arisen between America and Britain over cruisers. Everyone here is agreed on that.

MacDonald is staying with me tonight at Stanmore. If there is anything further tomorrow I shall report it.

The President will receive by the *Aquitania* a long personal letter which I sent last Tuesday.[42]

STIMSON

---

[40] *Foreign Relations*, 1929, vol. i, p. 299.
[41] Stanley Baldwin, leader of the Conservative Party; David Lloyd George, leader of the Liberal Party; Winston Churchill, former First Lord of the Admiralty and member of the House of Commons; Earl Grey of Fallodon, former Secretary of State for Foreign Affairs and member of the House of Lords.
[42] Not printed.

500.A15a3/705 : Telegram

The Ambassador in Japan (Castle) to the Acting Secretary of State

[Extract]

Tokyo, February 24, 1930—3 p. m.
[Received February 24—9 : 30 a. m.]

32. Repeat to London.[43] The elections have resulted in a decisive victory for the Government. The latest figures give the Minseito 273 seats, Seiyukai 174, balance of 19 seats being scattered among various proletarian groups and independents. . . .

The Government now has unassailable position and is expected to prosecute its policies both foreign and domestic in a decisive manner.

.   .   .   .

Castle

———————

500.A15a3/711 : Telegram

The Ambassador in Japan (Castle) to the Acting Secretary of State

[Paraphrase]

Tokyo, February 25, 1930—5 p. m.
[Received February 25—7 : 45 a. m.]

34. Please repeat to London.[44] Report in press. It is stated in *Neigo* that Stimson and MacDonald will propose that the Conference resolve itself into one of three powers should the French not agree to reduce demands. I questioned Shidehara whether Japan would, if this report is true, agree to this. Favorable consideration, he said, would certainly be given to the idea and he asked whether I believed a conference of three powers would be successful. My reply was that it seemed far more hopeful than at Geneva,[45] since the British cruiser demands were reduced, to which he was in agreement. The presence of Sarraut,[46] he believed, will make it almost impossible for the French to agree.

Castle

———————

[43] Transmitted to the American delegation as Department's telegram No. 137, February 24, 10 a. m.
[44] Transmitted to the American delegation as Department's telegram No. 140, February 25, 9 a. m.
[45] Three-Power Conference, June 20–August 4, 1927, *Foreign Relations*, 1927, vol. I, pp. 1 ff.
[46] Albert Sarraut, Minister of Marine in the French Ministry formed on February 21, 1930.

500.A15a3/717a : Telegram

The Acting Secretary of State to the Chairman of the American Delegation (Stimson)

[Paraphrase]

WASHINGTON, February 26, 1930—8 p. m.

149. Your personal letter to the President [46a] containing a résumé of affairs to February 17 has been received and read. Although the following course is not being recommended to you, we assume that you are considering whether or not a wise course may not be a three-power agreement with a political clause in event of menacing building. The reasons which make a step of that sort seem wise to us are (1) because in such a compact you can establish the present building programs at lower levels than you could if more governments were involved, particularly France; (2) because of apparent political instability of the French Government.

COTTON

500.A15a3/716 : Telegram

The Chairman of the American Delegation (Stimson) to the Acting Secretary of State

[Paraphrase]

LONDON, February 27, 1930—noon.
[Received February 27—8 : 06 a. m.]

91. The informal conversations with the Japanese were resumed by a conversation between Senator Reed and Ambassador Matsudaira [47] after a luncheon at the Japanese Embassy on Tuesday. A possible scheme of compromise on figures was worked out by the two of them together but as yet this delegation and as far as we know the Japanese delegation have not accepted these figures. Thus any possible figures which might appear in Tokyo either in press leaks or otherwise lack any official approval and are completely unofficial. When any definite progress has been made you will be informed.

Please repeat to Tokyo.[47a]

STIMSON

[46a] Not printed.
[47] Japanese Ambassador in Great Britain and member of the Japanese delegation.
[47a] Transmitted to the Embassy in Japan as Department's telegram No. 38, February 27, 10 a. m.

500.A15a3/718 : Telegram

The Chairman of the American Delegation (Stimson) to the Acting Secretary of State

[Paraphrase]

LONDON, February 28, 1930—2 p. m.
[Received February 28—11:55 a. m.]

95. A tentative agreement was reached with the British yesterday, the difference being split at 323,500 tons on total cruiser tonnage. The attempt to limit the size of 6-inch cruisers so far as America is concerned is withdrawn by them, while the *Rodney* option is withdrawn by us. The modernization of old ships including gun mountings is, by satisfactory exchange of notes withdrawing protests, legalized by them. Of course the tonnage proposed for destroyers and submarines depends directly on Japan and France, but Great Britain and the United States will try to reduce these tonnages as far as possible below our original offer which was sent to you in our telegram No. 35, February 4. We are encouraged by this settlement as being at least a definite step forward, although of course it may be jeopardized or modified by French or Japanese action. It is highly approved by Reed and unanimously by the whole delegation. With the Japanese active negotiations are taking place.

We have received your telegram No. 149, February 26. You will have been reassured as to our attitude on the three-power pact by my telegram No. 80, February 23; we still plan, however, to make strenuous efforts to get the French in.

STIMSON

500.A15a3/723a : Telegram

The Acting Secretary of State to the Chairman of the American Delegation (Stimson)

[Paraphrase]

WASHINGTON, February 28, 1930—5 p. m.

154. Apparently with the sympathetic support of Briand, and starting with certain of the American correspondents, a pretty definite drive appears to have developed demanding that the President make a public announcement of policies concerning the Kellogg Pact with a view to satisfying the French of some sort of political security assurance on the part of the United States. This movement has now taken the form of statements from European correspondents to the effect that the President should save the Conference by making some commitment, and that it will be the President's fault if the Conference fails on account of his not solving, even by so moderate assur-

ances, French security needs. Private advices that such action on his part would satisfy the French are also given the President.

Such steady reiteration that the future of the Conference depends on the President's courage, that he can save the Conference, and that on him rests the responsibility for failure—appears to us to be wholly French propaganda intended in the first place to see if it is possible to secure some American political assurances and in the second place to throw on the President or on the United States responsibility for failure.

These developments have been followed up here by considerable agitation from peace groups demanding that the President by such action save the Conference. Of course, the President has ignored all such activities entirely, but we thought that you ought to know what was going on, especially as there may possibly be an opportunity for this activity to be checkmated by you.

CARR

500.A15a3/721 : Telegram

The Chairman of the American Delegation (Stimson) to the Acting Secretary of State

[Paraphrase]

LONDON, February 28, 1930—7 p. m.
[Received February 28—6 : 29 p. m.[48]]

97. The lawyers representing the several powers have been meeting during the past week with a view to agreeing upon provisions of the treaty to regulate use of submarines in warfare.

Proposal has been made by us to adopt text of the first four articles, generally known as the Root resolutions, of treaty regulating use of submarines and noxious gases in warfare which all powers at Washington Conference in 1922 signed and which was subsequently ratified by all with exception of France.[49]

Being unable to obtain abolition of submarines we desired to obtain the most effective attainable restriction of their use. The best way to accomplish our object seemed to us to propose adoption of the first four articles of the 1922 submarine treaty on account of prestige they have derived from their acceptance by the Washington Conference, and from their ratification by the Senate of the United States and by the constitutional authorities of three of the other four powers.

It now seems clear, as a result of the preliminary discussions, that the French will not agree to article III of our proposal making pro-

---

[48] Telegram in three sections.
[49] *Foreign Relations*, 1922, vol. I, p. 267.

vision for trial and punishment, as if for an act of piracy, of persons who violate rules set forth in article I; and further that the French will not agree to article IV, which prohibits use of submarines as commerce destroyers as between the parties to the treaty.

The following clause has been proposed by the French representatives: "In operations against merchant vessels, submarines are bound to conform to the rules of international law which govern surface war vessels."

Our articles I, II, and IV might be acceptable to Italy, but objection is made to article III, which provides for punishment. The French clause quoted above is preferred by Italy to our article I.

Probably Japan would accept the four articles of the 1922 treaty as we have proposed, although the Japanese do not like article III. They may also have some suggestions in the way of verbal alterations.

Great Britain is willing to accept all four articles of the 1922 submarine treaty, but does not feel that article IV will be a real deterrent. The British think, moreover, that France cannot be induced to accept more than articles I and II.

My strong personal feeling is that the French proposal will be much less effective than articles I and II would be, in that the clause proposed would not make clear exactly what the rules of war required and, as a result, in the event of another war, it would not so strongly and promptly crystallize the public opinion of the world against possible submarine abuses. See speech by Mr. Elihu Root in support of articles I and II.[50] My personal inclination also is to favor article III, but I am keeping my mind open as to possible improvement.

If possible, I wish that you would consult Mr. Root and Mr. John Bassett Moore [51] and then give me the benefit of their views, as well as of your own, on the following questions:

1. Do you agree that articles I and II of the 1922 submarine treaty are a more desirable form of statement than is the proposed French clause?

2. Is inclusion of article III essential? Some hold opinion that the prescription of punishment of an individual for act ordered by his Government would not have much preventive effect.

3. In event that the number of powers participating in the submarine treaty were reduced from five to three, would you think desirable the inclusion of article IV, which prohibits use of submarines as commerce destroyers as between the three powers while other powers

---

[50] *Conference on the Limitation of Armament, Washington, November 12, 1921–February 6, 1922* (Washington, Government Printing Office, 1922), p. 268.

[51] Experts in international law. Mr. Root had been Secretary of State, 1905–1909; Mr. Moore had been Counselor of the Department of State, 1913–1914.

are not bound by this prohibition unless it be by later accession to the treaty? This last question is not to be considered from the standpoint of national policy but from that of the enforceability of articles I and II.

STIMSON

500.A15a3/728 : Telegram

The Ambassador in Japan (Castle) to the Acting Secretary of State

TOKYO, March 3, 1930—2 p. m.
[Received March 3—7: 52 a. m.]

35. Repeat to London.[52]
Telegram dated London, March 2, to the Tokyo *Nichi Nichi:*

"According to information gathered in various quarters, the Reed-Matsudaira conversations cover a discussion of the building of large cruisers after 1936. If the United States should increase its fleet to 18 after 1936, the United States would apparently be prepared to allow Japan to build one more large cruiser. It is believed that the United States proposes that until 1936 she should have 16 such cruisers. It is also receiving attention [that] the United States has proposed that with regard to submarines the United States should retain 60,000 tons and Japan about 50,000 tons."

Telegram dated March 1 from Dentsu Press Agency:

"The following is one of the important features of the proposal submitted by Mr. Reed to Mr. Matsudaira during the meetings which have been held since the 27th ultimo between these two delegates:

'Assuming that the United States were prepared to reduce the number of its 10,000 ton 8-inch cruisers and built instead a certain number of 9,000 ton cruisers armed with 6-inch guns, would Japan be satisfied with its present strength in 8-inch cruisers?'

It cannot be determined whether or not the foregoing is a definitive proposal; but the American naval authorities have been conducting investigations into the efficiency of 6-inch guns and are of the opinion that cruisers mounted with guns of this caliber could be profitably employed; in the light of which fact it is highly probable the report of Mr. Reed having made the foregoing proposal is correct."

For my confidential information I should be glad to know something of the nature of Reed's tentative proposals.

CASTLE

---

[52] Transmitted to the American delegation as Department's telegram No. 163, March 3, 9 a. m.

500.A15a3/728 : Telegram

The Acting Secretary of State to the Ambassador in Japan (Castle)

WASHINGTON, March 3, 1930—1 p. m.

41. I have repeated your 35 to London as I do not know the answer.

COTTON

500.A15a3/731 : Telegram

The Chairman of the American Delegation (Stimson) to the Acting Secretary of State

[Paraphrase]

LONDON, March 3, 1930—6 p. m.
[Received March 3—5:36 p. m.[53]]

103. For the President and the Acting Secretary of State. Your telegram No. 154, February 28, 5 p. m. The possibility of making any treaty may ultimately depend upon the question of political security and it may well become pivotal. I am sending this estimate of the situation on to you so that you may be fully prepared in case the necessity for quick decisions occurs. The French, we hear, will return to London next Thursday and the events will then undoubtedly move quickly. This is merely to prepare you for all eventualities and in laying the possibility of last measures before you, I do not mean to paint too dark a picture.

The French, at their last meeting before Tardieu left, demanded ten new and two old, 8-inch cruisers. MacDonald was not willing to concede any old ones and only seven new ones, which was one more than the British Admiralty advised. They had not reached the difficulties regarding the submarine program. Thus far no argument has made any impression upon the Italians, who are unyielding in their insistence upon parity with France. If Great Britain would offer them some kind of security in the Mediterranean, they could make concessions, they have privately indicated to us. The public anxiety and feeling against France suddenly aroused here by her demands is the serious factor in the situation and I am of the opinion that if France persists in her program MacDonald may find himself eventually unable to carry through even a three-power treaty on the basis of our present tentative agreement with a clause similar to article 21 of the Washington Treaty. MacDonald has stated that if necessary he is in favor of such a three-power treaty but it is possible, I believe, that in the last event public opinion may compel him either to demand a much higher building program than that

---

[53] Telegram in five sections.

now agreed upon between us or to remain entirely free. The following is the situation as to security proposals: The British originally declined to give a guaranty pact for the Mediterranean. Informally the British suggested a consultative Mediterranean Pact, but the French were of the opinion that it added nothing to the Covenant of the League of Nations. An alternative form of agreement along the lines of the Locarno Covenant [54] has been informally submitted by the French, and this alternative form of agreement is still under discussion between France and Great Britain. I have informed both Great Britain and France that, whether consultative or guaranty, America would not join in such a pact.

Briand has suggested on two occasions that eventually he would wish to discuss with me an amendment to the Kellogg Pact, a matter which had been broached last summer in conversations between Claudel and me.[54a] I told him that I should be glad to talk the whole matter over with him after these naval negotiations have ended. It is my surmise, though Briand has said nothing, that they will propose something in the nature of a *quid pro quo* for reductions in naval armament in the shape of an amendment to the Kellogg Pact. These are reasons why France might readily believe such a proposition on her part reasonable: (1) Because the need of additional machinery in the pact was brought up by me last summer, although what I had in mind was an investigative rather than a consultative clause; and (2) because the same suggestion for a consultative clause such as Briand now has in mind was made by Chief Justice Hughes last April.[55]

As you know, it is suggested by your cable that the proposal is being urged by the French indirectly through the press and otherwise. Our information is that the Locarno proposal is still under discussion and this proposal is much more according to France's wish. The danger to the naval treaty in the Senate, should any political agreement be presented as a condition, is recognized.

It does not seem to me, however, that the Kellogg Pact suggestion is inherently objectionable and if France should bring it forward its presentation to the Senate would almost necessarily have to be at a different time and as a different matter from the naval treaty, since much time for its negotiation with the other signatories would be required. I think, therefore, it should be given most careful consid-

---

[54] Treaty of Mutual Guarantee, signed at Locarno on October 16, 1925, by Great Britain, Belgium, France, Germany, and Italy; League of Nations Treaty Series, vol. LIV, p. 289.

[54a] See "Informal Suggestions for Further Implementing the Treaty for the Renunciation of War," *Foreign Relations*, 1929, vol. I, pp. 59 ff.

[55] Speech delivered by Charles Evans Hughes, President of the American Society of International Law, at the twenty-third annual meeting of the Society, Washington, April 24, 1929.

eration before rejection, should the point be reached where it offered the only solution to a complete failure of the Conference. The relations of the French with us make it easily possible to bring forward any such proposition directly and they should not be forced to use propaganda, and I am quite in harmony with the President's refusal to give attention to attempts made indirectly to get from him a pronouncement on the subject.

If the question of security arises when the French return, I plan, first, to encourage the making by the Mediterranean powers of a satisfactory pact among themselves; and, second, to urge the consultative features of article 21 of the Washington Treaty upon the French. These would probably have to be introduced into any new treaty in order to assure them of consultation with America as to naval problems which may in the future arise. The British will not consent to a three-power treaty if none of these steps are sufficient to save the treaty from failure. May I have the President's views as to how far a Conference resolution calling upon all the signatories of the Kellogg Pact for a consultative amendment to that pact can be supported by us? I append, in order that a full background of the matter may be before the President, a draft of the proposed treaty drawn up by us but which has been withheld awaiting a favorable opportunity to bring it forth at a time when final differences may be bridged by it. It has been shown to both MacDonald and Tardieu, but they have not been given copies. They are inclined to favor it. The consultative feature of article III has already been approved by the Senate, having been copied exactly from article 21 of the Washington Treaty. Here follows the present draft: [56]

"Article I. The contracting powers recognize the sovereign right of each power to determine for itself the amount and kind of naval armament necessary for its defense. They also recognize that in order to prevent competition in armaments and the international suspicion inseparable therefrom it is essential that each power in exercising its right should endeavor to adopt such a program of naval armament as will not alarm the other powers or be regarded by any of them as a menace, and such as to effect reduction of its naval armament to the lowest point consistent with national safety.

Article II. The programs of naval armament for the period ending December 31, 1936, herein below set forth have been adopted in accordance with the principles stated above. They are not intended to define the relative maritime interests of the several contracting powers.

Program of the United States of America:
Program of the British Empire:
Program of France:
Program of Italy:
Program of Japan:

---

[56] Quoted draft treaty not paraphrased.

Article III. The contracting powers agree not to exceed the programs herein set forth during the period ending December 31, 1936; provided, however, that if during the term of the present treaty the requirements of the national security of any contracting power in respect of naval defense are, in the opinion of that power, materially affected by any change of circumstances, the contracting powers will, at the request of such power, meet in conference with a view to the reconsideration of the provisions of the treaty and its amendment by mutual agreement.

Article IV. If at such conference a mutual agreement of the five contracting powers is not reached as to the amendment of the provisions of this treaty, then the power which has requested such conference may give six months' notice to the other contracting powers of its intention to alter its program and will inform the other powers of the exact nature of such alterations. Upon the expiration of said six months said power shall be free to alter its program accordingly. Upon receipt of such notice each of the other contracting powers, absolves itself from the obligations of this treaty and in such case may alter its program as it may determine for itself."

STIMSON

500.A15a3/731a : Telegram

The Acting Secretary of State to the Chairman of the American Delegation (Stimson)

[Paraphrase]

WASHINGTON, March 3, 1930—7 p. m.

167. [From the President.] Of course we are most anxious over the situation of the Conference. Due to French propaganda, the support of the American public is rapidly dividing. We could not hope to have the support of the war groups and we are rapidly losing support of the peace groups.

It appears to me that some vigorous leadership by the American group is needed. Unless France is prepared to take a real cooperative part we must prepare the way for three-power action, for it appears here that she has no intention of cooperating; and we must prepare for her isolation and assessment with responsibility.

Would you not consider making a definite proposal to the Conference, as a start, that parity should exist among all naval powers on destroyers and submarines, the latter at a maximum of 40,000 tons with an appropriate reduction, say 100,000 tons in destroyer fleets, both of these to be brought about prior to 1936 by obsolescence.

The following are the reasons:

1. Theory that the weaker naval powers do not need a large number of submarines unless they wish them for offensive purposes, because the submarine is the coast defense weapon for these weaker powers.

2. The American and British theory that we would be better off if submarines were abolished surely leads to the logic that we are proceeding to our objective if we can hold down the number of them.

3. Accomplishment of tonnage reduction is of great importance, economically.

4. It is important morally and the Conference would be saved from the present prospect of increasing world tonnage by attempts to limit instead of decreasing tonnage.

5. Parity should flatter Japan, France, and Italy. The responsibility will be placed squarely upon the shoulders of France for undermining the Conference should she oppose it. Japan and Italy should not oppose full parity and France would be isolated. It would restore confidence in this country back to the plane of our initial high purposes if such a position of the American delegation is made known and it would not seem necessary to await the return of the French delegation. The President submits the above.

COTTON

500.A15a3/731b : Telegram

The Acting Secretary of State to the Chairman of the American Delegation (Stimson)

[Paraphrase]

WASHINGTON, March 3, 1930—8 p. m.

168. [From the President.] Referring to the Department's telegram No. 154, February 28, 5 p. m., it is asserted here repeatedly and with assurance that you are personally in favor of expanding the Kellogg Pact by a Presidential declaration.

With regard to this question it is also asserted that the delegation is divided, and that Senator Robinson disapproves.

We do not believe either of these reports, but the agitation is assuming dangerous proportions, as witness the petition sent you this morning by the Foreign Policy Association. Such agitation will undoubtedly result in placing upon our shoulders the blame for the failure in relation to France.

From the beginning our assumption was that the Kellogg Peace Treaty marked a new era in international relations and that the provisions of this treaty warranted a reduction in strength by the naval powers of the world. Upon this thesis the whole Conference was launched and not upon the theory that before such a reduction could take place it would be necessary to have further political agreements. The Kellogg Pact would be repudiated if the Conference were launched on any other basis.

We are of the opinion that the American public in the end will resent French cooperation at the expense of expanding the Kellogg Pact and we are not disposed to expand it as the price of French cooperation. The objectives of such extension will be interpreted by our public as involving us directly in the politics of France for the purpose of giving them guarantees. The entanglement of political guarantees in these negotiations, though they may be indirect, is more dangerous than anything else to the whole American acceptance of results. We could expect only the most embarrassing and dangerous consequences if we were to make a declaration of what we believe to be the logical procedure under the Kellogg Pact in case of international controversy, under the present situation. If it were made at any other time than in connection with this Conference it might have no dangerous results.

The French, for instance, are bound to use it as a tangible justification for some action and this would in turn be proof to the people of this country of a dangerous involvement on our part with the Republic of France.

If any such political appendix is entered into by the Conference, Senator Robinson is being accepted by the Democratic Party to lead the opposition. Such a point of opposition would also be welcome to certain independent Republicans. I am of the opinion that even if the President were to make any coincidental declaration that could be interpreted as such a policy there would not be the remotest possibility of ratifying a naval agreement. Such a declaration independent of any naval agreement which might be entered into might have the effect of an acceptance of the naval agreement by the Senate, but it would certainly result in a reservation or a resolution denying the authority or binding character of any such declaration in order to humiliate the President or to serve political purposes. In order that you might fully understand our next telegram, the President has sent you the foregoing.

COTTON

500.A15a3/731 : Telegram

The Acting Secretary of State to the Chairman of the American Delegation (Stimson)

[Paraphrase]

WASHINGTON, March 4, 1930—7 p. m.

171. Your telegram No. 103, March 3.

1. Your position that the United States should join in no Mediterranean Pact but would not object to an agreement of this sort among other powers, is in accordance with our views.

2. In principle, we accept articles 3 and 4 of the form of treaty

proposed by you, and we agree that they follow article 21 of the Washington Treaty fairly closely. We are confident, however, that it would be an improvement if you could amend the concluding phrase of your article 3 to read "meet in conference with a view to agreement on alteration of the programs of naval armament." We also suggest omitting the words "the amendment of the provisions" in the first sentence of your article 4, and substituting "alteration of programs" in their place. It is our purpose by these changes to emphasize that the Conference is not to be on political matters or to cover joint naval action, but merely to deal with programs of construction or scrapping armament. We want, in other words, such a clause to be definitely different from the one in the Four-Power Pacific Treaty, thus making it impossible to misunderstand the clause as one under which there might creep into being a new Holy Alliance of the Allied and Associated naval powers.

3. With regard to amending the Kellogg Pact, it is our feeling that it is due to the pact that the state of the world has been so far changed as to permit this Conference to bring about a reduction in arms now. The United States feels proud of its share in initiating the pact with France and does not desire to be mixed up in efforts to amend it which may not be understood by some of its signatories and which may seem to go too far to some of them. We would, nevertheless, if France so desires, agree to take up and explore, entirely separately from the naval treaty, the possibility of a general agreement by all nations to initiate investigation of controversies which have not otherwise been settled, thus making public opinion more effective. On the other hand, we cannot agree to consult as to other coercive sanctions or to consult only with the allied naval powers. An agreement of this sort would be so diluted and attenuated as to be of no real value to the French even for temporary political purposes unless there were an exaggeration of its meaning. It cannot, moreover, be doubted that opponents of naval reduction would exaggerate it as an excuse for belaboring the results of the London Conference if the naval treaty included any agreement for consultation or conference.

Mowrer's [57] press reports and those of other correspondents close to Briand indicate that an all-round 25 percent cut in programs is likely to be proposed by the French. Such proposals are obviously put forward solely with a view to causing embarrassment and reinforcing in our mind the desirability of your taking some such action as indicated in our telegram of yesterday, No. 167.

We are not, as we see it, particularly interested in the size of the French fleet inherently, except in so far as it reflects on us through

---

[57] Paul Scott Mowrer, special correspondent for the *Chicago Daily News*.

boosting the British fleet, but it does seem to us that the Conference has reached a stage where our delegation is bound to be embarrassed by the French taking the offensive and raising serious disturbances in the United States, as they have already in various directions begun to do.

It seems to us from this distance improbable that there is any indication on the part of France of actually building a 725,000 ton fleet and that the British would be amply safe up to 1936 in proceeding with a program like the one we have outlined possibly even with such reduction in destroyers and submarines, and that a general provision that the British shall be free to take such steps as will give them protection in the event that the combined fleets of any two other powers, excepting the United States and Japan, shall exceed or threaten to exceed the British fleet.

Less even than France is Italy likely to build such a fleet and Britain would certainly be amply protected until 1936 under such an arrangement. It is not necessary to formulate in those terms the two-power condition.

The time has come, we strongly feel, for the American delegation to take the offensive against the French proposals by demanding a reduction in certain categories such as submarines and destroyers before the American public shall have become completely prejudiced against us through the French. The support of the American public would tend to be restored through any indicated demand on our part for limiting the tonnages now under discussion.

COTTON

500.A15a3/733 : Telegram

The Chairman of the American Delegation (Stimson) to the Acting Secretary of State

[Paraphrase]

LONDON, March 4, 1930—8 p. m.
[Received 9:11 p. m.[58]]

107. Department's No. 163, March 3, 9 a. m.[58a] Please transmit the following to Castle from Reed as the delegation's No. 27:[59]

The present situation in its bearing upon Japan is substantially as follows. The American naval proposal[60] and the subsequent Japanese proposal,[61] both made early in February, are the only formal proposals which have been submitted. There has been no recession on the part of either delegation from the positions outlined

---

[58] Telegram in two sections.
[58a] See footnote 52, p. 35.
[59] Transmitted to the Embassy in Japan as Department's telegram No. 43, March 4, midnight.
[60] See telegram No. 41, February 6, 7 p. m., p. 19.
[61] See *Proceedings of the London Naval Conference*, p. 244.

in these proposals, which you have received and which have also been published.

In the effort to devise suggestions to get around the deadlock, I have held frequent and informal meetings with Matsudaira. It has been suggested, but the suggestion has not yet been approved by either delegation, that the construction of our eighteen 8-inch-gun ships should be so planned that the last three should be laid down in the years 1933, 1934, and 1935, respectively. By this procedure Japan would be assured that we shall not have actually in service more than fifteen ships to her twelve when the next Conference will convene. We have worked out this schedule in connection with the general naval study of the possibilities of completing the construction called for under the proposals now being discussed between the Japanese, the British and our delegation. This suggestion is not inconsistent with the Japanese position and appears to preserve the American position. There seems to be no substantial dispute in regard to cruisers carrying 6-inch guns, as the Japanese demands are not in excess of what we are prepared to allow. They ask 105,000 tons in destroyers as against 150,000 tons for the British and Americans. Ninety thousand for Japan is our maximum. In view of the great preponderance in destroyers which we now have this appears fair.

The British apparently acquiesce in the suggestion concerning submarines which has been made to the effect that Britain and America should scrap down to 60,000 while all submarines becoming 13 years old between now and 1936 should be scrapped by Japan, thus giving the Japanese on that date 52,000 tons. The Japanese appear willing to accept the proposal on capital ships which was outlined in our original proposition for immediate scrapping and a construction holiday, it being understood that no new battleships to match the *Rodney* would be built by America or Japan. The fact that unless an agreement is reached on auxiliaries there can be no battleship holiday has been impressed upon them. Unless we can get a comprehensive treaty now, the Washington schedule must be adhered to as our delegation and the Washington administration will not yield at this point nor do I believe the British will do so. This fact should be strongly impressed on the Tokyo authorities.

A minimum of new construction outlay by Japan and the least possible scrapping of ships, which she now has, are called for by the suggestions now under consideration. Japan would be given by these suggestions in the two classes, which are its principal concern, 72 percent in 8-inch cruisers and 87 percent in submarines in actual commissioned tonnage at the time of the 1935 Conference. Naturally, however, at the completion of construction then under way if no change were made in the 1935 Conference Japan would be at approximately 60 percent in 8-inch-gun tonnage. If the Japanese insist on a flat 70 percent it can lead only to a disruption of the Conference and will necessarily arouse alarm in America and the demand that the treaty forbidding fortification of Manila be terminated. Our argument to the Japanese here is that our generous offer to scrap capital ships and half our destroyer fleet clearly shows our pacific intentions. It developed last night in conversation with the British that they are willing to go as far as, but no further than, the suggestions which have been made, especially with regard to the building of two additional 8-inch cruisers of 8,800 tons each by the Japanese. This proposal would clearly be cause for great alarm to Australia and New Zealand. It has been our effort to impress upon the Japanese that a large part of our cruiser, destroyer, and submarine fleet must remain in the Atlantic and at Hawaii and Panama. The Japanese would be given a clear supremacy over us in the Western Pacific by the suggestions we are now discussing. It is realized, I believe, by Ambassador Matsudaira that we have gone as far as it is possible to go in these suggestions and that even for this it will be difficult to get the unanimous approval of our delegation. Possibly Japan's naval officials think they can secure better terms by holding out, but you will be absolutely correct in assuring Tokyo officials that this is not the case, should the question be broached.

STIMSON

500.A15a3/734 : Telegram

The Chairman of the American Delegation (Stimson) to the Acting Secretary of State

[Paraphrase]

LONDON, March 4, 1930—9 p. m.
[Received March 4—8 : 20 p. m.]

108. For the President and the Acting Secretary of State. Your telegrams No. 167, March 3, 7 p. m., and No. 168, March 3, 8 p. m. Some of your inquiries have been answered in my telegram No. 103.[61a] I am glad to learn from your telegram No. 167 that you are willing to have parity in destroyers and submarines. Provided it can be done without precipitating a break with France, which we are still hopeful of avoiding, I agree with you that the present situation needs a new expression of the high purposes with which you initiated this movement toward naval limitation. Ambassador Edge,[62] who arrived today, is very confident that Tardieu and Briand will return to the Conference most anxious to reach an agreement. To reach any agreement, however, they regard some political pact as an essential condition. Morrow has been in continuous contact with Aubert,[63] who is the right-hand man of Tardieu during the interregnum, and Massigli,[64] who is the right-hand man of Briand. They are both hopeful that a satisfactory Mediterranean agreement can be reached with Great Britain and they assure him that the French desire to reach an agreement.

I am told that on Thursday Briand will be here to stay permanently and that MacDonald on Friday morning proposes to call the

---

[61a] *Ante,* p. 36.
[62] Walter E. Edge, American Ambassador in France.
[63] Louis Aubert, former Director of the Public Information Service, French High Commissioner's Office in the United States, and member of the delegation.
[64] René Massigli, head of the League of Nations Department, French Ministry for Foreign Affairs, and member of the delegation.

heads of delegations together. Tardieu cannot be absent from home continuously, for the position of the new French Government is not secure enough to permit it. He will be here for the coming week end and possibly subsequent week ends.

In view of the fact that MacDonald is Chairman and host of the Conference I believe he is entitled to be consulted before a step is taken which may vitally affect its outcome, therefore your proposition could hardly be put forward publicly by us without full previous conference with him for we already have different tentative agreement. Furthermore, we are not in the position to be sure that a three-power agreement is possible, although I have for 10 days been pressing him on the subject.

We think the Japanese attitude as to cruisers less defensible than that of the French; they have been adhering very stubbornly to position which we cannot accept. I think you will see, for all these reasons, that before your suggestion can be carried out it will require time and opportunity. I have not had an opportunity to confer with the delegation today for I have a cold and am confined to my house at Stanmore. I shall, however, confer with them and also Mac-Donald as soon as possible. I am glad to have your suggestions.

STIMSON

500.A15a3/738a : Telegram

The Acting Secretary of State to the Chairman of the American Delegation (Stimson)

[Paraphrase]

WASHINGTON, March 5, 1930—10 p. m.

178. Reference is made to your telegram No. 107, March 4, 8 p. m., and to our telegram No. 167, March 3, 7 p. m., regarding cuts in destroyer and submarine strength.

We would like to put the following before you merely for your consideration and without any final views on the subject:

(1) From our point of view a compromise with Japan giving her larger cruiser strength and reducing her strength in submarines and destroyers below present suggestions is a much less important concession than if the French were given any kind of direct or indirect political commitment.

(2) The Japanese fleet, assuming that it finally included 52,000 tons of submarines, 90,000 tons of destroyers, 6-inch cruisers in an amount which in your No. 107 is indicated as satisfactory to you, and with 8-inch cruisers in the amount even to that which in No. 107 you say is desired, would still be greatly inferior to the American fleet and no national anxiety as to our dominance in the Pacific in case of controversy need be caused by it.

COTTON

500.A15a3/737 : Telegram

The Chairman of the American Delegation (Stimson) to the Acting Secretary of State

[Paraphrase]

LONDON, March 5, 1930—7 p. m.
[Received March 5—4:20 p. m.[65]]

111. For the President and the Acting Secretary of State. Answering further your cables No. 167, and No. 171 to American delegation on March 3, 7 p. m., and March 4, 7 p. m., respectively. Both telegrams were carefully considered this morning by the delegation.

1. Your attitude regarding any proposal to amend the Kellogg Pact is clearly understood by us; it coincides entirely with our view. I have had a personal talk with MacDonald, since the arrival of your telegram; have explained to him our position on this matter; and have received his cordial agreement. We need not fear, therefore, that the British will add any pressure in support of such a proposal by France.

2. With regard to your submarine and destroyer-reduction proposal, contained in your telegram No. 167, the delegation is of the opinion that your suggestion with regard to an offer of parity at a very low figure in submarines may offer a valuable opportunity to improve our tactical situation. The whole delegation feels, however, that it cannot be done, without endangering the success of the Conference, before the French return to London. We will use it later after the Conference is under way and I have already begun to take such steps for its use.

I cannot explain at length at present but the delegation also felt that there were differences in the situation of the destroyer fleet which militated against taking a precisely similar situation as to destroyers.

3. MacDonald assured me today that he would go forward with the other powers in case the French would not join in an agreement. MacDonald is very anxious to make a four-power agreement, if possible, which would include Italy. We feel certain that Japan would not dare to remain out but in case they all prove obdurate he is willing to make a two-power agreement with us.

4. I am giving out tonight the following press statement in an attempt to relieve somewhat the pressure which is being brought upon you by peace supporters who are ignorant of the true situation: [66]

"There seems to be an impression that the work of the American delegation at this Conference is likely to result in an increase instead of a reduction in the tonnage of the navies of the world. The surest way to answer that is to give such results as seem to be within reach

---

[65] Telegram in two sections.
[66] Quoted statement not paraphrased.

up to date.   The plan which in its essentials appears to be acceptable to America and Great Britain provides for a net reduction in the tonnage of the American fleet, in capital ships, cruisers, destroyers and submarines, built, building or appropriated for, of over 200,000 tons and an even larger reduction on the part of the British fleet. If vessels authorized but not commenced were included in existing fleets the amount of the reductions would be much greater.

Of course these reductions are contingent upon some reductions being made in the fleets of other powers."

STIMSON

500.A15a3/739a : Telegram

The Acting Secretary of State to the Chairman of the American Delegation (Stimson)

WASHINGTON, March 5, 1930—8 p. m.

175. For Senator Reed from Huntley.[67]   Senator Moses told me today he does not share the view that a consultative treaty cannot be put through the Senate, and says that he does not see why anyone who subscribed to the Knox formula [68] in the League of Nations fight cannot support such a treaty if one should be signed as a by-product of the London Conference.   Considering Moses' prominence in anti-League fight, this statement is very significant.   Senator Watson says Fess sounded Senate key-note on Conference yesterday when, in the course of speech, he summarized administration achievements and reviewed Conference background.[69]

The principal features relating to this Conference of this speech are :

[Here follows a summary of the speech.]

COTTON

500.A15a3/741a : Telegram

The Acting Secretary of State to the Chairman of the American Delegation (Stimson)

[Paraphrase]

WASHINGTON, March 6, 1930—4 p. m.

181. I had a talk with Swanson and Borah, separately, today and I gave them a fair picture of my idea of the present situation of the Conference without showing them any of your cables.   They both

---

[67] T. A. Huntley, secretary to Senator Reed.

[68] The form of reservation proposed by Senator Knox of Pennsylvania on November 6, 1919, for consent to the ratification of the Treaty of Versailles (*Treaties, Conventions, etc., Between the United States of America and Other Powers*, 1910–1923 (Washington, Government Printing Office, 1923), vol. III, p. 3329) in such terms as would make the United States a consulting member of the League of Nations ; *Congressional Record*, vol. 58, pt. 8, p. 8000, pt. 9, p. 8742.

[69] Speech delivered by Simeon D. Fess, Senator from Ohio, on March 4, 1930 ; *Congressional Record*, vol. 72, pt. 5, p. 4666.

talked freely, although I told them I was not trying to commit them as to their views. Senator Borah stated that the best agreement would be with the five powers but a three-power agreement would be good. He also stated that a five-power agreement with any kind of a political pact would not be as good as a three-power agreement without a political pact. Borah stated that it is not so much the political pacts that he objects to but that the tonnage demands of France are impossible and France is behaving like a spoiled child. However, he is of the opinion that international trouble would more likely be created by a political pact than by giving Japan a couple of additional cruisers and France a great many more cruisers and submarines. Since he does not think they will build he does not care how many they have the right to build. Owing to the present conditions of the fleets and also the present trade conditions he cannot bring himself to fear Japan as an immediate potential enemy.

Swanson on the other hand dislikes political pacts and he fears the Senate's reactions and reservations on them. He would not consider a three-power agreement as bad. He does not like Japan and consequently does not want to give them much. On the whole, rather than political assurances and agreements, he would prefer to make concessions to France and Japan in cruisers.

COTTON

500.A15a3/741 : Telegram

The Ambassador in Japan (Castle) to the Acting Secretary of State

[Paraphrase]

Tokyo, March 7, 1930—9 p. m.

[Received March 7—12:40 p. m.[70]]

39. To be repeated to Reed in London.[71] I am grateful for your message, which was clear and interesting. I have been told by Shidehara that, with regard to your conversations, he had just received a personal message from Matsudaira. The figures were exactly those sent by you. This seemed extremely generous, I said, and if accepted by the delegations it surely was a basis for agreement. The several points were discussed and I made it very plain that the suggested revision of the capital ship program depended absolutely upon agreement on auxiliaries. He said, in regard to large cruisers, that since we were definitely allowed eighteen such an arrangement was a denial of the 10–7 ratio demanded by Japan. I told him that it seemed to leave the question open for the next Conference, and the fact that the requested ratio was more than maintained could be

---

[70] Telegram in two sections.

[71] Transmitted to the American delegation as Department's telegram No. 184, March 7, 11 a. m.

established in public opinion prior to that time by the Japanese Government. If our last three cruisers could be postponed until 1935, he said that agreement would be simple, that then another cruiser might also be asked for by Japan. My answer was that Great Britain would certainly have something to say in this regard and that American public opinion was of equal importance with Japanese; that if these demands which seemed excessive were insisted upon by Japan very bad feeling in America would certainly be caused, something far more to be feared than an extra cruiser or two; also that he was mistaken in saying that eighteen cruisers was what we wanted, for actually our minimum had been twenty-one, and furthermore in reducing to eighteen we had made a great sacrifice, and that the only compromise could not certainly be limited to ourselves. Shidehara is, I believe, personally willing to accept American suggestions in regard to the cruiser question but fears the opposition of the Navy. The telegram has been shown to no Navy men by him.

The submarine question Shidehara considered the most difficult and asked the reason for our great opposition to submarines. Our belief, I said, was that submarines were bound to be used in the way they had been used by the Germans. Denying that Japan would ever so use them, he stated that they were wanted by the Japanese Navy only for coast defense, that ratio was not a matter of concern inasmuch as Japan could never be attacked by American submarines, but that a certain number for coast defense was estimated as necessary. Japan, he said, not only would be ready to sign the Washington submarine treaty but, since France would not agree that submarines could not even be used for visit and search of merchant vessels, would gladly sign a new treaty with the United States alone. The London arrangement, I pointed out, involved more than Japan and the United States, and France would be encouraged in its demands by the large submarine tonnage for Japan. We were not discussing ratio, I pointed out, but only whether Japanese submarines should be scrapped down to 52,000 tons when they reached 13 years of age. The United States was offering to scrap at once a large part of its submarine fleet.

He heartily concurred when I told him that it would be a tragedy if the Conference should be disrupted by Japanese insistence on 70 percent. There was a clear understanding that our talk was as informal as yours and Matsudaira's. The suggestion made as to the submarine treaty was the only new one. Any discussion of fortifications was avoided because anything in the nature of a threat is not only ineffective but dangerous when dealing with the Japanese . . .

In addition, looking at it from the broader aspect, nothing would be more certainly disastrous to peace in the Pacific regions than the construction of further fortifications. Only as a last resort could this be justified.

CASTLE

500.A15a3/781

Mr. Elihu Root to the Acting Secretary of State

NEW YORK CITY, March 7, 1930.

DEAR MR. COTTON: I have your letter of March 3rd [72] enclosing the paraphrase of a cable despatch from Secretary Stimson saying that he would like my views upon three questions regarding the Washington treaty in relation to the use of submarines concluded February 6, 1922.

The first question is whether the first and second Articles of the Washington submarine treaty constitute a more desirable form of statement than the clause now proposed by the French in London, as follows:

"In operation against merchant vessels submarines are bound to conform to the rules of international law which govern surface war vessels."

My answer is a clear affirmative. The proposed French alternative is not merely a weaker statement but it is an abandonment of the chief and avowed purpose of the Washington provisions. That purpose is stated in Article Two of the Washington treaty in these words:

"so that there may be a clear public understanding throughout the world of the standards of conduct by which the public opinion of the world is to pass judgment upon future belligerents."

The rules of international law are known only to experts, who can always dispute about them indefinitely. Upon such a basis no clear public understanding can be reached and therefore no public condemnation can follow. If the French are unwilling to agree to the first two Articles, it would be infinitely better to have no treaty at all than to make a treaty in the form they propose, which would virtually be a retirement on the part of the United States, Great Britain, Italy and Japan from the statement of the rule and the effect of the rule contained in the treaty of Washington. About the only thing we could be sure of then would be that the statement of rules and the effect of them in the Treaty of Washington is not correct because all

---

[72] Not printed; see telegram No. 97, February 28, 7 p. m., from the chairman of the American delegation, p. 33.

the nations which joined in making that statement have given it up.

As to Articles Three and Four the situation is entirely different. They propose new provisions not yet forming a part of international law, and their omission from the new treaty would merely indicate that general acceptance of those provisions had not been reached, which is, of course, true. I think, however, that if a new treaty were made on the subject there should be a clause which prevented the new treaty from impairing in any way the obligations of Articles Three and Four between the powers which have entered into them.

I should think that the French would understand that a refusal to agree to Article Four of the Treaty of Washington was notice to the world that she intends to use submarines as commerce destroyers and that her refusal to agree to Article One is notice to the world that she intends to be as free as possible from any application of the rules of international law in the use of submarines as commerce destroyers.

To be more specific, I do not think the inclusion of Article Three is essential.

I do not think it desirable to include Article Four in a treaty to be signed by only three powers. The provision limited to three powers would necessarily be futile and it would rather tend to confuse the application of Article One.

If there is anything more I can do or say let me know and I shall be glad to do what I can.

Faithfully yours,   ELIHU ROOT

500.A15a3/742 : Telegram

The Chairman of the American Delegation (Stimson) to the Acting Secretary of State

[Paraphrase]

LONDON, March 8, 1930—11 a. m.
[Received March 8—9 : 15 a. m.]

121. Your telegrams No. 177, March 5,[72a] and No. 178, of March 5. We are making progress in our negotiations with Japan. We are close together and I believe that better results than in your telegram No. 178, March 5, can be had. Time, however, is necessary for such negotiations and no hurry is possible. There has been a basic change in the situation covered by your No. 178. Both the British Admiralty and Japan object to the 10,000-ton proposition and it is, therefore, not available. In addition serious aircraft carrier reduction is opposed by our entire delegation as well as Admiral Pratt, who has been most liberal on other matters; first, because the tonnage allotment of the Washington Treaty is probably low in proportion even to our proposed reduced fleet on account of the

---

[72a] Not printed.

development in aircraft in the last 10 years in which the American Navy has played a leading part; and second, because in the *Lexington* and *Saratoga* there is frozen a disproportionate amount of this tonnage and, since the expense of scrapping them would never be faced by Congress, there is practically no value in the theoretical suggestion of reserving a right to replace them. For a long time the matter has been carefully considered and we believe that to make a serious reduction without proportionate compensation would cripple the fleet in the feature in which it is most advanced. A slight reduction of 10,000 or 15,000 tons purely for moral purposes may eventually become possible but there is doubt even of that.

Yesterday the Kellogg Pact amendment was broached to me by Briand but my reply was that I considered such a suggestion wholly separate from the question of security in the Naval Conference and the subject was at once dropped by him.

I am informed by the British Government that they have practically abandoned the thought of giving any guarantee.

STIMSON

500.A15a3/743 : Telegram

The Chairman of the American Delegation (Stimson) to the Acting Secretary of State

[Paraphrase]

LONDON, March 8, 1930—2 p. m.
[Received March 8—11:40 a. m.]

122. The following to be repeated to Tokyo.[73] From Reed for the Ambassador.

With reference to your telegram (Department's No. 184, March 7, 11 a. m.),[73a] we continued negotiations yesterday with Wakatsuki and today with Matsudaira. The matter of the application of 20,000 tons is now the narrow margin of difference. All possible concessions have been made by us. We have offered to allow the Japanese to retain 20,000 tons of cruisers over 20 years of age but without the right to replacement in order that we may give apparent compliance with the Japanese popular insistence on 70 percent. Spreading this 20,000 tons over various categories of modern ships is asked by the Japanese. This would be fought bitterly by our Navy people, as well as by the British Admiralty and Dominions, and I know that it

---

[73] Transmitted to the Embassy in Japan as Department's telegram No. 44, March 8, noon.
[73a] See footnote 71, p. 49.

will not be acceptable to our delegation.   The actual effective strength of the Japanese will always be in excess of 70 percent during the life of the treaty on account of the proposed spread of our building program over the 6-year period of contemplated treaty.   It is hoped that this point will be conceded by the Japanese, for agreement seems impossible without this concession.

STIMSON

500.A15a3/782

Mr. John Bassett Moore to the Acting Secretary of State

WINTER PARK, FLORIDA, March 9, 1930.
[Received March 12.]

DEAR MR. COTTON: Your letter of the 3d inst. has just reached me.[74] I left New York on February 28th and have been traveling.

I have not read the Washington Submarine treaty since February 1923, and no copy of it is now at hand; but, speaking from memory, it is my impression that the proposed French substitute for Articles 1 and 2 may be taken to imply what those articles prescribe in detail.   I therefore assume that France would not hold out against those articles, although she might desire some changes in specifications or in phraseology.

Article 3 I have never myself been able to regard as sound or as practicable.   The word "piracy" has been and still is popularly and promiscuously used as an epithet to render odious things done on land as well as on the sea.   Take, for instance, the phrase "literary piracy."   But, to assume to classify and to punish as piracy acts done by individuals under public authority is contrary to the elementary legal conception of the pirate as a person who cruises and commits acts [not] authorized by a recognized government.   The article, in my opinion, is also incapable of just and effective execution, and, if its enforcement were attempted, would inevitably lead to reprisals.

The retention of the submarine as a commerce destroyer seems logically to exclude article 4.   The distinctive advantage claimed for the submarine, as a fighting machine, is, I believe, that it is the most effective means of discharging torpedoes, especially at battleships.   If there has been any proposal to abolish the use of torpedoes for offensive purposes, I have overlooked it.

Sincerely yours,   JOHN B. MOORE

---

[74] Not printed; see telegram No. 97, February 28, 7 p. m., from the chairman of the American delegation, p. 33.

500.A15a3/744 : Telegram

The Chairman of the American Delegation (Stimson) to the Acting Secretary of State

[Paraphrase]

LONDON, March 10, 1930—8 p. m.
[Received 8:40 p. m.]

126. For the President and the Acting Secretary of State. I took Morrow with me on Saturday morning and had a conference with Henderson. Henderson and Briand, I had learned, were about to meet and I wished Henderson to know clearly the American position in opposition to the consultative pact. A definite and clear statement of this was made to him. This precaution was a fortunate one, as it developed that he felt quite differently from MacDonald and such a pact had even been drafted by him.

That afternoon I had tea at Stanmore with Briand and Léger, with Morrow present, and had a long talk with them. I then told them that I had reached the conclusion that any blending of a successful naval treaty and the Kellogg Pact now would be disastrous to both; that I was a friend of both. I gave them a full and careful explanation of my position on the modification of the Kellogg Pact, filling in fully the background since last summer when the subject was first broached; and my reasons for the conclusion which I had reached. I told him why the papers in America relied on by him did not represent real public opinion on the subject and explained fully to him the situation as to that public opinion. The interview, which was long and friendly, terminated in his telling me that the matter was ended so far as he was concerned and that he fully understood my position.

Briand and Massigli had a long conference at Chequers on Sunday with Henderson and the Prime Minister, as I was told by the Prime Minister today. He had overruled Henderson, so he told me, on the subject of a consultative pact. The interview with Briand, he said, had been long and friendly, and any idea which Briand had had of a guarantee of military assistance was ended. The Prime Minister hoped that through some other formula an agreement with the French could still be worked out. He is thinking of inserting a preamble in the proposed naval treaty which would recite and reaffirm the Kellogg Pact as to the renunciation of war. The following sentence from the joint statement made at Rapidan [75] might possibly serve as the basis for such a preamble: [76]

"After full consideration our Governments resolve to accept the peace pact not only as a declaration of good intentions but as a positive obligation to direct national policy in accordance with its pledge."

[75] Foreign Relations, 1929, vol. III, p. 33.
[76] Quoted sentence not paraphrased.

Negotiations between the French and the British were resumed today, with Morrow, Robinson and myself present. This session later merged into a session of a subcommittee, which lasted all day and will continue tomorrow, for the purpose of analyzing the British-French figures. Morrow was present.

Morrow and I believe that a purely consultative pact would not help in reducing France's figures, unless the French people would falsely conceive such a pact to imply that we would give military assistance against an aggressor, and it seems to us that what France really wants is a security pact of mutual military assistance against an aggressor. We are convinced, in other words, that American newspapers such as the *Baltimore Sun*, the *World*, and the *New York Times*, which have been attacking the President for not favoring a purely consultative pact, are wrong in their belief that France would be satisfied with such a pact.

Reed, aided by me, has been carrying on negotiations with the Japanese contemporaneously with the foregoing negotiations. The negotiations with the Japanese are very tedious, as the Japanese, evidently in an endeavor to satisfy internal dissensions in their delegation, are bringing to us recurrent propositions which they know we will refuse; however, we believe we are slowly reaching a point of agreement with them which will be satisfactory.

The Italians remain noncooperative.

The reference to the Rapidan joint statement which the Prime Minister made last night in his broadcast was suggested to him by me in order that pressure on the President might be relieved by giving evidence that the Prime Minister did not expect America to cooperate in affairs in Europe.

STIMSON

500.A15a3/744 : Telegram

The Acting Secretary of State to the Chairman of the American Delegation (Stimson)

[Paraphrase]

WASHINGTON, March 11, 1930—4 p. m.

198. Just had a consultation regarding your telegram No. 126, March 10. There is no comment. The course which you are pursuing is all right; we do not well see how you could take any other.

If the information leaked out that what France wanted is a security pact of mutual military action against an aggressor and that a purely consultative pact would not help in reducing her figures, it might be helpful to public opinion here. It is impossible, of course, to do that here. The reporters who are supposed to represent the views of Briand give just the opposite impression in American papers. However, you will have to decide whether to follow this suggestion. You will understand that it is only a suggestion.

COTTON

500.A15a3/721 : Telegram

The Acting Secretary of State to the Chairman of the American Delegation (Stimson)

[Paraphrase]

WASHINGTON, March 11, 1930—5 p. m.

199. Your telegram No. 97, February 28, 7 p. m.

[Here follows the substance of Mr. Root's letter of March 7, printed on page 51.]

We have not yet heard from Mr. Moore. My feeling is that articles III and IV, to which Mr. Root refers, are of even less importance than he views them. To me, article III always seemed and still seems definitely unwise. I cannot imagine that a naval officer in command of a submarine would be affected by it in the least and I certainly do not believe in post-war trials. I should not think that it would be necessary to insert the clause he suggests preventing a new treaty from impairing in any way the obligations under articles III and IV of the powers which have entered into them. I agree with Mr. Root that inclusion of article IV in a three-power treaty is not desirable, and I do not regard it as essential in a five-power treaty.

With regard to articles I and II, I agree with Mr. Root that they are far better than the proposed French clause, but I would not agree that these articles could not be changed or modified in expression to meet the wishes of any of the powers; but because of its vagueness, the particular French expression seems to me very objectionable.

COTTON

500.A15a3/747 : Telegram

The Chairman of the American Delegation (Stimson) to the Acting Secretary of State

[Paraphrase]

LONDON, March 12, 1930—6 p. m.
[Received March 12—5 : 25 p. m.]

128. Your No. 198, March 11, 4 p. m. I had already had a conference with the press yesterday afternoon at which time I explained our position to them as to political pacts. I pointed out that America is already a party to many pacts which make consultations obligatory and that our objection to a consultative pact was not because of

its nature; that it was because the French would naturally feel, under the circumstances in which the proposed pact is presented, that it is an equivalent for their abandoned naval strength and they may claim reimbursement in kind in an emergency. All our best American reporters were present and they expressed themselves as understanding our position and as much gratified at having it explained to them.

MacDonald will not resign, though he lost an important vote in the House of Commons last night. His position has caused us some apprehension for some time for fear of a possible slip-up. It is quite possible that the Conservative leaders, though they are anxious to permit him to finish the Conference, might, by accident, lose control of their own followers.

I have come to the conclusion that both for the reason of the possible eventuality just mentioned and as a tactical maneuver against the delays which we are suffering from Japanese and French sources, we should proceed, therefore, with the drafting of a two-power treaty with Great Britain. I discussed the matter with MacDonald this morning, and he agreed with me. He also told me that he had specific information that the delays we have encountered during the past week with the Japanese were instigated by the French. Consequently, I had a conference with Wakatsuki this morning; after some further futile negotiations over figures, I told him that the adverse vote in the House of Commons last night had troubled me greatly, and that I was proceeding to close up with MacDonald. Although my statement was made under the usual pledge of secrecy, what I said will probably leak out and I advise you of it so that you may be prepared to back us up at home.

The proposed two-power treaty might cover all categories but carry a provision that the sections which relate to reductions under the Washington Treaty would not become effective unless and until a treaty with Japan is made by both Great Britain and the United States to cover all categories of fleets. An immediate treaty for a battleship equivalent or reduction between the British and ourselves would be just what the Japanese would most like, of course, as it would permit them to economize on battleship replacements and yet leave them free to proceed with their auxiliary construction.

Negotiations between Alexander for the British and Dumesnil[77] for the French with reference to the respective fleet figures are continuing, with Morrow sitting in. Alexander has been patient in handling the situation and has spoken very plainly to the French, but the latter are unyielding. Last evening he made them the offer

---

[77] Jacques-Louis Dumesnil, Minister of Marine in the French Ministry formed by Tardieu on March 2, 1930.

of 66,000 tons in submarines, that figure being the amount remaining in 1936 if they ceased all new construction. Dumesnil stated in reply that such figures were not even inside the zone of possible negotiation.

Tardieu is coming to London for the week end.

STIMSON

500.A15a3/747 : Telegram

The Acting Secretary of State to the Chairman of the American Delegation (Stimson)

[Paraphrase]

WASHINGTON, March 13, 1930—2 p. m.

207. Your telegram No. 128, March 12, 6 p. m.

(1) In regard to situation which has developed at the Conference, we agree, of course, that a two-power pact is better than nothing, but that a three-power pact would be very much stronger in all its implications. A serious question arises as to whether at the right moment, no doubt later on, we would not make some intermediate concession to the Japanese to bring them into the pact.

(2) We should also like to have your view as to whether the moment has not arrived when the President should issue a public notice in the nature both of an appeal and a definition of the American position. The reasons for the disavowal of a political pact under the setting staged by the French have appeared in the press here, but it would be desirable to have them formally and extensively rammed home to the American public. The pronouncement might be in the nature of an appeal for reduction and limitation, stating that these negotiations were undertaken in consequence of the Kellogg Pact, which is already a security pact of the first order; also a strong statement might be added on necessities of the world in the matter of naval arms. Then possibly a statement might be included to the effect that upon some entirely separate occasion when there could be no connection with question of French naval armament, the Government of the United States would be prepared to take part, as occasions arise, in investigatory processes, which would be for the general purpose of establishing public opinion but for no purpose of sanctions.

If it is your belief that such a statement as sketched would be advantageous, it is highly desirable that you formulate broad lines of it and send it to us.

(3) We assume that you still expect to draft a five-power treaty on humanization of use of submarines; in that regard, it does not seem to us to be important whether or not departure from the form of the Washington Treaty be made, nor do we believe that articles III and IV of that treaty are of real importance.

COTTON

500.A15a3/749 : Telegram

The Chairman of the American Delegation (Stimson) to the Acting Secretary of State

[Paraphrase]

LONDON, March 13, 1930—3 p. m.

[Received March 13—1 : 05 p. m.]

133. To be repeated to Tokyo.[78]

The following is the present situation : We have stood firm against allotting more than 108,400 tons of 8-inch-gun cruisers to Japan but our offer has been to defer until 1933, 1934, and 1935, respectively, the laying down of our last three cruisers. The offer of the Japanese has been to limit their 8-inch-gun cruisers to twelve in number, but they requested the privilege before 1936 of replacing the *Furutaka* class with 10,000-ton ships. Reed was told by Matsudaira that this had been suggested by you in Tokyo and in Washington. Reed's reply was that there must have been a misunderstanding.

We have stood fast at the present Japanese tonnage of 98,415 tons of 6-inch cruisers except when we agreed, in a talk between Stimson and Wakatsuki on Wednesday, to ascertain what view regarding a possible increase of Japanese 6-inch cruisers to 108,000 tons would be held by our Navy. Having discovered the bitter opposition of the Navy and the majority of our delegates to this increase, we are informing the Japanese delegates of its impossibilities today.

The Japanese appear satisfied with 97,500 tons of destroyers and the allotment of this much is agreeable to us.

Reed has held out in talks with Matsudaira for 60,000 tons of American submarines against 52,700 tons of Japanese, but yesterday in the Stimson-Wakatsuki talk it was intimated that parity at 52,700 might be acceptable. The Japanese would be satisfied with this we believe.

Particularly with regard to the French is the Conference situation at this moment critical. If Japan cannot agree with us within a few days, MacDonald has agreed with Stimson that we will prepare a two-power treaty establishing parity with Great Britain and America in auxiliary categories of fleets by which competitive building in them would be ended. The battleship program of the Washington Treaty will not be modified by this treaty since we will not do that unless by a treaty covering all categories in which Japan joins. You can readily see how favorable, in view of French difficulties, will be the public reaction in America and Great Britain if a three-power treaty covering all categories including battleships can be joined by Japan. An unfortunate effect correspondingly would

---

[78] Transmitted to the Embassy in Japan as Department's telegram No. 46, March 13, 2 p. m.

be caused by a Japanese refusal to join. It is essential to have an early decision.

That we have gone to the limit to accommodate Japan should be impressed upon Shidehara. The increase in speed limit of exempt vessels from 18 to 20 knots has been reluctantly agreed to by us. Maximum submarine displacement has been raised from 1,800 to 2,000 tons. Japan has been conceded the right to build two 5,000-ton minelayers in the special class, and we have agreed to allow her to retain in the special class for use as training ships five old cruisers of 43,690 tons. Parity in submarines and particularly 70 percent in 6-inch-gun cruisers has been agreed to by us. An agreement is impossible on the 70 percent ratio 8-inch-gun cruisers, as it would not be acceptable to Great Britain and our Senate. We can go no further.

STIMSON

500.A15a3/750 : Telegram

The Chairman of the American Delegation (Stimson) to the Acting Secretary of State

[Paraphrase]

LONDON, March 13, 1930—6 p. m.
[Received March 13—2:25 p. m.]

134. To be repeated to Tokyo.[79]   Our telegram of March 13, 3 p. m.
An agreement was reached with Wakatsuki and Matsudaira in further conversation with the Japanese this afternoon that the following limits for Japan will be recommended to their delegation and to Tokyo: 8-inch, 108,400; 6-inch, 100,450; destroyers, 105,500; submarines, 52,700. This will mean 60 percent in 8-inch, 70 in 6-inch, 70 in destroyers, and submarine parity. We have agreed to make the same recommendation to the British as well as to our delegation and to Washington. A reservation will be inserted by Japan to the effect that after the expiration of the treaty she may claim that 10,000-ton cruisers will replace the *Furutaka* class in 1943. A statement reserving the right to oppose this claim if then made will be signed by us.

STIMSON

---

[79] Transmitted to the Embassy in Japan as Department's telegram No. 47, March 13, 3 p. m.

500.A15a3/750 : Telegram

The Acting Secretary of State to the Chairman of the American Delegation (Stimson)

[Paraphrase]

WASHINGTON, March 14, 1930—3 p. m.

211. Your telegram No. 134, March 13, 6 p. m. We approve your recommendation to Japan.

COTTON

500.A15a3/755 : Telegram

The Chairman of the American Delegation (Stimson) to the Acting Secretary of State

[Paraphrase]

LONDON, March 14, 1930—3 p. m.
[Received March 14—2:10 p. m.]

136. For the President and the Acting Secretary of State. Your No. 207, March 13, 2 p. m.

1. Probably as result of my statement to Wakatsuki on Wednesday relative to a two-power pact, negotiations with the Japanese moved forward yesterday and culminated in an agreement supported by all our delegation and by the majority of Japanese delegation (see our telegram No. 134, last night). Settlement was submitted by us last evening to the British and approved by them. Wakatsuki and Matsudaira have agreed to use their earnest efforts to have it approved at Tokyo.

In view of the difficulties of negotiation we think this settlement very satisfactory. Admiral Pratt highly approves. By it the Japanese are held down to their existing construction of eight cruisers; they are allowed only about 2,000 tons additional 6-inch cruiser construction; their existing destroyer fleet is reduced by 17,000 tons and their submarine fleet is reduced to amount which it will reach in 1936 by obsolescence without any additional construction.

2. Alexander, Henderson, and Dumesnil on Wednesday afternoon reported to full committee on the negotiations as to the fleet figures of the British and the French. The committee was composed of the foregoing, with the addition of MacDonald for the British and Briand and Massigli for the French. Robinson, Morrow, and I sat in. Nothing came from the meeting but discouraging counter statements. The French adhered to their high figures and Dumesnil made unyielding statements of the absolute needs of the French. A tense atmosphere pervaded the meeting, and I said nothing as I

was afraid that the French might feel that our opposition amounted to a virtual combination with Britain. In all Conference circles on that evening there was great pessimism and Briand issued a pessimistic statement which indicated the impossibility of obtaining a substantial five-power treaty.

Morrow and I called on Briand and Dumesnil yesterday morning, at which time I stated as forcibly as possible our views on the impression which would be made on the American public by their figures. In an endeavor to maintain the friendly relations which we have had with the French and at the same time to impress them with the serious effect which would be produced upon relations with America by their attitude, I had made this statement the most carefully thought out one that I had yet made. At once Briand abandoned the assertions of absolute needs made by Dumesnil and limited himself to arguments which had as their basis relativity with Italy and the latter's stubborn position. Briand showed a much more hopeful attitude at the close of the conference and it found us joined in an effort to find means of accord with Italy.

3. Grandi,[80] in the meantime, had been worked upon by MacDonald, who reported to me that afternoon that Grandi had made some slight concessions toward giving figures for examination. At the close of the day a much more hopeful attitude prevailed than at the close of the previous day. There is much dependent on Tardieu's visit tomorrow.

During the conference Briand admitted that he had not expected me to yield to his suggestion of America's joining a consultative pact, but that he had made the application because he had been directed to do so. The possibility of securing a five-power pact which will be successful depends upon two things: (1) our ability to induce Italy to make some statement as to her needs; and (2) the possibility which still exists that Britain may give France some material assurance which would induce France to reduce her figures.

4. I think that a statement from the President along general lines suggested in our No. 128, March 12, 6 p. m., would possibly help. The delicate and critical situation may change with Tardieu's arrival. Will send suggestions as to what we think would be most likely to help situation here, after consultation with delegates, if it should be desired to make the statement.

STIMSON

---

[80] Dino Grandi, Italian Minister for Foreign Affairs, and head of the Italian delegation.

500.A15a3/752 : Telegram

The Ambassador in Japan (Castle) to the Acting Secretary of State

[Paraphrase]

Tokyo, March 14, 1930—6 p. m.
[Received March 14—7 : 07 a. m.]

44. Please repeat to London.[81] A personal suggestion made to you last February was the only reference I have ever made to the possibility of eventual replacement of the *Furutaka* class by 10,000-ton cruisers. It has never been mentioned here by me because I have never deviated from the original American program, except when conversing with Shidehara as fully reported in my telegram No. 39, March 7, 9 p. m., when I urged the generosity of Reed's attitude and stated that I was sure the limit of concession had been reached by the United States. This evening I will see Shidehara.

Castle

500.A15a3/760 : Telegram

The Chairman of the American Delegation (Stimson) to the Acting Secretary of State

[Paraphrase]

London, March 17, 1930—6 p. m.
[Received March 17—4 : 23 p. m.]

140. (1) A five-hour conference took place at Chequers yesterday between the French and British delegations. The true results of the situation are difficult to appraise, but Dawes and Morrow, both of whom have known Tardieu in past negotiations, share my impression that he hopes eventually to make a five-power agreement.

Tardieu is very stubborn in regard to his figures and is making great efforts to persuade both the British and us to help him to bring Italy down to a sufficient margin of naval inferiority. Whether he is doing this for domestic politics only or whether it masks some international order between the two nations, I am not yet able to determine. As our work progresses, the situation may be clarified. The French have stated the amount of tonnage superiority they demand over the Italians, and by taking old tonnage into consideration it is not impossible that such a tonnage superiority may be worked out from the *status quo*. Aside from this, however, Italy is trying to force France to concede formal naval parity, while

---

[81] Transmitted to the American delegation as Department's telegram No. 209, March 14, 10 a. m.

France is trying to force Italy to concede formal naval inferiority. Neither can hope to win this issue, yet neither one will yield.

MacDonald and I are trying to suggest some formula of mutual reservations and agreement upon a *modus vivendi* which is not to represent real maritime interests. I believe that if any solution is reached, it will be along some such line as this. I am assuming in all of this, however, that there is no secret military issue involved, and as to that I am not yet sure.

(2) In further answer to your No. 207, March 13, 2 p. m., I have consulted the delegation and we are clearly of the opinion that the situation would not be helped on this side by any Presidential statement. We are strongly opposed to any appeal, either here or at home, for reduction. Assuming that Japan ratifies the Japanese agreement, we shall have accomplished a three-power settlement which should receive, we believe, the hearty approval of the President and of the American public. When it was submitted to the President in February (our telegram No. 35, February 4), its adoption received his hearty approval. For him now to appeal for reduction would give, almost inevitably, the impression that he is in sympathy with the recent criticism of the pacifist press, which has of necessity been ignorant of the details of the settlement and of the difficulties against which we have labored. A result of that sort would be most unfair to the delegation.

As far as a statement regarding the consultative pact is concerned, my decision has been expressly accepted by both Briand and Tardieu, and accordingly there is no reason for such a statement here. The matter is no longer an issue in the Conference. The press summaries received from you seem to indicate that my statement has been accepted fairly well by the American press, even papers like the *Times* and the *World*, their former attitude being taken into consideration; but if the President wishes to ram home the subject still further, I perceive no great objection, from this end of the line, to doing so, except for the danger which always exists in stirring up a dead issue. It is our general impression that it would be better to withhold all Presidential statements until our negotiations are concluded, when a statement from him will undoubtedly be very helpful in bringing home the character of such a settlement as we may accomplish and the reasons for it.

STIMSON

500.A15a3/761 : Telegram

The Ambassador in Japan (Castle) to the Acting Secretary of State

[Paraphrase]

Tokyo, March 18, 1930—3 p. m.
[Received March 18—9:05 a. m.]

48. Please repeat to London.[82] There was published last night a statement alleged to have been made by the Japanese Navy Department which has undoubtedly been repeated to London. The statement gives fairly accurately the figures of the tentative agreement but it interprets them most unfairly and would appear to be intended to make difficult Japanese official consent. The final paragraph reads as follows: [83]

"The latest American proposal constitutes a concession in appearance but in contents it still adheres to its own contentions. Due to ignorance of this fact or due to propaganda for some ulterior purpose, reports are being circulated to the effect that the United States has recognized Japan's demand. This gives the people of Japan exceedingly erroneous information. The Japanese Navy by no means accepts such a proposal."

The Vice Minister of the Foreign Office, Yoshida, said that Shidehara immediately telephoned the Vice Minister of the Navy, who, it is stated, knows nothing of the statement and will issue a denial that it was of an official nature. The Vice Minister believes that some person in the "big navy" group gave out the statement. The papers are absolutely incorrect in alleging that the Premier passed on the statement. As the denials never have the effect of the original statement, the Foreign Office is very angry, for this makes its task more difficult. I told him that it utterly discouraged me when I saw it because it looked like a failure in London by which relations for years would be embittered. Without an agreement in London, I reminded Yoshida, the cruiser law presumably would be carried out as it stood. They knew this, he said, and Baron Shidehara was preparing a strong statement to be presented at the Friday meeting of the Cabinet. The necessity for prompt and favorable decision was again urged by me since the limit of concession has been reached by the United States. Anything further, I reminded him, would probably not in any case be acceptable to Great Britain since the question is by no means solely between the United States and Japan. Then he desired to know whether I believed England would sign a three-power treaty with the figures which the delegations have agreed to recommend to their Governments, if France persisted in the stand which it has taken. He was informed that I naturally

---

[82] Transmitted to the American delegation as Department's telegram No. 225, March 18, 9 a. m.
[83] Quotation not paraphrased.

could not interpret British views but that it appeared probable to me that Great Britain would accept either of them if a political clause calling for further discussion in case the French construction program became menacing, were added. I do not believe that the situation here is as bad as has been made out by the papers.

CASTLE

500.A15a3/762 : Telegram

The Chairman of the American Delegation (Stimson) to the Acting Secretary of State

[Paraphrase]

LONDON, March 19, 1930—5 p. m.
[Received March 19—1 : 03 p. m.]

145. In an effort to bring matters to a head, we are holding conferences constantly. However, there are no further definite results that I can report at this time. I learned on Monday through Japanese delegation representative that the French were endeavoring to get the Japanese to raise their figures regarding submarines. Castle in Tokyo confirmed this later. This effort was reported to us by a representative of the Japanese delegation and we together with the British are taking steps to accelerate this tentative agreement by the Japanese Government at Tokyo. We are still hopeful that the Japanese Government will ratify our tentative agreement without any substantial alterations but our informant here thinks that there is a real controversy between Japanese civil government and the naval party there.

As to whether the French are merely protecting their position to maintain their present high tonnage figures or whether they are making an effort to break up the Conference, there is a difference of opinion here. We are doing our utmost to combine patience with energy in bringing the situation to a focus. We are inclined toward the former hypothesis but we are not neglecting to prepare ourselves against the latter.

STIMSON

500.A15a3/765 : Telegram

The Chairman of the American Delegation (Stimson) to the Acting Secretary of State

[Paraphrase]

LONDON, March 19, 1930—7 p. m.
[Received March 19—5 p. m.]

147. The following as substitute for subdivisions 1 and 2 of article 1 of submarine treaty was suggested by Malkin, legal adviser of British Foreign Office: [84]

---

[84] Quoted passage not paraphrased.

"1. In their action with regard to merchant ships submarines must conform to the rules of international law to which surface war vessels are subject;

2. In particular except in the case of persistent refusal to stop on summons, or of active resistance to visit or search, a warship, whether surface vessel or submarine, may not sink a merchant vessel without having first placed the passengers, crew and ship's papers in a place of safety. For this reason the ship's boats are not regarded as a place of safety unless the safety of the passengers and crew is assured, in the existing sea and weather conditions, by the proximity of land, or the presence of another vessel which is in a position to take them on board."

Mr. Root's purpose of clearly defining for the benefit of public opinion the rules of international law preventing inhumane practices against merchant vessels are fully met, in the opinion of Malkin and my own adviser, Rublee, in the foregoing. Both Malkin and Rublee believe it an improvement in its definition of "a place of safety". In their opinion French criticism of Root's article for combining rules of visit and search with rules for protecting life is to a certain degree well founded and they feel that in that respect this proposal is superior.

The fact that it comes from the British who are chiefly interested in limiting submarine attack against commerce and the fact that it may satisfy the French who are actively opposing the Root form makes it worthy of careful consideration but I am not committed to this, however. Does Root see any serious objection to this substitute? I should like to know.

STIMSON

500.A15a3/766 : Telegram

The Ambassador in Japan (Castle) to the Acting Secretary of State

TOKYO, March 20, 1930—11 a. m.
[Received March 20—9:05 a. m.]

51. Repeat to London.[85] My 50, March 19, 4 p. m.[86] The *Nichi Nichi* this morning carries the following article:

"Admiral Kanji Kato, chief of the Naval Staff, and Vice Minister Admiral Kobayashi called on the Prime Minister yesterday afternoon. There was a full exchange of opinion, Admiral Kato going into the American proposal at great length and explaining the effect which it would have upon the disposition of Japanese naval forces. He pointed out that while there was virtual agreement over the demand for the global ratio in auxiliary vessels, the inferior ratio of 60

---

[85] Transmitted to the American delegation as Department's telegram No. 234, March 20, 9 a. m.
[86] Not printed.

percent in heavy cruisers and the inability of Japan to construct new submarines before 1936 made it impossible for Japan to accept the proposal. He then went on to say that as Japan had gone so far as to surrender parity and accept the 70 percent ratio, which is the minimum compatible with national security, as the basis of the agreement it now remained for the United States to make the next concession. After the Prime Minister had put several questions regarding the future of the Conference, Admiral Kato brought out his last and final plan. He proposed that the Government should explore the possibility of establishing a political treaty to cover the Pacific and to include Japanese-American relations with respect to China. Mr. Hamaguchi promised to give the suggestion the most careful consideration."

CASTLE

500.A15a3/766 : Telegram

The Acting Secretary of State to the Ambassador in Japan (Castle)

[Paraphrase]

WASHINGTON, March 20, 1930—5 p. m.

53. Last two sentences of your telegram No. 51, March 20, 11 a. m. We hope that the Japanese Government will not formulate any proposal along this line. The Department is of the opinion, in view of existing treaties already in force, that no useful purpose is likely to be served by a further political treaty with Japan relating to the Pacific. Furthermore, the Department considers, in view of the history of Anglo-Japanese Alliance and Lansing-Ishii notes, that it would be gratuitously offensive to China and a possible source of embarrassment to have relations with China determined or defined by a treaty between Japan and the United States in which China would not be included. If the matter is broached to you in any connection, you should not give any encouragement to this idea unless otherwise instructed by the Secretary of State.

Our delegation informed of the foregoing.

COTTON

500.A15a3/768a : Telegram

The Acting Secretary of State to the Ambassador in Japan (Castle)

[Paraphrase]

WASHINGTON, March 20, 1930—6 p. m.

54. You may emphasize the following: After conference with leaders, we are convinced that present naval proposals to Japan are all it would be possible for us to attempt to carry. Alternative is full twenty-three cruiser program.

COTTON

500.A15a3/768 : Telegram

The Ambassador in Japan (Castle) to the Acting Secretary of State

[Paraphrase]

Tokyo, March 21, 1930—noon.
[Received March 21—4 : 23 a. m.]

53. Yesterday Shidehara assured me that he was exploring every possibility to bring about acceptance by Japan; he stated that he was in communication daily with Hamaguchi and the Navy but that he was not optimistic. He promised to bring the contents of your telegram, which I gave him in writing, to Hamaguchi's attention immediately. He evidently was opposed to my approaching the Prime Minister directly; if I saw Hamaguchi personally, sensational articles might do great damage for the press is watching every move.

It is Shidehara's understanding that on replacement of *Furutaka* class it was agreed that at the next conference Japan should have the right to demand replacement by one 10,000-ton cruiser when our 16th had been built, another when our 17th had been built, and another when our 18th had been built. He stated he was not sure that the United States reserved the right to oppose but that England had reserved this right. I told him that we reserved the right to oppose; that the original idea had been that Japan would claim right to replace *Furutaka* class by large cruisers in 1943 but I would consult you as to whether the situation had changed any. He was of the opinion that only the British opposed the idea at present. I told him that the United States, I felt, was firm for the 10–6 ratio in 8-inch cruisers because these were associated, in some way, with capital ships, and that because Japan agreed to this ratio the United States had agreed not to fortify its Pacific possessions. Failure to reach agreement, I impressed upon him, could only lead to a full resumption of the building program of the United States.

With regard to the Reed-Matsudaira conversations, Shidehara stated that Japan did not have a full account of them and this was one difficulty because the Navy keeps asking if this or that proposition was advanced by them. I feel that decision cannot be reached until next week for he has not asked for full information on certain points.

Shidehara's vigor of presentation or willingness to take responsibility should not be distrusted for I am sure he fully realizes that his statesmanship is at stake.

Please repeat to London.[88]

CASTLE

---

[88] Transmitted to the American delegation as Department's telegram No. 238, March 21, 5 a. m.

500.A15a3/769 : Telegram

The Chairman of the American Delegation (Stimson) to the Acting Secretary of State

[Paraphrase]

LONDON, March 21, 1930—5 p. m.
[Received March 21—3 : 58 p. m.]

149. Repeat to Tokyo.[89] Agreement of the three delegations in regard to replacement of *Furutaka* class is that a reservation will be inserted by Japan to the effect that at the next conference she will be free to claim the right of replacement by a 10,000-ton cruiser of each vessel of that class when 20 years old. This right of replacement will not be conceded by Great Britain or America and if it is then asserted each will be free to oppose the claim. As your telegram stated, your understanding of the matter is still correct. We have been repeatedly asked by Matsudaira to surrender on this point and until it became clear that neither Great Britain nor ourselves could yield, he did not abandon his insistence.

Our agreement is here continually claimed by the newspapers as an American proposal and they say that in Japan a counterproposal is being considered. The lack of a public statement by either the Japanese delegation or the Tokyo authorities that this is not an American proposal but is in fact an agreement reached by the three delegations, is surprising to us. Should Tokyo repudiate this agreement we would have difficulty in continuing to negotiate with a delegation which is without power and which its Government does not support. If the proposal is repudiated by Tokyo or a so-called counterproposal is sent we will immediately commence preparation of a two-power agreement with Great Britain on auxiliary categories and the American delegation will return to Washington on the termination of that agreement.

Because we have been urgently requested by Wakatsuki and Matsudaira to say nothing until the Japanese Government has acted we have refrained from making any press statement.

STIMSON

---

[89] Transmitted to the Embassy in Japan as Department's telegram No. 55, March 21, 5 p. m.

500.A15a3/770 : Telegram

The Chairman of the American Delegation (Stimson) to the Acting Secretary of State

[Paraphrase]

LONDON, March 22, 1930—1 a. m.
[Received March 21—10: 30 p. m.]

152. Tyrrell [90] this evening has advised MacDonald from Paris that the following position has been decided upon by the French:

1. The French believe that their delegation cannot do anything more in London so long as France is being asked by Great Britain to lower her figures without entering into a Mediterranean agreement with her and so long as Italy's demand for parity continues.

2. Therefore, if the British have decided to refuse a Mediterranean agreement and can do nothing more with the Italians and also will agree to let the French figures stand as they are, the French will help wind up the Conference with a report to the League which would contain certain agreements with respect to the regulation of reduction, naval holiday for certain construction, methods of limiting naval armament, and so forth.

Of last two clauses the former refers evidently to a battleship holiday and the latter to certain recommendations of a minor character made by a subcommittee.

The British press is asked by Tyrrell to exercise restraint; he reports that the French press, though quiet, is well informed. He expects to have a conference with Briand tomorrow to confirm the foregoing. According to information which Tyrrell has received, Briand will not return to London for several days and Tardieu will be away until the 31st, unless given assurance of [security pacts?] along above lines. In the latter case they might return earlier.

A meeting of the heads of delegations will probably be called by MacDonald tomorrow afternoon to consider this. It is my belief, based upon my observations of the effect of the French attitude throughout the Conference on other delegations and on public opinion here, that this will end the attempt to secure a five-power agreement and that MacDonald will try for a smaller one. Owing to the restlessness of the public, there is grave doubt in my mind whether serious mutual press recriminations can be successfully prevented. In the light of MacDonald's efforts, through which some real but slight steps toward reconciling the figures of the French and Italians have been made, and also because of the setback to the cause of the desire of Europe for peace, this would be a great pity. MacDonald and Craigie think that tonight's decision will represent an effort by

[90] Sir William G. Tyrrell, British Ambassador in France.

Tardieu, under the influence of certain extremists, to force the issue in France's favor. If so, it will almost certainly not succeed and the result will probably be that the security France already has will be greatly diminished. Our refusal to enter a consultative pact, as you will notice, is not mentioned by the French as a reason for their action. The view which I formerly expressed that there was no intention on their part to rely upon such a pact from us is confirmed by this.

STIMSON

500.A15a3/771 : Telegram

The Ambassador in Japan (Castle) to the Acting Secretary of State

[Paraphrase]

TOKYO, March 22, 1930—11 a. m.
[Received March 22—4:31 a. m.]

54. Your telegram No. 53, March 20, 5 p. m. I think that there is no danger that this matter will arise unless it is mentioned in the press. The Government here has not considered it, so Shidehara tells me; one reason is that it would scarcely be possible to arrive at a formula by which China would not be irritated. We are not more sensitive than he is on this point. He was told that, despite anything the press might say, we should always consider the Kellogg Pact as effective as in any other connection so far as China was concerned and that there was no necessity of committing this to paper. Please repeat to London.[91]

CASTLE

500.A15a3/773a : Telegram

The Acting Secretary of State to the Chairman of the American Delegation (Stimson)

[Paraphrase]

WASHINGTON, March 22, 1930—1 p. m.

244. To press for three-power agreement is the only thing we can see to do.

COTTON

---

[91] Transmitted to the American delegation as Department's telegram No. 242, March 22, 10 a. m.

500.A15a3/765 : Telegram

The Acting Secretary of State to the Chairman of the American Delegation (Stimson)

[Paraphrase]

WASHINGTON, March 22, 1930—2 p. m.

245. Your No. 147, March 19, 7 p. m., last paragraph. It is Mr. Root's opinion:

1. That the Washington Treaty is superior to the proposal of Malkin in that the latter does not directly state the rules as a foundation for public opinion.

2. That the substance of what is most important is included, however, and

3. That a valuable addition is made by the clause as to what is meant by safety.

4. That the change would be compensated for by French ratification. At the same time he thinks that the criticism that the Washington provision joins search and seizure regulations with rules for protection of life has no merit.

The rights of search and seizure furnish the only foundation for the right to threaten lives on a merchant vessel, and the only basis for the protection of such lives rests upon definite rules pertaining to such rights.

COTTON

500.A15a3/774 : Telegram

The Ambassador in Japan (Castle) to the Acting Secretary of State

TOKYO, March 23, 1930—noon.
[Received March 23—4:33 a. m.]

55. Your 55, March 21, 5 p. m.[91a] Repeat to London.[92]

Wakatsuki gave out a statement that this is not an American proposal but an agreement which was reached by three delegations. His statement was published in all the Japanese newspapers yesterday morning.

CASTLE

[91a] See footnote 89, p. 71.
[92] Transmitted to the American delegation as Department's telegram No. 248.

500.A15a3/776 : Telegram

The Chairman of the American Delegation (Stimson) to the Acting Secretary of State

[Paraphrase]

LONDON, March 23, 1930—3 p. m.
[Received March 23—11: 20 a. m.]

155. Castle has been sent the following telegram:

"If Shidehara is satisfied and you think it advisable to deliver to Hamaguchi a message from me, you might do so along the following lines:

'It is my feeling that the greatest naval powers of the world are presented with an opportunity to consolidate the good relations existing between them. The removal of all question of competitive building would mean progress together in the direction of the pacific growth of the future welfare of these three great peoples. The stability of the peace of the whole world would be increased as well.'

You should tell Hamaguchi that Shidehara has seen this. I hope that I have made it clear that the delivery of the message is not to be made unless thought wise to do so by both you and Shidehara. It is our desire that nothing be done which the opponents of the agreement would misconstrue."

STIMSON

500.A15a3/777 : Telegram

The Chairman of the American Delegation (Stimson) to the Acting Secretary of State

[Paraphrase]

LONDON, March 23, 1930—9 p. m.
[Received March 23—7: 32 p. m.[93]]

156. The following is our survey of the situation.

(1) Negotiations as to the relative size of their fleets have been conducted by the French and the Italians and by the French and the British. On some of these negotiations, particularly those between the British and the French, we have sat in at the request of both sides. I have conferred many times with MacDonald, Briand, and Tardieu, in addition to which Morrow has kept in constant touch with Aubert and Massigli. The French, in coming to the Conference, we believe desired it to succeed; however, from the first they have insisted upon a mutual assistance security pact in which Britain would participate. France would have substantially reduced her figures, we think, had she gotten such a pact. Whether under Britain's two-power European standard such reduction would have been enough to meet the figures in the agreement we have had with Great

---
[93] Telegram in six sections.

Britain we cannot say, because negotiations between Great Britain and France have not gotten that far. We have never been asked directly by France to give her a consultative pact; and we are certain, on information we have gotten, that even had such a pact been offered she would not have, on that basis alone, reduced her figures.

(2) A pivotal point in preventing an agreement between the British and the French has been the unwillingness of MacDonald to satisfy the French on the subject of European security. In his former administration, you will remember, the protocol idea, so-called, with the purpose of strengthening the League of Nations sanctions even to military protection against an aggressor, was partly his doing. The subsequent Conservative Government repudiated this tentative arrangement for the protocol. Chamberlain substituted Locarno for this protocol idea. The French assert, in this regard, that the hope was held out to them by the British that the League would be strengthened not by a sweeping agreement for sanctions but by a series of regional pacts, the parties to which would be those countries having a vital interest in the particular regions to be protected.

Ten months ago when MacDonald entered office there was under way in England a decided reaction against that country entering into any further sanctions through which they might become involved in a continental struggle. With the coming of our negotiations, the French demand for security through a Mediterranean Pact, which was suggested by them in their December note, was refused by MacDonald, who has not since forsaken that position. Two weeks ago French disquiet was added to by his public statement in opposition to entangling alliances. The French claim that they cannot understand this change from Britain's former attitude toward them. It would now be difficult, and perhaps impossible, for the MacDonald Government to reverse itself completely in this position, as there seems to be an increasing volume of public opinion in Britain in support of MacDonald's attitude toward keeping free from further entanglement in continental affairs. Not all members of his own Cabinet, however, have heartily supported this position. Henderson, who was at Geneva for seven weeks negotiating the protocol in 1924, feels, and has always felt, that Britain, provided she could get in return definite naval reduction from France, should add to or at least reaffirm definitely her European obligations. He criticizes France on the ground that she does not offer great enough reduction of armament in return and not because she asks for more security. In brief, he feels that France never gave sufficient consideration in return for the Locarno Agreement, although he feels it was all right for Britain to join this agreement and even the protocol idea. The permanent officials of the British Foreign Office, who realize that they must continue to have France as their nearest neighbor, seem to share Henderson's feeling. Tyrrell, who is now in Paris and who has much weight with the permanent officials, we have been told, shares this view.

(3) The British effort, in place of the security pact, has principally been to endeavor to secure from Italy for France a reduction corresponding to or greater than that which she asks of France in order to force the latter's figures down. We have from time to time been invited to sit in on these negotiations by both sides as friendly impartial counselors, but have taken no part, though we have been present. No substantial success has come from these negotiations. France and Italy, both of whom have been very stubborn in their demands for parity in the one case or superiority in the other in naval strength, have toward the end shown some willingness to set aside their theoretical positions and instead to stand upon reservations thereof with the aim of adopting a *modus vivendi*. Willingness to make concessions with regard to over-age tonnage has been asserted by both, but as the matter stands neither has made any concessions in building programs or under-age tonnage.

British opinion considers France's submarine and perhaps her cruiser program a serious menace, though we do not believe she is consciously building against Great Britain. A series of unpleasant incidents, which have occurred recently, have been the basis of suspicion and fear of France and Italy toward each other. I have no evidence of any danger to peace between the countries which is specific and imminent.

(4) The outcome of the interview between Tardieu and MacDonald last Sunday, which was unfortunate, has complicated the situation during the past week. Apparently MacDonald gave the French some ground for their belief that he has appealed to Mussolini through the Ambassador to get more definite figures. It was apparently through a French source that the possibility of British influence at Rome leaked out to the press. Both the Italians and MacDonald were greatly irritated. A dispute on fact arose between the French and English as a result. There had already existed a distrust between MacDonald and Tardieu, which has been added to temporarily at least by this incident. The incident has also brought forth a strong statement from the Fascist Council giving unqualified support to insistence upon parity by Grandi. Of course we had no representative at the meeting at Chequers, and I did not know of any action which was being taken in Rome by MacDonald. I had, however, solely for his information, apprised Garrett of the situation.[96]

---

[96] John W. Garrett, American Ambassador in Italy.

(5) Since day before yesterday when I sent my No. 152, MacDonald and I have not talked; but on Sunday Craigie told me that Massigli has tried to soften the position taken by the French as reported by Tyrrell from Paris and claims that that report is exaggerated; that there is no intention by Tardieu and Briand to end negotiations, but that the latter will be back Tuesday.

(6) It will be seen from the foregoing that two fundamental controversies exist, the first between the British and the French and the second between the French and the Italians. We can properly take no leading part in either. The parties to the controversies must themselves work out their problem with such friendly help as we can give. A mistaken idea as to the fundamental nature of the controversies is the basis, we think, for the idea of the American press that by some simple act or statement we could bring about their solution.

(7) The following is our position with reference to a consultative pact:

I have made clear to Briand and Tardieu that a consultative pact is not inherently objectionable to us, as we have already joined many of them, of which the Washington Disarmament Treaty was one. I told them that there was little doubt that a consultative provision with respect to matters of naval program in a treaty growing out of the Conference would be favored by us. I have made clear that our objection was to a pact which, because of the circumstances under which it would be given, would be considered as a *quid pro quo* for French reduction in naval armament; that we objected to any pact which might be the basis of a future demand for military assistance. Tardieu and Briand have both told me that they fully appreciated that no pact could be given by us which was subject to any construction of an implied promise of military assistance. We have been assured by the French that what they wanted and must have as a condition precedent to reduction of their program was a treaty of mutual assistance with Britain, or at least that Britain's existing obligations under the Covenant of the League of Nations be amplified or clarified. They consider this especially important, because they believe that Britain apparently wishes to back away from the European commitments which she already has made. A reason or plausible excuse is thus afforded France for getting a navy of some kind with the possibility facing them of confronting a European situation with Great Britain neutral. French public opinion, from the best sources we have, is solidly behind Tardieu and Briand. What the French are asking of Great Britain is understandable if we consider the continental agreements of the past decade, though we have no sympathy with their action. Our belief is that France is seeking to force participation in European sanctions by Britain through a French naval program very alarming to public opinion in England. This is particularly true with reference to France's submarine program. Due to this the future of European politics gives us serious anxiety.

(8) Should Great Britain and France resume negotiations it is possible that a situation might arise in which it would be safe and appropriate to make a promise of some consultation. This is for your consideration. It might be of moment to both France and Great Britain if they had an assurance that we could be consulted when an emergency arose with respect to our method of exerting our peaceful influence toward maintaining the world's peace, in case Britain upon consideration, should try to reach an agreement with France based upon some security pact, or amplification or interpretation of their covenants under the League as a *quid pro quo* for the reduction of the French Navy. The matter has been discussed by the delegation and we feel that a consultative arrangement of this sort would have to be safeguarded (1) by a separate security pact between France and Great Britain, and (2) by specific clauses which would clearly and expressly deny any promise of military assistance. The Rapidan joint statement of October 9 [97] has been studied in this connection as a guide for a statement setting forth in their relation to Europe the different functions of Britain and America.

(9) With respect to our future action, we hope to confer with MacDonald on Monday. Confirmation of my views as to the effect of France's position, as stated in my No. 152, has been gotten as a result of a conference Saturday with our delegation.

A new and favorable factor in the situation may be introduced as a result of cables from Tokyo which indicate a probable approval of our agreement.

STIMSON

500.A15a3/785 : Telegram

The Chairman of the American Delegation (Stimson) to the Acting Secretary of State

[Paraphrase]

LONDON, March 25, 1930—5 p. m.
[Received March 25—1 : 35 p. m.]

161. Morrow, Robinson, and I conferred with Alexander, Henderson, and MacDonald yesterday. The conference was held at my suggestion, for I wished to be sure that there existed no misunderstanding

---

[97] See press release issued by the White House, October 10, 1929, *Foreign Relations*, 1929, vol. III, p. 33.

as to the positions of our respective delegations, especially where political pacts were concerned. The French in their December note, you will recall, called attention to the relationship existing between the questions of disarmament and security. I reviewed the French position since that note, speaking of the way in which they relied upon the Covenant of the League of Nations, and particularly of the manner of the sanctions to be used against an aggressor; also, of the desire of the French that a mutual assistance pact be made, to which all Mediterranean countries would be a party, as this would be a contributory reason toward armament reduction. I called the Prime Minister's attention to his reply to the French note and, as I understood it, to the British position that they would be unwilling to assume any continental obligations in addition to those they now had. I told him that the French had repeatedly made it clear to us that they wanted a treaty of mutual assistance as a condition of reduction of armament; that in the absence of a formal request from them asking for consultative provisions in the Pact of Paris, we had told them definitely that a consultative pact could not be given them as a substitute for the military mutual security which they desired.

I told MacDonald that we obviously could not, and had not, made any suggestion as to reconsideration of Britain's own situation with respect to France, as that was a question in which she and her neighbors on the continent were solely concerned. This situation seemed to be one of the things holding up a five-power agreement. I had previously pointed out to the Prime Minister the careful distinctions regarding the respective contributions our two countries could make toward world peace as set out in the Rapidan joint statement of October 9.

In the presence of Henderson and Alexander, MacDonald made two statements, the first of which was that Britain would be willing to make a formal statement of some sort to the French following the language in annex F to the Locarno Agreement,[98] which would make it clear that she would be bound to loyal and effective cooperation in support of the Covenant and in resistance of an act of aggression; but that France had not yet been advised of this intention. Second, that Great Britain would be willing to participate in a later conference of Mediterranean countries.

I then told the Prime Minister that if the other nations would take care of the question of mutual assistance in such a way as to secure a substantial reduction of armament, I should think it possible for us to consider with an open mind the question of a provision for

[98] Collective note to Germany, December 1, 1926, regarding art. 16 of the Covenant of the League of Nations, League of Nations Treaty Series, vol. LIV, p. 299.

consultation among the signatories to our agreement, with explicit denial of military action. Opinion was expressed by Henderson that he thought the conference should proceed along this line, provided substantial continental reduction in naval armament could be secured thereby. Approval of what I had said was expressed to the meeting by Senator Robinson, who afterward told me that under these circumstances he did not think the treaty would be weakened in the Senate by such a consultative provision.

STIMSON

500.A15a3/787a : Telegram

The Acting Secretary of State to the Chairman of the American Delegation (Stimson)

[Paraphrase]

WASHINGTON, March 25, 1930—7 p. m.

258. Peace societies yesterday received three telegrams asserting that statement was made by three American delegates in interviews that everything would be settled if the President would take action in offering a consultative pact. It is most embarrassing to have such pressure applied in a matter regarding which we have heard nothing as to wording or import.

It is asserted, they say, that if this were done Great Britain would be enabled to give guarantees of a more formal character. These reports are persistent and, obviously, annoying and the subject is being given much space in the press.

We should know exactly the terms proposed before such a subject is given consideration by you. Are you not able to reassure us as to the position of the delegates? It would be helpful under the circumstances if you could do so.

COTTON

500.A15a3/787b : Telegram

The Acting Secretary of State to the Chairman of the American Delegation (Stimson)

[Paraphrase]

WASHINGTON, March 25, 1930—8 p. m.

259. E. T. Stone, whose residence is given as 8 Park Place, St. James, London, has cabled to persons having a connection with the Foreign Policy Association that important members of your staff have given him information to the effect that dissatisfaction exists among the members of the delegation due to their not having received from the President constructive support, and that it is felt by them

that if he would follow the recommendations as to a consultative pact, etc., made by the American delegation, he could save the situation with the French.

We have stopped a move of the Foreign Policy Association to call a general meeting in New York for the purpose of protesting the action of the Administration and the President.

The advices in your No. 156, March 23, strictly contradict the foregoing. We believe that the whole idea of such a pact has been originated by those New York groups who have been trying to secure its advancement at the Conference. They have used propaganda here, and we think that some of the French delegation have contacts with Stone or other agents of theirs and from them have gotten some encouragement. Through such correspondents as James[99] and Mowrer these ideas have filtered back to the United States. Would it not be advisable for you or Morrow, or some other member of your delegation, to talk with Stone, giving him the facts which you have given us, and endeavor to find out which member of your staff has been giving out information which is being used against the work of the delegation and the Administration.

We think that dangerous ground is being trodden both in the interests of our country and delegation by outside groups who take it upon themselves to put forth ideas and to establish activities with other governments.

The President today, because of this agitation, stated to the press, not for publication nor to be attributed to any authority, that no government represented at the Conference had proposed a consultative pact to the United States. He said that the terms advocated by outside groups for such a pact would not reduce tonnage at all and that other governments know fully that the United States cannot enter any pact which implied either directly or indirectly the use of naval forces; that the pacts proposed by these groups were not of this nature and the situation was not met or assisted by them; and that it was an entirely unwarranted belief on their part that the United States' offering of such a pact would secure reduction of tonnage.

COTTON

500.A15a3/787c : Telegram

The Acting Secretary of State to the Chairman of the American Delegation (Stimson)

[Paraphrase]

WASHINGTON, March 25, 1930—9 p. m.

260. Our telegrams Nos. 258 and 259, March 25, 7 p. m. and 8 p. m., respectively, were written after we had read your No. 161,

---

[99] Edwin Leland James, press correspondent for the *New York Times*.

March 25, 5 p. m. The matter is assuming considerable seriousness over here, and the President is bothered. I am amazed at the cable advices of which Stone is the source.

COTTON

500.A15a3/787 : Telegram

The Chairman of the American Delegation (Stimson) to the Acting Secretary of State

LONDON, March 26, 1930—11 a. m.
[Received March 26—6 : 52 a. m.]

162. The following statement was issued last night by the delegation in view of the rumors current in certain of the British newspapers, particularly the *Daily Herald*, that the United States had changed its point of view on the matter of consultative pacts:

"Rumor was current last evening to the effect that the American delegation had made a change of their attitude toward consultative pacts and were willing to enter into such a pact for the purpose of saving the Conference. It was authoritatively denied at the headquarters of the American delegation that any change had taken place in the attitude of the American delegation, and its attitude remains as its spokesmen gave it out several weeks ago. At that time it was made clear [that] America had no objection to enter[ing] a consultative pact as such; on the contrary, the United States is already a party to a number of treaties involving the obligation of consulting with other powers. It will not, however, enter into any treaty, whether consultative or otherwise, where there is danger of its obligation being misunderstood as involving a promise to render military assistance or guaranteeing protection by military force to another nation. Such a misunderstanding might arise, if the United States entered into such a treaty as a *quid pro quo* for the reduction of the naval force of another power. That danger has hitherto inhered in the present situation, where France has been demanding mutual military security as a condition of naval reduction, as appears from her original statement of her case last December. If, however, this demand for security could be satisfied in some other way, then the danger of misunderstanding a consultative pact would be eliminated and in such case the question would be approached from an entirely different standpoint. In such a case the American delegation would consider the matter with an entirely open mind."

STIMSON

500.A15a3/788 : Telegram

The Chairman of the American Delegation (Stimson) to the Acting Secretary of State

[Paraphrase]

LONDON, March 26, 1930—5 p. m.
[Received March 26—3:10 p. m.]

163. 1. Nothing of the nature mentioned in your telegram No. 258, March 25, has been said by any American delegate. No attention should be paid to it, for it is nonsense. In my telegram No. 156, March 23, paragraphs 7 and 8, and in my telegram No. 161, March 25, I stated our position on a consultative pact and it has not changed. I can assure the President that nothing coming from this delegation is responsible for this situation and I am sorry he has been troubled.

.   .   .   .

3. Statement by President, mentioned in your telegram No. 259, March 25, is entirely in accord with our position and is accurate in every respect.

4. I learned that a story was to be published by the *London Herald* to the effect that owing to the intervention of the President our delegation had completely changed its position on a consultative pact, so I issued my press statement last evening. Today the situation changed in favor of a five-power treaty. I was told by MacDonald that my statement helped greatly. I believe Great Britain has at last changed its position with regard to security for France. Although I have discreetly refrained from inquiry I believe this to be a fact. I am informed by MacDonald that Briand will arrive tonight. He will discuss pacts with Henderson tomorrow. MacDonald also informed me that this morning the French had reduced their figures considerably; they are now within about 400,000 tons total tonnage of meeting the figures of the British. The trend for the last 24 hours has been more encouraging than anything we have experienced for a long time, but there are many difficulties still remaining in the road. I had lunch with Lloyd George. He has been pessimistic and seemingly antagonistic but he now seems to think the Conference will be successful. His statement is significant, as his coalition is a big factor in keeping MacDonald in office.

5. In view of this change and the possibility of a security agreement between Great Britain and France, it is very likely that a consultative pact of the nature suggested in my Nos. 156 and 161 will be brought to the front. I assume that if we adhere to the safeguards enumerated by me it will meet with the President's approval. Next week we shall probably have an important plenary session. There will be a review of the progress made to date, and it may well be that an opportunity will be presented at that time or later

at which a message to the American delegation from the President can be presented with powerful effect to the Conference. This possibility we will consider and we will let you know in time if it seems desirable.

6. Tokyo reports remain encouraging; they counsel patience on ground that Government is making progress towards a favorable conclusion. I am informed from British and American sources that French have worked hard to delay or disrupt an agreement with Japan, in submarine figures particularly.

STIMSON

500.A15a3/788a : Telegram

The Acting Secretary of State to the Chairman of the American Delegation (Stimson)

[Paraphrase]

WASHINGTON, March 26, 1930—6 p. m.

265. After reading your yesterday's press statement and after conference with the President, I send you the following:

It is our wish to call the following points to your attention with respect to the whole question of a consultative pact:

1. If the provisions of the Four-Power Pacific Treaty [1] are applied to a setting which is European, even though a reservation is made against military action, they become an entanglement of the first order in European affairs, this being particularly true of paragraph 2 of the Pacific Pact. The two settings present this essential difference: With respect to Europe, if included in the present treaty, it would apply to every European political disturbance which might affect any one of the five parties; with respect to the Pacific Pact, we have possessions in the East and the Pact refers solely to those possessions.

2. The supplementary agreement of December 13, 1921 [*February 6, 1922* [2]], by delimiting action further under those provisions, which cannot be included in the present treaty, modified the Pacific Pact.

3. To repeat the text of the Pacific Treaty as a part of the text of the present proposed treaty would be to incur, therefore, the greatest possible dangers. We would be drawn into questions into which we could not go if the pact were so drawn as to be confined to Europe; and if such a pact were not confined to Europe, other powers would be drawn into questions affecting the Western Hemisphere, and this we cannot allow.

4. To us it would appear that the provisions of any such pact

---

[1] Signed December 13, 1921, *Foreign Relations,* 1922, vol. I, p. 33.
[2] *Ibid.,* p. 46.

would necessarily have to be strictly limited to an agreement of mutual frank communication with the purpose of finding means for peaceful settling of any dispute apt to occasion war between those signing, and that such interchanges should be confined wholly to the ascertainment of peaceable methods and should leave out specifically all consideration of military or other sanctions, that no signatory shall be obliged to take part in such interchanges dealing with problems in which they say they have no concern, and it should contain an affirmation that it is this country's policy not to become involved in controversies with respect to Europe.

5. There are certain implications which some will draw if some of the Pacific Pact terms were included in this treaty. It would be interpreted as a declaration of the purpose to dominate the world by five naval powers. It is true that even the adoption of the above modified form if it employed the word "consultation" would be interpreted in all probability as leaving the implication of conference and it should not be "consultation" but rather "communication."

6. It appears to us important that, as early as possible and prior to further discussion as to a consultative pact, your Conference ascertain whether or not France will be satisfied enough with the sanctions which Great Britain is willing to offer to reduce her terms to an approved level before you discuss the terms of any arrangement which they may ask of you. As any arrangement which might be made by you would have to be so diluted as not to be particularly valuable, it would seem improbable that any consultative arrangement would be asked of you. We think the above course best because the whole matter in public discussion on this side has assumed undue importance.

7. It is our desire, in any event, to be consulted and informed as to the form in which you propose to put your commitments before you have discussion as to their terms.

COTTON

500.A15a3/790 : Telegram

The Chairman of the American Delegation (Stimson) to the Acting Secretary of State

[Paraphrase]

LONDON, March 27, 1930—3 p. m.
[Received March 27—11: 40 a. m.]

165. Referring to your telegram No. 265, March 26. We have no idea of following the form of the Four-Power Pacific Treaty, as we are already fully aware of the dangers. We have also been considering the advisability of ascertaining the extent to which the French would be willing to reduce their building program, before we bind ourselves

to any formal pact whatever. We are of the opinion that this is an express condition of the negotiations the British and French are now carrying on. I have had in mind, in addition to the limitation proposed in paragraph 4 of our cable [3] as to the discussion being limited to methods for pacific settlement, a limitation somewhat as follows:

"The United States' obligation shall extend only to an examination of the situation as it may affect the interests of her nationals and of herself".

Before consenting to the use of her fleet it is Britain's desire to ascertain the effect which such use would have upon United States trade and policy and the above would be in line with her desire to obtain this information.

This matter is being discussed by our delegation today; I shall consult you, of course, as to the form which seems most acceptable to us just as soon as we reach an agreement and I shall get your views before submitting or proposing it to other parties. I hope you will keep me promptly posted as to the President's views as they may develop, as matters are now moving rather rapidly.

STIMSON

500.A15a3/794 : Telegram

The Chairman of the American Delegation (Stimson) to the Acting Secretary of State

[Paraphrase]

LONDON, March 27, 1930—7 p. m.
[Received March 27—5 p. m.]

167. It was decided by the heads of delegations this afternoon to hold a plenary session on Friday, April 4, when full reports and discussions will be made of the progress of the Conference up to that date. Briand has been in conference during the day with the British and I understand that with respect to figures encouraging progress is being made. The pessimism that MacDonald had last week has changed and he is now hopeful for a treaty by the five powers.

Morrow, Robinson, Reed, and Dawes this afternoon produced a suggestion for a consultative clause to be placed in the naval treaty. This was done after a long and thorough conference. I examined it, upon my return from meeting, and I believe it the best suggestion thus far. I think it meets the limitations I had in mind.

The following is the suggestion:

"The signatories hereto shall settle all disputes between them by pacific means. As to what measures may be adopted to maintain peace among them, the high contracting parties shall consult with

---

[3] Presumably telegram No. 161, March 25, 5 p. m., p. 79.

one another frankly and fully but this agreement to consult or any consultation between the parties shall not imply a commitment on the part of the signatories or any of them to use military force or take any coercive action."

Senators Robinson and Reed feel sure that such a clause would be approved by the Senate; they also feel strongly that it would not be helped and might be harmed by a declaration "that the policy of the United States is not to entangle itself in European controversies."

I send the suggestion along to you for your consideration and any comment you may care to make.

STIMSON

500.A15a3/794b : Telegram

The Acting Secretary of State to the Chairman of the American Delegation (*Stimson*)

[Paraphrase]

WASHINGTON, March 27, 1930—8 p. m.

269. For your information the situation here is as follows:

1. With regard to a consultative pact, friends of the Administration in the Senate indicate an overwhelming Senate opposition. Intimations from Senators George and Swanson also indicate this to be true. They do not know the terms of such a pact, of course, but they contemplate that it is akin to the Pacific Pact. We are positive that a consultative pact in terms of the Pacific Pact would be impossible of ratification at present but if it were of a different nature and sufficiently limited there might be a change of opinion.

2. We are of the opinion that the British and French negotiations should be settled before any discussion of the text of the consultative pact is entered upon, although we do not wish our view on tactics to override your views. To put it another way, we should not engage in this problem until the British and French have settled their guarantees on one side and their tonnage on the other; for with the obvious leaks of every text and detail of your negotiations, the pact will become the battleground here and will overshadow the entire disarmament program. It is not desirable to have it develop unnecessarily to a serious question, for if the negotiations between Great Britain and France should fail it would unnecessarily consolidate opposition to any form of agreement. We take it that no such pact will be included in a three-power treaty. Moreover, we think it very desirable that the other delegations should present the form of the consultative clause and by stating your receptive position you have laid the groundwork for this already. They should be warned that nothing in the nature of the text of the Pacific Pact would be possible but this should be done at an appropriate time. It is

suggested that you might consider repeating from the Kellogg Pact the two important paragraphs as a preamble to any other undertaking.

In our view, the text of the pact ought to come from some other governments and the reason is that if we presented the text the effort of the other delegations, undoubtedly, would be to put more teeth in it and we might fail on the question of words, the import of which would be almost impossible to establish clearly in the mind of the public.

On the other hand, should they present a form of pact of as moderate a basis and we proceeded to take any teeth out, our position would be much stronger here.

We have received your telegram No. 165, March 27. The above was written before its receipt, but we do not think position is changed.

COTTON

500.A15a3/803a : Telegram

The Acting Secretary of State to the Chairman of the American Delegation (Stimson)

[Paraphrase]

WASHINGTON, March 28, 1930—4 p. m.

271. I think you should understand the President's position regarding a consultative pact and I, therefore, submit the following for your own personal information. From the very beginning, his attitude, as you know, has been against inclusion of any political undertaking as a part of disarmament agreement. Both of us were of the opinion that the Kellogg Pact was the political basis for reduction of arms at the present.

At the time this situation began to loom up as a result of peace society and French propaganda, we observed from your telegrams Nos. 126, 128, 136, and 152 [3a] a continuous refusal to agree to any consultative pact or any other political pact with the exception of consultation provisions with respect to a naval program in the treaty growing out of the Conference and of the general purport of the Washington Armament Treaty. We had no intimation that there was any possible change until we received your No. 156; [3b] then your No. 161, [3c] regarding the offer you had made to the British, was received before we were able to reply to your No. 156.

At his press conference the same day but before the receipt of your Nos. 156 and 161, the President made a strong statement to the

[3a] *Ante,* pp. 55, 57, 62, 72.
[3b] *Ante,* p. 75.
[3c] *Ante,* p. 79.

newspapers, not for quotation, to the effect that such a pact would be of no purpose or effect on reduction of tonnage, relying of course on your previous statements. He has continuously advised Senators, newspaper editors, and other persons who have been agitating this question that no political action could be taken by this Government. He is much pressed, therefore, on the inconsistency of the present situation. He does not intend to embarrass the negotiations, however, by explanations or other statements but he is of the opinion that any form of political pact would very likely strengthen the opposition of big navy people by including others.

We are of the opinion that this situation leads to some important considerations.

First, there should be strict limitation of our commitments within the spirit of the President's Armistice Day speech.[4]

Second, a political pact should be a separate treaty from the naval treaty as was the case of the Pacific treaties, so that if the political pact should not receive confirmation it would not put the disarmament program in danger; and at some appropriate time our colleagues in the Conference could be informed that it would be impossible for us to guarantee ratification and that two treaties must not be contingent upon each other.

Third, we should be fully advised as to any new departure in the negotiations even though it would mean delay, so we could have time to reflect on it before you indicate your position.

This is merely an explanation of the difficulties which confront us here and the things that should be safeguarded against, and the President does not wish you to think that this is in the nature of criticism.

The President and I suggest that you consider a repetition of the two vital clauses of the Kellogg Pact, instead of the formula in your No. 167 [4a] and then continue as follows:[5]

"In accordance with the spirit of this undertaking the signatories declare that in event of controversy among them they will advise with one another fully and frankly to the end that they may discover pacific means of settlement (it being the clear understanding that so far as it concerns the United States 'pacific means' shall exclude from discussion any military or other coercive action.)"

The foregoing formula does not necessarily represent our final opinion.

It is suggested further that the Bryan treaties[6] be considered by you as to the possibility of rendering them binding upon all parties.

COTTON

---

[4] Delivered on November 11, 1929; *Congressional Record*, vol. 72, pt. 1, p. 505.
[4a] *Ante*, p. 87.
[5] Quotation not paraphrased.
[6] For the Bryan treaties for the advancement of general peace, see *Foreign Relations*, 1914, index, p. 1130; *ibid.*, 1915, index, p. 1328; and *ibid.*, 1916, index, p. 1007.

500.A15a3/799 : Telegram

The Chairman of the American Delegation (Stimson) to the Acting Secretary of State

[Paraphrase]

LONDON, March 28, 1930—4 p. m.
[Received March 28—12 : 30 p. m.]

171. Have cabled following to Castle, today, 4 p. m.:

"Referring to your cable today, noon, and your question regarding actual part taken by Japanese delegation in the settlement now under consideration at Tokyo. At a meeting of the heads of delegations held on Tuesday, March 25, the following was adopted on Wakatsuki's suggestion as a correct statement of the facts:[7]

'In regard to Japan a compromise had emerged from the negotiations between the delegations of the United States of America, the United Kingdom, and Japan, which the Japanese delegation had agreed to recommend to its Government. It was incorrect to say as had been said that that compromise proposal was an American proposal since, as he had stated, it had emerged from the negotiations.' "

STIMSON

500.A15a3/801 : Telegram

The Chairman of the American Delegation (Stimson) to the Acting Secretary of State

[Extract–Paraphrase]

LONDON, March 28, 1930—6 p. m.
[Received March 28—1 : 20 p. m.]

172. The following telegram has been received from Castle, dated March 28, noon:

. . . .

I took your personal message for the Prime Minister[8] immediately to Shidehara, who said that it was very friendly and that he himself would give it to Hamaguchi. A message from MacDonald was delivered in the same manner by the British Ambassador. Both he and Shidehara urged me not to attempt to see Hamaguchi personally, as to do so would produce a dangerous public reaction. If you were here you would understand the need of extreme caution. It is most essential to prevent private conversations with many influential men.

Much discussion has taken place in the press over whether or not the Japanese delegation is actually back of the agreement; the Navy intransigents are still calling it "the American proposal", in spite of the fact that frequent denials have been made. The papers say that you discussed the question with Wakatsuki on March 25; I should find it very helpful to know the real attitude of the Japanese delegation."

STIMSON

---

[7] Quoted passage not paraphrased.
[8] See telegram No. 155, March 23, 3 p. m., from the chairman of the American delegation, p. 75.

500.A15a3/804a : Telegram

The Acting Secretary of State to the Chairman of the American Delegation (Stimson)

[Paraphrase]

WASHINGTON, March 29, 1930—2 p. m.

274. It has been suggested that a new formula draft be cabled to you for your consideration, as it contains a new idea. This new formula, which follows, does not represent my personal view:[9]

"In accordance with the spirit of this undertaking, i. e., the Kellogg Pact, the signatories declare that in the event of a controversy among them which cannot be settled by direct negotiation, those signatories not parties to the controversy will advise and use their good offices to the end that they may discover a pacific means of settlement—it being the clear understanding that 'pacific means' shall be interpreted as excluding all coercive action."

COTTON

500.A15a3/804 : Telegram

The Chairman of the American Delegation (Stimson) to the Acting Secretary of State

[Paraphrase]

LONDON, March 29, 1930—6 p. m.
[Received 7:44 p. m.[10]]

177. Your telegram No. 271, March 28.

1. An analysis and summary of the various forms of political pacts which in one form or another have been given support in respect to this Conference will help you best to understand the past week's events and to secure future coordination.

(*a*) Ambassador Houghton on his return from London brought to my attention almost a year ago the British desire for consultative arrangements with us as a precaution against a clash between our Navies when the British Fleet was serving as an ancillary to the League of Nations and might thus interfere with our trade. This danger is well known; it has been the subject of frequent discussion and the attention of British statesmen has been preoccupied by it. The purpose of such a consultative arrangement would be to obviate friction between the United States outside the League and a Europe organized under the League. Particularly as the British Navy will be supported by the navies of the other members of the League, it is important for us to know what course will be pursued by it in case of an impending emergency. Eventually such consultations are certain to take place; it would, however, appear of great advantage to all parties if they should occur prior to the creation of an irrevo-

---

[9] Quoted passage not paraphrased.
[10] Telegram in six sections.

cable situation fixed by the League Council's vote. It appears to me that a consultative pact of this kind is the only one having a direct connection with this Conference's problems, for the British have been embarrassed by the absence of such consultation in fulfilling their obligations under the League of Nations and the Locarno Agreement toward the French and therefore French security is impaired in the opinion of the French.

(b) At the time of the Russo-Chinese crisis last summer, Claudel, acting for Briand, suggested to me that, in order to provide machinery to meet such a situation, there be added to the Kellogg Pact a consultative clause based on the Four-Power Pacific Treaty. While I have always felt that a clause of this kind offered many difficulties to the Kellogg Pact and have had a preference for other machinery which I have had in mind, nevertheless I expressed myself as being ready to discuss the proposition.

(c) The French in their note to the British on December 20, on the subject of the Naval Conference, brought up their demand for an agreement as to mutual assistance. They suggested different forms which such assistance might take, for example, the amplification and clarification of the Locarno Agreements now existing and a Mediterranean Pact. Because of this demand and its temporary refusal by the British, as I have stated before, it was impossible for the United States to consider any political pact, even solely for consultation, as a substitute for the French demand, for fear that it would lead in the future to misunderstandings as to the scope of American obligations.

(d) Apparently the situation was further complicated and all distinction between these fundamentally different forms of political pacts was confused when the Foreign Policy Association and French propaganda entered into the discussion and it was taken up by the American press.

(e) My press conference of March 11 was prompted by this confusion of legitimate consultation with implied obligations. In that conference I made it clear that our objection was not to consultative pacts in themselves, but to the circumstances which surrounded the broaching of the question. In my many conferences with Mac-Donald I also made this plain, as well as to Tardieu and Briand; see my telegram No. 156, March 23, 9 p. m.

2. MacDonald's position on this matter, as stated in my telegram No. 156, has gradually shown a decided cleavage from that of his Foreign Office. Since he retained personal control over the negotiations and was decidedly in opposition to the granting of the French demand, those who thought otherwise could never discuss the question of a change in this attitude.

3. Upon receipt of advices from Tyrrell on the evening of March 21, as I reported in No. 152, March 22, MacDonald apparently thought it impossible to bring about an agreement between the five powers. I think such a feeling on his part was justified, in view of Tyrrell's advices and MacDonald's own views with respect to the French. On Saturday, March 22, there was a strong effort made, apparently by the permanent officials of the Foreign Office, to further, even on new lines, a five-power agreement. Apparently Henderson sympathizes with their view. That the Conference was on the brink of a precipice, with the consequent disastrous result to the whole European peace situation which would follow failure on such issues, was recognized by all parties. Consequently all parties attempted to canvass entire situation prior to a break which would be final. A meeting at one o'clock on Saturday, the 22d, was held by our own delegation, at which time the situation was discussed from all angles. Craigie told me last Saturday that Massigli's view of the situation was that it was not so hopeless as Tyrrell's report indicated. Therefore, we sent you our No. 156, on Sunday, March 23, containing our complete summary of the situation.

4. I sought the conference with Alexander, Henderson, and Mac-Donald on Monday morning, March 24, as reported to you in my telegram No. 161, March 25, because it had become clear to us that there were decidedly different points of view in the British delegation as to the proper course to pursue with respect to France and because we were unwilling to have any possibility of misunderstanding with us prevent the saving of the situation. This was the first real opportunity we had had to discuss with the Prime Minister and Henderson the question which seemed to be holding up the Conference. Obviously the question which the French regarded as fundamental was what was the true British position with respect to the clauses in the Covenant of the League of Nations providing for mutual assistance. The British had been a party to these clauses for more than a decade, but the apprehensions of the French had been aroused by MacDonald's attitude. Especially did his radio speech on "entangling alliances" disturb them.

5. French diplomatic and journalistic methods throughout the Conference have apparently irritated MacDonald, whose great patience, tact, and industry have characterized his conduct of the negotiations. We have felt, as we viewed the general peace problem of Europe, that Henderson's view toward France was the sounder one. I believe I am accurate in saying that the spirit of that portion

of the Rapidan statement of October 9 which follows: "the part of each of our Governments in the promotion of world peace will be different, as one will never consent to become entangled in European diplomacy and the other is resolved to pursue a policy of active cooperation with its European neighbors; but each of our Governments will direct its thoughts and influence towards securing and maintaining the peace of the world" is being adhered to by the Foreign Office and Henderson.

6. The importance of my statement made on March 24th to the British, which merely repeated what I had already said to Tardieu, Briand, and MacDonald (emphasized, however, by the impending crisis), was that it gave Henderson his first opportunity to urge upon MacDonald a reconsideration of the British position toward the French; and MacDonald had evidently been won over to Henderson's view by Tuesday morning, as the latter then was given authority by the Prime Minister to telephone to Briand at Paris that they would discuss the subject of mutual security with the French. The French themselves had, at the same time, evidently experienced the beneficial effect of the threatened failure of the Conference and the invitation to return to London was accepted by Briand. In the French afternoon papers of Tuesday incorrect and sensational accounts of the changes in the situation were already appearing; and the necessity of our midnight statement was occasioned by these incorrect accounts reaching London that same evening.

7. You can see from the foregoing the rapid course of events which the impending failure of the Conference produced and during which an opportunity for the British to change their position was furnished by our statement. I need not tell the President how much I regret that my statement, contained in my telegram No. 156, failed to reach him before he had given out his press statement on Tuesday. It was sent at 9 p. m. on Sunday, and there had been inserted sections (7) and (8) expressly to warn you that the matter of a consultative pact might come up, although we were surprised with the rapidity with which matters moved. I appreciate the fine sporting spirit of the President toward us in the face of the extreme difficulty into which he had been put. Please tell him so.

8. I will discuss with the delegation promptly your suggestion, in your telegram No. 271, for a consultative clause, and you will be kept advised of any changes in the negotiations.

STIMSON

500.A15a3/810 : Telegram

The Acting Secretary of State to the Chairman of the American Delegation (Stimson)

WASHINGTON, March 31, 1930—5 p. m.

280. [Paraphrase.] You may say to Briand and Tardieu, if you think it will help, that the President has sent a personal message for them. You may make any alterations or deletions you wish in the text which follows. It is our object to emphasize to the French that if American cooperation is to be secured, it should be accomplished by dealing with positive problems successfully and to build up gradually the principles and methods. The message reads: [End paraphrase.]

"At this distance from the Conference I cannot hope to know all its difficulties and problems, but I have, as well as I have been able, followed the course of argument and it is possible that my estimate of the American position may be of help to them now.

I have given a great deal of consideration to the position of our relations with Europe, especially with France, and the setting of the United States in the whole picture of international cooperation as affected by the current possibilities of the naval conference. You are well aware of my own intensely sympathetic feeling toward France and of the deep-rooted bonds which so profoundly unite the peoples of the United States and France together with my long and consistent devotion to the cause of world peace. I appreciate fully the logic of the French note of December 31st [20th?] to the British Government in which the French Government introduces questions of political agreement in connection with reduction of navies and sets out her view of the ineffectiveness of the Pact of Paris, her insistence upon more methodical procedure of pacific settlements to make it more effective, and her opinion that the absence of provisions of security against aggression makes her dependence on the League of Nations essential.

1. Following the World War we have had a period in the United States of strong reaction against any cooperation in general plans for methodical procedure in settlement of international controversies. The distance of our people from Europe, their inability to appreciate fully the difficulties of European statesmen, and the differences between European political constitutions and our own, together with deep dissensions and disappointments which have arisen here out of our participation in the great war—have all confirmed the inherited and deep instinct of our people against being involved in any international action with Europe.

Framed largely by the genius of Mr. Briand, the Pact of Paris gave a formula which found complete and ready acceptance in the American mind. The outlawry of war was a noble and simple basis for the preservation of peace in which this country was generally in agreement. There was general agreement also in the idea that there must be always sought pacific means for the settlement of international controversies and that public opinion, informed and enlightened, is a most potent power to that end. But the American mind has not come to the point of accepting any general plan of methodical procedure for the pacific settlement of international disputes and particularly, it is not ready to commit itself to any plan in cases of violation of the Pact of Paris or as to action in cases of aggression.

But the American mind is, I think, ready to take up and consider, and, I believe, approve certain immediate and obviously practicable steps which will do much to obviate and to remove the source of international controversies and thus help prevent war. The American people have before them the plan to enter the World Court [12] and become a party to an impartial international tribunal for the settlement of such legal questions as we may from time to time be ready to submit to the Court for decision. That is a simple proposal consonant with our traditional principles and acceptable to the American mind.

We could, no doubt, from time to time take up other definite, limited questions which bear on world peace. One we are ready now to take up as to naval arms.

2. We believe that the outstanding controversy of the world today is competition in naval arms and the excessive size of navies in the light of the presumed reorientation of world thought to a purely defensive basis through the Pact of Paris. In our participation in a conference of the naval powers to settle this question, the United States has joined in a practical instance in a possible methodical settlement of controversies by pacific means which, if successful, would pave the way for the natural development of cooperation in settlement of other age-old controversies which imperil the peace of the world. Success in such practical steps one by one seems the way the American people are prepared to accept more systematic or automatic methods of procedure of international cooperation.

3. In the matter of general security we had conceived that by our preliminary negotiation with the British (through which we had eliminated the hitherto primary bar to any settlement of the naval question) we were in fact making a very distinct contribution toward the security of France. The result of these negotiations promised a reduction of the British fleet by some 300,000 or 400,000 tons, a reduction of the American fleet by some 200,000 tons, substantial reduction of the Japanese fleet—which very reductions add materially to the security of France and the world. It was our feeling that these measures were the very fundamentals of practical progress toward security in the world and they were even more important as establishing the principle of cooperation with the other nations in the elimination of war.

It is the view of American public men that we have an obligation to serve in the cause of peace among nations and we believe it is the desire of other nations that we should so serve. Recognizing the realities of our situation, however, this cooperation can best be developed, as I have said, by dealing with limited and positive questions as they may arise."

COTTON

---

[12] See *Foreign Relations*, 1929, vol. I, pp. 1 ff.

500.A15a3/811 : Telegram

The Acting Secretary of State to the Chairman of the American Delegation (Stimson)

[Paraphrase]

WASHINGTON, March 31, 1930—6 p. m.

281. We assume that the statement issued by the British last night ends the possibility of any five-power pact.[13] If this is correct, it would seem to us most vital and urgent that every effort should be made by you in the direction of a three-power agreement. An agreement of this kind would accomplish the greater portion of that which we have tried to bring about in the stabilization and reduction of arms. A setting would be created by it and we believe that at a later date the other nations would have to adhere in practice, even though they never do so by signature. It is as important from a national point of view as it is to the world. Although all we wish might not be gotten under our final terms with the Japanese, at the same time our ultimate aims with respect to the world are advanced and the cause of world peace is saved from the great disaster of a break-down.

COTTON

500.A15a3/812 : Telegram

The Acting Secretary of State to the Chairman of the American Delegation (Stimson)

[Paraphrase]

WASHINGTON, March 31, 1930—7 p. m.

282. It would seem to us, if it is certain that there is no longer a possibility of a five-power agreement, that you might deem it advisable to convey a message to the Prime Minister from the President to the effect that the Rapidan conferences took cognizance of the possibility of a three-power treaty; that at that time such a treaty was thought feasible if the effort to induce the other powers to join was not successful; that it is the President's belief that such a step would in large measure fulfill the high purpose of both the Prime Minister and himself. A great advance in world stabilization would in itself be made by cooperation between Japan, Great Britain, and the United States.

---

[13] On March 30 a statement issued to the press from No. 10 Downing St., the residence of the British Prime Minister, and printed in the morning papers on March 31 said in part that "any further military or naval commitments are impossible, for that would be tantamount to tying ourselves down to military operations without being able to control the situation from which they have arisen. No British Government could undertake such commitments, which would be contrary to the whole feeling of the British people."

There can well be introduced into such a treaty provisions to protect the British in case of antagonistic naval building; the taking of such action by any nation, however, with consequent upsetting of a major plan of stability, would in all probability be brought to a halt by the feeling of world understanding. The President believes that a crisis has now been reached, when nothing should be left undone to prevent what may be a backward step in the world peace movement. It would be deplorable to have that movement checked.

COTTON

500.A15a3/806 : Telegram

The Chairman of the American Delegation (Stimson) to the Acting Secretary of State

[Paraphrase]

LONDON, April 1, 1930—1 p. m.

[Received April 1—7:15 a. m.]

181. Your telegrams Nos. 281 and 282, March 31, 6 p. m., and 7 p. m., respectively. Reports of our death are greatly exaggerated. Last evening at 5 o'clock the British submitted their proposal to the French for the clarification of the Covenant relations of the two powers, and the document was read to me at 6 o'clock. As I understand the British propositions, they so nearly approach the French demands that I doubt very much that the French will reject them. MacDonald expects a reply tomorrow; and this morning he tells me that he is very hopeful. He is of the opinion that the firmness of the British statement, to which you referred, has cleared the atmosphere and has made the French more amenable. I have been working for a three-power treaty as my second line of reserve since I arrived here. I shall continue to work for a five-power treaty as long as I deem it to be within the bounds of possibility, for I feel that the high purposes mentioned in your suggested message from the President to MacDonald will be far better served by a five-power treaty than by a three-power treaty.

STIMSON

500.A15a3/809 : Telegram

The Chairman of the American Delegation (Stimson) to the Acting Secretary of State

[Paraphrase]

LONDON, April 1, 1930—6 p. m.

[Received April 1—11:35 a. m.]

186. Following telegram dated April 1, noon, received from Castle:

"I was just told by Yoshida [14] that instructions to the Japanese delegation will probably go tonight. Cabinet is meeting. From con-

---

[14] Japanese Vice Minister for Foreign Affairs.

51329

versation with Count Makino [15] last night I believe agreement will be practically accepted. Of course I could not get the details from Yoshida, but he said that wonderful work had been done during the past few days by Shidehara, who now only dreaded reaction of the Navy. Insistence that agreement continue only until another conference is held, at which time the right is reserved by Japan to ask 70 percent, will be the only change, I think.

This morning's *Nichi Nichi* declares that threatening note was transmitted to Hamaguchi and that the conclusion is drawn from comment thereon that this was a joint *démarche* by the United States and England. Had this been published several days ago, it might have been disastrous, and would have been deeply resented. It is fortunate that this was not done, and even more so that the action was not attributed to me."

STIMSON

500.A15a3/819 : Telegram

The Chairman of the American Delegation (Stimson) to the Acting Secretary of State

[Paraphrase]

LONDON, April 2, 1930—7 p. m.
[Received 7:35 p. m.]

195. The reply of the Japanese Government was presented by the delegation at a meeting with the American and the British delegations this afternoon. It was substantially a complete acceptance of the compromise agreement submitted to Tokyo. The reply was accompanied by a note from the Japanese Government which was very good-spirited and considerate, and the British feel, as do we, that they have acted in the finest of spirit in the entire matter. Another meeting at 11 tomorrow was asked for by Wakatsuki in order that further details, evidently of minor character, might be discussed. After that meeting a full report of the settlement with the Japanese will be sent you.

Both the British and the French seem hopeful and encouraged, and negotiations between them are proceeding actively. Since last week there has been a change in the entire spirit of the Conference, and it now seems that even though the French and the Italians cannot be included in a five-power agreement at the present time, matters in which they are concerned could be left so that there would be a very good prospect of their prompt inclusion; it looks at present, however, as though they will be included in the settlement now.

Adjournment of the plenary meeting was made owing to the feeling of all of us that the negotiations between the British and the French were so hopeful that it would be advisable that they be given, without a public statement, a few days more, as in that time they

---

[15] Former Minister for Foreign Affairs, and member of the Japanese House of Peers.

may be able to come to an agreement which could be announced simultaneously with the Japanese result.

Tomorrow morning Briand is coming to see me, and I shall then give the President's message to him.

STIMSON

500.A15a3/821 : Telegram

The Chairman of the American Delegation (Stimson) to the Acting Secretary of State

[Paraphrase]

LONDON, April 3, 1930—5 p. m.

[Received April 3—1 : 40 p. m.]

199. Our meeting with the British and the Japanese took place this morning without bringing forth any serious obstacles to the prompt settlement of the agreement with Japan. The serious problem of unemployment in the Japanese shipyards might make it necessary for the Government to ask the privilege of premature replacement of a portion of their cruiser, destroyer, and submarine tonnage in order to give employment, without altering, however, the total tonnages. Neither the British nor we see any objection to this. The matter is now referred to an experts committee to outline a schedule. The Japanese have also asked us for permission to make a limited transfer between certain categories, but it is our impression that this request was made as a matter of form in order to satisfy their Navy party, and that it is not expected to be accepted by either the British or us.

This morning Briand called on me for an hour and a half. Morrow was present also. I read the President's message to Briand, and he expressed appreciation, saying that he quite understood the limitations of American action. He expressed his gratitude to us for our having given the push that broke the jam between the British and the French last week, and told us about his negotiations since that date with the British. These have been confined wholly to question of the redefinition and affirmation of British responsibilities under the League of Nations; Briand stated that he considered the two nations were very close together. Tonnage figures had not yet been discussed, however, and no further progress has been made with the Italians; but if the British and the French get together, the pressure upon the Italians will become very heavy.

Since our March 26 press statement [16] and our conference with the British on March 24,[17] no allusion has been made to consultative pacts with us.

STIMSON

---

[16] See telegram No. 162, March 26, 11 a. m., from the chairman of the American delegation, p. 83.

[17] See telegram No. 161, March 25, 5 p. m., from the chairman of the American delegation, p. 79.

500.A15a3/825a : Telegram

The Acting Secretary of State to the Chairman of the American Delegation (Stimson)

[Paraphrase]

WASHINGTON, April 4, 1930—3 p. m.

300. The press despatches lead us to believe that a three-power pact is the inevitable conclusion, in view of the improbability of finding a basis between the French and Italians or even the French and British. If the British are prepared to come along on the Rapidan figures and your subsequent battleship arrangements, we think that a three-power pact will be regarded as a distinct victory, and a reasonable political clause protecting the signatories in case of menacing construction will not be regarded as out of line.

A five-power pact, of course, is what we would all prefer but we are of the opinion that we run some danger in extending negotiations, for the failure of the five-power treaty is at present clearly upon the French and Italians but they might turn the tables by making such demands on the United States as would appear to place upon us the responsibility. Moreover the five-power treaty with consultative provision stronger than that which we telegraphed might cause breakdown of the Conference if demands were made for more teeth in the consultative pact than we could secure agreement for. I am sure it would create great opposition here if it were made stronger than that which we telegraphed.[18]

COTTON

500.A15a3/825 : Telegram

The Chairman of the American Delegation (Stimson) to the Acting Secretary of State

[Paraphrase]

LONDON, April 4, 1930—6 p. m.
[Received April 4—5:12 p. m.]

200. The negotiations between the French and the British, which have been going ahead steadily on question of security, culminated today in a four-hour session. The following propositions are under discussion:

1. Restatement of annex F of the Locarno Pact; this has been practically agreed upon;
2. Amendment of the League of Nations Covenant so as to prohibit wars in certain conditions which are not now prohibited;
3. General agreement of both Great Britain and France to improve all means of judicial and arbitrable settlement of disputes.

---

[18] See telegram No. 271, March 28, 4 p. m., to the chairman of the American delegation, p. 89.

Tomorrow the Conference will continue on proposition of: (1) French tonnage figures; (2) relations with Italy.

It is probable that Briand will then go to Paris to lay the plan before the French Government and will return on Monday.

The decision of the British Government is contingent upon a meeting of the Cabinet to be called on Monday.

We have taken no part in the conference, of course, but I have strongly urged upon MacDonald the necessity of expeditious settlement of the pivotal questions of the Conference in order that we may bring things to a close as soon as possible.

Conferences with the Japanese on details of settlement with them are progressing before the committee of experts.

STIMSON

500.A15a3/827 : Telegram

The Chairman of the American Delegation (Stimson) to the Acting Secretary of State

[Paraphrase]

LONDON, April 5, 1930—4 p. m.
[Received 4 : 28 p. m.[19]]

202. Your telegram No. 300, April 4. After conference with Briand this morning, MacDonald and Craigie informed Morrow and myself of the situation at luncheon. Briand is taking with him to Paris this afternoon security plan for the consideration of the French Government, as mentioned in my telegram No. 200, yesterday. Conferences will be resumed Tuesday afternoon upon his return from Paris. He refused to discuss tonnage figures, stating that the French Government would have to decide first how much the proposed security plan was worth in tonnage. After consultation with his Government he is to transmit figures by telegraph. The security plan will be considered by the British Cabinet when it meets Monday. Therefore, there is still hope of a five-power agreement, but MacDonald's mind, I can see, is influenced very much by the evident reaction in British opinion against further political commitments of whatever nature in the European situation. Therefore, we discussed at our luncheon a three-power agreement coupled with efforts to secure inclusion of France and Italy. I impressed upon MacDonald importance of at least beginning with Rapidan figures in the three-power agreement even though the British Government would soon be compelled to increase its tonnage, particularly in destroyers, in order to meet French submarine construction in the future. Mac-Donald stated emphatically that he would begin with the Rapidan figures although the French program, he feared, would compel a

---

[19] Telegram in two sections.

change within two years, if it were continued. I informed him of the substance of your views contained in your telegram No. 300, April 4, and he fully appreciated their force. I am of the opinion that the probable outcome will be a three-power treaty. You must remember, however, that although the present French-British and French-American atmosphere and relations are good and infinitely better now than 10 days ago, yet it will be rather difficult to preserve the atmosphere from deteriorating unless an agreement is decided upon by the five powers; therefore all of us feel that a much greater stability will be given to our work and the European situation in general if the French and Italians can be brought into the settlement. To secure that end, we are therefore continuing our efforts.

STIMSON

500.A15a3/832 : Telegram

The Chairman of the American Delegation (Stimson) to the Acting Secretary of State

[Paraphrase]

LONDON, April 9, 1930—11 a. m.
[Received April 9—9 : 50 a. m.]

207. MacDonald told me that on Monday the Cabinet had trimmed down his security proposal, and that the leaders of the Conservative and the Liberal Parties had also objected to parts of it. Consequently, he had slightly modified its language. I expected, therefore, that on Briand's return there would be a prompt decision against a five-power treaty. MacDonald told me, however, after his meeting with Briand last evening, that the security negotiations were not rejected, that the French were very conciliatory and were evidently anxious for an agreement. Negotiations are still on, and at last tonnage figures are to be taken up this morning by the British and the French, Alexander acting for the former and Dumesnil for the latter. The French-Italian deadlock still remains. The Prime Minister intimated that by this evening he would know the fate of the five-power treaty.

Nearly all of the questions raised by the Japanese have been settled, and today we hope to settle what remains. Yesterday all five powers in the First Committee adopted unanimously the form of the proposed declaration of international law as to protecting lives of the crew and passengers from submarine attack. The form is that which was last submitted to Root.[21] The First Committee is

---

[21] See telegram No. 147, March 19, 7 p. m., from the chairman of the American delegation, p. 67.

also finishing up other technical and procedural questions on which the other committees have been at work.

Morrow and I together with Gordon and Rublee are working on form of a five-power treaty to be used even should the five-power agreement on auxiliary tonnage fail. If that happens, there are still several important subjects for a five-power treaty and it is our purpose to provide a framework for keeping the five powers together for future interpellations.

I insert here a possible skeleton outline for such a five-power treaty:

Part I. Five-power agreement amending the Treaty of Washington construction schedule so as to provide for a capital ship holiday and for the scrapping of capital ships. Also broadening the definition of an aircraft carrier.

Part II. Three-power agreement dealing with auxiliary categories.

Part III. Five-power agreement regarding use of submarines.

Part IV. Five-power agreement as to certain future methods of procedure recommended by the First Committee.

Part V. (Or probably special resolution.) France and Italy to undertake to continue with their efforts to reach agreement on auxiliary category limitations; meanwhile, Conference adjourns.

Parts I, II, and III to take effect on ratification of the treaty by the United States, Great Britain, and Japan.

If the progress we are making seems to be distressingly slow, please remember that the British leaders, as result of their parliamentary and other work, are able to give only fraction of their time to the Conference itself, and that MacDonald is very despondent and very tired. I have made the President's suggestions regarding the advantages of a three-power treaty quite clear to the Prime Minister, but the decision, of course, as to when to cease efforts for a five-power agreement necessarily rests with him.

STIMSON

500.A15a3/833 : Telegram

The Chairman of the American Delegation (Stimson) to the Acting Secretary of State

[Paraphrase]

LONDON, April 10, 1930—4 p. m.
[Received April 10—12 : 55 p. m.]

211. We settled all questions with Japanese this morning, thus entirely closing the three-power agreement. MacDonald informed me later that, after conferring with Briand, the British had practically given up hope of agreement with Italy and France on auxiliary tonnage. In order to forestall any acrimonious termination of the Conference, we took up at once the proposition for the conclusion of a composite treaty on general basis outlined in my telegram No. 207,

yesterday. The British, Japanese, French, and Italians have given their assent to that method and it now appears as though the situation of closing in a friendly spirit was well in hand. We have a rough draft of proposed treaty completed and we are informed that the British have another partially completed. As matters now stand, I believe the Conference could adjourn with a fair degree of promptness, possibly before April 22, but owing to the final delays which are inevitable I advise against making any prophecy.

STIMSON

500.A15a3/835 : Telegram

The Chairman of the American Delegation (Stimson) to the Acting Secretary of State

[Paraphrase]

LONDON, April 10, 1930—5 p. m.
[Received April 10—2 : 55 p. m.]

212. This morning we reached an agreement with the British and the Japanese; we are now endeavoring to arrive at an agreement with the French and the Italians, so that the results of the work shall be embodied in single treaty. Following is the tentative program which we have accepted : [22]

"Skeleton of proposed five-power treaty.

Part I. A five-power agreement amending Washington Treaty so as to provide:

(1) For a capital ship holiday of all five powers; France and Italy to have the right to still lay down the tonnage which they were entitled to lay down in 1927 and 1929.

(2) Agreement for scrapping 3 capital ships by the United States, 5 by British Empire, and 1 by Japan.

(3) New definition of aircraft carrier.

Part II. Five-power agreement declaring the rules of international law as to the use of submarines.

Part III. Three-power agreement dealing with auxiliary vessels including therein provisions relating to exempt and special ships.

Entire treaty shall go into effect as to Great Britian, United States of America, and Japan when ratified by these three nations."

The Japanese have abandoned their position on the transference of tonnage from destroyer category into the submarine category, and have accepted definite limitation to 52,700 tons of submarine tonnage. In order to provide certain amount of work in Japanese dockyards, we have made allowance for some premature scrapping and replacement of light cruisers, destroyers, and submarines, always subject to provision that total tonnage limitations of these categories shall

---

[22] Quotation not paraphrased.

not be exceeded. We have also consented to retention by each of the three nations of one demilitarized battleship for a gunnery training ship and that three demilitarized cruisers of the *Kuma* class may be retained by Japan to be used as cadet training vessels to replace five over age ships now being used for that purpose.

Please repeat to Tokyo.[23]

STIMSON

500.A15a3/838b : Telegram

The Acting Secretary of State to the Chairman of the American Delegation (Stimson)

WASHINGTON, April 11, 1930—6 p. m.

323. By instruction of the President I transmit to you his congratulations on the success of the result which you have achieved and this expression of his admiration for your patience and determination through an arduous and difficult negotiation. This instruction is being made public here.[24]

COTTON

500.A15a3/864 : Telegram

The Chairman of the American Delegation (Stimson) to the Acting Secretary of State

LONDON, April 22, 1930.
[Received April 22—9:55 a. m.]

253. For the President. I am happy to tell you that the Naval Treaty which is the result of movement initiated by you last spring is signed. The form is satisfactory and the spirit of the occasion excellent.

STIMSON

Treaty Series No. 830

Treaty for the Limitation and Reduction of Naval Armament, Signed at London, April 22, 1930 [25]

The President of the United States of America, the President of the French Republic, His Majesty the King of Great Britain, Ireland and the British Dominions beyond the Seas, Emperor of India, His Majesty the King of Italy, and His Majesty the Emperor of Japan,

---

[23] Transmitted to the Embassy in Japan as Department's telegram No. 68, April 10, 3 p. m.
[24] *Proceedings of the London Naval Conference*, p. 246.
[25] In English and French; French text not printed. Ratification advised by the Senate, July 21, 1930; ratified by the President, July 22, 1930; ratifications deposited at London, October 27, 1930, by the United States of America, the United Kingdom of Great Britain and Northern Ireland and all parts of the British Empire which are not separate members of the League of Nations, the Dominion of Canada, the Commonwealth of Australia, the Dominion of New Zealand, the Union of South Africa, India, and Japan; December 31, 1930, by the Irish Free State; proclaimed by the President, January 1, 1931.

Desiring to prevent the dangers and reduce the burdens inherent in competitive armaments, and

Desiring to carry forward the work begun by the Washington Naval Conference and to facilitate the progressive realization of general limitation and reduction of armaments,

Have resolved to conclude a Treaty for the limitation and reduction of naval armament, and have accordingly appointed as their Plenipotentiaries:

The President of the United States of America:

Henry L. Stimson, Secretary of State;
Charles G. Dawes, Ambassador to the Court of St. James;
Charles Francis Adams, Secretary of the Navy;
Joseph T. Robinson, Senator from the State of Arkansas;
David A. Reed, Senator from the State of Pennsylvania;
Hugh Gibson, Ambassador to Belgium;
Dwight W. Morrow, Ambassador to Mexico;

The President of the French Republic:

Mr. André Tardieu, Deputy, President of the Council of Ministers, Minister of the Interior;
Mr. Aristide Briand, Deputy, Minister for Foreign Affairs;
Mr. Jacques-Louis Dumesnil, Deputy, Minister of Marine;
Mr. François Piétri, Deputy, Minister of the Colonies;
Mr. Aimé-Joseph de Fleuriau, Ambassador of the French Republic at the Court of St. James;

His Majesty the King of Great Britain, Ireland and the British Dominions beyond the Seas, Emperor of India:

for Great Britain and Northern Ireland and all parts of the British Empire which are not separate Members of the League of Nations:

The Right Honourable James Ramsay MacDonald, M. P., First Lord of His Treasury and Prime Minister;
The Right Honourable Arthur Henderson, M. P., His Principal Secretary of State for Foreign Affairs;
The Right Honourable Albert Victor Alexander, M. P., First Lord of His Admiralty;
The Right Honourable William Wedgwood Benn, D. S. O., D. F. C., M. P., His Principal Secretary of State for India;

for the Dominion of Canada:

Colonel The Honourable James Layton Ralston, C. M. G., D. S. O., K. C., a Member of His Privy Council for Canada, His Minister for National Defence;
The Honourable Philippe Roy, a Member of His Privy Council for Canada, His Envoy Extraordinary and Minister Plenipotentiary in France for the Dominion of Canada;

for the Commonwealth of Australia:

The Honourable James Edward Fenton, His Minister for Trade and Customs;

for the Dominion of New Zealand:

Thomas Mason Wilford, Esquire, K. C., High Commissioner for the Dominion of New Zealand in London;

for the Union of South Africa:

Charles Theodore te Water, Esquire, High Commissioner for the Union of South Africa in London;

for the Irish Free State:

Timothy Aloysius Smiddy, Esquire, High Commissioner for the Irish Free State in London;

for India:

Sir Atul Chandra Chatterjee, K. C. I. E., High Commissioner for India in London;

His Majesty the King of Italy:

The Honourable Dino Grandi, Deputy, His Minister Secretary of State for Foreign Affairs;
Admiral of Division The Honourable Giuseppe Sirianni, Senator of the Kingdom, His Minister Secretary of State for Marine;
Mr. Antonio Chiaramonte-Bordonaro, His Ambassador Extraordinary and Plenipotentiary at the Court of St. James;
Admiral The Honourable Baron Alfredo Acton, Senator of the Kingdom;

His Majesty the Emperor of Japan:

Mr. Reijiro Wakatsuki, Member of the House of Peers;
Admiral Takeshi Takarabe, Minister for the Navy;
Mr. Tsuneo Matsudaira, His Ambassador Extraordinary and Plenipotentiary at the Court of St. James;
Mr. Matsuzo Nagaï, His Ambassador Extraordinary and Plenipotentiary to His Majesty the King of the Belgians;

Who, having communicated to one another their full powers, found in good and due form, have agreed as follows:

PART I

ARTICLE 1

The High Contracting Parties agree not to exercise their rights to lay down the keels of capital ship replacement tonnage during the years 1931–1936 inclusive as provided in Chapter II, Part 3 of the Treaty for the Limitation of Naval Armament signed between them at Washington on the 6th February, 1922, and referred to in the present Treaty as the Washington Treaty.

This provision is without prejudice to the disposition relating to the replacement of ships accidentally lost or destroyed contained in Chapter II, Part 3, Section I, paragraph (c) of the said Treaty.

France and Italy may, however, build the replacement tonnage which they were entitled to lay down in 1927 and 1929 in accordance with the provisions of the said Treaty.

Article 2

1. The United States, the United Kingdom of Great Britain and Northern Ireland and Japan shall dispose of the following capital ships as provided in this Article:

United States:
"Florida".
"Utah".
"Arkansas" or "Wyoming".
United Kingdom:
"Benbow".
"Iron Duke".
"Marlborough".
"Emperor of India".
"Tiger".
Japan:
"Hiyei".

(a) Subject to the provisions of sub-paragraph (b), the above ships, unless converted to target use exclusively in accordance with Chapter II, Part 2, paragraph II (c) of the Washington Treaty, shall be scrapped in the following manner:

One of the ships to be scrapped by the United States, and two of those to be scrapped by the United Kingdom shall be rendered unfit for warlike service, in accordance with Chapter II, Part 2, paragraph III (b) of the Washington Treaty, within twelve months from the coming into force of the present Treaty. These ships shall be finally scrapped, in accordance with paragraph II (a) or (b) of the said Part 2, within twenty-four months from the said coming into force. In the case of the second of the ships to be scrapped by the United States, and of the third and fourth of the ships to be scrapped by the United Kingdom, the said periods shall be eighteen and thirty months respectively from the coming into force of the present Treaty.

(b) Of the ships to be disposed of under this Article, the following may be retained for training purposes:

by the United States: "Arkansas" or "Wyoming".
by the United Kingdom: "Iron Duke".
by Japan: "Hiyei".

These ships shall be reduced to the condition prescribed in Section V of Annex II to Part II of the present Treaty. The work of reducing these vessels to the required condition shall begin, in the case of the United States and the United Kingdom, within twelve months, and in the case of Japan within eighteen months from the coming into force of the present Treaty; the work shall be completed within six months of the expiration of the above-mentioned periods.

Any of these ships which are not retained for training purposes shall be rendered unfit for warlike service within eighteen months, and finally scrapped within thirty months, of the coming into force of the present Treaty.

2. Subject to any disposal of capital ships which might be necessitated, in accordance with the Washington Treaty, by the building by France or Italy of the replacement tonnage referred to in Article 1 of the present Treaty, all existing capital ships mentioned in Chapter II, Part 3, Section II of the Washington Treaty and not designated above to be disposed of may be retained during the term of the present Treaty.

3. The right of replacement is not lost by delay in laying down replacement tonnage, and the old vessel may be retained until replaced even though due for scrapping under Chapter II, Part 3, Section II, of the Washington Treaty.

ARTICLE 3

1. For the purposes of the Washington Treaty, the definition of an aircraft carrier given in Chapter II, Part 4 of the said Treaty is hereby replaced by the following definition:

The expression "aircraft carrier" includes any surface vessel of war, whatever its displacement, designed for the specific and exclusive purpose of carrying aircraft and so constructed that aircraft can be launched therefrom and landed thereon.

2. The fitting of a landing-on or flying-off platform or deck on a capital ship, cruiser or destroyer, provided such vessel was not designed or adapted exclusively as an aircraft carrier, shall not cause any vessel so fitted to be charged against or classified in the category of aircraft carriers.

3. No capital ship in existence on the 1st April, 1930, shall be fitted with a landing-on platform or deck.

ARTICLE 4

1. No aircraft carrier of 10,000 tons (10,160 metric tons) or less standard displacement mounting a gun above 6.1-inch (155 mm.) calibre shall be acquired by or constructed by or for any of the High Contracting Parties.

2. As from the coming into force of the present Treaty in respect of all the High Contracting Parties, no aircraft carrier of 10,000

tons (10,160 metric tons) or less standard displacement mounting a gun above 6.1-inch (155 mm.) calibre shall be constructed within the jurisdiction of any of the High Contracting Parties.

ARTICLE 5

An aircraft carrier must not be designed and constructed for carrying a more powerful armament than that authorised by Article IX or Article X of the Washington Treaty, or by Article 4 of the present Treaty, as the case may be.

Wherever in the said Articles IX and X the calibre of 6 inches (152 mm.) is mentioned, the calibre of 6.1 inches (155 mm.) is substituted therefor.

PART II

ARTICLE 6

1. The rules for determining standard displacement prescribed in Chapter II, Part 4 of the Washington Treaty shall apply to all surface vessels of war of each of the High Contracting Parties.

2. The standard displacement of a submarine is the surface displacement of the vessel complete (exclusive of the water in nonwatertight structure) fully manned, engined, and equipped ready for sea, including all armament and ammunition, equipment, outfit, provisions for crew, miscellaneous stores, and implements of every description that are intended to be carried in war, but without fuel, lubricating oil, fresh water or ballast water of any kind on board.

3. Each naval combatant vessel shall be rated at its displacement tonnage when in the standard condition. The word "ton", except in the expression "metric tons", shall be understood to be the ton of 2,240 pounds (10,016 kilos.).

ARTICLE 7

1. No submarine the standard displacement of which exceeds 2,000 tons (2,032 metric tons) or with a gun above 5.1-inch (130 mm.) calibre shall be acquired by or constructed by or for any of the High Contracting Parties.

2. Each of the High Contracting Parties may, however, retain, build or acquire a maximum number of three submarines of a standard displacement not exceeding 2,800 tons (2,845 metric tons) ; these submarines may carry guns not above 6.1-inch (155 mm.) calibre. Within this number, France may retain one unit, already launched, of 2,880 tons (2,926 metric tons), with guns the calibre of which is 8 inches (203 mm.).

3. The High Contracting Parties may retain the submarines which they possessed on the 1st April, 1930, having a standard displacement not in excess of 2,000 tons (2,032 metric tons) and armed with guns above 5.1-inch (130 mm.) calibre.

4. As from the coming into force of the present Treaty in respect of all the High Contracting Parties, no submarine the standard displacement of which exceeds 2,000 tons (2,032 metric tons) or with a gun above 5.1-inch (130 mm.) calibre shall be constructed within the jurisdiction of any of the High Contracting Parties, except as provided in paragraph 2 of this Article.

ARTICLE 8

Subject to any special agreements which may submit them to limitation, the following vessels are exempt from limitation:

(*a*) naval surface combatant vessels of 600 tons (610 metric tons) standard displacement and under;

(*b*) naval surface combatant vessels exceeding 600 tons (610 metric tons), but not exceeding 2,000 tons (2,032 metric tons) standard displacement, provided they have none of the following characteristics:

(1) mount a gun above 6.1-inch (155 mm.) calibre;
(2) mount more than four guns above 3-inch (76 mm.) calibre;
(3) are designed or fitted to launch torpedoes;
(4) are designed for a speed greater than twenty knots.

(*c*) naval surface vessels not specifically built as fighting ships which are employed on fleet duties or as troop transports or in some other way than as fighting ships, provided they have none of the following characteristics:

(1) mount a gun above 6.1-inch (155 mm.) calibre;
(2) mount more than four guns above 3-inch (76 mm.) calibre;
(3) are designed or fitted to launch torpedoes;
(4) are designed for a speed greater than twenty knots;
(5) are protected by armour plate;
(6) are designed or fitted to launch mines;
(7) are fitted to receive aircraft on board from the air;
(8) mount more than one aircraft-launching apparatus on the centre line; or two, one on each broadside;
(9) if fitted with any means of launching aircraft into the air, are designed or adapted to operate at sea more than three aircraft.

ARTICLE 9

The rules as to replacement contained in Annex I to this Part II are applicable to vessels of war not exceeding 10,000 tons (10,160 metric tons) standard displacement, with the exception of aircraft carriers, whose replacement is governed by the provisions of the Washington Treaty.

ARTICLE 10

Within one month after the date of laying down and the date of completion respectively of each vessel of war, other than capital ships, aircraft carriers and the vessels exempt from limitation under Article 8, laid down or completed by or for them after the coming into force of the present Treaty, the High Contracting Parties shall communicate to each of the other High Contracting Parties the information detailed below:

(a) the date of laying the keel and the following particulars:
classification of the vessel;
standard displacement in tons and metric tons;
principal dimensions, namely: length at water-line, extreme beam at or below water-line;
mean draft at standard displacement;
calibre of the largest gun.

(b) the date of completion together with the foregoing particulars relating to the vessel at that date.

The information to be given in the case of capital ships and aircraft carriers is governed by the Washington Treaty.

ARTICLE 11

Subject to the provisions of Article 2 of the present Treaty, the rules for disposal contained in Annex II to this Part II shall be applied to all vessels of war to be disposed of under the said Treaty, and to aircraft carriers as defined in Article 3.

ARTICLE 12

1. Subject to any supplementary agreements which may modify, as between the High Contracting Parties concerned, the lists in Annex III to this Part II, the special vessels shown therein may be retained and their tonnage shall not be included in the tonnage subject to limitation.

2. Any other vessel constructed, adapted or acquired to serve the purposes for which these special vessels are retained shall be charged against the tonnage of the appropriate combatant category, according to the characteristics of the vessel, unless such vessel conforms to the characteristics of vessels exempt from limitation under Article 8.

3. Japan may, however, replace the minelayers "Aso" and "Tokiwa" by two new minelayers before the 31st December, 1936. The standard displacement of each of the new vessels shall not exceed 5,000 tons (5,080 metric tons); their speed shall not exceed twenty knots, and their other characteristics shall conform to the provisions of paragraph (b) of Article 8. The new vessels shall be regarded as special

vessels and their tonnage shall not be chargeable to the tonnage of any combatant category. The "Aso" and "Tokiwa" shall be disposed of in accordance with Section I or II of Annex II to this Part II, on completion of the replacement vessels.

4. The "Asama", "Yakumo", "Izumo", "Iwate" and "Kasuga" shall be disposed of in accordance with Section I or II of Annex II to this Part II when the first three vessels of the "Kuma" class have been replaced by new vessels. These three vessels of the "Kuma" class shall be reduced to the condition prescribed in Section V, sub-paragraph (*b*) 2 of Annex II to this Part II, and are to be used for training ships, and their tonnage shall not thereafter be included in the tonnage subject to limitation.

Article 13

Existing ships of various types, which, prior to the 1st April, 1930, have been used as stationary training establishments or hulks, may be retained in a non-seagoing condition.

ANNEX I

Rules for replacement

Section I.—Except as provided in Section III of this Annex and Part III of the present Treaty, a vessel shall not be replaced before it becomes "over-age". A vessel shall be deemed to be "over-age" when the following number of years have elapsed since the date of its completion:

(*a*) For a surface vessel exceeding 3,000 tons (3,048 metric tons) but not exceeding 10,000 tons (10,160 metric tons) standard displacement:

    (i) if laid down before the 1st January, 1920: 16 years;
    (ii) if laid down after the 31st December, 1919: 20 years.

(*b*) For a surface vessel not exceeding 3,000 tons (3,048 metric tons) standard displacement:

    (i) if laid down before the 1st January, 1921: 12 years;
    (ii) if laid down after the 31st December, 1920: 16 years.

(*c*) For a submarine: 13 years.

The keels of replacement tonnage shall not be laid down more than three years before the year in which the vessel to be replaced becomes "over-age"; but this period is reduced to two years in the case of any replacement surface vessel not exceeding 3,000 tons (3,048 metric tons) standard displacement.

The right of replacement is not lost by delay in laying down replacement tonnage.

Section II.—Except as otherwise provided in the present Treaty, the vessel or vessels, whose retention would cause the maximum tonnage permitted in the category to be exceeded, shall, on the completion or acquisition of replacement tonnage, be disposed of in accordance with Annex II to this Part II.

Section III.—In the event of loss or accidental destruction a vessel may be immediately replaced.

ANNEX II

Rules for disposal of Vessels of War

The present Treaty provides for the disposal of vessels of war in the following ways:

    (i) by scrapping (sinking or breaking up) ;
    (ii) by converting the vessel to a hulk ;
    (iii) by converting the vessel to target use exclusively ;
    (iv) by retaining the vessel exclusively for experimental purposes ;
    (v) by retaining the vessel exclusively for training purposes.

Any vessel of war to be disposed of, other than a capital ship, may either be scrapped or converted to a hulk at the option of the High Contracting Party concerned.

Vessels, other than capital ships, which have been retained for target, experimental or training purposes, shall finally be scrapped or converted to hulks.

Section I.—Vessels to be scrapped

(a) A vessel to be disposed of by scrapping, by reason of its replacement, must be rendered incapable of warlike service within six months of the date of the completion of its successor, or of the first of its successors if there are more than one. If, however, the completion of the new vessel or vessels be delayed, the work of rendering the old vessel incapable of warlike service shall, nevertheless, be completed within four and a half years from the date of laying the keel of the new vessel, or of the first of the new vessels; but should the new vessel, or any of the new vessels, be a surface vessel not exceeding 3,000 tons (3,048 metric tons) standard displacement, this period is reduced to three and a half years.

(b) A vessel to be scrapped shall be considered incapable of warlike service when there shall have been removed and landed or else destroyed in the ship:

(1) all guns and essential parts of guns, fire control tops and revolving parts of all barbettes and turrets;
(2) all hydraulic or electric machinery for operating turrets;
(3) all fire control instruments and rangefinders;
(4) all ammunition, explosives, mines and mine rails;
(5) all torpedoes, war heads, torpedo tubes and training racks;
(6) all wireless telegraphy installations;
(7) all main propelling machinery, or alternatively the armoured conning tower and all side armour plate;
(8) all aircraft cranes, derricks, lifts and launching apparatus. All landing-on or flying-off platforms and decks, or alternatively all main propelling machinery;
(9) in addition, in the case of submarines, all main storage batteries, air compressor plants and ballast pumps.

(c) Scrapping shall be finally effected in either of the following ways within twelve months of the date on which the work of rendering the vessel incapable of warlike service is due for completion:

(1) permanent sinking of the vessel;
(2) breaking the vessel up; this shall always include the destruction or removal of all machinery, boilers and armour, and all deck, side and bottom plating.

SECTION II.—*Vessels to be converted to hulks*

A vessel to be disposed of by conversion to a hulk shall be considered finally disposed of when the conditions prescribed in Section I, paragraph (*b*), have been complied with, omitting sub-paragraphs (6), (7) and (8), and when the following have been effected:

(1) mutilation beyond repair of all propeller shafts, thrust blocks, turbine gearing or main propelling motors, and turbines or cylinders of main engines;
(2) removal of propeller brackets;
(3) removal and breaking up of all aircraft lifts, and the removal of all aircraft cranes, derricks and launching apparatus.

The vessel must be put in the above condition within the same limits of time as provided in Section I for rendering a vessel incapable of warlike service.

SECTION III—*Vessels to be converted to target use*

(*a*) A vessel to be disposed of by conversion to target use exclusively shall be considered incapable of warlike service when there have been removed and landed, or rendered unserviceable on board, the following:

(1) all guns;
(2) all fire control tops and instruments and main fire control communication wiring;
(3) all machinery for operating gun mountings or turrets;
(4) all ammunition, explosives, mines, torpedoes and torpedo tubes;
(5) all aviation facilities and accessories.

The vessel must be put into the above condition within the same limits of time as provided in Section I for rendering a vessel incapable of warlike service.

(*b*) In addition to the rights already possessed by each High Contracting Party under the Washington Treaty, each High Contracting Party is permitted to retain, for target use exclusively, at any one time:

(1) not more than three vessels (cruisers or destroyers), but of these three vessels only one may exceed 3,000 tons (3,048 metric tons) standard displacement;
(2) one submarine.

(*c*) On retaining a vessel for target use, the High Contracting Party concerned undertakes not to recondition it for warlike service.

SECTION IV.—*Vessels retained for experimental purposes*

(*a*) A vessel to be disposed of by conversion to experimental purposes exclusively shall be dealt with in accordance with the provisions of Section III (*a*) of this Annex.

(*b*) Without prejudice to the general rules, and provided that due notice be given to the other High Contracting Parties, reasonable variation from the conditions prescribed in Section III (*a*) of this Annex, in so far as may be necessary for the purposes of a special experiment, may be permitted as a temporary measure.

Any High Contracting Party taking advantage of this provision is required to furnish full details of any such variations and the period for which they will be required.

(c) Each High Contracting Party is permitted to retain for experimental purposes exclusively at any one time:

(1) not more than two vessels (cruisers or destroyers), but of these two vessels only one may exceed 3,000 tons (3,048 metric tons) standard displacement;

(2) one submarine.

(d) The United Kingdom is allowed to retain, in their present conditions, the monitor "Roberts", the main armament guns and mountings of which have been mutilated, and the seaplane carrier "Ark Royal", until no longer required for experimental purposes. The retention of these two vessels is without prejudice to the retention of vessels permitted under (c) above.

(e) On retaining a vessel for experimental purposes the High Contracting Party concerned undertakes not to recondition it for warlike service.

SECTION V.—*Vessels retained for training purposes*

(a) In addition to the rights already possessed by any High Contracting Party under the Washington Treaty, each High Contracting Party is permitted to retain for training purposes exclusively the following vessels:

United States: 1 capital ship ("Arkansas" or "Wyoming");
France: 2 surface vessels, one of which may exceed 3,000 tons (3,048 metric tons) standard displacement;
United Kingdom: 1 capital ship ("Iron Duke");
Italy: 2 surface vessels, one of which may exceed 3,000 tons (3,048 metric tons) standard displacement;
Japan: 1 capital ship ("Hiyei"), 3 cruisers ("Kuma" class).

(b) Vessels retained for training purposes under the provisions of paragraph (a) shall, within six months of the date on which they are required to be disposed of, be dealt with as follows:

1. Capital Ships.
The following is to be carried out:

(1) removal of main armament guns, revolving parts of all barbettes and turrets; machinery for operating turrets; but three turrets with their armament may be retained in each ship;

(2) removal of all ammunition and explosives in excess of the quantity required for target practice training for the guns remaining on board;

(3) removal of conning tower and the side armour belt between the foremost and aftermost barbettes;

(4) removal or mutilation of all torpedo tubes;

(5) removal or mutilation on board of all boilers in excess of the number required for a maximum speed of eighteen knots.

2. Other surface vessels retained by France, Italy and Japan.
The following is to be carried out:

(1) removal of one half of the guns, but four guns of main calibre may be retained on each vessel;

(2) removal of all torpedo tubes;

(3) removal of all aviation facilities and accessories;

(4) removal of one half of the boilers.

(c) The High Contracting Party concerned undertakes that vessels retained in accordance with the provisions of this Section shall not be used for any combatant purpose.

ANNEX III

Special vessels

UNITED STATES

Name and type of vessel	Displacement Tons
Aroostook—Minelayer	4, 950
Oglala—Minelayer	4, 950
Baltimore—Minelayer	4, 413
San Francisco—Minelayer	4, 083
Cheyenne—Monitor	2, 800
Helena—Gunboat	1, 392
Isabel—Yacht	938
Niagara—Yacht	2, 600
Bridgeport—Destroyer tender	11, 750
Dobbin—Destroyer tender	12, 450
Melville—Destroyer tender	7, 150
Whitney—Destroyer tender	12, 450
Holland—Submarine tender	11, 570
Henderson—Naval transport	10, 000
	91, 496

FRANCE

Name and type of vessel	Displacement Tons
Castor—Minelayer	3, 150
Pollux—Minelayer	2, 461
Commandant-Teste—Seaplane carrier	10, 000
Aisne — Despatch vessel	600
Marne " "	600
Ancre " "	604
Scarpe " "	604
Suippe " "	604
Dunkerque " "	644
Laffaux " "	644
Bapaume " "	644
Nancy " "	644
Calais " "	644
Lassigny " "	644
Les Éparges " "	644
Remiremont " "	644
Tahure " "	644
Toul " "	644
Épinal " "	644
Liévin " "	644
(——)—Netlayer	2, 293
	28, 644

BRITISH COMMONWEALTH OF NATIONS

Name and type of vessel	Displacement Tons
Adventure—Minelayer (United Kingdom)	6, 740
Albatross—Seaplane carrier (Australia)	5, 000
Erebus—Monitor (United Kingdom)	7, 200
Terror—Monitor (United Kingdom)	7, 200
Marshal Soult—Monitor (United Kingdom)	6, 400
Clive—Sloop (India)	2, 021
Medway—Submarine depot ship (United Kingdom)	15, 000
	49, 561

ITALY

Name and type of vessel	Displacement Tons
Miraglia—Seaplane carrier	4, 880
Faà di Bruno—Monitor	2, 800
Monte Grappa—Monitor	605
Montello—Monitor	605
Monte Cengio—Ex-monitor	500
Monte Novegno—Ex-monitor	500
Campania—Sloop	2, 070
	11, 960

JAPAN

Name and type of vessel	Displacement Tons
Aso—Minelayer	7, 180
Tokiwa "	9, 240
Asama—Old cruiser	9, 240
Yakumo " "	9, 010
Izumo " "	9, 180
Iwate " "	9, 180
Kasuga " "	7, 080
Yodo—Gunboat	1, 320
	61, 430

PART III

The President of the United States of America, His Majesty the King of Great Britain, Ireland and the British Dominions beyond the Seas, Emperor of India, and His Majesty the Emperor of Japan, have agreed as between themselves to the provisions of this Part III:

ARTICLE 14

The naval combatant vessels of the United States, the British Commonwealth of Nations and Japan, other than capital ships, aircraft carriers and all vessels exempt from limitation under Article 8, shall be limited during the term of the present Treaty as provided in this Part III, and, in the case of special vessels, as provided in Article 12.

ARTICLE 15

For the purpose of this Part III the definition of the cruiser and destroyer categories shall be as follows:

Cruisers.

Surface vessels of war, other than capital ships or aircraft carriers, the standard displacement of which exceeds 1,850 tons (1,880 metric tons), or with a gun above 5.1 inch (130 mm.) calibre.

The cruiser category is divided into two sub-categories, as follows:

(a) cruisers carrying a gun above 6.1-inch (155 mm.) calibre;

(b) cruisers carrying a gun not above 6.1-inch (155 mm.) calibre.

Destroyers.

Surface vessels of war the standard displacement of which does not exceed 1,850 tons (1,880 metric tons), and with a gun not above 5.1-inch 130 mm.) calibre.

ARTICLE 16

1. The completed tonnage in the cruiser, destroyer and submarine categories which is not to be exceeded on the 31st December, 1936, is given in the following table:

Categories	United States	British Commonwealth of Nations	Japan
Cruisers:			
(a) with guns of more than 6.1-inch (155 mm.) calibre.	180,000 tons (182,880 metric tons)	146,800 tons (149,149 metric tons)	108,400 tons (110,134 metric tons)
(b) with guns of 6.1-inch (155 mm.) calibre or less.	143,500 tons (145,796 metric tons)	192,200 tons (195,275 metric tons)	100,450 tons (102,057 metric tons)
Destroyers............	150,000 tons (152,400 metric tons)	150,000 tons (152,400 metric tons)	105,500 tons (107,188 metric tons)
Submarines............	52,700 tons (53,543 metric tons)	52,700 tons (53,543 metric tons)	52,700 tons (53,543 metric tons)

2. Vessels which cause the total tonnage in any category to exceed the figures given in the foregoing table shall be disposed of gradually during the period ending on the 31st December, 1936.

3. The maximum number of cruisers of sub-category (a) shall be as follows: for the United States, eighteen; for the British Commonwealth of Nations, fifteen; for Japan, twelve.

4. In the destroyer category not more than sixteen per cent. of the allowed total tonnage shall be employed in vessels of over 1,500 tons (1,524 metric tons) standard displacement. Destroyers completed or under construction on the 1st April, 1930, in excess of this percentage may be retained, but no other destroyers exceeding 1,500 tons (1,524 metric tons) standard displacement shall be constructed or acquired until a reduction to such sixteen per cent. has been effected.

5. Not more than twenty-five per cent. of the allowed total tonnage in the cruiser category may be fitted with a landing-on platform or deck for aircraft.

6. It is understood that the submarines referred to in paragraphs 2 and 3 of Article 7 will be counted as part of the total submarine tonnage of the High Contracting Party concerned.

7. The tonnage of any vessels retained under Article 13 or disposed of in accordance with Annex II to Part II of the present Treaty shall not be included in the tonnage subject to limitation.

ARTICLE 17

A transfer not exceeding ten per cent. of the allowed total tonnage of the category or sub-category into which the transfer is to be made shall be permitted between cruisers of sub-category (*b*) and destroyers.

ARTICLE 18

The United States contemplates the completion by 1935 of fifteen cruisers of sub-category (*a*) of an aggregate tonnage of 150,000 tons (152,400 metric tons). For each of the three remaining cruisers of sub-category (*a*) which it is entitled to construct the United States may elect to substitute 15,166 tons (15,409 metric tons) of cruisers of sub-category (*b*). In case the United States shall construct one or more of such three remaining cruisers of sub-category (*a*), the sixteenth unit will not be laid down before 1933 and will not be completed before 1936; the seventeenth will not be laid down before 1934 and will not be completed before 1937; the eighteenth will not be laid down before 1935 and will not be completed before 1938.

ARTICLE 19

Except as provided in Article 20, the tonnage laid down in any category subject to limitation in accordance with Article 16 shall not exceed the amount necessary to reach the maximum allowed tonnage of the category, or to replace vessels that become "over-age" before the 31st December, 1936. Nevertheless, replacement tonnage may be laid down for cruisers and submarines that become "over-age" in 1937, 1938 and 1939, and for destroyers that become "over-age" in 1937 and 1938.

ARTICLE 20

Notwithstanding the rules for replacement contained in Annex I to Part II:

(*a*) The "Frobisher" and "Effingham" (United Kingdom) may be disposed of during the year 1936. Apart from the cruisers under construction on the 1st April, 1930, the total replacement tonnage of cruisers to be completed, in the case of the British Commonwealth of Nations, prior to the 31st December, 1936, shall not exceed 91,000 tons (92,456 metric tons).

(*b*) Japan may replace the "Tama" by new construction to be completed during the year 1936.

(*c*) In addition to replacing destroyers becoming "over-age" before the 31st December, 1936, Japan may lay down, in each of the years 1935 and 1936, not more than 5,200 tons (5,283 metric tons) to replace part of the vessels that become "over-age" in 1938 and 1939.

(*d*) Japan may anticipate replacement during the term of the present Treaty by laying down not more than 19,200 tons (19,507 metric tons) of submarine tonnage, of which not more than 12,000 tons (12,192 metric tons) shall be completed by the 31st December, 1936.

ARTICLE 21

If, during the term of the present Treaty, the requirements of the national security of any High Contracting Party in respect of vessels of war limited by Part III of the present Treaty are in the opinion of that Party materially affected by new construction of any Power other than those who have joined in Part III of this Treaty, that High Contracting Party will notify the other Parties to Part III as to the increase required to be made in its own tonnages within one or more of the categories of such vessels of war, specifying particularly the proposed increases and the reasons therefor, and shall be entitled to make such increase. Thereupon the other Parties to Part III of this Treaty shall be entitled to make a proportionate increase in the category or categories specified; and the said other Parties shall promptly advise with each other through diplomatic channels as to the situation thus presented.

PART IV

ARTICLE 22

The following are accepted as established rules of International Law:

(1) In their action with regard to merchant ships, submarines must conform to the rules of International Law to which surface vessels are subject.

(2) In particular, except in the case of persistent refusal to stop on being duly summoned, or of active resistance to visit or search, a warship, whether surface vessel or submarine, may not sink or render incapable of navigation a merchant vessel without having first placed passengers, crew and ship's papers in a place of safety. For this purpose the ship's boats are not regarded as a place of safety unless the safety of the passengers and crew is assured, in the existing sea and weather conditions, by the proximity of land, or the presence of another vessel which is in a position to take them on board.

The High Contracting Parties invite all other Powers to express their assent to the above rules.

PART V

ARTICLE 23

The present Treaty shall remain in force until the 31st December, 1936, subject to the following exceptions:

(1) Part IV shall remain in force without limit of time;
(2) the provisions of Articles 3, 4 and 5, and of Article 11 and

Annex II to Part II so far as they relate to aircraft carriers, shall remain in force for the same period as the Washington Treaty.

Unless the High Contracting Parties should agree otherwise by reason of a more general agreement limiting naval armaments, to which they all become parties, they shall meet in conference in 1935 to frame a new treaty to replace and to carry out the purposes of the present Treaty, it being understood that none of the provisions of the present Treaty shall prejudice the attitude of any of the High Contracting Parties at the conference agreed to.

ARTICLE 24

1. The present Treaty shall be ratified by the High Contracting Parties in accordance with their respective constitutional methods and the ratifications shall be deposited at London as soon as possible. Certified copies of all the *procès-verbaux* of the deposit of ratifications will be transmited to the Governments of all the High Contracting Parties.

2. As soon as the ratifications of the United States of America, of His Majesty the King of Great Britain, Ireland and the British Dominions beyond the Seas, Emperor of India, in respect of each and all of the Members of the British Commonwealth of Nations as enumerated in the preamble of the present Treaty, and of His Majesty the Emperor of Japan have been deposited, the Treaty shall come into force in respect of the said High Contracting Parties.

3. On the date of the coming into force referred to in the preceding paragraph, Parts I, II, IV and V of the present Treaty will come into force in respect of the French Republic and the Kingdom of Italy if their ratifications have been deposited at that date; otherwise these Parts will come into force in respect of each of those Powers on the deposit of its ratification.

4. The rights and obligations resulting from Part III of the present Treaty are limited to the High Contracting Parties mentioned in paragraph 2 of this Article. The High Contracting Parties will agree as to the date on which, and the conditions under which, the obligations assumed under the said Part III by the High Contracting Parties mentioned in paragraph 2 of this Article will bind them in relation to France and Italy; such agreement will determine at the same time the corresponding obligations of France and Italy in relation to the other High Contracting Parties.

ARTICLE 25

After the deposit of the ratifications of all the High Contracting Parties, His Majesty's Government in the United Kingdom of Great Britain and Northern Ireland will communicate the provisions inserted in Part IV of the present Treaty to all Powers which are not signatories of the said Treaty, inviting them to accede thereto definitely and without limit of time.

Such accession shall be effected by a declaration addressed to His Majesty's Government in the United Kingdom of Great Britain and Northern Ireland.

ARTICLE 26

The present Treaty, of which the French and English texts are both authentic, shall remain deposited in the archives of His Majesty's Government in the United Kingdom of Great Britain and Northern Ireland. Duly certified copies thereof shall be transmitted to the Governments of all the High Contracting Parties.

In faith whereof the above-named Plenipotentiaries have signed the present Treaty and have affixed thereto their seals.

Done at London, the twenty-second day of April, nineteen hundred and thirty.

HENRY L. STIMSON.
CHARLES G. DAWES.
CHARLES F. ADAMS.
JOSEPH T. ROBINSON.
DAVID A. REED.
HUGH GIBSON.
DWIGHT W. MORROW.
ARISTIDE BRIAND.
J. L. DUMESNIL.
A. DE FLEURIAU.
J. RAMSAY MACDONALD.
ARTHUR HENDERSON.
A. V. ALEXANDER.
W. WEDGWOOD BENN.
PHILIPPE ROY.
JAMES E. FENTON.
T. M. WILFORD.
C. T. TE WATER.
T. A. SMIDDY.
ATUL C. CHATTERJEE.
G. SIRIANNI.
A. C. BORDONARO.
ALFREDO ACTON.
R. WAKATSUKI.
TAKESHI TAKARABE.
T. MATSUDAIRA.
M. NAGAI.

500.A15a3/905a : Telegram

The Secretary of State to the Ambassador in Great Britain (Dawes)[26]

[Paraphrase]

WASHINGTON, May 20, 1930—4 p. m.

127. In arguments before the Senate Foreign Relations Committee it has been contended by some of the "big Navy" opponents of the treaty, who thereby seek to confuse and discredit the treaty, that construction might be placed on article 19, second sentence, so as to permit replacements of tonnage in 6-inch cruisers with the same amount of tonnage in 8-inch cruisers or vice versa by any of the three parties. Since the word "replacement" necessarily implies the substitution of the same amount of tonnage in the same kind of ships, we believe there is no basis for such contention. We consider, more-over, that this contention is directly contrary to the fair implica-tions of the provision for transfer included in article 17, and also directly disregards division of cruisers into two sub-categories made by articles 15 and 16. We are anxious, nevertheless, that the treaty's enemies in the Senate may be given no possible excuse. Approach should be made therefore to the appropriate British authorities to inquire whether an exchange of notes on the following terms would be consented to:[27]

"It is the understanding of the Government of the United States that the word category in Article nineteen of the London Naval Treaty of 1930 means category or sub-category. The Government of the United States declares that it interprets the Treaty to mean that vessels becoming overage in either sub-category A or sub-category B of the cruiser categories (Article sixteen) shall be replaceable only in that sub-category.

"The American Government will be most happy to have the confir-mation of this understanding from His Majesty's Government."

Use your best efforts to obtain Foreign Office consent to an exchange of notes of this nature as soon as possible. A similar note will be addressed to the Imperial Japanese Government.

STIMSON

500.A15a3/1343

The Japanese Minister for Foreign Affairs (Shidehara) to the American Ambassador in Japan (Castle)[28]

[Translation]

No. 66/T1   TOKYO, May 24, 1930.

EXCELLENCY: I have the honor to acknowledge receipt of your Note dated May 21, 1930,[29] relative to the interpretation of the term "cate-

---

[26] Sent also to the Ambassador in Japan, *mutatis mutandis*, on the same date, as the Department's telegram No. 92.
[27] Quoted passage not paraphrased.
[28] Copy transmitted to the Department by the Ambassador as an enclosure to his despatch No. 109, January 20, 1931 ; received February 7.
[29] *Proceedings of the London Naval Conference*, p. 297.

gory" appearing in Article 19 of the London Naval Treaty of 1930.

The Imperial Government understands the word "category" appearing in Article 19 of the above-mentioned treaty to mean "category" or "sub-category;" thus, it interprets this treaty in the sense that ships belonging to either sub-category (*a*) or sub-category (*b*) of the cruiser category (Article 16) which shall become over age may be replaced only within that sub-category.

I avail myself [etc.]   BARON KIJURO SHIDEHARA

[SEAL]

500.A15a3/1325

The British Secretary of State for Foreign Affairs (Henderson)
to the American Ambassador in Great Britain (Dawes) [30]

A 3861/1/45   [LONDON,] June 5, 1930.

YOUR EXCELLENCY: In the note No. 611 [31] which Your Excellency was so good as to address to me on June 5th you stated that it was the understanding of the Government of the United States that the word "category" in Article 19 of the London Naval Treaty, 1930, meant category or sub-category. Your Excellency added that the Government of the United States declared that it interpreted the Treaty to mean that vessels becoming over-age of either sub-category A or sub-category B of the cruiser categories (Article 16) shall be replaceable only in that sub-category.

2. His Majesty's Government in the United Kingdom note the above understanding and interpretation of the London Naval Treaty of 1930 and concur therein. His Majesty's Government in the United Kingdom do so without prejudice to Article 20 (*a*) of that Treaty under which they understand that the tonnage to be scrapped and replaced in the case of the British Commonwealth of Nations by the 91,000 tons of 6″ cruiser tonnage which may be completed before 31st December, 1936, comprises partly 6″ gun cruiser tonnage and partly cruiser tonnage of the 7.5″ gun "Effingham" class.

I have [etc.]   (For the Secretary of State)
ROBERT VANSITTART

500.A15a3/1107a : Telegram

The Secretary of State to the Minister in the Irish Free State
(Sterling)

WASHINGTON, October 3, 1930—noon.

16. Now that the Japanese have ratified the Naval Treaty,[32] it is understood that Australia, New Zealand and India will ratify very

---

[30] Copy transmitted to the Department by the Ambassador as an enclosure to his despatch No. 1524, January 5, 1931; received January 14.
[31] *Proceedings of the London Naval Conference*, p. 297.
[32] On October 2, the Japanese Ambassador orally informed the Secretary of State that on October 2 the Emperor of Japan ratified the treaty (500.A15a3/1108).

promptly. In this case, Ireland would be alone in preventing the coming into effect of the Treaty. The Department, therefore, would be very glad to have you once more take up this matter with the Government of the Free State to see whether some means might not be discovered to bring about ratification immediately. If this cannot be done, this Government is suggesting that a ceremony be held at the time of the deposit of the Japanese and American ratifications, since the President feels it important that the world should know, prior to the meeting of the Preparatory Commission, what has been actually accomplished in one phase of disarmament.

STIMSON

500.A15a3/1173 : Telegram

The Ambassador in Great Britain (Dawes) to the Secretary of State

LONDON, October 22, 1930—6 p. m.
[Received October 22—3 : 10 p. m.]

265. My 262, October 22, 1 p. m.[33] Prime Minister's office has just communicated following press communiqué, which is to be published here tomorrow morning:

"It is understood that ratifications in respect of the London Naval Treaty will be deposited at the Foreign Office on Monday morning, October 27th, by representatives of all His Majesty's Governments, with the possible exception of the Irish Free State, whose ratification may be delayed a few days by technical difficulties, and of the United States and Japanese Governments.

In the afternoon President Hoover, Mr. Hamaguchi, the Prime Minister of Japan, and Mr. Ramsay MacDonald will broadcast speeches on the Naval Treaty which it is hoped will be audible in all three countries.[34]

Further details as to times will be announced later."

DAWES

Treaty Series No. 830

Procès-Verbal of the Deposit of Ratifications in Respect of the United States of America, Great Britain and Northern Ireland and all Parts of the British Empire Which Are Not Separate Members of the League of Nations, Canada, Australia, New Zealand, Union of South Africa, India and Japan

The Undersigned, having met together for the purpose of proceeding to the deposit of ratifications of the Treaty for the limitation and reduction of Naval Armament, signed at London the 22nd day of April, 1930;

---

[33] Not printed.
[34] For texts of speeches, see *Proceedings of the London Naval Conference,* pp. 299–303.

Having produced the instruments whereby the said Treaty has been ratified by the President of the United States of America, by His Majesty the King of Great Britain, Ireland and the British Dominions beyond the Seas, Emperor of India, in respect of the United Kingdom of Great Britain and Northern Ireland and all parts of the British Empire which are not separate members of the League of Nations, of the Dominion of Canada, of the Commonwealth of Australia, of the Dominion of New Zealand, of the Union of South Africa, and of India; and by His Majesty the Emperor of Japan;

And the respective Ratifications of the said Treaty having been carefully compared and found to be in due form, the said deposit in accordance with the provisions of Article 24 (1) of the Treaty took place this day in the customary form.

The representative of the United States of America declared that the instrument of ratification of the United States of America was deposited subject to the distinct and explicit understandings set forth in the resolution of July 21, 1930, of the Senate of the United States of America advising and consenting to ratification, that there are no secret files, documents, letters, understandings or agreements which in any way, directly or indirectly, modify, change, add to, or take from any of the stipulations, agreements or statements in said Treaty; and that, excepting the agreement brought about through the exchange of notes between the Governments of the United States, Great Britain and Japan, having reference to Article 19, there is no agreement, secret or otherwise, expressed or implied, between any of the parties to said Treaty as to any construction that shall hereafter be given to any statement or provision contained therein.

IN WITNESS WHEREOF they have signed this *procès-verbal*, and have affixed thereto their seals.

DONE at London, the 27th day of October, 1930.

[SEAL]	CHARLES G. DAWES
[SEAL]	J. RAMSAY MACDONALD
[SEAL]	R. B. BENNETT
[SEAL]	J. H. SCULLIN
[SEAL]	GEO. W. FORBES
[SEAL]	J. B. M. HERTZOG
[SEAL]	ATUL E. CHATTERJEE
[SEAL]	T. MATSUDAIRA

500.A15a/1198 : Telegram

The Minister in the Irish Free State (Sterling) to the Secretary of State

DUBLIN, October 27, 1930—3 p. m.
[Received October 27—11:40 a. m.]

25. Cosgrave informs me accommodation has been refused by De Valera's party.[35] He greatly regrets, therefore, treaty will not be ratified until the Dail meets next month.[36]

Repeated to London.

STERLING

[The following is a statement issued by the Department of State on September 30, 1941, concerning the Treaty for the Limitation and Reduction of Naval Armament, signed at London, April 22, 1930:

"Termination of Certain Parts of the Treaty

"With the exception of part IV which, under the first exception in article 23, 'shall remain in force without limit of time', and of the provisions of articles 3, 4, and 5, and of article 11 and annex II to part II so far as they relate to aircraft carriers, the Treaty for the Limitation and Reduction of Naval Armament, signed on the part of the United States of America, the British Empire, France, Italy, and Japan at London on April 22, 1930, and ratified by the United States, the British Empire, and Japan, ceased to be in force on December 31, 1936, in accordance with the provision of article 23 thereof, that the treaty should remain in force until that date.

"The provisions of articles 3, 4, and 5, and of article 11 and annex II to part II so far as they relate to aircraft carriers, terminated on December 31, 1936, under the second exception in article 23, that they should remain in force for the same period as the 'Washington Treaty' (Treaty for the Limitation of Naval Armament, between the United States of America, the British Empire, France, Italy, and Japan, signed at Washington on February 6, 1922), by reason of the termination of the 'Washington Treaty' pursuant to a notice given by Japan on December 29, 1934.

---

[35] William T. Cosgrave, President of the Irish Free State; the Fianna Fáil was the Opposition Parliamentary party led by Eamon de Valera.
[36] The ratification of the Irish Free State was deposited in London on December 31.

Parties to Part IV

"The Governments of France and Italy, which did not ratify the treaty of 1930 in its entirety, ratified part IV, and their instruments of ratification of part IV were deposited with the Government of the United Kingdom of Great Britain and Northern Ireland on November 6, 1936. Part IV of the treaty of 1930 therefore came into force without limit of time in respect of France and Italy as well as the United States of America, the British Empire, and Japan among whom it already was in force.

"In a procès-verbal signed at London November 6, 1936 by states signatories of the London Naval Treaty of 1930, the Government of the United Kingdom of Great Britain and Northern Ireland was requested to communicate to non-signatories of that treaty the rules regarding the action of submarines with respect to merchant-ships, inviting them to accede thereto definitely and without limit of time as provided in article 22 of the treaty.

"As a result of invitations extended pursuant to this procès-verbal, the following states adhered to the rules of international law to which submarines must conform set forth in part IV of the London Naval Treaty of 1930: Afghanistan, which acceded thereto on May 25, 1937; Albania, on March 3, 1937; Belgium, on December 23, 1936; Brazil, on December 31, 1937; Bulgaria, on March 1, 1937; Costa Rica, on July 7, 1937; Czechoslovakia, on September 14, 1937; Denmark, on April 21, 1937; Egypt, on June 23, 1937; El Salvador, on November 24, 1937; Estonia, on June 26, 1937; Finland, on February 18, 1937; Germany, on November 23, 1936; Greece, on January 11, 1937; Guatemala, on September 8, 1938; Haiti, on January 23, 1937; Hungary, on December 8, 1937; Iran, on January 21, 1939; Iraq, on February 3, 1938, effective as from December 27, 1937; Latvia, on March 7, 1938; Lithuania, on January 27, 1938; Mexico, on January 3, 1938; Nepal, on January 27, 1937; Netherlands, on September 30, 1937, including Netherlands Indies, Surinam, and Curaçao; Norway, on May 21, 1937; Panama, on February 26, 1937; Peru, on June 3, 1937; Poland, on July 5, 1937, effective as from July 21, 1937; Saudi Arabia, on June 11, 1937; Sweden, on February 15, 1937; Switzerland, on May 22, 1937; Thailand, on January 12, 1938; Turkey, on July 7, 1937; the Union of Soviet Socialist Republics, on December 27, 1936; Vatican City State, on March 16, 1937; and Yugoslavia, on April 19, 1937."]

NEGOTIATIONS LOOKING TOWARD A SOLUTION OF THE PROBLEM OF FRENCH AND ITALIAN NAVAL CONSTRUCTION

500.A15a3/902 : Telegram

The Minister in Switzerland (Wilson) to the Secretary of State

[Paraphrase]

BERNE, May 16, 1930—3 p. m.
[Received May 16—1:35 p. m.]

42. From Italian sources in the League Council, I learn that the British Prime Minister recently wrote to Grandi [37] asking information concerning the reasons for the Italian naval construction program announced by that Government after London Conference [37a] and expressing his apprehension regarding its magnitude.

In explanation, Grandi replied that the countries participating in the London Conference knew what Italy's intentions were; namely, to build on same scale as France; and that the program announced for 1930 and 1931 by Italy merely equaled the French program for the same period. Grandi added that the Royal Government was ready to retard building, reduce building, or stop building on its program while the two Governments were engaged in an effort to . solve the difficulties arising from their naval programs to the same extent that the French Government would retard, reduce, or stop its program during that period. According to what I was told, Mac-Donald expressed his satisfaction with the Italian proposal, but whether the proposal has yet reached French sources is not known.

I have commented on the French-Italian conversations at Geneva in my despatch No. 1447, of today's date.[38]

WILSON

500.A15a3/1038 : Telegram

The Ambassador in Great Britain (Dawes) to the Secretary of State

[Paraphrase]

LONDON, August 11, 1930—5 p. m.
[Received August 11—12:40 p. m.]

181. Saturday afternoon Craigie told Marriner [39] that the French and the Italians had arranged for informal conversations to begin between Massigli and Rosso,[40] each to be accompanied by a naval expert, in Paris on August 15. Craigie, together with Bellairs from

[37] Dino Grandi, Italian Minister for Foreign Affairs.
[37a] For correspondence relating to the London Naval Conference of 1930, see pp. 1 ff.
[38] Not printed.
[39] Robert L. Craigie, head of the American Department of the British Foreign Office; and J. Theodore Marriner, Chief of the Division of Western European Affairs, Department of State.
[40] René Massigli, chief, and Augusto Rosso, director general, of the League of Nations sections of the French and Italian Ministries for Foreign Affairs respectively.

the British Admiralty, will be touring in France and will be on call by the British Embassy in Paris in the event that the French-Italian conversations should bring forth any development calling for comment by the British before the meeting of the Council of the League of Nations at Geneva on September 5, at which time the results of these conversations will be discussed by the representatives of the countries present there. Craigie told Marriner that he would keep the latter informed if anything of significance happened before the meeting of the Council, and said that he himself would be in Geneva when the Council met.

DAWES

500.A15a3/1074 : Telegram

The Ambassador in France (Edge) to the Secretary of State

[Paraphrase]

PARIS, September 6, 1930—9 a. m.
[Received 1 : 03 p. m.]

281. The conversations which have been going on between Massigli and Rosso have now terminated, and yesterday Massigli left for Geneva. I learned that there was nothing definite accomplished as it was found impossible to surmount above all the essential obstacle presented, namely, Italy's insistence upon parity and France's inability to concede it.

The respective Governments gave carte blanche to Massigli and Rosso to talk freely and on a purely personal basis without fear of committing their Governments with a view to discovering, if possible, some formula whereby each, so to speak, would "save face". No such double-sided formula, however, has thus far appeared in the discussions and while it is still hoped that the conversations may possibly solve the difficulty, there is little optimism that much progress can be made either along this line or with regard to military or air questions, which both France and Italy assert to be intimately bound up with the naval.

Repeated to Embassies in London and Rome.

EDGE

500.A15a3/1098 : Telegram

The Minister in Switzerland (Wilson) to the Secretary of State

BERNE, September 26, 1930—5 p. m.
[Received 5 : 25 p. m.]

87. [Paraphrase.] Referring to my telegrams No. 80, September 10, 4 p. m., and No. 83, September 19, 3 p. m.[40a] I went to Geneva yesterday where I talked with British, French, Italian, and Japanese delegates attending the current League session. [End paraphrase.]

[40a] Neither printed.

On the 19th instant Massigli made a further counterproposal to Rosso. The proposal provided for two categories of surface craft not covered by the Washington Treaty [40b]: (*a*) 8-inch-gun craft; (*b*) less than 8-inch-gun craft of which an unspecified percentage shall not exceed 3,000 tons. Submarine two classes: (*a*) above 2,000 tons; (*b*) less than 2,000 tons of which not more than an unspecified percentage to be over 800 tons. Neither party to build units which exceed in tonnage any unit constructed by them within that category since 1924. Parity in numbers of ships but without mention of tonnage. The entire contract to be covered by a clause reading somewhat as follows: "If either high contracting party contemplates the construction of units exceeding by an unspecified percentage the maximum displacement of a unit of the same class [of] cruiser constructed by it since 1924, that Government will advise the other of its intention one year in advance and the other will have the right of denunciation."

[Paraphrase.] This French proposal is regarded by the Italians as a retrogression and they are, or purport to be, full of disillusionment. They call attention to the 6-inch-gun cruiser of approximately 7,800 tons which the French have built since 1924, whereas their maximum has been 4,400 tons. Estimating construction between present date and 1936 on basis of the maximum unit permitted under French proposal, France would have superiority in tonnage of approximately 3 to 2 in the 6-inch-gun class, whereas at present there is a practical equality.

The French offer was, nevertheless, transmitted to Grandi, who replied with an abrupt order to end the discussions; and Rosso so notified Massigli. Later on, Briand [40c] consulted Scialoja [41] and persuaded him to agree that both parties should state that the conversations had been temporarily interrupted.

The situation is now completely the reverse of that which existed ten days ago. The French are in some degree optimistic, and indicate that they have made a very generous offer, also hinting that there will be an immediate resumption of conversations. The mood of the Italians is the exact opposite.

It appears unlikely that any improvement in the situation is to be hoped for during present session of the Assembly. Massigli is going on a vacation very shortly, and unless the conversations are resumed soon by reponsible Cabinet officers the appearances are that we shall enter the Preparatory Commission with this irritating point still unsettled. [End paraphrase.]

WILSON

[40b] Signed February 6, 1922, *Foreign Relations*, 1922, vol. I, p. 247.
[40c] Aristide Briand, French Minister for Foreign Affairs.
[41] Vittorio Scialoja, Italian member (substitute) of the Council of the League of Nations.

500.A15a3/1165

The Ambassador in France (Edge) to the Secretary of State

No. 927   PARIS, October 8, 1930.
                                              [Received October 20.]

SIR: I have the honor to report as follows on that portion of a conversation which I had last evening with the President of the Council dealing with naval disarmament, particularly from the Franco-Italian angle.

I told M. Tardieu that I was returning to the United States on a visit and that I would like to be in a position to inform you and the President, knowing how great your interest was in the matter, of the present status of the Franco-Italian negotiations regarding naval disarmament.

M. Tardieu answered that at Geneva, as I had perhaps heard, a new proposition had been made by the French representatives, based on a five years program, but that this proposal had been rejected by the Italians who have always in the final analysis continued to insist upon parity with France. (He apparently had reference to the proposal of Massigli, set forth in Mr. Hugh Wilson's telegram from Berne to the Department No. 87, September 26, 5 P. M.) M. Tardieu said that he himself was somewhat relieved that the negotiations had broken down on the basis of this offer as he was convinced that the French Parliament would not have agreed to the proposal as a basis for settlement. In any case, the Italians had turned it down and now the situation was perhaps even less favorable than it had been at London. M. Tardieu then went on to discuss the general question. He said that he felt that the position of no country on any question could be clearer and more unassailable than France's position on the question of naval disarmament. All she asked was a navy sufficient to protect her communications with her outlying colonies, dispersed as they were over all parts of the globe. The United States and Great Britain were at liberty, so far as France was concerned, to build as many thousand tons as they desired, but he did not see why the mere fact of the United States and Great Britain having agreed between themselves upon a certain maximum tonnage should serve as a basis for establishing an arbitrary figure as representing the needs of France. He was afraid that, as a result of the Washington Conference,—he did not wish to criticize the handling of France's case there as that was a thing of the past,—the impression seemed to be general that France was willing to accept parity with Italy. This was most emphatically not the case. France could not accept parity with Italy and every unprejudiced student of the question with whom he had spoken was in agreement. He mentioned the British Prime Minister, Mr. MacDonald, yourself, Mr. Morrow, Mr. Gibson and others with whom he had spoken. But, he added, no one of the American or British delegates at London seemed to be willing, in the final analysis, to put it up squarely to the Italians: in other words, to bring pressure to bear on Italy to recede from the impossible position she had taken. He said that during the Conference, on one of the occasions when he had been forced to return to Paris, the British Ambassador had paid him a hurried visit and had insisted upon his returning to London as they had everything prepared for an agreement: that the American and British delegates were prepared to tell the Italians that they would have to accept reasonable terms and no longer insist upon parity with France. As a result of this, M. Tardieu had gone to London, spent a day at Chequers, but had found that no such pressure was to be brought to bear upon the Italians, as he had been led to believe, through the representatives of Great Britain and the United States at Rome.[44] He said that you had intimated to him that the British message, as transmitted to him through Lord Tyrrell, had been sent without your knowledge or approval.

M. Tardieu then went on to speak of the general situation of chaos that existed in Europe to-day. He said that France and Czechoslovakia were the only two countries that seemed to be weathering the storm; that they were oases in the desert. All of which would seem to justify the French Government in continuing with the policy which it had been pursuing. He said that in the forty years during which he had been a student and observer of international affairs he had never seen such a state of moral decomposition as existed in Europe today. So far as reaching an understanding with Italy was concerned, he reiterated that there was nothing that he desired more: that one had only to study the present situation in Europe to realize how important it was from France's point of view to reach such an agreement, but that it could not be accomplished at such a sacrifice as Italy demanded.

I did not attempt to argue with him, merely explaining that I had raised the question with the sole idea of being in a position to report the latest developments.

Respectfully yours,   WALTER E. EDGE

---

[44] See telegram No. 156, March 23, 9 p. m., from the chairman of the American delegation, p. 75.

500.A15a3/1145 : Telegram

The Ambassador in France (Edge) to the Secretary of State

[Paraphrase]

PARIS, October 14, 1930—5 p. m.
[Received 8 : 08 p. m.]

324. The following information from an official source believed to be accurate has been obtained by the Acting Military Attaché.

The plans of the Ministry of Marine for the French naval program for 1931 are completed and have been approved by Tardieu and by the Ministry of Finance.

Admiral Violette, the author of the program, is a close personal friend of both Herriot and Painlevé, and our information includes statement that the plan has approval of these two leaders of the Left, in event that an agreement with Italy is not obtained. Briand is now considering these plans, and they will be put into effect unless there is an Italian agreement, which seems impossible at the present time.

The proposed French naval plan is based on necessity of insuring unquestioned control of the western end of the Mediterranean and provides for construction of 50,000 tons of new ships in 1931. The keel of one 10,000-ton 8-inch cruiser will be laid on December 1, 1930, and on April 1, 1931, construction will start on the first of three 22,000-ton capital ships. These ships are within the 1.75 ratio allowed France by Washington Treaty, and will mount 13-inch guns and have a speed of 28 to 30 knots.

As a bid for British neutrality, the submarine construction will be reduced except in the 600-ton coast defense class.

EDGE

500.A15a3/1150a : Telegram

The Secretary of State to the Ambassador in Great Britain (Dawes)

[Paraphrase]

WASHINGTON, October 15, 1930—6 p. m.

258. This afternoon the Secretary saw the Japanese Ambassador, and at the same time Marriner and Gibson [45] talked with Campbell, Counselor of the British Embassy, as the Ambassador is ill.

The purpose of these conversations with Debuchi and Campbell was to explain that as the French are now on the verge of publishing their building program for 1931, it would seem desirable that the three powers who have ratified the London Naval Treaty [46] should

[45] Hugh S. Gibson, American Ambassador to Belgium, temporarily in the United States.
[46] Ante, p. 107.

make representations for the purpose of preserving the levels set down in that treaty from any disturbance arising from a failure on the part of France and Italy to come to some agreement.

In addition to imminence of publishing the French program for 1931, an action which would tend to aggravate the situation, it is felt to be important that France and Italy shall not come to the session of the Preparatory Commission set for November 6 in Geneva and there embark upon naval discussions calculated to complicate the situation still further.

Campbell is cabling to his Government the details of the conversation, the point of which is that the three powers should make the suggestion to France and Italy through all available channels that they abandon efforts to win diplomatic victories, each over the other, with respect to naval parity and defer that issue until 1936, in the meantime issuing unilateral declarations setting forth their respective naval programs. The terms of these declarations, naturally, would have to be worked out together beforehand, and they would constitute, presumably, a retarding or postponement of their building programs in such a way as not to risk bringing into play article 21 of the Naval Treaty.

The Secretary will emphasize to the French and Italian Ambassadors that their mutual attitude on naval armaments will not increase security; in particular, that a heavy increase over present establishments on the part of France which would necessitate any change in the London Treaty levels, would tend to alienate sympathy not only in Great Britain but in the United States as well, and presumably in Japan. The Government of the United States does not desire to be alone in its efforts as it feels that maximum influence can be exercised on France and Italy only after each realizes that the question is one which is of genuine world interest, not of interest to any one country alone.

The foregoing is for your information and your guidance should the matter be broached to you in London.

STIMSON

500.A15/1067a : Telegram

The Secretary of State to the Ambassador in Japan (Forbes)

[Paraphrase]

WASHINGTON, October 16, 1930—6 p. m.

190. Yesterday I had a conversation with the Japanese Ambassador which was based on conferences with the President and our delegates

to the Preparatory Commission.[47] I summarize the conversation as follows, for your information:

I told the Ambassador that the failure of France and Italy to make any progress in their naval negotiations troubled me. If progress were not made before the meeting of the Preparatory Commission, I felt that the likelihood would be very great that something would be said or done at the forthcoming session of the Commission which afterward would make a solution of the issue between the two countries more difficult or impossible. I feared that something might be said at any moment, furthermore, particularly on the part of France, which might make the granting of any concession more difficult for her.

What was required on France's part, I pointed out, was reduction in her naval program to which she had adhered continuously since 1924; and that what was required on the part of Italy was that she should refrain from insisting upon diplomatic victory for a theoretical parity to which she did not intend to build. Such a deadlock, it seemed to me, ought to be comparatively simple of solution. If France continued to insist rigidly upon her 1924 naval program, she would make it almost certain that Great Britain would have to invoke the so-called "escalator" clause in the London Naval Treaty and increase the British fleet; this action on Britain's part would make it probable that we and the Japanese should have to do likewise. It seemed to me that France would be taking a very grave responsibility if, at a time when all the rest of us were cutting down our navies, she would go ahead and build up a navy to such an extent that she would force the breaking of the Naval Treaty. I could not believe that France would wish to run the risk of such adverse world opinion as this course on her part would be sure to arouse.

As for the Italians, they admitted frankly that they did not wish to build up to a theoretical parity with France. The difficulty ought easily to be solved, therefore, by a *modus vivendi* until 1936. I told Mr. Debuchi that my suggestion would be that the two Powers in question should agree not to agree on theory, but that each should make a unilateral announcement of a reasonable program of naval construction until 1936, all questions of mutual parity or of superiority being reserved until after 1936.

Debuchi repeated my propositions after me carefully. He asked me whether it was our intention to go ahead by ourselves or to await an answer from Japan. I told the Ambassador that I was not seeking to force any joint action, but that in view of the pressure of time I felt that I should go ahead in the very near future; and I hoped that

---

[47] Hugh S. Gibson, Ambassador to Belgium, and Hugh R. Wilson, Minister to Switzerland. See pp. 187 ff.

if Baron Shidehara [48] agreed with me in my views he might do something of the same sort.

I told Debuchi that I was sending a similar message to the British Ambassador, and that I hoped to talk with the French and the Italian Ambassadors in the very near future. Debuchi thanked me for my action in notifying Japan, and said that he would communicate with his Government.

STIMSON

500.A15a3/1156e : Telegram

The Secretary of State to the Ambassador in France (Edge) [49]

[Paraphrase]

WASHINGTON, October 16, 1930—6 p. m.

260. This morning I had a long conversation with the French Ambassador which followed these lines:

I told Claudel that, with the date of the meeting of the Preparatory Commission set for November 6, the urgency became greater that some arrangement should be reached between France and Italy on the naval questions between them, lest inflammatory speeches be made at the forthcoming session.

I pointed out to him that if France and Italy should make no settlement, the British almost certainly would have to invoke the escalator clause of the Naval Treaty, a step which would have a profound effect on world public opinion and would discredit all efforts to reduce naval armament. The blame for any such alterations, furthermore, naturally would fall upon France and Italy.

I told the Ambassador that I felt that it was my duty to point out to him and to the Italian Ambassador as well that, without entering into a binding treaty, it might be possible for each country to make a unilateral declaration of a reasonable and nonprovocative program of naval construction up to 1936, reserving until that date, with full liberty of action, the theoretical questions which had brought about a deadlock.

I let Claudel know that this country, in the Preparatory Commission, had never put impediments in the way of the land defenses of France, as it was recognized that France's chief danger had always been from the land. In the case of the French naval program, however, the man in the streets might take the view that that was an element of provocation.

I asked the Ambassador to consider whether France, in reality, were not reducing her security through the effect that increases in

---

[48] Japanese Minister for Foreign Affairs.
[49] Sent also to the Ambassador in Great Britain as telegram No. 260.

her Navy would produce upon her neighbors and friends, Great Britain especially.

Claudel was not encouraging in his replies but he promised to communicate the entire conversation to his Government.

Yesterday I talked along similar lines with the Italian Ambassador, and today I had conversations with the British and the Japanese Ambassadors, urging that they join in representations of the character indicated, in the hope that concerted action of this sort would bring about some result.

STIMSON

500.A15a3/1156a : Telegram

The Secretary of State to the Ambassador in Italy (Garrett)

[Paraphrase]

WASHINGTON, October 16, 1930—7 p. m.

91. This morning I had a conversation with the Italian Ambassador in which I told him that if the Preparatory Commission for the Disarmament Conference should meet on November 6 without an agreement having been reached previously between Italy and France on the naval question, the situation as it is now might be inflamed and a subsequent agreement would be made more difficult. In all probability Great Britain would invoke, in that case, the escalator clause in the Naval Treaty, thus making necessary a change in the levels of naval armaments by the three powers which had already ratified the treaty.

I told the Ambassador that I had decided to make a final appeal to France and Italy that they try to reach some provisional agreement at once, and that I had communicated my intention of taking this step to the British and the Japanese Governments, who, no doubt, will make similar representations. I referred to a previous conversation I had had with him in which I had suggested that the possible solution of the problem might be, instead of a binding treaty between the two countries, a unilateral declaration by each announcing a reasonable, nonprovocative program of naval construction until 1936, reserving until that date the decisions on the theoretical questions still at issue.

I told the Ambassador that I had talked with the French Ambassador, and that I had said to Claudel, as I now said to him, that the security of the two powers was not being increased but on the contrary was being decreased by adding to their existing naval armaments.

STIMSON

500.A15a3/1156d : Telegram

The Secretary of State to the Ambassador in France (*Edge*) [50]

[Paraphrase]

WASHINGTON, October 16, 1930—7 p. m.

261. Gibson is sailing for Europe on October 18 and will arrive in Paris on the 24th. After his full consultation with the President and with the Secretary of State here, the Department desires that you take him to call upon the Prime Minister and the Minister for Foreign Affairs for the purpose of discussing Department's telegram No. 260, October 16, 6 p. m.

STIMSON

500.A15a3/1166 : Telegram

The Chargé in France (*Armour*) to the Secretary of State

[Paraphrase]

PARIS, October 20, 1930—6 p. m.
[Received October 21—8 : 50 a. m. [50a]]

334. This morning the Counselor of the British Embassy here called to say that the Embassy had received from London a copy of the telegram which Lindsay [51] had sent from Washington to the Foreign Office stating that you had taken up with the Embassy the rumored naval construction program of the French Government as it had been reported to you by us; and that you had made the suggestion that the British and Japanese Governments join with the American Government in an endeavor to persuade the Governments of France and Italy to come to an agreement on naval disarmament.

The Counselor said that you had hoped to receive a reply from London before Gibson sailed for Europe, but that the British Foreign Office had wished first to consult the Japanese Government but had found this impossible. The Counselor asked whether, in the meantime, I could give him the source of our information on the French naval program regarding which the British apparently had no information.

I said that we had received our information from a source which we deemed reliable and pointed out that in the issue of *Figaro* for October 18 an article appeared by Thomazi, the journal's naval expert, who is himself a reserve officer of the Marine, and is in close

---

[50] A similar telegram was sent to the Ambassador in Italy instructing him to take Mr. Gibson, who would arrive in Rome on October 29 or 30, to see the Italian Minister for Foreign Affairs.

The Embassy in Japan was informed of these steps by Department's telegram No. 191, October 16, 7 p. m.; not printed.

[50a] Telegram in two sections.

[51] Sir Ronald Lindsay, British Ambassador in the United States.

touch with the French Ministry of Marine; and that this article contained substantially the same information as that which had been set forth in our telegram to you four days before the appearance of the *Figaro* article referred to.

The Counselor and I agreed that we should both try to obtain official confirmation of the reported French program, using the *Figaro* article as a basis. As I am endeavoring to arrange for Gibson the interviews with Tardieu and Briand which you requested, I am particularly anxious to have something definite for him when he arrives four days from now.

Referring again to your No. 260, October 16, 6 p. m., I would draw your attention particularly to a conversation between the Ambassador and Tardieu just before the former left Paris and reported by him in the Embassy's despatch No. 927, October 8. The despatch should have reached you by this date. See also our telegram No. 325, October 14, 9 p. m.[51b]

ARMOUR

500.A15/1075 : Telegram

The Ambassador in Japan (Forbes) to the Secretary of State

[Paraphrase]

TOKYO, October 22, 1930—2 p. m.
[Received October 22—5 : 24 a. m.]

197. The Government yesterday instructed the Japanese Ambassadors in Italy and France to address inquiries to the Governments to which they are respectively accredited, and to express verbally the views which you outlined to Debuchi. I understand that the text of Government's instructions has been repeated to Debuchi for your information.[52]

FORBES

500.A15a3/1175 : Telegram

The Chargé in France (Armour) to the Secretary of State

[Paraphrase]

PARIS, October 22, 1930—3 p. m.
[Received October 23—11 : 30 a. m.]

337. Embassy's No. 334, October 20, 6 p. m. I have seen the Counselor of the British Embassy again and he tells me that yesterday the British Naval Attaché made inquiries at the Ministry of Marine, using the *Figaro* article as the basis for his inquiry. He was told

[51b] Not printed.
[52] On October 30, the Japanese Ambassador reported to the Department the steps which his Government had taken; memorandum of conversation not printed (500.A15a3/1219).

that while there had been some discussion inside the Ministry itself along the lines set forth in the article and in the Embassy's telegram No. 324, October 14, 5 p. m., and while the question may even have been brought up before the Supreme Defense Council with a view to deciding how the funds allocated to the Navy under the budget should be spent, the entire matter is far from being in definite shape.

The important point, the Counselor said, seemed to be that in any event the French had no intention for the present of making a public announcement in regard to any building program the effect of which might be unfortunate, particularly just before the meeting of the Preparatory Commission. He also said that another member of the staff of the British Embassy had called on Massigli in connection with the *Figaro* article, and that Massigli had confirmed, more or less, what had been obtained from the Ministry of Marine. In accordance with instructions from the British Foreign Office, which were to determine the accuracy of the report, the results of the investigations described above had been sent to London.

I gathered that the Embassy's report to the Foreign Office included a very emphatic expression of my opinion, et cetera, that representations by the three Powers (United States, Great Britain and Japan) to the French in the present mood of the latter would be of little avail unless some new formula could be devised by which parity would be avoided and which would at the same time offer some basis for discussion: That, after all, they had failed at London and no more reason existed now to suppose that they would be more successful at the present time unless some such formula could be devised, as the French were just as decided as ever not to grant parity to Italy.

I am inclined to share the Counselor's opinion. In a conversation I had yesterday with Léger [53] he referred to the decision taken recently at the Fascist Grand Council [54] not to negotiate with France along any other line except parity. His remarks were similar to those expressed by Tardieu to the American Ambassador as reported in Embassy's despatch No. 927, October 8.

Massigli telephoned me this evening to come over to see him. He told me that the Foreign Office had received a telegram from Claudel which indicated that you were in some measure perturbed over a report regarding a proposed French program of naval construction. I called his attention to the article by Thomazi in *Figaro*. He said that there was nothing new in the information the article contained; that it had all been talked over at London, but that, in actuality, the

---

[53] Alexis Léger, Director of Political and Commercial Affairs, French Ministry for Foreign Affairs.

[54] On October 7, the Grand Council pronounced approval of the report of the Italian Minister for Foreign Affairs relative to the recent (August–September) naval negotiations with France.

French Government had no intention of building up to the program set forth.

Massigli then referred to the French-Italian naval negotiations, discussing the offer which the French had made at Geneva [55] and the resolutions adopted by the Fascist Grand Council. He did not seem to be sanguine over the outlook for arriving at any solution.

ARMOUR

500.A15a3/1182 : Telegram

The Secretary of State to the Ambassador in Great Britain (Dawes)

[Paraphrase.]

WASHINGTON, October 23, 1930—8 p. m.

268. Department's No. 258, October 15, 6 p. m. This afternoon the British Ambassador handed me copy of a telegram from the Foreign Office, dated October 22, 1930,[56] which concludes with the statement that, in the circumstances, they fear that anything in the nature of joint representations at the present moment might do more harm than good.

Our suggestion was not for joint representations; we clearly informed the Embassy here that in all events we were proceeding to express our own views to France and Italy, but that we hoped that the British Government would realize the gravity of the situation as we view it, and on its own initiative would proceed to express its views while there is still time to preserve the levels set by the London Naval Treaty. Both the President and I feel keen disappointment at the British attitude. The communication we have received suggests that the rumors which have come to our ears to the effect that the French are on verge of announcing an extremely disappointing naval building program for 1931–1932 are unfounded, and also suggests that there is hope that the French will propose conciliatory steps during the Preparatory Commission conference. This optimism is not in the least corroborated by any of our information. On the contrary, our fears are strengthened by our conversations with both the French and the Italian Ambassadors, and we believe that the only hope of saving the French-Italian negotiations before they are crystallized in failure lies in the influence of a clearly expressed outside public opinion.

I should like to have you see the Prime Minister personally and discuss the foregoing with him, expressing the disappointment of

[55] On September 19. The conversations had continued between Rosso and Massigli, who were in attendance at the sessions of the Council and the Assembly of the League of Nations.
[56] Not printed.

this Government. You might also suggest to him that it might be possible for someone, Craigie perhaps, to get in touch with Gibson when he arrives tomorrow in Paris.

Repeated to Embassy in France.[57]

STIMSON

500.A15a3/1175 : Telegram

The Secretary of State to the Chargé in France (Armour)

[Paraphrase]

WASHINGTON, October 23, 1930—8 p. m.

270. Your No. 337, October 22, 3 p. m. The primary interest of the American Government is not whether the French naval building program is what is announced in *Figaro*, or elsewhere; it is solely whether or not the building program of the French Government is of such size and character as to threaten the stability in the naval levels set by the London Treaty.

While an exact formula for figures is not being suggested, the American Government has pointed out, and it has been informed that the Government of Japan will do likewise, the advisability of permitting the issue to be postponed during the lifetime of the present treaty. The interests of both France and Italy might be fully safeguarded, it would seem, by a unilateral statement by France to the effect that while the London Treaty remains in force, that is up to 1936, her building program could be reduced materially, subject, of course, to a similar and satisfactory unilateral declaration by Italy.

Similar representations accompanied by suggestion of the same formula of a unilateral declaration have been made to Italian Government together with suggestion that whole question of naval parity be postponed until 1936. The entire matter has been discussed with Claudel, and it has been pointed out, furthermore, that France was not in any way adding to her security by insisting on high levels in naval armament and by prolonging unduly the period of uncertainty on this subject through failing either to come to an agreement with Italy or to act simultaneously with that power along independent lines.

It is my belief that Claudel has not got across the true gist of my conversation with him on the subject; Gibson should be very careful, therefore, to emphasize every point as if the French Government had no previous knowledge of the subject he wishes to take up.

Repeated to Embassy at London.[58]

STIMSON

---

[57] Transmitted as Department's telegram No. 271, October 23, 9 p. m.
[58] Transmitted as Department's telegram No. 269, October 23, 9 p. m.

500.A15/1077 : Telegram

The Ambassador in Great Britain (Dawes) to the Secretary of State

[Paraphrase]

LONDON, October 24, 1930—6 p. m.
[Received October 24—3 : 35 p. m.]

271. Your No. 268, October 23, 8 p. m. I had an interview with the Prime Minister this evening. He told me that the matter had never been presented to him in the way in which I outlined it on the basis of your telegram. Henderson [59] is out of London but Mac-Donald will take the matter up with him directly and in detail next Monday, when you may expect further word from me.

DAWES

500.A15a3/1178 : Telegram

The Ambassador in Italy (Garrett) to the Secretary of State

[Paraphrase]

ROME, October 24, 1930—6 p. m.
[Received October 24—4 : 25 p. m.]

98. I am told by the Japanese Chargé here that he saw Grandi yesterday evening, and acting under instruction from his Government asked the Minister whether he had any information regarding a rumor that the French Government intended to announce a capital ship construction program, a rumor which, in the Chargé's belief, was communicated to the Japanese Government by its Ambassador at Washington following a conference with the Secretary of State on October 15. Grandi told the Japanese Chargé that he had no such information.

The Japanese Chargé then expressed the general interest that his Government felt in the consummation of a French-Italian naval agreement, and more specifically the concern of the Japanese Government that the failure of France and Italy to reach an agreement might lead Great Britain to invoke article 21 of the London Naval Treaty; in which event, the Government of Japan could not remain indifferent.

There was no intimation that the Chargé's representations were based on anything except the Japanese Government's own initiative. Grandi accorded a most agreeable reception to what the Chargé said. The Japanese Ambassador in Paris was sent identical instructions; he has notified his Government that he is holding back action on them until he has seen Gibson tomorrow in Paris. Gibson has been informed.

GARRETT

---

[59] Arthur Henderson, British Secretary of State for Foreign Affairs.

500.A15a3/1194 : Telegram

The Chargé in France (Armour) to the Secretary of State

[Paraphrase]

PARIS, October 25, 1930—8 p. m.
[Received 11 p. m.]

339. From Gibson and Wilson. It seems to be clear that British, French, and Japanese Governments have, at best, misunderstood your suggestion in that all of them have taken it to be in the nature of a protest to France against the completion of the French naval building program for 1931, as it was sketched in this Embassy's telegram No. 324, October 14, 5 p. m.

We called this morning on the British Ambassador, who had received instructions to investigate truth of report regarding the 1931 program with a view to making representations protesting it, but who had raised vigorous objection on the ground that to do this would do more harm than good. We explained to the Ambassador that the reference to the 1931 building program of France in the conversations which took place in Washington was not a determining factor but was merely an additional reason why it would be well that any action contemplated should be taken before existing situation was aggravated either by the discussion at the session of the Preparatory Commission or by the announcement by France of a building program which might no longer leave that Government in position of a free agent in deciding its future course.

We went on to explain that the possibility of such an announcement had come to your attention only after you had come to a decision on your general plan. We then outlined fully to the Ambassador the nature of my statement made in conversation with Tardieu.

Tyrrell said that this gave an entirely different aspect to the whole matter; that he felt that it was a wise course to pursue; and, to my astonishment, he seemed to feel that there was considerable chance of Tardieu's receiving it favorably. In this connection, Tyrrell suggested laying stress on two points: (1) That we were not questioning France's right to build within the limits of the Treaty of Washington, and were confining our suggestion to auxiliary craft, thus meeting the needs of the British as far as MacDonald was concerned; and (2) that we propose to urge the Italian Government to postpone effort to obtain a diplomatic victory on the question of naval parity.

Tyrrell said that the Japanese Ambassador had come to call on him, and, although not very communicative, had given him to understand that he had received instructions from Tokyo similar to those which Tyrrell has received from London; that the Ambassador had questioned the wisdom of acting upon them and had notified Tokyo of his views. Fortunately both Ambassadors had put off taking action until the situation had been clarified.

The British Ambassador said that a message from London had been received this morning stating that by evening he will probably receive a communication which he is to make to the French Govern-ment. We assume that he will inform his Government of substance of our conversation with him and will express himself satisfied as to wisdom of the course proposed.

Next we called on the Japanese Ambassador. It was evident that he was not at all familiar with the subject, and from the very meager instructions he had evidently received from the Japanese Foreign Office he had been unable to obtain any clear view of the situation.

We explained the matter fully to him. He asked us many questions, finally making a memorandum of the several points embodying a clear understanding of what our aims are. Then he said that he would present the matter along lines similar to our own, although I think that his statement will be more of a formal communication than an informal discussion of the problem. We believe that the matter has now been clarified satisfactorily with both the British and the Japanese Ambassadors.

Gibson goes to Brussels this afternoon so as to stop possible conjectures on the part of the press as to the reason for his continuing to stay in Paris. He will return here on Monday morning as he has an appointment to see Tardieu in the afternoon at 5 o'clock; this date is the earliest opportunity offered, as the Premier is fully occupied today in receiving the French aviators, Coste and Bellonte; and Briand is ill. Gibson will leave for Rome on Tuesday afternoon. Wilson will remain in Paris at least until Gibson has left.

ARMOUR

500.A15a3/1196

The British Ambassador (Lindsay) to the Secretary of State

WASHINGTON, October 26, 1930.

DEAR MR. SECRETARY: I think I ought to let you know at once that in response to your message to London, our Ambassadors in Paris and Rome have been instructed to make oral representations to the French and Italian Governments. I enclose copy of what they are to say, and they must have received their instructions this morning. They have been told that it is important that they should take action today if possible.

Believe me [etc.]   R. C. LINDSAY

[Enclosure]

Instructions Issued to the British Ambassadors in France and Italy

His Majesty's Government in the United Kingdom have been much concerned at rumours which continue to reach them in regard to a Franco-Italian deadlock in naval question. Assurances were given to Mr. Henderson at Geneva that conversations which had been suspended would be continued but up to the present nothing in this direction appears to have occurred. His Majesty's Government earnestly hope that the negotiations which at one time seemed to be progressing favourably may be resumed in some form at earliest possible moment. Prime Minister as chairman of naval conference offered his good offices when conference adjourned and Mr. Henderson made same offer to M. Briand and Signor Grandi in May last. The good offices of His Majesty's Government as party closely concerned in every aspect of this question remain open to the two Governments should they desire to make use of them.

500.A15a3/1195 : Telegram

The Ambassador in Italy (Garrett) to the Secretary of State

[Paraphrase]

ROME, October 26, 1930—11 a. m.
[Received October 26—9 : 40 a. m.]

100. I have been told by the British Ambassador that he received instructions this morning to represent to the Italian Government the great interest of Great Britain in the reaching of a naval accord between Italy and France and to tender the good offices of the British Government to that end.

The Ambassador added that his Government appeared to be reluctant to take this step, but feels that in view of your suggestions it cannot fail to do so. He is instructed to make his representations today so that they may precede the exchange of treaty ratifications tomorrow in London.[61] Gibson has been informed.

GARRETT

500.A15a3/1212

Memorandum by the Assistant Secretary of State (Castle) of a Conversation With the Italian Ambassador (De Martino), October 27, 1930

[WASHINGTON,] October 28, 1930.

The Italian Ambassador came to see me to read a telegram from his Government of comment on the conversations he had with the Secretary on the subject of French-Italian naval building.

---
[61] See p. 128.

Mussolini pointed out in the telegram that, in the last conversation with France, Italy took the initiative in presenting compromise proposals. Italy was perfectly willing to make compromises, but France was not willing to make any at all. No Italian concessions were matched by any French concessions.

I had told the Ambassador one day that it would be rather wonderful if Italy would have the courage to act alone and make an announcement that they had no intention of building before the next conference. I said that, if Italy would do a thing of this sort, it would gain the sympathy of the entire world and that France would practically be forced by public opinion to cut down its own program. Apparently the Ambassador had telegraphed this conversation also to Rome because the telegram he had pointed out, specifically referring to what I had said, that this practically was the Italian proposal of last May,[62] although, of course, the naval holiday was presupposed to be on the part of both countries. Mussolini feels that a onesided declaration of this kind might be altogether too dangerous because there was no proof that France would not gayly continue its building program.

W. R. CASTLE, JR.

500.A15a3/1197 : Telegram

The Chargé in France (Armour) to the Secretary of State

[Paraphrase]

PARIS, October 27, 1930—11 a. m.
[Received October 27—9 : 50 a. m.]

340. From Gibson and Wilson. The British Ambassador has informed Wilson that on Sunday morning, acting under instructions from his Government, he called on the Foreign Office and made the statement that the British Government viewed with concern the apparent check in the French-Italian naval conversations; that Mr. Mac-Donald in the London Conference, and Mr. Henderson at a later date, had already offered any possible British assistance in solution of the difficulty; that the British Government had now instructed him (the Ambassador) to reiterate that Great Britain's offer of assistance for mediation or other purposes was still open at any time that the disputing powers chose to avail themselves of it.

The Foreign Office official to whom Tyrrell was speaking replied that Massigli had taken the latest step in the discussions by the offer he made at Geneva; the Italians had not yet replied to it, although they had stated that the negotiations were still open; that Fascist Grand Council had subsequently adopted a resolution calling for

---

[62] See telegram No. 42, May 16, 3 p. m., from the Minister in Switzerland, p. 132.

parity, and that under these circumstances the first step toward resumption of negotiations must come from Italy and that it could lead to something only if they relaxed their attitude with regard to parity. Gibson is to see Tardieu at 5 o'clock. Embassy at Rome informed.

ARMOUR

500.A15/1079 : Telegram

The Ambassador in Great Britain (Dawes) to the Secretary of State

[Paraphrase]

LONDON, October 27, 1930—1 p. m.
[Received October 27—11 : 50 a. m.]

277. My No. 271, October 24, 6 p. m. Henderson told me that the British Embassy at Washington was instructed to show you the cable sent to the British Ambassador there reversing the position outlined in your telegram No. 268, October 23, 8 p. m. The cable was shown to me but I shall not repeat it as it is in your possession. I was also informed that instructions were issued immediately to the British Ambassadors at Rome and at Paris to carry out your suggestions, and that this morning the Foreign Office had received cables stating that the respective Ambassadors had made representations yesterday to the Italian and the French Governments. Grandi was away from Rome on Sunday, but a written statement was left at his office. I assume that this information will reach you through the British Ambassador. I have telegraphed to our Embassy at Paris requesting that the substance of the foregoing be conveyed to Wilson and Gibson. Craigie feels that, as things are, there will be no occasion for him to consult with Gibson in Paris.

The deposit of ratifications of the London Naval Treaty took place this afternoon with simple ceremony.

DAWES

500.A15a3/1192 : Telegram

The Secretary of State to the Chargé in France (Armour)

[Paraphrase]

WASHINGTON, October 27, 1930—5 p. m.

278. For Gibson. On Saturday morning the French Ambassador brought me a memorandum from his Government on the French naval program and the French-Italian difficulties.[63] The most significant passage stated that the French Government was still striving to reach a friendly agreement with Italy with regard to the limitation of the

---

[63] Not printed.

categories of warships not provided for in the Washington Treaty; that, however, such an agreement could not be effected on terms which would imply the superiority on the Mediterranean of the Italian fleet over the French fleet, the latter being required for the protection, on other seas and within the French colonies, of interests which do not fall to the care of the Italian Navy.

Claudel asked me, before I had time to read the memorandum, what kind of a compromise between France and Italy I would recommend. I said that of course I could not make any recommendation on figures; that they were a matter for negotiation between the two countries. I again made clear to him that my suggestion was that Italy should lay aside until 1936 her technical insistence on parity and that France should, in the meantime, abandon her insistence upon the exact figures of the *loi navale* between now and 1936. I told him that I thought if this could be done, a *modus vivendi* on construction in the meantime could be arranged and announced to the world in unilateral declarations. I likewise let him know that it seemed to us that Italy had thus far displayed a more conciliatory disposition than France. Claudel inquired whether or not the building of any of the reserve tonnage in the battleship category would adversely affect the situation; I told him that I realized that this right had been reserved to France in the London Naval Treaty.

STIMSON

500.A15a3/1200 : Telegram

The Chargé in France (Armour) to the Secretary of State

[Paraphrase]

PARIS, October 27, 1930—9 p. m.
[Received 10:20 p. m.[64]]

341. From Gibson. I called on Tardieu with Armour at 5 o'clock this afternoon. We found him in a very irritated state of mind, obviously caused by Claudel's failure to understand the character and the real purpose of your original proposal. As a matter of fact, Tardieu manifestly in no way realized that a definite proposal for a solution of the problem had been made by the Italian Government. In introducing my statement I said that I had a rather long communication to make to him and that I hoped he would hear me through to the end before giving me his comment, in order that my message might be delivered clearly and accurately. Tardieu agreed to this and made a successful effort not to interrupt during the following quarter of an hour.

---

[64] Telegram in two sections.

At the end of my statement [65] he said that some of the objections he had intended to raise had already been anticipated by me and that it had been his feeling that by this method nothing could be accomplished; he said the suggestion for unilateral declarations had been put forward by him very early in the London Conference but had been turned down by Henderson as negligible. The French Government, he continued, had repeatedly suggested this method but it had never been given favorable consideration. He felt, moreover, that the resolution of the Fascist Grand Council to the effect that no further negotiations would be undertaken until their claim to parity had been accepted, had blocked all hope of agreement effectively.

In reply, I pointed out how the proposed unilateral declarations would avoid this difficulty and leave both Governments free, without any loss of face, to announce restricted building programs, adding that I was going to repeat to Grandi in Rome the substance of what you had told the Italian Ambassador at Washington and to urge upon him that Italy defer until 1936 the idea of a diplomatic victory on parity. When I had explained this latter point to Tardieu in various ways, he at last showed his first favorable reaction and stated that this method might prove the means toward a solution.

On repeated occasions I expressly disclaimed any intention on our part to mediate or to lay down the figures which France was to have, saying that, up to the point where French construction might upset the London Treaty levels, her building program was a matter of indifference to us.

When he had heard all I had to say, Tardieu's irritation vanished and by successive stages he arrived at a point where he expressed definite approval of the idea I had laid before him and voiced the belief that the problem might be solved in this manner. Tardieu promised to give the possibilities of the situation immediate study in order to be prepared when he heard how Grandi received the suggestion.

Upon answering his question as to the opening date of the Preparatory Commission meeting, I was surprised to find that he considered the period up to November 6th left ample time for an agreement, provided Italy reacted favorably. In explanation he said that the two Governments had discussed figures exhaustively and that if agreement as to this method of avoiding the parity problem were reached, they should be able "within an hour" to come to a satisfactory understanding.

He also asked me to see Massigli and Berthelot [66] before leaving

---

[65] See telegram No. 344, October 28, 4 p. m., from the Chargé in France, p. 156.
[66] Philippe Berthelot, Secretary General of the Ministry for Foreign Affairs.

Paris tomorrow and to give them the whole story, in view of the misapprehension in regard to the character of our proposal. Owing to the possibility of further developments during the next few days, Armour and I have requested Wilson to remain in Paris at least until I can get in touch with him after seeing Grandi in Rome.

ARMOUR

500.A15a3/1205 : Telegram

The Chargé in France (Armour) to the Secretary of State

[Paraphrase]

PARIS, October 27, 1930—10 p. m.
[Received October 28—6 : 47 a. m.]

342. From Gibson. Tardieu this afternoon in the course of our conversation, and after some hesitation, said he felt he ought to tell me, very confidentially, about one difficulty: The real obstacle to naval agreement was, he said, to find levels which would satisfy the British; as soon as these levels were found, it would be relatively easy to come to terms with the Italians. He added that for several days discussions with Great Britain had been under way and he hoped they would be over shortly with a resultant material clarification in the situation. Indeed, it was his suggestion that I remain in Paris until the question had been settled but he subsequently agreed with me that I had better go on to Rome and prepare the ground there.

It would seem from this that the British have already gone along our lines about as far as they can while they themselves are engaged in direct negotiations; for this reason you may feel that we cannot in the immediate future ask them to do anything further.

Considering the present situation—which now seems adjusted as satisfactorily as can be hoped for here—do you not think it would be better to make any further communications through our Paris Embassy rather than through Claudel in order that they may be coordinated with the clear understanding now existing in Paris rather than show up any further misunderstandings resulting from possible failure of Claudel to understand the exact nature of your proposals.

ARMOUR

500.A15a3/1207 : Telegram

The Chargé in France (Armour) to the Secretary of State

[Paraphrase]

PARIS, October 28, 1930—2 p. m.
[Received October 28—1 : 40 p. m.]

343. From Gibson. The Japanese Ambassador, Yoshizawa, asked Wilson to call this morning and told him that he had seen Berthe-

lot last night and, in accordance with instructions, had asked Berthelot whether the French-Italian naval discussions were making any headway. Berthelot gave him a negative reply, whereupon Yoshizawa stated that the Japanese Government felt uneasy about the situation because good relations might be endangered by failure to reach agreement and invocation of article 21 of the London Treaty might be rendered unavoidable. Berthelot then stated that as long as Italy insisted on parity he could see little hope. The Japanese Ambassador inquired whether he could not envisage some means by which the deadlock might be broken, to which Berthelot replied that in his opinion the only way was for the United States, Great Britain, and Japan to consult with France with a view to fixing a level in auxiliary craft which would be satisfactory to parties of the London Treaty and to France. The Italian problem would be much simpler, he added, if this could be accomplished.

ARMOUR

500.A15a3/1214 : Telegram

The Chargé in France (Armour) to the Secretary of State

[Paraphrase]

PARIS, October 28, 1930—4 p. m.
[Received October 29—6 : 45 p. m.]

344. From Gibson. On account of the possibility that subsequent discussions may bring up details of my interview with Tardieu, I think it advisable to send you herewith, as a supplement to my telegram No. 341, October 27, the following full summary of my remarks to him, in the form of a free translation from the French:

"Inasmuch as I was going to Paris, the Secretary of State thought it desirable that I call on you and give you the substance of what he told M. Claudel on October 16, and also that I make use of the few days before the opening of the next meeting of the Disarmament Conference to call on Signor Grandi in order to give him the substance of Mr. Stimson's conversation on the same day with the Italian Ambassador.

My message being rather long, I venture to begin by stating that it will lead up to a suggestion as to how a solution might be found of the Franco-Italian naval difficulty.

It is our conviction that there is a necessity for completing at its next meeting the work of the Preparatory Commission for the Disarmament Conference. If this session ends without completing its labors, we feel this completion will be indefinitely retarded, and a situation fraught with unpleasant possibilities will arise. It is my understanding that this view is shared by the French Government.

There seems to be no insuperable obstacle in dealing with the questions on the agenda, the naval question excepted. The Secretary of State, however, is worried by the thought that if the Preparatory

Commission should meet without a prior solution of their naval controversy having been found by France and Italy, a distinct danger that the situation will be embittered as regards this and other problems will exist. The efforts largely under French guidance for finding a solution of the general disarmament problem have been followed with great interest by the United States Government, and Mr. Stimson's friendly feelings prompted him to express his uneasiness at the present situation to M. Claudel.

French concern for security in any move toward disarmament is fully understood by the American Government. As you will remember, we recognized, in the course of the work of the Preparatory Commission, that the French thesis concerning land armaments resulted from this concern for security, and we have therefore deferred to the French conception in this matter even to the extent of giving up our insistence upon the necessity for limiting trained reserves—a concession which subjected our Government in the United States to severe criticism. I remind you of this merely to emphasize our genuine desire to meet the French conception of security and to fall in with this point of view as far as it is practically possible.

Considering this attitude of the American Government—which has been proven in practical form—I am convinced you will not take amiss a frank statement of our views on the naval phase of the disarmament problem as it bears upon the security of France. To us it seems clear that if it were possible to remove the French-Italian question from the field of discussion, security would inevitably be enhanced by the resulting confidence and good will.

If, however, there is continued the present insistence on the principles of parity on the one hand, and of superiority on the other, there is danger that security will tend to become diminished as a result of increasingly bitter discussions. We are convinced for this reason that, if the present misunderstanding with Italy should lead France to a rapid and complete execution of her 1924 program, the result would not be increased security but exactly the opposite due to the repercussions in other countries which would probably follow.

It is necessary to bear in mind another consideration: Should the 1924 program be put into rapid execution, it is apparent that the British Government, when a certain point is reached, would invoke article 21 of the London Treaty, thus upsetting the existing three-power agreement. Naval competition between the three signatory powers has been eliminated by this agreement; any event which upsets the agreement would certainly give rise to misgivings among the peoples of these three countries. It was my desire to draw attention to this merely as a fact which is evident.

I should like to express another thought as regards this controversy. In analyzing the problems between your two countries, it has seemed to us that these problems are far from insoluble, and that by a single step of real leadership it would be easily possible materially to improve relations between France and Italy. There would appear to be little hope of an agreement if negotiations are to be continued on the present basis, according to such information as we have regarding the progress of these discussions. The Italian insistence on naval parity cannot be reconciled with French insistence on naval superiority. It seems to us, however, that as a practical matter this immediate difficulty could be put to one side by a gesture of real political leadership by means of a unilateral declaration by both countries, postponing, until 1936, the question of principle and announcing, for the intervening period, restricted programs of construction. These declarations would of course be entirely unilateral and spontaneous as regards their public effect. As a practical matter, however, it would be necessary to coordinate them between France and Italy beforehand, and to make sure that the declarations really meet the situation as far as concerns Great Britain.

I am under the impression that the French delegation made this suggestion informally during the London Conference and it is our belief that at this time this offers the one practical way toward a solution. You will recall that a similar idea has already proved very useful as regards the slowing up of this year's building programs; and we believe that if this French idea could be adopted, both countries could easily leave out of consideration, for the next five years, the parity problem. What is more, a gesture of this sort would produce an atmosphere of harmony which would increase the possibility of later on reaching the more lasting agreement.

In the event that the French Government could see its way to declaring that, in the absence of unforeseen factors, it proposed to hold up until 1936 its 1924 building program as regards auxiliary vessels, it may be hoped that Italy would respond with similar declarations thus assuring France the maintenance of the present difference in the two fleets in favor of France for the duration of the London Treaty, with the added advantage of good feeling between France and Italy. Such a declaration would make it easy for Italy to adopt a similar program in view of the fact that they also have maintained that it is their wish to avoid building and that, if given some help in the face of their own public opinion, they would gladly give up building. As you have no controversy with Italy concerning the building of capital ships within the Washington Treaty tonnage, the real problem is definitely restricted, thus leaving only new construction in auxiliary craft. Nor would replacements presumably be affected. What we propose, briefly, is that on the subject of parity there should be neither a diplomatic victory nor a diplomatic defeat, but that both countries should expressly reserve their position on this question until 1936, if they desire to do so, and that their declarations should be limited to a statement of their intentions during the period up to the expiration of the London Naval Treaty.

What I am saying to you bears especially on the French phase of the problem, naturally; but I am leaving for Rome in order to state the case to Grandi after my conversation with you. I have instructions to urge Italy to give up the idea of a diplomatic victory at this time, and to postpone the question of parity in order to facilitate any measure you may feel justified in taking in order to reach a solution of this difficulty.

I would like to say only one more thing: This is the first time in history that there has been a long, patient, and scientific effort to prepare the basis for a limitation and reduction of the armaments of all nations. The United States also recognizes that French initiative has been largely instrumental in bringing about this effort, and that a large role in the work has been played by the French delegations at

Geneva. The moment has now arrived when we can hope that what has been done may be practically applied. There will inevitably result a deep general discouragement and disillusionment if the enterprise collapses at this point, and a definite setback to the whole cause of disarmament would ensue. If, on the other hand, this dangerous problem can be set aside by a new evidence of French leadership, a new impulse will be given to a movement toward security just as much as to the movement toward disarmament. For this reason, the President and the Secretary of State, persuaded of the great importance of this problem, have regarded it as a friendly duty to send · me to call on you in order to submit this suggested solution and to ask you to give your careful and friendly consideration to our proposal."

You will recognize that this message is a somewhat attenuated version of your own, rendered necessary by the irritation in which I found the Prime Minister. I did not fail, nevertheless, to drive home points in subsequent conversation when I saw that he no longer was in an antagonistic attitude.

ARMOUR

500.A15a3/1208 : Telegram

The Chargé in France (Armour) to the Secretary of State

[Paraphrase]

PARIS, October 28, 1930—5 p. m.
[Received October 28—4 : 30 p. m.]

345. From Gibson. Wilson and I, following Tardieu's suggestion, today went over the naval question with Massigli. Evidently he was pleased with the possibility of an agreement; he urged me to tell the Italian Government that the French were ready and anxious to resume conversations at any moment. He said the French had been prevented from resuming conversations themselves by the Fascist Grand Council's resolution.

Massigli informed us further that he had called on the British Ambassador this morning in order to discuss an arrangement concerning tonnage levels in auxiliary vessels and he hoped that a solution might be arrived at with the British along lines somewhat as follows:

(a) In addition to the seven 8-inch-gun cruisers she already possesses, France should have "the right to build" a further cruiser of this type to replace the *Edgar Quinet*, it being his idea that should it be possible to persuade Italy not to duplicate this new vessel the combined Franco-Italian force would remain within the limits of the present two-power standard of the British.

(b) No difficulties existed with regard to destroyers.

(c) While the submarine question presented more difficulties, Massigli hoped that a solution might be found by slowing up replacements in order to achieve a gradual decrease in French strength in this category thus putting Great Britain in 1936 in a better relative position.

These figures, for the first time, seem to us to offer definite hope that an all-round agreement might be reached.

Massigli repeatedly emphasized in the course of our conversations the earnest desire of the French Government to solve this troublesome problem. He thereby confirmed the remark of Tardieu, which I omitted in my telegram No. 341 yesterday, to the effect that really vital problems beset him to such an extent that he would be the first to welcome any method of getting rid of this one problem which was troublesome out of all proportion to its real importance. This was repeated by him with obvious sincerity and in several different ways.

ARMOUR

500.A15a3/1217 : Telegram

The Chargé in France (Armour) to the Secretary of State

PARIS, October 30, 1930—6 p. m.
[Received October 30—2:10 p. m.]

349. Following telegram for Gibson at Rome from Wilson repeated to you for your information:

"New York *Herald* has received following telegram from New York: 'Washington says Gibson has free hand to try to bring France and Italy together and may visit Rome.'
I have declined all comment. If you have any suggestion as to comment, telegraph Armour.
Unless you have special task for me here I think it better under present circumstances to leave Paris."

Could the Department inform me as soon as possible whether it has authorized any such statement and what response if any it desires to be made to the many inquiries from the correspondents here that will undoubtedly result from this story.

ARMOUR

500.A15a3/1217 : Telegram

The Secretary of State to the Chargé in France (Armour)

[Paraphrase]

WASHINGTON, October 30, 1930—5 p. m.

283. Yesterday the Secretary declined either to affirm or to deny press inference that because Gibson had had conversations in Paris it was probable that he was going to Rome, or that he had any instructions. It would be better, no doubt, that Wilson absent himself from Paris and that you avoid discussion of the subject as far as possible.

STIMSON

500.A15a3/1220

Memorandum by the Secretary of State

[WASHINGTON,] October 30, 1930.

The Italian Ambassador came to say that he had reported what took place between him and me when he brought me Signor Grandi's answer to my first conversation with him (de Martino), and that Signor Grandi said that Italy had proposed concessions and proposed a holiday and had received no answer. What more could she do? I then said that since I had sent my first message to Signor Grandi we had been making progress with France; that Mr. Gibson had had conferences in Paris with Monsieur Tardieu which made me more hopeful than I was a week ago; that Mr. Gibson was going to Rome to have conferences with Signor Grandi, and I hoped that the Ambassador would say to Mr. Grandi that I trusted that Grandi would hear him with sympathy and with the attention which I thought the importance of the situation demanded. I said that I regarded the situation as extremely important and hopeful. He said he would report that to Grandi.

I told him that I had been troubled by Signor Mussolini's speech [67] but had been encouraged by the fact that the French press and the French Government had seemed to take it temperately. He said, "Why that speech was made in the American way," and that he had been congratulated by Americans on the fact that Mussolini brought out the facts into the light of public opinion and that that was the only way they could be settled. He said, too, that the speech was most pacific, that Mussolini said that Italy would attack no one. I then asked him, laughing, whether I was to understand from him that when in Italy a man shook his fist at another he intended to blow a kiss to that other. If that was so, that was not the American method of speech to which he alluded. He laughed but made no reply. When we parted, I went back to Gibson's visit to Grandi and renewed my injunction that he should tell Grandi that I regarded that as a most important visit and that the situation was hopeful and I prayed that Grandi would give it most careful attention.

He read me something which he said came from German newspaper sources, suggesting that if America would reduce the interest on the French debt, France would reduce her navy. I told him I had heard nothing of that sort and could not discuss it.

He referred to the French contention that France was compelled to defend herself on two seas, whereas Italy only on one, and he handed me a memorandum which had been prepared in answer to

---

[67] Delivered at Rome on October 27.

that subject, which is annexed hereto as "A". I glanced over it and told him of course I did not want to get into a discussion of naval strategy with him, but from my hasty examination of it it would seem to me that France would answer that this memorandum was based upon the assumption that France was fighting only Italy alone, whereas the French would say that they were compelled to face the very strong possibility that they might be fighting with two enemies at the same time. He replied that that was the same with Italy, but we would not discuss naval strategy at this meeting.

I recalled to him my speech of last June, in which I had said that the naval officer saw only one-half of the horizon of national defense and failed to see that portion of national defense which depended upon the cultivation of such moral defense as good will; that the statesman must see the whole horizon and that I hoped that France and Italy in their situation would not shut their eyes to this important one-half of the horizon and would not descend to the situation of the naval strategist. He said he agreed with me.

H[ENRY] L. S[TIMSON]

[Annex A]

Memorandum by the Italian Ambassador (*De Martino*)

With reference to the French contention that France is compelled to defend herself on two seas, the following considerations shall be taken into account:

1) It is absurd to think of the possibility of an Italian naval attack against the French coast in the British Channel or in the Atlantic, in view of the absence of Italian naval bases in these waters: therefore, an eventual war could only be fought by the two Navies in the Mediterranean.

2) Italy is entirely dependent upon the sea for her material existence in contrast with France who in the first place has much greater resources in her own territory than Italy, and in the second place she can depend for her supplies on her ports in the British Channel and in the Atlantic, which are safe from attack from Italy.

3) Italy has 4.300 nautical miles of coasts and metropolitan islands to defend, while France has only 960. Taking also into consideration the colonies (speaking only of the territories with Mediterranean coasts) Italy has a total of 5.425 nautical miles of coasts to defend, while France has only 2.578.

4) The Italian coasts are much more vulnerable than the French coasts. On the Italian coasts, or at gun range from same, are located industrial centers of vital importance and large open cities, more numerous and important than the French. As regards the

Adriatic, the situation is even tragic for Italy, as it was again demonstrated in the world war. The Italian coast is completely open, while the opposite coast is protected by natural defenses almost insurmountable.

500.A15a3/1218 : Telegram

The Ambassador in Italy (Garrett) to the Secretary of State

[Paraphrase]

ROME, October 30, 1930—7 p. m.
[Received 9:20 p. m.[68]]

101. From Gibson. At half past five this afternoon Garrett took me to call on Grandi. When I had concluded my message, which I delivered in considerable detail, Grandi expressed no views as to possibility of finding a solution by the method we have suggested, but he gave me a detailed recital of the French-Italian negotiations since the termination of the London Conference. His story contained nothing new of importance; it was unfortunately like the opposite side of the question as I had heard it in Paris.

Grandi said that evidently the French Government, thanks to the interest we had shown in the subject, had taken steps to explain that their failure to send a further communication to Italy after Briand's consultation with the Cabinet did not constitute a rupture in the French-Italian discussions, but was due wholly to the fact that the French were precluded from making further advances by the resolution of the Fascist Grand Council on parity. He added that he had informed the French Ambassador that as far as the Italian Government was concerned the resolution merely reiterated the consistent position held by Italy and that not in any sense need it be considered an obstacle to further discussions.

The French Ambassador told Grandi that the Government of the Republic was anxious to take up the discussions again, and he suggested that possibly Rosso might be sent back to Paris for that purpose. Grandi told him that Rosso could hardly be sent a second time to Paris on an errand of this kind, but that in any event Rosso or someone else with other Italian experts would be in Geneva next week for the meeting of the Preparatory Commission, and at that time would be ready to meet the French representatives there.

Grandi added bluntly, that Italy was obliged to "save her face;" that she had, as a matter of fact, surrendered the essence of parity in her own proposals at Geneva while at the same time trying to maintain a semblance of parity with a view to satisfying public opinion.[69] Several times, Grandi repeated that Italy would be re-

---

[68] Telegram in two sections.
[69] See telegram No. 42, May 16, 3 p. m., from the Minister in Switzerland, p. 132.

luctant to build up to any French program and would begrudge money taken from other more urgent enterprises to spend on naval building, but, on the other hand, some semblance of parity must be insisted on for the sake of Italian public opinion.

In conversation with the French Ambassador, Grandi had spoken of the approaching end of the naval holiday for 1930 with misgiving and had told him that he looked forward with concern to the possible need, if no accord was reached by January 1931, of laying down forty-odd thousand tons.

Grandi confined himself to repeating that Italy ardently desired an agreement, although I offered him several opportunities to express his views as to the possibilities of our suggestion. He stated that Italy would welcome any possible solution, but said nothing which gave us ground for feeling that the next move might come from Italy. Finally, he expressed gloom almost amounting to hopelessness as to achieving any agreement satisfactory to the French Government.

I am to see Mussolini tomorrow or Saturday according to arrangements which Grandi is making. At that time an opportunity for getting further light on the Italian attitude may or may not be afforded.

GARRETT

500.A15a3/1222 : Telegram

The Ambassador in Italy (Garrett) to the Secretary of State

[Paraphrase]

ROME, October 31, 1930—7 p. m.
[Received 8 : 05 p. m.]

102. From Gibson. The American press correspondents here, having been advised from Washington that I was in Rome, asked to be received today. They arrived in a body after lunch, and several of them produced messages from their offices in Washington to the effect that I had been sent to Rome on special mission as the personal representative of the President and had been given a free hand to bring about a naval understanding between Italy and France. In some of the messages the terms good offices and mediation were used.

Through their representatives these messages from the American press were so wholly inaccurate that I was able to deny them, confining what I said to the statement that both in Paris and here I had discussed particularly important questions on the agenda of the Preparatory Commission in the hope that we might be able to speed matters so as to make this meeting the last.

This statement is entirely accurate, as, both in Paris and here, I have gone over the agenda in considerable detail, and in such conversations as I have had in both capitals I have made it clear to the respective Governments that I was not on any special mission, that I did not have any mandate to offer mediation or good offices, and that my role was limited to repeating substance of your conversations with the French and the Italian Ambassadors at Washington.

GARRETT

500.A15a3/1223 : Telegram

The Ambassador in Italy (Garrett) to the Secretary of State

[Paraphrase]

ROME, October 31, 1930—8 p. m.
[Received October 31—6 : 44 p. m.]

103. From Gibson. Rosso came to see me this morning under instructions from Grandi and asked me to go over the whole naval problem with him. After full explanations Rosso expressed himself as inclined to feel that the plan you have suggested offered the best way out for Italy yet devised, at the same time holding advantages for the French which they would not find it easy to resist.

Rosso repeated what Grandi had said yesterday, to the effect that the Italians were anxious to avoid building up to parity with the French, and he added that the solution suggested would enable Italy to forego building without incurring the reproach that the principle of parity had been abandoned.

Today Grandi lunched at the Embassy and talked over the naval problem for a short time in terms which seemed to us distinctly more optimistic than were those he used yesterday regarding the possibility of solving the present problem.

This afternoon at 5 o'clock he took me to make a courtesy call on Mussolini. We discussed the general work of the Preparatory Commission for the Disarmament Conference for about 20 minutes, but no reference was made to the French-Italian naval problem. (I gathered the impression that this silence may have been so that Mussolini might be in a position to say to the press that we had not discussed French-Italian relations, in view of the sensational reports from Washington appearing in the press to which I referred in my telegram No. 102, October 31, 7 p. m.; I emphasize fact that this subject was not discussed so that you may be in position to handle any erroneous press despatches.)

I expect to leave Rome either Monday or Tuesday, going directly to Geneva.

GARRETT

500.A15a3/1225 : Telegram

The Secretary of State to the Ambassador in Italy (*Garrett*)

[Paraphrase]

WASHINGTON, November 1, 1930—11 a. m.

95. For Gibson. Constantine Brown, correspondent of the *Chicago Daily News*, has reported to me, from a conversation he had had with the French Naval Attaché here, Sablé, that the British had intervened in the French-Italian naval negotiations with a suggestion which Tardieu had been advised by the French Naval Staff would make a satisfactory solution of the problem and upon which, as a basis, negotiations between the French and the Italians could be resumed.

Essential feature of the reported suggestion was that the French had been persuaded that by building three battle cruisers of 22,000 tons each, with 13-inch guns and speed of 34 knots, as they can do under the Washington Treaty, the superiority they desire can be obtained; while at the same time the Italians who do not wish to build such ships can rest on the theoretical parity given them by the same treaty.

The Naval Attaché is reported to have said, however, that the French would require a definite private understanding with Mussolini that Italy would not build. Were this arrangement made, the auxiliary tonnage would remain on basis suggested last summer by the Italians.

STIMSON

500.A15a3/1224 : Telegram

The Ambassador in Italy (*Garrett*) *to the Secretary of State*

[Paraphrase]

ROME, November 1, 1930—1 p. m.
[Received November 1—11:30 a. m.]

104. From Gibson. I should like to have your reassurance that the line I have taken with the press agrees with yours.

GARRETT

500.A15a3/1224 : Telegram

The Secretary of State to the Ambassador in Italy (*Garrett*)

[Paraphrase]

WASHINGTON, November 1, 1930—6 p. m.

97. For Gibson. Your 104, November 1, 4 [*1*] p. m. I have not denied categorically that you are discussing French-Italian difficulties, although I have made denial of any suggestion of good offices, mediation, and set formulae. The first story published on the subject came

from Stowe, Paris correspondent of the *Herald Tribune*, and was inadvertently corroborated here to Drew Pearson by the British Ambassador.

The French Embassy here, furthermore, has told enough to Constantine Brown for him to be able to piece out a story with the information he has received from the same paper's correspondent in Paris.

I have also tried to emphasize the connection between your visit and the meeting of the Preparatory Commission at Geneva this month.

STIMSON

500.A15a3/1226 : Telegram

The Ambassador in Italy (Garrett) to the Secretary of State

[Paraphrase]

ROME, November 2, 1930—1 p. m.
[Received November 2—10 a. m.]

105. From Gibson. Last night the British Ambassador said that Grandi had told him that your suggested method of solution seemed to be less advantageous for Italy than it was for France. You will remember Grandi's great deliberation in the assimilation of new ideas. His attitude in this instance may not be taken, perhaps, as final.

The Italian press comment so far has been more favorable than that which has been telegraphed from Paris.

Grandi told the French Ambassador that he had not reported his conversation with me to Mussolini before I called on the Duce.

The French Ambassador has gone to Paris. It is our impression, which is confirmed by that of the British Ambassador here, that Beaumarchais is so filled with pessimism over possibility of achieving any agreement with Italians that he will be a wet blanket on present hopeful situation in Paris.

GARRETT

500.A15a3/1226 : Telegram

The Secretary of State to the Ambassador in Italy (Garrett)[70]

[Paraphrase]

WASHINGTON, November 3, 1930—1 p. m.

98. For Gibson. Your No. 105, November 2, 1 p. m. In view of what appears to be Italian reluctance to take any decisive steps, the fact that France has been drawing closer to Britain as far as actual figures go might make desirable the suggestion to the French of

---

[70] Repeated to the Ambassador in Great Britain for his information as telegram No. 285.

issuing a unilateral declaration on basis of figures acceptable to the British, with proviso that the terms of the declaration would be observed up to 1936, unless some other power's actual naval construction should render alteration in the program necessary; in other words, a declaration along lines of article 21 of the Naval Treaty. By this course the onus of the situation would be put firmly on Italy, and as any change in the French figures would be based on Italy's actual construction, it should be quite as acceptable to the signatories of the Naval Treaty as the "escape" clause itself of that treaty. Also, such an act on France's part, not involving an agreement with Italy, should not meet, it would seem, with any difficulty in the French Parliament. I should be willing, if you think the step desirable, for you to go to Geneva by way of Paris and talk over this possibility with Tardieu. As to informing Grandi that such a possibility might be considered, use your own discretion.

It seems to us that to obtain an agreement for proper armament levels by France is the most important item, and that it would be a pity to have the efforts to that end nullified by wave of what seems to be professional pessimism on the part of the Ambassadors concerned, the Foreign Offices, and the press.

STIMSON

500.A15a3/1230 : Telegram

The Ambassador in Italy (Garrett) to the Secretary of State

[Paraphrase]

ROME, November 3, 1930—9 p. m.
[Received November 4—1:52 a. m.[71]]

107. From Gibson. At Grandi's request Garrett and I called on him at 5 o'clock this afternoon. He stated that although he wished to tell us something of how our suggestion impressed the Italian Government, he felt somewhat embarrassed in stating anything definite. He said that he had still felt rather optimistic when he had last seen us, because he believed that my conversation in Paris had at least prompted steps to be taken by the French for reopening conversations. (See my telegram No. 101, October 30, 7 p. m.)

Grandi went on to state that since that time the French Ambassador has made him feel extremely pessimistic by a further call on Friday evening. Beaumarchais stated that the French Government was glad to hear that Grandi was prepared to continue conversations on the naval question, and that if the Italian Government would as a precedent condition abandon the idea of parity, the French Government was ready to acquiesce.

---

[71] Telegram in four sections.

In reply Grandi stated that, although they were prepared to make substantial concessions as to substance, they could not agree to abandon their principle previous to discussion. Beaumarchais said that in that case all he could do was to refer the matter back to the French Government.

He went on to say that information from several sources indicated that the building of two or three 15,000-ton capital ships was being contemplated by France, who were assuming that Italy could be depended upon not to duplicate their construction inasmuch as this was outside the auxiliary classes. He felt that they would almost inevitably have to duplicate French construction in this class on account of the popular outcry to the effect that their cruiser units would be outclassed by even one of these ships. He indicated by inference that, without reaching such a high figure as 15,000 tons—he mentioned 12,000—the French might construct something to deal with the German *Ersatz Preussen*. He added that, in dealing with this question by means of statements which paradoxically announce a program of capital ship construction that would have to be duplicated by Italy, he feared that it might result in an increase in French and Italian naval armaments instead of a decrease and that careful consideration must be given to this matter.

Grandi then brought up the subject of the reports coming from Paris and London intimating that France was making ready to come to terms with the parties to the three-power treaty and to complete a four-power agreement. Grandi stated that these reports had caused considerable resentment in Italy as it was felt that purpose of the move was to make Italy appear to be responsible for any future difficulties. When the Italian Ambassador in London had inquired at the Foreign Office regarding the basis of the report, Craigie had told him that "there was nothing official yet" on this subject, that it was nevertheless quite possible, and that he felt it might be rather a good thing as it would tend to force Italy to come to agreement of some sort.

Grandi said that he had been bewildered, when our suggestion was under consideration, by the move of the French Government in insisting, as a preliminary to discussion, that Italy surrender her parity principle, as well as by the somewhat ominous allusion to a four-power pact. If he were obliged to give his real thoughts, he told us, he would have to be rather disagreeable as regards other people. We could see plainly that the present French attitude bewilders him.

Grandi stated that instructions have been given to the Italian experts on the Preparatory Commission to maintain the offers which Rosso has already made and to examine any other proposals which may be made in a friendly way. Rosso, who was present, interrupted at this point. Since he himself was the one who was going to handle the problem at Geneva, he wished to clarify what he considered to be Grandi's views. His statement was that they would maintain his proposals and would examine any others, and that they were quite prepared to examine, through the method we had suggested, whether a solution could be found—a statement from which Grandi did not dissent.

Perfect understanding of our helpful attitude in this problem was expressed by Grandi, who stated, however, that we would understand that, his position with the Grand Council being difficult, he would have to be prudent in view of French intransigence.

Rosso, after we had left Grandi's room, asked us to remain so that the situation might be still further clarified. Rosso said that, while he had hoped Grandi would be more outspoken as to his real attitude, he did not hesitate to elaborate it in his own words since it was so definite. He stated that if a direct agreement could be reached with France making possible the completion of the five-power agreement by continuing the conversations after reaching Geneva, this would be preferred as a better arrangement by Italy. In reply to my statement that we would much prefer that the five-power treaty be completed and that our suggestion has been made in the event that this was impossible, he stated that they quite understood this, but that if in Geneva it became obvious that agreement could not be reached by direct negotiations, the Italian Government desired that our method of unilateral declarations be adopted. At my request Rosso repeated this part of the conversation in the same words to Garrett, who had not heard it.

This afternoon I talked with the head of the Italian delegation at Geneva, General de Marinis, and as a result of this conversation and conversation with Grandi and Rosso, Garrett and I are convinced that the Italians sincerely desire an agreement and that if they can avoid the appearance of a diplomatic defeat and thus allow Grandi to defend the agreement before the Grand Council, they are willing to make substantial sacrifices. No good effect, we are convinced, would result from any maneuvers to force them into foregoing the principle of parity or, by leaving them out of a four-power agreement, to make them appear responsible.

It is clear that, apart from what Grandi has said as to their reluctance to begin a building program, they have every interest in reaching an agreement and consequently avoiding heavy naval expenditure, in view of the fact that the financial situation here is becoming acute. Nevertheless the possibility that something might be put over on them clearly worries them, and if no attempt is made to meet them they may feel that they must duplicate the French program.

The French might be inclined to make exacting terms, we fear, if the foregoing were communicated to them.

We do not think, in any event, that anything can be done here to deal with this phase of the problem. You may, however, wish to use some moderating influence on France either directly or through the British, making clear to the latter that if the Italians were allowed to infer that they were being maneuvered into an awkward position by the Franco-British negotiations (telegram No. 342, from Paris, October 27, 10 p. m.) which have been reported in the press, it would have an unfortunate effect.

GARRETT

500.A15a3/1239 : Telegram

The Chairman of the American Delegation on the Preparatory Commission (Gibson) to the Secretary of State

[Paraphrase]

GENEVA, November 5, 1930—11 p. m.
[Received November 6—2 : 25 a. m.]

2. We have been turning over in our own minds various possible ways of reconciling the French desire for naval superiority in auxiliary craft with Italian desire for the appearance of parity, and we should like to submit the following for your consideration as one possible means of achieving this. If you approve the suggestion, it might be held in reserve to be put forth informally in the event that the pending French-Italian negotiations are deadlocked again.

In view of the French ships which are still in commission, a considerable portion of any French naval construction program could be described as "replacement." It might be possible, therefore, for the French to declare a program of replacement to end in 1936, which might amount practically to a holiday on "construction." Besides this, the French might announce a unified program of construction, and if any question were to be raised in the Fascist Grand Council, Grandi could say that he had obtained full parity in "construction" and that Italian replacements obviously were not governed by French "replacements" but by age and condition of Italian ships.

Of course, we have not tried any suggestions of this sort while the efforts of France and Italy to reach an agreement in their own way are continuing, but if we were in a position to offer an informal suggestion at the right moment we might promote agreement.

The statement made by Grandi that Italy would feel obliged to duplicate France's construction in capital ships is due, in our opinion, to present acute disagreement over auxiliaries, and it may well turn out that, if agreement is reached on auxiliaries, the Italians will no

172

longer feel that they must duplicate French building under the Washington Treaty in view of fact that their parity in this heavier craft is clearly recognized.

In any event, we assume that construction under the Washington Treaty does not concern us directly, as we are not in a position to question it. Wholly apart from this, as participation by France and Italy in the 1936 conference is essential, we believe that we must be careful to avoid at this time any action which will leave either power with the feeling that treaty rights of either were called into question, and thereby make for a reluctance on their part to undertake further decrease in 1936.

We should find it very helpful if you would let us have your views on the feasibility of suggested division of programs into two parts, and if you would give us any alternative suggestions which might, in case of need, be advanced informally.

GIBSON

500.A15a3/1242 : Telegram

The Chairman of the American Delegation on the Preparatory Commission (Gibson) to the Secretary of State

[Paraphrase]

GENEVA, November 6, 1930—11 a. m.
[Received November 6—10 : 30 a. m.]

3. Reference is made to my telegram No. 107, November 3, from Rome. This morning I was visited by Massigli. I said to him that I thought that there was obviously a misunderstanding between the French and Italian Governments in regard to the message which was delivered last Friday by the French Ambassador, and I repeated this message as Beaumarchais gave it to me and also as Grandi had repeated it to me. Thereupon I stated that the effect had been most unfortunate but that the Italian Government had nevertheless declared that they desire that direct agreement should be reached or that, if this proves impossible, the proposed program of unilateral declarations should be carried out.

The telegram to Beaumarchais from the Foreign Office in Paris, which contained his instructions for this conversation, was next read to me by Massigli. The telegram opened by saying that France would gladly resume naval conversations with the Italian Government, but it would be necessary, if any practical result was to be expected, that the conversations be directed to the subject of concrete figures, the question of parity being set aside. The French Government, the message continued, desired to emphasize to him that they wish nothing which could in any way embarrass my mission or which would create anything but a favorable atmosphere for a negotiation.

They desired to make things as easy as possible for Italy and to afford a graceful way out for the Italian Government. The matter is being taken up with Rome this morning by Massigli who will no doubt put matters right with the Italian Government.

Repeated to Rome.

GIBSON

500.A15a3/1251

Memorandum by the Secretary of State

[WASHINGTON,] November 6, 1930.

The French Ambassador called today and first asked whether I had read his note of two days ago. I told him that I had received a verbal report of it through Mr. Marriner but had not read it myself. I sent for Mr. Marriner who came in with the report and the Ambassador then said he did not have anything further to discuss about it.

It then developed what his real mission was. He asked me about his suggestion the other day of having France build battleships under her rights in the Washington Treaty and asked whether I had reported that to Mr. Gibson. The information which I had just received from Mr. Constantine Brown about a half an hour before, as to the difference between the French Admiralty and the French Government, at once recurred to my mind. I asked the French Ambassador whether I correctly understood his proposition to be that if France built these 3 battleships, as she had a right to do under the Treaty, this would serve to establish the superiority over Italy which she desired and would permit France to be generous to Italy in the other categories, namely, the auxiliary ships? He at once said that that was his idea. I said, of course if his proposition merely was that France would build the battleships and then also insist upon her contention of superiority over Italy in the auxiliary vessels, it would be of no assistance. He said, "Oh, no. My proposition was the first one that you mentioned." I then said in response to his question that I did not report this to Mr. Gibson because I had thought that this suggestion came from the French Government and that in that case of course Mr. Gibson would already have it from Mr. Tardieu. The French Ambassador at once said, "No, that was my suggestion. Not my Government's. It is to be taken as originating in the air and was suggested as a means of helping." I thanked him warmly for his kindness in coming to correct the error which I had made and said that I would report it to Gibson at once.

The foregoing would seem to be a clear confirmation of Constantine Brown's statement about Sablé's attitude, namely, that the French

Admiralty has a plan which they would agree to and they have been trying to get it to us in this indirect way. In view of this, his statement to the effect that Tardieu is opposed to this proposition on account of its expense and prefers to try to maintain French superiority in auxiliary construction in order to achieve his aim of superiority over Italy and still keep his budget lowered, may also be correct.

H[ENRY] L. S[TIMSON]

500.A15a3/1239 : Telegram

The Secretary of State to the Chairman of the American Delegation on the Preparatory Commission (Gibson)

[Paraphrase]

WASHINGTON, November 6, 1930—5 p. m.

1. Your No. 2, November 5, 11 p. m. This morning the French Ambassador called on me and brought up the suggestion, which had previously come to me indirectly through a well-known press correspondent, that France should exercise her rights under the Washington Treaty and should build three battle cruisers, all of high speed, and that if this construction could be accomplished on some tacit understanding that the Italians would not build, at the same time retaining their rights under the Washington Treaty, it might be possible to reach a practical parity in auxiliary craft.

Claudel asked me whether I had informed you of this suggestion. I said that I had not, as I assumed you had heard of it from Tardieu in Paris; I refrained from mentioning your discussion of it with Grandi (telegram No. 107, November 3, 9 p. m., from Rome). Claudel said that in all probability Tardieu had not discussed this proposition as it was his, the Ambassador's, own idea which he had put forward merely to be helpful.

To give you further background, it appears that the suggestion must have emanated originally from the Naval Attaché of the French Embassy, who discussed it with one of the press correspondents about a week ago. The latter reported it to the Department. As no comment was elicited from the Department, the Naval Attaché again urged his press acquaintance to tell the Department that comment on the suggestion was desired. The inference was also drawn by the correspondent in question that the proposition was viewed very favorably by the French Admiralty, although it was less acceptable to the Prime Minister, who did not see in it any possibility of economy.

Referring to your suggestion in event of French-Italian negotiations approaching deadlock, it seems wholly satisfactory here that each side consider the possibility of differentiating between replacement and new construction, and that a parity in new construction might be reached, always taking into account the fact that the new building together with any replacement construction must still be within bounds which are acceptable to the parties to the London Naval Treaty.

STIMSON

500.A15a3/1253 : Telegram

The Chairman of the American Delegation on the Preparatory Commission (Gibson) to the Secretary of State

[Paraphrase]

GENEVA, November 7, 1930—9 p. m.
[Received November 7—8 : 22 p. m.]

9. From several sources it is reported that the French Government and the French delegation feel that the American delegation can exercise, in their negotiations with Italy, a very favorable influence. We are inclined to believe that they may have instructions along this line since this has been made so clear. A similar hope that we will exercise friendly influence has been expressed here by the Italians.

It may be possible, on account of this attitude on the part of the two delegations, for us to exercise a helpful conciliatory influence when occasion arises. However, I feel that you ought to know that we are leaning over backward to make it clear that we have no desire to exercise mediation or good offices, and that we think that in their fortunate resumption of direct negotiations lies the best hope at present.

GIBSON

500.A15a3/1254 : Telegram

The Chargé in France (Armour) to the Secretary of State

[Paraphrase]

PARIS, November 8, 1930—11 a. m.
[Received 11 : 30 a. m.]

361. Information, which seems reliable, has been received to the effect that the French Ministry of Marine and Louis Aubert, who was at the London Naval Conference with Tardieu, have every confidence in Gibson's ability and disinterestedness and very much hope that his good offices may be available in any negotiations looking to a solution of the naval situation that may be carried on between France and Italy. Information has also been received that Aubert,

in view of the above, has advised Tardieu that instructions to keep Gibson fully informed of all developments should be given to the French delegation at Geneva.

My own knowledge of Tardieu's friendship for and confidence in Gibson confirms the above. As the Department is aware, I was present at the interview between Gibson and Tardieu on October 27 of this year. On that occasion it was very evident that this confidence of Tardieu in Gibson and in his sincerity largely contributed to the favorable reception which the new suggestions received from Tardieu and the French.

Feeling that these impressions might be useful as background in case they should fit in with your information from other sources, I take the liberty of submitting them to you.

ARMOUR

500.A15a3/1262 : Telegram

The Chairman of the American Delegation on the Preparatory Commission (Gibson) to the Secretary of State

[Paraphrase]

GENEVA, November 11, 1930—8 p. m.
[Received 11:58 p. m.]

14. I received a call this afternoon from Massigli. He stated that he had had a talk with Rosso in order to ascertain whether there was any basis for profitable resumption of naval conversations. In reply to the question whether Italy would insist, in laying down figures, on maintaining the appearance of parity, it was suggested by Rosso that such was the effect of his instructions. It was next stated by Massigli that at the present time this subject of conversation did not seem to be a profitable one and inquiry in regard to other alternatives was made, in reply to which Rosso stated that, while preferring that the five-power treaty be completed, if it should prove impossible the Italian Government would be ready to consider unilateral declarations'as an alternative.

Having been asked by Massigli whether Italy would feel obliged to announce the same program, if France laid down a program in its declarations, Rosso replied in the affirmative. After which it was stated by Massigli that in this case it might be more profitable if the discussion were approached from another angle. He asked whether Rosso was willing that the question of levels as between the British and the French Navies should be discussed with Craigie by Massigli, to which Rosso agreed rather reluctantly. The above is confirmed by Craigie who talked with both Massigli and Rosso. He adds that, awaiting certain instructions requested by Massigli, the discussions between Britain and France cannot take place until the end of this week.

The possibility of a distinction between replacements and new construction is being examined by Britain and France in the meantime, to see if anything can be done toward having both France and Italy announce a holiday in new construction so that the question of parity may be avoided and a satisfactory French superiority in replacement worked out. The possibility of declarations to cover the period up to and including 1933, which may simplify the problem, has been discussed by Craigie and Massigli as a last resort.

GIBSON

500.A15a3/1266 : Telegram

The Chairman of the American Delegation on the Preparatory Commission (Gibson) to the Secretary of State

[Paraphrase]

GENEVA, November 13, 1930—3 a. m.
[Received 5 : 10 a. m.]

17. This evening I received a call from Rosso, who stated that he wanted to tell us about his conversations with Craigie and Massigli, so as to explain his own thoughts to us and to ask our opinion in the matter.

Rosso stated that he had, in his talk with Massigli, very frankly explained the Italian political situation, one element being impatient of any efforts to conciliate France, an attitude tending to throw them into the camp of those who desire existing treaties to be revised; and another element, which included Grandi, being sincerely anxious that a more farsighted course, which involved finding a solution of the existing difficulties with France, should be followed; that even on questions of naval figures he felt that, in order to strengthen the element which favors a saner course, this should be borne in mind.

In reference to the possibility of unilateral declarations, Rosso had told Massigli that naturally any figures used by France must be forwarded to Rome, and that undoubtedly the Admiralty would press for duplication of France's program, presumably in disguised form to render it more difficult of comparison. It would in its essence, however, have to contain equality in construction tonnage, a policy which for six years had already been followed. This would enable Italy to justify the declarations, yet it must not be forgotten by France that this would involve approval of France's present superiority until 1936, clearly postponing the thesis of acknowledging full parity with France held by the Admiralty.

In his talk with Craigie, Rosso said that he had been concerned by Craigie's insistence that our suggestion envisaged an agreement. upon the levels to be achieved in 1936, and not a statement of programs for the next 5 years. The readiness of Italy to consider unilateral declarations, Rosso said, was based on the fact that the virtue of this expedient for Italy lay in its avoidance of the question of levels which could be compared. Italy would be left in a visibly inferior position, which Grandi would have difficulty in justifying, by specification of levels.

It was further stated by Rosso that the good understanding as a result of satisfactory unilateral declarations might, of course, subsequently render possible that some formula for entering the treaty between now and 1936 would be found. I stated, in reply to a direct question as to my views, that I felt it was important that unnecessary complications should not disturb the present hopeful atmosphere; that it was the present desire of the French and the British, so far as I knew from my conversations with them, that they should devote themselves to finding a possible agreement with the Italians, regular French adherence to the treaty not being pressed at this time; that our suggestions had been made, so far as we were concerned, with the desire that both France and Italy should reach some sort of agreement that would carry forward the idea of a five-power understanding; and that we were anxious, in our rather detached position as regards figures, that all the parties to the London negotiations should be able to reach a general agreement in a contented frame of mind, so that in 1936 they would be disposed to come back willingly to a conference.

Rosso expressed his intention to have a further talk with Massigli. He proposed to state that, if the French would declare their program up to 1936, he would transmit the figures to Rome, and would recommend, in order to make comparison as difficult as possible, the distribution of the tonnage of the Italian program in a different way among the categories; fruitful exploration, he hoped, might be made along these lines.

GIBSON

500.A15a3/1269

Memorandum by the Secretary of State

[WASHINGTON,] November 13, 1930.

The Italian Ambassador had a long telegram which he did not read to me, nor give me the contents of. But he said that Signor Grandi was doubtful whether the French will wish to make an agreement or will refrain from insisting upon recognition of inferiority by Italy.

The Ambassador mentioned the statements of Beaumarchais. I told him that I remembered what he had reported Beaumarchais to have said to Signor Grandi and had no reason to discredit Signor Grandi's report of it as being accurate [73] but I knew those were not the instructions of the French Government [74] and they no longer stood in the way of an agreement. I told him that whereas I was a little afraid at first that the French were not anxious to make an agreement, that apprehension on my part had been removed and I was confident now that the French were ready to make a fair agreement. I said that my apprehension had now shifted to whether Italy was ready to do its part and that I was inclined to fear that she was not. I told him that I was keeping in touch with the conversations which were going on in Geneva and I wished he would convey to Signor Grandi what I said, namely, that I felt sure that the French were ready to make a fair agreement and that I hoped Italy would not block it. He said he would do so.

H[ENRY] L. S[TIMSON]

500.A15a3/1270 : Telegram

The Chairman of the American Delegation on the Preparatory Commission (Gibson) to the Secretary of State

[Paraphrase]

GENEVA, November 13, 1930—midnight.
[Received November 14—10 : 40 a. m.]

20. I received a call this evening from Craigie, who stated that he sees, from his various conversations, three possibilities to the solution of the naval difficulty between France and Italy. He enumerated them in order of preference as follows:

First point: Tonnage agreement which will enable the five-power treaty to be entered.

Second point: Building program unilateral declarations—the possibility that after such declarations the treaty might be entered on building programs alone without translating the figures into tonnage levels, the disparity of total tonnages of the two fleets thus not being thrown into relief, was not excluded by him.

Third point: The treaty to be entered by France after a level acceptable to the three signatories has been worked out; this should be envisaged only if agreeable to Italy, in his opinion.

The first point, obviously the most desirable, is the one on which efforts are now being concentrated, and various possibilities are being explored which do not warrant detailed report since they are too

---

[73] See telegram No. 107, November 3, 9 p. m., from the Ambassador in Italy, p. 168.
[74] See telegram No. 3, November 6, 11 a. m., from the chairman of the American delegation on the Preparatory Commission, p. 172.

nebulous as yet. We cannot, however, be sure that at any time an abrupt turn in the direction of the third point will not take place. The procedure to be followed if this should materialize is being envisaged by us.

It is plain from Rosso's remarks, and those of other Italians here, that the Italian Government is nervous over press reports of such an impending change in events and it fears that French entrance into the treaty, if she lays down figures agreeable to Britain, will enable her to veto adherence by Italy except on France's terms, for the reason that the other three Powers naturally, without the consent of the fourth party to the treaty, could not admit Italy. If France is admitted and Italy later requests admission on the same tonnage levels, it seems to us that the position of the three original signatories might become embarrassing. In case they should agree to France's veto on Italian admission, they run the risk of seeming to favor France by making themselves judges of the issue of parity; they would be accused, on the other hand, of deciding in favor of Italy in case they should bring pressure on France to admit Italy on similar terms.

It is difficult to envisage a situation in which France can accept the treaty without aggravating the situation with Italy, after direct agreement has failed. We feel that it would be a mistake, no matter how important and desirable it may be to complete the five-power agreement, for us to lose sight of the fact, which we have consistently maintained, that naval limitation is a continuing process and that we have a general interest in bringing all five naval powers back into succeeding conferences both confidently and willingly.

We have kept these misgivings to ourselves, reporting them to you only to give you the whole picture as our conversations have shown it to us. We have been careful in talking with the Italians not to dispel their anxiety that, should other efforts fail, the above possibility exists.

GIBSON

500.A15a3/1276 : Telegram

The Chairman of the American Delegation on the Preparatory Commission (Gibson) to the Secretary of State

[Paraphrase]

GENEVA, November 20, 1930—11 p. m.
[Received 11 : 58 p. m.]

31. We have learned from Craigie who has called that, in a lengthy conversation with Rosso, he, Craigie, had suggested to the Italian delegate a plan for auxiliary vessels which would work out along the following lines:

1. Other than the completion of the 1930 program, no 8-inch-gun cruisers to be constructed between now and 1936.

2. In 6-inch-gun cruisers, replacement only; that is, no new construction.

3. For destroyers, the same policy as laid down in point 2.

4. Upon completion of the 1930 program, no construction of submarines.

Briefly, this adds up to a naval holiday with regard to points 1 and 4, and the construction of replacements only under points 2 and 3.

On points 1 and 2 this amounts to an approximate parity, and on points 3 and 4 France is left a considerable margin of superiority.

Rosso did not at all commit himself but raised no objection to Craigie's suggestion that he, Craigie, go over this matter with Massigli. Rosso merely requested that the fact that he had even heard of it should not be mentioned.

Massigli, whom Craigie saw next, showed the latter a new offer which he, Massigli, had just received from Dumesnil. The new offer essentially provides that the two fleets remain on their present levels. There should be replacement only, no new construction. Craigie states that the French would plan replacements to the extent of about 50,000 tons annually. Having less replaceable material, the Italians would have to be satisfied with a considerably smaller program. This, Craigie indicated to Massigli, was a considerably worse offer than the French had made at London. There the French had included about 100,000 tons of over-age material in their proposal of 685,000 tons.

Thereupon Craigie introduced the plan outlined in the first paragraph of this telegram. After hours of discussion an agreement was reached. Until he had had further talks with Massigli concerning the Craigie proposal, the British delegate would not submit the Dumesnil plan to Rosso.

The essential points of what Craigie had told us were confirmed by Massigli when he called. Massigli declared, however, that under the Dumesnil plan the French building program would not be 50,000 tons per annum but approximately 40,000.

It has become more and more obvious that both the Italians and French, rather than negotiating by means of direct conversations, prefer negotiating through the intermediary of Craigie.

GIBSON

500.A15a3/1286 : Telegram

The Chairman of the American Delegation on the Preparatory Commission (Gibson) to the Secretary of State

[Paraphrase]

GENEVA, December 6, 1930—11 p. m.
[Received 11:25 p. m.]

58. Owing to illness of both Craigie and Rosso, the French-Italian naval discussions have been delayed and are now definitely adjourned

while the French Cabinet is being reconstituted. In conversation today, Rosso brought the matter up to date.

A messenger was sent to Rome to explain Craigie's latest proposal and to recommend on Rosso's behalf that the Italian Government accept it as a basis for discussion. Some days ago a reply was received to the effect that Italy would accept the proposal as a basis for discussion, provided that France also accepted it in its present form.

Rosso has analyzed Craigie's proposal and has picked out certain points which, unless they are altered, present insuperable obstacles for Italy. Reducing proposal to figures, Rosso finds that it works approximately as follows:

1. 8-inch cruisers. France and Italy 70,000 tons each.
2. 6-inch cruisers and destroyers. France, 199,000 tons; and Italy, 157,000 tons.
3. Submarines. France, 77,000 tons; and Italy, 44,000 tons.

For technical reasons, Rosso said, a navy can keep on effective service only one submarine out of three; for this reason, the Italian Admiralty is definitely opposed to accepting any figure lower than 52,700 tons while French figures remain at something over 77,000 tons. Rosso is also of the opinion that the 1930 program must be considered as a program of replacement for which obsolete tonnage, if any, is to be scrapped, not as additional program which is to be added on to existing fleet.

Rosso has drawn up the following formula with these two considerations in mind:

No further construction of 8-inch cruisers after completion of the 1930 program;

Completion of the 1930 program for 6-inch cruisers and destroyers, and construction for replacement of over-age vessels after January 1, 1930 (on being replaced, vessels are to be scrapped, except certain surface craft of more than 3,000-ton displacement, which will be kept as "special");

No further construction of submarines except for replacement when the total tonnage is below 52,700 tons, after completion of the 1930 program, when the tonnage passes this figure, over-age vessels will be scrapped.

The auxiliary fleets reduced to tonnage of 1936 will reach the following levels: (a) Both France and Italy will have 70,000 tons for 8-inch cruisers; (b) France will have 187,352 tons for 6-inch cruisers and destroyers, and Italy will have 155,309 tons; (c) France will have 77,541 tons for submarines, and Italy will have 52,700 tons.

Rosso proposes to discuss this formula with Craigie this afternoon. He believes he can obtain his Government's consent for these figures, although the formula is his own personal proposal. Due to the French Cabinet crisis, this will probably be the last important discussion of this matter. Rosso does not think that his Government will make an insuperable obstacle of conceding additional small amounts of tonnage. He called attention to his statement of acceptance applying to 6-inch cruisers and destroyers which is as follows:[75]

"With the exception of (blank) number of pre-Washington light surface craft of more than 3,000 tons displacement which may be retained as 'special vessels' ".

He explained that this clause was intended to make acceptance easier for France by permitting them to keep certain old cruisers for colonial use.

Desire to discuss building of auxiliary ships along with discussion of building of capital ships has been indicated by the French. Their intention is to build *pari passu* with Germany in capital ships and they wanted to have an understanding with Italy on construction to be done by latter. Italy replied stating willingness to talk matters over in friendly spirit, but that it was Italy's feeling that no agreement involving a limitation of their indubitable rights under the Washington Treaty could be undertaken before a satisfactory agreement had been reached regarding auxiliaries.

Rosso invited our attention to the fact that in the past 6 years the French and Italian Navies had each built 197,000 tons. In another 10 years of construction, if this pace were continued, they would reach real parity. Naturally Rosso recognized that the French had money and that the Italians had not, and that that was one of the real reasons why the Italians saw definite advantage to their accepting some formula even though it did not accord them satisfaction in matter of recognition of parity.

GIBSON

500.A15a3/1288 : Telegram

The Chairman of the American Delegation on the Preparatory Commission (Gibson) to the Secretary of State

[Paraphrase]

GENEVA, December 9, 1930—11 a. m.
[Received December 9—6:50 a. m.]

59. Craigie has confirmed what Rosso told me 3 days ago (telegram No. 58, December 6, 11 p. m.). Craigie thinks the additional submarine tonnage of 8,000 tons which the Italians are demanding is the only important point between France and Italy.

While the French Cabinet crisis has unfortunately halted proceedings at this time, all three negotiators believe that greater possibilities than before are offered by the present situation; as soon as French

---
[75] Quotation not paraphrased.

conditions make it possible they will continue to explore these possibilities. It has been recognized by all of them that the discussions were started again by the initiative of the United States, and they highly appreciate our help.

GIBSON

500.A15a3/1295 : Telegram

The Minister in Switzerland (Wilson) to the Secretary of State

[Paraphrase]

BERNE, December 16, 1930—5 p. m.
[Received December 16—2 p. m.]

101. Delegation's telegrams No. 58, December 6, 11 p. m., and No. 59, December 9, 11 a. m. I am informed by Craigie, who is now in Berne, that Rosso went to Rome with the intention of discussing with Grandi the possibility of accepting Craigie's formula regarding 6-inch cruisers and destroyers, and thus narrowing the conversations regarding auxiliary craft to Italy's right to build submarines up to 52,700 tons.

Rosso told Craigie in Geneva that if the situation were hopeful, he would ask the latter to go to Rome to talk with Grandi. Craigie has now received such an invitation and is going to Rome this evening.

Japan's attitude, at least as Craigie heard it expressed at Geneva, has created, he says, a new difficulty. The Japanese representative feared that the Privy Council would interpose very serious objections to any treaty figures calculated at a higher level than 52,700 tons in submarine category, such as would be permitted by allocating 77,000 tons for French submarines.

Repeated to Brussels and Rome.

WILSON

500.A15a3/1299 : Telegram

The Ambassador in Italy (Garrett) to the Secretary of State

[Paraphrase]

ROME, December 21, 1930—10 a. m.
[Received December 21—9:30 a. m.]

124. I am informed that Craigie, who is leaving for Paris today, is taking with him the personal and private assurance of Rosso that he considers that his Government will be able, provided France does the same, to accept with two exceptions the proposal which Craigie submitted to them. The exceptions are:

First, that, instead of the 44,000 tons proposed in the original plan, Italy must have a minimum of 52,700 tons for submarines;
Second, the idea, which had been proposed in connection with the suggested capital ship settlement, of scrapping pre-Washington cruiser tonnage is opposed by Italy.

It is Craigie's feeling, nevertheless, that a very good basis for submission to the French Government has now been obtained. It is suggested that if an agreement is now reached the two Ministers of Marine should embody it in an exchange of unofficial letters. While it is feared by Craigie that there is not enough time to conclude the negotiations before the meeting of the Council of the League of Nations on January 16, it is nevertheless his hope that such a result may be achieved.

Repeated to Brussels and Berne.

GARRETT

500.A15a3/1301 : Telegram

The Chargé in France (Armour) to the Secretary of State

[Paraphrase]

PARIS, December 23, 1930—1 p. m.
[Received 1 : 30 p. m.]

424. Craigie, who last evening arrived from Rome and is today leaving for London, informs me that since his talk with Mr. Garrett in Rome (a résumé of which has, I understand, been sent to the Department) there is little to report. He also says that the French have expressed a willingness to study the questions further, although they are not entirely satisfied with what he was able to bring them from Rome. He states that submarines and the question of capital ships continue to present the principal difficulties. It is difficult for the French, because of the overthrow of the Government and the political crisis here, to concentrate on the negotiations. Some further delay may be caused by the fact that Sarraut, the new Minister of Marine, has not yet had an opportunity to give his attention to questions other than political ones.

I am also informed by Craigie that they hope to decide how and when they are to resume any further negotiations that may be held; it is his belief that this will not be in any case until about January 3, after the Christmas holidays. He repeated, in conclusion, that he himself was reasonably hopeful and that he felt that difficulties were being eliminated and the eventual solution brought nearer by each exchange of ideas.

Repeated to Brussels, Berne, and Rome.

ARMOUR

500.A15a3/1306a : Telegram

The Secretary of State to the Ambassador in Belgium (Gibson)

[Paraphrase]

WASHINGTON, December 30, 1930—4 p. m.

41. Yesterday Mr. Castle was informed by the Italian Ambassador that the suggestions for an agreement made to them by Craigie were

being considered in the most cordial way by the Italian Government, and that the interest of the British and American Governments in bringing about such an agreement was greatly appreciated by the Italian Government. It was further stated by the Ambassador that Mr. Grandi, however, wished to point out that things were made much more difficult by the malevolent attitude taken toward these conversations by the French press. I have stated at different times, in reply to questions from the press, that you were authorized to do anything, in the interests of settling this question, that in your judgment you thought might be helpful.

It might be well, therefore, if you think it wise, for you to get in touch with the appropriate people in London and go down for a talk with the appropriate people in the new Government in Paris. Authorization is hereby given you to proceed to London and/or Paris, and should you do so, you may furnish a copy of this telegram to the Embassy there.

STIMSON

500.A15a3/1308 : Telegram

The Ambassador in Belgium (Gibson) to the Secretary of State

[Paraphrase]

BRUSSELS, January 1, 1931—2 p. m.
[Received 2 : 30 p. m.]

1. Reference is made to telegram No. 41, December 31 [*30*], 4 p. m., from the Department. A letter from Massigli, who is now on leave, states that he will come to see me here next week, in order to bring me up to date on recent negotiations and on the steps which, with a view to reaching agreement, he contemplates urging upon his Government. Through Atherton I am communicating with Craigie to learn whether there are any new developments at London which render it desirable for me to proceed there. I question the desirability, unless some way is disclosed in which I can be useful, of going either to London or Paris at this time in view of the way in which the press in both France and Italy have complicated the situation. It is my desire that anything which might introduce fresh conjectures should be avoided and I feel that it is better for me to keep in the background and hold myself in reserve in case of a hitch here and there, so long as direct negotiations continue. Your authorization for me to visit London and Paris is welcome, however, and if the situation warrants it will be acted upon.

GIBSON

PARTICIPATION OF THE UNITED STATES IN THE WORK OF THE PRE-
PARATORY COMMISSION FOR THE DISARMAMENT CONFERENCE,
SIXTH SESSION, SECOND PART, NOVEMBER 6–DECEMBER 9, 1930 [76]

500.A15/1075a

*The Secretary of State to the American Delegates to the Preparatory
Commission (Gibson and Wilson)* [77]

WASHINGTON, October 16, 1930.

SIRS: I am directed by the President to inform you of his desire
that you represent this Government at the forthcoming continuation
of the Sixth Session of the Preparatory Commission for the Disarmament Conference. You will be assisted by the following advisers:

Mr. Jay Pierrepont Moffat,
First Secretary of the American Legation, Berne.
Mr. Pierre de L. Boal,
Assistant Chief, Division of Western European Affairs.
Lieutenant-Colonel George V. Strong, U. S. A.
Captain William W. Smyth, U. S. N.
Commander Thomas C. Kinkaid, U. S. N.

and by the following technical assistants:

Major Robert Le G. Walsh, U. S. A.
Assistant Military Attaché, American Embassy, Paris.
Lieutenant Commander George D. Murray, U. S. N.
Assistant Naval Attaché, American Embassy, London.

In view of the progress made at previous meetings and especially
in regard to naval questions at the London Naval Conference,[78] it is
hoped that the forthcoming meeting may dispose of the questions
still remaining on the agenda and result in the elaboration of a final
draft in which all the countries represented on the Preparatory
Commission can concur. The President is heartily desirous of seeing
the work of the Preparatory Commission brought to an early and
successful conclusion in order that the general problem of the reduction of armaments may pass from the theoretical to the practical
phase. While it is not expected that problems of major importance
to the United States will be brought forward in this session, you
will, nevertheless, have constantly as your goal the furtherance of

---

[76] For correspondence concerning the first part of the sixth session, see *Foreign
Relations*, 1929, vol. I, pp. 65 ff.

The proceedings of the sixth session, second part, together with other documents relating to the work of the Preparatory Commission are printed in League
of Nations, *Documents of the Preparatory Commission for the Disarmament
Conference Entrusted With the Preparation for the Conference for the Reduction
and Limitation of Armaments*, Series X (C.4.M.4.1931.IX). See also Department
of State Conference Series No. 7, *Report of the Preparatory Commission for the
Disarmament Conference and Draft Convention* (Washington, Government Printing Office, 1931).

[77] Hugh S. Gibson, Ambassador in Belgium, and Hugh R. Wilson, Minister in
Switzerland.

[78] See pp. 1 ff.

effective general disarmament, and it is desired that you lose no opportunity to contribute to this end.

Regarding naval problems, you will be guided in general by the findings of the First Committee of the London Conference [79] which were transmitted to the Secretary General of the League of Nations by the President of that Conference. It may be found necessary to modify the terms in so far as they apply to nations possessing smaller navies. The United States is not disposed to maintain an attitude so rigid as to prevent the inclusion of those foreign navies within the framework of limitation and reduction, and it may be necessary therefore to make such minor adjustments for their benefit as you deem advisable. It is well understood, however, that no such modifications would affect the treaty already existing between the principal naval powers.

Among the questions which will come up for discussion is Chapter II, Section III, Article AD, "Air Armaments." [80] This would be examined in connection with Article ZD.[81] This Government could not agree to any draft which contained a reference to civil aviation as an arm of war or as one of the factors on which the calculation of armed forces is based. Indeed it appears that Article AD would serve merely as a justification for large figures in this field. Furthermore, it would seem that such a statement would have no proper place in the text of an international treaty. Nevertheless, we recognize that to many other States this matter is of paramount importance and if such States feel that they desire to attach to the draft a resolution embodying their own views and not that of all members of the Preparatory Commission, the American Delegation need take no exception thereto.

The discussion of Chapter III will bring up the question of budgetary limitation of military expenditures. This Government is of the decided opinion that the acceptance by the United States of any form of direct budgetary limitation is impracticable and on this point the Delegation must stand firm. When defining the Delegation's position in this matter, it should be clearly stressed that the fullest publicity is given by this Government not only on expenditure, but also on numbers, weights, and units of matériel.

The question of a standard account may be discussed. This Government feels that the labor involved in changing the budgetary methods of fifty-odd states would prove very difficult in practice and hardly calculated to produce proportionate results. So far as this

---

[79] See Department of State Conference Series No. 6, *Proceedings of the London Naval Conference of 1930*, pp. 123 ff.
[80] For text of the draft convention, see League of Nations, *Documents of the Preparatory Commission*, Series X, Annex 1 (C. P. D. 211), pp. 423, 440.
[81] *Ibid.*, p. 458.

Government is concerned, full and detailed information is given, which could be embodied in any form of presentation or comparison.

Chapter V, Section I, Organization. It is understood that fresh plans in this connection will be introduced by the French and British Delegations. This Government is, of course, willing to enter into international cooperation for the fullest exchange of information and for such elucidation of fact as may be contributory to the cause of peace. The American Government is pleased to note that the present tendency of the Preparatory Commission is to move rather in the direction of "information and inquiry" than of "supervision and control" and abandon any form of control in the usually accepted English sense. It is noted with satisfaction that the draft agenda states that in examining this question the Commission will have to take into account the special situation of the United States, which is not a member of the League of Nations. While this Government would, of course, be unable to accept provisions for reference of such matters to the Council of the League of Nations, it would find no difficulty in accepting reference to a body set up by the Treaty which, in addition to a representative of the United States, might contain representatives of those countries represented on the Council.

10–Chapter V, Section III, will bring up the question of derogations, or methods of being freed from the obligations of the Treaty in cases of emergency. It is the belief of this Government that the obligations of such a Treaty will be more readily accepted by the various Powers if they feel that in case of genuine need they will not be bound. It is believed by this Government that the States will more voluntarily assume and more scrupulously observe obligations as to armament if they are free in cases of emergency to take adequate measures to protect themselves. We also believe that the states will go much further in the drastic reduction of armament if they are not bound by too long and too rigid terms. This Government is therefore in favor of including a broad escape clause which will merely specify that the nation which believes its security threatened shall, after a public statement of the reasons for this belief, be freed from its obligations, which would leave the decision and responsibility for the invocation of the clause solely to the Signatory Power concerned. In this connection, it may be possible to induce those states bordering on Russia to withdraw their reservation in view of the fact that they may adopt measures for their protection any time occasion demands. Furthermore, the argument for the necessity of including a clause justifying the consideration of the state of civil aviation of neighboring countries, loses a large portion of its value if every state is free to denounce the terms of the Treaty when it feels its security menaced.

In connection with the preparation of a report of the Preparatory Commission to the Council of the League of Nations, it is noted that this report will contain recommendations as to the date of the first General Disarmament Conference. It would seem sufficient for the American Delegation to state that this Government hopes for early and effective progress and will be prepared to participate at any date which the Powers are able to agree on as the most efficacious.

I have [etc.]   HENRY L. STIMSON

500.A15/1113 : Telegram

The Chairman of the American Delegation (Gibson) to the Secretary of State

GENEVA, November 15, 1930—8 p. m.
[Received November 15—5 p. m.]

23. We have been contemplating what form of escape clause would be efficacious and have borne in mind your views to the effect that it should be very liberal in scope. We are of the opinion that a broad escape clause will aid the states bordering on Russia especially to enter a convention and will make it easier for all states to apply lower figures of limitation. In view of these considerations, we have drafted a text on which we would like to have your advice. Inasmuch as we may reach this debate early in the week I would appreciate a reply as soon as convenient. The text of the amendment which we propose to submit to the Secretariat to be circulated in advance as a proposed "American amendment," is as follows:

"(1) If during the life of the present convention a change of circumstances constitutes, in the opinion of any high contracting party, a menace to its national security, such high contracting party may denounce or modify in so far as concerns itself any article or articles of the present convention, other than those expressly designed to apply in the event of war, provided

(*a*) That such high contracting party shall immediately notify the other high contracting parties of such denunciation or modification, and in the latter event, of the extent thereof.

(*b*) That simultaneously with the notification referred to in point (*a*) the high contracting party shall make to the other high contracting parties full explanation of the 'change of circumstances' referred to above."

GIBSON

500.A15/1113 : Telegram

The Secretary of State to the Chairman of the American Delegation
(Gibson)

WASHINGTON, November 17, 1930—5 p. m.

6. Your 23, November 15, 8 p. m. Department approves of your text with suggestion of two possible changes:

(1) It would seem preferable to omit the words "denounce" and "denunciation" wherever they occur since they seem to imply a wider latitude with respect to changes in the proposed convention than the escape clause is intended to cover. In other words, there will be separate provisions for the denunciation of the treaty and changes in any articles thereof would come under the head of modification.

(2) Add after Paragraph B of the draft the following sentence "thereupon the other High Contracting Parties shall promptly advise with each other as to the situation thus presented".

You will note that this is a modification of the phrase used in the London Naval Treaty [82] on this point, which in turn was modified from the Washington Treaty. All reference to the channels for advising in accordance with the terms of the article has been omitted.

STIMSON

500.A15/1120 : Telegram

The Chairman of the American Delegation (Gibson) to the Secretary
of State

GENEVA, November 18, 1930—4 p. m.
[Received November 18—11:50 a. m.]

26. Your No. 6, November 17, 5 p. m. We propose to circulate the proposed amendment on derogations during Thursday meeting.

In view of the insertion of the final sentence proposed by you at the end of paragraph B and in view of the President's Armistice Day speech,[83] it would be very helpful to receive, at the earliest possible moment, any comment on this resolution that you propose to make or have made to the press.

GIBSON

---

[82] See art. 21, *ante*, p. 123.
[83] *Address Delivered on November 11, 1930, at the Annual Conference and Good-Will Congress of the World Alliance for International Friendship Through the Churches* (Washington, Government Printing Office, 1930).

500.A15/1120 : Telegram

The Secretary of State to the Chairman of the American Delegation
(Gibson)

[Paraphrase]

WASHINGTON, November 18, 1930—6 p. m.

7. Your telegram No. 26, November 18, 4 p. m. In view of your misgivings that the phraseology on this subject as modified from the London Naval Treaty would arouse undue comment, I think that it would be preferable to make the phraseology identical, that is to say, "shall promptly advise with each other through diplomatic channels as to the situation thus presented."

Any comment that might be aroused from doing this could be answered by a statement to the effect that this was the principle embodied in the London Naval Treaty, which had received the consent of the United States Senate to ratification. On the other hand, if you think that any proposition of this character would arouse too much comment and too much speculation, I perceive no special reason why the United States should be the one to offer a redraft of the escape clause at all. Is there any reason why debate on the old draft should not be allowed to lead gradually to changes without any specific proposal which could be designated as the American proposal?

STIMSON

500.A15/1121 : Telegram

The Chairman of the American Delegation (Gibson) to the Secretary
of State

GENEVA, November 18, 1930—7 p. m.
[Received November 18—4 : 35 p. m.]

27. Department's 6, November 17, 5 p. m. The sentence added by you to our draft reads as follows: "Thereupon the other high contracting parties shall promptly advise with each other as to the situation thus presented." Taken in conjunction with the preceding sentence of paragraph B, it would appear that the high contracting party seeking to modify its treaty obligations would be excluded from the exchange of views. This phraseology, a modification of that used in article 21 of the London Treaty, is applicable in that treaty to two powers only and the "new construction" leading to invocation of the escape clause can be initiated only by a nonsignatory. I submit for your consideration that in the present instance we are dealing with what is intended to be a universal treaty or one which in any case will have a large number of signatories. Under this treaty, problems arising from action taken by nonsignatory states will be the exception and not the rule. Under the proposed phraseology it

is possible to envisage a situation in which the state modifying a clause or clauses of the treaty is the only state in the world excluded from consultation about this condition. If we maintain the word "other," state A which has announced its intention of modifying the treaty as a result of some action of state B, the initiator of the trouble, will nevertheless participate. It may seem to you more practical to suppress the word "other," thus providing consultations with all interested states.

In view of this inquiry we will postpone circulating the resolution until we can hear from you on this point. We will then advise regarding the date of circulation.

GIBSON

500.A15/1121 : Telegram

The Secretary of State to the Chairman of the American Delegation (Gibson)

[Paraphrase]

WASHINGTON, November 19, 1930—5 p. m.

8. Your No. 27, November 18, 7 p. m. The Department is still of the opinion, as it suggested in its No. 7, November 18, 6 p. m., that either you should use phraseology of the London Naval Treaty, or, if you think effect of that phraseology would be unfortunate, you should refrain from making any proposal whatever regarding escape clause.

The omission of word "other" would imply right to "advise" as to whether or not the party desiring to make use of escape clause is justified in doing so or not; we desire to avoid this implication, just as we did at the London Naval Conference, in order that the freedom to make use of it shall not be hampered.

STIMSON

500.A15/1125 : Telegram

The Chairman of the American Delegation (Gibson) to the Secretary of State

GENEVA, November 19, 1930—9 p. m.
[Received November 19—8:18 p. m.]

29. Your No. 7, November 18, 6 p. m. Under the circumstances I think it would be better for the time being to withhold any circulation by us of an escape clause. In all probability in view of the several divergent views now existing regarding derogations, there will be a prolonged debate on this subject. At some period in this debate

it might be well for us to advance the escape clause as contained in our 23, November 15, noon [*8 p. m.*], and modified by your paragraph under (1) in No. 6, November 17, noon [*5 p. m.*], but omitting the sentence contained in your paragraph (2) of that telegram.

Regarding the escape clause without the final sentence, unless you see reasons to the contrary, we think it may be advantageous to sponsor the proposal as we believe it will be of great value in working out a solution.

We are inclined to believe that any discussion on an escape clause will invariably induce some form of suggestion as to consultation on the situation thereby created. In the event that the suggestion is made by another delegation we believe that acquiescence on our part would avoid in a large measure the undue comment which initiative of the American delegation on this subject would incite. Such procedure might cover the thought that is conveyed in the question contained in your last sentence of telegram 7, November 18, 1 [*6*] p. m.

We fear that the words used in article 21 of the London Treaty "through diplomatic channels" would be impractical in a treaty which may have forty or more signatories, particularly as the time element will probably be a factor in any case of derogation. Probably we could restrict the phraseology to the phrase "thereupon the high contracting parties shall promptly advise with each other in every situation thus presented." Would much appreciate your comment on these matters.

GIBSON

500.A15/1125 : Telegram

The Secretary of State to the Chairman of the American Delegation (Gibson)

WASHINGTON, November 20, 1930—2 p. m.

9. Your 29, November 19, 9 p. m. Constant crossing of telegrams makes comment difficult. Department does not wish to quibble over words but prefers, first, that if an Escape Clause is proposed by the American Delegation, it be modelled as closely as practicable on the London Naval Treaty, and, second, that any Escape Clause finally adopted contain some provision for "advice" along the lines of the last clause of Article 21 of that Treaty.

From this point of view, the alternatives suggested in the telegrams exchanged, beginning with your 23 of November 15, 8 p. m., present themselves to the Department in the following order of preference:

(1) Proposal by American Delegation of Escape Clause along lines of your 23, November 15, 8 p. m., as modified by Department's

6, November 17, 5 p. m.,—with or without reference to "diplomatic channels";

(2) No proposal at all by American Delegation, thus permitting the situation to develop in the course of debate on the old draft of Article ZE toward preferred version;

(3) proposal as under (1) above but omitting the paragraph relating to "advice", as suggested in the first paragraph of your No. 29, November 19, 9 p. m., provided you are reasonably certain that some other delegation will propose the addition of a clause similar in effect to the one omitted;

(4) proposal as under (1) above, but modified as suggested in the last paragraph of your 29, November 19, 9 p. m. This would omit the word "other" and take no account of the objections voiced in the Department's 8, November 19, 5 p. m. Department will not insist on its position in this matter, however, if you are still convinced that this is the best alternative.

Please report to the Department which of the above four alternatives you finally decide on. In the event that you adopt the second one, we are prepared to approve any Escape Clause resulting from the debate which is similar in substance to any one of the above texts.

The Department has purposely avoided using the word "consultation" in its telegrams on this subject and believes that the Delegation had best refrain from using it so far as possible in the discussions, since we do not desire this issue confused with the question of a Consultative Pact.

STIMSON

500.A15/1129 : Telegram

The Chairman of the American Delegation (Gibson) to the Secretary of State

GENEVA, November 21, 1930—noon.
[Received 11:58 p. m.]

33. We have during the past day or two had several private conversations with delegates concerning the general subject of derogations in an effort to elicit their general views as to how the escape clause can be made most effective and acceptable. We have found that one of their main preoccupations was to reconcile any possible draft with the obstacle constituted for League members by the provision in paragraph 4 of article 8 of the Covenant to the effect that when a disarmament agreement is reached "the limits of armaments therein fixed shall not be exceeded without the concurrence of the Council."

We have found a considerable measure of sympathy with our view that an escape clause should be drafted so broadly as to avoid the defects of an itemized statement of reasons for modification (such as rebellion, menace of aggression, technical development, growth of civilization, et cetera) and to afford reassurance to the signatories in accepting low figures in the knowledge that they can, in the case of real need, modify them so far as strictly necessary.

In view of the wording of the Covenant above referred to it seems to be generally felt that the best hope of a solution lies in the stipulation that modifications are to be temporary in character, and we have therefore felt justified in inserting language and adding a final paragraph to this effect. We are in full accord as to the analysis given in your 9, November 20, 2 p. m., and after our conversations are confirmed in the belief that the best course is the one indicated by you as first in the order of preference.

As various alternative drafts are being submitted for consideration by a special subcommittee which is to meet tomorrow in preparation for general debate which will probably take place Monday, and since there seems to be a general feeling that a draft submitted by us would be most helpful, we are circulating tomorrow a draft of which the following is the text:

"If, during the life of the present convention, a change of circumstances constitutes, in the opinion of any high contracting party, a menace to its national security, such high contracting party may modify temporarily, in so far as concerns itself, any [article] or articles of the present convention, other than those expressly designed to apply in the event of war, provided:

(a) That such high contracting party shall immediately notify the other high contracting parties of such temporary modification, and of the extent thereof;

(b) That simultaneously with the notification referred to in point (a) the high contracting party shall make to the other high contracting parties full explanation of the change of circumstances referred to above.

Thereupon the other high contracting parties shall promptly advise as to the situation thus presented.

When the reasons for such temporary modification have ceased to exist, the said high contracting party shall reduce its armaments to the level agreed upon in the convention, and shall make immediate notification to other high contracting parties".

You will note that article EA of chapter V of the draft convention (document 211) [84] precludes any possible modification by this draft of existing treaties dealing with armament including those of Washington and London.

GIBSON

---

[84] League of Nations, *Documents of the Preparatory Commission*, Series X, pp. 423, 458.

500.A15/1129 : Telegram

The Secretary of State to the Chairman of the American Delegation
(Gibson)

WASHINGTON, November 22, 1930—2 p. m.

10. Your 33, November 21, noon. Department considers the draft quoted satisfactory and appreciates the reasons cited for the additions.

STIMSON

500.A15/1139 : Telegram

The Chairman of the American Delegation (Gibson) to the Secretary
of State

GENEVA, November 26, 1930—11 a. m.
[Received November 26—10:20 a. m.]

39. I am sending in my telegram No. 40, November 26, 1 p. m.,[85] some texts drawn up by the special subcommittee dealing with chapter V of the convention relating to the Permanent Disarmament Commission and to the general procedure with respect to complaints, derogations, and revision.[86] These texts will now be submitted to the Plenary Commission.[87]

In this subcommittee there was at first a decided tendency toward giving the Permanent Disarmament Commission judicial or quasi-judicial powers to enable it to determine when and if the convention had been violated and what action should be taken by high contracting parties in the case of a violation by a contracting party.

(*b*) [*sic*] Acts of another contracting party not in violation of the treaty but of a nature to give concern.

(*c*) Similar acts of a nonsignatory state estimate. [*sic*]

There was a further tendency toward linking it closely with League machinery and the obligations under the Covenant. This situation became so involved that we took occasion to make a statement of our position along the following lines:

That we had envisaged a Permanent Disarmament Commission designed to receive, collect, and disseminate information, to follow in a broad way the progress of disarmament, and to make preliminary studies for future disarmament conferences. When, however, it came to giving the Commission actual powers as indicated in the preceding paragraph we felt bound in frankness to say that we could not follow their lead.

---

[85] Not printed.
[86] League of Nations, *Documents of the Preparatory Commission*, Series X, p. 210.
[87] *Ibid.*, p. 243.

518625—45——18

That we recognized in logic the distinction between the various classes of violations referred to above but felt that the remedy should be the same for all and should follow in broad lines the escape clause we had proposed.

That it was not always easy to find a formula that would meet the preoccupations of both League members and non-League members and if the subcommittee did not see its way to following along the path we outlined we suggest that the League members frame the provisions which would satisfy them. The non-League members could then consider to what degree and with what modifications they could adhere to the system proposed.

A considerable modification of views became apparent in the course of subsequent debate evidently due on the one hand to a growing realization of the impracticability of other alternative drafts, and on the other hand to the growing desire to have us included in the system from the beginning and as will be seen from the text our views appear to have been met in regard to most, at least, of the essentials.

In general the text outside of our particular amendment is more detailed and specific than we would have preferred. Indeed from the start it became evident that, opposed to the Anglo-Saxon desire for a brief and simple text which would permit the logical growth of the Permanent Commission through experience, was the rather general desire to foresee every contingency and specify in detail and with rigidity a rigid and binding procedure. In view of the fact that this desire for rigidity was based on apprehension as to the future, the acceptance of broader and simpler views seems to us to constitute a very material concession even though it be in the direction of common sense.

Studying the text it would seem that the only article of doubtful acceptability is article ZB dealing with the report to be made by the Commission upon receipt of complaints. We made it clear that we wished to give this article further study. We incline however to the belief that as finally phrased (it having been twice attenuated to meet our special preoccupation) it should present no difficulties particularly as the text remains subject to further modification at the Conference itself.

The Department will note two or three minor alterations made by the committee in our escape clause, notably that the Permanent Disarmament Commission should be notified of any temporary suspension of the convention together with the reasons therefor at the same time as the other high contracting parties.

The provisions of article OA concerning the status of members of the Commission seem somewhat open to criticism. These represent a compromise between the views held by the French and the British delegations. In view of the divergences of views on this point, this will undoubtedly be reopened at the Conference and meanwhile would not appear of sufficient importance to us to warrant a strong stand as there could in no event be an obligation on the part of the United States to accept membership on the Permanent Disarmament Commission if it did not so desire.

These articles will come up for discussion before the full Commission this afternoon or tomorrow and will probably be somewhat modified in text, although there is no reason to foresee that they will not be accepted for their broad outline.

We should greatly appreciate it if the Department would permit us to express general approval of the texts outlined, bearing in mind that this is a draft only open to modification and indeed complete review at the final conference. The delegates of the major powers have made very substantial modification of their thesis to meet our views and have shown an earnest desire and [sic] to meet our difficulties. It would have a happy effect if we could express appreciation at the third reading as well as a readiness to take this text as the basis of our discussions at the General Disarmament Conference.

GIBSON

500.A15/1145 : Telegram

The Chairman of the American Delegation (Gibson) to the Secretary of State

GENEVA, November 28, 1930—10 a. m.
[Received November 28—8 : 50 a. m.]

45. At the speed at which we are at present progressing the second reading will in all probability be terminated this week. The third reading which is expected to be purely formal will take place presumably early next week, possibly Monday.

The text is practically complete on second reading with the exception of a possible provision for revision under restricted circumstances, ratification, and denunciation.

These are being prepared and will probably be passed this afternoon or tomorrow morning.

In considering the texts which have been sent you, please bear in mind that they are considered in no sense a finished product but that they represent the most practical method of stating the resultant views of conflicting schools of thought among 25 delegations. They really should be regarded as constituting a memorandum as a starting point for discussion in the final conference and in no sense as a binding text. This has been repeatedly stated and remains uncontested so that we have not felt it necessary to prolong this session by insistence on perfected drafting such as would be essential for signature.

GIBSON

500.A15/1145 : Telegram

The Acting Secretary of State to the Chairman of the American Delegation (Gibson)

WASHINGTON, November 28, 1930—2 p. m.

13. Your 39, 40, 41, 42, of November 26, your 44 of November 27 and your No. 45 of November 28.[88] Department approves of texts as telegraphed on the clear understanding that such approval does not prejudice its attitude at the final conference, when figures are under discussion.

COTTON

500.A15/1150 : Telegram

The Chairman of the American Delegation (Gibson) to the Secretary of State

GENEVA, December 1, 1930—8 p. m.
[Received December 1—5 p. m.]

49. Commission this afternoon completed chapter on ratification, revision, and denunciation of the convention. Inasmuch as it is distinctly understood that all texts are subject to revision at the general conference and as no new amendments are in order, I shall not telegraph texts of these articles unless you so instruct.

A few pending amendments to the second reading text are still to be considered but it is anticipated that all amendments of substance will be disposed of in tomorrow morning's session and that the remainder of our time will be spent in approving the final drafting and the report.

GIBSON

500.A15/1167 : Telegram

The Chairman of the American Delegation (Gibson) to the Secretary of State

[Paraphrase]

GENEVA, December 4, 1930—7 p. m.
[Received December 4—4:39 p. m.]

54. A number of general statements will be made at the final session of the Preparatory Commission and there will be an excessive amount of self-congratulation on the results which our draft convention has achieved, if past experience can be relied on. The undue optimism shown in America in regard to the reduction which the London Conference would achieve greatly embarrassed us there, as

---

[88] Nos. 40, 41, 42, and 44 not printed.

you will remember. Serious disillusionment, will, we fear, face the American people if they have similar high hopes of the results to be achieved by the General Disarmament Conference, and our failure to inform them of the meager results which are to be expected may consequently be criticized. In order to sound a note of warning as to realities, a step which you may consider advisable, I have prepared a speech which I am sending for your consideration in my telegram No. 55 (December 4, 9 p. m.).

In paragraph 3 a reference to the concern which some powers have for national security has been inserted in order that French criticism may be disarmed and so that in our attempts to put the final discussions on an honest basis the French may be given an opportunity to cooperate. The quotation from Lincoln has been inserted with the belief that it will have a good effect among those who urge reduction in the United States and on the Continent; we recognize, however, that the Continental press may possibly remove this from its context in an effort to show that Germany's contention that the Allied Powers have no real intention of reducing armaments is being supported by us. It is important to have your comments or approval at the earliest possible date for the reason that the general statements may come by Saturday of this week.

GIBSON

500.A15/1168 : Telegram

The Chairman of the American Delegation (Gibson) to the Secretary of State

GENEVA, December 4, 1930—9 p. m.
[Received 10 p. m.]

55. Following is draft of speech referred to in my 54, December 4, 7 p. m.:

"In the course of our debates we have heard numerous estimates as to the value of our work. But it is only now that our deliberations are coming to an end that we can effectively judge to what degree we have succeeded in our task.

For four years we have been endeavoring to reach an agreement. There have been long and direct conflicts of opinion; views have been maintained with vigor; and yet our friendship with those who have differed from us has grown as steadily and as surely as our friendship with those who have shared our views. I take this as a good omen for the spirit in which all the nations will enter the General Disarmament Conference and try to convert our text from a theory to a reality.

I have, throughout, been sensible of the very real difficulties under which many members of this Commission have labored. Overshadowing our discussions, though seldom spoken, have been the anxieties and worries that have arisen from the special preoccupations felt by numerous governments for their national security.

We have now completed a draft convention which, after study by the Governments, will go forward to the general conference. I should not be frank if I did not say that this draft falls far short of our hopes and expectations. It fails to contain many factors in which we have always believed and which, in our opinion, would lead to a real reduction of armaments. What we have achieved does not hold out the promise of bringing about that immediate reduction of armaments we would like to see. Make no mistake; it is not my purpose to belittle what we have done. Although our hopes may thus be disappointed, we can find comfort in the measure of agreement which has been reached in this Commission. We can at least foresee a stabilization of armaments, the setting up of a machinery to receive and disseminate information on armaments, to educate public opinion, and to prepare systematically for the work of future conferences, as successive milestones in the continuing process of disarmament. If these things can be achieved by the coming conference, and from present indications I think we are justified in assuming that they can be achieved, we shall have a situation obviously better than we have at present and, while we cannot claim to have built the edifice, we shall at least have laid the foundation upon which the edifice can be erected.

It is possible that the coming conference will accomplish more than this, but, if so it will be because our labors have been improved upon and because, after mature study of the problems involved and after weighing the consequences of failure, the governments come to the conference resolved on greater measures of concession than the delegates here have been authorized to make.

I feel that we should be rendering a poor service to the cause of reduction of armaments if we were to lead our peoples to believe that this work carried the movement further than it does. We have been repeatedly told during the past four years of the role of public opinion in connection with disarmament. It has been repeatedly said that real achievement by the Conference can be reached only by an aroused public opinion. This is partly true, but it is not enough that public opinion be aroused. It is first of all necessary that it should be informed, for an aroused and uninformed public opinion may do infinitely more harm than good. Public opinion will not be informed in such a way as to exercise an intelligent influence if, through a desire to create confidence, we adopt too optimistic a tone as to what can be accomplished on the basis of our present draft. Such exaggeration can really tend only to lull public opinion into a false sense of confidence, render it incapable of exercising its salutary influence, and prepare it for inevitable disillusionment. Exaggerated statements have their inevitable reaction because, in the words of Abraham Lincoln, 'you can fool all of the people some of the time and some of the people all of the time but you cannot fool all of the people all of the time.'

We are all in agreement that an immense amount of preparatory work remains to be done before the meeting of the General Conference. The technical preparation for that Conference is in all conscience great enough; but a more difficult and more responsible task lies ahead of all our governments in informing public opinion as to the facts, as to the difficulties, and as to the possible measures which may, with mutual concession, help us toward the goal we all desire to reach. This end can be served only by stating our achievements and our difficulties with moderation.

I hope that in separating at the conclusion of our labors we shall not yield to the temptation to indulge in mutual congratulation, that we may separate with becoming modesty, and, on reporting to our various governments, that we do so with a full and frank recognition of the shortcomings of our present draft, and of the duties and responsibilities still before our governments to lead the General Disarmament Conference to the success which our peoples earnestly desire."

GIBSON

500.A15/1168 : Telegram

The Secretary of State to the Chairman of the American Delegation (Gibson)

[Paraphrase]

WASHINGTON, December 5, 1930—4 p. m.

20. Your telegrams No. 54 and No. 55, December 4, 7 p. m., and 9 p. m., respectively. I approve tenor and purpose of your speech, but I feel that inclusion of Lincoln quotation makes it slightly too denunciatory. That would probably be the particular bit on which the press would seize, and give rise to statements that American delegation was announcing that Preparatory Commission had been engaged in fooling the world for many years.[89]

STIMSON

500.A15/1173 : Telegram

The Chairman of the American Delegation (Gibson) to the Secretary of State

GENEVA, December 9, 1930—10 p. m.
[Received December 9—6:51 p. m.]

60. Commission adjourned this morning [*afternoon*].[90] Delegation pouch will be forwarded via Paris.

GIBSON

---

[89] By telegram No. 57, December 6, 10 p. m., Mr. Gibson informed the Department that at the end of the sixth paragraph the entire last sentence beginning "Exaggerated statements" had been eliminated. Mr. Gibson's speech as delivered on December 9 is printed in League of Nations, *Documents of the Preparatory Commission*, Series X, p. 408.
[90] The 27th and last meeting was held at 3:30 p. m.

CONFERENCE FOR THE CODIFICATION OF INTERNATIONAL LAW, HELD AT THE HAGUE, MARCH 13–APRIL 20, 1930, AND TEXT OF PROTOCOL RELATING TO MILITARY OBLIGATIONS IN CERTAIN CASES OF DOUBLE NATIONALITY [91]

504.418A2/37

The Secretary General of the League of Nations (Drummond) to the Secretary of State [92]

C. L. 271.1929.V.   GENEVA, October 15, 1929.

SIR: By my circular letter of July 15th, last [93] (C. L. 142.1929.V.), I had the honour to inform you that the Council of the League of Nations had decided in principle that the first Codification Conference, which is to consider the questions of Nationality, Territorial Waters, and the Responsibility of States for Damage caused in their territory to the person or property of foreigners, should meet at The Hague on March 13th, 1930.

My letter of July 15th explained the origin of the Conference and the measures which had been taken to prepare for it and gave the list of the Governments which the Council had decided to invite to the Conference, namely:

The members of the League, Brazil, Costa Rica, Free City of Danzig, Egypt, Ecuador, United States of America, Iceland, Mexico, Monaco, San Marino, Turkey and the Union of Soviet Socialist Republics.

I at the same time forwarded to your Government the documentation submitted to the Conference, namely:

1. Bases of Discussion drawn up by the Preparatory Committee for the Conference upon the question of Nationality. (Doc. C 73.M. 38.-1929.V. Bases of Discussion Volume I).

This volume contains the two reports presented to the Council by the Preparatory Committee for the Codification Conference, the list of the points which were submitted to the Governments, the replies of the Governments on each particular point and the full text of these replies, the observations of the Preparatory Committee and the bases of discussion which it has drawn up.

2. Bases of discussion drawn up by the Preparatory Committee

---

[91] The preliminaries to the Conference are printed in League of Nations, *Bases of Discussion Drawn up for the Conference by the Preparatory Committee*, 3 vols. (I. Nationality; II. Territorial Waters; III. Responsibility of States for Damage Caused in Their Territory to the Person or Property of Foreigners), (Geneva, 1929).

The proceedings of the Conference are printed in League of Nations, *Acts of the Conference for the Codification of International Law*, 4 vols. (I. Plenary Meetings; II. Minutes of the First Committee; III. Minutes of the Second Committee; IV. Minutes of the Third Committee), (Geneva, 1930).

[92] Transmitted to the Department by the Minister in Switzerland in despatch No. 1139 (L. of N. No. 1517), October 17, 1929; received October 26.

[93] Not printed.

for the Conference upon the question of Territorial Waters. (Doc. C. 74.M. 39.1929.V. Bases of Discussion Volume II).

This volume is arranged in the same manner as volume I.

3. Bases of discussion drawn up by the Preparatory Committee for the Conference upon the question of Responsibility of States for damage done in their territory to the person or property of foreigners. (Doc. C. 75.M. 69.1929.V. Bases of Discussion, Volume III).

This volume is arranged in the same manner as volumes I and II.

Various replies from Governments received after the communication of the above-mentioned three documents to the Council have been printed and circulated to the Governments invited to the Conference as addenda to the three main documents.

4. Draft Rules of Procedure for the Conference for the Codification of International Law (Doc. C. 190(1).M. 93.1929.V.).

5. Letter from the President of the Advisory and Technical Committee for Communications and Transit, dated March 26th, 1929, formulating certain desiderata on the subject of Territorial Waters (Doc. C. 218(1).M. 96.1929.V.).

In execution of a further decision taken by the Council on September 25th last, I have now the honour, on behalf of the Council, to convey to your Government a formal invitation to be represented at the Conference by a delegation furnished with the full powers necessary to sign such conventions or declarations as the Conference may draw up.

I beg to enclose a copy of the report made to the Council on September 25th by the representative of Italy and the resolution adopted by the Council (Document C. 480.1929.V.).[94]

You will observe that the Governments are invited to send to the Conference delegations sufficiently numerous to permit of the three questions on the agenda being discussed simultaneously in the committees appointed by the Conference, and that the Council has requested me specially to call the attention of the Governments to the desirability of appointing without delay their representatives at the Conference, whether plenipotentiary delegates, substitute delegates, or technical delegates, in order that the members of the Conference may be able to make a thorough study of the documentation already assembled.

As regards the composition of the delegations, I venture further to call attention to the resolution adopted by the Assembly of the League of Nations on September 24th, 1928, in the following terms:

"The Assembly, considering that the question of nationality which is on the agenda of the Conference is of special interest to women, and that Article 7 of the Covenant embodies the principle that all positions under or in connection with the League shall be open equally to men and women, expresses the hope that the Members of the League, when invited to the forthcoming Conference, will consider

---

[94] Enclosure not printed.

the desirability of taking these considerations into account in composing their delegations."

As regards the subjects to be discussed by the Conference, M. Scialoja in his report to the Council thought it desirable to make special mention of the following passage in the second report of the Preparatory Committee:

"The suggestion that the Conference should deliberate on the bases |of discussion prepared by the Preparatory Committee was also prompted by a desire to facilitate the work of the Conference. In point of fact these bases of discussion were furnished by the Governments themselves, which replied to the requests submitted to them for information. The Committee merely collated their replies and brought out the points in which they are in agreement. The individual delegations will, moreover, have the fullest liberty to submit amendments. The reason why proposals which do not come within the scope of the bases of discussion can only be dealt with if this is allowed by a previous decision is to obviate the necessity for the Conference to handle questions on which, as a result of the work of the Committee of Experts and the replies received from Governments, agreement would appear to be very unlikely. Moreover, the Conference will have the fullest possible powers to allow any question to be considered."

Finally, you will observe from the enclosed document that the Council, in agreement with the Assembly, requests those Governments which have not replied to the Preparatory Committee's questionnaire to be so good as to do so.

The Council has appointed as President of the Conference M. Heemskerk, Netherlands Minister of State, former Prime Minister and former Minister of Justice.

The Conference will sit at the Peace Palace at The Hague but the opening meeting will be held at 11 a. m. on March 13th at the Ridderzaal.

I shall be grateful if your Government would be so good as to inform me, if possible before the end of February 1930, of the names of its delegates to the Conference.

I have [etc.]   ERIC DRUMMOND

504.418A2/49½

The Secretary of State to President Hoover

WASHINGTON, December 12, 1929.

THE PRESIDENT: This Government has received from the Secretary General of the League of Nations an invitation dated October 15, 1929, to attend an International Conference to be held at The Hague beginning March 13, 1930, for the purpose of considering the Codification of International Law. The subjects to be taken up at this

Conference are (1) Nationality, (2) Territorial Waters, and (3) Responsibility of States for damage caused in their territory to the person or property of foreigners.

Each of these subjects is of great importance in the conduct of the foreign relations of this Government. Troublesome questions of dual nationality are constantly arising in connection with our efforts to protect American citizens abroad. It is frequently found that the persons whom we endeavor to protect or assist, although American citizens under our law by birth, are also regarded as citizens or subjects of the foreign States concerned under their laws. Like difficulties are frequently encountered in the case of naturalized citizens. Several countries do not recognize the expatriation of their nationals by naturalization in foreign countries. The result is that naturalized American citizens, formerly nationals of those countries, on returning to their native lands are still regarded as nationals and frequently find themselves in difficulties under the laws pertaining to military service, taxation, etc. It is, therefore, very desirable that these conflicts between the national laws of the various countries should, in so far as is possible, be reconciled.

The question of Territorial Waters is likewise important. The Conference will consider, among other things, the breadth of the territorial waters under the sovereignty of the coastal State; the distance to which the coastal State may exercise authority on the high seas to prevent the infringement within its territory or territorial waters of its customs or sanitary regulations, or interference with its security; the points from which the belt of territorial waters is to be measured; methods by which territorial waters of islands and groups of islands are to be determined; questions pertaining to the right of innocent passage of foreign merchant vessels and of foreign war ships through the territorial waters of a State; the right of local authorities to make arrests on board foreign merchant vessels within or passing through such territorial waters; and the continuation on the high seas of pursuit begun within territorial waters.

It will readily be appreciated that, in view of the extent of the coast line of the United States and the magnitude and importance of American shipping, these questions are of vital interest to this Government.

The third question, namely, that of Responsibility of States for damage caused in their territory to the person or property of foreigners, is of tremendous importance to this Government. The Conference will consider, among other subjects involving questions of State, responsibility, the repudiation by legislative or executive acts of debts of the State, and failure to comply with obligations resulting from debts; refusal to allow foreigners access to judicial tribunals;

delays on the part of such tribunals, ill-will manifested toward foreigners, and procedure resulting in a miscarriage of justice; acts and omissions of officials, including those of diplomatic and consular officers, and political subdivisions of a State, such as communes, provinces, etc.; acts of armed forces, such as the requisitioning, occupation, and damage to or destruction of property; insurrection, riot, mob violence, and other disturbances; and responsibility of a State entrusted with the conduct of the foreign relations of another State or political unit for damages suffered by foreigners in the territory of the latter State or political unit.

In view of the effect upon the conduct of our foreign relations, particularly the protection of American life and property in foreign countries, of conclusions which may be reached at this Conference on the various subjects to be considered, I think it most important that this Government should be represented at the Conference by delegates, technical advisers, and other necessary personnel.

I therefore, submit the enclosed draft of a Joint Resolution for which I recommend that the favorable consideration of the Congress be requested.[95]

Respectfully submitted,   HENRY L. STIMSON

504.418A2/159½

The Acting Secretary of State to Mr. David Hunter Miller, Editor of Treaties, Department of State

WASHINGTON, February 27, 1930.

DEAR MR. MILLER: I am asking you to act as Chairman of the Commission which is going to The Hague and in case of your inability at any time to act, ask Mr. Hackworth [96] to act as Chairman.

Written instructions cannot be given this delegation. You, Mr. Hackworth, and I have talked the matter over and I shall have to ask that if at any time there are differences in the delegation where any delegate takes a serious position which is opposed to the position that you and Mr. Hackworth take, it be referred to Washington by telegraph; or, if you and Mr. Hackworth differ on any matter, that that be referred to Washington, and that, I think, will cover all differences. You will know that in some of the subjects at least the Department does not expect conventions.

The Technical Assistants are people of substantial value in con-

---

[95] Not printed; for text of the resolution as approved, see 46 Stat. 85.
[96] Green H. Hackworth, Solicitor for the Department of State.

nection with the various subjects, but you will use entire discretion about appointing them on committees. Speaking generally, I should think you would expect Mr. Flournoy to serve on any special committee on Naturalization; Mr. Hackworth on Responsibility of States, and yourself on Territorial Waters. You will understand, of course, that the delegates are in no sense to approve the Harvard drafts [97] as a whole or to approve the League bases as a whole.

Sincerely yours, J. P. COTTON

504.418A2/159½

The Acting Secretary of State to the Chairman of the American Delegation (Miller) and the Alternate Chairman (Hackworth)

WASHINGTON, February 27, 1930.

GENTLEMEN: In addition to your formal instructions, I want to give you one private one.

As at present advised, we do not expect the delegates to sign conventions and you will regard it as an instruction not to sign a convention without prior cable authorization.

Sincerely yours, J. P. COTTON

504.418A2/159 : Telegram

The Acting Secretary of State to the Minister in Switzerland (Wilson)

WASHINGTON, March 1, 1930—2 p. m.

16. Your despatch 1139, October 17.[98] Please address a communication to Sir Eric Drummond as follows:

"With reference to your letter of October 15, 1929, to the Secretary of State, I am instructed by the Acting Secretary of State to inform you that my Government is sending a delegation to the Codification Conference composed of five plenipotentiary delegates as follows: Mr. David Hunter Miller, Mr. Green H. Hackworth, Mr. Theodore G. Risley, Mr. Richard W. Flournoy, junior, and Mrs. Ruth B. Shipley, accompanied by five technical advisers as follows: Mr. Jesse S. Reeves, Mr. Edwin M. Borchard, Mr. Manley O. Hudson, Mr. S. W. Boggs and Miss Emma Wold."

CARR

---

[97] See Research in International Law, Harvard Law School, *Nationality, Responsibility of States, Territorial Waters, Drafts of Conventions Prepared in Anticipation of the First Conference on the Codification of International Law, The Hague, 1930* (Harvard Law School, Cambridge, 1929).

[98] Not printed; see footnote 92, p. 204.

504.418A2/212 : Telegram

The Minister in the Netherlands (Diekema) to the Acting Secretary of State

THE HAGUE, March 24, 1930—10 a. m.
[Received 10:45 a. m.]

37. [From Miller.]   Conference No. 5.   After one week of the daily meetings of each of the three committees I think the result to date may be generally summarized as follows: The progress made has been very limited and slow as the discussions have been confined to a few principles in each committee.   In territorial waters, unless the three Magyar [*three-mile?*] states admit an exception for such countries as Italy, Norway, Sweden, and Portugal, any agreement seems remote.   In responsibility of states, any general agreement if reached would be of very small scope.   In nationality, I see almost no chance of an agreement.   Our policy for the right of expatriation is opposed by a majority and I cannot now see any compromise form of formula which we could accept in view of the act of 1868.[1] Furthermore the vital difference in this subject between France and Italy is one of real political importance which cannot be met in a general convention.   The foregoing were my views prior to a talk I had last evening with Giannini, chief Italian delegate, and are confirmed by that interview.   There will be a strong effort made this week to speed up work of Conference and there is great pressure to end by April 12 and no earlier date seems now possible.   Miller.

DIEKEMA

504.418A2/225 : Telegram

The Minister in the Netherlands (Diekema) to the Acting Secretary of State

[Extract—Paraphrase]

THE HAGUE, March 31, 1930—11 p. m.
[Received March 31—10:20 a. m.]

42. From Miller.   Conference No. 10.

.   .   .   .

There is not the slightest possibility that the Conference will adopt the proposal of the National Woman's Party as a clause of a convention.[2]   A very large majority of the delegations are opposed to it,

[1] 15 Stat. 223.
[2] The clause which it was desired to insert in the proposed convention of nationality provided that on the part of the contracting parties there should be no distinction based on sex in their law or practice relating to nationality.

as Miss Stevens [3] herself has stated. Under the circumstances the obvious course, which the women have in mind, is for them to seek a resolution or recommendation of the Conference which would be favorable to the proposal; our attitude on such a resolution, of course, would be one of great importance. In talking with Miss Stevens I reserved any answer on the point. I think that the Chilean delegation, which has brought forward the proposal, would be disposed to accept any suggestion which we may make in the matter.

I suggest following as form of such a resolution: [4]

"The Conference recommends to the study of the Governments the principle that in their law and practice relating to nationality there shall be no distinction based on sex with particular consideration of the interests of children involved in the application of that principle."

In support of such a proposal a statement might be made to the effect that the Government of the United States had gone very far in its nationality laws in removal of discrimination based on sex, but that it is our feeling that questions relating to children and their interests are closely bound up with the complete application of the principle and therefore should be considered in connection therewith.

Subject to the day-to-day developments here which are impossible to forecast in detail, I recommend that we favor a resolution in the form given above and support it along lines of statement indicated. I await instructions. [5] . . .

DIEKEMA

504.418A2/237 : Telegram

The Minister in the Netherlands (Diekema) to the Acting Secretary of State

[Extract]

THE HAGUE, April 5, 1930—11 p. m.
[Received April 6—2:26 a. m.]

46. [From Miller.] Conference No. 13. In my 12 of this date [6] I have sent you the text of seventeen articles of the proposed convention on nationality which are now before the commission on nationality. These seventeen articles represent almost exactly the definitive text adopted by a two-thirds majority vote of the commission on each

---

[3] Doris Stevens, chairman of the Inter-American Commission of Women. The Commission was created pursuant to a resolution of the Sixth International Conference of American States, Habana, 1928.
[4] Quoted passage not paraphrased.
[5] By telegram No. 23, April 1, 1 p. m., the Department approved the suggested form of resolution.
[6] Not printed.

article.[7] In addition to these seventeen articles there is now a proposed preamble and there are also various general articles which are or will be proposed and the text of which I do not now transmit.

. . . .

The major question of policy is our attitude toward the prestige [protocol?] of convention containing the seventeen substantive articles above mentioned as well as the other general articles. . . . Of course it would be possible for the United States to sign this convention and by preferring reservations to cut out, so far as we are concerned, all the objectionable features. I do not favor that course.

The proposed convention does little toward the removal of dual nationality or the prevention of statelessness. Our policy of expatriation receives no recognition at all. I think that we should refuse to sign the convention and make a statement to the effect that while the discussions have been very valuable and helpful, the convention as proposed contains a number of features which the United States could not accept and while it contains certain clauses to which we have no objection an acceptance of these by the United States would involve such extensive reservations to the agreement as a whole that we consider it better to await a further and more progressive agreement which we hoped the discussion of the present Conference would facilitate.

Hackworth, Risley, and Mrs. Shipley concur. Flournoy asked me to add this expression of his views with which the rest of us do not agree.

Flournoy thinks that article 1 is useful and that, with reference to statements in articles 3 and 4 and other articles concerning double nationality, a reservation to the effect that the United States cannot admit that a person who obtains naturalization in the United States retains his former allegiance, would sufficiently safeguard the position of our Government. He believes that as the articles of the convention so far agreed to are inadequate it would be desirable to recommend that the signing of any convention be postponed until further consideration shall have been given by all concerned. However, if it is decided that a convention shall be signed, he thinks that it would be preferable for us to sign with reservations thus getting the advantage of the articles of which we approve. Miller.

DIEKEMA

---

[7] League of Nations, *Acts of the Conference for the Codification of International Law*, vol. II, Minutes of the First Committee, annex III, p. 298.

504.418A2/241 : Telegram

*The Minister in the Netherlands (Diekema) to the Acting Secretary
of State*

[Extract]

THE HAGUE, April 6, 1930—4 p. m.
[Received 8 : 17 p. m.]

49. From Miller.   Conference No. 17.

. . . One of the general clauses adopted Saturday night permits signature until December 31, 1930, but even so I think it better to say at this Conference that we will not sign.   The objections are obvious now and we might as well make our position clear.   A new and to my mind fatal objection to the whole convention is that the committee Saturday night voted down a clause permitting future special agreements on nationality between particular states.   It is quite impossible for us to tie our hands in this regard by any general convention.

I shall not cable the general clauses at length unless you wish as they are pages long and mostly are not material on the question of signature.   Some of them are not yet definitive.

DIEKEMA

504.418A2/239 : Telegram

*The Minister in the Netherlands (Diekema) to the Acting Secretary
of State*

THE HAGUE, April 6, 1930—5 p. m.
[Received 6 : 31 p. m.]

50. [From Miller.]   Conference No. 18.   I think the general result of this Conference will be a set-back to the whole idea of the codification of international law; this opinion is subject to revision but it expresses my views at the moment.

In nationality, the agreement reached will be very limited and if you agree with our views it will be one which the United States will never sign.

In responsibility, any agreement will be quite limited in any case and even such a limited agreement is not now definitely in sight. This is the only one of the three subjects which presents primarily questions of existing international law for codification.

In territorial waters, there appears no possibility of agreement with views more openly divergent than they were when discussions commenced.

There is this much to be said on the other side.

The difficulties on all three questions have been explored and have been found to have been more real than was supposed when the Governments agreed on this Conference. The study of the three questions and the interchange of views will be valuable regardless of the present result and may perhaps lead gradually to some result later on some points although more probably in the near future along the lines of particular conventions than by general agreement. Miller.

DIEKEMA

504.418A2/248 : Telegram

The Acting Secretary of State to the Minister in the Netherlands (Diekema)

WASHINGTON, April 7, 1930—4 p. m.

25. For Miller. Your 46, Conference No. 13.[8] We think you should refuse to sign convention and make statement to the effect indicated by you. We do not think you should sign with reservations. Proposed Articles 1 and 2 seem to us more objectionable even than you indicate.

Your 17.[9] We think it better to say at the conference that your delegation has recommended against signature and you do not expect signature even if the general clause permits signature until end 1930.

COTTON

504.418A2/247 : Telegram

The Minister in the Netherlands (Diekema) to the Acting Secretary of State

THE HAGUE, April 7, 1930—9 p. m.
[Received April 7—8 : 08 p. m.]

53. Conference number 21. From Miller. At commission on territorial waters April 7, I proposed that the commission abandon all idea of a signed convention and submit to the Governments for their future consideration and study a report of the studies and deliberations of the commission; that action will be followed. There will be no convention or draft convention on territorial waters but merely a report of the commission which will contain an account of the proceedings, the points of agreement and of difference and drafts of certain articles provisionally agreed upon and hoping for a further conference on the subject in the future.

DIEKEMA

[8] *Ante,* p. 211.
[9] *Ante,* p. 213.

504.418A2/252 : Telegram

The Minister in the Netherlands (Diekema) to the Acting Secretary of State

THE HAGUE, April 8, 1930—6 p. m.

[Received 11 : 58 p. m.]

54. From Miller. Conference 22. The commission on nationality has adopted the following recommendations:

1. The Conference is unanimously of the opinion that it is very desirable that the various states should, in the exercise of their power of regulating questions of nationality, make every effort to reduce so far as possible cases of statelessness and that the League of Nations should continue the work which it already has in hand for the purpose of arriving at an international settlement of this serious question.

2. The Conference is also unanimous in declaring that it is very desirable that the various states should, in the exercise of their power of regulating questions of nationality, make every effort to reduce so far as possible cases of dual nationality and that steps should be taken by the League of Nations to prepare the way for a settlement by international agreement of the various conflicts which arise from the possession by individuals of two or more nationalities.

In particular it is recommended that the various states adopt legislation designed to facilitate renunciation by persons born with dual nationality of the countries in which they are not residing and that such renunciation be not made subject to the fulfillment of unnecessary conditions. The wording of the second paragraph of the foregoing recommendation is provisional.

3. It is desirable that states should give effect to the principle that the acquisition of a foreign nationality through naturalization involves the loss of the previous nationality.

At the same time so long as the principle is not universally applied it is desirable that before conferring their nationality by naturalization, states should endeavor to ascertain that the person concerned has fulfilled, or [is] in a position to fulfill, the conditions required by the law of his country for loss of nationality.

4. The Conference recommends to the Governments the study of the question whether it would not be possible:

(1) To introduce into their law the principle of the equality of the sexes in matters of nationality, taking particularly into consideration the interests of the children, and

(2) Especially to decide that in principle the nationality of the wife should not be affected without her consent either by the mere fact of marriage or by any change in the nationality of her husband.

5. The Conference is of the opinion that a woman who in consequence of her marriage has lost her nationality without acquiring that of her husband, should be able to obtain a passport from the state of which her husband is a national.

6. (Very tentatively adopted.) The Conference recommends to the Governments the study of the question whether it would not be desir-

able that in the case of a person losing his nationality without acquiring another the state whose nationality he last possessed shall at the request of the country where he is residing and under certain conditions admit him to its territory.

7. The Conference, with the view of facilitating the progressive codification of international law, expresses the [understanding?] that, in the future, states shall be guided as far as possible by the provisions of the acts of the first Conference for the Codification of International Law in any special conventions which they may conclude amongst themselves.

8. The first Conference for the Codification of International Law draws attention to the advisability of examining at a future conference questions connected with the proof of nationality. It would be highly desirable to determine the legal value of certificates of nationality which have been, or may be, issued by the competent authorities, and to lay down the conditions for their recognition by other states.

My comments on the foregoing recommendations follow:

To numbers 1, 2, 6 and 8, I see no objection.

Number 3. The first paragraph is in accord with our policy but I object very strongly to the second paragraph which in effect nullifies the first. In my opinion we could never accept and consequently cannot accept the recommendation.

Number 4. Clause (1) is our proposal. As to clause (2), there is at least some doubt in view of the provisions of the Cable Act [10] regarding loss of nationality of a woman marrying an ineligible alien. However, the recommendation only recommends study of the question, and in view of clause (1), which we proposed, and in view also of the fact that clause (2) raises a very delicate question, it is my view that we should accept number 4.

Number 5. I oppose as we cannot issue passports to persons not owing allegiance.

Number 7. Necessarily I object to this as the general convention, which is one of the acts of the Conference, is unacceptable to us.

The question remains whether any statement should be made regarding these recommendations when they come before the plenary session of the Conference where they can be adopted by a majority vote. I think that a statement should be made opposing numbers 3 and 7 and that we should merely vote against number 5.

All our delegates concur.   DIEKEMA

---

[10] 42 Stat. 1021.

504.418A2/249 : Telegram

The Minister in the Netherlands (Diekema) to the Acting Secretary of State

THE HAGUE, April 8, 1930—7 p. m.
[Received 10:27 p. m.]

55. From Miller. Conference number 23. The commission on nationality has adopted a protocol to be annexed to the general convention and consisting of the following three articles:

Article 1. A person possessing two or more nationalities who habitually resides in one of the countries whose nationality he possesses, and [who] is in fact most closely connected with that country, will be exempt from all military obligations in the other country or countries.

This exemption may involve the loss of allegiance to the other country or countries.

Article 2. Without prejudice to the provisions of article 1, if a person possesses the nationality of two states and under the law of either state has the right to renounce or decline the nationality of that state on attaining his majority, he shall be exempt from military service in that state during his minority.

Article 3. Similarly the individual who has lost the nationality of a state according to the law of that state and has acquired another nationality, will be exempt from military obligations in the country whose nationality he has lost.

The said commission also adopted another protocol to be annexed to the general convention and consisting of one article as follows:

Article. In a state whose nationality is not conferred by the mere fact of birth in its territory, a child born in its territory of a mother possessing the nationality of that state and of a father without nationality or of unknown nationality shall have the nationality of the said state.

The said commission also adopted a special separate protocol of one article as follows:

Article. If a person after entering a foreign country loses his nationality without acquiring another nationality, the state whose nationality he last possessed remains bound to admit him at the request of the country where he is residing:

(1) If he is permanently indigent either as a result of an incurable disease or for any other reason; [or]
(2) If he has been sentenced in the country where he is residing to not less than one month's imprisonment and has served his sentence or obtained total or partial remission thereof.

In the first case the State whose nationality he last possessed may refuse to receive him, on undertaking to meet the cost of relief in the country where he is residing as from the thirtieth day from the date on which the request was made. In the second case the person must be sent back to the territory of the State whose nationality he last possessed at the expense of the country where he is residing.

I make the following comments on foregoing protocols:

Annexed protocol of three articles. So far as these provide for exemption from military service they are desirable. But there are two serious objections to them: (1) Article 1 and 2 by implication, and article 3, expressly admit dual nationality of naturalized citizens which we strongly oppose; (2) an annexed protocol is closely bound up with the general convention. It is possible to meet at least the first objection and perhaps the second by appropriate reservations. I think that we should take the course here of not signing the protocol but saying that it will be considered by our Government.

Flournoy thinks it preferable to sign here with reservations as he believes article 1 of great practical value.

Annexed protocol of one article. This is of no particular interest to us although there is a conceivable case where it might apply to an American mother in another country who had two nationalities. However, the objection that it is an annexed protocol and so connected with the general convention seems to me conclusive.

A special separate protocol. I oppose this as I think we would be worse off with such qualifications in returning undesirable aliens than we are now. All our delegates concur.

DIEKEMA

504.418A2/258 : Telegram

The Acting Secretary of State to the Minister in the Netherlands
(Diekema)

WASHINGTON, April 9, 1930—5 p. m.

28. [For Miller.] Your 54, Conference 22. Your recommendations approved.

Your 55, Conference 23. Your recommendations approved.

I have had considerable doubt as to the point Flournoy raises; but because of considerable criticism going on here by a certain group of women, I should prefer that there be no signing of conventions at all at The Hague and prefer to have our Government's signature affixed, if at all, after you return. I am aware that this course may mean that other nations will not be following your example by signing promptly, but I regard that difficulty as unavoidable.

COTTON

504.418A2/261 : Telegram

The Minister in the Netherlands (Diekema) to the Acting Secretary of State

THE HAGUE, April 10, 1930—noon.
[Received April 10—11 a. m.]

60. [From Miller.] Conference 28. The question as to our signature of the document called the Final Act of the Conference is now presented for decision.

The Final Act will be a formal and quite summary statement of the proceedings of the Conference reciting the invitation, the names of the delegates, the officers of the Conference and the three commissions; then will follow a list of the conventions drawn up mentioning them only by title and a reference to the reports on territorial waters and responsibility; then a statement that the Conference had adopted various resolutions which will be set forth *in extenso;* and finally a *testimonium* clause.

The Final Act has not yet been written but I think the foregoing is a correct statement of the substance of the document.

In any case there will be nothing in the Final Act which will be in any sense of a contractual nature. It is intended merely as a formal and official record of the proceedings.

Both Hackworth and I feel strongly that the United States should sign the Final Act and we recommend we should be authorized accordingly. The United States has taken a prominent part in the proceedings here and sometimes a decisive part and it seems, to us, particularly in view of the small result of the Conference as a whole, that it would be a great pity if we refused to sign a document that is merely a record and binds nobody to anything.

If you agree in principle with our recommendation I shall have to ask that will you not include also discretion to us regarding the form of the Final Act. The signature of that document is now set for Saturday afternoon April 12 and I doubt if it will be at all possible for me to telegraph you its text even in skeleton form in time for you to answer before the hour of signature.

Accordingly I hope you will find it possible to instruct us upon receipt of this telegram.

All our delegates concur. Miller.

DIEKEMA

504.418A2/264 : Telegram

The Acting Secretary of State to the Minister in the Netherlands
(Diekema)

WASHINGTON, April 10, 1930—noon.

30. For Miller. Following telegram received from Doris Stevens:

"United States delegation Codification Conference making no effective fight prevent adoption Nationality convention based on sex discrimination. On contrary supporting two articles based on principle inequality. Do you approve? If not urge send immediately precise instructions Miller."

Please tell me what the two articles are as I would like to counteract unpleasant publicity here. Certain women have been making most unfair criticisms which I believe to be without any reason whatsoever.

COTTON

504.418A2/269 : Telegram

The Acting Secretary of State to the Minister in the Netherlands
(Diekema)

WASHINGTON, April 10, 1930—3 p. m.

32. For Miller. The organized feminine lobby has persuaded a large part of the Foreign Affairs Committees and their leaders publicly to express the view that the United States should attempt to get a postponement of any convention on nationality in the same way that you expect to postpone as to the other topics. As you fully understand I have never thought that any of these subjects was ready for world codification and have never expected a satisfactory convention. We would prefer not to see a great majority of the other nations crystallize their views on nationality in a way which we do not approve. We cannot of course attempt for a moment to dictate the views of other nations as to whether or not they deem it wise to enter into conventions but I think you might express the view that we deem it unwise that the conference should attempt in any degree to legislate on questions where there is real conflict of opinion.

COTTON

504.418A2/270 : Telegram

The Acting Secretary of State to the Minister in the Netherlands
(Diekema)

WASHINGTON, April 10, 1930—4 p. m.

33. [For Miller.] Your 60, Conference No. 28. You are authorized to sign any formal and official record of the proceedings

which you deem in proper form and you are the judges of what is proper form, provided it is merely a record and binds nobody to anything.

Cotton

504.418A2/276 : Telegram

The Minister in the Netherlands (Diekema) to the Acting Secretary of State

[Paraphrase]

THE HAGUE, April 11, 1930—3 p. m.
[Received 10 : 25 p. m.]

67. [From Miller.] Your telegram No. 30, April 10, noon. The two articles to which Miss Stevens refers read as follows in text adopted at plenary session of Conference yesterday: [11]

"Article 10. Naturalization of the husband during marriage shall not involve a change in the nationality of the wife except with her consent.

Article 11. The wife who under the law of her country lost her nationality on marriage shall not recover it after the dissolution of the marriage except on her own application and in accordance with the law of that country. If she does recover it, she shall lose the nationality which she acquired by reason of the marriage."

The convention was voted on as a whole at the plenary session, not by articles, and, as I informed you earlier today,[12] the United States delegation voted against the convention as a whole; we were the only delegation that voted against it.

At one of the commission's previous meetings when convention was voted on article by article, the delegation with my express approval and direction voted in favor of articles 10 and 11, quoted above, which then had different numbers. Before that vote was taken the delegation had offered amendments to the two articles which would have made them general in language; as, for example, saying in No. 10: [11]

"Naturalization of one spouse during marriage does not of itself involve a change of nationality for the other spouse."

The amendments had been rejected by the commission, so it seemed to me not only proper but desirable that the United States should vote affirmatively on the two articles quoted above. That naturalization of a husband shall not automatically and without the consent of the wife bring about her naturalization is wholly in accord with

---

[11] Quoted passage not paraphrased.
[12] Telegram No. 65; not printed.

United States law and policy. That a wife upon dissolution of her marriage shall not recover a former nationality which she had except upon her own application and in accordance with law is also wholly in accord with United States law and policy. In my view it was impossible for the United States to vote against such proposals. I was quite aware that Miss Stevens wanted me to vote against them and I refused to do so because I refused to put the United States in position to have it said that we supported views that consent of wife in either of two cases which I mentioned was necessary. To say that this Government should vote against such proposals merely because their language in terms does not apply to both sexes when we all know that in practical application and in fact only one sex is concerned would be to make a fetish of words. I fully believe that my action was right, and in accordance with your views. As you know, the Conference has acted on the nationality question. On the point, however, that we should have attempted to prevent the adoption here of any convention at all, it is quite obvious that any such attempt would have been fruitless. At an international conference the United States is not in the position of a dictator and the vote last night of 40 to 1 on this convention shows in itself what were the views of the other countries including all the other great powers except Russia.

The views of the United States on expatriation and married women, the subjects which I regard as the two major issues, were put before the Conference here definitely and very strongly—the first in my declaration on expatriation which had Department's approval;[14] and the second in the resolution offered by our delegation, also approved by Department, regarding the principle of equality of sex, the substance of which is first part of recommendation No. 4 in my telegram Conference No. 22, April 8, 6 p. m. and which passed last night by the Conference as recommendation No. 6[15] in language almost identical with that reported in my No. 22.

. . . .

I do not hold the opinion that action of the Conference here regarding nationality has altogether crystallized the views of other countries in opposition to our policy. I believe, on the contrary, that discussions here have shown that world sentiment on the whole question of nationality is in state of flux and that the trend is our way despite fact that at this time various countries have other views which are based partly on social and economic conditions and partly on religion. Miller.

DIEKEMA

---

[14] Telegram No. 25, April 7, 4 p. m., to the Minister in the Netherlands, p. 214.
[15] League of Nations, *Acts of the Conference for the Codification of International Law*, vol. I, p. 163.

504.418A2/278 : Telegram

The Minister in the Netherlands (Diekema) to the Acting Secretary of State

THE HAGUE, April 12, 1930—9 p. m.
[Received April 12—7 : 30 p. m.]

73. [From Miller.] Conference 38. There were two plenary sessions of the Conference on April 12.[16] At the morning session the somewhat elaborate report of the commission on the territorial waters was received. There were then adopted without dissent three recommendations: The first related to future work of codification; the second to the international regime of ports; the third to the protection of products of the sea.

All of these appear to be harmless and I shall not cable their text in full unless you request it.

The afternoon session was devoted to the signing of five documents namely: The nationality convention; protocol relating to military obligations; protocol relating to case of statelessness; special protocol relating to statelessness; and the Final Act of the Conference.

Of course we signed neither the convention nor any one of the protocols. After consideration we thought the form of the Final Act proper and constituting merely a formal record and in no way binding as an agreement in any sense. Accordingly the Final Act was signed on behalf of the United States by our four delegates,[17] Flournoy having left. Therefore [*Thereupon?*] the Conference finally adjourned. Miller.

DIEKEMA

504.418A2/338 : Telegram

The Secretary of State to the Minister in Switzerland (Wilson)

WASHINGTON, December 27, 1930—6 p. m.

112. You are instructed to proceed to Geneva and to sign the protocol relating to military obligations in certain cases of double nationality, concluded at The Hague, April 12, 1930. The last day on which the protocol remains open for signature is December 31, 1930.

Please inform the Acting Secretary General of the League of Nations that the President's full power to sign the protocol has been issued to you and will be forwarded by the next mail. It is hoped that the exhibition to the Acting Secretary General of the present telegraphic instruction will be accepted by him as sufficient authority for you to sign the protocol of April 12, 1930.[18]

STIMSON

---

[16] League of Nations, *Acts of the Conference for the Codification of International Law*, vol. I, pp. 50, 55.
[17] *Ibid.*, p. 138.
[18] Signed on the part of the United States on December 31, 1930.

Treaty Series No. 913

Protocol Relating to Military Obligations in Certain Cases of Double Nationality, Signed at The Hague, April 12, 1930 [19]

The undersigned Plenipotentiaries, on behalf of their respective Governments,

With a view to determining in certain cases the position as regards their military obligations of persons possessing two or more nationalities,

Have agreed as follows:

ARTICLE 1

A person possessing two or more nationalities who habitually resides in one of the countries whose nationality he possesses, and who is in fact most closely connected with that country, shall be exempt from all military obligations in the other country or countries.

This exemption may involve the loss of the nationality of the other country or countries.

ARTICLE 2

Without prejudice to the provisions of Article 1 of the present Protocol, if a person possesses the nationality of two or more States and, under the law of any one of such States, has the right, on attaining his majority, to renounce or decline the nationality of that State, he shall be exempt from military service in such State during his minority.

ARTICLE 3

A person who has lost the nationality of a State under the law of that State and has acquired another nationality, shall be exempt from military obligations in the State of which he has lost the nationality.

ARTICLE 4

The High Contracting Parties agree to apply the principles and rules contained in the preceding articles in their relations with each other, as from the date of the entry into force of the present Protocol.

The inclusion of the above-mentioned principles and rules in the said articles shall in no way be deemed to prejudice the question whether they do or do not already form part of international law.

It is understood that, in so far as any point is not covered by any of the provisions of the preceding articles, the existing principles and rules of international law shall remain in force.

---

[19] Ratification advised by the Senate, June 18 (legislative day of June 15), 1932; ratified by the President, July 5, 1932; ratification of the United States deposited at Geneva, August 3, 1932; proclaimed by the President, April 26, 1937.

ARTICLE 5

Nothing in the present Protocol shall affect the provisions of any treaty, convention or agreement in force between any of the High Contracting Parties relating to nationality or matters connected therewith.

ARTICLE 6

Any High Contracting Party may, when signing or ratifying the present Protocol or acceding thereto, append an express reservation excluding any one or more of the provisions of Articles 1 to 3 and 7.

The provisions thus excluded cannot be applied against the High Contracting Party who has made the reservation nor relied on by that Party against any other High Contracting Party.

ARTICLE 7

If there should arise between the High Contracting Parties a dispute of any kind relating to the interpretation or application of the present Protocol and if such dispute cannot be satisfactorily settled by diplomacy, it shall be settled in accordance with any applicable agreements in force between the Parties providing for the settlement of international disputes.

In case there is no such agreement in force between the Parties, the dispute shall be referred to arbitration or judicial settlement, in accordance with the constitutional procedure of each of the Parties to the dispute. In the absence of agreement on the choice of another tribunal, the dispute shall be referred to the Permanent Court of International Justice, if all the Parties to the dispute are Parties to the Protocol of the 16th December, 1920,[19a] relating to the Statute of that Court, and if any of the Parties to the dispute is not a Party to the Protocol of the 16th December, 1920, the dispute shall be referred to an arbitral tribunal constituted in accordance with the Hague Convention of the 18th October, 1907, for the Pacific Settlement of International Conflicts.[20]

ARTICLE 8

The present Protocol shall remain open until the 31st December, 1930, for signature on behalf of any Member of the League of Nations or of any non-Member State invited to the First Codification Conference or to which the Council of the League of Nations has communicated a copy of the Protocol for this purpose.

[19a] *Foreign Relations*, 1920, vol. I, p. 17.
[20] *Ibid.*, 1907, pt. 2, p. 1181.

ARTICLE 9

The present Protocol is subject to ratification. Ratifications shall be deposited with the Secretariat of the League of Nations.

The Secretary-General shall give notice of the deposit of each ratification to the Members of the League of Nations and to the non-Member States mentioned in Article 8, indicating the date of its deposit.

ARTICLE 10

As from January 1st, 1931, any Member of the League of Nations and any non-Member State mentioned in Article 8 on whose behalf the Protocol has not been signed before that date may accede thereto.

Accession shall be effected by an instrument deposited with the Secretariat of the League of Nations. The Secretary-General of the League of Nations shall give notice of each accession to the Members of the League of Nations and to the non-Member States mentioned in Article 8, indicating the date of the deposit of the instrument.

ARTICLE 11

A procès-verbal shall be drawn up by the Secretary-General of the League of Nations as soon as ratifications or accessions on behalf of ten Members of the League of Nations or non-Member States have been deposited.

A certified copy of this procès-verbal shall be sent by the Secretary-General to each Member of the League of Nations and to each non-Member State mentioned in Article 8.

ARTICLE 12

The present Protocol shall enter into force on the 90th day after the date of the procès-verbal mentioned in Article 11 as regards all Members of the League of Nations or non-Member States on whose behalf ratifications or accessions have been deposited on the date of the procès-verbal.

As regards any Member of the League or non-Member State on whose behalf a ratification or accession is subsequently deposited, the Protocol shall enter into force on the 90th day after the date of the deposit of a ratification or accession on its behalf.

ARTICLE 13

As from January 1st, 1936, any Member of the League of Nations or any non-Member State in regard to which the present Protocol is then in force, may address to the Secretary-General of the League of Nations a request for the revision of any or all of the provisions of this Protocol. If such a request, after being communicated to the other Members of the League and non-Member States in regard to which the Protocol is then in force, is supported within one year by at least nine of them, the Council of the League of Nations shall decide, after consultation with the Members of the League of Nations and the non-Member States mentioned in Article 8, whether a conference should be specially convoked for that purpose or whether such revision should be considered at the next conference for the codification of international law.

The High Contracting Parties agree that, if the present Protocol is revised, the new Agreement may provide that upon its entry into force some or all of the provisions of the present Protocol shall be abrogated in respect of all of the Parties to the present Protocol.

Article 14

The present Protocol may be denounced.

Denunciation shall be effected by a notification in writing addressed to the Secretary-General of the League of Nations, who shall inform all Members of the League of Nations and the non-Member States mentioned in Article 8.

Each denunciation shall take effect one year after the receipt by the Secretary-General of the notification but only as regards the Member of the League or non-Member State on whose behalf it has been notified.

Article 15

1. Any High Contracting Party may, at the time of signature, ratification or accession, declare that, in accepting the present Protocol, he does not assume any obligations in respect of all or any of his colonies, protectorates, overseas territories or territories under suzerainty or mandate, or in respect of certain parts of the population of the said territories; and the present Protocol shall not apply to any territories or to the parts of their population named in such declaration.

2. Any High Contracting Party may give notice to the Secretary-General of the League of Nations at any time subsequently that he desires that the Protocol shall apply to all or any of his territories or to the parts of their population which have been made the subject of a declaration under the preceding paragraph, and the Protocol shall apply to all the territories or the parts of their population named in such notice six months after its receipt by the Secretary-General of the League of Nations.

3. Any High Contracting Party may, at any time, declare that he

desires that the present Protocol shall cease to apply to all or any of his colonies, protectorates, overseas territories or territories under suzerainty or mandate, or in respect of certain parts of the population of the said territories, and the Protocol shall cease to apply to the territories or to the parts of their population named in such declaration one year after its receipt by the Secretary-General of the League of Nations.

4. Any High Contracting Party may make the reservations provided for in Article 6 in respect of all or any of his colonies, protectorates, overseas territories or territories under suzerainty or mandate, or in respect of certain parts of the population of these territories, at the time of signature, ratification or accession to the Protocol or at the time of making a notification under the second paragraph of this article.

5. The Secretary-General of the League of Nations shall communicate to all the Members of the League of Nations and the non-Member States mentioned in Article 8 all declarations and notices received in virtue of this article.

ARTICLE 16

The present Protocol shall be registered by the Secretary-General of the League of Nations as soon as it has entered into force.

ARTICLE 17

The French and English texts of the present Protocol shall both be authoritative.

IN FAITH WHEREOF the Plenipotentiaries have signed the present Protocol.

DONE at The Hague on the twelfth day of April, one thousand nine hundred and thirty, in a single copy, which shall be deposited in the archives of the Secretariat of the League of Nations and of which certified true copies shall be transmitted by the Secretary-General to all the Members of the League of Nations and all the non-Member States invited to the First Conference for the Codification of International Law.

Germany
  GÖPPERT
  HERING
United States of America
  HUGH R. WILSON
Austria
  LEITMAIER
Belgium
  J. DE RUELLE
  Sous réserve d'adhésion ultérieure pour la Colonie du

Congo et les Territoires sous mandat.[21]
Great Britain and Northern Ireland and all parts of the British Empire which are not separate Members of the League of Nations.
MAURICE GWYER
OSCAR F. DOWSON
Canada
PHILIPPE ROY
Irish Free State
JOHN J. HEARNE
India

In accordance with the provisions of Article 15 of this Protocol I declare that His Britannic Majesty does not assume any obligation in respect of the territories in India of any Prince or Chief under His suzerainty or the population of the said territories.
BASANTA KUMAR MULLICK
Chile
MIGUEL CRUCHAGA
ALEJANDRO ALVAREZ
H. MARCHANT
Colombia
A. J. RESTREPO   FRANCISCO JOSÉ URRUTIA
Cuba
    Ad referendum
DIAZ DE VILLAR
CARLOS DE ARMENTEROS
Denmark
F. MARTENSEN-LARSEN   V. LORCK.
Egypt
A. BADAOUI.
M. SID AHMED
Spain
A. GOICOECHEA
France
PAUL MATTER
A. KAMMERER
Greece
    Ad referendum
N. POLITIS
MEGALOS CALOYANNI
JEAN SPIROPOULOS

---

[21] Translation: Subject to accession later for the Colony of the Congo and the mandated territories.

518625—45——20

Luxemburg
    CONRAD STUMPER
Mexico
    EDUARDO SUAREZ
The Netherlands
Les Pays-Bas:
    1° Excluent de leur acceptation l'article 3;
    2° N'entendent assumer aucune obligation en ce qui con-
cerne les Indes néerlandaises, le Surinam et Curaçao.[22]
    V. EYSINGA
    J. KOSTERS
Peru
    M. H. CORNEJO
Portugal
    JOSÉ CAEIRO DA MATTA
    JOSÉ MARIA VILHENA BARBOSA DE MAGALHAES.
    Prof. Doutor J. LOBO D'AVILA LIMA
Salvador
    J. GUSTAVO GUERRERO
Sweden
    Sous réserve de ratification de S. M. le Roi de Suède avec
l'approbation du Riksdag.[23]
    K. J. WESTMAN
Uruguay
    E. E. BUERO

Treaty Series No. 913

*Procés-Verbal Regarding the Deposit of the Ten Ratifications or
Accessions Referred to in Article 11 of the Protocol Relating to
Military Obligations in Certain Cases of Double Nationality, Signed
at The Hague, April 12th, 1930* [24]

In accordance with Article 11, paragraph 1, of the Protocol relating
to Military Obligations in certain cases of double nationality, signed
at The Hague on April 12th, 1930, the undersigned hereby certifies
that the following instruments were deposited with the Secretariat of

---

[22] Translation: The Netherlands:
    1. Exclude from acceptance Article 3;
    2. Do not intend to assume any obligation as regards Netherlands Indies,
        Surinam and Curaçao.
[23] Translation: Subject to ratification by his Majesty the King of Sweden with
the approval of the Riksdag.
[24] The instrument of ratification by the Netherlands (including the Netherlands
Indies, Surinam, and Curaçao) was deposited at Geneva on April 2, 1937. At
the time of depositing the ratification the Netherlands Government withdrew
the reservation regarding art. 3 made at the time of signature of the protocol.
In accordance with the second paragraph of art. 12 of the protocol, the protocol
entered into force in respect of the Netherlands (including the Netherlands Indies,
Surinam, and Curaçao) on the 90th day after the date of the deposit.

the League of Nations in connection with the above-mentioned Protocol:

(1) Instrument of accession of Brazil, deposited on September 19th, 1931;

(2) Instrument of ratification for Great Britain and Northern Ireland and all parts of the British Empire which are not separate Members of the League of Nations, deposited on January 14th, 1932;

(3) Instrument of ratification by the United States of America, deposited on August 3rd, 1932;

(4) Instrument of ratification by India, deposited on September 28th, 1932;

Subject to the following reservation:

In accordance with the provisions of Article 15, His Britannic Majesty does not assume any obligation in respect of the territories in India of any Prince or Chief under His Suzerainty or the population of the said territories.

(5) Instrument of ratification by Sweden, deposited on July 6th, 1933;

(6) Instrument of accession of Australia, deposited on July 8th, 1935;

This accession includes also the territories of Papua and Norfolk Island and the mandated territories of New Guinea and Nauru.

(7) Instrument of accession of the Union of South Africa, deposited on October 9th, 1935;

The accession of the Government of the Union of South Africa to this Protocol is subject to the express reservation, in terms of Article 6 of the Protocol, that the provisions of Article 2 be excluded.

(8) Instrument of ratification by Salvador, deposited on October 14th, 1935;

(9) Instrument of ratification by Cuba, deposited on October 22nd, 1936;

Subject to the following reservation:

The Government of Cuba declares that it does not accept the obligation imposed by Article 2 of the Protocol when the minor referred to in that Article, although he has the right, on attaining his majority, to renounce or decline Cuban nationality, habitually resides in the territory of the State and is in fact more closely connected with the latter than with any other State whose nationality he may also possess.

(10) Instrument of ratification by Colombia, deposited on February 24th, 1937.

In order to give effect to the second paragraph of the same Article, the undersigned has drawn up the present procès-verbal.

Done at Geneva on the twenty-fourth day of February, one thousand nine hundred and thirty-seven.

The Secretary-General
J. AVENOL

ATTITUDE OF THE UNITED STATES REGARDING A PROPOSED
AMENDMENT TO THE COVENANT OF THE LEAGUE OF NATIONS

500.C Covenant/62

The British Embassy to the Department of State

AIDE-MÉMOIRE

In execution of the resolution of the Assembly of the League of
Nations of September 24th 1929,[26] a Committee met recently in Geneva
to consider amending the Covenant of the League in order to bring
it into harmony with the Pact of Paris.[27]   The resolution of the Assembly declared that "it is desirable that the terms of the Covenant
of the League should not accord any longer to members of the League
a right to have recourse to war in cases in which that right has been
renounced by the provisions of the Pact of Paris."

The Committee produced a report dated March 8th 1930,[28] proposing that amendments be made in certain articles of the Covenant.
These proposed amendments have been discussed by His Majesty's
Government in the United Kingdom and it has been decided to instruct the British Delegation at the next Assembly of the League of
Nations, subject to the concurrence of His Majesty's Governments in
the Dominions, to support the inclusion of the proposed amendments
in the Covenant. This decision was brought to the notice of the
Secretary of State of the United States by His Majesty's Principal
Secretary of State for Foreign Affairs in a letter dated April 8th,[28a]
with which Mr. Henderson enclosed a copy of the above-mentioned
report of the League Committee.

From page 10 of the report it will be observed that amongst other
amendments the Committee proposed the addition of a new paragraph
to Article 15 of the Covenant, entitled paragraph 7 bis. The effect
of this new paragraph is to provide that in a dispute likely to lead
to a rupture the Council of the League of Nations may *by a majority*
ask for an advisory opinion on any point of law involved. In the
present state of the Covenant such an opinion can only be asked for
by unanimity.

In Article 5 of the Protocol of Accession of the United States of
America [29] to the Protocol of Signature of the Statute of the Permanent Court of International Justice it is stated that: "With regard to
requesting an advisory opinion of the Court in any case covered by

---

[26] League of Nations, *Official Journal*, Special Supplement No. 75, Records of the
Tenth Ordinary Session of the Assembly, pp. 167–169.

[27] Treaty for the Renunciation of War, signed at Paris, August 27, 1928,
Foreign Relations, 1928, vol. I, p. 153.

[28] League of Nations, *Report of the Committee for the Amendment of the
Covenant of the League of Nations In Order To Bring It Into Harmony With
the Pact of Paris* (A.8.1930.V.).

[28a] Not printed.

[29] *Foreign Relations*, 1929, vol. I, p. 53.

the preceding paragraphs, there shall be attributed to an objection of the United States the same force and effect as attaches to a vote against asking for an opinion given by a Member of the League of Nations in the Council or the Assembly."

The effect of the adoption by the Assembly of the new paragraph to Article 15 of the Covenant will be to diminish the power of Members of the League to prevent an advisory opinion from the Court being requested, and will therefore similarly diminish the power of the United States in this respect, because if the paragraph is adopted the United States will not be able, as they would be if the proposed paragraph is rejected, to block any such request being made to the Court, seeing that the matter will be decided by a majority and not by unanimity.

His Majesty's Government are therefore anxious to ascertain whether the insertion of the proposed new paragraph 7 bis in Article 15 is likely adversely to affect the prospects of the Senate of the United States accepting the Protocol of Accession of the United States to the Permanent Court of International Justice. Although His Majesty's Government have decided to support the inclusion of the proposed amendments in the Covenant, the proposed new paragraph 7 bis can well be omitted without affecting the rest of the amendments, and should objection be taken to it in the United States, His Majesty's Government would for their part be disposed to move that the new paragraph 7 bis should not be accepted.

WASHINGTON, May 22, 1930.

500.C Covenant/62

The Department of State to the British Embassy

AIDE-MÉMOIRE

With reference to the inquiry which you made during your call on May 22, 1930, at the time the United States Senate reservations of January 27, 1926,[30] were formulated, there existed no provision in the Covenant specifically empowering the Council to request an advisory opinion from the Court by other than unanimous vote. The adoption of an amendment to the Covenant specifically providing that the Council may request an advisory opinion from the Court by majority rather than unanimous vote in cases arising under Article 15, would effect a fundamental change in the situation which existed at the time the Senate reservations were formulated, as well as at the time the Protocol of Accession of the United States to the Protocol of Signature of the Statute of the Permanent Court of International Justice was signed.

WASHINGTON, May 27, 1930.

---

[30] *Foreign Relations*, 1926, vol. I, p. 1.

500.C Covenant/65

Memorandum by the Chief of the Division of Western European Affairs (Marriner)

[WASHINGTON,] May 27, 1930.

I handed Mr. Campbell, Counselor of the British Embassy, a memorandum in reply to a memorandum which the Ambassador left with the Secretary of State on May 22, 1930, on the subject of the amendments to the Covenant of the League of Nations, concerning unanimity of the majority of the requests for advisory opinions. I pointed out to him that the point of the memorandum was that any such alteration of the Covenant would change the conditions under which the reservations of the Senate to the Protocol of Signature of the Statute of the World Court were made and that this was our only observation in the matter, as we did not, under any circumstances, wish to interfere with any action the members of the League of Nations might care to take with respect to altering the Covenant. I told him that I felt that the matter should not be given undue publicity and that the United States would not, under any circumstances, wish to be put in the position of preventing the League from carrying out its wishes in the matter.

Mr. Campbell said he understood fully and would report the matter immediately to the Ambassador.

J[AMES] M[ARRINER]

POLICY OF THE UNITED STATES REGARDING THE BANK FOR INTERNATIONAL SETTLEMENTS [31]

462.00R296 Bank for International Settlements/71

The Chargé in Switzerland (Moffat) to the Acting Secretary of State

No. 1336

BERNE, March 5, 1930.
[Received March 29.]

SIR: Referring to my despatch No. 1308 of February 14, 1930,[32] I have the honor to report that the convention concerning the Bank of International Payments [33] was ratified by the Swiss Federal Chambers on February 25, 1930. This took the form of the approval of two decrees, the one putting the convention into force insofar as Switzerland is concerned for fifteen years, the other prolonging the terms of the convention for the life of the Bank. This second decree is subject to a referendary delay which expires on May 27; except for the improbable event of a demand for a national referendum, final

---

[31] For previous correspondence concerning the Bank for International Settlements, see *Foreign Relations*, 1929, vol. II, pp. 1032–1073, *passim*.
[32] Not printed.
[33] League of Nations Treaty Series, vol. CIV, p. 441.

ratification of the convention for the duration of the Bank will have been completed on that date.

Preparations are now afoot in Basel for opening the Bank on April 1. In the circumstances, and with a view to receiving advance rulings from the Department I respectfully request instructions as to:

1. The nature of reports desired with regard to the work or position of the Bank.

2. Whether the Consulate at Basel should cover such reporting or whether there are certain phases which the Department desires the Legation to follow.

3. What attitude the Legation should adopt in the event that the American members of the Bank should request assistance.

4. Whether the Legation should grant such American members any special facilities over and above customary courtesies accorded to all distinguished Americans.

I have [etc.] PIERREPONT MOFFAT

462.00R296 Bank for International Settlements/86

The Acting Secretary of State to the Chargé in Switzerland (Moffat)

No. 873 WASHINGTON, April 29, 1930.

SIR: With reference to your despatch No. 1336 dated March 5, 1930, there is enclosed a copy of an instruction of this date to the American Consul at Basel regarding the Bank for International Settlements.[34] The Legation should exercise a general supervision over the Consulate's execution of this instruction, carefully reviewing the Consulate's reports and making to the Consul such suggestions as may seem appropriate.

It is presumed that the American members of the Board of Directors of the Bank will report primarily to the American banking group interested in the establishment of the Bank and will not have occasion to request the assistance of the Legation in their capacity as Directors or officers of the Bank. They should be granted the customary courtesies accorded to all distinguished Americans. Any request from them for any special facilities over and above such courtesies should be carefully considered in each case and not treated as a matter of routine.

I am [etc.] J. P. COTTON

462.00R296 Bank for International Settlements/85

The Acting Secretary of State to the Consul at Basel (Hitch)

WASHINGTON, April 29, 1930.

SIR: The Department has received the Consulate's despatch No. 329 dated February 4, 1930,[35] requesting instructions regarding the

[34] *Infra.*
[35] Not printed.

attitude of the Consulate toward the Bank for International Settlements.

The establishment at Basel of so important an institution as the Bank for International Settlements will make it a particular duty of the Consul there to study the Bank and its operations; it may make it possible for the Consulate to submit valuable economic and political reports; the Consul will naturally maintain the most cordial possible relations with the Bank, its officers, directors and personnel; however, the Consul is charged with no special mission toward the Bank and should avoid any attitude which might be misconstrued as evidencing such a mission.

The Department has hitherto designated an officer as an Acting American Observer with the Reparation Commission; the Bank succeeds to some of the functions of the Reparation Commission, but not in a way that will admit of the participation of Government representatives in its activities. The United States is not a party to the international agreements pursuant to which the Bank is founded, nor will it have contractual relations with the Bank such as will be established between the Bank and several other governments by the Trust Agreement (Annex VIII to The Hague Agreement of January 1930 [36]). The United States has negotiated an agreement with Germany which contemplates direct payment by Germany of its indebtedness to the United States.[37] Similar arrangements are in force with the other European debtors of the United States. The Secretary of State on May 16, 1929, issued a statement (copy of which is enclosed) [38] that the American Government will not permit any officials of the Federal Reserve System either to themselves serve or to select American representatives as members of the proposed International Bank.

In some respects the position of the Consulate will not be dissimilar from that of the other Consulates at Basel. As stated in the preamble to the Constituent Charter of the Bank, the Bank is founded by Central Banks pursuant to a Plan [39] adopted by the Powers signatory to The Hague Agreement of January 1930. The Plan (Young Plan, paragraph 148) "recommended the creation of the Bank for International Settlements in order to provide machinery for the removal of the Reparation obligation from the political to the financial sphere." The Plan states (paragraph 72) that "the

[36] Agreement regarding the complete and final settlement of the question of reparations, signed at The Hague, January 20, 1930, League of Nations Treaty Series, vol. CIV, pp. 243, 328.

[37] See vol. III, pp. 106 ff.; for text of the agreement signed at Washington, June 23, 1930, see *Annual Report of the Secretary of the Treasury for the fiscal year ended June 30, 1930* (Washington, Government Printing Office, 1931), p. 341, or League of Nations Treaty Series, vol. CVI, p. 121.

[38] *Foreign Relations*, 1929, vol. II, p. 1070.

[39] See Great Britain, Cmd. 3343 (1929): *Report of the Committee of Experts on Reparations*, p. 10.

Bank excludes from its procedure all political influences" and again (paragraph 54) "its organization will be outside the field of political influences." The British Chancellor of the Exchequer stated in the House of Commons February 20, 1930:

"While His Majesty's Government welcome the creation of the Bank for International Settlements, it is, as I have previously stated, a non-political institution, and national Governments will not be concerned with the direction of the policy of the Board. Neither the action of individual directors, nor the action of a Central Bank under Article 20 of the Statutes requires the prior approval of the Treasury of the country to which the director of the Central Bank belongs. . . . There will be no Treasury representatives at Basel."

In view of these antecedents and of the traditions of the Central Banks represented on the Board of Directors of the Bank, the Consul should avoid over-ambitious initiatives in informing himself regarding its operations.

It is not known what reports the Bank will issue regarding its activities.

It is presumed that on mere request, the Bank will furnish the Consulate in a routine way, such information and notices as it makes available generally to other consulates and information agencies in Basel. While such routine information will probably receive wide publicity, the Department, and other Departments in Washington, will wish to build up files of information on the Bank which should include the texts of the more important formal announcements which the Consulate can make available. The Consul will, of course, not refuse such additional economic information as comes to him, with due regard to the proprieties, through personal contacts in view of the known interest of the United States Consular Service in economic reporting.

In spite of the desire of the founders of the Bank to minimize political influences, it is obvious that the operations of the Bank, and particularly the annual election of Directors, will not be devoid of international political interest. The Consul's opportunities for observation and study may enable him to render reports in this regard which will be of interest both to the Department and to its several missions.

The Consulate should address its despatches and reports regarding the International Bank to the Legation at Berne, which will forward them to the Department and provide for their further distribution through the European Information Center at Paris and assure the Consulate the reciprocal delivery of information from other European missions.

I am [etc.] J. P. COTTON

PRESENCE OF AMERICAN UNOFFICIAL OBSERVERS AT GENEVA DURING THE INTERNATIONAL CONFERENCES FOR A TARIFF TRUCE, FEBRUARY–MARCH 1930 AND NOVEMBER 1930

560.M5/33

The Secretary General of the League of Nations (Drummond) to the Acting Secretary of State [40]

C. L. 9. 1930. II.   GENEVA, January 18, 1930.

SIR: I have the honour to inform you that the Council of the League of Nations decided at its meeting on January 14th, 1930, to convene for Monday, February 17th, 1930, at 11 a. m. at Geneva, the Conference contemplated in the first part of the Tenth Assembly's resolution dealing with the economic work of the League (A.68. 1929. II).[41]

The object of this Conference is defined in the resolution, which states that "in order that this concerted action may be pursued on a firm basis and in an atmosphere of confidence, the Assembly recommends that States which are prepared to participate therein should agree not to increase their protective tariffs above the present level for a period of from two to three years, or to impose new protective duties or create new impediments to trade." It therefore recommends "the establishment, if necessary, of a programme of subsequent negotiations for facilitating economic relations by all practicable means and especially by reducing hindrances to trade".

As the representative of Germany pointed out in his report to the last session of the Council, the Assembly defined its ideas concerning the character of the conference in the following paragraph of its resolution: "no effective action will be possible in the future unless the Governments are now requested to examine in their turn the questions left in suspense by the Consultative Committee and by the Economic Committee, availing themselves of the work accomplished by those Committees to assist them in their decisions". In the report introducing the resolution the Assembly expressed "the conviction that negotiations for an economic *rapprochement* must not be left entirely in the hands of technical experts, but that, on the contrary, it is essential for Governments to participate more directly than they have hitherto done".

The text of this resolution was communicated to you on September 30th, 1929, by my circular letter No. 258.1929.II.[42] On November 7th, 1929, by my circular letter No. 305.1929.II,[42] I had the honour to send you the text of a preliminary draft convention intended to serve as a basis for the conference's discussions and prepared by the Eco-

---

[40] Transmitted to the Department by the Minister in Switzerland in despatch No. 1264 (L. of N. No. 1585), January 20, 1930; received January 30.
[41] Not reprinted.
[42] Not printed.

nomic Committee in accordance with the instructions contained in the Assembly resolution.

I take this opportunity to send you a copy of the report by the representative of Germany,[43] who is *Rapporteur* to the Council on economic questions. This report was approved by the Council on January 14th, 1930. I should in addition inform you that since that date the Japanese and Lithuanian Governments have notified me that they also will take part in the projected conference.

Further, I feel that I should let you know that the Governments of Belgium, Bulgaria, Great Britain, Greece, Spain, Hungary and Poland, have informed me of the composition of their delegations. The delegations of Belgium, Great Britain, Spain, Hungary and Poland will be headed by responsible Members of the Cabinet.

Lastly I have the honour to inform you that at its meeting on January 14th the Council appointed Count Carl Moltke, Minister Plenipotentiary and ex-Minister for Foreign Affairs of Denmark, to preside over the Conference.

I have [etc.]   ERIC DRUMMOND

560.M5/38 : Telegram

The Acting Secretary of State to the Chargé in Switzerland (*Moffat*)

WASHINGTON, February 8, 1930—noon.

12. You will convey in the customary manner the following note to the Secretary General of the League:

"The Acting Secretary of State of the United States of America has received, with appreciation, the note of the Secretary General of the League of Nations, dated January 18, 1930, with which he was good enough to enclose the report on the economic work of the League of Nations (Document A.68.1929.II) and a copy of the report submitted to the Council of the League by the *Rapporteur* on economic questions which was approved by the Council at its meeting on January 14, 1930 (Annex to C. L. 9.1930.II), and with which the Secretary General conveyed the information that the Council of the League of Nations had decided, at its meeting on January 14, 1930, to convene at Geneva on February 17, 1930, the Conference contemplated in the first part of the Tenth Assembly's resolution dealing with the economic work of the League.

The American Government notes that the object of this Conference is defined in the resolution, which states that 'in order that this concerted action may be pursued on a firm basis and in an atmosphere of confidence, the Assembly recommends that States which are prepared to participate therein should agree not to increase their protective tariffs above the present level for a period of from two to three years, or to impose new protective duties or create new impedi-

---

[43] Annex to C.L.9.1930.II, C.L.9 (a) ; not reprinted.

ments to trade.' The American Government likewise notes that the resolution of the Tenth Assembly recommends 'the establishment, if necessary, of a programme of subsequent negotiations for facilitating economic relations by all practicable means and especially by reducing hindrances to trade.'

The American Government views with approbation any endeavor to facilitate world-wide economic relations and to remove discriminatory economic measures and has, with this object, signed and ratified the Convention for the Abolition of Import and Export Prohibitions and Restrictions [44] and has cooperated with other international activities looking to the betterment of economic conditions throughout the world. The Government of the United States does not feel, however, that it could at this time usefully participate in the Conference to which the Secretary General's note makes reference.

The American Government will, nevertheless, follow with sympathetic interest any action which may be taken by the States participating in this Conference to promote by non-discriminatory measures their economic welfare."

Please inform the Secretary General that Mr. Edwin C. Wilson, First Secretary attached to the American Embassy at Paris, has been instructed to be present in Geneva during the period of the Conference and to associate himself with the American Consulate at Geneva with a view to obtaining information regarding the developments of the Conference. At the same time you will request his good offices that the Conference authorities may understand the nature of Mr. Wilson's duties and may afford to him such facilities as may be practicable.

Repeat by mail to American Consul at Geneva and to Edwin Wilson.

COTTON

560.M5/41 : Telegram

The Acting Secretary of State to the Ambassador in France (Edge)

WASHINGTON, February 8, 1930—1 p. m.

31. Your February 4, February 6.[45] For Edwin C. Wilson. You are instructed to proceed to Geneva at such a time as may be convenient to you prior to the opening of the Conference for the Discussion of a Tariff Truce on the morning of February 17, 1930, and to remain at Geneva during the period of the Conference and for such a time following the Conference as you may find necessary for completing inquiries and preparing reports to the Department.

. . . .

The Department desires that at Geneva you associate yourself with the Consulate assuming charge of the political and economic work of

---

[44] *Foreign Relations*, 1928, vol. I, p. 336.
[45] Neither printed.

the Consulate insofar as it relates to the Conference and cognate matters. Consul Everett is being instructed to render you full assistance in this respect.

Inasmuch as the Department's note declines the League's invitation to be represented at this Conference, your "association with the Consulate", as well as its serving practical ends, is designed to forestall possible interpretation of your duties as those of an "official observer".

The Department attaches great importance to this Conference, not so much because it is likely to lead to any immediate results in line with its announced agenda, as because it is regarded as the first step in a possible reorientation of European trade and tariff policy of vital concern to American commercial and financial interests. It is thought, on this account, that private expressions of opinion from responsible individual delegates as to present and prospective trends in European economic policy may be fully as significant as any formal action which the Conference itself may determine. You should report fully to the Department your observations and all developments of importance, especially those affecting American interests. Reference is made to Diplomatic Serial No. 886, December 5, 1929.[46]

In this connection, the Department leaves to your discretion entirely the extent to which you will go in attending sessions of the Conference and in establishing relations with the delegates. The Department, however, perceives no objection to your entering into extensive and frank relations with the delegates at the Conference with the natural limitation that it does not desire to be placed in the position of taking part, and you should, of course, take due care that nothing which you may say be interpreted as commitments on the part of this Government.

CotTon

560.M5/72 : Telegram

The Consul at Geneva (Blake) to the Acting Secretary of State

GENEVA, February 28, 1930—10 a. m.
[Received 2 p. m.]

From Wilson. The question of principal interest to the United States which is being discussed here seems to me clearly to be that concerning the effect of multilateral economic agreements upon the most-favored-nation clause in bilateral treaties. The following is a summary of the position of the question in the light of discussions in subcommittees and private conversations:

There is general acceptance of the view that existing rights based on the most-favored-nation clause cannot be affected or modified

---

[46] Not printed.

without the consent of the parties concerned. Thus it was agreed to make no attempt to restrict the advantages of the tariff truce convention, if one should be adopted here, to signatory states only. As regards the future, there is a division of opinion. On the one side, the Belgians, French, Dutch, Swiss and Germans hold that the application of the most-favored-nation clause in an unrestricted and unconditional form constitutes a serious obstacle to the economic work of the League as regards the conclusion of collective agreements. They desire that future commercial treaties should contain a provision excluding from the effect of the most-favored-nation clause the advantages of multilateral conventions of a general character concluded under the auspices of the League of Nations and open to all countries (for example, see article 2 of treaty between France and Switzerland of July 8, 1929,[47] and article 1 of treaty between the Belgo-Luxemburg and Switzerland of August 26, 1929 [48]). They also favor the modification in this sense, by mutual agreement, of existing most-favored-nation treaties as has been done by Belgium and Holland in an exchange of letters in January 1930. On the other side, Great Britain, Italy and Norway oppose any limitation on the most-favored-nation clause and insist that no recommendation in this sense should be made by the present Conference but that on the contrary every state must be left free to decide its own policy in the matter.

On the whole, the question is being discussed in a moderate manner. Even those states which hold the problem lies at the heart of the future economic work of the League appear to recognize that they have nothing to gain by trying to force the acceptance of their idea and that they must leave each state free to decide the question according to its own interests. They will, however, of course continue to urge at every appropriate occasion the adoption of the restrictive clause referred to above.

BLAKE

560.M5/101 : Telegram

The Consul at Geneva (Blake) to the Acting Secretary of State

GENEVA, March 25, 1930—10 a. m.
[Received March 25—9 a. m.]

From Wilson. The Conference held final plenary session yesterday. The following three documents have been adopted:[49]

A. Commercial convention (this contains the obligation not to denounce existing treaties),
B. Protocol to the convention, and
C. Protocol concerning the program of future negotiations.

---

[47] League of Nations Treaty Series, vol. CXIV, p. 189.
[48] *Ibid.*, vol. CV, p. 9.
[49] For texts of these documents, see League of Nations document C.203.M. 96.1930.II (Geneva, April 15, 1930).

In the past two weeks there has been a consistent whittling down of the obligations originally contemplated in the two main documents. The commercial convention follows in general the main lines mentioned in my telegrams of March 10, 11 a. m., and March 17, 11 a. m.,[50] but has been weakened all along the line. It was signed yesterday by eleven countries including Great Britain, France, Germany and Italy and will remain open for signature until April 15th. A conference will be held in November of states which have ratified in order to determine whether and when it is to come into force.

The protocol regarding future negotiations recommends that the states represented at the Conference reply as soon as possible to a questionnaire concerning methods of improving trade in agricultural and manufactured products and the movement of European raw materials; the economic organization will formulate proposals based on these replies to be submitted as early as possible for the examination of the Governments on the basis of replies from the Governments; the League Council will draw up the subsequent procedure. Until a few days ago fixed and early dates had been laid down for the various stages. However, at the last minute the French and Italian delegations against the opposition of the British insisted that the Governments should not be obliged to take action under the protocol until parliaments had first ratified the commercial convention and that the subsequent procedure should be left to the League Council in order to avoid holding conference of mediocre success such as the present one. In addition to the foregoing proposal for future negotiations, the protocol also recommends action on many questions dealt with by the 1927 Economic Conference and now under examination by the economic organization.

The Chairman in his final speech stressed the European character of the Conference, pointed out that its results represent not the work of the League but of the Governments themselves, and said that future developments from this "first hesitating step" will obviously depend upon the spirit in which it will be regarded and executed.

BLAKE

560.M5/151

The Chargé in Switzerland (Moffat) to the Secretary of State

No. 1692　　　　　　　　　　　　　BERNE, October 9, 1930.
L. N. No. 1824　　　　　　　　　　　[Received October 20.]

SIR: Referring to my telegram No. 96 dated October 9, 10 a. m.,[51] I have the honor to transmit herewith the letter of the Deputy Secretary General of the League of Nations (C.L. 279 (c) 1930. II)[52] dated

[50] Neither printed.
[51] Not printed.
[52] Not reprinted.

October 8, 1930, whereby he informs you that he has convened the States that participated in the Conference of February–March 1930 to a second Conference of Concerted Economic Action to meet at Geneva on November 17, 1930, and further points out that should the United States Government desire to designate an official observer or other representative to follow the proceedings of the Conference, as at the February–March Conference, he would be glad to give him the necessary facilities.

Respectfully yours,   PIERREPONT MOFFAT

560.M5/150 : Telegram

The Secretary of State to the Minister in Switzerland (Wilson)

WASHINGTON, October 14, 1930—2 p. m.

98. Legation's telegram 96, October 9, 10 a. m.[53] Express to Secretary General appreciation of offer of facilities and advise him that American Consul at Geneva will be instructed to follow the proceedings. Inform Gilbert.

STIMSON

560.M5/162 : Telegram

The Consul at Geneva (Gilbert) to the Secretary of State

GENEVA, November 18, 1930—3 p. m.
[Received November 18—12:45 p. m.]

The Second International Conference on Concerted Economic Action convened yesterday with 26 European countries sending delegates and 6 overseas countries represented by observers. The Conference first considered the question of the coming into force of the commercial convention of March 24, 1930. Of the 9 countries which have so far ratified this convention, none apparently was willing to put it into effect among themselves. In view of the impending ratification of France and Italy, the Conference will probably decide to extend the date when ratifications may be received and postpone fixing the time of the coming into force of this convention until the January meeting of the Conference. Conference now considering position of countries with reference to the protocol of future negotiations, particularly the replies made to the questionnaire attached thereto.

GILBERT

---

[53] Not printed; see despatch No. 1692, October 9, *supra*.

560.M5/171 : Telegram

The Consul at Geneva (Gilbert) to the Secretary of State

GENEVA, November 28, 1930—5 p. m.
[Received November 29—9:25 a. m.]

Economic Conference ended this morning. In view of uncertainties present in the Conference, it has seemed expedient to defer reporting until the various situations had become clarified.

All states signed or announced their intention of signing Final Act. Final Act being forwarded as a League document.[54]

Conference considered to have been a failure as far as negotiations with a view to ameliorating present tariff conditions are concerned. The general air has been pessimistic throughout. A summary of the relatively meager results of the Conference are as follows:

1. Commercial convention. States which have ratified, agreed to extend time limit for deposit of ratifications to January 25, 1931. The question of the putting into force of this convention has been postponed until a later meeting. This may take the form of a very short meeting late in January for this particular purpose.

2. British proposal for reductions on groups of commodities. As far as collective negotiations are concerned the Final Act of the Conference flatly declared that they "could not be entered upon by all of the signatory states en bloc". The possibility of bilateral negotiations was "noted with satisfaction" by the Conference and the hope expressed that some improvement might possibly result from this method. This obviously means very little, unless Germany and other Continental countries, fearful of Great Britain turning to protection, make some concessions in the way of tariff reductions in direct negotiations with Great Britain.

3. Preferential treatment for cereal exports of agricultural countries of Eastern Europe. These negotiations exaggerated completely as far as conceded action was concerned, the Final Act simply "notifying" the proposal of the agricultural countries. Of the five countries from whom preference was requested, France, Italy, and Austria refused to consider a preferential regime, Czechoslovakia doubtful, and only Germany willing to negotiate on basis. It is understood that Germany has already begun preliminary negotiations with Roumania for a general commercial treaty. It is not improbable that in these treaty negotiations the question will be raised of granting possible preferences on cereal products in return for tariff reductions on industrial products in the exportation of which Germany is particularly interested. Similar negotiations on Germany's part with Hungary and Yugoslavia are foreshadowed.

4. Convention for abolition of import and export prohibitions and restrictions. Situation unchanged from consulate's November 26, 10 a. m.[55]

---

[54] League of Nations document C.655.M.270.1930.II (Geneva, December 9, 1930) was forwarded to the Department by the Minister in Switzerland in his despatch No. 1820 (L. of N. No. 1902), December 19, 1930; received January 5, 1931.

[55] Not printed.

5. Treatment of foreigners. No formal action taken. Private conversations however took place with a view to advancing this project.

6. Technical questions such as indirect protection, unfair competition, customs nomenclature, etc. No action taken beyond expressing the hope that the League would expedite the pertinent studies.

Although the work of this Conference was considered as preliminary, the idea of collective action in tariff matters appears to have been allowed to lapse at least for some time to come.

The third Economic Conference,[55a] if called, will now probably not take place before March in order to allow time for negotiations which have been envisaged to proceed.

GILBERT

CRITICISM OF CERTAIN PROVISIONS IN AMERICAN TARIFF LEGISLATION [56]

611.003/2244

The Acting Secretary of State to Senator Reed Smoot [57]

WASHINGTON, April 11, 1930.

MY DEAR SENATOR SMOOT: Referring to previous correspondence regarding the so-called countervailing duty provisos in the tariff bill which are inconsistent with most-favored-nation treaties, I hope that the conference committee can give consideration to reconciling such provisos with our treaty obligations. The pending bill as passed by the Senate and by the House, respectively, contained such provisos in their mandatory form, as follows:

As Passed by the House	As Passed by the Senate
Par.	Par.
369, automobiles etc.	401, lumber
371, bicycles etc.	1402, paperboard etc.
1402, paperboard etc.	1621, bread
1640, calcium acetate	1650, coal etc.
1649, coal etc.	
1686, gunpowder, etc.	

As suggested in my letter of February 4, 1930,[58] if it is considered necessary to retain any of these provisos the treaty obligations could

---

[55a] A second session of the Second International Conference with a view to Concerted Economic Action was held at Geneva March 16–18, 1931. Its proceedings were followed informally by officers of the American Consulate at Geneva and reported in despatch No. 88 Political, March 21, 1931 (560.M5/216). The commercial convention of March 24, 1930, failed to be put into effect.

[56] For previous correspondence, see *Foreign Relations*, 1929, vol. I, pp. 985 ff. Additional representations, not printed, regarding certain tariff rates were received from a number of governments and transmitted to the appropriate committees of Congress.

[57] Chairman of the Senate Finance Committee.

[58] Not printed.

be saved from impairment by adding to each paragraph in which any such proviso appears a provision that nothing in the paragraph shall be construed or permitted to operate in any manner to impair or affect the provisions of any treaty between the United States and any foreign nation.

It is understood that those who favored the reenactment of such provisos had primarily in view their use in connection with our trade with Canada, a country with which we have no treaty guaranteeing most-favored-nation treatment in customs matters. It is estimated that not less than 80 per cent. of our total importations of products which would be affected by the countervailing duty provisos come from that country, and that of the remainder a very considerable proportion comes from other countries with which the United States has no treaties providing for most-favored-nation treatment. Thus it is evident that provisions such as those suggested would not prevent the countervailing duty provisos from serving their intended purpose, and yet would make manifest the intention of this Government fully to meet the obligations accepted in its treaties.

Sincerely,

J. P. COTTON

611.003/2248

The Under Secretary of State (Cotton) to the Secretary of State

[WASHINGTON,] May 6, 1930.

THE SECRETARY: The attached memorandum is all correct. I took this up with the President some time ago and also with the Chairman of the Conference Committee. I have letters [59] from both Smoot and Hawley [60] saying it is impossible to make the changes. The Department has done all it can to this end and has a clear record. There is no excuse for these countervailing duties, but I do not recommend further action.

J. P. C[OTTON]

[Enclosure]

Memorandum by the Chief of the Treaty Division (Barnes)

[WASHINGTON,] May 6, 1930.

MR. COTTON:
MR. SECRETARY:

The tariff bill as reported to the two houses of Congress by the Conference Committee, on April 28, 1930, still contains five provisos, in Paragraphs 369, 371, 1402, 1650 and 1687, referring, respectively, to automobiles, bicycles, paperboard, coal and gunpowder, which re-

---

[59] Not printed.
[60] Representative Willis C. Hawley, Chairman of the House Ways and Means Committee.

quire discriminatory duties and would operate in violation of the most-favored-nation clause of our commercial treaties.

The violation of the treaties could be avoided by the insertion in the bill of a section expressly exempting the treaties from the operation of the provisos. A draft section which would meet this situation is attached. It is suggested that you give consideration to the question of bringing the situation to the attention of the President with a view to his asking Congress to insert the section herein suggested in the bill before final passage.

The section suggested is as follows:

Sec. ——. Nothing in the provisos in Paragraphs 369, 371 and 1402 of Title I, Section 1, and Paragraphs 1650 and 1687 of Title II, Section 201, of this Act shall be construed or permitted to operate in any manner to impair or affect the provisions of any treaty between the United States and any foreign nation.

[The paragraphs referred to are numbered according to the bill as it passed the Senate; paragraph 369 refers to automobiles; 371, bicycles; 1402, paperboard; 1650, coal; 1687, gunpowder.] [61]

C[HARLES] M. B[ARNES]

611.003/2112

The German Embassy to the Department of State

The latest legislative developments regarding the determination of rates of duty provided for in the bill now in the final stage of parliamentary consideration and entitled:

"71st Congress, 2nd Session, H. R. 2667, An Act to provide revenue, to regulate commerce with foreign countries, to encourage the industries of the United States, to protect American labor, and for other purposes",

have caused much anxiety among German industries and commerce engaged in trade with the United States. The existing fear for the future of their trade seems well justified in view of the fact that the proposed increases in rates of American duty would affect to the point of practical import prohibition with respect to Germany, a great majority of just such articles as the German Government enumerated in the enclosure to its Memorandum, submitted to the Government of the United States on July 25, 1929,[62] and in which certain economic reasons for consideration in connection with the revision of the respective rates of duty were set forth in detail.

It may be stated that particularly grave concern is felt by the

---

[61] Brackets appear in the original memorandum.
[62] Printed in *Tariff Act of 1929:* Hearings before the Committee on Finance, United States Senate, 71st Cong., 1st sess., on H. R. 2667 . . . vol. XVIII (Washington, Government Printing Office, 1929), p. 221.

interested German industries over the effect on their trade of the American rates of duty now proposed for the following merchandise:

clocks (par. 368, Tariff Act of 1922),
upholstery cloth and tapestry (par. 909/10 Tariff Act of 1922),
jewelry (par. 1428, Tariff Act of 1922),
leather (par. 1606, Tariff Act of 1922) and
leather goods (par. 1432, Tariff Act of 1922).

Exhaustive studies have definitely convinced German Authorities on leather trade, for instance, that the item in German exports to the United States covering leather and leather-goods, amounting to approximately 45.000.000 RM p. a. at present, would completely disappear if the tariff bill in its present form were enacted into law by the United States.

The seriousness of the economic situation of Germany, resulting from her constantly unfavorable trade balance with the United States, her most unfavorable position in the system of the world's balances of payment and particularly with respect to her balance of payment with the United States, would be further aggravated to a considerable extent, should the proposed new rates of duty go into effect against most of the products shipped today from Germany to the United States.

WASHINGTON, May 12, 1930.

611.003/2280

The Ambassador in France (Edge) to the Secretary of State

No. 676   PARIS, July 3, 1930.
                                           [Received July 14.]

SIR: The latest incident in connection with the French protests and criticisms of the new tariff bill is a rather disquieting letter I received yesterday from M. Flandin, the French Minister of Commerce, in direct charge of tariff and customs matters. I am enclosing a copy and translation of his letter, together with a copy of my reply.

As M. Flandin indicates, and as I have already advised the Department in previous despatches, he has been very helpful in preventing actual legislative reprisals on the part of the French Parliament. He clearly suggests, however, in the letter enclosed, that if raises, particularly on laces, which furnished such an acute situation here, are contemplated by the Tariff Commission, he will be helpless in his efforts to prevent unfortunate results.

I am drawing this specially to the attention of the Department as I feel it is of such importance that some consideration should be given to this matter if a possible tariff war is to be prevented. It is only necessary to go back to the French motor tariff legislation to realize that if the lace schedule, for instance, should be raised above existing law, it would probably be a signal for retaliation all along the line. I am presenting the situation as it apparently exists on this side and have the honor [etc.]

WALTER E. EDGE

[Enclosure 1]

The French Minister of Commerce (Flandin) to the American Ambassador (Edge)

PARIS, July 2, 1930.

MY DEAR AMBASSADOR: I read with surprise, in this morning's "La Journée Industrielle," the following news item dated Washington, July 1st:

"The Senate has voted Mr. Bingham's resolution ordering the Tariff Commission to make an investigation into the cost of production in the United States and abroad of laces, various fabrics, etc."

You know with what calm I set out to study the situation created for French economy by the publication of the new American customs tariff, nor are you unaware that I have encountered great difficulty in having my point of view shared in parliamentary circles: many representatives of agricultural and industrial circles demanded purely and simply that, as regards American imports, the general tariff be substituted for the minimum tariff.

If the item quoted above, destroying the happy effect of your recent efforts, should be confirmed, I fear I should not be able any longer to resist the pressure being brought to bear against me.

Knowing how much you yourself are endeavoring to reach a conciliatory solution, I wanted, my dear Ambassador, to inform you, in a strictly friendly and private way, of the unfortunate repercussion on French opinion of the decision of the Senate, and beg you to believe in my most friendly sentiments.

P. E. FLANDIN

[Enclosure 2]

The American Ambassador (Edge) to the French Minister of Commerce (Flandin)

PARIS, July 3, 1930.

MY DEAR MINISTER: I have your letter of July 2nd and hasten to reply thereto. At the outset, permit me again to emphasize the deep appreciation I feel for the generous and helpful cooperation you have given in your desire to alleviate criticism of the new tariff.

I am of the opinion that you are unnecessarily disturbed over the reported action of the United States Senate directing the Tariff Commission to investigate production costs of laces, cloths, etc. It is now very simple under the new law to obtain a cost of production investigation by the United States Tariff Commission, and it can be obtained by a request of the President, either House of Congress, or any interested party. As you, of course, understand, the Tariff Commission is charged with the responsibility of investigating production costs either for the purpose of raising or lowering duty to a maximum of 50% over or under existing rates. Therefore, it is impossible to prevent interested parties from asking the Commission to investigate tariffs that may be considered too low any more than to investigate tariffs that may be considered too high. The result of the Tariff Commission's inquiry must be based upon the actual facts, irrespective of the wishes of the applicant.

The mere fact that Senator Bingham requested the Tariff Commission to make this investigation is evidence that the rates as passed were lower than some members of the Senate desired, thus demonstrating that real consideration has been given to the French protests against higher tariffs.

I had an informal conference yesterday with Ambassador Claudel at which time I renewed my assurances given you and others that I would gladly refer to the State Department requests for review by the Tariff Commission of the new rates on any commodities in which French exporters were particularly interested and where they believed the rates unjust. Of course, I must repeat that the result of such inquiries, whether the rates should be lowered, increased, or remain as specified, is entirely a matter which must be controlled by the facts adduced.

Both France and the United States have adopted a policy of protection. The tariff is supposed to represent a fair estimate of the difference between the cost of production in competing countries. If the Tariff Commission finds the duty is greater than the difference in cost, it naturally recommends a reduction in tariff. If, on the other hand, it finds the tariff insufficient to represent the difference in cost, it just as naturally recommends an increase. I am afraid speculation as to the final recommendation of the Tariff Commission would be resultless but I repeat that, based on the well known formula and policy of protection, the reorganized Tariff Commission is given increased authority over the old law to reach decisions fair and equable to both countries.

With further assurances of my desire to cooperate in every possible consistent manner, I beg to remain,

Sincerely yours, WALTER E. EDGE

REPRESENTATIONS BY FOREIGN GOVERNMENTS REGARDING SENATE BILLS FOR THE DEPORTATION OF CERTAIN ALIEN SEAMEN [63]

150.071 Control/23

The British Embassy to the Department of State [64]

AIDE-MÉMOIRE

Senate Bill S–1941, copy of which is attached,[65] is understood to be identical with Senate Bill S–717, of the 70th Congress, and almost identical with S–3574 which failed to pass the House of Representatives in 1927. This bill appears to be open to serious objection on the part of foreign nations.

In the first place, the bill provides for interference with the composition of the crews of foreign vessels while in United States ports. It is the general international understanding that when private ships of a foreign state are in port the territorial authorities should refrain from interference with the interior economy of the vessel. The composition of the crew is a matter which affects the interior economy of a vessel, and the proposed clauses if enacted, would therefore conflict with a well-established, well-recognized and useful international practice.

Further, the bill would in effect discriminate against foreign vessels trading in American ports. It would cause great embarrassment to all ships in which Chinese labor and Lascars are employed, and in particular to British Tramp Steamers trading with American ports in the course of their world voyages. The technical difficulties of eliminating from the crews of tramp steamers the Asiatic elements against which this bill is aimed would, in practice, probably result in the masters of such vessels being compelled to cut out American ports from their sailing schedules. In this way freight rates on American exported produce would automatically rise, prices of American grain and cotton and other produce would be increased in the countries of consumption and British consumers of such produce would be obliged to curtail their purchases with resulting damage to themselves and their trade with the United States.

Even stronger objection may be taken to the proposed legislation on the ground that it constitutes a direct interference with trade, its effect being to dictate to other countries how they are to carry goods to and from the American market. At the same time, the proposed interference with the composition of the crews of foreign vessels and

[63] Continued from *Foreign Relations*, 1928, vol. I, pp. 838–844.

[64] Left at the Department by the Third Secretary of the British Embassy on March 7, 1930. A copy was transmitted by the Department to the Chairmen of the Senate Committee on Immigration and the House Committee on Immigration and Naturalization.

[65] Introduced by Senator King of Utah, September 30 (Calendar day October 24), 1929, 71st Cong., 1st sess. See *Congressional Record*, vol. 71, pt. 5, p. 4830.

in particular the difficulty of complying with section 6 of the Bill which refuses clearance to vessels departing from the United States unless carrying a crew of at least the same number as on arrival, are likely to lead to much inconvenience, and in many cases to long delays involving the alteration of sailing schedules and serious loss to business. Further, the bill would prohibit the employment of Lascars and Chinese on ships registered outside their own States, and countries such as India might well consider this as a direct and unwarrantable interference with the employment of their subjects on the high seas. Active apprehensions have in fact been caused in the Legislative Assembly in India by the legislation proposed, and they have been in communication with His Majesty's Government in Great Britain on the subject.

At the same time, protests have been received from many of the principal shipping interests in Great Britain. The opinion was expressed before the House Committee in 1927 that the bill would in practice constitute a discrimination in favor of Japanese and other Asiatic vessels at the expense of the merchant marine of Great Britain and all other maritime countries, since whereas vessels of these countries would be prevented from employing Japanese and Asiatic labour, Japanese or other Asiatic merchant vessels would be free to call at United States ports with crews of their own nationality on board. At the same time, as pointed out above, there would appear to be discrimination against Asiatic seamen serving in European or other vessels not of their own country.

Detailed objections to the bill on technical grounds were laid before the House Committee on Immigration by representatives of the shipping interests in previous years.

WASHINGTON, January 23, 1930.

150.071 Control/26

The Canadian Legation to the Department of State [66]

AIDE-MÉMOIRE

Senate Bill S. 1941 and House Bill H. R. 7763, which are identical measures "to provide for the deportation of certain alien seamen, and for other purposes", are re-introductions of legislative proposals which failed to pass the 69th and 70th Congresses. The possibility of the enactment of these Bills is causing concern to foreign countries, both because they diverge in certain important respects from accepted international practice, and because their provisions would create serious difficulties for foreign shipping.

---

[66] A copy was transmitted by the Department to the Chairmen of the Senate Committee on Immigration and the House Committee on Immigration and Naturalization.

The general ground on which objection may be based is that the proposals would result in drastic interference with the composition of crews of foreign vessels in United States ports; they would thus infringe on the accepted principle which provides against interference with the domestic economy of a foreign vessel, except in extraordinary circumstances, by the authorities of the States which it visits in the ordinary course of trade.

Furthermore, the Bills would have the effect of discriminating against foreign vessels trading to the United States, and this discrimination would be particularly severe in the case of vessels the crews of which were in part composed of Oriental seamen. These vessels, unless they were registered in the country of the nationality of their crews, probably would be debarred from entering a port of the United States by the effect of Section 7 of the Bills.

Specific objections may be made to the provision of Section 2 which authorizes a United States Immigration Inspector to determine whether any member of a vessel's crew is or is not a bona fide seaman; also to the provision of Section 3 that an alien who has been found to be not a bona fide seaman by the Immigration Service, and who is not admissible as an immigrant, must be deported as a passenger on a vessel other than that by which he arrived; and to the provision of Section 6 that every vessel, the majority of the crew of which has been engaged abroad, should not be granted clearance unless it takes out from the United States a crew at least equal in number of that with which it entered.

It may be noted also that the Bills apparently would apply to shipping on the Great Lakes as well as to shipping at ocean ports. Several of their provisions, and those of Section 6 especially, might easily cause substantial delay, trouble and expense to Canadian lines maintaining regular passenger and freight services on the Great Lakes.

Representations have been received from shipping interests in Canada complaining of the hardship which would be inflicted on them by the passage of the Bill for the reasons which are briefly summarized above, and on additional technical grounds.

WASHINGTON, April 1, 1930.

150.071 Control/22

The Netherlands Legation to the Department of State

No. 1280

The Royal Netherland Legation presents its compliments to the Department of State and has the honor to enclose herewith copy of its *Note Verbale* of January 17, 1928, No. 170,[67] with the request

---

[67] See *Foreign Relations*, 1928, vol. I, p. 842.

that the State Department will kindly consider the contents of said note applicable to the bill (S. 202) providing for the deportation of certain alien seamen, which was ordered reported favorably from the Committee on Immigration of the Senate on April 7th, 1930.[68]

The Royal Legation presents its anticipated thanks to the Department of State for what might be done in this respect.

WASHINGTON, April 8, 1930.

150.071 Control/24

The German Embassy to the Department of State

MEMORANDUM

On January 21st 1928 the Embassy had the honor to inform the Department of State [69] of the apprehension felt by the German Government with regard to the former Senate Bill 717 "to provide for the deportation of certain Alien seamen, and for other purposes".

The considerations submitted in this respect also pertain to the bills S. 202, S. 1941 and H.R. 7763 introduced in the present 71st Congress, as any such legislation would, in the opinion of the German Government, entail serious difficulties to the German American shipping trade.

WASHINGTON, April 15, 1930.

INTERNATIONAL CONFERENCE ON LOAD LINES, HELD AT LONDON, MAY 20–JULY 5, 1930

585.61B1/5

The British Ambassador (Howard) to the Secretary of State

No. 664   WASHINGTON, December 21, 1929.

SIR: When the International Conference on the Safety of Life at Sea met in London in 1913, it was expected that it would be followed and completed by an international conference on the subject of load-line, and a committee was appointed by the President of the British Board of Trade in 1913 to review the whole subject of loadline and prepare a report which would serve as a basis for international discussion and agreement. The intention was that the Safety of Life at Sea Conference should deal with the safety of the passenger ship, with the provision of wireless and with the rules of general naviga-

---

[68] Congressional Record, vol. 72, pt. 6, p. 6561.
[69] Foreign Relations, 1928, vol. I, p. 843.

tion, and that a conference on loadline should cover the question of the seaworthiness of the cargo ship.

2. Owing to the war this programme could not be carried out. The Safety of Life at Sea Convention signed in 1914[70] could not be brought into effect and no steps could be taken to arrange for the international discussion on the question of loadline.

3. The Convention on the Safety of Life at Sea of 1914 has now been revised and expanded into the Convention on Safety of Life at Sea signed in London on May 31st, 1929,[71] and there is good reason to hope that this convention will be generally adopted. In the meantime progress has been made with the subject of loadline, and His Majesty's Government in the United Kingdom of Great Britain and Northern Ireland are now in a position to submit proposals for the consideration of foreign maritime Governments.

4. An expert committee was appointed by the President of the British Board of Trade two and a half years ago to review all the work which had previously been done on the subject of loadline, to revise the regulations in force, and to consider certain special problems which had arisen with regard to certain classes of ships. The committee has now produced its report, which is being communicated to the Governments of all maritime States.

5. I have the honour to inform you that I have been instructed by His Majesty's Principal Secretary of State for Foreign Affairs, when addressing you in the above sense, to transmit to you the enclosed copies of the committee's report[72] and to enquire whether, in the opinion of the United States Government, the report would form a suitable basis for international discussion.

I have [etc.]   ESME HOWARD

585.61B1/12

The Acting Secretary of State to the British Ambassador (Howard)

WASHINGTON, February 7, 1930.

EXCELLENCY: I have the honor to refer to Your Excellency's communication of December 21, 1929, inquiring whether in the opin-

---

[70] *British and Foreign State Papers*, vol. CVIII, pt. 2, p. 283.
[71] *Treaties, Conventions, etc.*, 1923–1937, vol. IV, p. 5134; for correspondence concerning the international conference at London, April 16–May 31, 1929, see *Foreign Relations*, 1929, vol. I, pp. 368 ff.
[72] *Report of the Committee Appointed by the President of the Board of Trade To Advise on Load Lines of Merchant Ships and Special Load Lines for Steamers Carrying Timber Deck Cargoes and for Tankers* (London, His Majesty's Stationery Office, 1929); not reprinted.

ion of the United States Government a report submitted by the President to the British Board of Trade on the subject of load line would form a suitable basis for international discussion.

This Government considers that an international meeting to discuss load line legislation will be desirable and believes that the proper course will be to have the British Committee's report form the basis of an international discussion.

If an invitation to such a conference is contemplated, this Government will be pleased to be notified at the earliest possible moment, preferably by cable, in order that the authority to attend the conference, and later an appropriation to pay the expenses of a delegation thereto may be requested of the Congress.

Accept [etc.]   For the Acting Secretary of State:
WILBUR J. CARR.

585.61B1/13

The British Ambassador (Howard) to the Acting Secretary of State

No. 63   WASHINGTON, February 7, 1930.

SIR: I have the honour to inform you that His Majesty's Government in the United Kingdom of Great Britain and Northern Ireland propose to convene in London in May next a conference of representatives of the Governments of all maritime States with a view to the conclusion of an international convention on load-lines covering all the questions dealt with in the report of which copies were enclosed in my note No. 664 of December 21st last.

2. His Majesty's Principal Secretary of State for Foreign Affairs has instructed me to convey an invitation to the United States Government, on behalf of His Majesty's Government in the United Kingdom, to send representatives to this conference which will open in London on May 20th next, and to request that the reply of the United States Government may be communicated as soon as possible. In the event of the present invitation being accepted, His Majesty's Government will be glad to receive notification at an early date of the names of the United States delegates who should be supplied with such full powers as will enable them to negotiate and sign whatever instrument may be drawn up at the conference.

3. I am to state that an invitation to be represented *ad audiendum* at the conference is being addressed to the Advisory and Technical Committee for Communications and Transit of the League of Nations.

I have [etc.]   ESME HOWARD

585.61B1/48

The Acting Secretary of State to the American Delegation [73]

WASHINGTON, April 29, 1930.

SIRS: An International Conference on Load Lines will be held in London beginning May 20, 1930. You have been appointed as delegates on the part of the United States of America and certificates designating you in that capacity, have already been delivered to you.

There is enclosed the President's instrument conferring upon you, jointly and severally, plenary powers to negotiate, conclude and sign a Convention on Load Lines.[74] This instrument should be deposited with the Secretariat of the Conference, or the Committee on Credentials, whichever may be the procedure adopted.

The formal invitation to the Government of the United States to send representatives to the Conference was contained in a note dated February 7, 1930, to the Acting Secretary of State from the British Ambassador, in which it was stated that the Conference would convene at London on May 20 next. A copy of this invitation is enclosed.[75]

There is also enclosed a copy of the *Report of the United States Load Line Committee, 1928, for Merchant Vessels Engaged in Foreign Voyages by Sea (Great Lakes excepted)*.[76] This report is the result of the work during the past two years of a committee of nine technical advisers and representatives of the shipping interests of the country and contains concrete proposals which the Department of Commerce believes have the approval of all the American interests concerned. At the specific request of the Secretary of Commerce, you are instructed that this report with its enclosures is to form the basis of the American proposals at the Conference.

For your further guidance, there are quoted the following paragraphs from a memorandum submitted by the Secretary of Commerce to the Secretary of State:

"The fixing of load lines on merchant vessels in the foreign trade is essentially international in its character and uniformity in the rules governing the placing of such load lines is essential to the proper administration of the law by the several nations involved.

"It is important that United States practices, particularly those pertaining to tankers and to lumber-carrying vessels, be properly presented to the Conference as otherwise, the regulations adopted to which our vessels would be subject while in foreign ports, might seriously handicap American vessels and trade, and the initiative and

---

[73] For list of the American delegates, see note of May 8 to the British Ambassador, p. 260.
[74] Enclosure not printed.
[75] *Supra.*
[76] Not printed.

ability of our shipbuilders and ship operators would be adversely affected in such trade.

"To obtain acceptance of the American proposals will require determined effort and absolute unanimity on the part of the American delegation. It is imperative that the American delegation present a united front if the desired results are to be obtained. The individuals composing the delegation must be guided and abide by the decisions of the delegation as a whole, and individual opinions in opposition to the delegation's decisions must be restrained if the influence of the American delegation is not to suffer seriously. To assure that the American proposals are couched in well-chosen words which give exactly the intent desired, it would appear that, except in informal committee discussion, they should be prepared in advance. Important questions of policy and general principle should be determined by vote of the delegation. These should follow as far as possible the recommendations agreed to in the preparatory work.

"It should be borne in mind at all times that the delegation has a three-fold responsibility; first, to uphold the prestige and dignity of the United States; second, to obtain the highest practicable standard of safety at sea for American citizens traveling in ships flying its flag and those of other nations; and third, to obtain an agreement to facilitate trade between the United States and foreign countries, bearing in mind at all times that no load line shall be established or marked on any vessel which load line is above the actual line of safety."

It would seem to be desirable that English as well as French should be the official language of the International Conference on Load Lines, not only as a compliment to the British Government, in whose territory the Conference is to be held, but also because of the richness of the English language in commercial and nautical terminology. For the same reasons it is believed that any Convention or other instrument signed at the Conference should be signed in English as well as in French. As, however, the Conference will be held at London, it would seem to be more appropriate for the British delegates to make proposals in regard to this matter. You may confer with them informally concerning it, and should they propose to the Conference the adoption of English as an official language of the Conference, you will give the proposal your support. This will conform to the procedure recently adopted at the Conference on the Safety of Life at Sea.

You will be assisted in your work at the Conference by the following technical advisers:

Mr. G. A. Smith
Mr. David W. Dicky

You are instructed to inform the American Embassy at London of your arrival and to maintain contact with the Embassy during the progress of negotiations. A copy of your instructions is being forwarded to the Embassy, which is being requested to afford the delegation appropriate assistance. It is particularly desired that should questions of a political, rather than a technical, nature arise you will consult the Embassy and be guided by its suggestions in this connection.

I am [etc.]   J. P. COTTON

585.61B1/56

The Secretary of State to the British Ambassador (Lindsay)

WASHINGTON, May 8, 1930.

EXCELLENCY: I have the honor to refer to Sir Esme Howard's note No. 63 of February 7, 1930, and subsequent correspondence, extending on behalf of your Government an invitation to this Government to send delegates to an International Conference on Load Lines to be held at London beginning May 20, 1930.

I have the honor to inform you that this Government is pleased to accept the invitation of His Majesty's Government to send representatives to this Conference. The following have been designated as delegates on the part of the United States with plenary powers to sign such instrument or instruments as may be drawn up at the Conference:

> Mr. H. B. Walker, President of the American Steamship Owners' Association.
> Mr. David Arnott of the American Bureau of Shipping.
> Mr. Laurens Prior of the Bureau of Navigation, Department of Commerce.
> Mr. H. C. Towle of the Bethlehem Shipbuilding Corporation.
> Mr. S. D. McComb of the Marine Office of America.
> Captain A. F. Pillsbury of Pillsbury and Curtis.
> Mr. Robert F. Hand of the Standard Oil Company.
> Mr. James Kennedy, General Manager, Marine Department, Gulf Refining Company.
> Mr. H. W. Warley of the Ore Steamship Company.
> Rear Admiral J. G. Tawresey, United States Navy, Retired, United States Shipping Board.

The technical advisers to the American delegation are:

> Mr. David W. Dicky
> Mr. G. A. Smith.

Accept [etc.]   For the Secretary of State:
                                                              J. P. COTTON

585.61B1/57

The Secretary of State to the Ambassador in Great Britain (Dawes)

No. 357 WASHINGTON, May 8, 1930.

SIR: On February 7, 1930, this Government received through the British Embassy at Washington an invitation to send delegates to an International Conference on Load Lines, to be held at London beginning May 20, 1930.

The invitation has been accepted and the Congress has authorized the appropriation of the sum of $20,000 for the expenses of participation. Instructions dealing with the fiscal matters of the delegation will be furnished you at a later date.

A list of the American delegates and technical advisers is enclosed,[77] together with a copy of their instructions.[78]

As the members of the delegation have been given plenary powers to sign such instrument or instruments as may be drawn up at the Conference, and as the Department of State is not represented on the delegation, you are instructed to follow the proceedings of the Conference with care. It is suggested that an officer be detailed to cooperate with the delegation and that the Embassy keep itself informed with regard to any political questions which may arise during the progress of the negotiations. Should any such question appear likely to cause serious difficulty you may inform the Department and request specific instructions.

I am [etc.] For the Secretary of State:
J. P. COTTON

Treaty Series No. 858

International Load Line Convention and Final Protocol, Signed at London, July 5, 1930 [79]

INTERNATIONAL LOAD LINE CONVENTION

PREAMBLE

The Governments of Germany, the Commonwealth of Australia, Belgium, Canada, Chile, Cuba, Denmark, the Free City of Danzig, Spain, the Irish Free State, the United States of America, Finland, France, the United Kingdom of Great Britain and Northern Ireland, Greece, India, Iceland, Italy, Japan, Latvia, Mexico, Norway, New Zealand, Paraguay, the Netherlands, Peru, Poland, Portugal,

---

[77] Enclosure not printed.
[78] *Ante*, p. 258.
[79] Ratification advised by the Senate, February 27 (legislative day February 17), 1931; ratified by the President, May 1, 1931; ratification of the United States deposited at London, June 10, 1931; proclaimed by the President, January 5, 1933.

Sweden, and the Union of Socialist Soviet Republics; desiring to promote safety of life and property at sea by establishing in common agreement uniform principles and rules with regard to the limits to which ships on international voyages may be loaded, have resolved to conclude a Convention for that purpose and have appointed as their Plenipotentiaries:—

[Here follows list of names of plenipotentiaries.]

Who, having communicated their full powers, found in good and due form, have agreed as follows:—

CHAPTER I.—*Preliminary*

ARTICLE 1

GENERAL OBLIGATION OF CONVENTION

So that the load lines prescribed by this Convention shall be observed, the Contracting Governments undertake to give effect to the provisions of this Convention, to promulgate all regulations, and to take all other steps which may be necessary to give this Convention full and complete effect.

The provisions of this Convention are completed by Annexes,[80] which have the same force and take effect at the same time as this Convention. Every reference to this Convention implies at the same time a reference to the Rules annexed thereto.

ARTICLE 2

SCOPE OF CONVENTION

1. This Convention applies to all ships engaged on international voyages, which belong to countries the Governments of which are Contracting Governments, or to territories to which this Convention is applied under Article 21, except—

    (a) ships of war; ships solely engaged in fishing; pleasure yachts and ships not carrying cargo or passengers;

    (b) ships of less than 150 tons gross.

2. Ships when engaged on international voyages between the near neighbouring ports of two or more countries may be exempted by the Administration to which such ships belong from the provisions of this Convention, so long as they shall remain in such trades, if the Governments of the countries in which such ports are situated shall be satisfied that the sheltered nature and conditions of such voyages between such ports make it unreasonable or impracticable to

---

[80] The annexes, which are printed in Department of State Treaty Series No. 858 and 47 Stat. 2228, are not reprinted here.

apply the provisions of this Convention to ships engaged in such trades.

3. All agreements and arrangements relating to load line or matters appertaining thereto at present in force between Contracting Governments shall continue to have full and complete effect during the terms thereof as regards—

(a) ships to which this Convention does not apply;
(b) ships to which this Convention applies in respect of matters for which it has not expressly provided.

To the extent, however, that such agreements or arrangements conflict with the provisions of this Convention, the provisions of this Convention shall prevail.

Subject to any such agreement or arrangement—

(a) all ships to which this Convention does not apply; and
(b) all matters which are not expressly provided for in this Convention;

shall remain subject to the legislation of each Contracting Government to the same extent as if this Convention had not been made.

ARTICLE 3

DEFINITIONS

In this Convention, unless expressly provided otherwise—

(a) a ship is regarded as belonging to a country if it is registered by the Government of that country;
(b) the expression "Administration" means the Government of the country to which the ship belongs;
(c) an "international voyage" is a voyage from a country to which this Convention applies to a port outside such country, or conversely, and for this purpose, every colony, overseas territory, protectorate or territory under suzerainty or mandate is regarded as a separate country;
(d) the expression "Rules" means the Rules contained in Annexes I, II and III;
(e) a "new ship" is a ship, the keel of which is laid on or after the 1st July, 1932, all other ships being regarded as existing ships.
(f) the expression "steamer" includes any vessel propelled by machinery.

ARTICLE 4

CASES OF "FORCE MAJEURE"

No ship, which is not subject to the provisions of this Convention at the time of its departure on any voyage, shall become subject to the provisions of this Convention on account of any deviation from its intended voyage due to stress of weather or any other cause of *force majeure.*

In applying the provisions of this Convention, the Administration shall give due consideration to any deviation or delay caused to any ship owing to stress of weather or to any other cause of *force majeure.*

CHAPTER II.—*Load Line: Survey and Marking*

ARTICLE 5

GENERAL PROVISIONS

No ship to which this Convention applies shall proceed to sea on an international voyage after the date on which this Convention comes into force, unless the ship, being—

A—a new ship,

(*a*) has been surveyed in accordance with the provisions of Annex I;
(*b*) complies with the provisions of Part II of Annex I; and
(*c*) has been marked in accordance with the provisions of this Convention.

B—an existing ship,

(*a*) has been surveyed and marked (whether before or after this Convention comes into force) in accordance with the conditions prescribed either in paragraph A of this Article or in one of the sets of Rules for the Assignment of Load Line particularised in Annex IV; and
(*b*) complies with the provisions of Part II of Annex I in principle, and also in detail, so far as is reasonable and practicable, having regard to the efficiency of (i) the protection of openings; (ii) guard rails; (iii) freeing ports, and (iv) means of access to crews' quarters provided by the existing arrangements, fittings and appliances on the ship.

ARTICLE 6

PROVISIONS FOR STEAMERS CARRYING TIMBER DECK CARGOES

1. A steamer which has been surveyed and marked under Article 5 shall be entitled to be surveyed and marked with a timber load line under Part V of Annex I if, being—

A—a new ship, it complies with the conditions and provisions prescribed in Part V of Annex I;
B—an existing ship, it complies with the conditions and provisions of Part V of Annex I other than Rule LXXX, and also in

principle, so far as is reasonable and practicable, with the conditions and provisions prescribed by Rule LXXX provided that in assigning a timber load line to an existing ship the Administration shall make such addition to the freeboard as shall be reasonable, having regard to the extent to which such ship falls short of full compliance with the conditions and provisions prescribed in Rule LXXX.

2. A steamer when using the timber load line shall comply with Rules LXXXIV, LXXXV, LXXXVI, LXXXVIII and LXXXIX.

ARTICLE 7

PROVISIONS FOR TANKERS

A steamer which has been surveyed under Article 5 shall be entitled to be surveyed and marked as a tanker under Part VI of Annex I if, being—

A—a new ship, it complies with the conditions and provisions prescribed in Part VI of Annex I;

B—an existing ship, it complies with the conditions and provisions in Rules XCIII, XCVI, XCVII, XCVIII and XCIX, and also in principle so far as is reasonable and practicable with Rules XCIV, XCV and C, provided that in assigning a tanker load line to an existing ship the Administration shall make such addition to the freeboard as shall be reasonable having regard to the extent to which such ship falls short of full compliance with the conditions and provisions prescribed in Rules XCIV, XCV and C.

ARTICLE 8

PROVISIONS FOR SHIPS OF SPECIAL TYPES

For steamers over 300 feet in length, possessing constructional features similar to those of a tanker which afford extra invulnerability against the sea, a reduction in freeboard may be granted.

The amount of such reduction shall be determined by the Administration in relation to the freeboard assigned to tankers, having regard to the degree of compliance with the conditions of assignment laid down for these ships, and the degree of subdivision provided.

The freeboard assigned to such a ship shall in no case be less than would be assigned to the ship as a tanker.

ARTICLE 9

SURVEY

The survey and marking of ships for the purpose of this Convention shall be carried out by officers of the country to which the ships belong, provided that the Government of each country may entrust the survey and marking of its ships either to Surveyors nominated for this purpose, or to organisations recognised by it. In every case the Government concerned fully guarantees the completeness and efficiency of the survey and marking.

ARTICLE 10

ZONES AND SEASONAL AREAS

A ship to which this Convention applies shall conform to the conditions applicable to the zones and seasonal areas described in Annex II to this Convention.

A port standing on the boundary line between two zones shall be regarded as within the zone from or into which the ship arrives or departs.

CHAPTER III.—*Certificates*

ARTICLE 11

ISSUE OF CERTIFICATES

A certificate, called "International Load Line Certificate," shall be issued to every ship which has been surveyed and marked in accordance with this Convention, but not otherwise.

An International Load Line Certificate shall be issued either by the Government of the country to which the ship belongs or by any person or organisation duly authorised by that Government, and in every case the Government assumes full responsibility for the certificate.

ARTICLE 12

ISSUE OF CERTIFICATES BY ANOTHER GOVERNMENT

The Government of a country to which this Convention applies may, at the request of the Government of any other country to which this Convention applies, cause any ship which belongs to the last-mentioned country, or (in the case of an unregistered ship) which is to be registered by the Government of that country, to be surveyed and marked, and, if satisfied that the requirements of this Convention are complied with, issue an International Load Line Certificate to such ship, under its own responsibility. Any certificate so issued must contain a statement to the effect that it has been issued at the request of the Government of the country to which the ship belongs, or of the Government by whom the ship is to be registered, as the case may be, and it shall have the same force and receive the same recognition as a certificate issued under Article 11 of this Convention.

ARTICLE 13

FORM OF CERTIFICATE

The International Load Line Certificates shall be drawn up in the official language or languages of the country by which they are issued.

The form of the certificate shall be that of the model given in Annex III, subject to such modifications as may, in accordance with Rule LXXVIII, be made in the case of ships carrying timber deck cargoes.

ARTICLE 14

DURATION OF CERTIFICATES

1. An International Load Line Certificate shall, unless it is renewed in accordance with the provisions of paragraph 2 of this Article, expire at the end of such period as may be specified therein by the Administration which issues it: but the period so specified shall not exceed five years from the date of issue.

2. An International Load Line Certificate may be renewed from time to time by the Administration which issued it for such period (not exceeding five years on any occasion) as the Administration thinks fit, after a survey not less effective than the survey required by this Convention before the issue of the certificate, and any such renewal shall be endorsed on the certificate.

3. An Administration shall cancel any International Load Line Certificate issued to a ship belonging to its country:

A. If material alterations have taken place in the hull and superstructures of the ship which affect the calculations of freeboard.

B. If the fittings and appliances for the (i) protection of openings, (ii) guard rails, (iii) freeing ports and (iv) means of access to crews' quarters are not maintained in as effective a condition as they were in when the certificate was issued.

C. If the ship is not inspected periodically at such times and under such conditions as the Administration may think necessary for the purpose of securing that the hull and superstructures referred to in Condition A are not altered and that the fittings and appliances referred to in Condition B are maintained as therein provided throughout the duration of the certificate.

ARTICLE 15

ACCEPTANCE OF CERTIFICATES

International Load Line Certificates issued under the authority of a Contracting Government shall be accepted by the other Contracting

Governments as having the same force as the certificates issued by them to ships belonging to their respective countries.

ARTICLE 16

CONTROL

1. A ship to which this Convention applies, when in a port of a country to which it does not belong, is in any case subject to control with respect to load line as follows: An officer duly authorised by the Government of that country may take such steps as may be necessary for the purpose of seeing that there is on board a valid International Load Line Certificate. If there is such a certificate on board the ship, such control shall be limited to the purpose of securing—

(a) that the ship is not loaded beyond the limits allowed by the certificate;
(b) that the position of the load line on the ship corresponds with the certificate; and
(c) that the ship has not been so materially altered in respect to the matters dealt with in conditions A and B (set out in paragraph 3 of Article 14) that the ship is manifestly unfit to proceed to sea without danger to human life.

2. Only officers possessing the necessary technical qualifications shall be authorised to exercise control as aforesaid, and if such control is exercised under (c) above, it shall only be exercised in so far as may be necessary to secure that the ship shall be made fit to proceed to sea without danger to human life.

3. If control under this Article appears likely to result in legal proceedings being taken against the ship, or in the ship being detained, the Consul of the country to which the ship belongs shall be informed as soon as possible of the circumstances of the case.

ARTICLE 17

PRIVILEGES

The privileges of this Convention may not be claimed in favour of any ship unless it holds a valid International Load Line Certificate.

CHAPTER IV.—*General Provisions*

ARTICLE 18

EQUIVALENTS

Where in this Convention it is provided that a particular fitting, or appliance, or type thereof, shall be fitted or carried in a ship, or that any particular arrangement shall be adopted, any Administration may accept in substitution therefor any other fitting, or appliance, or type thereof, or any other arrangement, provided that such Administration shall have been satisfied that the fitting, or appliance, or type thereof, or the arrangement substituted is in the circumstances at least as effective as that specified in this Convention.

Any Administration which so accepts a new fitting, or appliance, or type thereof, or new arrangement shall communicate the fact to the other Administrations, and, upon request, the particulars thereof.

ARTICLE 19

LAWS, REGULATIONS, REPORTS

The Contracting Governments undertake to communicate to each other—

(1) the text of laws, decrees, regulations and decisions of general application which shall have been promulgated on the various matters within the scope of this Convention;

(2) all available official reports or official summaries of reports in so far as they show the results of the provisions of this Convention, provided always that such reports or summaries are not of a confidential nature.

The Government of the United Kingdom of Great Britain and Northern Ireland is invited to serve as an intermediary for collecting all this information and for bringing it to the knowledge of the other Contracting Governments.

ARTICLE 20

MODIFICATIONS, FUTURE CONFERENCES

1. Modifications of this Convention which may be deemed useful or necessary improvements may at any time be proposed by any Contracting Government to the Government of the United Kingdom of Great Britain and Northern Ireland, and such proposals shall be communicated by the latter to all the other Contracting Governments, and if any such modifications are accepted by all the Contracting Governments (including Governments which have deposited ratifications or accessions which have not yet become effective) this Convention shall be modified accordingly.

2. Conferences for the purpose of revising this Convention shall be held at such times and places as may be agreed upon by the Contracting Governments.

A Conference for this purpose shall be convoked by the Government of the United Kingdom of Great Britain and Northern Ireland whenever, after this Convention has been in force for five years, one-third of the Contracting Governments express a desire to that effect.

CHAPTER V.—*Final Provisions*

ARTICLE 21

APPLICATION TO COLONIES

1. A Contracting Government may, at the time of signature, ratification, accession or thereafter, by a notification in writing addressed to the Government of the United Kingdom of Great Britain and Northern Ireland, declare its desire that this Convention shall apply to all or any of its Colonies, overseas territories, protectorates or territories under suzerainty or mandate, and this Convention shall apply to all the territories named in such notification, two months after the date of the receipt thereof, but, failing such notification, this Convention will not apply to any such territories.

2. A Contracting Government may at any time by a notification in writing addressed to the Government of the United Kingdom of Great Britain and Northern Ireland express its desire that this Convention shall cease to apply to all or any of its colonies, overseas territories, protectorates or territories under suzerainty or mandate to which this Convention shall have, under the provisions of the preceding paragraph, been applicable for a period of not less than five years, and in such case the Convention shall cease to apply twelve months after the date of the receipt of such notification by the Government of the United Kingdom of Great Britain and Northern Ireland to all territories mentioned therein.

3. The Government of the United Kingdom of Great Britain and Northern Ireland shall inform all the other Contracting Governments of the application of this Convention to any Colony, overseas territory, protectorate or territory under suzerainty or mandate under the provisions of paragraph 1 of this Article, and of the cessation of any such application under the provisions of paragraph 2, stating in each case the date from which this Convention has become or will cease to be applicable.

ARTICLE 22

AUTHENTIC TEXTS.—RATIFICATION

This Convention, of which both the English and French texts shall be authentic, shall be ratified.

The instruments of ratification shall be deposited in the archives of the Government of the United Kingdom of Great Britain and

Northern Ireland, which will notify all the other signatory or acceding Governments of all ratifications deposited and the date of their deposit.

ARTICLE 23

ACCESSION

A Government (other than the Government of a territory to which Article 21 applies) on behalf of which this Convention has not been signed, shall be allowed to accede thereto at any time after the Convention has come into force. Accessions shall be effected by means of notifications in writing addressed to the Government of the United Kingdom of Great Britain and Northern Ireland, and shall take effect three months after their receipt.

The Government of the United Kingdom of Great Britain and Northern Ireland shall inform all signatory and acceding Governments of all accessions received and of the date of their receipt.

ARTICLE 24

DATE OF COMING IN FORCE

This Convention shall come into force on the 1st July, 1932, as between the Governments which have deposited their ratifications by that date, and provided that at least five ratifications have been deposited with the Government of the United Kingdom of Great Britain and Northern Ireland. Should five ratifications not have been deposited by that date, this Convention shall come into force three months after the date on which the fifth ratification is deposited. Ratifications deposited after the date on which this Convention has come into force shall take effect three months after the date of their deposit.

ARTICLE 25

DENUNCIATION

This Convention may be denounced on behalf of any Contracting Government at any time after the expiration of five years from the date on which the Convention comes into force in so far as that Government is concerned. Denunciation shall be effected by a notification in writing addressed to the Government of the United Kingdom of Great Britain and Northern Ireland, which will notify all the other contracting Governments of all denunciations received and of the date of their receipt.

A denunciation shall take effect twelve months after the date on which notification thereof is received by the Government of the United Kingdom of Great Britain and Northern Ireland.

In faith whereof, the Plenipotentiaries have signed hereafter.

Done at London this fifth day of July, 1930, in a single copy, which shall remain deposited in the archives of the Government of the United Kingdom of Great Britain and Northern Ireland, which shall transmit certified true copies thereof to all signatory Governments.

[Here follow the signatures of plenipotentiaries on behalf of the Governments of Germany, the Commonwealth of Australia, Belgium, Canada, Chile, Cuba, Denmark, the Free City of Danzig, Spain, the Irish Free State, the United States of America, Finland, France, the United Kingdom of Great Britain and Northern Ireland, Greece, India, Iceland, Italy, Japan, Latvia, Mexico, Norway, New Zealand, Paraguay, the Netherlands, Peru, Poland, Portugal, Sweden, and the Union of Soviet Socialist Republics.]

FINAL PROTOCOL

At the moment of signing the International Load Line Convention concluded this day, the under-mentioned Plenipotentiaries have agreed on the following:—

I

Ships engaged solely on voyages on the Great Lakes of North America and ships engaged in other inland waters are to be regarded as outside the scope of the Convention.

II

This Convention is not applied to the existing ships of the United States of America and of France of the lumber schooner type propelled by power, with or without sails, or by sails alone.

III

The Government of the United Kingdom of Great Britain and Northern Ireland shall convoke a Conference of the Contracting Governments of the countries to which tankers belong, upon request of the United States of America, at any time within the five-year period mentioned in Article 20, for the purpose of discussing matters relating to tanker freeboard.

The Contracting Governments will not raise any objection to the provisions contained in this Convention in regard to tanker load line being altered as may be determined at such Conference, provided that the conclusions then reached are communicated forthwith to the Governments signatory to the present Convention and that no objection is received by the Government of the United Kingdom of Great Britain and Northern Ireland within six months of the despatch of such communication.

In Witness whereof the Plenipotentiaries have drawn up this Final Protocol which shall have the same force and the same validity as if the provisions thereof had been inserted in the text of the Convention to which it belongs.

Done at London this fifth day of July, 1930, in a single copy which shall be deposited in the archives of the Government of the United Kingdom of Great Britain and Northern Ireland, which shall transmit certified true copies thereof to all signatory Governments.

[Here follow the signatures on behalf of the Governments signatory to the convention.]

Treaty Series No. 858

Final Act of the Load Line Conference, Signed at London, July 5, 1930

The Governments of Germany, the Commonwealth of Australia, Belgium, Canada, Chile, Cuba, Denmark, the Free City of Danzig, Spain, the Irish Free State, the United States of America, Finland, France, the United Kingdom of Great Britain and Northern Ireland, Greece, India, Iceland, Italy, Japan, Latvia, Mexico, Norway, New Zealand, Paraguay, the Netherlands, Peru, Poland, Portugal, Sweden and the Union of Soviet Socialist Republics;

Desiring to promote safety of life and property at sea by establishing in common agreement uniform principles and rules with regard to the limits to which ships on international voyages may be loaded;

Having decided to participate in an international conference which, upon the invitation of the Government of the United Kingdom of Great Britain and Northern Ireland, was held in London;

Appointed the following delegations:—

[Here follows list of names of delegates.]

Who accordingly assembled in London.

Admiral of the Fleet Sir Henry F. Oliver was appointed President of the Conference, and Mr. A. E. Lee, Secretary-General.

For the purposes of its work the Conference set up the following Committees, of which the under-mentioned were Presidents:—

Administration Committee: Mr. Koenigs.
Main Technical Committee: Sir Charles Sanders.
Tankers Committee: Mr. Kennedy.
Timber Ships Committee: Mr. Emil Krogh.
Special Types of Ship Committee: Vice-Admiral Fock.
Zones Committee: General Ingianni.
Drafting Committee: Mr. Haarbleicher.
Credentials Committee: Mr. Nakayama.

In the course of a series of meetings between the 20th May, 1930, and the 5th July, 1930, a Load Line Convention, dated the 5th July 1930, was drawn up.

I

The Conference takes note of the following declarations, made by the undermentioned delegation:—

The Plenipotentiaries of the United States of America formally declare that the signing of the International Load Line Convention by them, on the part of the United States of America, on this date, is not to be construed to mean that the Government of the United States of America recognizes a régime or entity which signs or accedes to the Convention as the Government of a country when that régime or entity is not recognized by the Government of the United States of America as the Government of that country.

The Plenipotentiaries of the United States of America further declare that the participation of the United States of America in the International Load Line Convention signed on this date does not involve any contractual obligation on the part of the United States of America to a country, represented by a régime or entity which the Government of the United States of America does not recognize as the Government of that country, until such country has a Government recognized by the Government of the United States of America.

II

The Conference also adopts the following recommendations:—

SHIPS OF LESS THAN 150 TONS GROSS ENGAGED ON INTERNATIONAL VOYAGES

The Conference recommends that such regulations as may be made by any of the Contracting Governments relating to ships of less than 150 tons gross engaged on international voyages should, so far as practicable and reasonable, be framed in accordance with the principles and rules laid down in this Convention, and should whenever possible be made after consultation and agreement with the Governments of the other countries concerned in such international voyages.

STRENGTH

As under the Rules attached to this Convention, ships which comply with the highest standard laid down in the rules of a classification society recognised by the Administration are regarded as having sufficient strength for the minimum freeboards allowed under the rules, the Conference recommends that each Administration should request the Society or Societies which it has recognised to confer from time to time with the Societies recognised by other

Administrations, with a view to securing as much uniformity as possible in the application of the standards of strength on which freeboard is based.

ANNUAL SURVEYS

The Conference recommends that, if possible, each Administration should make arrangements for the periodical inspections referred to in paragraph (3) (c) of Article 14 to be held at intervals of approximately twelve months so far as concerns the maintenance of the fittings and appliances referred to in Condition B of paragraph 3 of that Article (*i.e.*, the fittings and appliances for the (i) protection of openings, (ii) guard rails, (iii) freeing ports and (iv) means of access to crews' quarters).

INFORMATION REGARDING DAMAGE TO TANKERS

The Conference recommends that the Governments of the countries to which tankers belong shall keep records of all structural and deck damage to these ships caused by stress of weather, so that information with regard to these matters may be available.

In faith whereof the undersigned have affixed their signatures to the present Act.

Done in London this fifth day of July, 1930, in a single copy which shall be deposited in the archives of the Government of the United Kingdom of Great Britain and Northern Ireland, which shall transmit certified true copies thereof to all signatory Governments.

[Here follow the signatures on behalf of the Governments signatory to the Final Act.]

DISINCLINATION OF THE UNITED STATES TO ACT TO SECURE RATIFICATION OF DRAFT CONVENTION ON OIL POLLUTION OF NAVIGABLE WATERS [81]

501.45A2/427

The British Embassy to the Department of State

MEMORANDUM

The British Embassy have for some time past corresponded semi-officially with the Department of State in regard to the draft Convention on Oil Pollution prepared as a result of the conference held at Washington in the summer of 1926.

A member of the Embassy staff who discussed the present position respecting this Convention with an official of the Department in May last, understood that the German and Japanese Governments

---

[81] For final act of the Preliminary Conference on Oil Pollution of Navigable Waters held at Washington, June 8–16, 1926, and annexed draft of convention, see *Foreign Relations*, 1926, vol. I, pp. 238 and 245, respectively.

still maintained certain objections to the draft and that the Italian Government were not altogether satisfied with it. Moreover, there appeared to be no strong demand in the United States for bringing the Convention into force, and in these circumstances the Department of State were disposed to let the matter rest unless His Majesty's Government or one of the other interested Powers moved the United States Government to take some further action.

The Embassy have now learned that His Majesty's Government in the United Kingdom attach importance to the conclusion of the proposed Convention since this alone would enable the problem of oil pollution to be dealt with by international agreement. It will be remembered that at the Washington Conference in 1926 two measures were proposed, viz, the carrying of oil separators on all ships, or the fixing of zones round the coasts within which the discharge of oil or oily water should be prohibited. Neither of these measures would necessarily be a complete cure because it would, from the nature of the case, be impossible to be certain that the separators on board the ships would be used as they should be used on all occasions, and it would equally be impossible to secure evidence of the improper discharge of oil within prohibited zones. They were, however, the only measures which Governments, as such, could take to deal with this nuisance, and it was clear that international agreement could not be obtained for the first of these remedies, the carrying of separators.

The second remedy, the establishment of zones, is the one embodied in the draft Convention, and His Majesty's Government consider it very desirable that every effort should be made to secure the adoption of that Convention. It is true that the shipowners in the United Kingdom, and it is believed, also in the United States and in Holland, have voluntarily adopted the principle of the Convention, and it cannot be said that the adoption of the Convention by the remaining Powers would necessarily put an end to the nuisance in any of the countries where it still exists; but it is the only international method of dealing with this nuisance which at present has any chance of success at all, and if the negotiations for the Convention are dropped or fail, there will be renewed pressure for the adoption of national measures by individual Governments. This, His Majesty's Government consider, would be undesirable in the interests of all concerned.

The Embassy have therefore been instructed to enquire whether the United States Government, if officially approached, would be disposed to exert their good offices on behalf of the draft Convention with the other Governments interested.

WASHINGTON, August 22, 1929.

501.45A2/435

The British Ambassador (Lindsay) to the Secretary of State

WASHINGTON, May 23, 1930.

MY DEAR MR. SECRETARY: On August 22nd last my predecessor left at the Department of State an *aide-memoire* on the subject of the draft convention on oil pollution stating that the Embassy had received instructions to enquire whether the United States Government, if officially approached, would be disposed to exert their good offices on behalf of the draft convention with the other governments interested. A copy of this *aide-memoire* is enclosed for convenience of reference.[82]

As we do not appear to have any record of a reply to this enquiry and as my government have again intimated that tney would be glad of one at an early date, I should be grateful for an answer in the near future.

Believe me [etc.]   R. C. LINDSAY

501.45A2/437

Memorandum by the Chief of the Division of Far Eastern Affairs (Hornbeck)

[WASHINGTON,] June 7, 1930.

In regard to this matter of a proposed agreement on the subject of oil pollution in navigable waters,—

The outstanding question is whether or not to go forward with the effort to conclude an international agreement based on the Draft of a Convention drawn up under the terms of the Final Act signed in Washington June 16, 1926. The British and the Danish Governments have been prodding us about it.[83] Mr. Culbertson and I have explored the subject and we are of the opinion that it would be best for the present to let the matter continue to lie on the table.

I should like to call in an officer from the British Embassy and one from the Danish Legation and explain orally to each of them that the American Government is not disposed at present to make any move in regard to the matter.

May I request authorization or disapproval?[84]

S. K. H[ORNBECK]

---

[82] *Supra.*
[83] Communications from the Danish Government not printed.
[84] At this point the memorandum is noted by the Under Secretary of State: "O. K.   J. P. C[OTTON]."

518625—45——23

501.45A2/438

Memorandum by the Chief of the Division of Far Eastern Affairs
(Hornbeck)

[WASHINGTON,] June 12, 1930.

Mr. Torr [85] called by appointment.

Mr. Hornbeck said that he wished informally to explore the ground with regard to the British Government's attitude in reference to questions raised in the British Embassy's *aide-mémoire* of August 22, 1929, referred to in the Ambassador's letter to the Secretary of May 23, 1930. The communications in question conveyed inquiry whether the American Government, if officially approached, would be disposed to exert its "good offices on behalf of the draft Convention with the other Governments interested". He would like to know how great importance the British Government attached to this matter at this time.

Mr. Torr said that he must base his opinion on the views expressed in the *aide-mémoire* of August 22, 1929. There the British Government stated that it considered it very desirable that every effort be made to secure the adoption of the Convention "since that alone would enable the problem of oil pollution to be dealt with by international agreement". Mr. Torr said that he did not know what was the situation in British territorial and adjacent waters, whether it had improved or whether it was worse than in 1926 and before, but that he knew that the Board of Trade frequently brought up the question of the desirability of having an international agreement.

Mr. Hornbeck said that the situation in American coastal waters, in relation to oil pollution, appears to have improved materially in recent years and that there is not the amount of complaint that there formerly was and not the amount of agitation in reference to legislation and/or international agreement. He explained that certain parties particularly interested in both questions have apparently concentrated on the question of domestic legislation and have advanced the view that it would be well for the United States first to get the matter regulated in reference to its own waters by domestic legislation and then, thereby being in better position to enter or take the lead in international action, to revert to discussion of an international agreement. Therefore, it was the thought of the Department that it might be best to let the matter of the draft agreement continue to lie on the table.

Mr. Torr inquired whether we knew anything about the views of Canada. Mr. Hornbeck replied that we did not. After some discus-

---

[85] C. J. W. Torr, Second Secretary of the British Embassy.

sion, Mr. Torr said that he thought he might endeavor informally to see whether the views of Canada could be ascertained.

Mr. Torr said again that he thought his Government attached quite a little importance to the matter and asked what countries were standing out or indifferent. Mention was made of Japan, Italy and Germany. Mr. Torr advanced, tentatively, the view that the subject might be one which might be taken up by the League of Nations as a question susceptible of practical solution by and among the countries of Europe, inasmuch as the United States and Japan are remote from European waters. But, he said, that did not dispose of the question of acts in the neighborhood of European waters by vessels of countries not party to such agreement as might be concluded. There followed some discussion of the possibility that the United States and Japan would find it convenient to become parties to an agreement first concluded by and among European states.

Mr. Hornbeck said that we had also had inquiries from the Danish Legation, and that we would like to get such information as could be had with regard to the view of the Danish Government. Mr. Torr suggested that inquiry might be made with regard to the view of the Japanese Government. Mr. Hornbeck said that he would endeavor to discuss the matter informally with an officer of the Danish Legation and an officer of the Japanese Embassy.

The conversation then turned to the question of extraterritoriality (see separate memorandum of even date).[86]

COOPERATION OF THE UNITED STATES WITH SEVERAL OTHER GOVERNMENTS IN RECONNAISSANCE SURVEYS FOR AN INTER-AMERICAN HIGHWAY

810.154/228

The Secretary of State to the Minister in Panama (Davis)

No. 31   WASHINGTON, July 1, 1930.

SIR: There is being forwarded herewith the original of an instruction addressed, in care of your Legation, to Messrs. Thomas A. Forbes, D. Tucker Brown, and Marcel Bussard, Highway Engineers, who have been appointed members of a technical committee to make effective, in accordance with instructions to be issued from time to time by the Secretary of State, this Government's cooperation with several other Governments, members of the Pan American Union, in reconnaissance surveys pertinent to the building of an inter-American highway or highways. Accompanied by Mr. E. W. James of the

---

[86] Not printed.

Bureau of Public Roads of the Department of Agriculture, they departed from New York on June 21 by the steamship *Virginia* expecting to reach Cristobal on June 27 and to call at your Legation soon after their arrival. Please deliver their instruction to them as soon as you conveniently can. A copy of it is attached hereto for your information and the files of your Legation.

There is also enclosed a copy of a proposed budget of the expenditures which it is supposed will be necessary in connection with their work during the remainder of the present year.[87] You are authorized to make payments during this time, and at the same rate for eighteen months thereafter, upon vouchers approved by the chairman of the committee, consistent with such budget, and to draw on the Secretary of State for the required amounts, citing on the drafts the appropriation chargeable and rendering a separate account therefor.

You are requested to render to these gentlemen such other assistance in the performance of their duties as may be possible and proper.

In this connection your attention is especially called to the fifth, sixth and seventh paragraphs of their instruction, from which you will note that the Government to which you are accredited is not one of those which have hitherto requested this Government's cooperation in the reconnaissance surveys and that they are, therefore, asked to refrain from offering their services to that Government until they shall be informed that this Government's cooperation has been requested. You are instructed to bring this matter as soon as possible to the attention of the appropriate officials of the Government to which you are accredited, assuring them that your Government is, however, both willing and ready to make available its cooperation with their Government in these surveys as soon as information shall reach the Secretary of State through the Director General of the Pan American Union that such cooperation is desired. You, also, will be promptly informed thereafter and will be authorized to present the Engineers to the appropriate authorities of the Panamanian Government so that they may properly offer their services to it. If that Government's failure to request this Government's cooperation should have been due merely to inadvertence and should it be the desire of that Government that the cooperation should begin in the near future, the necessary preliminary correspondence can of course be attended to in a very few days by cable or by air mail.

I am [etc.]   For the Secretary of State:
                                                    WILBUR J. CARR

---

[87] Not printed.

[Enclosure]

The Secretary of State to the Members of the Technical Committee on the Inter-American Highway Reconnaissance Surveys [88]

[WASHINGTON, July 1, 1930.]

SIRS: In a letter dated June 19, 1930,[89] the Secretary of Agriculture was requested to inform you that the President had approved your designation as members of a technical committee to make effective, in accordance with instructions which will from time to time be issued by the Secretary of State, this Government's cooperation with several other Governments, members of the Pan American Union, in reconnaissance surveys pertinent to the building of an inter-American highway or highways. In the same communication authorization was given for making the necessary expenditures in connection with the work upon which you will be engaged. Since you are proceeding first to Panamá and since the time intervening between your appointment and your departure was insufficient for its preparation, this instruction is being addressed to you in care of the Legation of the United States at Panamá.

The following is the text of the pertinent portion of the Act of the Congress of the United States (Deficiency Act for the fiscal year ending June 30, 1930, approved by the President March 29, 1930) which has enabled the Secretary of State to make available through you, this Government's cooperation with other interested Governments in these reconnaissance surveys:

"To enable the Secretary of State to cooperate with the several Governments, members of the Pan American Union, when he shall find that any or all of such States having [*have?*] [90] initiated a request or signified a desire to the Pan American Union to cooperate, in the reconnaissance surveys to develop the facts and to report to Congress as to the feasibility of possible routes, the probable cost, the economic service and such other information as will be pertinent to the building of an inter-American highway or highways, to be expended upon the order of the Secretary of State, including the additional cost incident to the assignment by the President of personnel in the Government service, as now authorized, additional compensation of such personnel for foreign service, compensation of employees and rent in the District of Columbia and elsewhere, contingent expenses, official cards, printing and binding, purchase of necessary books and documents, transportation and subsistence or per diem in lieu of subsistence (notwithstanding the provisions of any other Act), stenographic and other services by contract if deemed necessary, without regard to section 3709 of the Revised Statutes (U. S. C., title 41,

---

[88] Thomas A. Forbes, Senior Highway Engineer; D. Tucker Brown, Senior Highway Engineer; and Marcel Bussard, Associate Highway Engineer.
[89] Not printed.
[90] Brackets appear in the original instruction.

sec. 5), and such other expenses as may be deemed necessary by the Secretary of State in furtherance of the projects described, fiscal year 1930, to remain available until expended, $50,000." [91]

The brief review, in this paragraph, of antecedent related events, which you may already have in mind, is inserted merely for convenience. The Sixth International Conference of American States, by a Resolution adopted at Habana on February 7, 1928,[92] entrusted the Pan American Union with the preparation of projects for the construction of an inter-American highway. The Governing Board of the Pan American Union, acting through the Pan American Federation for Highway Education, requested the cooperation of the several Governments, members of the Union, in the formulation of such projects. The Congress of the United States, by a Joint Resolution, approved May 4, 1928,[93] requested the President to direct the several agencies of this Government to cooperate with the other interested states in the preparation of such projects. In his annual message to Congress on December 4, 1928, the President of the United States said: "In my message last year I expressed the view that we should lend our encouragement for more good roads to all the principal points on this hemisphere south of the Rio Grande. My view has not changed." [94] He recommended that the necessary Congressional authorization for this Government's cooperation in the project should be given. The Senate and the House of Representatives of the United States by Joint Resolution No. 104, of the 70th Congress, approved by the President on March 4, 1929,[95] "authorized to be appropriated, out of any moneys in the Treasury not otherwise appropriated, the sum of $50,000 to enable the Secretary of State to cooperate with the several Governments", etc., following almost verbatim the language of the Appropriation Act of a year later which is quoted above. At the invitation of the Government of Panamá, the delegation of the United States returning from the Second Pan American Highway Congress, which had been held at Rio de Janeiro, Brazil, from August 16 to August 28, 1929, attended a conference at Panamá from October 7 to 12 with representatives of the Canal Zone, Costa Rica, El Salvador, Guatemala, Honduras, Nicaragua, and Panamá, for the purpose of considering the measures to be taken to complete an international highway from the United

[91] 46 Stat. 90, 115.
[92] See *Report of the Delegates of the United States of America to the Sixth International Conference of American States, Held at Habana, Cuba, January 16 to February 20, 1928, With Appendices* (Washington, Government Printing Office, 1928), pp. 36, 282; and *Sixth International Conference of American States, Havana, 1928, Final Act, Motions, Agreements, Resolutions* (Habana, 1928), p. 14.
[93] 45 Stat. 490.
[94] *Foreign Relations*, 1928, vol. I, p. xviii.
[95] 45 Stat. 1697.

States to Panamá. After a full discussion the conference adopted several resolutions. A copy of a document containing them is enclosed for your convenience.[96] It was the sentiment of the conference, you will observe, that a highway should be opened between Panamá and the United States within five years and that in order to expedite this work, the Pan American Union should appoint an Inter-American Highway Commission whose task it should be to make a field study of the project; and all Governments interested were requested to cooperate with the Union and the Commission in this task.

The enactment of the legislation, quoted in the second paragraph above, appropriating funds to meet the expense of its participation in the projected reconnaissance surveys, is one of the important steps recently taken by this Government in the requested cooperation. Another is your designation as the agency through which the Secretary of State is to make effective this Government's cooperation in these surveys. In this connection it is appropriate to allude to the fact that, on May 27, 1930, the President affixed his approval to the Act passed by the Congress of the United States (No. 269, 71st Congress) [97] to authorize and provide for the construction and operation of a ferry across the Panamá Canal and a highway across the Canal Zone, which were also recommended by the Inter-American Highway Conference at Panamá last October, as will be seen by referring to the enclosed copy of the text of the Resolutions of that conference. A copy of the legislation just referred to is also enclosed.[96]

The Director General of the Pan American Union has informed the Department of State that the Governments of Guatemala and Nicaragua have expressed a desire to have reconnaissance surveys undertaken to determine the most desirable route for the proposed inter-American highway across their respective territories. The chiefs of the diplomatic missions of this Government in those countries had previously informed the Department that they had been apprised of the fact that those Governments had taken the steps mentioned. The steps taken by these two Governments appear to have complied fully with the conditions which the Act appropriating the $50,000 and also the Act approved March 4, 1929, authorizing such an appropriation make a necessary prerequisite to the Secretary of State's cooperating with the other interested Governments in these reconnaissance surveys. Referring to the resolution adopted by the Inter-American Highway Conference at Panamá recommending the creation of an Inter-American Highway

[96] Not printed.
[97] 46 Stat. 388.

Commission, the Director General also stated that, in accordance with the terms of that resolution, the Governments of Costa Rica, El Salvador, Guatemala, and Panamá had designated their representatives on that Commission. The actions just mentioned appear to indicate that these four Governments also expect to cooperate in the construction of the inter-American highway; but the Director General has not yet informed the Department that any Governments other than Guatemala and Nicaragua have actually requested this Government's cooperation in the reconnaissance surveys.

In view of the fact that the Act approved March 29, 1930, quoted in the second paragraph above, which makes available the appropriation for the reconnaissance surveys, and also the Joint Resolution approved on March 4, 1929, authorizing such an appropriation both clearly contemplate that the cooperation of the Secretary of State in the reconnaissance surveys shall be made available only when the other interested Governments shall have "initiated a request or signified a desire to the Pan American Union" for such cooperation, and since this Government has of course no desire to participate in the contemplated reconnaissance surveys in any country whose Government has not unmistakably indicated a desire to have this Government's participation, you are instructed to offer your services, for the present at least, only to the two Governments mentioned above as having complied fully with the conditions made by law a necessary prerequisite to the Secretary of State's making available this Government's cooperation. As soon as the Director General shall have informed the Secretary of State that the other interested Governments, or any of them, have requested this Government's cooperation, you will be promptly informed and will be instructed to offer your services also to them. The chief of this Government's diplomatic mission in each of the countries concerned whose Governments have not hitherto requested this Government's cooperation is being instructed to embrace an early opportunity to bring this matter to the attention of the appropriate authorities of the Government to which he is accredited, assuring them that his Government is both willing and ready to make available its cooperation with their Government in these surveys as soon as information shall reach the Secretary of State through the Director General of the Pan American Union that such cooperation is desired. To the Minister at Panamá it is being suggested that if that Government's failure to request this Government's cooperation should have been due merely to inadvertence and should it be the desire of that Government that the cooperation should begin in the near future the necessary preliminary correspondence can of course be attended to in a very few days by cable or by air mail.

Before offering your services to any interested Government, or any official thereof, you are instructed to call upon the chief of the diplomatic mission of the United States at the capital of the country concerned in order that you may be properly introduced to the appropriate officials of that Government. The chief of each such diplomatic mission is being apprised of the fact that you have been designated and instructed to make effective this Government's cooperation with the Government to which he is accredited, in case, or as soon as, such cooperation shall have been requested. He is also being informed that you will call upon him before establishing any official relations with the Government to which he is accredited; and he is being instructed to introduce you to the proper authorities and to render to you such other assistance as may be possible and proper.

You are instructed to submit written reports to the Secretary of State from time to time, through the diplomatic mission of the United States at the capital of the country where you may be at the time each report is made, regarding your progress in the performance of the task which has been entrusted to you. These progress reports should be submitted not less frequently than once every three months; and they may be made as much more frequently as you may deem it desirable to make them. If, as it is understood you contemplate doing, you establish and maintain an office for your headquarters at or near the city of Panamá, the Legation of the United States at that capital will of course be the medium through which you will communicate with the Secretary of State, not only while cooperating with the Government of that country, should you be informed that it has requested your cooperation, but also while establishing your headquarters, if they are to be in that country or the Canal Zone, and, also, should there be such a time, whenever you shall not actually be engaged in cooperation with the Government of any other country.

A copy of this instruction is being attached to the instruction which, as indicated above, is being addressed to the Minister at Panamá. A copy of the budget which was enclosed with the letter addressed to the Secretary of State on June 7, 1930, by the Secretary of Agriculture, requesting your appointment, is also being sent to the Legation at Panamá and the Minister is being authorized to make payments, upon vouchers approved by the chairman of your committee consistent with such budget, and to draw on the Secretary of State for the required amounts.

Copies of this instruction to you are also being enclosed with the instructions which are being sent to the chiefs of the diplomatic missions of this country in Costa Rica, El Salvador, Guatemala, Honduras, Mexico, and Nicaragua.[99] Copies of the same are also being

---

[99] The instructions were sent on July 22 to the American diplomatic missions in Costa Rica (No. 21), El Salvador (No. 96), Guatemala (No. 22), Honduras (No. 13), Nicaragua (No. 40) ; and on July 23 to Mexico (No. 1192).

furnished to the Director General of the Pan American Union and to the Secretary of Agriculture for the Chief of the Bureau of Public Roads.

Upon completion of your task and your return to the United States you should reasonably promptly submit to the Secretary of State three copies of a comprehensive report of your entire work, one for the records of the Department and two for communication by the Secretary of State to Congress in compliance with the provisions of the law, quoted above, authorizing and making provision for the work.

Very truly yours,   For the Secretary of State:

WILBUR J. CARR

810.154/235 : Telegram

The Minister in Panama (Davis) to the Secretary of State

PANAMA, July 11, 1930—11 a. m.
[Received 12:25 p. m.]

46. Reference Department's mailed instruction No. 31, July 1st.

1. Instructions have been delivered to Commission.

2. Copy of budget mentioned in paragraph 2 Department's instruction did not accompany instruction.

3. Panaman Minister for Foreign Affairs has today cabled Panaman Minister in Washington to request cooperation of Commission through channels mentioned in Department's instruction.

4. Panaman Government offered office quarters in National Palace through Director of Pan American Union. Does Department perceive any objection to acceptance of this offer by Commission?

DAVIS

810.154/235

The Secretary of State to the Minister in Panama (Davis)

No. 33   WASHINGTON, July 12, 1930.

SIR: In the Department's telegraphic response [1] to your telegram No. 46 of July 11, 11 a. m., which you will of course have already received, you have been informed that the Department perceives no objection to the Commission's acceptance of the office quarters offered by the Panamanian Government. In that instruction it was suggested that should an appropriate occasion offer you might express through the proper officials your Government's appreciation of their Government's offer.

---

[1] Not printed.

There are transmitted herewith two copies of the budget [2] mentioned in the second paragraph of the Department's instruction to you of July 1, no copy of which, your telegram under acknowledgment states, accompanied that instruction. The second copy of the budget is for delivery by you to the engineers since, from the copy of their instruction enclosed with the instruction of July 1 to you, you will observe a copy of that budget should have gone also to them. Possibly their copy also failed to go.

The Department would like to have you ascertain whether the instruction to the engineers bore a date and, if not, wishes you to affix to it the date July 1, 1930. The reason for making this request is that the Department's file copy of the instruction to the engineers has been found to be undated. It should of course bear the same date as the instruction to you with which it was sent for delivery by you.

As soon as the Panamanian Government's request for this Government's cooperation, to which the third numbered paragraph of your telegram of July 11 relates, shall have reached the Department from the Director General of the Pan American Union you will be requested by telegraph officially to present the engineers to the appropriate Panamanian authorities so that they may properly offer to cooperate with the Panamanian Government in the reconnaissance surveys.

Very truly yours,

For the Secretary of State:

FRANCIS WHITE

810.154/237 : Telegram

The Secretary of State to the Minister in Panama (Davis)

WASHINGTON, July 16, 1930—6 p. m.

49. Third numbered paragraph your telegram 46, July 11, 11 a. m. and Department's mail instruction 31, July 1.

The Director General of the Pan American Union has just informed the Department [3] that the Minister of Panama in Washington has apprized the Pan American Union of the fact that his Government desires the cooperation of this Government in the projected reconnaissance survey of the Panamanian section of the proposed Inter-American Highway.

Please inform this Government's cooperating highway engineers and officially introduce them to the appropriate Panamanian authorities in order that the engineers may properly make available this Government's cooperation.

---

[2] Not printed.
[3] Letter of July 14; not printed.

The Director General also states that, as reported in the fourth numbered paragraph of your telegraphic despatch, he has been informed that the Government of Panama is prepared to offer adequate office accommodations for the engineers.

STIMSON

810.154/238

The Minister in Panama (Davis) to the Secretary of State

No. 119   PANAMA, July 21, 1930.
                                           [Received July 30.]

SIR: I have the honor to acknowledge the receipt of the Department's mailed instruction No. 33 of July 12, 1930, and the Department's telegraphic instruction No. 49, dated July 16, 6 P. M.

In accordance with instructions, I have introduced the members of the Technical Commission on the Inter-American Highway Reconnaissance Surveys to the appropriate Panamanian authorities. In presenting the members of the Commission I stated that the Technical Commission is now prepared to offer its cooperation to the Panamanian Government in making the survey of the Panamanian section of the proposed Inter-American Highways. At the same time, I expressed appreciation orally on behalf of my Government for the Panamanian Government's kind offer of office quarters to the Technical Commission and accepted the offer.

With reference to the second paragraph of the Department's instruction No. 33 of July 12, 1930, the two copies of the budget mentioned therein have been received and one copy has been delivered to the Chairman of the Technical Commission. In this connection may I state that it is my understanding that I am to draw only that part of their salary accounts which comes under the special appropriation, and that it is my understanding that salary accounts paid from bureau funds will be paid directly to the members of the Technical Commission from their office in Washington.

I have investigated the question raised in paragraph three of the Department's instruction No. 33 dated July 12, 1930, and find that the copy of instructions addressed to the Technical Commission is dated July 1. The carbon copy thereof which I have kept for my files was, however, dated July 2, 1930. I have changed this date to read July 1, in accordance with instructions.

I have [etc.]   ROY T. DAVIS

810.154/250

The Minister in Nicaragua (Hanna) to the Secretary of State

No. 133   MANAGUA, August 27, 1930.
                                             [Received September 22.]

SIR: With reference to the Department's instruction No. 40 of July 22, 1930,[5] concerning assistance to the Government of Nicaragua in a reconnaissance survey pertinent to the building of the projected Inter-American Highway, I have the honor to report that the Nicaraguan Foreign Office in a note dated August 20, 1930, informed the Legation that it would be agreeable to the Government of Nicaragua to have the reconnaissance survey begin here as soon as, or whenever, the engineers referred to in the Department's instruction might be able, or find it convenient, to proceed to Nicaragua. The Minister for Foreign Affairs at the same time requested that the Legation express to the Government of the United States Nicaragua's gratitude for its generous and useful cooperation.

Respectfully yours,   MATTHEW E. HANNA

810.154/246 : Telegram

The Minister in Honduras (Lay) to the Secretary of State

                              TEGUCIGALPA, September 2, 1930—3 p. m.
                                             [Received 6 : 30 p. m.]

83. Department's instruction No. 13, July 21 [*22*].[5] Government of Honduras accepts cooperation American engineers. Have suggested that Minister of Public Works so advise Pan American Union direct.

                                             LAY

810.154/249

The Secretary of State to the Minister in Honduras (Lay)

No. 40   WASHINGTON, October 1, 1930.

SIR: Referring to your telegram of September 2, 1930, regarding the Honduran Government's indication to you that it desired to avail itself of the proffered cooperation of this Government in the Inter-American Highway Reconnaissance Surveys, you are informed that, in a letter dated September 19, 1930,[6] the Director General of the Pan

---

[5] See footnote 99, p. 285.
[6] Not printed.

American Union has reported that he had received a communication from the Secretary of Promotion, Agriculture and Labor of Honduras indicating that the Government of that country desires this Government's cooperation in the survey of the Honduran section of the Inter-American Highway.

The Chairman of the Technical Committee of the United States on the Inter-American Highway Reconnaissance Surveys has been informed, through the Minister of the United States in Panamá,[8] that the Honduran Government has indicated this desire and he has been instructed to offer his Committee's services to the Honduran Government at the appropriate time in the manner prescribed in the seventh paragraph of the Committee's instruction, dated July 1, 1930, a copy of which was enclosed for your information with the Department's instruction to you of July 22.[9]

Please ascertain and report to the Department, so that it may inform the engineers, whether it will be agreeable to the Government of Honduras to have the reconnaissance surveys begun within that country as soon as, or whenever, this Government's cooperating highway engineers may be able or find it convenient to proceed to that country.

Very truly yours,   For the Secretary of State:

FRANCIS WHITE

810.154/254

The Chargé in Mexico (Lane) to the Secretary of State

No. 2834   MEXICO, October 7, 1930.
                                                  [Received October 13.]

SIR: Referring to the Department's instruction No. 1192 of July 23, 1930,[9] concerning the projected Inter-American Highway, I have the honor to transmit herewith a copy and translation of Foreign Office note No. 14971 of October 2, 1930,[10] in which it is stated that the Department of Communications and Public Works thanks the Government of the United States for its offer of cooperation in this matter which, however, it is obliged to decline since the National Commission of Roads has made and will continue to make the necessary studies and projects relative to the part of this work which corresponds to Mexico. The Department of Communications and Public Works likewise communicates that the points where the Inter-American Highway will cross the Mexican frontiers are in the north,

---

[8] Instruction No. 69, October 1; not printed.
[9] See footnote 99, p. 285.
[10] Not printed.

Nuevo Laredo; in the south, Suchiate, Chiapas; as well as having international traffic on the northern frontier at Reynosa and Matamoros, Tamaulipas; Ciudad Juarez, Chihuahua; Nogales, Sonora; Mexicali, Lower California, and Piedras Negras, Coahuila.

Respectfully yours,   ARTHUR BLISS LANE

810.154/253 : Telegram

The Minister in Panama (Davis) to the Secretary of State

PANAMA, October 10, 1930—5 p. m.
[Received 6:26 p. m.]

69. Referring to Department's instruction No. 31, July 1. Press reports Government of Honduras has requested cooperation highways survey. Chairman of committee has requested me to inform Legation at Tegucigalpa that engineers can begin survey about November first. Please inform me by cable whether Honduras has requested cooperation.

DAVIS

810.154/258

The Minister in Guatemala (Whitehouse) to the Secretary of State

No. 195   GUATEMALA, October 10, 1930.
[Received October 22.]

SIR: In accordance with your instruction No. 22 of July 22nd last [11] (File No. 810.154/228) the Guatemalan Government was duly informed of the presence in Panama of the American Highway Engineers, and of their readiness to begin active cooperation with the other interested Governments in making reconnaissance surveys for the projected Inter-American Highway.

I have the honor to report that I am now in receipt of a note from the Foreign Office quoting the pertinent part of the reply received from the Guatemalan Minister of Agriculture, which reads as follows:

"Regarding this matter, I have the honor to inform you that this Office appreciates the important collaboration of the three engineers mentioned, and, if their coming does not occasion expenses—which at present it is not possible to defray—they will be received with the greatest pleasure in order that they may carry out this interesting study."

Respectfully yours,   SHELDON WHITEHOUSE

---

[11] See footnote 99, p. 285.

810.154/253 : Telegram

The Acting Secretary of State to the Minister in Honduras (Lay)

WASHINGTON, October 11, 1930—4 p. m.

61. Please telegraph as soon as possible response to request in last paragraph of mail instruction 40, dated October 1.

The Legation at Panama telegraphs that engineers can begin survey in Honduras about November first.

CASTLE

810.154/253 : Telegram

The Acting Secretary of State to the Minister in Panama (Davis)

WASHINGTON, October 11, 1930—4 p. m.

68. Your 69, October 10, 5 p. m. Honduras has requested cooperation. See mail instruction 69 dated October 1 [12] and enclosed instruction same date to Chairman Forbes of Committee.

On same date the Legation at Tegucigalpa was instructed also by mail to ascertain and report so that the engineers might be informed whether it will be agreeable to the Government of Honduras to have the survey begun within that country as soon as or whenever this Government's engineers may be able or find it convenient to proceed to that country. No reply has yet been received. As soon as it is, you will be informed.

CASTLE

810.154/256

The Minister in Panama (Davis) to the Secretary of State

No. 227   PANAMA, October 11, 1930.
                                        [Received October 18.]

SIR: I have the honor to transmit herewith copy of a communication addressed to me by Mr. Thomas A. Forbes, Chairman of the Technical Committee of the Inter-American Highway Reconnaissance Surveys,[13] relative to the plans of the Committee. It will be noted that the Commission would find it convenient, according to Mr. Forbes, if it could continue its survey into Costa Rican territory when it completes its work in Panama.

---

[12] See footnote 8, p. 290.
[13] Not printed.

If the Department has any information as to the attitude of the Costa Rican Government toward the proposed survey which would be of interest to Mr. Forbes, I shall be pleased if the Department will furnish this information to me, together with any information it has relative to the attitude of the Government of Salvador.

The local press has reported that the Government of Honduras has requested the cooperation of the Survey Committee. If this is the case, I assume that I will be advised by the Department of the action taken by the Government of Honduras.

Respectfully yours,

Roy T. Davis

810.154/257 : Telegram

The Minister in Honduras (Lay) to the Secretary of State

TEGUCIGALPA, October 19, 1930—noon.
[Received 10:52 p. m.]

102. Department's telegram No. 61, October 11, 4 p. m. Minister of Fomento states agreeable if engineers come about November 1st but not later, during rainy season.

LAY

810.154/258a

The Secretary of State to the Minister in Panama (Davis)

WASHINGTON, October 21, 1930—6 p. m.

74. Your 69, October 10, 5 p. m. and the Department's reply 68 October 11, 4 p. m. The Legation at Tegucigalpa cabled October 19, noon: "Minister of Fomento of Honduras states agreeable if engineers come about November 1st but not later during rainy season".

Please communicate the foregoing to Chairman Forbes and telegraph directly to the Legation at Tegucigalpa when the engineers expect to reach that capital.

Please ask the Chairman whether the Committee has mailed its first quarterly report to the Secretary of State. If not invite his attention to the eighth paragraph of the general instructions of July 1. No report from the Committee has yet reached the Department, other than its letter to you enclosed with your No. 227 of October 11.[13a]

Costa Rican Government has not yet requested cooperation. Department will discuss this with Eberhardt who is expected about November first.

STIMSON

[13a] Enclosure to despatch No. 227 not printed.

810.154/261

The Minister in Panama (Davis) to the Secretary of State

No. 248   PANAMA, October 28, 1930.
                                                        [Received October 31.]

SIR: Referring to the last paragraph of the Department's telegraphic instruction No. 74, dated October 21, 6 P. M., relative to the participation of the Government of Costa Rica in the survey of the proposed Inter-American Highway, in which American engineers are cooperating, I have the honor to report that the Costa Rican Minister to Panama, Mr. Enrique Fonseca, recently discussed this survey with me. I had an opportunity to explain to Minister Fonseca the conditions under which American engineers are cooperating in this survey. He indicated an active interest in the matter, and later informed me that he had forwarded an air mail despatch to his Government, recommending that the cooperation of the American engineers be requested at an early date.

Respectfully yours,   ROY T. DAVIS

810.154/266

The Chargé in Panama (Merrell) to the Secretary of State

No. 274   PANAMA, November 20, 1930.
                                                   [Received November 29.]

SIR: I have the honor to enclose as of possible interest to the Department a copy of a memorandum of a conversation between the Costa Rican Minister to Panama and Mr. Thomas A. Forbes, Chairman, Inter-American Highway Reconnaissance Surveys, Technical Committee.

Respectfully yours,   GEORGE R. MERRELL, JR.

[Enclosure]

Memorandum by the Chairman of the United States Technical Committee on the Inter-American Highway Reconnaissance Surveys (Forbes)

The Costa Rican Minister to Panama called at the office of the Inter-American Highway Reconnaissance Surveys, Technical Committee, on Saturday, November 15th, 1930 during my absence. Upon return to the office, I immediately proceeded to the Costa Rican Legation in order that I might ascertain the reason for the call.

The Costa Rican Minister said that his Government had authorized him to inform the Technical Committee that his Government was anxious to render all assistance necessary in furthering the reconnaissance in Costa Rica, and that they would cooperate with us in all ways and are most desirous of furthering the work of the Inter-American highway.

The Costa Rican Minister said that he had been in conversation with the American Minister to Panama, Hon. Roy T. Davis, previous to his departure to the United States, about this matter. The Costa Rican Minister inquired into the details of our work in order that he might familiarize himself with what we would wish to do in Costa Rica.

I explained to the Costa Rican Minister that our work would consist of a reconnaissance in Costa Rica in order to ascertain a feasible route for the proposed Inter-American highway and make an estimate of the cost of construction of the same. That we were also particularly interested in the country adjoining the Panama and Nicaragua borders insofar that we would be unable to complete our work in northern Panama until we had made a survey of the frontier region of Costa Rica in order that the proposed Inter-American highway in the two countries would join at a common point on the border.

The selection of the junction point at the border between Costa Rica and Panama will necessitate a study of the terrain in both countries adjacent to the border in order to select a feasible route of equal advantage to both Panama and Costa Rica.

Since the Costa Rican Minister had been one of the delegates from Costa Rica to the conference held here in Panama in the fall of 1929, I was sure that he was familiar with the procedure necessary to arrange for the services of the Technical Committee in Costa Rica. I stated to the Costa Rican Minister that it would be a pleasure to cooperate with the authorities of Costa Rica in a reconnaissance survey within their borders, and that I assumed that he was fully informed as to the proper procedure before our cooperation could be given, namely that his Government through the Pan-American Union in Washington, would make a request or signify a desire to have the cooperation of the Technical Committee to the United States State Department. The State Department would after receiving such request, promptly notify the Technical Committee, who would then immediately make plans to offer their services to Costa Rica.

I told the Costa Rican Minister that during rainy season we had been forced to abandon our reconnaissance in northern Panama and were working at present in Honduras. However within a month or six weeks we expected to return to northern Panama to complete the reconnaissance there, and it would be of particular advantage to us if we were able to reconnoitre the country in Costa Rica adjacent to the Panamanian border in order that we might select a proper junction point on the border.

810.154/266

The Secretary of State to the Minister in El Salvador (Robbins)

No. 132   WASHINGTON, December 27, 1930.

SIR: There is enclosed for your information a copy of an instruction addressed on December 16, 1930, to the Chairman of the United States Technical Committee on the Inter-American Highway Reconnaissance Surveys,[14] in care of the Legation at Panamá, regarding the attitude of El Salvador toward requesting this Government's cooperation in those surveys.

Your attention is especially invited to the next to the last paragraph of the instruction of which a copy is enclosed; and you are requested to bring this matter again to the attention of the appropriate authorities of the Government to which you are accredited and to submit an early report containing such pertinent information as you may be able to obtain in addition to that contained in your Legation's two despatches cited in the instruction to the engineers. You will note the importance of their being informed at least regarding the points where the Salvadoran section of the Inter-American Highway reaches the frontiers of Guatemala and Honduras.

Referring to the last paragraph of the instruction to the engineers you are authorized in your discretion to inform the appropriate Salvadoran authorities that your Government's cooperating engineers would appreciate an invitation to inspect the Salvadoran section of this Highway even though it has already been located and partially, or completely, constructed especially the portions of it near the frontiers of the two neighboring countries in order that the engineers may be better prepared to cooperate with the Governments of Guatemala and Honduras in planning the connecting portions of the Highway in those countries.

Very truly yours,   For the Secretary of State:
                                     FRANCIS WHITE

---

[14] Not printed.

CONVENTION ON THE REGULATION OF AUTOMOTIVE TRAFFIC, SIGNED AT WASHINGTON, OCTOBER 6, 1930

515.4D2A/12

Convention on the Regulation of Automotive Traffic, Signed at Washington, October 6, 1930 [15]

The Governments of the American Republics, desirous of establishing uniform rules among themselves for the control and regulation of automotive traffic on their highways;

Have decided to conclude a convention for that purpose and to that end have conferred the necessary powers upon their respective representatives;

Who, having met at the Pan American Union in Washington on October fourth, one thousand nine hundred and thirty, have agreed upon the following provisions:

ARTICLE I

It is recognized that each State has exclusive jurisdiction over the use of its own highways, but agrees to their international use as specified in this Convention.

ARTICLE II

All vehicles before admission to international traffic shall be registered in the manner prescribed by the State of origin. In addition to the registration plate of the State of origin, each vehicle shall carry a plainly visible international registration marker, of the form and type of plaque markers provided for by the International Convention for the Circulation of Automobiles, 1909, as amended in 1926,[16] as follows:

The distinctive plaque is composed of an oval plate, 30 centimeters wide by 18 centimeters high, bearing from 1 to 3 letters painted black on a white background. These letters shall be capital Latin

---

[15] "The 1930 Convention was never submitted to the Senate for its advice and consent to ratification. The principal objections raised to the 1930 Convention, so far as this Government was concerned, were:

1. It would have overridden State laws dealing with subjects theretofore within the exclusive control of the various States.

2. It would have required Federal legislation creating an official agency for the administration of detailed obligations assumed by the Federal Government under the Convention, or the authorization of the performance of official duties by a private organization for the purpose of such administration, or both. . . . "—The Acting Chief of the Treaty Division (McClure) to the Chief of the Division of International Conferences (Kelchner), August 20, 1941. (515.4D2A/68)

[16] Convention with respect to the international circulation of motor vehicles, signed at Paris, October 11, 1909, Great Britain, Treaty Series No. 18 (1910), p. 311; international convention relative to motor traffic, Paris, April 24, 1926, Great Britain, Treaty Series No. 11 (1930), p. 1.

letters and must be at least 10 centimeters high and their profile 15 millimeters. For motorcycles, the distinctive plaque shall be only 18 centimeters wide and 12 centimeters high. The letters themselves shall measure at least 8 centimeters high and their profile 10 millimeters.

The distinctive letters for the different countries are the following:

Argentina	RA	Haiti	HA
Bolivia	R. B.	Honduras	HS
Brazil.	BR	Mexico	MEX
Chile	R. Ch.	Nicaragua	NIC
Colombia	CO	Panama	R. P.
Costa Rica	C. R.	Paraguay	PY
Cuba	C	Peru	PE
Dominican Republic	R. D.	United States of	
Ecuador	EC	America	U. S. A.
El Salvador	E. S.	Uruguay	R. O. U.
Guatemala	GU	Venezuela	V

ARTICLE III

Evidence of proper registration in any of the Contracting States shall entitle all such vehicles to international reciprocity.

ARTICLE IV

All motor vehicle operators shall have such driving certificates as may be required by the laws of their State. A special international traveling pass in the form and containing the information prescribed by the International Convention for the Circulation of Automobiles, 1909, as amended in 1926, shall also be required for admission to international traffic.

The international automobile certificate issued in any one of the Contracting States shall be worded in the language prescribed by the legislation of the said State.

The final translation of the certificate into the official languages of the Contracting States shall be communicated to the Pan American Union by each of the Governments party to this Convention.

ARTICLE V

Each State or its subdivisions shall maintain central bureaus of registration for purposes of exchange of information with other States as to registration of vehicles and operators.

ARTICLE VI

The rule of the road shall be to pass on the right when meeting another vehicle and to pass to the left when overtaking.

Article VII

All vehicles approaching an intersection shall yield the right of way to vehicles which have entered the intersection. When two vehicles enter an intersection at the same time the vehicle on the left shall yield to that on the right.

Article VIII

All vehicles admitted to international traffic shall have the following equipment:

(1) Brakes adequate to control the movement of and to stop and to hold such vehicle, including two means of applying the brakes, each of which means shall be effective to apply the brakes to at least two wheels and so constructed that no part which is liable to failure shall be common to the two. A motorcycle shall be equipped with at least one brake.

(2) Suitable horn or other warning device satisfactory to the regulatory authorities, which shall not make excessive noise.

(3a) Every motor vehicle other than a motorcycle, road roller, road machinery or farm tractor shall be equipped with two head lamps, at the front of and on opposite sides of the motor vehicle, which shall at all time, under normal atmospheric conditions and on a level road, produce a driving light sufficient to render clearly discernible a person 200 feet ahead, but shall not project a glaring or dazzling light to persons in front of such lamp.

(3b) Every motor vehicle and every trailer or semi-trailer which is being drawn at the end of a train of vehicles shall carry at the rear a lamp which exhibits a red light plainly visible under normal atmospheric conditions from a distance of 500 feet to the rear of such vehicle and so constructed and placed that the number plate carried on the rear of such vehicle shall under like conditions be so illuminated by a white light as to be read from a distance of 50 feet to the rear of such vehicle.

(4) No person shall drive a motor vehicle on a highway unless such motor vehicle is equipped with a muffler in good working order and in constant operation to prevent excessive or unusual noise.

Article IX

Any vehicle entering another State shall register at the point of entry, but shall not be required to post bond until a lapse of 90 days since it last entered the country.

Article X

All vehicles and drivers in international traffic are subject to the regulations, not in conflict with the articles of this Convention, of the State in which they are operating.

ARTICLE XI

Danger, restriction and direction signs shall be made uniform as between the several States.

ARTICLE XII

The size of vehicles and loads shall be limited to the following:

(1) No vehicle shall exceed a total outside width, including any load thereon, of 8 feet, except that the width of a farm tractor shall not exceed 9 feet, and excepting further, that the limitations as to size of vehicles stated in this section shall not apply to implements of husbandry temporarily propelled or moved upon the public highway.

(2) No vehicle with or without load shall exceed a maximum height of 12 feet.

(3) No vehicle shall exceed a length of 33 feet, and no combination of vehicles coupled together shall exceed a total length of 85 feet.

(4) No vehicle or train of vehicles shall carry any load extending more than 3 feet beyond the front thereof.

(5) No passenger vehicle shall carry any load extending beyond the line of the fenders on the left side of such vehicle nor extending more than 6 inches beyond the line of the fenders on the right side thereof.

(6) Special permits for vehicles or combinations of vehicles exceeding these limits may be issued by the competent authority of the State.

ARTICLE XIII

The present Convention shall be deposited with the Pan American Union, which shall furnish a certified copy thereof to each Government, member of the Union.

The Convention shall be ratified by the Contracting States and the instrument of ratification shall be deposited with the Pan American Union, which shall communicate notice of each deposit to all the Contracting States.

The Convention shall come into effect for each Contracting State on the date of the deposit of its ratification with the Pan American Union.

The American Republics which have not subscribed to this Convention may adhere thereto by depositing with the Pan American Union an instrument evidencing such adherence, a certified copy of which shall be furnished by the Pan American Union to each State member thereof.

This Convention may be denounced by any Contracting State and the denunciation shall take effect twelve months after the receipt of

the corresponding notice by the Pan American Union, which shall
communicate notice of such denunciation to the other Contracting
States. Such denunciation shall not affect the validity of the Convention as between the other Contracting States.

IN WITNESS WHEREOF, The undersigned delegates have signed this
Convention in English, Spanish and Portuguese, and thereto have
affixed their respective seals.

Done in the City of Washington on the sixth day of October in
the year one thousand nine hundred and thirty.

For Argentina:	J. A. VALLE	[SEAL]
	JOSE I. GIRADO	[SEAL]
For Bolivia:	GEO. DE LA BARRA	[SEAL]
For Brazil:	S. GURGEL DO AMARAL	[SEAL]
	Presidente da Delegação Brazileira, *ad referen-dum* do Governo Brazileiro.	
	G. M. DE MENEZES	[SEAL]
	S. ARNALDO A. DA MOTTA	[SEAL]
For Chile:	ALBERTO FERNÁNDEZ R.	[SEAL]
	O. TENHAMM V.	[SEAL]
For Colombia:	CARLOS DE NARVÁEZ	[SEAL]
	ENRIQUE CORONADO SUÁREZ	[SEAL]
For Costa Rica:	J. P. ARANGO	[SEAL]
For the Dominican Republic:	PERSIO C. FRANCO *ad referendum*	[SEAL]
For Ecuador:	HOMERO VITERI L.	[SEAL]
For Guatemala:	ADRIÁN RECINOS	[SEAL]
	RAMIRO FERNÁNDEZ	[SEAL]
	ED. JEANNEAU	[SEAL]
For Honduras:	FELIX CANALES SALAZAR	[SEAL]
For Mexico:	A. BECERRIL COLÍN	[SEAL]
	LEOPOLDO FARÍAS	[SEAL]
For Nicaragua:	JUAN B. SACASA	[SEAL]
For Panama:	J. R. GUIZADO	[SEAL]
For Paraguay:	PABLO M. YNSFRAN	[SEAL]
For Peru:	EDUARDO DIBOS D.	[SEAL]
For El Salvador:	JULIO E. MEJÍA	[SEAL]
	F. A. REYES, H.	[SEAL]
For Uruguay:	MARIO COPPETTI	[SEAL]
	JUAN P. MOLFINO	[SEAL]
	CARLOS A. RABASSA	[SEAL]
For Venezuela:	FCO. J. SUCRE	[SEAL]
For the United States of America:	J. WALTER DRAKE	[SEAL]

515.4D2A/14

The Chairman of the American Delegation to the Pan American Conference on the Regulation of Automotive Traffic (Drake) to the Secretary of State [17]

SIR: I beg to submit herewith a report on the Pan American Conference on the Regulation of Automotive Traffic, held at the Pan American Union in Washington, from October 4th to 6th, 1930, and the text of the Convention signed on the latter date.[17a] Certified copies of the Convention have been sent by the Pan American Union to the Government of the United States as well as to the Governments of the other American Republics.

The Conference was convened by the Governing Board of the Pan American Union, with representatives of the following States in attendance, all of whom signed the Convention.

Argentina	Honduras
Bolivia	Mexico
Brazil	Nicaragua
Chile	Panama
Colombia	Paraguay
Costa Rica	Peru
Dominican Republic	United States of America
Ecuador	Uruguay
El Salvador	Venezuela
Guatemala	

The Delegation appointed to represent the Government of the United States at the Conference consisted of Messrs. Tasker L. Oddie, Cyrenus Cole, Francis White, Thos. H. MacDonald, Frank Sheets, Frederick Reimer, H. H. Rice, A. B. Barber, Robert Hooper, and the undersigned.

Of this group, Messrs. Oddie, Cole, MacDonald, Sheets, Reimer, Rice and the undersigned represented the United States at the Second Pan American Highway Congress at Rio de Janeiro in August, 1929, at which the draft convention on the regulation of automotive traffic was formulated.[18]

ANTECEDENTS OF THE CONVENTION

It has occurred to me that it might be desirable to set forth the antecedents, and give a brief review of the steps preceding the signing of the Convention.

The initial step toward the regulation of international automotive

---

[17] Transmitted to the Department by the chairman of the American delegation in covering letter of December 5.

[17a] *Supra.*

[18] *Report of the Delegation From the United States of America, Second Pan American Highway Congress, Rio de Janeiro, August 16 to 28, 1929* (Washington, Government Printing Office, 1930), p. 16.

traffic in the Republics of the Western Hemisphere was taken at the Sixth International Conference of American States, held at Havana, Cuba, in 1928.[19] At that time a resolution was adopted recommending that the Second Pan American Highway Congress "formulate the bases of a convention for the international regulation of automotive traffic between the countries that are members of the Pan American Union."

To facilitate the work of the Second Pan American Highway Congress, and in order that the delegates to that meeting might have something to serve as a basis of discussion, the Governing Board of the Pan American Union requested the Pan American Confederation for Highway Education to undertake a study of the subject and to formulate a project that might be transmitted by the Governing Board to the Highway Congress at Rio de Janeiro. The Confederation for Highway Education was organized in 1924 by a group of highway engineers of Latin America who were invited to visit the United States as guests of the Highway Education Board and undertake a study of highway construction, administration and finance as practiced in this country.[20] On the termination of the tour, conferences were held at the Pan American Union, at which the Highway Confederation was created, with National Federations in each country and with the headquarters of the Executive Committee established at the Pan American Union. As the purpose of the Confederation is to promote by every possible means all phases of highway activity, the Executive Committee of the Confederation immediately accepted the invitation of the Governing Board.

The Executive Committee of the Confederation made a thorough study of the existing conventions on the regulation of automotive traffic, including the Paris Conventions of 1909 and 1926, and also availed itself of the studies made by the National Conference on Street and Highway Safety appointed by President Hoover while Secretary of Commerce. The results of these studies were incorporated into a draft convention submitted to the Pan American Union, and in turn transmitted to the Second Pan American Highway Congress at Rio de Janeiro. At that Congress the draft convention was approved with virtually no modifications, but as the delegates did not possess the necessary powers to sign a convention, the Congress limited itself to the adoption of a resolution approving the draft and forwarding it to the Pan American Union.

The Governing Board of the Pan American Union appointed a

[19] *Report of the Delegates of the United States of America to the Sixth International Conference of American States, Held at Habana, Cuba, January 16 to February 20, 1928, With Appendices* (Washington, Government Printing Office, 1928), appendix 40, p. 274.

[20] See *The Pan American Confederation for Highway Education, Its Aims and Purposes, Constitution and By-Laws* (Washington, Pan American Union, [1927]).

Special Committee to consider the resolutions adopted at the Second
Pan American Highway Congress, and with respect to the draft convention on the regulation of automotive traffic recommended that
the Director General be authorized to transmit the draft to the
Governments, members of the Union; and further, that the delegates of the American Republics to the Sixth International Road
Congress be authorized to sign the Convention at a special conference to be held at that time at the Pan American Union. This recommendation was unanimously approved by the Board, and communications were dispatched to the Governments of the American Republics,
transmitting the draft convention and requesting that the necessary
authority be conferred upon the delegates of the respective countries
to the Sixth International Road Congress [21] to meet in special session
at the Pan American Union to consider and, if found acceptable, to
sign the Convention on the Regulation of Automotive Traffic.

THE CONFERENCE AT WASHINGTON

The Conference at the Pan American Union was convened on Saturday, October 4th, at 10 o'clock by the Director General of the
Union, Dr. L. S. Rowe, who spoke as follows:

"Gentlemen of the Conference:
I deem it a very real privilege to extend to you the warmest possible welcome on behalf of the Pan American Union. You are assembled to fulfill a most important mission. In giving final and
definite form to the great work accomplished by the Second Pan
American Highway Congress which met at Rio de Janeiro in August,
1929, you are laying the foundation for important steps in the development of closer communication between the nations of the
American Continent. The Convention on the Regulation of Automotive Traffic which is to be submitted to you is destined to be one
of the most important influences in giving the fullest measure of
efficiency to that great factor in inter-American communication,
namely, the motor highway. The successful operation of a Pan
American Highway, which is no longer in the realm of speculation,
but has come within the confines of reality, requires uniform standards of regulation, which the proposed convention is intended to
supply.
Permit me to congratulate you on the services which you are
rendering to the entire Continent in considering this important matter, and at the same time to wish you the fullest measure of success
in your deliberations."

Nominations for Permanent Chairman were then opened, and the
undersigned, as Chairman of the Delegation of the United States,
was elected. After expressing appreciation for the honor conferred

---

[21] See Sixth International Road Congress, Washington, D. C., 1930, *Proceedings of the Congress* (Washington, Government Printing Office, 1931). The
official opening session of the Congress took place on October 6, 1930.

upon him, the Chairman stated the purpose of the Conference and suggested that the Convention be taken up article by article.

In the interval between the Second Pan American Highway Congress and the meeting at the Pan American Union, the Pan American Confederation for Highway Education had given further study to the draft convention, and had proposed modifications intended to bring the provisions of the convention into harmony with the latest practices and to correlate the terms thereof with those contained in the International Conventions for the Circulation of Automobiles, signed at Paris in 1909 and 1926.

After all the articles of the Convention had been examined and discussed, a Drafting Committee was appointed to prepare the Convention for signature. This Committee consisted of the following delegates:

For the Spanish version . . . . Juan Agustín Valle, of Argentina
                              Homero Viteri Lafronte, of Ecuador
                              Adrian Recinos, of Guatemala
For the Portuguese version . . Godofredo M. de Menezes and Arnaldo M. [A.] da Motta, of Brazil
For the English version . . . . Thomas H. MacDonald, of the United States.

The session of Monday, October 6th, was called to order by the Chairman at 5:00 P. M. The Convention was submitted by the Drafting Committee in English, Spanish and Portuguese, and was thereupon signed by the representatives of the nineteen countries in attendance.

In accordance with the suggestion of the Chairman of the Brazilian Delegation, His Excellency, Dr. S. Gurgel do Amaral, Ambassador to the United States, that a study be made of road signs in order that they might be made uniform throughout the American Continent, the Drafting Committee submitted the following resolution which was unanimously adopted:

"Whereas Article XI of the Convention on the Regulation of Automotive Traffic provides that 'Danger, restriction and direction signs should [shall] be made uniform as between the several States,'

"The Pan American Conference on the Regulation of Automotive Traffic, RESOLVES:

"To recommend that the question of uniform danger, restriction and direction signs be given preferential consideration by the Pan American Union, in cooperation with the Pan American Confederation for Highway Education and other interested bodies, and that this subject be submitted for the consideration and approval of the delegates to the Third Pan American Highway Congress." [22]

The signing of the Convention and the adoption of the foregoing resolution completed the work for which the Conference was convened. In declaring the Conference adjourned, the Chairman spoke as follows:

"The signing of the Convention today by the delegates of the Pan American States, establishing uniform regulations of international highway use, marks an important practical step in bringing the peoples of those countries into closer relations and understanding through the medium of modern motor transportation. The countries whose representatives have signed the Convention have said to each other, in effect, 'The gate at the frontier is open; the latch-string is out.'

"During the past few years, the efforts of leading men of the various Pan American countries have been devoted to the stimulation of highway building, which will offer to all the advantages in social and economic ways that grow out of the opening of modern highways and the flow of modern motor traffic. Through long and patient effort upon the part of these men, devoted to these highways of friendship, this Convention has been evolved, which represents a large measure of progress toward the ultimate development of widespread modern highway transportation facilities connecting the Pan American States, and it is a vital prerequisite to that end, because adequate highway transportation cannot be developed unless it is free from the influence of widely divergent regulations affecting the use of vehicles upon the highways connecting the various countries. There are countless matters of an intricate, technical, and practical nature that bear upon the operation of vehicles and the use of highways in a safe and effective manner, and it is no easy task to bring the minds of nineteen countries to agree upon uniformity. To accomplish that end, a large degree of concession and compromise is required. Probably no convention would ever have been agreed upon which would embody all the proposals that might have been put forward for the regulation and safeguarding of motor transportation and highway use. But in a fine spirit of consideration for the views of each other, the representatives of the signatory states have come to an accord upon the minimum and essential requirements and have thereby made possible this Convention. This Convention, therefore, represents a tremendous gain for those countries, not only in the economic and social advantages toward which its operation will assist, but in a larger sense, it is a demonstration of enduring valuable friendships between the Pan American countries and peoples and of their willingness and eagerness to meet upon the common ground of practical affairs in the interests of closer acquaintance and understanding. The Convention is indeed a tangible and practical affair that reduces to concrete terms the real intent of the Pan American countries to cooperate for the mutual benefit of their peoples in making modern highways and motor transportation available to all of them.

"Under the auspices of the Pan American Union and through the

---

[22] Held at Santiago de Chile, January 11–19, 1939; *Tercer Congreso Panamericano de Carreteras* (Santiago de Chile, Imprenta Universitaria, 1940).

agency of the Pan American Confederation for Highway Education the encouragement and promotion of modern highway building is proceeding rapidly with marked results in the Pan American countries. The signing of this Convention is tangible evidence on which to base the belief that in the not distant future those countries will be enjoying the advantages of modern highway transportation from one to the other without let or hindrance."

The discussions at the Conference were inspired by the utmost good will, and with a profound appreciation of the significance of the subject under discussion. The subject of highway construction has only within recent years received serious attention in any of the Republics of Latin America, but in that time rapid progress has been made in all the countries, and today every nation of the American Continent has a constructive program of highway expansion.

The Inter-American Highway

In the highway programs of the several countries one of the items of major importance is that of a road or system of roads that will connect all the Republics of the American Continent, and extend from the United States on the north to Argentina and Chile on the south—in other words, Inter-American Highways. Since the Fifth International Conference of American States adopted a resolution recommending the holding of a Pan American Highway Congress,[23] the subject of roads in the American Republics has received preferential attention at a number of international conferences. As already stated, a commission of Pan American highway engineers visited the United States in 1924 as guests of the Highway Education Board, to study highway construction, administration and finance as practiced in the United States. The outcome of this visit was the creation of the Pan American Confederation for Highway Education, which has ever since been an instrumental factor in promoting road construction on the American Continent. Two Pan American Highway Congresses have also been held, the First at Buenos Aires in October, 1925,[24] and the Second at Rio de Janeiro in August, 1929.

At both of these Congresses, approval was given to the idea of an Inter-American Highway or system of highways that will connect the countries of the Western Hemisphere. As a practical step in the fulfillment of this plan, particularly that portion extending from Panama northward to the United States, an Inter-American Highway

[23] *Report of the Delegates of the United States of America to the Fifth International Conference of American States, Held at Santiago, Chile, March 25 to May 3, 1923, With Appendices* (Washington, Government Printing Office, 1924), pp. 14, 167–168.
[24] *Report of the Delegates of the United States [to the First] Pan American Congress of Highways, Buenos Aires, October 5–16, 1925* (Washington, Government Printing Office, 1927).

Conference met at Panama in October, 1929, with representatives in attendance from Panama, the Republics of Central America and the United States. At that time an Inter-American Highway Commission was created, to be composed of members appointed by the several Governments. Prior to that time, and as a demonstration of the interest of the Government of the United States in the construction of an Inter-American Highway, the cooperation of engineers of the Bureau of Public Roads of the Department of Agriculture had been offered to any Latin American Republic which might request such cooperation through the Pan American Union. Subsequently an appropriation of $50,000 was made available by the Congress of the United States to provide for such cooperation. Pursuant to requests from a number of the Central American countries for assistance in locating the route of the Inter-American Highway through their respective countries, engineers of the Bureau of Public Roads have been sent to Panama for the purpose of establishing an office and making the necessary preparations to undertake reconnaissance surveys to determine the most feasible route of the Inter-American Highway.[25] It is expected that the Inter-American Highway Commission created by the Conference which met at Panama in October, 1929, will meet shortly at Panama to discuss questions connected with the reconnaissance surveys.

An evidence of the interest of all the Republics of the Continent in the Inter-American Highway or system of highways was afforded at the Conference on the Regulation of Automotive Traffic, at which an informal conference of all the delegates was arranged after the Convention had been formally signed. The purpose of this informal gathering was specifically to discuss the question of the Inter-American Highway. After a lengthy exchange of views, in which Mr. Thomas H. MacDonald of the United States Bureau of Public Roads, who has been an earnest worker in this whole movement, explained the central organization that has been established for the prosecution of the work, the following resolution was submitted and unanimously adopted:

"Whereas, the representatives of the various Governments, members of the Pan American Union, who are attending the Sixth International Road Congress at Washington and who have just signed a Convention covering the regulation of international motor traffic between those countries, now wish to record their approval of the work already begun in furthering the realization of the great Pan American system of highways; be it

RESOLVED, That they urge the Pan American Union and the Pan American Confederation for Highway Education to proceed as expeditiously as possible with the work recommended by the Road Conferences of Buenos Aires, Rio de Janeiro and Panama, and

[25] See pp. 279 ff.

further, that they pledge their support to all activities leading toward the early realization of the great Pan American system of highways."

The extension of the system of highways in the Republics of the American Continent should prove of great importance in the development of international automotive traffic between the several Republics, and emphasizes the need of adequate regulations to govern the movement of such traffic. It is felt, therefore, that it is a matter of paramount importance to the United States, which will be the recipient of a large proportion of this international highway traffic, that the Convention signed at Washington on October 6th, 1930, receive the favorable approval and ratification of the Government of the United States.

Respectfully submitted, J. WALTER DRAKE

[WASHINGTON,] December 1, 1930.

THE CHACO DISPUTE BETWEEN BOLIVIA AND PARAGUAY [26]

Acceptance by Bolivia and Paraguay of the Uruguayan Formula for Carrying Out the Terms of the Conciliation Agreement of September 12, 1929 [27]

724.3415/923

The Chargé in Uruguay (Gade) to the Secretary of State

No. 957 MONTEVIDEO, December 12, 1929.

[Received January 2, 1930.]

SIR: With reference to the negotiations being carried on in Montevideo between the Bolivian and Paraguayan Ministers and the Uruguayan Minister for Foreign Affairs regarding the manner of exchanging Forts Vanguardia and Boquerón, I have the honor to report the following information.

The Bolivian Minister, Señor Diez de Medina, in a conversation on December 9th, informed me that his Government considered that the terms of the agreement should be carried out in the order in which these terms were set forth, namely, reëstablishment of the *status quo ante* in the Chaco before the renewal of diplomatic relations; and restoration of the buildings of Fort Vanguardia by Paraguay before the abandonment of Fort Boquerón by Bolivia. In this connection he declared that the Paraguayan Government held that one of the two designated Uruguayan officers should proceed to Fort Vanguardia and the other to Fort Boquerón, and that Bolivia should abandon the latter Fort upon the commencement of the work of restoration of the buildings of Fort Vanguardia by Paraguay. The Bolivian Government, on the contrary, believed that Fort Van-

---

[26] Continued from *Foreign Relations*, 1929, vol. I, pp. 818–933.

[27] For text of agreement, see telegram No. 50, September 12, 1929, to the Chargé in Bolivia, *ibid.*, p. 860.

guardia should first be restored and the two forts then exchanged simultaneously.

After an unsuccessful three-hour meeting held at the Foreign Office here on the 9th instant by the Uruguayan Minister for Foreign Affairs and the Bolivian and Paraguayan Ministers, the following self-explanatory statement (which I telegraphed to the Department)[28] was made by the Minister of Foreign Affairs:

(Translation) "In view of the position taken by the representatives of the contending parties, I thought it advisable to present in the name of the Uruguayan Government a formula of conciliation, which was submitted to the Paraguayan and Bolivian Governments for study. Certain objections were made by the latter, and many of the conclusions were rejected by the former.

"Tomorrow the Uruguayan Ministry of Foreign Affairs will submit for the consideration of the Governments of both countries a formula which is enlarged and in part revised, taking into consideration the desires of each in such a manner that without friction or injury to susceptibilities we might arrive at a definite agreement.

"This formula provides that the Uruguayan officers divide their tasks, one proceeding to Fort Vanguardia and the other to Fort Boquerón, where the latter will await the reconstruction of the structures destroyed in that military post. Upon completion of this, the Bolivians will take possession of Vanguardia and the Paraguayans of Boquerón on the same day.

"As the non-acceptance of this formula would signify a lack of good will, since there is only opposition to unimportant details, the Uruguayan Ministry of Foreign Affairs in that event would withdraw from any further intervention. This would be most deplorable, for all the high aspirations of confraternity which have been manifested in the consideration of the problem and all the extensive work done to reach a happy solution in the meetings of the neutrals held in the United States capital would fall to the ground.

"The discrepancies consist, I repeat, in slight details regarding the form in which the evacuation of Boquerón and the delivery of Vanguardia should be carried out. Our Government understands that as a proof of friendship and as the first act of a new era of peace this should be effected simultaneously.

["]It is to be hoped that the Uruguayan proposal will be accepted, since on the contrary it would mean a return to the moment of the beginning of the conflict, and this would be a constant menace to continental harmony."

The Bolivian Minister informed the press that his Government would accept the proposal of the Uruguayan Government. The Paraguayan Minister declined to comment, merely declaring that he was duly forwarding the proposal to Asunción.

I shall not fail to keep the Department fully informed of future developments in the matter.

GERHARD GADE

---

[28] Telegram No. 56, December 10, 1929. noon, *Foreign Relations*, 1929, vol. I, p. 862.

724.3415/925 : Telegram

The Chargé in Uruguay (Gade) to the Secretary of State

MONTEVIDEO, January 3, 1930—1 p. m.
[Received 1 : 30 p. m.]

2. My telegram number 56, December 10, noon.[29] The Minister for Foreign Affairs today informed me that in view of the Paraguayan Government's continued refusal to accept the Uruguayan formula for carrying out the terms of the Washington protocol,[30] which has been accepted by Bolivia, the Bolivian Government recently declared that it would break off negotiations here. Uruguayan Minister for Foreign Affairs has requested the Bolivian Government to postpone such action for a couple of weeks in order that an attempt might be made to induce Paraguay to accept the formula.

Uruguayan Minister for Foreign Affairs is sending Sampognaro, Uruguayan member of the Brazilian-Uruguayan boundary commission, to Asunción tomorrow on a special mission. He is to urge Paraguayan Minister for Foreign [Affairs?] to cooperate in preventing break-down of the negotiations which would mean the collapse of all the work accomplished at Washington.

In this connection the Minister for Foreign Affairs expressed the hope that the Government of the United States would make similar representations to Paraguay.

GADE

724.3415/925 : Telegram

The Acting Secretary of State to the Chargé in Uruguay (Gade)

WASHINGTON, January 6, 1930—5 p. m.

5. Your 2, January 3, 1 p. m. Department has cabled the substance of your message to the Legation at Asunción [31] outlining also the Uruguayan formula as contained on page 3 of your despatch No. 957 of December 12 and then instructed the Legation as follows:

"You may say to the Minister for Foreign Affairs that this Government considers that the Uruguayan proposal offers a practicable solution of the difficulty and that it feels sure the Paraguayan Government would not wish to have the negotiations break down when a practicable solution is offered. This Government therefore hopes that Paraguay will find it possible to accept the proposal offered by the Uruguayan Government."

You may so advise the Uruguayan Minister for Foreign Affairs.

COTTON

---

[29] *Foreign Relations,* 1929, vol. I, p. 862.
[30] Reference is to the conciliation agreement of September 12, 1929; for text, see telegram No. 50, September 12, 1929, to the Chargé in Bolivia, *ibid.,* p. 860.
[31] Telegram No. 1, January 6, 5 p. m.; not printed.

724.3415/937 : Telegram

The Minister in Paraguay (Kreeck) to the Acting Secretary of State

Asunción, January 8, 1930—9 a. m.
[Received January 9—1 a. m.]

3. In my despatch 976, December 23rd,[32] the difficulties arising at Montevideo between Paraguay and Bolivia are outlined, and mention was made that the Foreign Office has in preparation an official note dealing with these. This morning I received the note accompanied by copies of the following official correspondence:

First, memorandum Bolivian proposals;
Second, memorandum Paraguayan proposals;
Third, the Uruguayan formula;
Fourth, modifications requested by Bolivia;
Fifth, proposal offered by Paraguay;
Sixth, Bolivian refusal;
Seventh, new proposal by Paraguay.

Copy of note and enumerated documents sent to the Department by air service. Quoting pertinent passages:

"I cherish the conviction that the Government of the United States seeing these documents will be well aware of the sincere respect which Paraguay gives to the terms of the protocol and of its decided disposition to fulfill them honorably. In the Conference of Montevideo the difficulty which has arisen consists in the exigency of Bolivia backed up by the Uruguayan Government that the work of reconstruction of Fort Vanguardia take place first; all that relates to the obligation in regard to Boquerón being suspended until that is all accomplished. The proposals made by the Paraguayan Government do not involve any provision of treaty for either interested parties."

Article number 5 of the conciliatory resolution [32a] is then quoted declaring Paraguay's position in complete harmony thereto.

"There is not in that diplomatic document (conciliatory resolution) a single word, a single concept from which there could be logically inferred the preference of one obligation over the other. It is desired unduly to transform a resolution of purely conciliatory character into a penal resolution."

The note closes by saying that Paraguay is working constantly to reach an understanding of equal treatment as evidenced by their proposals.

Kreeck

---

[32] Not printed.
[32a] Of September 12, 1929; see telegram No. 50, September 12, 1929, to the Chargé in Bolivia, *Foreign Relations*, 1929, vol. I, p. 860.

724.3415/925 : Telegram

The Acting Secretary of State to the Chargé in Uruguay (Gade)

WASHINGTON, January 9, 1930—6 p. m.

6. Department's 5, January 6, 5 p. m. Department's only information regarding Uruguayan formula is your despatch No. 957, December 12, and so transmitted it to the Legation at Asunción. The Minister there states that the Minister for Foreign Affairs insists that the Uruguayan formula as presented to the Paraguayan Government is not exactly in accord with the understanding outlined by the Department. Please obtain and cable text of Uruguayan proposal as made to Paraguay.

COTTON

724.3415/938 : Telegram

The Chargé in Uruguay (Gade) to the Acting Secretary of State

MONTEVIDEO, January 10, 1930—2 p. m.
[Received 4 : 08 p. m.]

5. Department's telegram No. 6, January 9, 6 p. m. The following is the text in full of the Uruguayan proposal to Paraguay as handed to me by the Minister for Foreign Affairs this morning:

1. Major X will proceed to Puerto Suarez, arriving at Fort Vanguardia where he will witness the restoration by Paraguay of the structures which existed at this fort on December 5, 1928. To this end Major X will make an inspection and obtain such prior information as he may deem necessary regarding the position, situation and conditions in which the building, materials, et cetera, of the said fort were on the date mentioned. When this information has been obtained and the inspection completed, Major X will so inform the Bolivian and the Paraguayan authorities in order that the latter may order the execution of the work. In order to carry out the work, the Paraguayan Government will have in readiness the personnel necessary to proceed with the reconstruction of the fort.

2. Major Y will proceed to Puerto Pinasco, arriving at Fort Boquerón where, at the time determined in the following paragraph, he will witness its abandonment by the Bolivian forces and its occupation by the Paraguayan forces. Major Y will obtain such prior information as he may deem necessary regarding the conditions in which Fort Boquerón was found upon being occupied by the Bolivian troops and proceed to make an appropriate inspection.

3. As soon as the restoration of Fort Vanguardia has been finished, Majors X and Y will agree upon the date on which the records of proceedings of the termination of the work at Fort Vanguardia and the abandonment of Boquerón shall be simultaneously and officially drawn up.

4. As soon as Fort Boquerón has been abandoned, Major Y will so inform commander of the nearest Paraguayan fort in order that the commander may order occupation."

GADE

724.3415/941 : Telegram

The Minister in Paraguay (Kreeck) to the Acting Secretary of State

[Paraphrase]

Asunción, January 13, 1930—3 p. m.
[Received January 14—3 : 54 a. m.]

6. The Uruguayan mission, convinced that its viewpoint regarding Paraguay was in error, accepted at this morning's conference the proposal offered by Paraguay, and a new arbitration agreement is now being drafted accordingly. The Uruguayan mission has telegraphed its Government stating that it favored acceptance in preference to former formulas. The mission and the Foreign Office of Paraguay are in complete accord.

KREECK

724.3415/959 supp. : Telegram

The Acting Secretary of State to the Minister in Paraguay (Kreeck)

Washington, January 30, 1930—6 p. m.

5. Department's 1, January 6, 5 p. m., and 4, January 27, 6 p. m.[33] Paraguayan Chargé d'Affaires showed Department today a telegram from his Government stating that it could not agree to the Uruguayan formula because it would create a very bad precedent if Paraguay should accept something that Bolivia wanted in order that Bolivia might accept some other suggestion. To do this Paraguay would continually have to give up its position on the theory that otherwise Bolivia would not cooperate in bringing about a settlement. You will please point out to the Minister for Foreign Affairs that this Government first suggested the acceptance of the Uruguayan proposal on January 6, and that the present supposed outbreak in the Chaco did not take place until January 20,[33a] hence there could be no connection between the two.

The Department suggested the acceptance of the Uruguayan proposal because it felt that that proposal offers a practicable solution of the difficulty; that a refusal to carry it out would bring about an impasse in the execution of the conciliation agreement signed by both Paraguay and Bolivia on September 12, last. Bolivia having accepted the Uruguayan suggestion, a refusal on the part of Paraguay might make the latter appear as refusing to carry out the conciliation agreement duly signed by it. Department therefore hopes that the Paraguayan Government will see its way clear to accepting the Uruguayan proposal. Please report by cable.

COTTON

[33] Neither printed.
[33a] See telegrams No. 7, January 22, 6 p. m., to the Chargé in Bolivia, and No. 3, January 24, noon, from the Chargé in Bolivia, p. 330.

724.3415/980a : Telegram

The Acting Secretary of State to the Minister in Paraguay (Wheeler)

[Paraphrase]

WASHINGTON, February 11, 1930—5 p. m.

7. The following is for the consideration of the Minister. It is the desire of the Department that you familiarize yourself as soon as possible with the Bolivia–Paraguay situation in the Chaco. Please report action taken on telegrams No. 1, January 6, 5 p. m.,[34] No. 4, January 27, 6 p. m.,[35] and No. 5, January 30, 6 p. m., and whether in your opinion there is a likelihood that Paraguay will now accept the Uruguayan suggestion. While this suggestion of Uruguay to carry out the conciliation agreement of September 12, 1929 is not accepted by Paraguay, Bolivia advances that as a reason for not considering the note sent by the neutral Governments to Bolivia on January 9 [36] with a view to bringing about a settlement of the basic question in dispute. It had been the hope of the Department that the Government of Paraguay would not feel that its objection to the Uruguayan proposal was of sufficient importance to allow it possibly to jeopardize a settlement of the Chaco question.

COTTON

724.3415/982 : Telegram

The Chargé in Uruguay (Gade) to the Acting Secretary of State

MONTEVIDEO, February 13, 1930—2 p. m.
[Received 3 : 30 p. m.]

7. My telegram No. 6, January 25, 6 p. m.[35] The Minister for Foreign Affairs today informed me that he has just received a letter from Paraguayan Minister for Foreign Affairs containing two formulas. One formula, which had already been rejected by both Uruguay and Bolivia, proposed that Boquerón be turned over to Paraguay before the completion of Vanguardia. This will not even be reconsidered. The other formula merely proposes that the Uruguayan Government appoint two army officers to proceed, with the consent of the Governments of Bolivia and of Paraguay, to Forts Vanguardia and Boquerón and to be present at the execution of the measures designed to restore the state of things which existed prior to December 5, 1928. As this is nothing more than a repetition of article 5 of the resolution of conciliation and completely ignores the whole dispute as to the manner of carrying out the protocol, the Uruguayan

---

[34] See telegram No. 5, January 6, 5 p. m., to the Chargé in Uruguay, p. 311.
[35] Not printed.
[36] See telegram No. 2, January 6, 5 p. m., to the Chargé in Bolivia, p. 327.

Minister of Foreign Affairs has telegraphed to the Paraguayan Minister of Foreign Affairs inquiring whether this is to mean that the Paraguayan Government consents to give the Uruguayan Government ample authority to carry out the terms of the protocol according to the Uruguayan formula. Sampognaro when in Asunción received some oral proposal to this effect, but the Uruguayan Minister for Foreign Affairs wishes a definite commitment in writing from the Paraguayan Minister for Foreign Affairs in order to prevent misunderstanding or possible later repudiation on the part of the Paraguayan Government.

GADE

724.3415/982 : Telegram

The Acting Secretary of State to the Chargé in Uruguay (Gade)

WASHINGTON, February 14, 1930—6 p. m.

10. Your 7, February 13, 2 p. m., repeated to Asunción. Please keep Legation there advised of all developments; it has been instructed to keep you informed.

You may say to the Minister for Foreign Affairs that the Department, through the Legation at Asunción and through the Paraguayan Chargé in Washington, has been constantly urging on the Paraguayan Government acceptance of the Uruguayan formula and it has suggested to the other neutral Governments that they do likewise. Please say to the Minister that the Department also feels that it would be very helpful if the Uruguayan Government would urge the Bolivian Government to accept one of the proposals made in the neutral Governments' communication of January 9th. This Government has done so and is informing the other neutrals thereof and is suggesting that they also could help the situation materially by making similar representations. Please cable action taken by Uruguay.

COTTON

724.3415/987 : Telegram

The Minister in Paraguay (Wheeler) to the Acting Secretary of State

ASUNCIÓN, February 15, 1930—3 p. m.
[Received February 16—3 : 34 a. m.]

22. Your telegram No. 7, February 11, 5 p. m. My informal call on the Minister for Foreign Affairs, preceding my formal reception by the President, developed into a prolonged conversation on the Chaco situation. I expressed the continued concern of my Government and its profound hope that peace would be maintained and he

repeated with the greatest earnestness that Paraguay had made every reasonable concession and desired nothing further so much as a quick settlement. The Legation lacks record of action taken on the Department's telegrams numbers 1, 4, and 5 of January 6th,[38] 27th,[39] and 30th, but he shows familiarity with them. As to telegram number 1, he states that the Department somewhat misunderstood the Uruguayan proposal which in fact provided not that the Uruguayan officers should divide their tasks but that they should proceed together, first to Vanguardia and then to Boquerón. As to telegram number 4, he remarked that the rains unfortunately would not prevent attacks on isolated outposts and that regarding reduction Bolivia's forces at certain forts it is the expectation that the troops withdrawn will be replaced by new. His point of view is that if the neutral commissioners did not contemplate simultaneous action neither is there any indication that they contemplated that Vanguardia should be restored before Boquerón. I believe this Government is too strongly committed to the principle of simultaneous action to yield this point. What could have been waived at the outset without great difficulty has become more difficult to yield since the agreement upon the new formula was reached here by the Uruguayan Special Mission and the Paraguayan Foreign Office. (See Legation's telegrams No. 6, January 13, 5 [*3*] p. m.; and 7 [*8*], January 15 [*19*], 8 a. m.; and despatch 982 of the latter date).[40]

This morning the Minister for Foreign Affairs informed me, in strictest confidence, the Uruguayan Foreign Office has now accepted this new formula but that in so doing it expresses the desire "that there be added to the Paraguayan formula the declaration that the Uruguayan Government shall retain complete liberty to give to its officials such instructions as it deems appropriate". To this he is at present disposed to object on the ground that proper liberty of action is given them by the terms of the agreement itself. Dr. Higinio Arbo, the newly appointed Minister to Uruguay, left for his post today. In the face of the rumors of continued activity of Bolivian patrols in the Vanguardia sector the Government here shows complete patience and calmness. The movement reported in the Legation's telegram number 16, January 24, 8 p. m.,[39] does not appear to be a wide one. A further telegram will be sent tomorrow.

Repeated to La Paz and Montevideo.

WHEELER

---

[38] See telegram No. 5, January 6, 5 p. m., to the Chargé in Uruguay, p. 311.
[39] Not printed.
[40] Telegram No. 8, January 19, and despatch No. 982, January 15, not printed.

724.3415/991 : Telegram

The Chargé in Uruguay (Gade) to the Acting Secretary of State

MONTEVIDEO, February 18, 1930—2 p. m.
[Received 4 : 05 p. m.]

8. Referring to the Department's telegram of February 14, 6 p. m., No. 10. I have today informed the Minister for Foreign Affairs as directed. He declared that he believes from various previous conversations with Bolivian Minister that the Bolivian Government would make no reply to the neutral governments' communication of January 9th until agreement has been reached with Paraguay regarding manner of exchanging forts. However, he agreed to make oral representations, as suggested by the Department, to the Bolivian Government tomorrow, pointing out that in case the negotiations here regarding fulfillment of Washington protocol should be unsuccessful it would be advisable to have a commission to fall back upon in order to prevent serious developments.

With reference to telegram of February 15, 3 p. m., from the Legation at Asunción to the Department, the Minister for Foreign Affairs again confirmed that Uruguayan proposal is, as transmitted in my telegram of January 10, 2 p. m., No. 5, namely, that one officer should proceed to Vanguardia and one officer to Boquerón dividing their tasks. Since the restoration of Vanguárdia would take several weeks and the relinquishment of Boquerón only a few minutes, he did not see how more simultaneous action could be devised than as provided in the Uruguayan formula by which means the acts of proceedings of the completion of Vanguardia and the abandonment of Boquerón would be drawn up simultaneously.

The new Paraguayan Minister to Uruguay, Señor Arbo, is expected to present his credentials some time next week and bring with him a reply to the Uruguayan Minister for Foreign Affairs' last telegram.

Repeated to Asunción.

GADE

724.3415/1016b : Telegram

The Acting Secretary of State to the Chargé in Uruguay (Gade)

WASHINGTON, March 6, 1930—4 p. m.

11. The Bolivian Government's answer to the neutral Governments' note of January 9, was handed to Chargé d'Affaires at La Paz on the 25th ultimo.[42] The second paragraph reads as follows:

.   .   .   .

Then follows a résumé of the events from December 28, to date

---

[42] See telegram No. 16, February 27, 5 p. m., from the Chargé in Bolivia, p. 338.

including the incident of January 16, last,[43] and Bolivia's reasons why it cannot accept the so-called double arbitration. It reiterates Bolivia's adherence to the principle of arbitration and its willingness to arbitrate the present dispute once the extent of the territory to be submitted to the arbitrator is agreed upon. Note terminates with following paragraph:

.   .   .   .

You will note that this reply is favorable to a discussion of the matter between Bolivian and Paraguayan representatives in Washington as soon as the conciliation agreement of September 12, is carried out. It is the Department's understanding that the Minister for Foreign Affairs of Paraguay suggested to Sampognaro, the Uruguayan agent, that a protocol be signed in Montevideo which will be limited merely to designating the Uruguayan officers and the date of their departure for Boqueron and Vanguardia and will mention the commission's object quoting clause 5 of the Resolution of Conciliation of September 12. In proposing this statement to Sampognaro the Minister for Foreign Affairs for Paraguay stated that, "If the Uruguayan Government wishes the protocol to lay down in detail the procedure of the execution of the obligations, although this is unnecessary, the Paraguayan Government will be obliged to insist on its previous formula whereby on the day the work commences at Fort Vanguardia Bolivia will abandon Boqueron which will not be occupied by Paraguay until the work at Vanguardia terminates. The Uruguayan Government has those to choose from." The Department understands that Sampognaro expressed his preference for the former. Department feels that through the first proposal Paraguay in effect puts the matter back in the hands of Uruguay and thereby tacitly consents to have Uruguay proceed on the basis of the Uruguayan formula. The Conciliation Agreement of September 12, gave full latitude to Uruguay as to the manner of its execution. This freedom of action was somewhat trammelled by the recent negotiations but now that Paraguay accepts in its first formula to return to the exact wording of the Conciliation Agreement Department feels that a way out of the difficulty is now offered through the acceptance of the Paraguayan suggestion, which it presumes is acceptable to Bolivian representative in Montevideo as it is nothing more than a return to the Conciliation Agreement and that if the proposed protocol is promptly signed in Montevideo the Uruguayan Government could then proceed to send its officers to Boqueron and Vanguardia and carry out the provisions of the Conciliation Agreement through the repair of Vanguardia and the return of that Fort and Fort Boqueron to Bolivia and Paraguay respectively.

---

[43] See telegram No. 3, January 24 noon, from the Chargé in Bolivia, p. 330.

By this action Uruguay would contribute greatly to the establishment of permanent peace between the two countries by removing this obstacle to the discussion of the settlement of fundamental question at issue between Bolivia and Paraguay.

Please discuss the matter in this sense with the Minister for Foreign Affairs of Uruguay and report the results.

COTTON

724.3415/1019 : Telegram

The Chargé in Uruguay (Gade) to the Acting Secretary of State

MONTEVIDEO, March 10, 1930—10 a. m.

[Received 1:55 p. m.]

10. Department's telegram number 11, March 6, 4 p. m. I have duly discussed Paraguayan suggestion to Sampognaro with the Minister of Foreign Affairs and informed him of the Department's views thereon. He declared that in view of the words "with the consent of the Governments of Bolivia and of Paraguay" in article No. 5 of the conciliation agreement he did not consider that Uruguayan Government ever had such full liberty of action in carrying out the terms of the protocol. He believed that specific consent to the Uruguayan officers' instructions was necessary from Bolivia and Paraguay. While displaying keen interest in the Department's interpretation of article 5, he expressed doubt as to whether the two contending Governments and the neutrals' tribunal unreservedly agree as to the scope of Uruguay's authority and expressed regret that the protocol was not clearly defined.

The Minister for Foreign Affairs finally declared that he would propose to the Bolivian and Paraguayan representatives here that they make a declaration to the effect that they interpret article 5 of the conciliation agreement as permitting Uruguay to give the necessary instructions in the matter to its officers. If the Bolivian and Paraguayan Ministers accept this proposal, the Uruguayan Minister for Foreign Affairs will immediately instruct the officers to proceed to Boquerón and Vanguardia to assist in fulfilling the protocol according to the Uruguayan formula.

The Minister for Foreign Affairs promised to inform me of the results of his proposal.

Repeated to Asunción.

GADE

724.3415/1020 : Telegram

The Chargé in Uruguay (Gade) to the Acting Secretary of State

MONTEVIDEO, March 10, 1930—8 p. m.
[Received 10:47 p. m.]

11. My telegram 10, March 10, 10 a. m. Uruguayan Minister for Foreign Affairs has just informed me that, in lieu of proposing that the Bolivian and Paraguayan Ministers make a declaration interpreting article No. 5 of the conciliation agreement, he had deemed it preferable to make the following proposals this afternoon: That the Bolivian and Paraguayan Ministers sign a protocol to the effect that in accordance with article No. 5 of the conciliation agreement they thereby grant the Uruguayan Government authorization to give ample instructions to its officers with respect to the fulfillment of the terms of the Washington protocol.

Uruguayan Minister for Foreign Affairs also proposed that in this or in a second protocol the Bolivian and Paraguayan Ministers agree that their countries renew diplomatic relations by appointing Ministers on April 10th, transmitting the agreements through the Uruguayan Ministry of Foreign Affairs.

While both the Bolivian and Paraguayan Ministers expressed approval of these proposals, they wished to telegraph their Governments for and [*authorization?*] to conclude the agreement.

Minister for Foreign Affairs is highly optimistic that the protocol will be signed within a few days. He allowed me to read formula but declined to furnish copy of the text pending the Bolivian and Paraguayan replies as slight changes may be necessary.

Repeated to Asunción.

GADE

724.3415/1023 : Telegram

The Chargé in Uruguay (Gade) to the Acting Secretary of State

MONTEVIDEO, March 14, 1930—6 p. m.
[Received 10:32 p. m.]

12. My telegram No. 11, March 10, 8 p. m. The Minister for Foreign Affairs informed me this afternoon that the Paraguayan Government has accepted his proposal. A favorable reply from the Bolivian Government is expected at any time.

The following is the text of the proposed protocol, handed to me by the Minister for Foreign Affairs:

"For the purpose of hastening execution of the stipulations of the Bolivian-Paraguayan protocol signed in Washington, in accordance with the terms decided upon by the Commission of Conciliation, formed with a view to procuring a friendly solution of the conflict which occurred in the Chaco Boreal, the Governments of both countries agree to accord Uruguay ample authority to give instructions to the officers whom it is good enough to designate, in accordance with article No. 5 of the said resolution, in order to fulfill the provisions of the agreement concluded in September, 1929, determining therefor the procedure in conformity with the conditions and the context of the same.

In view of the friendly suggestions proposed by the Government of Uruguay, the Governments of Paraguay and Bolivia resolve to fix April 10th next as the date for the effective reestablishment of diplomatic relations between one another, designating the respective chiefs of mission.

The Uruguayan Ministry of Foreign Affairs is requested to obtain from the two Governments the agreements for the appointment of the persons who are to take charge of the respective missions."

Repeated to Asunción.

GADE

724.3415/1031 : Telegram

The Chargé in Uruguay (Gade) to the Acting Secretary of State

MONTEVIDEO, March 22, 1930—11 a. m.
[Received 1:35 p. m.]

13. Department's telegram No. 14, March 21, 5 p. m.[44] Protocol has not yet been signed. As the Minister for Foreign Affairs has been ill the last few days I have been unable to see him. Bolivian Minister informed me this morning that his Government has authorized him to sign protocol but amending it to fix May 1 instead of April 10 as the date for the renewal of diplomatic relations between Bolivia and Paraguay.

I believe delay in signing is due either to the illness of the Minister for Foreign Affairs or to possible desire of the Paraguayan Minister to refer question of the changed date to his Government.

Repeated to Asunción.

GADE

724.3415/1033 : Telegram

The Chargé in Uruguay (Gade) to the Acting Secretary of State

MONTEVIDEO, March 27, 1930—2 p. m.
[Received 4:23 p. m.]

17. My telegram number 13, March 22, 5 p. m. [*11 a. m.*]. The Minister for Foreign Affairs informed me today that owing to slight changes in wording of the draft of protocol as accepted by Bolivia,

---

[44] Not printed; it asked whether the Bolivia-Paraguay protocol had been signed and if not, the cause of the delay.

Paraguayan Minister, although admitting that texts were substantially the same, transmitted amended text to his Government 9 days ago for authorization to sign (see telegram March 20, 4 p. m., from the Legation at Asunción [45]). Uruguayan Minister for Foreign Affairs considers Paraguayan objection is made with a desire to repudiate former acceptance. He expressed keen disappointment and disapproval of Paraguayan attitude and declared that unless Paraguay accepted, his Government would make no further efforts in the matter.

Repeated to Asunción.

GADE

724.3415/1033 : Telegram

The Acting Secretary of State to the Chargé in Uruguay (Gade)

WASHINGTON, March 28, 1930—4 p. m.

15. Your 17, March 27, 2 p. m. Department sincerely hopes that a settlement between Bolivia and Paraguay will not be jeopardized by a quibble over wording. Department confidently hopes that the Government of Uruguay will not wish to imperil a settlement by taking any such categorical stand in the matter as last sentence of your telegram would seem to indicate.

Department does not understand why the formula was changed after it had been accepted by Paraguay. Paraguay accepted the Uruguayan formula and if Paraguay does not accept a modified form thereof Department hopes that the Uruguayan Government will not stand out for that change but will revert to original suggestion which was accepted by Paraguay and the Department understands by Bolivia also. Please clarify the situation.

COTTON

724.3415/1038 : Telegram

The Chargé in Uruguay (Gade) to the Acting Secretary of State

MONTEVIDEO, March 29, 1930—5 p. m.
[Received 9:11 p. m.]

20. Department's telegram 15, March 28, 4 p. m. I have just seen the Minister for Foreign Affairs who informed me that the Paraguayan reply was delivered to him by Arbo this morning. Paraguayan Government therein accepts proposed Uruguayan protocol with the Bolivian amendment as to the date in the following form:

"For the purpose of hastening the execution of the stipulations of the Bolivian-Paraguayan protocol signed in Washington, on Septem-

---

[45] Not printed.

ber 12, 1929, the Governments of both countries agree to accord the Government of Uruguay sufficient authority to give instructions or suitable rules of procedure to the officers whom it is to designate, in accordance with article No. 5 of the resolution, to be present at the fulfillment of the terms of the same, those instructions having to be in conformity with the provisions and text of the said resolution of September 12th.

The date accepted by the two Governments for appointing the plenipotentiaries shall be May 1st, next."

The Minister for Foreign Affairs declared that the Bolivian Minister found this entirely acceptable but insisted upon obtaining definitive authorization from his Government to sign.

Delay in receiving Paraguayan answer was due to Arbo's absence in Buenos Aires. Bolivian Minister confidentially expects favorable reply from La Paz.

The Minister for Foreign Affairs expressed a wish that the foregoing be kept confidential pending Bolivian acceptance.

Repeated to Asunción.

GADE

724.3415/1061

The Chargé in Uruguay (Gade) to the Acting Secretary of State

No. 1018   MONTEVIDEO, April 10, 1930.
                                                        [Received May 8.]

SIR: In confirmation of my telegram No. 25 of April 4 (1930) 5 p. m.,[46] I have the honor to report that the protocol according the Uruguayan Government sufficient authority to give its officers instructions with respect to carrying out the terms of Article 5 of the protocol of Washington and setting May first as the date for the renewal of diplomatic relations between Bolivia and Paraguay, was signed by the Bolivian and Paraguayan Ministers and the Uruguayan Minister for Foreign Affairs in Montevideo on the fourth instant.

Copies of the Spanish text of the protocol and an English translation thereof are enclosed for the information of the Department.

In this connection it will be observed that several slight changes in wording have been made in the protocol as finally signed.

As reported in my telegram No. 11, of March tenth, the Uruguayan Minister for Foreign Affairs on March tenth submitted to the Ministers of Bolivia and Paraguay a draft protocol (For text see my telegram No. 12 of March 14, 6 p. m.) providing that Bolivia and Paraguay grant the Uruguayan Government ample authority to give

[46] Not printed.

instructions to its officers with respect to the fulfillment of the terms of the protocol of Washington and fixing April 10, 1930, as the date for the renewal of diplomatic relations. This proposal was accepted by Paraguay on March 14th. On March 18th the Bolivian Government authorized its Minister to sign the protocol but with slight changes in wording and amending it to fix May first instead of April 10th as the date for the renewal of diplomatic relations. The Paraguayan Minister, Dr. Higinio Arbo, agreed that the changes in wording were immaterial but objected to the date May first as being too distant, and declared that he would have to submit the text of the Bolivian acceptance to his government.

In an interview on March 27th, the Uruguayan Minister for Foreign Affairs, Senor Dominguez, informed me that the Paraguayan Government had not yet replied . . . He felt that the date May first was not unreasonable in view of the fact that the ministers would need a short time to wind up their affairs before proceeding to their respective posts. While no objections to the wording had been received from the Paraguayan Government, Senor Dominguez had confidentially learned from the Uruguayan Chargé d'Affaires at Asuncion that such would probably be made. He expressed keen disappointment and disapproval over the Paraguayan attitude and informed me that if the Paraguayan Government did not accept, the Uruguayan Government would make no further efforts in the matter.

The *Diario del Plata*, a Nacionalista newspaper of Montevideo, on March 28th contained an editorial criticizing Paraguay for not replying. On the following day the Paraguayan Minister in an open letter answered that his government had sent a reply but owing to his absence in Buenos Aires it had not been delivered. He presented the Paraguayan acceptance with slight changes in wording to the Minister for Foreign Affairs the same day (My telegram No. 20, March 29, 1930).

As already stated, the protocol was duly signed on April fourth. After the ceremony, which was attended by the Minister for Foreign Affairs, the Bolivian and Paraguayan Ministers, the Uruguayan Under-Secretary of Foreign Affairs, the Chief of Protocol, General Ruprecht, Senor Sampognaro, the two majors assigned to proceed to the Chaco, and others; the Minister for Foreign Affairs and the Bolivian and Paraguayan Ministers requested me to express the warm thanks of their respective governments to my government for its friendly interest and assistance in the matter and for the services of its Chargé d'Affaires here.

I have [etc.] GERHARD GADE

[Enclosure—Translation]

Act of April 4, 1930, Signed on Behalf of Bolivia, Paraguay, and Uruguay

On April fourth, nineteen hundred and thirty, convened in the office of the Minister for Foreign Affairs of Uruguay, Don Rufino T. Dominguez, and in his presence, the Envoys Extraordinary and Ministers Plenipotentiary of Bolivia and Paraguay, Doctors Alberto Diez de Medina and Higinio Arbo, respectively, with the object of continuing the conversation begun on November thirteenth last, regarding the instructions which should be furnished the Uruguayan officers who in accordance with the fifth article of the resolution drafted by the Commission of Investigation and Conciliation Bolivia and Paraguay, should proceed to Forts Vanguardia and Boquerón, both diplomats declare that "with the purpose of hastening the execution of the stipulations of the Bolivian-Paraguayan protocol signed in Washington on September 12, 1929, the Governments of both countries agree: To accord the Government of Uruguay sufficient authority in order that it may give the instructions to the officers whom it is to designate, in accordance with Article 5 of the resolution, to be present at the execution of the terms of the same, those instructions having to be in conformity with the provisions and text of the above-mentioned resolution of September 12, 1929." Both diplomats further agree that in view of the friendly suggestions offered by the Government of Uruguay, the Governments of Paraguay and Bolivia resolved to fix the date of May first next for the effective renewal of diplomatic relations between both, designating the respective Chiefs of Mission, with the request to the Ministry of Foreign Affairs of Uruguay that it be good enough to obtain from the two Governments the *agréments* for the appointment of the persons who are to carry out the said duties. The Minister for Foreign Affairs thanks the Governments of Bolivia and Paraguay in the persons of their present worthy representatives, in the name of the President of the Republic, Doctor Juan Campisteguy, and in his own, for the proof of confidence shown to Uruguay. The Minister for Foreign Affairs also expresses in the name of the President of the Republic and in his own, their hearty congratulations to the Governments of Paraguay and Bolivia, as well as to the Ministers Doctors Higinio Arbo and Alberto Diez de Medina, on the agreement concluded, and very especially desires to put on record the good will evinced by both parties from the time this agreement was initiated, as the intention invariably inspired by the sincere desire to reach friendly solutions was shown in the Bolivian and Paraguayan points of view which were unfolded during the debate.

In faith of which and for due record, these presents are signed on the date above indicated, the Minister for Foreign Affairs ordering certified copies thereof to be furnished to the Ministers of Bolivia and Paraguay.

ALBERTO DIEZ DE MEDINA   HIGINIO ARBO   RUFINO T. DOMINGUEZ

724.3415/1088 : Telegram

The Chargé in Bolivia (Hibbard) to the Acting Secretary of State

LA PAZ, July 24, 1930—5 p. m.
[Received 6 p. m.]

51. I have been officially informed by the Acting Minister for Foreign Affairs that yesterday the final act in accordance with the Washington agreement was signed and that Forts Boquerón and Vanguardia were returned in the presence of Uruguayan officers.

HIBBARD

Acceptance by Bolivia and Paraguay of the Proposal of the Neutral Nations To Institute Direct Negotiations in Washington for the Settlement of the Basic Question [47]

724.3415/931a : Telegram

The Acting Secretary of State to the Chargé in Bolivia (Hibbard)

WASHINGTON, January 6, 1930—5 p. m.

2. Department's 72, December 6, 4 p. m. [48] The neutral Governments have agreed to present the note to Bolivia on Thursday, January 9. You will accordingly present the note on that date. The Mexican Government suggested a modification in the ninth paragraph of the note and this modification has been accepted by all the neutral Governments. Paragraph nine of the note transmitted in the Department's December 6, 4 p. m. should therefore be changed to read as follows: "Noting with pleasure that the Government of Bolivia expects to inform them of its acceptance of their offer of good offices, should the direct negotiations fail, the five Governments are glad to state their readiness to appoint at that time members to form a friendly neutral Commission whose good offices it hopes will be of service to the two Governments concerned. In the meantime, in order that their services may be more easily available to the two contending Governments, they take pleasure in stating that they are willing that their diplomatic representatives in Washington keep in

[47] For previous correspondence concerning proposals for the settlement of the basic question, see *Foreign Relations*, 1929, vol. I, pp. 863 ff.
[48] *Ibid.*, p. 930.

touch with the situation as it develops in order that when proper they may be utilized for the organization of the Commission in question, which should be composed of delegates especially appointed thereto."

COTTON

724.3415/943 : Telegram

The Chargé in Bolivia (Hibbard) to the Acting Secretary of State

LA PAZ, January 14, 1930—4 p. m.
[Received 5 : 17 p. m.]

2. Department's telegram number 2, January 6, 5 p. m. I presented the note as instructed but I do not believe it will receive serious consideration from the President for some time due to the internal political situation. During the past two weeks the President has had continuous conferences with members of his own party and it now seems certain that in place of calling for elections he will endeavor to remain in office. No announcement has yet been made, as apparently he has not decided the exact method nor is he sure of the entire support of the army. There is a strong feeling against his continuance but the pressure is so great in his own party, which has no other candidate, in addition to his own ambition, that he has been persuaded. There is no way of making such a step constitutional. Should he in fact endeavor to continue in office there are certain to be political disturbances between now and May which, unless he can count on the entire army, he will be unable to control.[49] In any case they would seriously affect any negotiations over the Chaco question.

Meantime the Minister for Foreign Affairs and Abelli are prepared to accept the suggestion contained in penultimate paragraph of the last note of the neutral Governments and will attempt to persuade the President to this course when they can secure his attention. The delay of Paraguay in carrying out the provisions of the conciliation agreement signed in Washington[50] is playing into Siles' hand as it is being made to appear a national danger here and a strong reason to persuade the army for the continuance of the present administration.

HIBBARD

---

[49] See "Revolution in Bolivia," pp. 415 ff.
[50] See telegram No. 50, September 12, 1929, to the Chargé in Bolivia, *Foreign Relations,* 1929, vol. I, p. 860.

724.3415/951 : Telegram

The Minister in Paraguay (Kreeck) to the Acting Secretary of State

Asunción, January 21, 1930—10 a. m.
[Received January 22—7 a. m.]

11. The Minister for Foreign Affairs informs me that the Cabinet believes it necessary to notify League of Nations of the late Bolivian movement toward war, as neutrals unfortunately are to date without organization. He will advise therefore the Secretariat this morning.

KREECK

724.3415/953 : Telegram

The Chargé in Peru (Mayer) to the Acting Secretary of State

[Paraphrase]

Lima, January 22, 1930—3 p. m.
[Received 6 : 47 p. m.]

14. (1) When Mr. Robert Woods Bliss, Ambassador in Argentina, paid his respects to President Leguia, accompanied by me, the President spoke at considerable length regarding the Chaco dispute. He had been informed of the engagement in the Chaco which had resulted in a number of casualties and felt that this precipitated a most difficult and unfortunate situation. He several times repeated his considered opinion that the Government of the United States should take matters in hand and address the Governments of Bolivia and Paraguay very firmly to the effect that this situation must cease and that the questions involved should be settled by arbitration with plenary powers to determine all matters in dispute once and for all. The President observed, in this connection, that he was firmly of the opinion that despite newspaper reports and statements to the contrary and apparent attitudes dictated by local political consideration the Latin American Republics at heart believed that the United States of America was the one disinterested power capable of exercising a beneficent influence on Latin American affairs.

(2) President Leguia stated in continuation that if, as he considered not unlikely, an actual state of war resulted from present conditions in the Chaco, the prestige of the United States in Latin America, as well as in Europe, could not but suffer immeasurably. He added, that as the Government of the United States must know, he stood ready to give wholehearted support to any move we might make.

(3) Ambassador Bliss felt as I did that this conversation should be brought immediately to the attention of the Department.

MAYER

724.3415/945 : Telegram

The Acting Secretary of State to the Chargé in Bolivia (Hibbard)

[Paraphrase]

WASHINGTON, January 22, 1930—6 p. m.

7. Department's No. 5, January 20, 1 p. m., and No. 6, January 20, 6 p. m.[51] The Department has been receiving from Paraguayan sources reports which indicate the imminence of a general attack by Bolivian troops in the Chaco. Unless the result of the investigation which you are making in accordance with the Department's No. 5, January 20, 1 p. m., indicates that it would be inadvisable or inappropriate to do so, the Department desires you to express to the Government of Bolivia the very deep concern with which the Government of the United States has received numerous reports indicating that further armed conflict may occur in the Chaco and the confident hope of the Government of the United States that the reports regarding an imminent Bolivian attack on Paraguay are unfounded.

Report immediately any information obtainable regarding what is occurring in the Chaco.

COTTON

724.3415/956 : Telegram

The Chargé in Bolivia (Hibbard) to the Acting Secretary of State

LA PAZ, January 24, 1930—noon.
[Received 5 : 19 p. m.]

3. Department's telegram No. 5, January 20, 1 p. m.[52] and 7, January 22, 6 p. m. Official Bolivian communiqué states that on January 16 a squadron of 60 Paraguayan troops armed with machine guns attacked Bolivian observation post of 12 men north of Fort Boquerón dispersing them and killing one. Bolivian troops from Boquerón later repelled the attack. All blame for the aggression has been placed on Paraguay. The general opinion here, in which I concur, is that the attack was provoked by Bolivia on account of the internal political situation. As previously reported President Siles desires to continue in office. In order to postpone elections and justify such action a national emergency must be declared. An attack by Paraguay can be used as a pretext for such a declaration. Before the publication here on January 20 of news of the attack in the Chaco the Cabinet met and decided to call Congress for the purpose of declaring a national emergency. The reception of the news, however, was so apathetic in spite of attempts by the Government press to

---

[51] Neither printed.
[52] Not printed.

arouse public feeling that this decision has been temporarily suspended. President Siles now seems undecided as to his next move as the last has been too transparent even in Bolivia. The Nationalist Party and a large part of the army on which he must depend for continuance in office are strongly urging him to take further drastic action. The desire of the Military Party is obviously not altogether patriotic, as further military action in the Chaco requires money and the army is the first to be paid at all times. 250,000 bolivianos have already been drawn since January 16 from the extraordinary budget for the use of the army.

There are two Bolivian divisions scattered through the Chaco approximating 4,000 men. Much of the war material purchased from Vickers has been concentrated there. Five planes equipped with bombs have been ordered there from La Paz but have been unable to proceed due to weather and mechanical difficulties. It is admitted here that radio messages from the General Staff have been intercepted and deciphered by Paraguay. My opinion is that some of these were for use in case of further hostilities and that others were fabricated as a ruse. I do not think there is danger of further armed action by Bolivia immediately as the effect of the last has not been what Siles anticipated either here or abroad. However, troops in the Chaco are far from central control, communications are bad and hotheaded officers acting irresponsibly may precipitate trouble at any time.

With regard to the publication of the notes I believe that it would jeopardize Bolivia's acceptance of the good offices or of the suggestion contained in the last paragraph of the note of January 9 as it would be made to appear here that Bolivia was being forced; that the neutrals were in fact favorable to Paraguay and that Bolivia must stand alone. This might strengthen Siles' hand by concentrating opinion behind him.

In connection with this telegram please read the last paragraph of my telegram No. 76, October 2, 11 a. m.;[53] 2, January 14, 4 p. m.; and despatch No. 361, January 18.[53]

HIBBARD

724.3415/954 : Telegram

The Chargé in Switzerland (Moffat) to the Acting Secretary of State

BERNE, January 24, 1930—4 p. m.
[Received January 24—2 : 40 p. m.]

10. Drummond [54] last night repeated by telegraph to the Governments of Bolivia and Paraguay and to all members of Council the

---

[53] Not printed.
[54] Sir Eric Drummond, Secretary General of the League of Nations.

following message from Zaleski, Minister of Foreign Affairs of Poland:

"Concerned at news regarding Chaco Boreal. Requesting you in my capacity Acting President of the Council of the League of Nations to recall to Bolivian and Paraguayan Governments that after the session of December 1928, the then Acting President of the Council, Aristide Briand, and last September the League Assembly, congratulated the two noble nations on having adopted a pacific procedure for the settlement of their dispute in conformity with the undertakings of the Covenant. I believe I am interpreting the feeling of the Council and of the whole League of Nations in requesting you to express to both Governments our confidence that no serious incident will compromise success of pacific procedure in progress."

MOFFAT

724.3415/956 : Telegram

The Acting Secretary of State to the Chargé in Bolivia (Hibbard)

WASHINGTON, January 25, 1930—1 p. m.

9. Your 3, January 24, noon. You do not state whether you made the representations authorized in the first paragraph of the Department's 7, January 22, 6 p. m., and if so the reaction of Bolivian Government. In view of your statement that you concur in the opinion, which you state is general in La Paz, that the attack was provoked by Bolivia on account of the internal political situation, the Department desires you to call at once on the Minister for Foreign Affairs and tell him that the Department has been watching the situation developing in the Chaco with much concern and that it feels sure that Bolivia will not desire a renewal of hostilities there which cannot be of benefit to either country but is bound to react disastrously on both countries and that this Government therefore earnestly hopes that the Bolivian Government will find it possible to accept now one of the suggestions made by the neutral governments in their note of January 9. Please cable immediately result of your representations.

The Department considers the situation serious and wants to impress upon you the importance of following it closely and of keeping the Department promptly and frequently advised of all developments.

COTTON

724.3415/962 : Telegram

The Chargé in Bolivia (Hibbard) to the Acting Secretary of State

LA PAZ, January 27, 1930—noon.
[Received 5:05 p. m.]

4. Department's telegram No. 9, January 25, 1 p. m. I spoke to the Minister for Foreign Affairs this morning at 10, not having been able to see him yesterday. I repeated to him the contents of the telegram under acknowledgment and left with him an *aide-mémoire* in the same sense. I stated that the present seemed a most propitious time to accept one of the suggestions made by the neutral Governments and that such action would place Bolivia in a most favorable light. He replied that the Bolivian Army was under the complete control of the Government and that there was no danger of any hostilities on the part of Bolivia. Orders had been sent to all contingents in the Chaco to be ready to repulse any attack but to provoke or make none. All alarming messages had been sent out by Paraguay to prejudice the situation and for reasons of internal politics. The Bolivian War Office also had intercepted Paraguayan messages which could be made to appear equally damaging but the Bolivian Government refused to publish them. He stated that he attached no importance to a brief encounter of patrols in a disputed territory as it had been common all over the world where such conditions existed. The agitation of Paraguay was due to the fear that Bolivia would make reprisals as she had done in the case of Boquerón. This fear was unfounded as Bolivia would maintain peace but was prepared to repel any aggression.

I asked if the Bolivian Government had as yet had time to study the note of the neutral Governments of January 9. He replied that it had not as the results of the representations of the Uruguayan Government relative to the completion of the terms of the conciliation agreement were being awaited. I asked if the present incident would further delay consideration of the note and he agreed.

The press is strictly censored but the tone has been very moderate in the last few days. The public is not excited. Business circles are exerting pressure against military action because of the already depressed financial condition. Siles has not yet announced his plans but as elections must be called according to the electoral law on February 2nd some announcement may be made this week.

Two Vickers vespa [*bombing?*] planes have reached Santa Cruz and will probably go on to Puerto Suarez. Three Breguets are flying south to the Pilcomayo but have not arrived.

HIBBARD

724.3415/962 : Telegram

The Acting Secretary of State to the Chargé in Bolivia (Hibbard)

WASHINGTON, January 28, 1930—3 p. m.

11. Your 4, January 27 noon. Second paragraph. There is no connection whatsoever between the Uruguayan proposal for the exchange of Forts Vanguardia and Boquerón [58] and the suggestions of the neutral Governments for a settlement of the fundamental question at issue between Bolivia and Paraguay. Neither is dependent upon the other. Please call this to the attention of the Minister for Foreign Affairs in reply to his statement that the Bolivian Government has not yet studied the neutral note as it is awaiting the results of the representations of the Uruguayan Government relative to completion of the terms of the conciliation agreement. Cable result.

COTTON

724.3415/975 : Telegram

The Chargé in Bolivia (Hibbard) to the Acting Secretary of State

LA PAZ, February 1, 1930—noon.
[Received 2:45 p. m.]

8. My telegram No. 5, January 30, 10 a. m.[59] In spite of President Siles' statements and promises he has not yet considered the note of January 9. I have used every argument I can muster . . . The Minister for Foreign Affairs is in favor of acceptance but is unable to persuade the President. Public opinion as far as I am able to ascertain is also in favor. The President is still so occupied with the internal political situation that he can think of nothing else. What he will do is still a matter of conjecture. He leaves tomorrow for Potosi and will be away a week. There is no chance that the note will be considered until after his return. The situation in the Chaco appears to be quiet and there has been no further troop movement there. Three Breguet planes have now reached Villazon.

HIBBARD

---

[58] See pp. 309 ff.
[59] Not printed.

724.3415/994

The Brazilian Ambassador (Gurgél do Amaral) to the Acting Secretary of State [60]

AIDE MÉMOIRE

The Brazilian Government have adopted the invariable method of not assuming in the Bolivian-Paraguayan controversy any ostensible role. The Government are of the opinion that the Brazilian contribution to a pacific settlement of the dispute between the two neighbors will be more efficient as a result of our unassuming attitude in the matter. Such attitude allows Brazil to speak frankly both to Bolivia and Paraguay, as well as to the other intervening friendly countries, with the most perfect cordiality, without even the semblance of any suspicion or giving cause to misplaced interpretations. The Brazilian Government, whenever approached by Bolivia and Paraguay, in informal conversations, have always tried to support the diplomatic action of the United States Government. This has been done recently in conversations with Bolivia.

We deem it proper that our feelings in the matter should be known by the United States Government although we are convinced that any amount of success to which we could be a factor derives precisely from the fact that we do not actually intervene for reasons of neighborhood and on account of recent Treaties, which are well-known, so as to place us entirely without the range of the slightest appearance of urging for ourselves any attitude of evidence.

In bringing our views to the knowledge of the United States Government in an informal conversation, it is our desire, for the sake of historical truth, as well as in a testimony of the friendly interest we attach to the actions of the enlightened and friendly diplomacy of the United States in the pending controversy between Bolivia and Paraguay, to acquaint the Government in Washington with our views and to express that our action, no matter how quiet it has been and in fact is, finds its efficiency in our sincere wishes for the success of the diplomatic action of the United States in the Bolivian-Paraguayan controversy.

WASHINGTON, February 8, 1930.

---

[60] Handed to the Acting Secretary of State by the Brazilian Ambassador, February 10, 1930.

724.3415/983 : Telegram

The Chargé in Bolivia (Hibbard) to the Acting Secretary of State

LA PAZ, February 13, 1930—noon.
[Received 3:20 p. m.]

12. My telegram No. 8, February 1, noon. The President returned from Potosi Tuesday after what the Government newspapers call a triumphal reception. He has not taken up the matter of the neutral note either during his absence or since his return.

A [The] Nationalist Party has issued a manifesto containing the following statement:

"The Nationalist Party unanimously, with the sole exception of its founder, Dr. Hernando Siles, who has not yet been convinced, believes that, in view of the grave international situation provoked by Paraguay and the present chaotic state of internal politics, it is of the greatest public advantage in order to prevent anarchy and maintain peace which will assure the external defense of the country to execute a legal extension of the Presidential term of Dr. Siles until the situation becomes normal and the Nationalist Government is able to advance its wide constructive program and national consolidation."

It is evident that the Nationalist Party intends to prolong the Presidential term and the reluctance of Siles is only a pretense. The party has recovered from the first fright produced by the repercussion of the last Chaco incident and will now carry out its original program. The press is more rigidly censored and the most restrictive measures have been taken against all who express any opinion against the administration or are even suspected of doing so. For this reason the Republican Party has temporarily abandoned its convention to choose a Presidential candidate and it will probably never be held.

I believe the President will continue to delay consideration of the last neutral note since the principal reason for his continuance in office is the grave international crisis provoked by the alleged Paraguayan attack and any acceptance of good offices on his part would be construed as weakening his party's position.

Although in urging him to accept I have always pointed out that the United States is only animated by a friendly desire to see this old controversy amicably settled, I am constantly confronted with the expressed or implied feeling that the United States is exerting pressure for reasons of its imperialistic South American policy. As far as I can learn I am the only representative in La Paz who has urged acceptance. Would it be possible to suggest to the other neutral Governments that their representatives also be instructed to keep this matter actively before the President?

HIBBARD

724.3415/994

The Acting Secretary of State to the Brazilian Ambassador
(Gurgél do Amaral)

WASHINGTON, February 19, 1930.

EXCELLENCY: I have duly noted Your Excellency's *Aide Memoire* of February 3 [*8*], 1930, setting forth the views of the Government of Brazil with respect to the Bolivia–Paraguay question.

Your Excellency may be assured that the Government of the United States highly appreciates the friendly interest and cordial attitude which the Government of Brazil has maintained toward the efforts made by this Government and the friendly Governments associated with it to bring about a settlement of this controversy.

Accept [etc.]   For the Acting Secretary of State:
FRANCIS WHITE

724.3415/999 : Telegram

The Chargé in Bolivia (Hibbard) to the Acting Secretary of State

LA PAZ, February 25, 1930—6 p. m.
[Received 7 p. m.]

13. My telegram No. 12, February 13, noon. The Minister for Foreign Affairs has been ill in bed for the past 10 days. The Under Secretary for Foreign Affairs informs me that a special Cabinet meeting had been called to draft an answer to the note of the neutral Governments of January 9, but that it has been postponed until the Minister for Foreign Affairs is able to attend. As the President is well aware of the Foreign Minister's views, this in my opinion is only another excuse for delay.

Last night the central committee of the Nationalist Party and all departmental representatives met formally and unanimously declared themselves in favor of the continuance of the present administration, thus formalizing the manifesto previously circulated. All that is needed now is the President's consent which will probably be given within the next week. The delay is due to a desire to find some way by which such a step can produce a semblance of constitutionality or, failing that, to permit artificially stimulated propaganda make such a move appear to be the unanimous will of the people.

Conditions in the Chaco appear to be quiet. Two of the planes sent there are now out of commission. The floods are reported to be heavy.

HIBBARD

724.3415/1003 : Telegram

The Chargé in Bolivia (Hibbard) to the Acting Secretary of State

LA PAZ, February 27, 1930—3 p. m.
[Received 7 p. m.]

15. My telegram No. 14, February 26, 5 p. m.[63] The President in his conversation with me last night stated that Bolivia accepted the proposal of the neutral Governments to begin conversations between the diplomatic representatives of Bolivia and Paraguay Embassies. In my opinion this is not clear in the note which I have now translated in full and am coding. He further stated that he had entire confidence in the justice of the United States but would naturally take every precaution to safeguard the rights of Bolivia.

HIBBARD

724.3415/1013 : Telegram

The Chargé in Bolivia (Hibbard) to the Acting Secretary of State

LA PAZ, February 27, 1930—5 p. m.
[Received February 28—6:10 p. m.[64]]

16. My telegram No. 14, February 26, 5 p. m.[63] The following is a translation of the reply of the Bolivian Government to the note of the neutral Governments dated January 9:

"La Paz, February 25, 1930.   Note number 134.

Sir: I have the honor to acknowledge receipt of your esteemed note dated January 9th, last, in which the Governments of the United States, Mexico, Colombia, Uruguay and Cuba refer to the communication addressed to them by the Government of Bolivia on November 13th, last,[65] with regard to the suggestion of good offices for the settlement of the Bolivian-Paraguayan controversy over the Chaco Boreal. In the note under reference, the Governments of the five neutral nations deem it justifiable to formulate some opinions regarding the scope of the negotiations initiated, making clear certain opinions in order to avoid ambiguous interpretations.

The motive that guides the neutral Governments to induce Bolivia and Paraguay to an immediate settlement of the dispute is a noble one, but the Bolivian Government nevertheless considers that to proceed logically both as a safeguard of her right, of the promise given, and of the respectability of the extinct Commission of Conciliation at Washington, it is a primary matter before any exchange of ideas regarding the basis of the controversy to fulfill the decisions of the Commission of Washington.

---

[63] Not printed; in it the Chargé reported that he had just been handed Bolivia's reply to the note of January 9 from the neutral Governments.
[64] Telegram in two sections.
[65] See telegram No. 85, November 15, 1929, 6 p. m., from the Chargé in Bolivia, *Foreign Relations*, 1929, vol. I, p. 920.

When the unfortunate incident of the attack on Fort Vanguardia took place in December, 1928,[66] it was possible to avert a crisis through the Washington Protocol of January 3, 1929,[67] instituting the Commission of Inquiry and Conciliation. After a lengthy trial and a contradictory examination of facts, Bolivia and Paraguay subscribed to the conciliatory pact of September 12th, 1929, whose text establishes that the events of Vanguardia preceded those which took place in the Boquerón sector; that the use of coercive methods by Paraguay were responsible for reaction on the part of Bolivia; and as a consequence states that Paraguay must restore the buildings of Vanguardia and Bolivian troops abandon Fort Boquerón.

Having circumscribed the authority of the Commission at Washington to the procedure of investigation of the events of the Chaco at the end of 1928, excluding study and judgment of the territorial controversy, by clause 9 of the protocol of January 3rd, 1929, will it be practicable to initiate discussions of the case if the resolutions, the subject of its exclusive jurisdiction, have not been fulfilled?

In the course of the lengthy debate over the ownership of the Chaco, Bolivia has shown her desire to find just solutions. She has subscribed to pacts and submitted herself to procedure which prove it. Recent incidents in themselves are an unquestionable proof of her sincere desire to disentangle the difficulties. On January 16th of the current year an unfortunate incident took place on the Bolivian-Paraguayan military frontier; a patrol of Paraguayan soldiers, composed of 60 men armed with machine guns fired on and scattered a small Bolivian detachment in the neighborhood of Boquerón, causing one death. This new aggression is inexplicable at a time when peace was asserting itself, and proves the deliberate intention of Paraguay to rebel against the conciliation pact of Washington and to frustrate an agreement to which the good faith of the contending parties and that of the supreme authority of the neutrals intervening therein, was bound. Paraguay and Bolivia almost simultaneously carried their complaints to the League of Nations. My Government did so because Bolivia, as a signatory to the Treaty of Versailles, has certain international legal obligations to the League. Faithful to her pacifist traditions, she agreed to form part in [of] an organism destined to banish acts of violence in the intercourse of nations, to raise amongst them the empire of justice and to solve their difficulties by the conciliatory methods proclaimed by the rights of peoples.

The Ministry in my charge has noted with most [much] interest and attention the contents of the aforementioned note from Your Excellency, dated January 9th, and is pleased to express satisfaction with the statements contained therein, to the effect that the procedure of double arbitration to determine first the territory under dispute and on that basis to pronounce judgment later on the boundary question itself, is discarded. Bolivia only reaffirms the reserve with which she signed the general treaty of arbitration of January 5th of last year,[68] confirming the precedent established in the conferences of Buenos Aires[69] when the Bolivian delegation made known their

[66] See *Foreign Relations*, 1928, vol. I, pp. 680 ff.

[67] *Ibid.*, 1929, vol. I, p. 835.

[68] *Ibid.*, p. 653.

[69] See *ibid.*, 1928, vol. I, pp. 673–678; also *Proceedings of the Commission of Inquiry and Conciliation, Bolivia and Paraguay, March 13, 1929–September 13, 1929* (Washington [1929]), pp. 265 ff.

refusal to accept double arbitration, definitely suggested by the Paraguayan delegation.

Bolivia on different occasions in her history has shown her enthusiasm for and faith in the international institution of arbitration and in spite of the fact that numerous authors of treatises on international law agree that controversies affecting the honor or sovereignty of nations cannot be subject to arbitration, entrusted to the judgment of friendly nations differences of territorial sovereignty. At present, in her dispute with the Republic of Paraguay, not only does she agree but has definitely decided to resort to those means. But her adherence to the principles of arbitration cannot reach the extreme of submitting territorial zones, unquestionable part of the national patrimony, to the decision of third parties, although she greatly appreciates their probity and Pan American spirit, as in the case under reference, she has particular satisfaction in doing.

Neither the nation nor the Bolivian Government could accept such an arbitration, nor in general terms could any Bolivian public servant be capable of undertaking such a great responsibility.

Concerning territorial sovereignty, that is to say of the country itself, it is not possible in any way to leave to an unrestricted judgment the determination of the territory under litigation. Bolivia cannot follow blindly, without previously knowing what territory she delivers to the judgment of the arbitrators, or without establishing this as a basis first in an absolute and undoubted manner.

In the Gutierrez-Diaz Leon protocol,[71] Bolivia and Paraguay agreed that the parties 'would determine the exact zone on which the judgment of [the] tribunal of arbitration, chosen by common accord, would be given.' Therefore, the direct negotiations were charged with determining in concrete form the boundaries of the territory under litigation, and on this basis previously decided, the tribunal of arbitration should pronounce judgment. But as it is possible that the determining of such a zone will be the obstacle which will defeat the negotiations, [the] Government of Bolivia, filled with a desire for a sincere agreement, has proposed a formula which takes into consideration not only equity but the historic tradition of the controversy. This arbitration, proceeding from the law of treaties, consists, as I made known to Your Excellency in my note of November 13th, in taking the middle point of the demarcation established in the three agreements signed between Paraguay and Bolivia in 1879, in 1887, and in 1894.[72] Those unfinished agreements form something in the nature of a visible mark showing the final compromise attained by the parties at different times and the opinion of the statesmen of both nations during the course of half a century of negotiations to arrive at a Bolivian-Paraguayan agreement.

From a historical point of view, as well as one of equity and respect for territorial right which within certain limits cannot be discussed, such a formula would supply the means which would make arbitration practicable.

---

[71] Signed April 22, 1927; for text, see despatch No. 275, April 29, 1927, from the Chargé in Argentina, *Foreign Relations*, 1927, vol. I, p. 316.

[72] For texts, see Paraguay, Ministerio de Relaciones Exteriores, *Paraguay-Bolivia, Tratados y Protocolos . . .* (Asunción, Imprenta Nacional, 1927), pp. 3–10.

The arguments stated above will justify before the enlightened opinion of the neutral nations the attitude of Bolivia which is making an effort to find an equitable solution of a litigation and the justice of the objections made to unlimited arbitration. As regards the latter, an antecedent which gives greater force to the argument is worthy of mention. The Commission of Conciliation at Washington, unable by article 9 of the protocol of January 3, 1929, to discuss the territorial side of the question, in a laudable endeavor to solve the litigation completely, proposed a compromise frontier line from Puerto Leda on the Paraguay River to Fort D'Orbigny on the Pilcomayo River. A careful examination of the suggestion shows that it possesses nothing in the nature of a compromise. To compromise means mutual renouncement and common sacrifice in pursuit of an ideal of concord. In this proposal summary [such a] course was only expected of Bolivia. Taking the line of the Quijarro-Decoud Treaty as a basis of comparison, Paraguay preserved her penetration in the Chaco authorized by it, but without granting to Bolivia an equivalent advance up to the mouth of the River Apa, the western line being granted to Paraguay. The compensations of a river coast were expressly denied to Bolivia, and she had to renounce about one and a half geographic degrees on the banks of the Paraguay River.

The so-called compromise line suggested does not take into consideration strict right nor conventional right which it destroys, nor even equity. It seriously impairs the situation of Bolivia, disposes freely of her territory without offering her the compensation of an equivalent fluvial territory. If such a suggestion had its origin in the heart of a Commission not empowered to examine the fundamental issue, what may transpire before an organization empowered by definite authority to exert its influence in the delineation of the territory which must be submitted to arbitration?

It is true that in order to remove any doubts, Your Excellency is good enough to state the right of each of the parties to retire from the negotiations should the formula of the understanding be unsatisfactory. My Government believes that such a step would seriously affect the authority of the neutral nations and the prestige of the country which might try it. The formula, though adverse to the one damaged by it, would establish a precedent which due to the strength of its high origin would weaken legal titles, jealousy defended, and the Government who would dissent from such opinions would appear refractory to the ideas of international concord.

These reasons, which will be appreciated to the full by the neutral governments, induce Bolivia to reaffirm irrevocably the reserves set forth in her note of November 13th, 1929, regarding the necessity to establish concrete grounds for the functioning of the Commission.

My Government wishes to place on record its gratitude for the generous and disinterested efforts made by the five neutral powers to solve the difficulties unhappily existing between Bolivia and Paraguay. Bolivia recognizes the lofty aims of the five sister nations. And it is thus that she receives with pleasure the suggestion to initiate conversations between the diplomatic representatives of Bolivia and Paraguay accredited to the Government of the United States. Notwithstanding the fact that for reasons foreign to Bolivia, Bolivian-Paraguayan relations have not yet been reestablished, my Government has the hope that as soon as the act of conciliation at Washington is executed, it will not be long before they are resumed. The practical means arrived at by the neutrals will probably lead us to the terms of an agreement. The conversations between the diplomats of Bolivia and Paraguay taking place in the quiet and propitious atmosphere of Washington, cooperating with those which will be begun in La Paz or Asunción, will give satisfactory results. My Government has faith and confidence in them and if they do not settle the territorial litigation itself, they will at least offer in concrete form the correct material upon which a subsequent arbitration may offer the last word.

Begging Your Excellency to convey to the knowledge of the Government of the United States of America the tenor of this note and to reiterate Bolivia's deepest gratitude for her laudable and generous effort, I have the honor to offer to Your Excellency the assurance of my distinguished consideration.

Signed F. Vaca Chávez."

HIBBARD

724.3415/1016a : Telegram

The Acting Secretary of State to the Chargé in Bolivia (Hibbard)

WASHINGTON, March 5, 1930—5 p. m.

16. Department feels that progress is being made and that the penultimate paragraph of the note of February 25,[73] coupled with the statement of the President reported in your 15, February 27, 3 p. m. and a similar statement made to the Department by the Bolivian Minister on the third instant means that Bolivia will, as soon as the conciliation agreement of September 12 is carried out, initiate direct negotiations in Washington, supplemented by similar negotiations in La Paz and/or Asunción. Please call on the President and express the gratification of this Government at the decision of the Bolivian Government in the premises. At the same time you may discreetly point out that (1) the settlement of the fundamental question at issue is not linked up with the conciliation agreement, and (2) the conciliation agreement offers no basis for delaying the establishment of diplomatic relations pending the settlement of the questions of Boquerón and Vanguardia.

In carrying out the above you will be very careful to avoid any appearance of pressure on Bolivia or of attempting to hasten it unduly in instituting direct negotiations in Washington.

For your information the Department interprets the recent statement of Paraguay as giving complete freedom of action to Uruguay and tacitly accepting the Uruguayan formula for carrying out the agreement of September 12, as regards Boqueron and Vanguardia. The Department is advising the Uruguayan Government of its views

---

[73] See telegram No. 16, February 27, 5 p. m., from the Chargé in Bolivia, *supra.*

in the premises and is suggesting that it proceed by sending its officers to the Forts in question. The Department hopes that this last obstacle to prompt initiation of direct negotiations will, therefore, soon be removed.

COTTON

724.3415/1018 : Telegram

The Chargé in Bolivia (Hibbard) to the Acting Secretary of State

LA PAZ, March 8, 1930—noon.
[Received 1 p. m.]

18. Department's telegram No. 16, March 5, 5 p. m. I spoke to the President this morning in accordance with the Department's instructions. He expressed great pleasure at the message and stated that he was sure direct negotiations in Washington were the most practical means to reach a satisfactory solution and that he could never have accepted another commission. He added that he was prepared to start these negotiations as soon as the conciliation agreement was fulfilled and that he would send Abelli to Washington as Counselor of Legation with full powers to conduct them.

HIBBARD

724.3415/1110 : Telegram

The Minister in Paraguay (Wheeler) to the Secretary of State

ASUNCIÓN, August 19, 1930—10 a. m.
[Received 3:10 p. m.]

67. My Bolivian colleague has received a telegram from his Foreign Office stating that the Government junta does not favor beginning the boundary conversations in Washington till after the installation of the civil government but that if the United States especially desires that they begin without delay the point will be yielded. He has so informed Zubizarreta.[74]

WHEELER

724.3415/1120 : Telegram

The Minister in Paraguay (Wheeler) to the Secretary of State

ASUNCIÓN, September 12, 1930—3 p. m.
[Received September 13—6:55 a. m.]

70. My telegram No. 65, August 14, 3 p. m.[74a] Zubizarreta has several times asked me if I have received any word from you giving your opinion as to the best time for the opening of the conversations at Washington.

WHEELER

[74] Paraguayan Minister for Foreign Affairs.
[74a] Not printed.

724.3415/1120 : Telegram

The Acting Secretary of State to the Minister in Paraguay
(Wheeler)

WASHINGTON, September 13, 1930—3 p. m.

22. Your 70, September 12, 3 p. m. Bolivian note of February 25, 1930,[74b] intimates readiness of that Government to undertake conversations with Paraguayan representative in Washington after the Conciliation Agreement of September 12, 1929, has been complied with. The Conciliation Agreement having now been fulfilled by the reestablishment of diplomatic relations between Paraguay and Bolivia and the exchange of forts, it would appear that the conversations may be entered into at any time convenient to the two Governments concerned. So far as this Government is concerned any time agreeable to Paraguay and Bolivia will be satisfactory to it. This is a matter which could perhaps best be discussed, in the first instance at least, directly between the Paraguayan and Bolivian Governments.

COTTON

BOUNDARY DISPUTES

Guatemala and Honduras [75]

714.1515/1068a : Telegram

The Acting Secretary of State to the Minister in Guatemala
(Whitehouse)

WASHINGTON, April 25, 1930—6 p. m.

47. The negotiations between Guatemala and Honduras have been carried on now for somewhat over three months in a spirit of friendliness but with little or no flexibility on the part of either delegation.[76] Both delegations apparently have very categoric and rigid instructions. While very considerable advance has been made, namely, tentative agreement on the line from Cerro Brujo to Cerro Mirador, progress beyond that point has been hampered by the unyielding position taken by both delegations under instructions from their Governments.

While the Honduran delegation for some time maintained an intransigent position in demanding the Rio Motagua from Rio Jubuco to the sea it now seems possible that they would consent to a line running from Cerro Mirador to Cerro Jubuco, to Cerro Morjá, to

---

[74b] See telegram No. 16, February 27, 5 p. m., from the Chargé in Bolivia, p. 338.
[75] Continued from *Foreign Relations*, 1929, vol. I, pp. 946–975.
[76] The conference was held in Washington, January 20–July 16, 1930; see *Informe del Doctor don Mariano Vasquez Sobre la Conferencia de Limites Celebrada en Washington, D. C., del 20 de enero al 16 de julio de 1930* (Tegucigalpa, Tipografia Nacional, 1930).

Plaza Playitas, to Plaza de las Quebradas, to Quebrada Grande, and from there the Motagua to the sea.

Should this line be acceptable to the Guatemalan Government it seems likely that the question could be settled very shortly. The Guatemalan delegation has rejected this line but has consented to its being submitted to the Guatemalan Government. You will therefore please take the matter up as soon as possible with the President, setting forth the matter to him fully, as outlined above, and inquire whether this line would be acceptable to the Guatemalan Government.

[Paraphrase.] Should Guatemala definitely reject this line you will then endeavor to have as much latitude as possible given to the Guatemalan delegation to arrive at a solution. You understand that while the Department would be glad should Guatemala accept this line, as it would result in a settlement of the question, yet the Department desires you carefully to avoid giving the impression that this line is one proposed by the Government of the United States. Confidentially it may be said that the Department rather expects this line to be rejected, and then a Guatemalan line of the Cordillera from Cerro Elencia to Cerro San Ildefonso and thence to the Rio Tinto and the Motagua to be rejected by Honduras. With more liberal instructions a definite line could be agreed upon somewhere in between the two. Telegraph Department the result of your conversation and any counterproposals or suggestions made by the President. [End paraphrase.]

COTTON

714.1515/1069 : Telegram

The Minister in Guatemala (Whitehouse) to the Acting Secretary of State

[Paraphrase]

GUATEMALA, April 28, 1930—noon.
[Received 7 : 11 p. m.]

56. Department's 47, April 25, 6 p. m. I have just seen the President and the Minister for Foreign Affairs; they reject definitely the line mentioned and they are also unfavorably disposed to White's [77] last suggestion of the Rio Tepescuintla. They, moreover, claim that Salazar has full powers and that Guatemala is making all the concessions. The only suggestion offered was the Minister's remark that the best procedure seemed to be to continue working on the frontier section by section.

I think they would, of course, accept White's line, but are afraid to concede anything even at the mouth of the Motagua until they know what further concessions will be necessary to reach a settlement,

---

[77] Presumably Francis White, Assistant Secretary of State.

the political consequences of which the President gave me the clear impression of being afraid of. They did not dispute my statement as to the worthlessness of the entire territory and the real value of a settlement.

WHITEHOUSE

714.1515/1078a : Telegram

The Secretary of State to the Chargé in Honduras (Merrell)

WASHINGTON, May 21, 1930—6 p. m.

24. Negotiations between Honduras and Guatemala have been carried on now for somewhat over four months in a spirit of friendliness but with little or no flexibility on the part of either delegation. Both delegations apparently have very categoric and rigid instructions. While very considerable advance has been made, namely, a tentative agreement on the line from Cerro Brujo to Cerro Mirador, progress beyond that point has been hampered by the unyielding position taken by both delegations under instructions from their Governments.

While the Guatemalan delegation for sometime has maintained an intransigent position in demanding the Merendon range from Cerro Elencia to the sea, it now seems possible that if Honduras is prepared to deal with the matter in a more liberal spirit, not maintaining an intransigent position on the lines it has heretofore taken, that Guatemala will consent to renounce its claim to a portion of the right bank of the lower Motagua River.

The Honduran delegates state that they are bound by very rigid instructions limited to listening informally to any proposals that are made. They are thus prevented from entering into any serious negotiations with a view to a settlement. The Department relied upon the statements of the Minister for Foreign Affairs to the Legation as set forth in your telegrams 114, 117, and 118, of November 26, 10 a. m., November 30, 11 a. m., and December 3, 6 p. m.,[78] respectively, as indicating that the Honduran delegates would have full powers to negotiate a settlement of this question. The Department therefore desires you to recall these statements very earnestly to the attention of the Honduran Government and say that it feels that the two Governments are now nearer a settlement than they have been in the past and that if it will give more latitude to its delegation not binding it to stand out for any particular line but authorizing it to enter into a full and frank discussion with the Guatemalan delegation and the Department it feels that a settlement can be reached. In this connection, I may say that the Guatemalan Government informed the American Minister in Guatemala that the Guatemalan delegate

[78] *Foreign Relations*, 1929, vol. I, pp. 972, 974, and 975.

has been given full powers. Please take this matter up actively with the President and Minister for Foreign Affairs and cable the results. Also cable any indication you may get as to concessions that Honduras would be willing to make to arrive at a settlement.

You will of course point out that this Government has no interest in the matter other than to help two friendly Governments arrive at a just settlement of their difficulty and this Government has been expending a great deal of time and effort for the last four months in an endeavor to bring about a satisfactory settlement. If the delegates of the two Governments, however, do not have ample authority to negotiate a settlement this Government's helpfulness in the matter is limited and an agreement under such circumstances is improbable.

[Paraphrase.] The following is strictly confidential. While the Honduran delegation did suggest a line running from Cerro Mirador to Cerro Jubuco, Cerro Morjá, Las Playitas, Las Quebradas, and thence to the Motagua at Quebrada Grande, following the Motagua thence to the sea, they have, nevertheless, very informally indicated in conversation to members of the Department that they might be willing to support a line from Cerro Morjá to the Cordillera and thence along the northern slope to Cerro Chachagualia, leaving Jocornal and Cerro Jocornal in Honduras and from Cerro Chachagualia to the Rio Chachagualia, thence to the Motagua. However, if a settlement is to be made, it will be necessary for Honduras to agree to a line farther east than the Rio Chachagualia. This seems evident from the situation developed in our conversations with the Guatemalan delegation.

The Department desires that Minister Lay, immediately upon his arrival in Tegucigalpa, follow up the representations of the Chargé in the same manner indicated in this telegram and report the results. [End paraphrase.]

STIMSON

714.1515/1079 : Telegram

The Chargé in Honduras (Merrell) to the Secretary of State

TEGUCIGALPA, May 22, 1930—9 p. m.
[Received May 23—1 p. m.]

29. Your telegram No. 24, May 21, 6 p. m. In the presence of the Minister for Foreign Affairs and myself the President of the Republic this afternoon telegraphed instructions to the Honduran delegation in Washington which were in translation substantially as follows:

"I instructed you that you had ample powers to discuss the boundary question with Guatemala in all of its aspects. I now confirm these instructions."

MERRELL

714.1515/1082 : Telegram

The Minister in Honduras (Lay) to the Secretary of State

TEGUCIGALPA, June 4, 1930—4 p. m.
[Received June 5—9 : 35 a. m.]

34. Your telegram No. 24, May 21, 6 p. m. The President has given me to understand that while he would not concede the town of Chachahualia he is willing that Honduran delegation submit to him a proposed line east of the Rio Chachahualia and after consultation with members of his Government and certain deputies he will advise the delegation. The President insists that the Honduran delegation has ample powers to do this without further instructions.

The President told me that to cede any of the territory east of the Chachahualia River south of the Motagua River would be the greatest sacrifice Honduras could make and would be very unpopular in Honduras. He intimated that an exchange for other territory southwest of Rio Chachahualia would be better than ceding any of this area. He does not recognize that Guatemala has any legitimate claim to the right bank of the lower Motagua River. [Paraphrase.] The Foreign Minister, in the presence of the President, proposed that the Department of State suggest a line to the delegates. The President and the Foreign Minister undoubtedly believe that a line suggested by the Department of State would stand a much better chance of acceptance here than a line demanded or claimed by Guatemala especially in the area where Hondurans feel they are sacrificing their sovereignty. [End paraphrase.] [79]

LAY

714.1515/1084 : Telegram

The Minister in Honduras (Lay) to the Secretary of State

TEGUCIGALPA, June 17, 1930—5 p. m.
[Received June 18—9 : 05 a. m.]

46. The President of the Republic, in the presence of the Minister for Foreign Affairs, requested me to telegraph you his appreciation for your suggestion to the delegates in Washington that the Arbitral Commission be composed of one delegate proposed by Honduras, one by Guatemala, presided over by the Chief Justice of the United States Supreme Court and that a commission composed in this way would be most acceptable to Honduras. The President added that his

[79] Discussions to reach an agreement on a boundary line continued until June 12, when the chairman of the conference announced that on the following day the conference would pass to a discussion of a possible treaty of arbitration to put an end to the boundary question. See *Informe del Doctor don Mariano Vasquez sobre la Conferencia de Limites*, p. 12.

Government would willingly accept any award of such a Commission since it has the utmost confidence in the fairness and justice of the Chief Justice of the Supreme Court.

Repeated to Guatemala.

LAY

714.1515/1084 : Telegram

The Secretary of State to the Minister in Honduras (Lay)

WASHINGTON, June 19, 1930—3 p. m.

29. Your 46, June 17, 5 p. m. The suggestion was not made by the Department that the Arbitral Commission be composed of one delegate proposed by Honduras, one by Guatemala, and presided over by the Chief Justice of the United States. The Department's representative at the meeting of the Commission first asked the Honduran delegates who would be acceptable as Arbitrator and they listed the President of the United States, the Chief Justice, or one of the American Judges on The Hague Tribunal. Guatemala insisted upon the Central American Tribunal as the Treaty of 1923 [80] is binding on both Guatemala and Honduras. Honduras was not favorable to the Central American Tribunal. Inquiry was then made whether that Tribunal would be acceptable if agreement was had in advance as to who would preside over it. The Guatemalan delegate said that the Chief Justice of the United States would be eminently satisfactory to Guatemala as the third and presiding member. The Honduran delegation immediately accepted this proposal but stated it desired to have a Tribunal of three, one appointed by Guatemala, one by Honduras, to be presided over by the Chief Justice. The Guatemalan delegation insists that as the Treaty of 1923 is in effect and binding between the two countries that Tribunal should be accepted with the agreement made in advance, if necessary, as to the members who will compose the Tribunal. Honduras, while admitting that the Convention is in effect, maintains that it does not apply to this one particular case because Article I excepts cases in which the parties have "accepted some other form of arbitration". The Honduran position is that the Treaty of 1914 [81] was in effect when this Treaty was signed in 1923 and constituted acceptance of some other form of arbitration. The Honduran delegation maintains that the Treaty of 1914 was in effect at the time of the Central American Conference

---

[80] Convention for the establishment of an international Central American Tribunal, signed at Washington, February 7, 1923, *Conference on Central American Affairs, Washington, December 4, 1922–February 7, 1923* (Washington, Government Printing Office, 1923), p. 296.

[81] See *Foreign Relations*, 1917, p. 786.

in 1923 and that as the Convention signed at that time might not be ratified for some months, Mr. Hughes' suggestion that the boundary matter be settled in accordance with the 1914 Convention was perfectly proper and acceptable to Guatemala. As you know, the Governments did not agree, however, on the formula for arbitration and no action was taken under the 1914 Treaty before it expired by limitation in 1925. That Treaty being now of no effect, Guatemala maintains that it can not be alleged that they have accepted some other form of arbitration and hence can not submit their boundary dispute to the Central American Tribunal. The Department considers that this view is correct and if you can persuade the Honduran Government to accept the Central American Tribunal, with an agreement that the Chief Justice of the United States be asked to preside at its deliberations, it will make an agreement very much easier.

The difference between the two delegations is one of form; both are agreed upon the composition of the Tribunal and it is merely this technicality as to whether they have accepted some other form of arbitration or not which is delaying an agreement. This technicality could in any event be waived by the Honduran Government, even should its position be correct, and the Department very much hopes it will do so in the interest of a prompt agreement.

STIMSON

714.1515/1088 : Telegram

The Minister in Honduras (Lay) to the Secretary of State

TEGUCIGALPA, June 25, 1930—noon.
[Received 3:50 p. m.]

51. I have just received a note from the President of the Republic, dated June 23, stating that he has received a telegram from the Honduranean delegation in Washington to the effect that the Department's proposal that the competency of the Central American Tribunal to try the boundary question be submitted to a special tribunal has been accepted with the understanding that both parties will abide by the decision of the special tribunal.

The President's note then adds that although the Honduranean delegates have ample powers to act as they think best he has recommended that they observe the greatest harmony with the impartial opinion of the Department of State "principally with reference to the acceptance of the special treaty of juridical arbitration".

In view of the above message from the Honduranean delegation he states that he has decided not to call for the present the meeting mentioned in my telegram No. 49, June 22, 7 p. m.[82]

LAY

---

[82] Not printed.

714.1515/1090a : Telegram

The Secretary of State to the Ambassador in France (Edge)

WASHINGTON, July 7, 1930—6 p. m.

151. Please communicate following as soon as possible to the Honorable Charles E. Hughes, Chief Justice of the United States, who is now motoring in northern France, Belgium or the Rhineland, and whose address is care of Bankers' Trust Company, 5 Place Vendome, Paris:

"After six months negotiations in an endeavor to settle the boundary dispute between Guatemala and Honduras, a direct settlement not having been possible, the Delegates of the two countries have agreed on an arbitration treaty.

There is a difference between them as to whether the International Central American Tribunal established at the Conference on Central American Affairs, February 7th, 1923, has jurisdiction or not, but they have agreed to submit this question of competency to a Special Tribunal to be composed in the same manner as the International Central American Tribunal, provided that the Chief Justice of the United States is the third and presiding member. This Special Tribunal will determine the competency of the Central American Tribunal. If the Special Tribunal decides that the Central American Tribunal has jurisdiction, it will immediately constitute itself as the Central American Tribunal to determine the question at issue between them. If it decides that the Central American Tribunal has not jurisdiction, then the Special Tribunal will proceed to a consideration of the boundary dispute. It is provided that the Special Tribunal will meet, if it is possible, within sixty days following the exchange of ratifications of the Convention which they hope to sign on or about the fifteenth of this month. Provision is made that while the Parties are bound by the dates fixed the Tribunal can change them in order to meet with your convenience if you will accept to act as Presiding Judge. In other words, should the sixty days fall within your holiday next year, the court would not meet until the date fixed by you at your convenience in the following autumn.

I have been requested by both Parties to communicate with you and inquire whether you will permit them to provide in the treaty that the Chief Justice of the United States shall be the third arbitrator who will preside over the Tribunal.

I may say that there was very considerable difficulty in bringing them to an agreement on the Tribunal in view of their difference of opinion as to whether or not the Central American Tribunal is competent. Guatemala insisted upon the competency of the Central American Tribunal whereas Honduras desired the arbitration to be before a Special Tribunal presided over by you. Guatemala stated that it would accept the compromise arrangement of arbitrating the competency of the Central American Tribunal on the condition that the third arbitrator should be the Chief Justice of the United States. This was readily accepted by Honduras. After six months of negotiations it was the first point on which they were able to agree.

May I ask you to be so good as to transmit your reply to me through any of our diplomatic or consular officers who will cable it to me."

STIMSON

714.1515/1092 : Telegram

The Ambassador in France (Edge) to the Secretary of State

PARIS, July 11, 1930—11 a. m.
[Received July 11—5:36 a. m.]

214. Department's 151, July 7, 6 p. m. Following telegram received today from Chief Justice Hughes:

"I shall be happy to accept designation as third arbitrator to preside over tribunal established for purposes stated in your telegram July 7th. Hughes."

EDGE

714.1515/1097

Memorandum by the Assistant Secretary of State (White)

[WASHINGTON,] July 19, 1930.

I attach hereto, for the Department's confidential files, (until the texts are made public by the Guatemalan and Honduran Governments) the carbon copies of the texts of the Arbitration Treaty and Supplementary Convention, signed by the representatives of Guatemala and Honduras on the afternoon of July 16, 1930. These carbons are the exact copies of the Guatemalan and Honduran copies as signed. I also attach copies of the English translations of this Treaty and Convention, as agreed upon by the Guatemalan and Honduran Delegations.

FRANCIS WHITE

[Enclosure 1—Translation]

Treaty of Arbitration Between Guatemala and Honduras, Signed at Washington, July 16, 1930

The Governments of the Republics of Guatemala and Honduras, being desirous of settling the question of territorial boundaries which is unfortunately pending between the two Republics, have agreed to submit the said question to arbitration through the conclusion of this treaty, for which purpose they have appointed the following as their respective plenipotentiaries, to wit:

the Government of Guatemala:
    Licenciado Don Carlos Salazar and Licenciado Don Eugenio
    Silva Peña,
and the Government of Honduras:
    Dr. Mariano Vasquez,

who, having examined their respective Full Powers, which they found to be in good and due form,

Have agreed upon the following articles:

ARTICLE I

The High Contracting Parties agree that the Convention for the Establishment of an International Central American Tribunal, signed at Washington February 7, 1923, is in effect between them, in accordance with Article XXVI of the same Convention. The Government of Guatemala makes this declaration without reservations. The Government of Honduras affirms that that Convention is obligatory as to all controversies with the exception of the boundary dispute between Guatemala and Honduras, taking as a basis the wording of Article I of the said Convention, which does not include questions with regard to which the parties shall have "accepted some other form of arbitration". The Government of Honduras believes that this provision excludes from the jurisdiction of the International Central American Tribunal its boundary question pending with Guatemala, by virtue of the fact that the Convention for the Establishment of an International Central American Tribunal was signed February 7, 1923, while the Boundary Convention signed August 1, 1914, was in effect between the two countries.

The Government of Guatemala maintains that the International Central American Tribunal is fully competent to pass judgment, in judicial arbitration proceedings, on the pending boundary question, because its jurisdiction extends, in accordance with Article I of the respective Convention, invoked by the Government of Honduras, to "all controversies or questions which now exist between them or which may hereafter arise, whatever their nature or origin", a wording which covers and includes every question of territorial limits, without the competence of the tribunal being affected by the reservation alleged by the Government of Honduras, because there is no agreement between the parties, as to any other form of arbitration, since the willingness manifested in 1923 to submit the question to the President of the United States of America lapsed with the treaty of 1914 on which it was based.

The Government of Guatemala believes that the divergence existing between the points of view of the two governments, with respect to the application of the Convention for the Establishment of an International Central American Tribunal, can and must be adjusted in conformity with Article XIII of the said pact.

The Government of Honduras is of the opinion that the International Central American Tribunal is not authorized to determine its original competence, but only to decide the incidental competence, with the restrictions of Article I of the said Convention.

Both parties, however, agree that the tribunal which takes cognizance of the boundary question between the two countries, shall be organized in the same form prescribed in the Convention for the Establishment of an International Central American Tribunal.

In order to settle the conflict between the opposing points of view of the two governments, they have decided to establish in the city of Washington, a Special Tribunal, constituted in the form prescribed by the Convention for the Establishment of an International Central American Tribunal and to submit to this Special Tribunal in the first place, the following question:

Is the International Central American Tribunal created by the Convention of February 7, 1923, competent to take cognizance of the boundary question pending between Guatemala and Honduras?

If the decision of the Special Tribunal denies the competence of the International Central American Tribunal to take cognizance of the pending boundary question, the same tribunal, as Special Boundary Tribunal, shall proceed to take cognizance of the frontier dispute which is maintained by the High Contracting Parties.

If, on the other hand, the Special Tribunal recognizes, in its decision, the competence of the International Central American Tribunal, the said Special Tribunal shall take cognizance, as International Central American Tribunal, of the boundary question pending between Guatemala and Honduras and will sit at the said city of Washington.

In both cases, the stipulations of the present Treaty shall be observed.

ARTICLE II

The Special Tribunal referred to by the preceding article shall be constituted as follows:

The Government of Guatemala appoints Dr. Luis Castro Ureña from the permanent list of jurists established by Article II of the Convention for the Establishment of an International Central American Tribunal.

The Government of Honduras appoints Señor Dr. Don Emilio Bello Codesido from the same list.

The two Governments, by common agreement, appoint as Third Arbitrator the Chief Justice of the United States, who shall preside over the Tribunal.

ARTICLE III

The Special Tribunal shall meet, if possible, within the sixty days following the exchange of ratifications of the present Treaty; and each of the High Contracting Parties shall submit to it, within the three days following its organization, the pleas relative to the competence or incompetence of the International Central American Tribunal to take cognizance of the boundary question between Guatemala and Honduras.

In the light of the pleas the Special Tribunal shall pronounce its judgment, which shall be final and without appeal.

ARTICLE IV

Within the thirty days following notification of the decision which settles the question of competence, the High Contracting Parties shall submit to the Special Tribunal, or to the International Central American Tribunal, as the case may be, the pleas, proofs, and documents of whatever kind they may deem expedient to support their points of view and claims in the boundary question.

ARTICLE V

The High Contracting Parties are in agreement that the only juridical line which can be established between their respective countries is that of the *Uti Possidetis* of 1821. Consequently, they are in accord that the Tribunal shall determine this line. If the Tribunal finds that one or both parties, in their subsequent development have established, beyond that line, interests which should be taken into account in establishing the definitive boundary, the Tribunal shall modify as it may see fit the line of the *Uti Possidetis* of 1821 and shall fix the territorial or other compensation which it may deem just that either party should pay to the other.

ARTICLE VI

The pleas, the proofs, and the documents, shall be presented by the parties to the Tribunal in four copies, in English and in Spanish, one copy of which in both languages shall be for each of the members of the Tribunal and the remaining copy shall be delivered by the Tribunal to the other party in the dispute.

ARTICLE VII

The Tribunal shall deliver the plea of the other party to the representative of each Government for sixty days for examination and reply and shall exhibit to him, if he should so request, the documents presented.

ARTICLE VIII

Each party shall have the right to submit for the consideration of the Tribunal, together with its reply, plans (sketches), maps, proofs, and other documents which have not been presented with the initial plea. These shall be communicated to the other party, which may refute them within the fifteen days following the date on which it receives them.

ARTICLE IX

The time limits established in the present treaty shall be peremptory; but the Tribunal is expressly empowered by the Contracting Parties to extend them on sufficient grounds therefor.

ARTICLE X

All decisions of the Tribunal shall be arrived at by a majority of votes. In case the votes are scattered, the vote of the President of the Tribunal shall be decisive.

ARTICLE XI

Each party shall be represented by an attorney who, for the performance of his duty, may have such assistants as his Government may deem necessary.

ARTICLE XII

The High Contracting Parties confer on the Tribunal the necessary authority to settle by itself any difference which may arise with regard to the interpretation or carrying out of this Treaty and the decisions of the said Tribunal.

ARTICLE XIII

The High Contracting Parties empower the Tribunal to appoint committees of investigation, to utilize the service of experts and resort to other means of information which it may deem necessary for ascertaining the facts. They also empower it to organize the subordinate personnel of the Tribunal, in such form as it may deem desirable. To this end the parties undertake to place at the service of the Tribunal such facilities as may be necessary.

ARTICLE XIV

The award of the Tribunal shall be handed down as soon as possible and it shall set forth the points of fact and of law involved in the controversy, and the reasons and grounds which are considered valid for the decision. This award shall decide the boundary controversy finally and without appeal and shall be faithfully executed by the High Contracting Parties.

ARTICLE XV

The High Contracting Parties have agreed that the physical demarcation of the frontier shall be performed by a Technical Commission, in conformity with the provisions of the Convention supplementary to the present Treaty, signed on this same date.

ARTICLE XVI

Until the demarcation is made, each of the High Contracting Parties shall maintain the possessions which it at present has in the frontier zone, but may carry on agricultural, industrial, and commercial activities within the limits of its present possessions. Each undertakes not to make any new advance and to avoid all hostile acts between the two parties.

ARTICLE XVII

It is understood and agreed between the High Contracting Parties that private properties acquired under legitimate title prior to the date of the present Treaty, which may remain on either side of the dividing line, must be respected and shall have the benefit of all the guarantees provided in each country for the property of its nationals, by its constitution and laws, to which said properties shall then be subject.

ARTICLE XVIII

In case one or both of the arbitrators appointed separately by each of the High Contracting Parties resigns or is incapacitated, the respective government shall immediately take steps to replace him, selecting the new arbitrators from the lists established by Article II of the Convention for the Establishment of an International Central American Tribunal. Such substitution shall not affect the validity and force of this Treaty.

ARTICLE XIX

Each party shall pay the honorarium and expenses of the arbitrator which it appoints and the expenses incurred in preparing and prosecuting its action. Half of the general costs of the arbitration proceedings, as well as the honorarium and expenses of the President of the Tribunal, shall be paid by each of the Contracting Parties.

ARTICLE XX

The present Treaty shall be submitted, as soon as possible, in Guatemala and in Honduras, for ratification in the manner provided by their constitutions; and the exchange of ratifications shall take place in this city of Washington, capital of the United States of America, within the sixty days following the date of the last ratification.

In faith whereof, the plenipotentiaries of Guatemala and Honduras sign the present Treaty, in two copies of the same tenor, which they authenticate with their respective seals, in the city of Washington, D. C., on the sixteenth day of the month of July, one thousand nine hundred and thirty.

CARLOS SALAZAR   MARIANO VASQUEZ
EUGENIO SILVA PEÑA

[Enclosure 2—Translation]

Supplementary Convention to the Treaty of Arbitration Between Honduras and Guatemala, Signed at Washington, July 16, 1930

The Governments of the Republics of Honduras and Guatemala, in accordance with Article XV of the Treaty of Arbitration signed this day, in this city, have deemed fit to conclude the present Supplementary Convention to the said Treaty; and for that purpose have appointed as their respective plenipotentiaries,

The Government of Honduras: Dr. Mariano Vasquez; and the Government of Guatemala, Licenciado Don Carlos Salazar and Licenciado Don Eugenio Silva Peña, who, after having communicated to each other their respective full powers, which they found to be in good and due form, have agreed upon the following articles:

ARTICLE I

Within one hundred and twenty days, counting from the date on which the Arbitral Tribunal, set up by the Treaty of Arbitration aforementioned, shall have notified the High Contracting Parties of the award which shall determine the boundary line between Guatemala and Honduras, a Technical Commission shall proceed to carry out the demarcation of the said line.

ARTICLE II

The Commission referred to in the preceding article shall be composed of five engineers, of whom, one shall be designated by the President of the Arbitral Tribunal, in consultation with the United States Coast and Geodetic Survey; two shall be appointed by the

Government of Honduras and two by the Government of Guatemala, each Party having the right to appoint the complementary personnel which it may consider advisable. The work shall be carried on under the direction of the engineer designated by the President of the Arbitral Tribunal, who shall be the Head of the Commission, with sufficient authority to give in the field the final decision with regard to any differences whatsoever of a geodetic or topographical character which might arise between the engineers of Honduras and Guatemala.

Article III

If, after the lapse of the time limit of one hundred and twenty days referred to in the first article, one of the High Contracting Parties shall not have appointed the two engineers who, on its behalf, are to be members of the Technical Commission, the work of demarcation of the boundary line shall be started and carried to conclusion by the engineer designated by the President of the Arbitral Tribunal and those who shall have been appointed at the proper time by the other Party. In this case the Engineer at the head of the Technical Commission is authorized to appoint substitute engineers if he should deem it necessary.

Article IV

Once the appointment of the engineers has been made, they shall meet as soon as possible, in the town nearest to either of the terminal points of the line fixed by the decision of the Arbitral Tribunal and shall begin their work. The Head of the Commission shall advise the Governments of Honduras and Guatemala of this fact.

Article V

The Technical Commission shall establish at the extreme points of the boundary line and at the important points thereof, monuments which shall be located astronomically as to latitude and longitude. The latter shall refer to the meridian of Greenwich. It shall also construct monuments along the line on the summits of the hills, at the crossings of roads, rivers and ravines, and at other conspicuous places, in order that the inhabitants of each country may easily recognize the boundary.

The monuments shall be constructed of such material as may be considered most satisfactory by the Technical Commission, and the latter shall determine their dimensions and inscriptions.

Article VI

The Commission of Engineers shall remain in the region where the work of demarcation is performed. The latter can not be suspended except fortuitously, when the rainy season or other substantial reason does not permit of its performance.

ARTICLE VII

The Technical Commission shall have all the time that may be necessary to complete the work of demarcation.

If any of the members of the Commission should become incapacitated or unable, for any reason, to continue to render service, he shall be replaced immediately by another engineer who shall be appointed by the respective Government, upon mere notification by the Head of the Commission.

ARTICLE VIII

The Technical Commission shall endeavor, so far as possible, to draw the line of demarcation which must join the points indicated by the arbitral award, through such natural or mutually visible landmarks as the terrain may offer.

ARTICLE IX

After finishing the field and office work, the Technical Commission of Engineers shall draw up in triplicate a detailed report and send it, together with the general map and the detail maps, to the Governments of both Honduras and Guatemala and to the President of the Arbitral Tribunal.

ARTICLE X

The Governments of Honduras and Guatemala undertake to furnish the Technical Commission every assistance and facility for the accomplishment of its task.

ARTICLE XI

The general expenses caused by the demarcation, as well as the honorarium and expenses of the Engineer Head of the Technical Commission, shall be paid in equal parts, by the Governments of Honduras and Guatemala. In any case, the honoraria and expenses of the two engineers of each of the High Contracting Parties and their assistants shall be paid by each of the Parties individually.

ARTICLE XII

The High Contracting Parties undertake to recognize, maintain and respect perpetually and forever, as the boundary line between Honduras and Guatemala, the line demarcated by the Technical

Commission, in conformity with the award handed down by the Arbitral Tribunal, set up by the Arbitration Treaty concluded by the said High Contracting Parties, today, in this city.

Article XIII

The present Convention, supplementary to the Arbitration Treaty concluded on this same date between the Governments of Honduras and Guatemala, shall be submitted, together with the latter, for ratifications in accordance with the constitutional provisions of the two countries; and the exchange of ratifications shall take place in the city of Washington, capital of the United States of America, within the sixty days following the date of the last ratification.

In faith whereof, the plenipotentiaries of Honduras and Guatemala sign this Convention, in two copies of the same tenor, which they authenticate with their respective seals, in the city of Washington, D. C. on the sixteenth day of July, one thousand nine hundred and thirty.

[The ratifications of the treaty of arbitration and of the supplementary convention were exchanged on October 15, 1931, at Washington. In a letter of the same date to the Secretary of State, the Ministers of Guatemala and of Honduras requested that the Secretary communicate to the Chief Justice of the United States the latter's appointment to form and preside over the Arbitral Tribunal composed of himself and Doctors Emilio Bello Codesido of Chile and Luis Castro Areña of Costa Rica. Mr. Hughes accepted the appointment in a letter to the Secretary of State dated October 19, 1931. (714.1515/1192, 1196.)]

Honduras and Nicaragua[83]

715.1715/366a

The Secretary of State to the Minister in Honduras (Lay)[84]

No. 1   Washington, May 21, 1930.

Sir: The Department understands that the Governments of Honduras and Nicaragua are now in substantial agreement with respect to the method to be followed in adjusting the dispute which prevails with respect to a portion of their common boundary. The procedure apparently contemplated by the two Governments embraces the sign-

---

[83] Continued from *Foreign Relations*, 1929, vol. I, pp. 975–984.
[84] The same, *mutatis mutandis*, on the same date to the Minister in Nicaragua as instruction No. 16.

ing of a protocol of agreement, based upon the award of the King of Spain and providing for the appointment of a commission of engineers, to be formed of one Honduran engineer and one Nicaraguan engineer and to be presided over by an American engineer, who shall act as President.

Inasmuch as both Governments have expressed the desire that the Government of the United States shall thus cooperate in the settlement of the difficulty, the Department is prepared, if such action would be agreeable to the two Governments concerned, to lend its further cooperation by authorizing the American representatives at Tegucigalpa and Managua to collaborate in the preparation of the protocol of agreement.

A similar instruction is being addressed to the American Minister at Managua. Upon its receipt he will determine whether it is opportune and appropriate to undertake the action it contemplates and, if so, he will inform you of that fact and inquire whether the situation at Tegucigalpa likewise is propitious for the initiation of similar negotiations. When your respective Legations are in agreement as to the advisability of opening negotiations and the date upon which they shall be initiated and it has been ascertained by informal inquiry of both Governments that the assistance of this Government in the elaboration of the protocol of agreement would be acceptable, you may then submit the following general outline of the protocol of agreement for consideration, stating that similar action is being taken by the American Legation at Managua:

"Whereas, the Governments of the Republics of Honduras and Nicaragua are desirous of strengthening the fraternal ties of friendship which have traditionally bound them, through the removal of the only obstacle to complete harmony which now exists;

"And whereas on December 23, 1906, His Majesty the King of Spain rendered an arbitral award designating the boundary line between the two Republics from the Atlantic to the Pass of Teotecacinte (the remainder of the line, from the Pass of Teotecacinte to the Gulf of Fonseca having been definitively accepted by both Governments);

It is hereby agreed:

"1. The Governments of Honduras and Nicaragua mutually pledge their acceptance of the award of the King of Spain as handed down by him on December 23, 1906;

"2. The Governments of Honduras and Nicaragua hereby unconditionally agree that the delineation of the boundary determined by the award of the King of Spain, to which the preceding article refers, shall be entrusted to a Joint Commission, consisting of an engineer appointed by each Government and presided over by an American engineer designated by the Government of the United States of America;

"3. The Governments of Honduras and Nicaragua agree that the Commission of engineers described in the preceding article shall have full authority to establish the boundary line between the two Republics from the Atlantic Ocean to the Pass of Teotecacinte, in accordance with the award of the King of Spain, establishing that line at points where the award of the King of Spain may require clarification and interpreting the meaning of the award in such instances as its meaning may not be clear;

"4. In the event that the two Commissioners cannot reach an agreement, the President of the Commission shall render a decision which shall be final; and

"5. The Governments of Honduras and Nicaragua agree that the decisions, findings, and recommendations of the Joint Boundary Commission hereinbefore mentioned shall be accepted as final and without appeal, and that the boundary line as laid down by the Joint Commission shall be accepted by both Governments as their true and definitive common frontier."

Should alterations in the protocol be suggested, you should bear in mind that the essential points of agreement are that the Commission shall be established, that it shall function under the award of the King of Spain, and that its decisions and demarcation of the line shall be accepted by both Governments as final.

This Government would view with gratification the early settlement of this dispute, and it is desired that you report frequently and fully the progress of your representations.

I am [etc.] For the Secretary of State:
FRANCIS WHITE

715.1715/367 : Telegram

The Minister in Nicaragua (Hanna) to the Secretary of State

MANAGUA, June 13, 1930—4 p. m.
[Received 10 p. m.]

70. Department's instruction No. 16, May 21 [85] concerning the reopening of negotiations, the Nicaragua-Honduras boundary matter. When I called upon President Moncada yesterday to keep him informed of developments in connection with recent incidents on the border which have provoked protest from the Government of Honduras, I asked him what would be the effect on the existing situation if negotiations in the boundary dispute should be reopened. He replied that he is convinced that the creation of a boundary commission as heretofore proposed is the best if not the only way by which a permanent solution of the difficulty along the frontier including the suppression of banditry can be attained. He said he has been of this opinion all along and that he is more convinced than ever that negotiations should be reopened as soon as possible. He said I might so inform you if I cared to do so and that he is prepared to carry out his part of whatever program may be decided upon.

[85] See footnote 84, p. 361.

I was guarded in my comment on his views and told him it was a matter I wanted to consider maturely. I am, however, in full accord with his views and think there should be no delay in reopening negotiations if the Government of Honduras sees the matter in the same light. I believe that if a commission is created and sent to the border both Governments will be under obligations to afford it protection and that military cooperation between the forces of the two countries will thus be automatically insured. I am convinced that the Government will reply in a friendly and conciliatory tone to the recent protests of the Government of Honduras and it seems probable that the friendly atmosphere which should exist if negotiations are reopened can be created.

In view of the fact that the recent incidents involving charges that the *guardia* has entered Honduranean territory occurred along the portion of the frontier not embraced in the award of the King of Spain, it may be desirable in the course of the prospective negotiations to discuss broadening the terms of the protocol and the duties of the commission to include re-marking the boundary to the west of the Pass of Teotecacinte. Moreover, if this is not done, a new controversy is liable to arise in the future with respect to this portion of the boundary.

I am repeating this to Tegucigalpa and will await the Department's further instructions.

HANNA

715.1715/368 : Telegram

The Minister in Honduras (Lay) to the Secretary of State

TEGUCIGALPA, June 14, 1930—4 p. m.
[Received 10:38 p. m.]

111. Referring to the Department's instruction No. 1, May 21, and telegram from American Legation, Managua, to the Department June 13, 4 p. m. President Mejia Colindres told me this morning that he would be pleased if negotiations in the boundary dispute were reopened and a boundary commission created as soon as possible. He said that the fixing of the boundary between Honduras and Nicaragua promptly in this way would accomplish much to avoid the disputes along the frontier and thereby create a better understanding between the two countries.

I am awaiting instructions from the Department and further advices from American Legation at Managua before taking further steps mentioned in Department's instruction.

Repeated to Nicaragua.

LAY

715.1715/369 : Telegram

The Minister in Nicaragua (Hanna) to the Secretary of State

MANAGUA, June 19 [*sic*], 1930—9 p. m.
[Received June 18—11:20 p. m.]

71. My telegram No. 70, June 13, 4 p. m. The Minister for Foreign Affairs told me this afternoon that President Moncada had instructed him to draft a protocol to submit the boundary dispute to a commission. I fear that this will complicate matters and hope that you will authorize me to proceed with carrying out the program laid down in the Department's mail instruction No. 16, May 21, 1930.[85a]

HANNA

715.1715/369 : Telegram

The Secretary of State to the Minister in Nicaragua (Hanna)

WASHINGTON, June 19, 1930—7 p. m.

54. Legation's 70, June 13, 4 p. m. and 71, June 19, 9 p. m. You may proceed immediately with the program laid down in the Department's mail instruction No. 16, dated May 21, 1930,[85a] notifying the American Legation at Tegucigalpa of the action taken by you.

For your personal information and for such use as in your opinion should be made of the information, you are advised that the Department will discuss with the Navy Department the feasibility of an aerial survey of the Nicaraguan Honduran boundary region which would also embrace that portion of the frontier extending from the Gulf of Fonseca to the Pass of Teotecacinte.

A similar instruction is being sent to Tegucigalpa.[86]

STIMSON

715.1715/370 : Telegram

The Minister in Nicaragua (Hanna) to the Secretary of State

MANAGUA, June 25, 1930—4 p. m.
[Received 5:14 p. m.]

74. Department's telegram 54, June 19, 7 p. m. President Moncada told me this morning that in his opinion the draft protocol of agreement will be more favorably received by the Government of Honduras if prepared by the Department of State than if prepared by the Government of Nicaragua and that he will welcome the Department's

---

[85a] See footnote 84, p. 361.
[86] Telegram No. 30 of the same date; not printed.

assistance in preparing and submitting the draft. Accordingly I have sent the following telegram to the American Legation at Tegucigalpa:

"June 25, 3 p. m. Department's mail instruction of May 21, 1930, concerning reopening of negotiations in the Nicaraguan Honduranean boundary matter. The assistance of the Government of the United States in the elaboration of the protocol of agreement is acceptable to the Government of Nicaragua and I will submit the outline of the protocol of agreement for the consideration of this Government when you advise me that you are prepared to take similar action with the Government of Honduras.

Repeated to Department of State."

HANNA

715.1715/371 : Telegram

The Minister in Honduras (Lay) to the Secretary of State

TEGUCIGALPA, June 27, 1930—4 p. m.
[Received 10 : 15 p. m.]

53. The following telegram was sent to Nicaragua:

"June 27, 4 p. m. Department's instruction of May 21 and your June 25, 3 p. m.[87] The offer of assistance of the United States in elaborating the protocol of agreement is gratefully accepted by the Government of Honduras and if I do not hear to the contrary from you I shall submit the outline."

LAY

715.1715/372 : Telegram

The Minister in Nicaragua (Hanna) to the Secretary of State

MANAGUA, July 2, 1930—6 p. m.
[Received 9 : 15 p. m.]

80. Department's 54, June 19, 7 p. m. The draft protocol of agreement transcribed in Department's mail instruction No. 16 of May 21 [88] was submitted to the Nicaraguan Government today.

Repeated to Tegucigalpa.

HANNA

715.1715/373 : Telegram

The Minister in Honduras (Lay) to the Secretary of State

TEGUCIGALPA, July 3, 1930—9 a. m.
[Received 1 p. m.]

57. The draft protocol of agreement transmitted in Department's instruction No. 1 of May 21 was submitted to the Honduran Government yesterday.

Repeated to Managua.

LAY

---

[87] See telegram No. 74, June 25, 4 p. m., to the Secretary of State, *supra.*
[88] See footnote 84, p. 361.

715.1715/374 : Telegram

The Minister in Honduras (Lay) to the Secretary of State

TEGUCIGALPA, July 7, 1930—5 p. m.
[Received 10 : 45 p. m.]

58. Department's instruction No. 1, May 21, 1930, and my telegram No. 57, July 3, 9 a. m. I have now received a report from the Minister for Foreign Affairs, dated July 5, which after repeating the substance of my note is in translation as follows:

"In reply and with instructions from His Excellency, the President of the Republic, I am gratified to inform Your Excellency that my Government accepts in its entirety, and without any modification, the outline of the protocol of agreement for the execution [of the Award] of His Majesty the King of Spain which you have been good enough to send to this Secretariat of State for the definitive settlement of the boundary question between Honduras and Nicaragua; and that in case the Government of Nicaragua accepts it as is hoped, you will be good enough to inform me whether the protocol will be signed in Tegucigalpa or in Managua in order that this Secretariat may dictate the appropriate measures."

Repeated to Nicaragua.

LAY

715.1715/374 : Telegram

The Secretary of State to the Minister in Honduras (Lay)

WASHINGTON, July 8, 1930—6 p. m.

34. Legation's 58, July 7, 5 p. m. The selection of the place at which the boundary protocol is to be signed is a matter for agreement between the Governments of Honduras and Nicaragua. Should you find that they are unable to reach an agreement on this point, however, perhaps the difficulty might be solved by signature in Washington. The Department of course, prefers that the protocol be signed either in Honduras or Nicaragua.

A similar telegram is being sent to Managua.

STIMSON

715.1715/375 : Telegram

The Minister in Nicaragua (Hanna) to the Secretary of State

MANAGUA, July 9, 1930—3 p. m.
[Received 6 : 50 p. m.]

83. Department's 62, July 8, 6 p. m.[89] I expect to receive soon this Government's reply concerning the draft protocol. The Minister for

[89] See last paragraph of telegram *supra*.

Foreign Affairs has just told me that his Government probably will propose the addition of a provision to the effect that the Government of Honduras will guarantee property rights legally acquired by Nicaraguans and others under Nicaraguan law in territory heretofore considered as Nicaraguan but which the Boundary Commission may decide to be Honduranean territory, and that the Government of Nicaragua will give a similar guarantee under similar conditions. He said that this would be the only material change in the draft protocol that his Government will suggest.

Repeated to Tegucigalpa.

HANNA

715.1715/376 : Telegram

The Minister in Nicaragua (Hanna) to the Secretary of State

MANAGUA, July 14, 1930—5 p. m.
[Received 9 : 30 p. m.]

88. The following telegram was sent to the American Legation at Tegucigalpa:

July 14, 5 p. m. My telegram July 9, 3 p. m.[91] It appears that some of President Moncada's advisers hold the opinion that this Government, in accepting the Award of the King of Spain and the draft protocol, will make great concessions, whereas the Government of Honduras will make no concession in a similar acceptance. If you can advise me of any such concessions which the Government of Honduras claims to be making in this matter, I may be able discreetly to use the information you may give me to advantage. Repeated to the Department of State.

HANNA

715.1715/377 : Telegram

The Minister in Honduras (Lay) to the Secretary of State

TEGUCIGALPA, July 14, 1930—9 p. m.
[Received July 15—10 : 55 a. m.]

60. The following telegram was sent to Nicaragua, July 14, 9 p. m.:

"Your July 9, 3 p. m., to the Department. The Minister for Foreign Affairs informs me that Honduran Government would have no objection to the additional provision mentioned in your telegram. He intimated that the President desires that the protocol be signed at an early date and in Tegucigalpa. Would the Government of Nicaragua be disposed to accept an invitation direct from Honduras to sign the protocol at Tegucigalpa? If so, at the appropriate time I can suggest to President that he extend such an invitation. An invitation was extended to Honduras to sign a similar protocol here (see your telegram of November 8, 3 p. m., 1929, to the Department [92])."

LAY

---

[91] See telegram No. 83 of the same date to the Secretary of State, supra.
[92] Foreign Relations, 1929, vol. I, p. 983.

715.1715/380 : Telegram

The Minister in Nicaragua (Hanna) to the Secretary of State

MANAGUA [, July 31, 1930—5 p. m.]
[Received August 1—3 : 07 a. m.]

95. The following telegram was sent to the Legation at Tegucigalpa:

July 31, 5 p. m. Your July 14, 9 p. m.[93] This Government accepts the draft protocol with the following changes and additions.

In article 1, insert "as a basis" after the word "pledge".

In article 2, substitute "jointly" for "unconditionally", and the words "an arbitral boundary" for the words "a joint".

To article 3, add the sentence "In all doubtful cases, moreover, the President of the Commission shall decide and his decision shall be without appeal".

In article 4, insert the words "Nicaraguan and Honduranean" after the word "commissioners".

Add the following eight articles after article 5.

"6. The delivery of the territories which Honduras or Nicaragua is to receive through the fulfillment of the present agreement will be carried out within six months following the demarcation of the border.

7. The inhabitants of the territories which pass to a new sovereignty will retain their previous nationality but will have one year from the date of the delivery of the respective territories within which to choose either of the two nationalities. Silence at the expiration of the period will indicate a will not to change nationality.

8. The territorial property of the indigenous tribes, whether individual or collective, will not be altered by the change in sovereignty. If the territorial property of the tribes inhabiting the territory subject to a change in sovereignty has not been legalized, the state which may acquire said territory will be obligated to establish collectively or individually a legal regime of property in favor of said tribes by the terms of which they will be given gratuitously lots of ground in sufficient quantity to provide for their necessities.

9. Neither the agrarian regime in general nor that of private property will be altered in any way, and the latter shall be respected provided that it has been duly legalized in the country which may have possessed the territory affected in fact or by right prior to this agreement.

10. The Government of Nicaragua reserves the right to transfer to Nicaraguan territory the indigenous settlements located on the left bank of the river Coco or Segovia, and those which may be located to the north of said river in territory which on the date of the signing of the present agreement may have been in fact or by right subject to the jurisdiction of Nicaragua, including the

---

[93] See telegram No. 60 of the same date to the Secretary of State, *supra*.

settlement of Cruta at the mouth of the river of the same name. The Government of Nicaragua will exercise this right with the consent or on the petition of the inhabitants of said settlements and indigenous tribes.   This right will terminate five years from the date on which Honduras has received the territory situated to the north of the river Coco or Segovia.

11. Concessions granted to nationals or foreigners by either of the contracting states which are valid on the date of the present agreement and which apply or may apply to territory subject to a change in sovereignty by the execution of the award and of this agreement will continue in effect; that is, the state which may acquire the affected territory will reinvest the other in all the obligations and rights of the respective contract.

12. For the purposes of the preceding article and of the provisions of articles 8 and 9, the owners of lands or concessions acquired by virtue of acts of sovereignty of either of the contracting states, executed and perfected prior to the date of this agreement, will have the right to register their respective titles in the state which is to exercise sovereignty within the territory affected within a period of two years counting from the date of the delivery of said territory, made in compliance with the present agreement.

13. The present agreement will be submitted to the approval of the Congress of Nicaragua and will be ratified by the Government of Honduras in conformity with the terms of its political constitution; and the exchange of ratifications will be made in Managua or Tegucigalpa within the least possible time."

The changes in articles 1 and 2, in the opinion of President Moncada, will make the protocol less objectionable to the Nicaraguan public without altering the force of protocol, and the purpose of the addition to article 3 is to eliminate all doubt as to the power of the President of the Commission.

I will immediately transmit to you by radio *en clair* the original Spanish text of the foregoing eight additional articles and will await your report as to whether they are acceptable to the Government of Honduras.

HANNA

715.1715/381 : Telegram

The Minister in Nicaragua (Hanna) to the Secretary of State

MANAGUA, July 31, 1930—6 p. m.
[Received August 1—2 : 20 a. m.]

96. Department's telegram No. 62, July 8, 6 p. m.;[94] and telegram of July 14, 9 p. m., from the American Legation in Tegucigalpa. President Moncada does not agree to signing the protocol in Tegucigalpa because in his opinion it would create an unfavorable impression here.   He thinks that his Government will be in a much

---

[94] See last paragraph of telegram No. 34, July 8, 6 p. m., to the Minister in Honduras, p. 367.

stronger position if the protocol is signed in Managua and has asked me to make this known to the Department and the Government of Honduras. He appears to think that the Government of Honduras should not insist on this point but if it does he will consider signing in neutral territory or in both Tegucigalpa and Managua if this is admissible. I believe this small concession on the part of Honduras to sentiment here might have a beneficial effect now and when the protocol is before the Nicaraguan Congress, and I hope we may induce the Government of Honduras to concede this point. I will postpone suggesting signature in Washington until I am advised as to the decision of the Government of Honduras. If the protocol is signed in the near future it probably will be submitted to an extra session of the Nicaraguan Congress.

Repeated to Tegucigalpa.

HANNA

715.1715/382 : Telegram

The Minister in Honduras (Lay) to the Secretary of State

TEGUCIGALPA, August 1, 1930—4 p. m.
[Received 8:25 p. m.]

69. If Department perceives no objection I will submit to Honduranean Government for approval changes and additions to draft protocol embodied in Hanna's telegram of July 31, 5 p. m.

LAY

715.1715/382 : Telegram

The Acting Secretary of State to the Minister in Honduras (Lay) [95]

WASHINGTON, August 4, 1930—5 p. m.

39. Legation's 69, August 1, 4 p. m. The Department perceives no objection to your submitting to the Honduran Government for approval the changes in the boundary protocol suggested by the Nicaraguan Government.

CARR

715.1715/386 : Telegram

The Minister in Honduras (Lay) to the Secretary of State

TEGUCIGALPA, August 18, 1930—9 p. m.
[Received August 19—12:45 p. m.]

76. Referring to telegram from American Legation, Managua, to the Department, July 31, 5 p. m., and Department's telegram to this Legation number 39, August 4, 5 p. m. The Honduranean Minister

---

[95] Repeated to the Minister in Nicaragua as telegram No. 78.

for Foreign Affairs has submitted counterproposal of a protocol with several modifications and additions which I have sent by air mail to Hanna and Department.

The points upon which there is likely to be greatest disagreement between the two Governments are:

1. Honduras states it cannot accept insertion words "as a basis" after the word "pledge" in article 1 since this modification would fundamentally alter the character of the protocol which should treat only with execution of the Award of the King of Spain without permitting any actuation which might extend it to other conceptions, and,

2. The insertion of words "an arbitral boundary commission" in article 2, Honduras preferring the words "technical commission".

The Honduranean Government contend they cannot accept this modification as it would affect the essence of the protocol.

Lay

715.1715/386 : Telegram

The Acting Secretary of State to the Minister in Nicaragua (Hanna)[96]

Washington, August 20, 1930—3 p. m.

86. The Department perceives no objection to your submitting to the Nicaraguan Government for approval the changes in the boundary protocol suggested by the Honduran Government and being forwarded to you from Tegucigalpa by air mail.

Castle

715.1715/389 : Telegram

The Minister in Nicaragua (Hanna) to the Secretary of State

Managua, September 16, 1930—2 p. m.
[Received 10 : 50 p. m.]

115. Department's telegram 86, August 20, 3 p. m. The following telegram has just been sent to the American Legation at Tegucigalpa:

"September 16, 2 p. m. The full text of the boundary protocol as proposed by the Government of Honduras and transmitted with your air mail letter of August 17th is accepted by the Government of Nicaragua with the omission of article 5 which this Government deems unessential to the execution of the protocol.

Confidential for your information and discreet use: The Minister for Foreign Affairs has told me informally that this Government thinks that article 5 indicates doubt on the part of the Government of Honduras of the good faith of the Government of Nicaragua and he said that consequently the article is not acceptable.

Article 5 would certainly arouse bitter opposition in the Nicaraguan

---

[96] Repeated to the Minister in Honduras as telegram No. 43.

Congress and might defeat ratification of protocol. I have suggested no substitute for article 5 because the point covered by it seems unimportant, as compliance with the provision of law will be a matter of good faith on the part of both Governments.

The Department's telegram July 8, 6 p. m., to your Legation and my telegram to the Department July 31, 6 p. m., repeated to you concerning place at which the protocol is to be signed: I anticipate opposition to the protocol which may seriously endanger its ratification. The impression here will be much more favorable if the protocol is signed in Managua than it would be if signed in Tegucigalpa or [Washington?]. Signing in Tegucigalpa probably would greatly strengthen the opposition."

HANNA

715.1715/390 : Telegram

The Minister in Honduras (Lay) to the Secretary of State

TEGUCIGALPA, September 18, 1930—8 p. m.
[Received September 19—12 : 50 p. m.]

87. The following telegram was sent to the Legation at Managua:

"September 18, 8 p. m. Referring to your telegram of September 16, 2 p. m.,[97] stating that full text of the boundary protocol, proposed by the Government of Honduras and transmitted with my air mail letter of August 17, is accepted by the Government of Nicaragua with the omission of article 5. I take great pleasure in informing you that after explaining to the President that the omission of article 5 would improve chances of ratification in the Nicaraguan Congress he agreed to this text of the protocol in full without article 5.

Believing the moment opportune and for reasons you mention, I urged him to reconsider his previous objection to signing in Managua. A copy of a note from the Honduranean Foreign Office to this Legation agreeing to text of protocol in full with omission of article 5 and stating that Honduranean Government would have no objection to signing in Managua will be sent you by marine air mail tomorrow".

LAY

715.1715/393 : Telegram

The Minister in Nicaragua (Hanna) to the Secretary of State

MANAGUA, September 25, 1930—3 p. m.
[Received 5 : 33 p. m.]

120. The following telegram has just been sent to the American Legation, Tegucigalpa:

"September 25, 3 p. m. Your September 18, 8 p. m.[98] This Government considers it advisable to postpone signing the boundary protocol until after the Congressional elections of October [*November*], and President Moncada would like if possible to delay any publicity until after the signature. These suggestions arise out of

---

[97] See telegram No. 115 of the same date to the Secretary of State, *supra*.
[98] See telegram No. 87 of the same date to the Secretary of State, *supra*.

the Government's desire that the protocol be not injected into this approaching campaign and made a matter of party politics, since such a development would seriously endanger the approval of the protocol by the Nicaraguan Congress. I concur in these suggestions.

The ready acceptance by Honduras of Nicaragua's suggestion that the protocol be signed in Managua is greatly appreciated here. This Government will prepare the protocol for signature and I will communicate further arrangements in due time."

HANNA

715.1715/396 : Telegram

The Minister in Nicaragua (Hanna) to the Secretary of State

MANAGUA, November 21, 1930—11 a. m.
[Received 5 : 35 p. m.]

157. Department's 127, November 8, 5 p. m.[98a] The Minister for Foreign Affairs told me late yesterday that President Moncada desires to have some definite assurance of effective cooperation by the Government of Honduras in the suppression of banditry before signing the boundary protocol and had asked the Minister for Foreign Affairs to discuss the matter with me in an effort to find some acceptable way to attain that desire. The Minister for Foreign Affairs said that President Moncada thinks this a favorable opportunity to ask for such assurance which if given would help to meet opposition of the Conservative Party which has consistently opposed the Award of the King of Spain for a long period of years as well as the opposition of many Liberals who think Nicaragua is conceding too much and Honduras nothing. The Minister for Foreign Affairs stoutly maintained that his Government is not trying to evade signing the protocol and would sign as soon as the assurance mentioned was granted.

I told the Minister for Foreign Affairs that while I appreciated President Moncada's desire I would not like to submit to either my Government or the Government of Honduras a proposal to attain the desired assurance if acceptance thereof would be a condition precedent to signing the protocol. I told him a proposal made in such fashion could certainly be misinterpreted and would place this Government in an equivocal position in spite of protestations that it is not trying to evade signing the protocol. He said he thought President Moncada would insist upon having the assurance and I told him that I believe he could count upon the Department's assistance if the matter is presented to the Government of Honduras in an appropriate manner and at the proper time, but that I did not believe my Government would care to give its cooperation if this Government should now attach some condition to signing the protocol or even delay signing pending consideration of this new point.

[98a] Not printed.

I pointed out that the presence of the Boundary Commission on the frontier would place upon the Government of Honduras an equal share of responsibility for the adequate protection of the Commission and thus automatically bring about the desired cooperation and I reminded him that President Moncada had told me some months ago that he viewed the matter in that sense. I also pointed out that the probability of getting the desired assurance would be improved by signing the protocol. The Minister for Foreign Affairs said he would present my views to President Moncada and advise me further.

I deem President Moncada's desire reasonable if properly presented. The Boundary Commission must be given protection and the presence of an American on the Commission would appear to justify our arranging for Honduras to give an appropriate share of such protection but there should be no delay in signing the protocol pending that arrangement. The political difficulties mentioned by President Moncada exist and merit consideration. I may have some success in minimizing opposition by the Conservative Party but that party is now seeking issues on which to attack the Liberal administration. Please instruct.

Repeated to Tegucigalpa.

HANNA

715.1715/397 : Telegram

The Minister in Nicaragua (Hanna) to the Secretary of State

MANAGUA, November 22, 1930—11 a. m.
[Received 1:50 p. m.]

158. The American Minister in Tegucigalpa telegraphed me yesterday that the President of Honduras had just increased Honduran forces on the border from 30 to 70 men. The Minister stated that "vigorous pursuit of bandits in Honduras can be expected."

I am withholding this information from the Government here pending receipt of instructions requested in my telegram 157, November 21, 11 a. m.

HANNA

715.1715/400 : Telegram

The Minister in Nicaragua (Hanna) to the Secretary of State

MANAGUA, November 29, 1930—1 p. m.
[Received 3:45 p. m.]

163. Your telegram number 134, November 26, 2 p. m.[99] When I communicated to the Minister for Foreign Affairs this morning (President Moncada being out of town) the information summarized in my 158, November 22, 11 a. m., he expressed his gratefulness and said that he believed the boundary protocol would be signed before

[99] Not printed.

the end of this year and hoped that after seeing President Moncada he would be able to fix a date on which to base further arrangements.

HANNA

715.1715/396 : Telegram

The Secretary of State to the Minister in Nicaragua (Hanna)

WASHINGTON, December 5, 1930—5 p. m.

135. Your 157, November 21, 11 a. m.   Please seek earliest opportunity to confer with President Moncada and informally state that the Department regrets, in view of the antecedents in the case, that any suggestion of further delay in the signing of the Nicaragua-Honduras boundary protocol should arise, and the Department sincerely hopes that he may see his way clear to have the protocol as already agreed upon signed in Managua at an early date.

The Department feels that the recent actions of the Government of Honduras, especially as mentioned in your telegram No. 158, November 22, 11 a. m., indicate the favorable attitude of that Government.

[Paraphrase.]   The following is confidential.   The Department appreciates the political difficulties which face the President and it hopes that you may be successful in minimizing opposition by Conservative leaders.   The Department further hopes that the President himself will be able to avert opposition within his own party.   [End paraphrase.]

Your actions as outlined in the second paragraph of your telegram are approved and you should continue negotiations along the same lines.

Please repeat this message to the Legation at Tegucigalpa as No. 83 for its information.

STIMSON

715.1715/402 : Telegram

The Minister in Nicaragua (Hanna) to the Secretary of State

MANAGUA, December 6, 1930—3 p. m.
[Received 4:46 p. m.]

167. Department's 135, December 5, 5 p. m.   When I called upon the Minister for Foreign Affairs this morning concerning other matters, he told me he had conferred with President Moncada as promised in his previous conversation with me (reported upon in my telegram No. 163, November 29, 1 p. m.) and that President Moncada had authorized him to inform me that this Government is prepared to sign the protocol in Managua at the end of this month and that the Department may so inform the Government of Honduras to the end that the Government of Honduras may appoint its representative

and have him proceed to Managua with powers to sign the protocol. I told the Minister for Foreign Affairs I would advise you immediately by cable of the President's decision in this matter and he concurred.

The Minister for Foreign Affairs said that he personally thinks that publicity in this matter should be delayed as long as possible and that in his opinion this Government will maintain secrecy in this matter until the protocol is actually signed unless it is forced to make some statement to meet reports originating here or elsewhere concerning the negotiations. He said he thought it desirable to make every effort to avoid arousing opposition in the interval before the protocol is signed. I told him I would so advise you. President Moncada is absent from Managua and is not expected to return until December 8, his birthday. I will confer with him at the earliest practical moment thereafter; but, in view of the foregoing, I assume the Department will wish me to modify appropriately the instruction given in its telegram 135, December 5, 5 p. m.

I will repeat this telegram to Tegucigalpa, but I assume the Department will give the American Legation there appropriate instruction in the matter. With reference to the Department's No. 84, December 5, 6 p. m., to Tegucigalpa,[1] I suggest that Major Geyer's proposed visit to Managua be postponed pending developments.

HANNA

715.1715/402 : Telegram

The Secretary of State to the Minister in Nicaragua (Hanna)

WASHINGTON, December 8, 1930—6 p. m.

136. Your 167, December 6, 3 p. m. Please orally inform President Moncada that the Department is gratified with his decision to have the boundary protocol signed without further negotiations the end of this month,[2] and that in accordance with his suggestion the Legation at Tegucigalpa is being instructed by cable to inform the Government of Honduras and to suggest that the Honduran representative be appointed in order that he may proceed to Managua with full powers to sign the protocol as has now been fully agreed upon between the two Governments.

The desire of the Government of Nicaragua to avoid publicity is being brought to the attention of the Honduran Government.

Please modify appropriately such action as you take under the Department's telegram 135, December 5, 5 p. m.

The Department believes it now will be unnecessary for Major Geyer to go to Managua on this matter.

STIMSON

---

[1] Not printed.
[2] The protocol was signed at Managua January 21, 1931.

ARGENTINA

REVOLUTION IN ARGENTINA

835.00/461

The Chargé in Argentina (White) to the Secretary of State

No. 899   BUENOS AIRES, June 26, 1930.

[Received July 17.]

SIR: I have the honor to report that the cumulative results of hard times and the partial paralysis of the normal functions of government are stimulating the feeling that before many months elapse a change will come about.

The peso continues to depreciate daily as compared with foreign currencies. In the face of this phenomenon one possibility mentioned is to print more paper money, which would make the situation far worse. The other is to resort to a foreign loan. But the administration continues to delay and the terms of the financiers presumably grow stiffer as conditions get worse. . . . Labor is in an exceptionally refractory temper.

Any administration would be in a serious predicament in the face of such conditions. The present regime is held to be exceptionally dictatorial and extraordinarily inactive. The opposition within the Government party is growing.

Rumors are consequently current that the President may soon resign. If he did so his natural successor would be the Vice-President who is reported to be a good man. The latter, however, owes his selection to and is identified closely with the Minister of the Interior, who is considered the leader of one faction of the Radical Party, even as the Oyhanartes are prominent in the other wing, which represents the younger element; hence there is a rumor that both President and Vice-President might resign and that Congress would elect Dr. Alcorta, a former President of the Republic and a member of the Supreme Court.

While I do not at the moment of writing take much stock in reports of presidential or vice-presidential resignations, it is the general opinion that conditions are exceptionally bad and that the President's age, mentality and the state of his health render his continuation in office, if not problematical, at any rate a serious problem.

I have [etc.]   J. C. WHITE

835.00/464 : Telegram

The Ambassador in Argentina (Bliss) to the Secretary of State

[Paraphrase]

BUENOS AIRES, August 29, 1930—5 p. m.
[Received 6 : 55 p. m.]

111. The *coup d'état* in Peru [1] made a strong impression here and it may have been used by party chiefs in an endeavor to influence the President to believe that his life is in danger, that his only safeguard is to resign. The reinforcement of the guards at the Government House and President's residence in the last three days may have been done for the same purpose, though it is alleged to be the results of the discovery of plots against the Government. Nervousness has noticeably increased among officials and public. It is said that the military and naval forces favor the elimination of the provisions as to his successor. According to a fairly reliable report which came to me today, the President has consented to resign within the next few days. The situation is very tense but nothing definite has appeared.

BLISS

835.00/470 : Telegram

The Ambassador in Argentina (Bliss) to the Secretary of State

BUENOS AIRES, September 5, 1930—7 p. m.
[Received September 5—6 : 45 p. m.]

120. Foreign Office confirms that President has on account of ill health delegated his authority to the Vice President and that martial law is expected shortly to be declared.

BLISS

835.00 Revolutions/2 : Telegram

The Ambassador in Argentina (Bliss) to the Secretary of State

BUENOS AIRES, September 7, 1930—12 p. m.
[Received September 8—6 : 08 a. m.]

124. The text of the proclamation issued yesterday by the Provisional Government as well as the names of its personnel having been transmitted by press agencies I shall only forward them by pouch.

The overthrow of the Irigoyen Government yesterday which I reported by phone to the Department was accomplished expeditiously amid great public enthusiasm. At about 5 p. m. the white flag was hoisted at Government House and about an hour later General

[1] See "Revolution in Peru," vol. III, pp. 720 ff.

Uriburu cut off from his troops by the rejoicing civilians was triumphantly brought there by the populace, the Vice President at once signing his resignation as Acting President. The Cabinet officers who had already deserted their posts are at liberty.

Asylum had been asked for Irigoyen of the Chilean Ambassador and was accorded though not availed of, Irigoyen fleeing to La Plata where he surrendered himself to the military and resigned. He has not been held under restraint and is as free as his enfeebled physical condition permits.

Despite the change of government being effected by the Military, no resistance was offered though a certain number of civilians and soldiers have been killed and wounded by random machine gun firing from Irigoyenist houses. Except for the regrettable though understandable destruction of the personal effects of Irigoyen Oyhan [*Irigoyen Oyhanarte?*], several of their intimates and the office of the two *personalista* newspapers, no cases of vandalism have been reported. This is a credit to the Argentine populace as well as to military discipline and Uriburu is much gratified at having consummated his coup without serious bloodshed.

Immediately after assuming control the military junta issued a warning against excesses, dissolved Congress, and in Government proclamation stating that the Provisional Government would remain in power only until elections could be held, Government members pledging [*pledged?*] themselves neither to present nor accept their candidacy to the Presidency of the nation. The Uruguayan Ambassador tells me that he called informally this morning on Uriburu who said one of his principal concerns was how foreign countries would envisage his act and the attitude they would assume toward the new Government, for which reason he had selected Bosch as Minister of Foreign Affairs feeling sure a man of his high standing would produce a favorable effect abroad. [Paraphrase.] At the request of Bosch, who desires to talk with me before receiving the other foreign representatives, I am meeting him tomorrow morning at the residence of Adolfo Bioy, the new Under Secretary for Foreign Affairs. I shall then make the suggestion, as my personal opinion, that, in the official notification to the Chiefs of Missions of the establishment of a Provisional Government, he should not include a request for recognition. Recognition by the Government of the United States, however, would give not only great satisfaction to the new Government and its many adherents but would also help our situation in Argentina. I believe that the Provisional Government will be able to maintain itself in power until it has realized its declared purpose of holding, at the earliest possible date, elections for national Senators and Deputies and for President and Vice President. The preparation of the necessary machinery toward this end in the capital and provinces will require a considerable time. The Provisional Government is comprised of honest patriots, the Minister of the Interior and head of Cabinet being especially competent. All of them are Conservatives and represent the political minority of recent years. Nevertheless, the venality and blatant abuses of the Irigoyen Government have aroused such widespread indignation that it has been possible for Conservatives to overthrow it with the genuine approval of the majority of the population.

While following closely the developments of the next few days I recommend that the Government of the United States be ready to recognize this Provisional Government at an early date, and as soon as, if not before, any other important power. [End paraphrase.]

BLISS

835.00 Revolutions/3 : Telegram

The Ambassador in Argentina (Bliss) to the Secretary of State

[Extract—Paraphrase]

BUENOS AIRES, September 8, 1930—5 p. m.
[Received 8:30 p. m.]

125. . . . This morning there was published a declaration of the Independent Socialists giving their approval and adherence to the Provisional Government. Additional indications show that the overthrow of President Hipólito Irigoyen is warmly accepted throughout the country, and my belief that the new Government will be able to maintain itself and hold fair elections is being strengthened constantly by the news received from all parts of the country.

Early in the morning of September 6 a delegation of minority members of Congress [went to?] Campo de Mayo urging General Uriburu and exhorting troops to overthrow the Government. I again desire to emphasize the civilian composition of the new Government and that the Irigoyen Government was overthrown by a popular outburst of indignation and to renew the recommendation I made previously that the Government of the United States consider an early recognition believing that it would contribute toward the creation of a pleasant feeling on the part of the general public toward the United States.

BLISS

835.00 Revolutions/5 : Telegram

The Ambassador in Argentina (Bliss) to the Secretary of State

BUENOS AIRES, September 9, 1930—3 p. m.
[Received 4:51 p. m.]

126. Have received official note, signed Ernesto Bosch and dated yesterday, advising me that, as a result of event of public note, Gen-

eral Uriburu has assumed "Provisional Presidency of the nation" with the aims set forth in manifesto of the 6th and giving a list of his Cabinet. He also states: "It is the purpose and desire of the Provisional Government to maintain and develop as far as possible the cordial relations which happily unite the Argentine Republic with the nation that you so worthily represent."

BLISS

835.01/7 : Telegram

The Acting Secretary of State to the Ambassador in Argentina (Bliss)

[Paraphrase]

WASHINGTON, September 11, 1930—1 p. m.

100. Your personal conversation with Assistant Secretary of State Castle was fully considered by President Hoover. There appears to be no possibility of immediate recognition. I may say in the strictest confidence that a proposal has been made that the United States and Great Britain discuss the matter of recognition with each other. The Department will keep you informed.

COTTON

835.01/6 : Telegram

The Ambassador in France (Edge) to the Secretary of State

PARIS, September 11, 1930—1 p. m.
[Received September 11—12 : 38 p. m.]

286. According to Foreign Office press statement today France will await the action of the United States Government before deciding whether to recognize the new regimes in Argentina and in Peru.

[Paraphrase.] I understand that discussions over this matter have taken place between the British Embassy and the French Government and that the British Government also will probably await the decision of the United States before taking action. [End paraphrase.]

EDGE

835.01/8 : Telegram

The Ambassador in Argentina (Bliss) to the Secretary of State

[Paraphrase]

BUENOS AIRES, September 11, 1930—midnight.
[Received September 12—6 : 12 a. m.]

129. The Department is already aware of the fact that the revolution has resulted in favorable advance of exchange and an offer of a

loan double the amount asked by the Provisional Government; there are, however, other indications of immediate return of confidence; i. e., trade is resuming liabilities eliminated during the past years, commercial houses are making contributions to organizations previously refused in 1930, and in all probability the Supreme Court will manifest its adhesion to the Provisional Government within a few days.

The report of the embarkation of Irigoyen on an Argentine warship today is correct.

This afternoon the Spanish Ambassador called to inform me that he had received authorization to recognize the Provisional Government; that both he and the Italian Ambassador were desirous of proceeding at once but were disposed to wait if there were any likelihood of the United States taking similar action. I have learned confidentially that Uruguay is also ready to extend recognition. Yesterday the British Ambassador called to inquire about our attitude toward recognition, and I learned that he too had recommended it to his Government.

With reference to the Department's 100, September 11, 1 p. m., it would aid me to know whether the suggestion of American-British cooperation in matters of recognition originated with the British. It appears to me that England as the traditional friend of Argentina gains by keeping the United States from obtaining marked advantage in being first to extend recognition while her own nonrecognition loses her nothing as long as the United States is also withholding recognition. On the other hand, by simultaneous recognition the United States loses an advantage which becomes a British gain.

The United States, as the most feared and envied nation, has an opportunity to assist Argentina at a moment when moral support would be particularly appreciated, and would unquestionably benefit our position here. American business interests desire recognition in order to hasten recuperative business.

While I am not unmindful of Pan American interests, the situation created by the Bolivian revolution [2] and Peruvian revolution, or the possibility that a too prompt American recognition might be interpreted as of predatory intent, my handling of the delicate situation here would be strengthened were I to be informed what considerations are weighing against recognition.

BLISS

---

[2] See "Revolution in Bolivia," pp. 415 ff.

835.01/12 : Telegram

The Ambassador in Argentina (Bliss) to the Secretary of State

BUENOS AIRES, September 13, 1930—noon.
[Received 1 : 35 p. m.]

131. At 11 o'clock this morning Chile recognized the Provisional Government.

Norwegian Chargé d'Affaires told me this morning that he has received instructions to recognize when other important powers do so and that as soon as United States recognizes he will do likewise.

.   .   .   .

BLISS

835.00 Revolutions/7 : Telegram

The Acting Secretary of State to the Ambassador in Argentina (Bliss)

[Paraphrase]

WASHINGTON, September 13, 1930—3 p. m.

101. The Department desires to obtain promptly any reliable information with respect to the control exercised by the Provisional Government over the provinces, particularly those parts of Argentina where the party of President Irigoyen has been successful, e. g., the Province of Buenos Aires.

Also the Department desires to be kept informed with respect to the relations of the Provisional Government, which is understood to be made up largely of members of the Conservative Party and other political elements.

COTTON

835.00 Revolutions/8 : Telegram

The Ambassador in Argentina (Bliss) to the Secretary of State

BUENOS AIRES, September 14, 1930—12 p. m.
[Received September 15—2 : 43 a. m.]

132. Your 101, September 13, 3 p. m. Immediately after the overthrow of the Irigoyen Government the military authorities took charge of all provincial governments, civilian interventors having since been named for seven, military for two, naval for one and remaining two unannounced. In the two other provinces, Entre Rios and San Luis, the normal government machinery is functioning, anti-inte [*sic*] Irigoyenists having triumphed in recent elections.

The interventors appointed are men of highest type and are qualified to dominate the situation, such as Carlos Ibarguren for Cordoba,

Diego Saavedra for Santa Fe, Marco Aurelio Avellaneda for San Juan and Carlos Meyer Pellegrini, the last named having already assumed control of Buenos Aires Province with marked public approval. All the others will take office this week.

The Socialist Party has declared that while registering the illegality of the Provisional Government it acknowledges it and expresses faith in its intentions though, it will not collaborate with it. The Independent Socialist Party has made a like but more explicitly favorable declaration. The leaders of both parties have conferred with the Government and expressed confidence in the new Government. A majority of the members of the Senate, including all parties except the Radical, and the Deputies of all parties except the Radical met separately and declared in favor of dissolution. All parties in the Capital and the provinces except the Radical approve and support the Provisional Government. The overthrow of Irigoyen may justly be described as restoration rather than revolution. It is unquestionably civilian or popular rather than military, a constitutionalist movement unconstitutionally born.

BLISS

835.01/30

The Assistant Secretary of State (Castle) to the Under Secretary of State (Cotton) and the Assistant Secretary of State (White)

[WASHINGTON,] September 15, 1930.

The British Ambassador called at my house yesterday morning to say that his Government appreciated our friendly attitude in taking up with him the question of recognition of the new government of Argentina. He had just received a telegram, in which he was instructed to say that the British had studied the question very seriously in the light of reports from South America and had decided that clearly the governments of both Peru and Argentina should be recognized at the same time. The Foreign Office feels that conditions in the two countries are very similar and that it would be invidious to recognize one without recognizing the other. The Foreign Office feels, furthermore, that these governments, having displayed a reasonable stability and having expressed the determination to protect foreigners and to fulfill international relations, that they should be promptly recognized. The British Government wants us to know that Great Britain will recognize both Peru and the Argentine next Wednesday.[3] He hopes that this will be agreeable to us and that we shall be willing to recognize at the same time. The Ambassador tells me that, in the meantime, if the question is raised, their

---

[3] September 17.

Ambassadors have been told to say that, although there has not yet been formal recognition, they have been authorized to carry on diplomatically exactly as in the past.

In the light of the telegrams we have received, it seems to me we should be exceedingly unwise not to do this. I told the Ambassador that I would telephone him some time this morning what we should do.

W. R. C[ASTLE, JR.]

835.01/32

The Assistant Secretary of State (Castle) to the Secretary of State

[WASHINGTON,] September 16, 1930.

THE SECRETARY: Last night I telephoned the British Ambassador that you had the question of recognition of the governments of Argentina and Peru under consideration, that you would presumably take it up this morning with the President and that we should undoubtedly let him know the decision some time today. I also told him that this was merely for his information, that we understood that Great Britain was to recognize on the 17th and that we were not asking for delay. The Ambassador said that he fully understood.

This morning Mr. Campbell telephoned me to say that they had just received a cable from Mr. Alexander instructing the Embassy to inform the Department that Great Britain was delaying recognition for one day and would act on the 18th.

W. R. CASTLE, JR.

835.01/16 : Telegram

The Ambassador in Argentina (Bliss) to the Secretary of State

BUENOS AIRES, September 16, 1930—1 p. m.
[Received 1:26 p. m.]

134. Germany and Paraguay have today recognized the new Government. [Paraphrase.] I have just been informed by the British Ambassador that he has received instructions to recognize on September 18. [End paraphrase.]

BLISS

835.01/18 : Telegram

The Secretary of State to the Ambassador in Argentina (Bliss)

[Paraphrase]

WASHINGTON, September 16, 1930—2 p. m.

104. On Thursday, September 18, you will please inform the Foreign Minister that you are instructed by the Government of the

United States to enter into full diplomatic relations with the new Argentine Government, thus constituting recognition thereof.

An announcement of this will be made here late Wednesday afternoon. Until released here, the above should be treated as confidential. Similar action will be taken as to Bolivia and Peru.

STIMSON

835.01/20 : Telegram

The Minister in Colombia (Caffery) to the Secretary of State

[Paraphrase]

BOGOTÁ, September 16, 1930—6 p. m.
[Received 9 : 35 p. m.]

114. Department's telegram No. 47, September 16, 2 p. m.[4] Olaya told me that he would recognize Argentina, Bolivia, and Peru on Thursday, September 18.

CAFFERY

835.01/28

Press Release Issued by the Department of State on September 17, 1930

The Secretary of State stated:[5]

"I have directed Mr. Bliss, our Ambassador to Argentina, to resume normal diplomatic relations with the provisional Argentine Government; and have directed Mr. Dearing, our Ambassador to Peru, to resume normal diplomatic relations with the provisional Peruvian Government; and have directed Mr. Feely, our Minister accredited to Bolivia, to present his letters of credence and resume normal diplomatic relations with the provisional Bolivian Government. This is to be done tomorrow, September eighteenth.

"In reaching the conclusion to accord recognition to these three governments, the evidence has satisfied me that these provisional governments are *de facto* in control of their respective countries, and that there is no active resistance to their rule. Each of the present governments has also made it clear that it is its intention to fulfill its respective international obligations and to hold, in due course, elections to regularize its status.

"The action of the United States in thus recognizing the present Argentine, Peruvian and Bolivian Governments does not represent

---

[4] Not printed.

[5] The statement was transmitted to the American diplomatic missions in Costa Rica, Cuba, Dominican Republic, El Salvador, Guatemala, Haiti, Honduras, Nicaragua, and Panama in circular telegram of September 17, 4 p. m. The first four paragraphs of the statement were transmitted to the American diplomatic missions in Argentina, Bolivia, and Peru in another circular telegram of September 17, 4 p. m.

any new policy or change of policy by the United States toward the nations of South America or the rest of the world.

"I have deemed it wise to act promptly in this matter in order that in the present economic situation our delay may not embarrass the people of these friendly countries in reestablishing their normal intercourse with the rest of the world."

(The Secretary was asked to clarify his statement that this does not represent any change in policy. In reply he stated:)

"In acting towards these three Governments, which we are recognizing tomorrow, we are following the regular rules of international law, and the regular policy which has characterized this country ever since the first Secretary of State announced it—Mr. Jefferson in the Administration of President Washington. But with certain countries there are differences made by treaty either with us or between each other. For example, the five Central American countries have entered into a treaty between themselves in which they agreed not to recognize any Government which came into office by virtue of a *coup d'état* or a revolution. That was done in 1923,[6] and although we were not a party to the treaty, we were in hearty accord with it and we agreed on our part that we would follow the same policy with respect to the five Republics who had agreed upon it.

"I think in order that you may get this clear I will give you a statement Mr. Hughes made in June, 1923, and which represents the present policy of this Government. Mr. Hughes stated the attitude of our Government in regard to these five Central American Governments as follows:

" 'The attitude of the Government of the United States with respect to the recognition of new Governments in the five Central American Republics whose representatives signed at Washington on February 7, 1923, a general Treaty of Peace and Amity, to which the United States was not a party, but with the provisions of which it is in the most hearty accord, will be consonant with the provisions of Article II thereof which stipulates that the contracting parties will not recognize any other Government which may come into power in any of the five Republics through a *coup d'état* or a revolution against a recognized Government, so long as the freely elected representatives of the people thereof have not constitutionally reorganized the country. And even in such a case they obligate themselves not to acknowledge the recognition if any of the persons elected as President, Vice-President or Chief of State designate should fall under any of the following heads:

" '1) If he should be the leader or one of the leaders of a *coup d'état* or revolution, or through blood relationship or marriage, be an ascendent or descendent or brother of such leader or leaders.

---

[6] General treaty of peace and amity signed at Washington, February 7, 1923, *Conference on Central American Affairs, December 4, 1922–February 7, 1923* (Washington, Government Printing Office, 1923), pp. 287, 288.

" '2) If he should have been a Secretary of State or should have held some high military command during the accomplishment of the *coup d'état*, the revolution, or while the election was being carried on, or if he should have held this office or command within the six months preceding the *coup d'état*, revolution, or the election.'

"Those were very stringent restrictions which the different countries entered into by treaty between themselves with the object evidently of discouraging a revolution or *coup d'état* within the five Republics, and we endorsed that policy so far as those five countries are concerned. It is quite different from the general policy of this country and of the general policy of international law towards the recognition of Governments in the world at large. There are also other exceptions based on treaties although I am not going to go into them in detail. Of course, we have a special treaty with Cuba [7] which also changes the general rule of international law and imposes on this country greater obligations in regard to Cuba than we have toward other nations, and we have treaties with other nations like Haiti [8] and there may be others. I am not trying to give you an exclusive list, but those are all exceptions to the general policy which we are carrying out with regard to the three Governments in South America."

835.01/23 : Telegram

The Ambassador in Argentina (Bliss) to the Secretary of State

BUENOS AIRES, September 17, 1930—7 p. m.
[Received 8 : 30 p. m.]

136. I have appointment with Minister for Foreign Affairs at 11 o'clock tomorrow morning when I shall comply with instructions contained in your 104 of September 16, 2 p. m.

In addition to countries already reported, recognition was made yesterday by Sweden, Italy, the Vatican, Norway and Denmark, and today France and Spain.

BLISS

---

[7] Treaty of May 22, 1903, *Foreign Relations*, 1904, p. 243.
[8] Treaty of September 16, 1915, *ibid.*, 1915, p. 449.

835.01/33

The Chargé in Cuba (Reed) to the Secretary of State

No. 362   HABANA, September 18, 1930.
                                  [Received September 22.]

SIR: Referring to the Department's telegram No. 104 of September 16, 2 p. m.,[9] I have the honor to report that I duly informed the Cuban Secretary of State that the Government of the United States would recognize the provisional governments of Argentina, Bolivia and Peru on September 18.

.   .   .   .

Later in the afternoon, the President called me aside at a reception given by the Mexican Ambassador and told me that his Government was most anxious to act in complete harmony with the Government of the United States in this and in all other matters and that . . . he would nevertheless recognize all three governments at the same time as did the Government of the United States.

Accordingly, late yesterday afternoon, instructions were dispatched to the Cuban legations in Argentina, Bolivia and Peru to enter into official relations with the provisional governments of those countries.

Respectfully yours,   EDWARD L. REED

835.01/31 : Telegram

The Chargé in Brazil (Washington) to the Secretary of State

                    RIO DE JANEIRO, September 20, 1930—noon.
                    [Received September 20—11 : 40 a. m.]

57. I am reliably informed that today Brazil "will enter into friendly relations" with the Governments of Argentina and Bolivia.

The attitude of the Peruvian Government towards ex-President Leguia and towards persons who have sought asylum in the Brazilian Legation in Lima will probably cause Brazil to postpone its recognition for a few days.[10]

                                                    WASHINGTON

---

[9] Not printed.
[10] In telegram No. 58, September 20, 2 p. m., the Chargé in Brazil reported that he had just been informed that Brazil would recognize the Government of Peru that day; vol. III, p. 759.

AUSTRIA

CONSENT TO SUBORDINATION OF THE AUSTRIAN RELIEF LOAN TO A PROPOSED NEW AUSTRIAN LOAN [1]

863.51 Relief Credits/204 : Telegram

The Consul at Geneva (Blake) to the Acting Secretary of State

GENEVA, March 12, 1930—11 a. m.
[Received 2:40 p. m.]

From Wilson:[2] Reference Department's telegram reparation 79, June 15, 2 p. m., 1929, to Embassy Paris[3] regarding Austrian debt settlement. The question now arises whether the Department prefers that this matter be dealt with by the Reparation Commission as contemplated in article 6 of the draft agreement[4] or whether the Commission should take no action in view of the fact that the Hague agreement of January 20, 1930, concerning Austria[5] (which will doubtless be ratified shortly by the required number of countries) provided that the first charge upon Austrian assets and revenues in favor of reparation will cease to be operative. If the Department desires the Commission to act in the matter, such action had better be taken at the next meeting which will be held towards the end of this month and which will perhaps be the last meeting at which the Commission would still possess power to take the action called for under the draft agreement. I recently asked George of my office in Paris to submit informally the following draft decision to the principal delegations at the Reparation Commission; I am now advised that the British and French have no objections and that the Italian representative said he personally was in agreement and that he felt his Government would probably have no objections since recent difficulties between Italy and Austria had now been arranged, but that he would consult with his Government to confirm this:

"The Reparation Commission,
Considering the contingent agreement (annex 3505 H 1, 2) between

[1] For previous correspondence concerning the negotiations, see *Foreign Relations*, 1928, vol. I, pp. 858 ff.

[2] Edwin C. Wilson, First Secretary of Embassy in France, and American unofficial representative on the Reparation Commission.

[3] See footnote 66, *Foreign Relations*, 1928, vol. I, p. 923.

[4] *Austrian Debt Settlement:* Hearings before the Committee on Ways and Means, House of Representatives, 70th Cong., 2d sess., on H. J. Res. 340, etc. (Washington, Government Printing Office, 1928), pt. 2, p. 13.

[5] League of Nations Treaty Series, vol. CIV, p. 413.

the Federal Government of the Republic of Austria and the Government of the United States of America relative to the refunding of the principal and interest of the relief bonds, series B of 1920, by which Austria is indebted to the United States in the principal amount of $24,055,708.92,

Takes note that the bonds to be issued by Austria to the United States under this agreement are in substitution for and in refunding of the above-mentioned relief bond, series B of 1920, in the principal amount of $24,055,708.92 and accrued interest, and agrees that these bonds shall enjoy the same security as the bonds of relief series B 1920, and shall be a first charge upon all the assets and revenues of Austria, and shall have priority over costs of reparation under the Treaty of St. Germain [6] or under any treaty or agreement supplementary thereto, or under any arrangements concluded between Austria and the Allied and Associated Powers during the armistice, signed on November 3, 1918." [7]

It is possible that some delegation may insist on adding to the foregoing the phrase appearing at the end of the penultimate paragraph of the text of the original relief bond of 1920, beginning "without prejudice to the obligations of Austria" and ending "by an interested power". If this should be insisted on, I assume there could be no objection from our point of view.

I therefore respectfully request early instructions by telegraph as to (1) whether the Department desires the Commission to act in the matter, and (2), if so, whether the suggested draft decision is satisfactory. The foregoing is of course all subject to the Italian Government concurring in the action of the Commission.

BLAKE

863.51 Relief Credits/205 : Telegram

The Acting Secretary of State to the Consul at Geneva (Blake)

WASHINGTON, March 15, 1930—4 p. m.

For Wilson. Your March 12, 11 a. m.

(1) As draft agreement with Austria was submitted to Congress, it is desirable that the Reparation Commission take decision which will place Austria in a position to meet the requirements of Article 6 of the draft agreement.

(2) Suggested draft decision is satisfactory.

COTTON

---

[6] *Treaties, Conventions, etc.*, 1910–1923, vol. III, p. 3149.
[7] *Foreign Relations*, Paris Peace Conference, 1919, vol. II, p. 175.

863.51 Relief Credits/206 : Telegram

The Ambassador in France (Edge) to the Acting Secretary of State

PARIS, March 29, 1930—noon.
[Received March 29—9 : 25 a. m.]

92. Reparation No. 302. At a meeting held today the Reparation Commission:

1. Unanimously approved, as far as it is concerned, the plan for the repayment of the relief credits granted to Austria between 1919 and 1923 by nine relief bond holding governments (including the Government of the United States).

2. Having taken cognizance of the letters of March 12 and 23, 1929,[8] and appended documents (annexes 3505 F to H) by which the Austrian Government notified the contingent agreement concluded with the Government of the United States of America with a view to the funding and repayment of American relief credits, unanimously adopted decision in the terms of the suggested draft telegraphed to Department by Mr. Wilson from Geneva on March 12, 1930, and approved by the Department's telegraphic reply to Mr. Wilson dated March 15, 1930.

The adhesion of the Italian Government to the settlement agreement of London of June 15, 1928 [8] (see annexes 3505 A and E) is the subject of my letter to the Department of March 25, 1930,[8] transmitting copies annexes 3605 [*3505*] I and J.

EDGE

863.51 Relief Credits/207

The Austrian Minister (Prochnik) to the Acting Secretary of State

No. 47/R   WASHINGTON, March 31, 1930.

SIR: At the instance of the Federal Government of the Republic of Austria I have the honor to ask your kind intermediary with a view of bringing the following communication to the attention of the Secretary of the Treasury.

With Public Resolution No. 81 dated February 4th 1929,[9] the Secretary of the Treasury is authorized, if he determines that substantially similar action has been taken by each of the Governments of Denmark, France, Great Britain, Italy, the Netherlands, Norway, Sweden and Switzerland in respect of the Austrian relief bonds held by them and that the Reparation Commission has given an appropriate release in respect to such loan, to subordinate the lien of the United States upon the assets and revenues of Austria for the payment of the Austrian relief bond held by the United States (but without prejudicing the priority over costs of reparation stipulated in

---

[8] Not printed.
[9] 45 Stat. 1149.

the relief bond) to a lien upon such assets and revenues as may be pledged for the payment of one or more loans floated by Austria in an aggregate net amount of not more than 725,000,000 Austrian Schillings and for a period of not more than thirty years from July 1st 1929.

The Relief Bond Committee representing the Governments of the aforementioned countries expressed with note ddo December 12th 1927 [10] their consent in principle to the release from the prior charge in favor of the Relief Bonds, for the period of the new loan, not exceeding 30 years, of such securities as may be necessary for said loan provided that

1.) similar consent is obtained from any other Powers interested as holders of Austrian Relief Bonds;

2.) consent is also obtained from the Reparation Commission for the release of the securities in question from the charge for reparation and other Treaty Costs;

3.) the specific securities which it is desired to release, are in due course, submitted to the Chairman of the Relief Bond Committee who is authorized to approve them.

The first proviso referring to the United States of America was taken care of by the aforecited Public Resolution.

To satisfy the second proviso, although after coming into force of the Hague Convention of January 20th 1930, it will become obsolete, the Austrian Government has taken the necessary steps to obtain formal consent of the Reparation Commission.

It is now in respect to the third proviso that the Federal Government of the Republic of Austria by this present notifies the Government of the United States of America that it intends to pledge for the new Investment Loan the following resources, to wit:

1.) the revenues of the customs;

2.) the gross receipts of the Tobacco Monopoly;

3.) such parts of the other revenues and receipts of the Federal Government of Austria which for the full protection of the new loan may be considered necessary as a supplement in case the two previously referred to sources of income should be considered insufficient.

For further explanation my Government wishes to state, that it considers the probability of resorting to the additional securities mentioned on the third place very remote, nay almost out of question, as the receipts from customs and tobacco monopoly are four times the amount needed to take care of the service of the League of Nations-Loan and will be thrice the amount required for covering interest and sinking fund on both loans (the League of Nations-Loan and the new Investment Loan).

---

[10] *Foreign Relations, 1927*, vol. I, p. 470.

In view of the fact, however, that the new Investment Loan, unlike the first one, will not be vouched by an international guaranty, it seems inadvisable to my Government to strengthen this unavoidable discrepancy in the value of these two loans by restricting beforehand the volume of securities accessible for the new Investment Loan.

The Federal Government of Austria requests, therefore, the Government of the United States of America to consent to the release from the prior charge in favor of the Relief Bonds, of the custom-revenues, the gross receipts of the tobacco monopoly and of such other revenues and receipts of the Federal Government of Austria as may in future and under certain circumstances be required to cover the service.

A similar request was submitted to Sir Frederick Leith Roth [Ross] Chairman of the International Relief Bonds Committee by the Minister of the Austrian Republic in London.

Accept [etc.] EDGAR PROCHNIK

863.51 Relief Credits/212 : Telegram

The Acting Secretary of State to the Ambassador in Great Britain (Dawes)

WASHINGTON, April 15, 1930—6 p. m.

93. (1) Public Resolution No. 81 approved February 4, 1929, reads in part as follows:

"Resolved by the Senate and House of Representatives of the United States in Congress assembled, That in order that the United States may cooperate with the Governments of Denmark, France, Great Britain, Italy, the Netherlands, Norway, Sweden, and Switzerland in making it possible for Austria to obtain by means of a loan the additional funds necessary in the furtherance of its reconstruction program, the Secretary of the Treasury is hereby authorized, if he determines that substantially similar action has been taken by each of such Governments in respect of the Austrian relief bonds held by it (hiatus) to subordinate the lien of the United States upon the assets and revenues of Austria pledged for the payment of the Austrian relief bond held by the United States (hiatus) to a lien upon such assets and revenues as may be pledged for the payment of one or more loans floated by Austria in an aggregate net amount of not more than 725 million Austrian schillings and for a period of not more than 30 years from July 1, 1929."

The Federal Government of the Republic of Austria has notified the Government of the United States that it intends to pledge for the new investment loan the following resources, to wit: (1) the revenues of the customs; (2) the gross receipts of the tobacco monopoly; (3) such parts of the other revenues and receipts of the Federal Government of Austria which for the full protection of the new loan may be considered necessary as a supplement in case the two previously referred to sources of income should be considered insufficient.

Within the limits of the authority conferred by the above resolution, the Secretary of the Treasury is willing to subordinate the lien of the United States upon the above-mentioned Austrian assets and revenues, but in view of the proviso contained in the resolution the Secretary of the Treasury will not be in a position to take such action unless and until substantially similar action has been taken by the Governments of Denmark, France, Great Britain, Italy, the Netherlands, Norway, Sweden and Switzerland. In this connection you will note that the Resolution empowers the Secretary of the Treasury to determine when the proviso has been substantially complied with.

(2) The Department understands that Sir Frederick Leith-Ross, Chairman of the International Relief Bonds Committee, is acting for the other creditor Powers on an Austrian request to subordinate their liens. Please ascertain terms of such reply as may have been made through him.

(3) To enable the Secretary of the Treasury to determine whether the conditions set forth in Public Resolution No. 81 have been fulfilled, the Department desires a direct statement from each of the Relief Creditor Governments regarding the action taken with respect to subordinating their liens.

(4) A brief summary of Government's reply should be cabled, full text following by pouch.

(5) Repeat foregoing as Department's instruction to Copenhagen, Paris, Rome, The Hague, Oslo, Stockholm and Berne after substituting for paragraph (2) a statement of information received from Leith-Ross.

COTTON

863.51 Relief Credits/213 : Telegram

The Ambassador in Great Britain (Dawes) to the Acting Secretary of State

LONDON, April 17, 1930—3 p. m.
[Received April 17—1 : 10 p. m.]

69. Last paragraph of Department's 93, April 15, 6 p. m., complied with, with the following substituted for paragraph 2:

"2. Sir Frederick Leith-Ross states that he sent the following letter to the Austrian Minister in London on April 16, 1930:

'Sir: In the *aide-mémoire* which you were good enough to hand to me on the 19th [of] March, 1930, the Austrian Government submitted the specific securities for which a release is desired to me as Chairman of the International Relief Bonds Committee, representing the Governments of Denmark, France, Great Britain, Italy, the Netherlands, Norway, Sweden, and Switzerland.

In reply I request you to inform the Austrian Government that in [the] exercise of the mandate conferred upon me by the Committee, I approve on their behalf the specific securities proposed, namely, the customs and tobacco monopoly, and such of the other revenues and receipts of the Austrian Government as may from time to time be required by the trustees of the bondholders of the proposed development loan.

It is understood that the release of these securities is subject to (1) the Hague agreements of 20th January, 1930, coming into force, and (2) a similar release of these [the same] specific securities being given by the United States Government in respect of the relief bonds which they hold.

I am, Sir, et cetera, et cetera'."

Leith-Ross added that in his opinion British Government would ratify Young Plan [11] Wednesday next.

DAWES

863.51 Relief Credits/214

The Austrian Minister (Prochnik) to the Acting Secretary of State

No. 60/R   WASHINGTON, April 19, 1930.

SIR: The Federal Government of the Austrian Republic proposed final settlement of their indebtedness in respect of Relief Bonds of the series "Relief Bonds Series B of 1920" (Renewal Bonds) to all creditor Governments on an identical basis.

This proposal was accepted on behalf of the Governments of Denmark, France, Great Britain, Netherlands, Norway, Sweden and Switzerland by the International Relief Bonds Committee in London on June 15th 1928.

With note ddo. November 14th 1928, No. 158/R.[12] an offer of settlement was likewise submitted by this Legation to the Government of the United States on behalf of the Federal Government of Austria, and to the pertaining note were annexed the terms offered to and accepted by the aforementioned creditor nations [13] showing that neither of them received more favorable terms and conditions than those embodied in a draft agreement between the United States of America and Austria, submitted to the 70th Congress and approved by said legislative body with Public Resolution No. 81.

Negotiations were pending with Italy for her adherence to the agreements made with the other Governments of the Relief-Creditor-Nations which negotiations were brought to a successful conclusion

---

[11] For correspondence relating to plan for the final settlement of German reparations recommended by the Committee of Experts, June 7, 1929, see *Foreign Relations*, 1929, vol. II, pp. 1025 ff.

[12] *Ibid.*, 1928, vol. I, p. 917.

[13] Enclosures not printed.

in an exchange of notes effected in the Hague on January 19th 1930, between Dr. Johann Schober, the Federal Chancellor, representing Austria and Signor Antonio Mosconi, Finance Minister of the Kingdom of Italy, representing the latter country.

I have the honor to submit copies of the last mentioned notes[14] setting forth that also this agreement reached with the last outstanding Creditor-Government does not contain more favorable terms and conditions than those embodied in the draft agreement between the United States of America and the Republic of Austria.

Having thus proved to a conclusion that my Government fully complied with the provisions under which Congress authorized the settlement of the indebtedness of Austria to the United States of America and having previously submitted to you a power of attorney executed in my name for the purpose of signing said agreement on behalf of the Austrian Government I beg to request you to kindly set a time and place for the exchange of signatures on said instrument.

You would greatly oblige me by bringing the contents of this note to the attention of the Secretary of the Treasury.

Accept [etc.]   EDGAR PROCHNIK

863.51 Relief Credits/220 : Telegram

The Minister in Sweden (*Morehead*) *to the Acting Secretary of State*

STOCKHOLM, April 26, 1930—11 a. m.
[Received April 26—9:15 a. m.]

13. Department's telegram No. 93, to London, April 15, 6 p. m., repeated to this Mission.

I have received a note from the Minister for Foreign Affairs this morning in part as follows:

"I have the honor to inform you that the statement made by Sir Frederick Leith-Ross in his letter of April 16, 1930, to the Austrian Minister at London was issued with the authorization of the Royal (Swedish) Government and approved by it."

MOREHEAD

863.51 Relief Credits/221 : Telegram

The Ambassador in Great Britain (*Dawes*) *to the Secretary of State*

LONDON, May 2, 1930—11 a. m.
[Received May 2—6 a. m.]

88. Department's 93, April 15, 6 p. m. In letter dated May 1, 1930, Foreign Office refers to the letter, dated April 16, 1930, sent

---

[14] Enclosures not printed.

by Sir Frederick Leith-Ross to the Austrian Minister (text of which was contained in Embassy's 69, April 17, 3 P. M.), and states:

"Sir Frederick Leith-Ross, besides being Chairman of the International Relief Bonds Committee, is of course the representative of His Majesty's Government on the Committee and the letter which he wrote was written with their authority and embodies their intention."

DAWES

863.51 Relief Credits/222 : Telegram

The Ambassador in France (Edge) to the Secretary of State

PARIS, May 2, 1930—4 p. m.
[Received May 2—1 p. m.]

126. Department's 93, April 15, 6 p. m., to London. The French Government states that the terms of the letter of April 16 last from Leith-Ross to the Austrian Minister at London express the conditions to which it especially has subordinated its adhesion to the emission of the Austrian loan.

EDGE

863.51 Relief Credits/223 : Telegram

The Minister in Switzerland (Wilson) to the Secretary of State

BERNE, May 2, 1930—4 p. m.
[Received May 2—2 p. m.]

35. Department's 93, April 15, 6 p. m. [to London.]

[Federal Political] Department [reply], dated May 1st, just received. Final paragraph reads in translation as follows:

"Informed in 1927 of the desire of the Austrian Government to conclude in the United States a new loan of 725 million schillings, the Federal Council, by decision of December 12, 1927, authorized the Swiss representative in the International Committee of Relief Credits at London to acquiesce in the request made of the states participating in the 1920 loan to renounce, in favor of the projected loan, the assertion of its claim to the privilege of priority which the relief credit enjoys. Thus we can fully confirm the declarations made concerning this matter by Sir Frederick Leith-Ross."

Note follows by mail.[15]

WILSON

---

[15] Not printed.

863.51 Relief Credits/224 : Telegram

The Minister in Norway (Swenson) to the Secretary of State

OSLO, May 6, 1930—1 p. m.
[Received May 6—9 : 25 a. m.]

8. The Department's telegram No. 93, April 15, American Embassy at London. Foreign Office informs me that the Norwegian Government has agreed to subordinate the lien in question on the conditions named in Sir Frederick Leith-Ross' letter to Austrian Minister in London, dated April 15, last.

SWENSON

863.51 Relief Credits/229 : Telegram

The Chargé in Denmark (Ives) to the Secretary of State

COPENHAGEN, May 15, 1930—4 p. m.
[Received May 15—2 : 11 p. m.]

25. Department's 93, April 15, 6 p. m., to the Embassy, Paris [*London*]. I am in receipt of a note, dated May 14th, signed by Minister of Foreign Affairs, wherein it is stated that Denmark, by the declaration made on April 16, last, by the Chairman of the International Relief Bond Committee, has renounced its liens upon the revenues of the Austrian Government derived from customs and tobacco monopoly, on the condition that the Hague agreement of January 20, 1930, come into force and that a similar renunciation is made by the United States.

IVES

863.51 Relief Credits/231 : Telegram

The Secretary of State to the Chargé in Denmark (Ives)

WASHINGTON, May 19, 1930—5 p. m.

25. Your 25, May 15, 4 p. m. Does Danish note state that Denmark has renounced liens on all revenues mentioned in Leith-Ross' letter of April 16 or only on customs and tobacco revenues? United States Treasury must have unambiguous statement on which to base its action.

STIMSON

863.51 Relief Credits/233 : Telegram

The Chargé in Denmark (Ives) to the Secretary of State

COPENHAGEN, May 22, 1930—4 p. m.
[Received May 22—2 : 15 p. m.]

26. Department's 25, May 19, 5 p. m. Danish note May 14 mentioned only customs and tobacco revenues.

In a further note, dated May 20, Foreign Office states that by declaration of Leith-Ross, dated April 16, last, Denmark has renounced its liens on the revenues of the Austrian Government derived from the customs and tobacco monopoly as well as such of the other revenues as may from time to time be required as guarantee in favor of the creditors of the new loan.

IVES

863.51 Relief Credits/235

The Austrian Minister (Prochnik) to the Secretary of State

No. 75/R WASHINGTON, May 22, 1930.

EXCELLENCY: The London Relief-Agreement of June 15th, 1928, provides that Austria must obtain the consent of the Governments of the Relief-Creditor-Nations prior to settling certain indebtedness incurred by it through the so-called Forfait-agreement entered upon for the execution of Art. 184 of the Treaty of St. Germain. These obligations which were not affected by the Hague-Convention of January 20, 1930 (Art. IV), are as follows:

to Rumania	362. 700 gold-kronen
to Poland	54. 812 " "
to Yugoslavia	346. 280 " "
to France	16. 237 " "
total	780. 029 " "

Of these the debt to France amounting to 16.237 gold kronen is secured by a Treasury note, originally due on July 1st 1929 but subsequently deferred to July 1st 1930. As this amount may in the course of pending negotiations be subjected to some minor alteration, the Federal Government of Austria, wishing to provide for a safe margin, places the total amount of the Forfait-indebtedness at 850.000 gold kronen, for the payment of which amount it asks the consent of the Governments of the Relief-Creditor-Nations.

A major portion of this indebtedness will not be settled in cash but credited in way of compensation against certain claims which Austria is holding against the aforementioned countries.

At the instance of my Government I have the honor to ask Your

Excellency's kind intermediary with a view of obtaining the consent of the Government of the United States to the settlement by Austria of the so-called Forfait-debts not exceeding the total amount of 850.000 gold kronen.

To avoid delays in pending negotiations and in view of the fact that the above referred to Treasury Note to France falls due on July 1st, an early action on this request will be highly appreciated.

An identical request was submitted to the Relief Committee by our Minister in London.

Accept [etc.]   EDGAR PROCHNIK

863.51 Relief Credits/234

The Secretary of State to the Ambassador in France (Edge)

No. 170   WASHINGTON, May 23, 1930.

SIR: The Department has received your despatch No. 517, dated May 2, 1930,[16] transmitting the reply of the French Government to the Embassy's inquiry regarding the Austrian loan pursuant to the Department's cabled instruction No. 93 of April 15, 6 p. m., to the Embassy at London.

The reply of the French Government is not directly responsive to the Department's inquiry on behalf of the Treasury Department. The Embassy is requested to endeavor to obtain from the French Government a statement in substance that Sir Frederick Leith-Ross' letter of April 16, 1930, to the Austrian Minister at London is approved by the French Government and was made pursuant to its authority.

I am [etc.]   For the Secretary of State:
                                                          FRANCIS WHITE

863.51 Relief Credits/236 : Telegram

The Chargé in Italy (Kirk) to the Secretary of State

ROME, May 26, 1930—noon
[Received 12:50 p. m.]

37. Department's 93, April 15, 6 p. m., to London. Following statement received from Foreign Office in reply to representations made by this Embassy based on above-mentioned telegram:

Italian Ministry of Finance concurs with declarations made by Chairman of Relief Bond Committee to Austrian Government in note of April 16th, 1930, approving guarantees proposed by Government of Austrian Republic, with special reference to customs and

---

[16] Not printed; see telegram No. 126, May 2, 4 p. m., from the Ambassador in France, p. 399.

tobacco monopoly and such other revenues and receipts of Austrian Government as may from time to time be required by trustees of bondholders of the proposed reconstruction loan. It is understood that the release of these guarantees is subject to the Hague agreements and to the condition that similar approval be given by American Government, which appears to be contained in representations based on Department's above-mentioned telegram.

Statement concludes by declaring that Italy's decisions are subordinated to analogous decisions by other interested states.

Copy and translation of Foreign Office Note follows by pouch.[17]

KIRK

863.51 Relief Credits/237 : Telegram

The Secretary of State to the Chargé in Italy (Kirk)

WASHINGTON, May 29, 1930—5 p. m.

43. Your 37, May 26, noon. What is the meaning of the phrase "the release of these guarantees is subject to the Hague agreements," particularly as the Hague agreements are understood to have come into force before date of Italian statement?

STIMSON

863.51 Relief Credits/238 : Telegram

The Chargé in Italy (Kirk) to the Secretary of State

ROME, June 3, 1930—5 p. m.
[Received June 3—1:55 p. m.]

41. Department's 43, May 29, 5 p. m. Foreign Office official informs me that according to interpretation by Ministry of Finance of phrase referred to, Italian Government does not wish to agree to any proposals the conditions of which are contrary to the terms of the agreements reached at The Hague, some of which have already been ratified and some of which are still in the process of ratification. For the Department's further information, Italian text of above-mentioned phrase reads:

"il rilascio di queste garenzie è subordinato agli Accordi dell' Aja".

It would appear that *garenzie* may properly be translated either as "guarantees" or as "securities" and consequently wording of phrase referred to in Department's above-mentioned telegram seems to conform to last paragraph of letter of Sir Frederick Leith-Ross quoted in Department's telegram to London No. 93, April 15, 6 p. m.

KIRK

---

[17] Not printed.

863.51 Relief Credits/244

The Netherlands Minister (Van Royen) to the Under Secretary of State (Cotton)

WASHINGTON, June 20, 1930.

MY DEAR MR. SECRETARY:—The Minister of Foreign Affairs at The Hague has advised me, that the Minister of the United States has informed him, that the Department of State in Washington would appreciate receiving from Her Majesty's Government a confirmation of its assent to the suspension of its lien upon certain Austrian revenues, pledged for the payment of the Austrian Relief bonds. The American Minister referred in his note to Public Resolution No. 81 of February 4th, 1929.

Pursuant to instructions received, I take pleasure in informing you, that on the 19th of this month the Minister of Foreign Affairs has communicated by writing the assent of Her Majesty's Government to Mr. Diekema.[18]

Believe me [etc.]   J. H. VAN ROYEN

863.51 Relief Credits/245 : Telegram

The Chargé in Italy (Kirk) to the Secretary of State

ROME, June 21, 1930—11 a. m.
[Received June 21—9 : 55 a. m.]

50. My telegram No. 40 [41?], June 3, 3 [5?] p. m. Following is translation of urgent *note verbale*, dated June 20th, received today from Foreign Office with request that contents be cabled to the Department:

"With reference to *note verbale* No. 199 of April 19th of the American Embassy the Minister of Foreign Affairs learns that the Government of the United States of America has interpreted the consent given by Italy in its *note verbale* of May 20th, last, No. 217089–34 as an adherence which is not absolute and unconditional as regards the attitude of the Royal Government concerning the subordination of the liens and the acceptance of the guarantees (*garenzie*) proposed by Austria for the issuance of the new loan.

The Ministry of Foreign Affairs has the honor therefore to assure the American Embassy that by its above-mentioned *note verbale* of May 20th, last, the Royal Government had in fact intended to act unconditionally to the communication made by the chairman of the International Relief Bond Committee and to the request of the American Embassy with a view to facilitating the conclusion of the loan without in any way intending to prejudice the replies of the other Governments."

---

[18] Gerrit John Diekema, Minister in the Netherlands.

As meaning of phrase beginning "without in any way intending, et cetera" was doubtful I made an oral inquiry at the Foreign Office and was told that this phrase was intended merely to make it clear that the Italian adherence was not contingent upon the replies of the other Governments.

[Paraphrase.] I have been told by Austrian Minister here in Rome that the *note verbale*, dated June 20, was sent as a result of conversations held recently with officials of the Italian Foreign Office in which the Minister called attention to certain inaccuracies which he states were contained in the note of May 20. He believes these inaccuracies were based on misunderstandings between the Ministry of Finance and the Foreign Office. The hope has also been expressed by the Austrian Minister that the explanations contained in this last note may be cabled immediately to London where the Austrian Minister of Finance is arriving to confer regarding the Austrian loan. I have told him that I would send the Department information to that effect. [End paraphrase.]

KIRK

863.51 Relief Credits/260

The French Ministry for Foreign Affairs to the American Embassy in France [19]

[Translation]

PARIS, June 21, 1930.

By note dated the 10th of this month, the American Embassy inquired of the Ministry for Foreign Affairs if the reply addressed on April 16, 1930, by the Chairman of the Relief Credits Committee to the Austrian Minister at London concerning the authorisation solicited by the Austrian Government to issue a new loan of 750 million schillings, had been approved by the French Government, and whether he had acted on this occasion with the authority of this Government.

In reply to this communication, the Ministry for Foreign Affairs has the honor to inform the American Embassy that Mr. Leith-Ross acted in the matter as the representative of the Governments constituting the Relief Credits Committee, and that the letter of April 16, 1930, received the approval of the French Government.

---

[19] Copy transmitted to the Department by the Ambassador in France as an enclosure to his despatch No. 649, June 25, 1930; received July 7.

863.51 Relief Credits/247 : Telegram

The Ambassador in France (Edge) to the Secretary of State

PARIS, June 26, 1930—noon.
[Received June 26—8 : 45 a. m.]

195. Reparation 312. The Commission has just received a letter from the Austrian Minister at Paris to the effect that in the negotiations taking place in London for the projected Austrian loan the American bankers have stated that United States Treasury before subordinating its relief bond lien on Austrian assets in favor of the new loan would insist on the formal fulfillment of the condition expressed in Public Resolution Number 81, approved February 4, 1929, "that the Reparation Commission has given an appropriate release in respect of such loan". The Austrian section of the Commission is meeting this afternoon to consider the question and will probably recommend the Commission to adopt at its meeting on the 28th instant a decision to the effect that as of the date of putting into force of the Hague agreement of January 20, 1930, concerning Austria, the first charge on Austrian assets created by article 197 of the Treaty of Saint Germain ceases to have any effect.

EDGE

863.51 Relief Credits/248 : Telegram

The Ambassador in France (Edge) to the Secretary of State

PARIS, June 27, 1930—noon.
[Received June 27—9 : 20 a. m.]

199. Reparation 313. Following meeting Austrian section yesterday the Reparation Commission in order to avoid any delay in loan negotiations sent letter to Austrian Minister at Paris in sense indicated my reparation 312, June 26, noon. Letter will receive retroactive approval by Commission tomorrow.

EDGE

863.51 Relief Credits/251

The Secretary of State to the Austrian Minister (Prochnik)

WASHINGTON, June 27, 1930.

SIR: I have the honor to refer to your note No. 75/R, dated May 22, 1930, requesting the consent of the Government of the United States to the settlement by Austria of the so-called Forfait-debts not exceeding the total amount of 850,000 gold kronen, and to inform you that the Government of the United States offers no objection to the settlement by Austria of the so-called Forfait-debts in the manner set forth in your note under reference.

Accept [etc.]   H. L. STIMSON

863.51 Relief Credits/252 : Telegram

The Ambassador in France (Edge) to the Secretary of State

PARIS, June 28, 1930—6 p. m.
[Received June 29—7 : 44 a. m.]

202. Reparation 314. Reparation Commission this morning took decision indicated my reparation 313; [19a] that is, it approved retroactively the letter sent to the Austrian Minister on June 26, stating that as from the coming into force of the Hague agreement of January 20, 1930, between the creditor powers and Austria, the first charge on the assets and revenues of Austria created by Article 197 of the Treaty of Saint Germain ceases to be operative.

The Austrian Minister in Paris has just left with me a certified copy of the procès-verbal of deposit of ratification of the agreement of January 20, 1930, with Austria, drawn up at noon today at the Ministry for Foreign Affairs, which states that the instruments of ratification of the following countries have been deposited: Austria, Belgium, Great Britain, France, Italy, Greece, Rumania, Czechoslovakia and Yugoslavia. The Austrian Minister has asked me to cable the foregoing to the Department.

EDGE

863.51 Relief Credits/253

The Austrian Legation to the Department of State

MEMORANDUM

The Austrian Minister is in receipt of a cable from the Austrian Federal Minister of Finances from London June 28, 1930, transmitting the following note from the chairman of the Relief Committee:

"With reference to my letter of 16th April 1930, I have the honor to state for the information of the Austrian Government that the first proces verbale of the deposit of ratifications of the agreement signed at the Hague on 20th January 1930, having been drawn up on the 28th instant, and the agreement having come into force between the contracting parties who have ratified as from the last mentioned date of the release of the securities referred to in the letter of sixteenth April 1930, by the Governments of Denmark, France, Great Britain, Italy, Netherlands, Norway, Sweden and Switzerland which hold Austrian Relief Bond has come into operation subject to a similar release of the same securities being given by the United States Government in respects of the Relief Bonds which they hold.

"I am Your Excellency your obedient servant,

Leith Ross."

The Austrian Minister has been instructed to communicate the con-

---

[19a] See telegram No. 199, June 27, noon, from the Ambassador in France, p. 406.

tents of the above letter to the Secretary of the Treasury and to request that a declaration of release by the United States Government be issued at the earliest possible date and transmitted by cable.

WASHINGTON, June 30, 1930.

863.51 Relief Credits/256

The Secretary of the Treasury (Mellon) to the Secretary of State

[Extract]

WASHINGTON, July 2, 1930.

MY DEAR MR. SECRETARY:

.   .   .   .

Acting, therefore, under the authority conferred on me as Secretary of the Treasury of the United States by Public Resolution of Congress No. 81, approved February 4, 1929, having first determined that substantially similar action has been taken by each of the relief creditor governments in respect of the Austrian relief bonds held by it and that the Reparation Commission has given an appropriate release in respect of such loan, I hereby declare that the lien for the payment of the Austrian relief bonds held by the United States upon the customs and tobacco monopoly and such of the other revenues and receipts of the Austrian Government as may from time to time be required by the trustees of the bondholders of the proposed development loan, is subordinated to a lien upon such of said assets and revenues as may be pledged for the payment of one or more loans floated by Austria in an aggregate net amount of not more than 725,000,000 Austrian schillings for a period of not more than thirty years from July 1, 1929.

Very truly yours,

A. W. MELLON

TREATY AND EXCHANGE OF NOTES BETWEEN THE UNITED STATES AND AUSTRIA FOR EXTRADITION AND COMMUTATION OF DEATH PENALTY, SIGNED JANUARY 31, 1930

Treaty Series No. 822

Treaty Between the United States of America and Austria, Signed at Vienna, January 31, 1930 [20]

The United States of America and Austria desiring to promote the cause of justice, have resolved to conclude a treaty for the extradition of fugitives from justice, between the two countries and have appointed for that purpose the following Plenipotentiaries:

---

[20] In English and German; German text not printed. Ratification advised by the Senate, June 16, 1930; ratified by the President, June 28, 1930; ratified by Austria, August 9, 1930; ratifications exchanged at Vienna, August 12, 1930; proclaimed by the President, August 14, 1930.

The President of the United States of America:

Mr. Albert Henry Washburn, Envoy Extraordinary and Minister Plenipotentiary to Austria, and

The Federal President of the Republic of Austria:

Mr. Johann Schober, Federal Chancellor,

who, after having communicated to each other their respective full powers, found to be in good and due form, have agreed upon and concluded the following articles:

ARTICLE I. It is agreed that the Government of the United States and the Federal Government of Austria shall, upon requisition duly made as herein provided, deliver up to justice any person, who may be charged with, or may have been convicted of any of the offenses specified in Article II of the present Treaty which are designated in the laws of the surrendering state as crimes other than misdemeanors and which were committed within the jurisdiction of one of the High Contractings Parties, whenever such person shall seek an asylum or shall be found within the territories of the other; provided that such surrender shall take place only upon such evidence of criminality, as according to the laws of the place where the fugitive or person so charged shall be found, would justify his apprehension and commitment for trial if the offense had been there committed.

ARTICLE II. Persons shall be delivered up according to the provisions of the present Treaty, who shall have been charged with or convicted of any of the following offenses:

1. Murder, comprehending the crimes designated by the term parricide, assassination, manslaughter when voluntary, poisoning or infanticide.

2. Rape, abortion, carnal knowledge of children under the age of fourteen years.

3. Abduction or detention of women or girls for immoral purposes.

4. Bigamy.

5. Arson.

6. Wilful and unlawful destruction or obstruction of railroads, which endangers human life.

7. Crimes committed at sea:

   a) Piracy, as commonly known and defined by the law of nations, or by statute.

   b) Wrongfully sinking or destroying a vessel at sea.

   c) Mutiny or conspiracy of two or more members of the crew or other persons on board of a vessel on the high seas, for the purpose of rebelling against the authority of the Captain or Commander of such vessel, or by fraud or violence taking possession of such vessel.

   d) Assault on board ship upon the high seas with intent to do bodily harm.

8. Burglary, defined to be the act of breaking into and entering the house of another in the night time with intent to commit a felony therein.

9. The act of breaking into and entering the office of the Government and public authorities or the offices of banks, banking houses, savings-banks, trust-companies, insurance and other companies, or other buildings not dwellings with intent to commit a felony therein.

10. Robbery, defined to be the act of feloniously and forcibly taking from the person of another goods or money by violence or by putting him in fear.

11. Forgery or the utterance of forged papers.

12. The forgery or falsification of the official acts of the Governments, or public authority, including Courts of Justice, or the uttering or fraudulent use of any of the same.

13. The fabrication of counterfeit money, whether coin or paper, counterfeit titles or coupons of public debt, created by National, State, Provincial, Territorial, Local or Municipal Governments, bank notes or other instruments of public credit, counterfeit seals, stamps, dies and marks of State or public administrations, and the utterance, circulation or fraudulent use of the above mentioned objects.

14. Embezzlement or criminal malversation committed within the jurisdiction of one or the other party by public officers or depositaries, where the amount embezzled exceeds one hundred dollars or the Austrian equivalent.

15. Embezzlement by any person or persons, hired, salaried or employed, to the detriment of their employers or principals, when the crime is punishable by imprisonment or other corporal punishment by the laws of both countries, and where the amount embezzled exceeds one hundred dollars or the Austrian equivalent.

16. Kidnapping of minors or adults, defined to be the abduction or detention of a person or persons, in order to exact money from them, their families or any other person or persons, or for any other unlawful end.

17. Larceny, defined to be the theft of effects, personal property, or money, of the value of one hundred dollars or more or the Austrian equivalent.

18. Obtaining money, valuable securities or other property by false pretences or receiving any money, valuable securities or other property knowing the same to have been unlawfully obtained, where the amount of money or the value of the property so obtained or received exceeds one hundred dollars or the Austrian equivalent.

19. Perjury or subornation of perjury.

20. Fraud or breach of trust by a bailee, banker, agent, factor, trustee, executor, administrator, guardian, director or officer of any company or corporation, or by any one in any fiduciary position, where the amount of money or the value of the property misappropriated exceeds one hundred dollars or the Austrian equivalent.

21. Crimes against the laws of both countries for the suppression of slavery and slave trading.

22. Wilful desertion or wilful non-support of minor or dependent children.

The extradition is also to take place for participation in any of the aforesaid crimes as an accessory before or after the fact or for any attempt to commit any of the aforesaid crimes; provided such participation or attempt be punishable by imprisonment by the laws of both Contracting Parties.

ARTICLE III. The provisions of the present Treaty shall not import a claim of extradition for any offense of a political character, nor for acts connected with such offenses; and no person surrendered by or to either of the High Contracting Parties in virtue of this Treaty shall be tried or punished for a political offense committed before his extradition.

The State applied to or Courts of that State shall decide whether the offense is of a political character or not.

When the offense charged comprises the act either of murder or assassination or of poisoning, either consummated or attempted, the fact that the offense was committed or attempted against the life of the Sovereign or Head of any State or against the life of any member of his family, shall not be deemed sufficient to sustain that such offense was of a political character; or was an act connected with offenses of a political character.

ARTICLE IV. No person, except with the approval of the surrendering State, shall be tried for any crime committed before his extradition other than that for which he was surrendered, unless he has been at liberty for one month after having been tried for that offense, to leave the country, or, in case of conviction, for one month after having suffered his punishment or having been pardoned.

ARTICLE V. A fugitive criminal shall not be surrendered under the provisions hereof, when, from lapse of time or other lawful cause, either according to the laws of the country within the jurisdiction of which the crime was committed or according to the laws of the surrendering State, the criminal is exempt from prosecution or punishment for the offense for which the surrender is asked.

ARTICLE VI. If the person whose extradition has been requested, pursuant to the stipulations of this Convention, be actually under prosecution for a crime in the country where he has sought asylum, or shall have been convicted thereof, his extradition may be deferred until such proceedings be terminated, or until such criminal shall be set at liberty in due course of law.

ARTICLE VII. If a fugitive criminal claimed by one of the parties hereto, shall be also claimed by one or more powers pursuant to treaty provisions, on account of offenses committed within their jurisdiction, such criminal shall be delivered to that State whose demand is first received, unless its demand is waived. This Article shall not affect such treaties as have already previously been concluded by one of the Contracting Parties with other states.

ARTICLE VIII. Under the stipulations of this Treaty, neither of the

High Contracting Parties shall be bound to deliver up its own citizens.

ARTICLE IX. The expense of transportation of the accused shall be paid by the Government which has preferred the demand for extradition. No claim other than for the board and lodging of an accused prior to his surrender arising out of the arrest, detention, examination and surrender of fugitives under this Treaty shall be made against the Government demanding the extradition; provided, however, that any officer or officers of the surrendering Government, who shall in the course of their duty, receive no salary or compensation other than specific fees for services performed, shall be entitled to receive from the Government demanding the extradition the customary fees for the acts or services performed by them, in the same manner and to the same amount as though such acts or services had been performed in ordinary criminal proceedings under the laws of the country of which they are officers.

These claims for board and lodging and for fees are to be submitted through the intermediary of the respective Government.

ARTICLE X. Everything found in the possession of the fugitive criminal at the time of his arrest, whether being the proceeds of the crime, or which may be material as evidence in making proof of the crime, shall so far as practicable, according to the laws of either of the High Contracting Parties, be delivered up with his person at the time of surrender. Nevertheless, the rights of a third party with regard to the articles referred to, shall be duly respected.

ARTICLE XI. The stipulations of the present Treaty shall be applicable to all territory wherever situated, belonging to either of the High Contracting Parties or in the occupancy and under the control of either of them, during such occupancy or control.

Requisitions for the surrender of fugitives from justice shall be made by the respective diplomatic agents of the High Contracting Parties. In the event of the absence of such agents from the country or its seat of Government, or where extradition is sought from territory included in the preceding paragraph, other than the United States or Austria, requisitions may be made by superior consular officers. Requisitions for surrender with accompanying documentary proofs shall be required to be translated by the Government which has preferred the demand for extradition into the language of the surrendering Government.

The arrest and detention of a fugitive may be applied for on information, even by telegraph, of the existence of a judgment of conviction or of a warrant of arrest.

In Austria, the application for arrest and detention shall be addressed to the Federal Chancellor, who will transmit it to the proper department.

In the United States, the application for arrest and detention shall be addressed to the Secretary of State, who shall deliver a mandate certifying that the application is regularly made and requesting the competent authorities to take action thereon in conformity to statute.

In case of urgency, the application for arrest and detention may be addressed directly to the competent magistrate in conformity to the statutes in force.

The person provisionally arrested shall be released, unless within three months from the date of commitment in the United States—or from the date of arrest in Austria, the formal requisition for surrender, with the documentary proofs hereinafter described, be made as aforesaid by the diplomatic agent of the demanding Government, or in his absence, by a consular officer thereof.

If the fugitive criminal shall have been convicted of the crime for which his extradiction is asked, a copy of the sentence of the court before which such conviction took place, duly authenticated, shall be produced. If, however, the fugitive is merely charged with crime, a duly authenticated copy of the warrant of arrest in the country where the crime was committed, and of the depositions upon which such warrant may have been issued, shall be produced, with such other evidence or proof as may be deemed competent in the case.

ARTICLE XII. In every case of a request made by either of the High Contracting Parties, for the arrest, detention or extradition of fugitive criminals, the appropriate legal officers of the country where the proceedings of extradition are had, shall assist the officers of the Government demanding the extradition before the respective judges and magistrates, by every appropriate legal means within their power.

ARTICLE XIII. The present Convention shall be ratified by the High Contracting Parties, in accordance with their respective constitutional methods and shall take effect on the thirtieth day after the date of the exchange of ratifications, which shall take place at Vienna as soon as possible, but it shall not operate retroactively.

On the day when the present Convention takes effect, the Convention of July 3, 1856 shall cease to be in force except as to crimes therein enumerated and committed prior to the date first mentioned.

The present Convention shall remain in force for a period of six months after either of the two Governments shall have given notice of a purpose to terminate it.

In witness whereof the above named Plenipotentiaries have signed the present Treaty and have hereunto affixed their seals.

Done in duplicate at Vienna this 31rst day of January nineteen hundred and thirty.

ALBERT HENRY WASHBURN
[SEAL]
[SEAL] SCHOBER

Treaty Series No. 822

The American Minister in Austria (Washburn) to the Austrian Federal Chancellor (Schober)

VIENNA, January 31, 1930.

EXCELLENCY: At the moment of signing the Treaty of Extradition between the United States of America and the Republic of Austria, I have the honor to state that I have been duly authorized to inform Your Excellency that in the event of the conviction in the United States of a person extradited from Austria where such conviction is followed by a sentence of death, the Government of the United States will undertake to recommend to the appropriate authorities the exercise of mercy by way of the commutation of the sentence to life imprisonment.

Accept [etc.]   ·   ALBERT H. WASHBURN

Treaty Series No. 822

The Austrian Federal Chancellor (Schober) to the American Minister in Austria (Washburn)

[Translation]

VIENNA, January 31, 1930.

MR. MINISTER: I have the honor, in the name of the Federal Government, to acknowledge the receipt of the note which Your Excellency sent me on the occasion of the signing of the treaty between the Republic of Austria and the United States of America for the extradition of criminals, and to take note of the declaration therein contained according to which Your Excellency has been empowered to inform me that the Government of the United States, in the event of a person delivered by Austria being found guilty in the said State and sentenced to death, the gracious commutation of the death penalty to a life imprisonment will be recommended.

Accept [etc.]   SCHOBER

BOLIVIA

REVOLUTION IN BOLIVIA

824.00/495 : Telegram

The Chargé in Bolivia (Hibbard) to the Secretary of State

LA PAZ, May 29, 1930—11 a. m.
[Received 11 : 15 a. m.]

31. My telegram No. 30, May 28, 4 p. m.[1] President Siles resigned last night turning over the Executive power to the Cabinet. Elections for a constituent assembly to revise the Constitution have been called for June 29. The assembly will be composed of the usual number of Senators and Deputies making up Congress and will meet on July 28th.

HIBBARD

824.00/496 : Telegram

The Chargé in Bolivia (Hibbard) to the Secretary of State

LA PAZ, May 29, 1930—6 p. m.
[Received May 30—2 : 25 p. m.[2]]

32. My telegram No. 31.[3] I have received the following note from the Minister of Foreign Affairs.

"La Paz, May 28, 1930.

Mr. Chargé d'Affaires: The decree, copy of which I have the honor to enclose herewith, will inform you that today His Excellency, the President of the Republic, Dr. Hernando Siles, has resigned his high constitutional office and that the Cabinet (Council of Ministers) has assumed the functions of the Government.

I also have the honor to inform you that while the National Convention is being assembled, the Council of Ministers will continue the functions of the Executive power in all normality, respecting international conventions and all obligations of the state.

Requesting you to be so kind as to inform your Government of the contents of this note, I am pleased to offer you the assurance of my high consideration. Signed F. Vega."

---

[1] Not printed.
[2] Telegram in two sections.
[3] *Supra.*

415

Decree.

"The Council of Ministers considering:

That the President of the Republic, Dr. Hernando Siles, basing his opinion on the grave condition of the state and desiring to consolidate the institutionality of the country, has resigned today irrevocably his high office, thus preventing himself from intervening in the solution of the political problem raised by parliamentary and popular manifestations soliciting his continuance in the Government;

That it is necessary to normalize the institutional progress of the Republic, giving the Nation the possibility of resolving its own problems by itself with high civic spirit;

That the majority of the Nation has manifested the urgent necessity of proceeding with the constitutional reform for which it is indispensable to have recourse to the popular will, fountainhead of sovereignty;

That the ordinary National Congress is not endowed with sufficient power to resolve the existing problems nor to fix the standard conducive to the normalization of the institutional life of the Republic;

That the public administration cannot remain unattended without producing grave disorder and jeopardizing the stability of the Nation;

That the merely transitory functions imposed upon the Council of Ministers, by the exceptional circumstances of the present time, should last only for the time strictly necessary to consult the desire of the country, meanwhile [directing] the administration and fulfilling the external obligations which the Republic has incurred,

Decrees:

Article 1. The Council of Ministers assumes the functions of the Executive power.

Article 2. The conventional elections are convoked for Sunday, June 29th, next, for the purpose of electing Senators and Deputies in the entire Republic, who will jointly constitute the National Convention.

Article 3. The National Convention will begin its functions on July 28 of this year, in the city of La Paz, and will proceed immediately to resolve the political problem and to consider the constitutional reforms which may be proposed. Their work finished as members of the convention, the Senators and Deputies will exercise the functions of the ordinary Legislative power until they complete their term of office.

Article 4. A supplementary decree will regulate the elections.

Done in the Palace of Government in the city of La Paz, this 28th day of May 1930. Signed G. Antelo Araúz, Minister [of Government] and Justice; F. Vega, Minister for Foreign Affairs and Worship (ad interim) and War; F. Mercado, Minister of Hacienda; J. Aguirre Achá, Minister of Public Instruction; Lieutenant Colonel Toro, Minister of Fomento and Communications; Colonel Banzer, Minister of Agriculture and Colonization."

I have acknowledged the receipt of this note, stating that in accordance with the request contained therein I have informed my Government of its contents.

This afternoon there was a meeting of the diplomatic corps to discuss what attitude should be taken toward the new Government. Three points were raised:

(1) Whether, in view of the fact that this Government is in reality a continuation of President Siles' administration although unconstitutional, relations should not be continued normally with the exception of treaty negotiations.

(2) Whether if relations are continued normally this does not give tacit recognition to an unconstitutional government which might prove embarrassing later, particularly as there is a grave possibility that the power may be seized by an individual before the Constituent Assembly meets.

(3) Whether a formal act of recognition should be made and if so to whom should it be addressed.

The consensus of opinion was that nothing should be done which would embarrass the present administration and that it was therefore desirable to have uniformity of action by all representatives. However no one was prepared to commit his Government and it was decided that each should cable for instructions. I therefore respectfully request instructions as soon as possible as there will be another meeting of the corps on Monday afternoon in view of the arrival of the new Minister for Foreign Affairs.

As far as American interests are concerned the question of recognition has importance as the bankers must decide whether they will permit this Government to draw on funds now deposited in New York for future payments on the service of the Bolivian external debt.

HIBBARD

824.01/1 : Telegram

The Chargé in Bolivia (Hibbard) to the Secretary of State

LA PAZ, May 31, 1930—11 a. m.
[Received May 31—10:45 a. m.]

33. My telegram No. 32, May 29, 6 p. m. The Brazilian Minister has just called to inform me that he has received instructions from his Government in the following sense concerning the recognition of the present Bolivian Government. Brazil will assume the same attitude as that taken in 1920 at the time of the Saavedra revolution when Brazil and the United States acted in unison in maintaining cordial relations with the Provisional Government but refused to recognize Government constitutionality or to negotiate with it.[4] Brazil hopes that the United States will also take this attitude, as it is felt that to do otherwise would establish a dangerous precedent.

HIBBARD

---

[4] See *Foreign Relations*, 1920, vol. I, pp. 372, 381, and 382.

824.01/4 : Telegram

The Acting Secretary of State to the Chargé in Bolivia (Hibbard)

WASHINGTON, June 2, 1930—noon.

20. Your 32, May 29, 6 p. m., and 33, May 31, 11 a. m. The Department does not desire to raise any question regarding the recognition of the new regime in Bolivia. It desires that you should continue normal diplomatic relations with the Government and that you should not take part in any joint action of the diplomatic corps. You may inform the Brazilian Minister confidentially regarding the above.

CARR

824.01/4 : Telegram

The Chargé in Bolivia (Hibbard) to the Secretary of State

LA PAZ, June 3, 1930—11 a. m.
[Received 11 : 40 a. m.]

34. All diplomatic representatives received practically the same instructions as contained in Department's telegram 20, June 2, noon.

There are signs of dissension among the members of the Cabinet Council and reports from the interior indicate that some of the departments, particularly Cochabamba and Potosi, are not satisfied with the present regime. Fidel Vega appears to be strongest Minister and it is commonly expected that he will place himself at the head of the Provisional Government, thus becoming a formidable rival for Siles should elections actually be held. Both the Liberal and Republican Parties have invited Saavedra to return, but so far he has given no indication of his plans.

I gather from conversations with the Paraguayan Minister that his Government will not begin direct negotiations on the Chaco question until there is a constitutional government here.[4a]

HIBBARD

824.00/498 : Telegram

The Chargé in Bolivia (Hibbard) to the Secretary of State

LA PAZ, June 18, 1930—noon.
[Received 3 : 25 p. m.]

35. During the past week there have been several demonstrations of the Nationalist Party in favor of Siles and his reelection. They have been fairly orderly although the windows of Saavedra's house have been broken. There have been smaller counter-demonstrations, during one of which the headquarters of the Nationalist Party were

---

[4a] For correspondence relating to entrance by Bolivia and Paraguay into direct negotiations for settlement of the Chaco dispute, see pp. 327 ff.

destroyed. For not controlling the latter, the Chief of Police and his assistant have been transferred to the provinces.

An official report this morning announces that Villazon on the Argentine frontier was attacked yesterday by Communists but that the situation is well under control. There is much Communist activity at present particularly among unemployed miners in the Oruro district. Headquarters are said to be in Montevideo.

The Minister of the Interior and Justice Department has resigned and his position filled by Lieutenant Colonel Toro, formerly Minister of Public Works and Communications. Colonel Banzer, previously Minister of Agriculture, has taken the position left vacant by Toro thus giving the Army possession of the two most important Cabinet positions for controlling elections. Ezekiel Romecin has been made Minister of Agriculture.

HIBBARD

824.00/500 : Telegram

The Chargé in Bolivia (Hibbard) to the Secretary of State

LA PAZ, June 22, 1930—3 p. m.
[Received June 23—8 : 55 a. m.]

37. My telegram No. 36, June 20, noon.[4b] The situation in La Paz and throughout the country remains very tense. Last night an attempt against the Government here, including plans for Siles' assassination, was frustrated. There were street demonstrations last night and this morning. In the latter two students agitating against the Government were killed. There is no doubt that the Government exaggerates these demonstrations for the purpose of putting on heavier military restrictions but the situation is serious and there may be grave trouble before the elections next Sunday, particularly as those opposed to the Government are lining up with Communist elements.

HIBBARD

824.00/503 : Telegram

The Chargé in Bolivia (Hibbard) to the Secretary of State

LA PAZ, June 25, 1930—3 p. m.
[Received 3 : 10 p. m.]

41. My telegram No. 40, June 25, noon.[4b] Oruro has been taken by revolutionists. Federal troops there refused to take any action against the rebels. There is dissatisfaction among troops here and the Government fears to send any to Oruro for this reason and because the situation is too critical in La Paz. All regular communications are cut between La Paz and Oruro. It is expected that there will be a movement against the Government here tonight or tomorrow.

HIBBARD

[4b] Not printed.

Press Release Issued by the Department of State on June 30, 1930 [5]

The Department has received a telegram, dated June 27, 10 a. m.,[6] which was delayed in transmission from Mr. Frederick P. Hibbard, the American Chargé d'Affaires at La Paz, to the effect that on Wednesday night, June 25, at 9 o'clock, the cadets of the military college revolted against the Government following the receipt of the news of the successful revolt in Oruro. There was heavy street fighting all during the night and Thursday morning in which other elements opposed to the Government joined and during which the military college was bombarded. The Government troops were able to put down the uprising temporarily, although the majority of the cadets and their sympathizers had not yet surrendered and were barricaded on the outskirts of the city. Several members of the Diplomatic Corps appealed to General Kundt in the interest of humanity to halt the firing, which he did. The telegram adds that the Army has taken control of the Government and a military junta of six ranking colonels is in charge. Most of the members of the cabinet and the nationalist leaders have taken refuge in foreign legations. Ex-President Siles and his family are in the Brazilian Legation. However, the Nationalist Party still refuses to concede control to a military régime, and Mr. Hibbard stated that until this was settled there might be further trouble. Oruro, Cochabamba, Sucre, and Potosi are all in control of military juntas. Everything is quiet in those cities, although there has been street fighting. They are prepared to join La Paz in temporary Army control of the country, but insist that the Nationalist control of the country be broken and that Siles be exiled. Their program is to maintain the present constitution and, when tranquillity is established, to hold the elections in a normal manner. The telegram added that the atmosphere in La Paz was still tense, that shops and public utilities were closed, and that, although the American Legation was in the direct line of firing, no damage had been done to it or to any American property.

The Department has received a further telegram, dated June 28, 1 p. m., from Mr. Hibbard, stating that the cadets, students, and other elements opposed to the Government, who were barricaded on the Altiplano Thursday were joined by the aviation forces and several regiments. Meanwhile, there were continued demonstrations against the Government at La Paz, the crowds demanding the release of political prisoners. The Prefect, Colonel Julio Sanjines, also a member of the military junta, was eventually forced to resign, and the prefecture,

---

[5] Reprinted from Department of State, *Press Releases*, July 5, 1930, p. 1.
[6] Telegrams from the Chargé in Bolivia, upon which this release is based, are not printed.

as well as all other Government offices, was taken over by the mob. All political prisoners were released amid a wildly enthusiastic reception. The cadets, aviation troops, line regiments, and armed civilians marched into La Paz where they were joined by the crowd and other military units. During the day there was spasmodic firing. Mr. Hibbard adds that for the time being the Government is controlled by Colonel Pando as military chief, Otero as prefect, with Bustamante, President of the Banco Central, and Elio, former Minister for Foreign Affairs, as advisers. They are awaiting the arrival of military representatives from the other provinces when a new military junta will be formed to govern until constitutional elections can be called. The telegram adds that Friday afternoon the houses of ex-President Siles, Taborga, Romecin, Sanjines, Vega, Kundt, and other Nationalist leaders were sacked and the contents destroyed. Ex-President Siles' grand piano was burned in the street before the Brazilian Legation. The telegram adds that the battle cries have been for the constitution without mention of individual names and that a white flag is carried with the Bolivian flag. The Army has turned against General Kundt, and he has taken refuge in the German Legation along with the other German military instructors. The majority of the Army is being concentrated at La Paz. Except for enthusiastic street parades with bands, the city is quiet, although many shops are closed and rail and wire communications are irregular. Those in control are taking every measure to prevent further reprisals.

Mr. Hibbard adds that every legation excepting the American and the Italian have political refugees and that it is presumed that arrangements will shortly be made to take them out of the country, or else guarantees will be given them. On Wednesday and Thursday of last week, Bustamante, President of the Banco Central, was in the American Legation. Mr. Hibbard adds that the fact that the American Legation is next to the military college and has been in the center of the trouble, with troops surrounding it, has prevented it from being the asylum of other refugees.

Walter I. Gholz, an American teacher in the American Institute, was slightly wounded in the leg by machine-gun fire during the night of Wednesday, June 25, but no other Americans or American property have been injured.

A telegram, dated June 28, 4 p. m., from Mr. Hibbard, states that the following junta will govern the country for the present: Colonels Osorio, Pando, Lanza, González Quint, and Bilbao, with Doctor Bustamante as adviser.

The telegram states that the junta declares that it will respect the constitution of the nation calling shortly for free elections for deputies and senators and the consequent formation of a constitutional cabinet, and furthermore that it will comply strictly with the internal and external obligations of the Republic. The telegram added that everything was quiet during the afternoon of June 28, although the people were enjoying a holiday and all shops and offices remained closed.

824.01/5 : Telegram

The Ambassador in Chile (Culbertson) to the Secretary of State

SANTIAGO, July 1, 1930—6 p. m.
[Received 9 p. m.]

51. Foreign Office informs me that Siles will arrive in Arica tomorrow afternoon escorted by Brazilian Secretary and Chilean Military Attaché and that Chilean Minister in La Paz has been instructed to express good will privately to the junta, but recognition for the present is not contemplated.

CULBERTSON

824.00/514 : Telegram

The Chargé in Bolivia (Hibbard) to the Secretary of State

LA PAZ, July 2, 1930—5 p. m.
[Received July 3—4 : 22 a. m.]

47. The military junta remains well in control of the situation. On Sunday there were threatening demonstrations before those Legations in which political leaders had taken refuge and it was necessary for the diplomatic corps to call on the junta to demand greater protection. This was granted at once and there has been no further trouble. Siles left by automobile at 4 o'clock this morning accompanied by the Secretary of the Brazilian Legation and the Military Attaché of the Chilean Legation and with the protection of the junta. The troops at first refused to let him leave but were pacified and he was taken outside the city and placed on a special train for Arica, where he is now. The other refugees remain where they are but some will leave tomorrow with full guarantees. General Kundt offers the greatest problem. The feeling against him is intense and if he leaves the German Legation it will be difficult for the Government to protect him. On the other hand they do not wish him to leave the country, as it is feared he will sell or divulge Bolivian military plans to neighboring countries. The junta intends to proceed legally against members of the previous Government for malfeasance in office in an effort to secure the return of Government funds. Should the money not be returned, property will be confiscated. Charges are being prepared now.

All politicians exiled by Siles are returning but it is interesting to note that there is no mention of party or individuals. For the time being the country is solidly behind the junta. A decree giving the plans of the junta has been issued and has received general approbation. Freedom of the press is guaranteed, martial law, which has been in force for thirty-three months, is lifted and each member of the junta pledges himself not to run for any office.

With the aid of the banks, the Government has today telegraphed funds to New York to cover the June 5th and June 15th service payments on the external loan. The Chambers are cooperating fully with the Government in every way. The junta is reducing the number of public employees 25 percent and promises to reduce army expenditure. An economic council has been formed to study the needs of the country and make recommendations. Each Ministry is in charge of a member of the junta with a high-class civilian technical adviser. Decrees will be signed by the Under Secretary, the officer in charge, and General Galindo.

Elections will be called as soon as there is complete calm. I believe this will not be for some months as it is the desire of the junta and the people in general that all traces of the previous regime be removed and a new start made. Certainly there is an opportunity for a fine example to Bolivia and other South American republics if the junta can follow its original intentions.

I am informed that the junta has approached Chile, Brazil, Argentina and Peru for recognition. No answers have yet been received. The question has not yet been raised with the Embassy [*Legation*] although I know the junta is eager for the recognition of the United States. My impression is that the United States will not be asked until they know what reception the request has received in the countries mentioned.

HIBBARD

824.00/520 : Telegram

The Chargé in Bolivia (Hibbard) to the Secretary of State

LA PAZ, July 9, 1930—6 p. m.
[Received July 10—10 : 10 a. m.]

48. My telegram No. 47, July 2, 5 p. m. In conversation with an individual in the confidence of the junta, I was informed that the present Government has made no overtures to any neighboring Governments for recognition. The junta, while desirous of recognition, hoped that it would come "spontaneously". I was asked whether the United States would accord recognition. I stated that I could only reply personally but that my opinion was that the United States would continue normal diplomatic relations with Bolivia; that as far

as I was aware it had not been customary for the United States to grant *de jure* recognition to governments constituted as the present Bolivian Government and I advised against raising a question which might prove embarrassing, particularly in view of the announcement of the junta that constitutional elections would be called shortly. I added however that should the Government desire to make a formal request I would, of course, transmit it to the Department at once.

This afternoon I called on General Blanco Galindo in accordance with the Department's telegram No. 24, July 8, 6 p. m.[7] He expressed the warm admiration of Bolivia for the United States and a hope that relations would always remain cordial. He added that he hoped relations would shortly be closer between the two countries but that he understood it was not customary for the United States to grant recognition under the circumstances. I made no comment.

I have conferred with my Brazilian and Peruvian colleagues who state that in spite of repeated expressions by the junta of the desire to maintain normal and cordial relations with their countries the question of recognition has not been raised. They do not intend to take any action. The Chilean Minister is more vague and my impression is that Chile will endeavor to find some way to strengthen her relations here either by recognition or otherwise in order to hold a predominating influence later.

.   .   .   .

HIBBARD

824.00/539

The Chargé in Bolivia (Hibbard) to the Secretary of State

No. 505   LA PAZ, August 22, 1930.
                                           [Received September 20.]

SIR: I have the honor to report that the Junta Militar of Bolivia has announced elections for the 4th, 5th, and 6th of January, next. On January 4th the electorate will vote on certain amendments or changes in the Bolivian Constitution which have not yet been announced but are now being prepared. These will probably include an extension of the presidential term from four to six years as well as an extension of the congressional term, the inclusion of an article protecting the financial institutions of the country, particularly those established by the recommendations of Professor Kemmerer, such as the Banco Central de Bolivia, the Contraloría General de la República, the National Tax Collecting Company, etc., an article guaranteeing more effectively freedom of speech and action, an article

---

[7] Not printed.

making the continuance of martial law impossible beyond a limited time, certain educational reforms and other reforms in the electoral law making the control of one party impossible.

Elections for the presidency and vice presidency will be held on January 5th and elections for the Senate and the Chamber of Deputies on January 6th. The old civil registers have been abolished and the citizens of the country will shortly be permitted to re-register. The registration will be controlled by military officers as well as the actual voting though in the latter there may be civil assistants appointed. The stamp tax on cards of identity, which are required of all voters has been abolished and only the voting requirements specified in the Constitution will be demanded. It is expected thus to secure a more popular and representative vote.

During the past week representatives of the three political parties, the Liberal, Republican and Genuine Republican, have met at the invitation of the Junta Militar to discuss plans for a representative election which would make possible the accomplishment of the revolutionary ideals and a popular government. There has been much speculation as to what means could be taken to avoid party rivalry and whether the party leaders would be able to submerge their personal ambitions for the benefit of the country. After much discussion of a highly patriotic character, a solution has been reached which seems to be the only one possible. The official representatives of the three parties have officially committed themselves to the following ticket. For the Presidency, Doctor Daniel Salamanca, first vice president, Doctor Ismael Montes, second vice president, Doctor Bautista Saavedra. In this way each party has a representative, although such a system will necessitate a slight change in the Constitution which was amended in 1920 to abolish the position of second vice president. It is presumed that the Congress and Cabinet will likewise be coalition in character.

The announcement of this program has been received with universal pleasure. Doctor Salamanca has occupied a unique position in the political life of the country as he has always remained free of party affiliations in spite of his service in various governmental offices. He is honest and intelligent but lacks the force to lead the country from its present crisis. The weakness of his health is a great handicap both physically and temperamentally. His aloofness from party affiliations will also be a handicap as it is impossible for the political life of the country to remain on such an elevated plane and he will be unable by temperament to combat party struggles which must necessarily arise in such a coalition.

Respectfully yours,　　　　　　　　　　　　FREDERICK P. HIBBARD

824.00/533

Memorandum by the Assistant Chief of the Division of Latin American Affairs (Thurston)

[WASHINGTON,] August 23, 1930.

The Bolivian Minister called this morning to read a telegram received from the Military Junta at La Paz announcing the coalition of the political parties in Bolivia and their selection of the following gentlemen as candidates for President, First Vice President and Second Vice President in the elections which are to be held January 5 and 6, 1931:

For President . . . . Daniel Salamanca
For First Vice President . . . . Ismael Montes
For Second Vice President . . . . Bautista Saavedra

The Minister stated that the telegram instructed him to inform this Government of the foregoing and he stated that if he might he would report that he had complied with the instructions and that the Department had expressed gratification at the developments cited. I told him that he could of course make such a statement, as we were indeed gratified by any developments which seemed, as this does, to hold promise for the future stability of Bolivia. I told him that we have not as yet received any report from the Legation at La Paz on this subject.

W. C. T[HURSTON]

824.01/10 : Telegram

The Chargé in Bolivia (Hibbard) to the Secretary of State

LA PAZ, August 30, 1930—noon.
[Received 2 : 35 p. m.]

57. I am reliably informed that the military junta in Bolivia is negotiating with the military junta in Peru for mutual recognition.[8] Bolivia hopes thus to secure favorable modification of the terms of the treaty between Chile and Peru.[9] A member of the junta or a confidential agent will probably leave for Lima early next week. The Peruvian Chargé leaves for Lima Monday. He tells me he will endeavor to prevent any modification of the treaty.

Repeated to Lima.

HIBBARD

---

[8] See "Revolution in Peru," vol. III, pp. 720 ff.
[9] See *Foreign Relations*, 1929, vol. I, pp. 720 ff.

824.01/12 : Telegram

The Minister in Ecuador (Dawson) to the Secretary of State

QUITO, September 9, 1930—11 a. m.
[Received 5 : 45 p. m.]

25. Ecuadorean Government has decided to give full recognition to existing Governments of Bolivia and Peru and sent yesterday telegraphic instructions to this effect to its mission in La Paz and a note to Peruvian Minister in Quito.

DAWSON

824.01/13 : Telegram

The Minister in Bolivia (Feely)[10] to the Secretary of State

LA PAZ, September 10, 1930—4 p. m.
[Received 9 : 30 p. m.]

59. During the past week there have been several demonstrations of unemployed, many of which have been inspired by Communists. In the southern districts, particularly Oruro and Potosi, several mining camps have been damaged. While the Government is apparently well in control, there is a distinct feeling of uneasiness, especially as there is good reason to believe that members of the former Government are aligning themselves with Communist elements.

In view of this situation, I have not yet made informal contacts with members of the junta as I have not wanted to make any move which might be interpreted as even tacit recognition. The question of recognition by the United States frequently arises, especially since the recognition of this Government by Peru and Ecuador and the probable recognition by Argentina. For these reasons my position here is embarrassing and I would prefer to leave La Paz until such time as the situation is more normal. I respectfully request the Department's instructions.

FEELY

824.01/14 : Telegram

The Chargé in Bolivia (Hibbard) to the Secretary of State

LA PAZ, September 11, 1930—4 p. m.
[Received 5 : 20 p. m.]

60. Chile officially recognized the present Bolivian Government yesterday afternoon.

HIBBARD

---

[10] Assigned June 4, 1930, but had not yet presented his credentials.

824.01/15 : Telegram

The Secretary of State to the Minister in Bolivia (Feely)

[Paraphrase]

WASHINGTON, September 16, 1930—2 p. m.

38. On Thursday, September 18, you will please inform the Foreign Minister, or the official in charge of that Ministry, that you are instructed by the Government of the United States to enter into full diplomatic relations with the governmental junta of Bolivia, and that you are ready to present your letters of credence to the person indicated by them as empowered to receive the credentials of foreign Ministers.

An announcement of this will be made here late Wednesday afternoon.[11] Until released here the above should be treated as confidential. Similar action will be taken as to Argentina [12] and Peru.

STIMSON

824.01/19 : Telegram

The Chargé in Bolivia (Hibbard) to the Secretary of State

LA PAZ [, undated].
[Received September 18, 1930—5 : 52 p. m.]

63. Department's telegram number 38, September 16, 2 p. m. In accordance with the Department's instructions I called on Colonel Osorio with Mr. Feely this morning at 10 and informed him that I had been instructed by the Government of the United States to enter into full diplomatic relations with the Government of Bolivia. I also handed him a note confirming this and requesting him to set the date for Mr. Feely to present his credentials. In discussing the question of credentials, I informed Colonel Osorio that these documents were addressed to the President of Bolivia and inquired whether it would be inconvenient to present them in that form and was informed that the Junta would prefer to have the credentials addressed to His Excellency General Carlos Blanco Galindo, President of the Military Junta of Government of Bolivia. However the Junta is anxious to avoid delay in receiving Mr. Feely. Accordingly it is being arranged for him to be received by General Galindo probably Saturday. Upon receipt of new credentials these will be deposited at the Ministry for Foreign Affairs. If the Department approves it will be appreciated if new credentials can be sent by the next pouch.

HIBBARD

---

[11] For press statement by the Secretary of State of September 17, 1930, regarding the policy of recognition, see p. 387.
[12] See "Revolution in Argentina," pp. 378 ff.

DISINCLINATION OF THE UNITED STATES TO APPOINT OFFICIAL
REPRESENTATIVE ON AMERICAN BANKERS COMMISSION TO DEAL
WITH BOLIVIAN ECONOMIC AND FINANCIAL PROBLEMS

824.51/564 : Telegram

The Minister in Bolivia (Feely) to the Secretary of State

La Paz, October 13, 1930—4 p. m.
[Received 6 : 15 p. m.]

70. In view of increasing difficulty in meeting foreign debt service
and critical financial outlook, this Government is planning to invite
a commission of interested American bankers to visit Bolivia for the
purpose of discussing plans of consolidation of outstanding indebtedness and for recommending other steps toward avoidance of financial
collapse, moratorium, etc. Government will suggest that one member
of commission to [*sic*] represent State Department or Commerce Department, and also plans the appointment of Bolivian representatives,
probably Martínez Vargas and Carlos Arimayo, to proceed to New
York for the same purpose.

Former Minister for Foreign Affairs Elio in an article yesterday's
La Razon recommends the suspension of foreign debt service; and
pressure is apparent to reduce gold value of boliviano from 18 pence to
12 pence which, in my opinion, might result in collapse of entire
financial structure.

Financial situation grows more critical daily and unless some plan
can be evolved to reduce debt service materially a long period of default
seems inevitable beginning with heavy payments due in December
and January.

Respectfully suggest that bankers should be notified of forthcoming
invitation.

Feely

824.51/565 : Telegram

The Minister in Bolivia (Feely) to the Secretary of State

La Paz, October 18, 1930—10 a. m.
[Received 2 : 30 p. m.]

71. My telegram No. 70 of October 13, 4 p. m. Minister for Foreign
Affairs today handed me legalized copy of the Supreme Economist
Council, saying that this memorandum represented the views of his
Government as to practical remedies for the threatening financial
crisis. Memorandum which is being forwarded by air mail recites
at length causes for present depression, including fall in prices of
Bolivia's principal exportable products, large budget deficit, heavy
foreign debt service and unemployment, and points out danger of

spread of communism as a result, and probable inability to meet December and January quotas of debt service in spite of Government's desire to maintain its credit abroad.

Memorandum arrives at certain conclusions which Minister for Foreign Affairs requested I transmit as an official invitation to the bankers concerned, at the same time intimating that the Bolivian Government would welcome the appointment of an official representative of the United States Government on the proposed commission.

The conclusions are as follows: That a commission made up of representatives of the American bankers interested be immediately organized and that the Republic of the United States be requested to appoint an official representative on the commission; that said commission recommend a plan of consolidating foreign debt; investigate the possibility of investment American and Bolivian capital in new industries; that the organization of the commission be negotiated simultaneously with the United States Government and American bankers by the American Minister in La Paz and Martínez Vargas already appointed Bolivian Special Agent in New York and Washington; that if Martínez Vargas decides consolidation can be arranged in New York commission need not come to La Paz; that as December-January debt service amounts to $1,838,000 negotiations should be undertaken immediately so that commission's recommendations may be made effective and if possible short-term credit accorded by bankers for December-January service if consolidation plan is not completed then.

In accepting the memorandum I expressed the opinion that, while the Department would undoubtedly be pleased to transmit the invitation to the bankers and would follow the course of any negotiations with interest, I could not assure him that my Government would accept an invitation to participate officially. The Minister for Foreign Affairs then suggested that invitation be transmitted to the bankers and that I ask what the Department's attitude would be toward the appointment of an official representative on the commission. Telegraphic instructions would be appreciated.

FEELY

824.51/565 : Telegram

The Secretary of State to the Minister in Bolivia (Feely)

WASHINGTON, October 20, 1930—5 p. m.

45. Your 71, October 18, 10 a. m. This Government does not desire to have a representative on the proposed Commission which is to deal with Bolivian economic and financial problems. Please so inform the appropriate Bolivian authorities orally and in-

formally, making it clear that while this Government is keenly sympathetic with the Government of Bolivia in the difficulties which confront it, the active participation of this Government in their solution would be contrary to usual practices. This does not mean that Department would not welcome any cooperation by you with the Bolivian officials in any way you can be helpful and which will be welcomed by the Bolivian Government.

Department will transmit project to bankers and will be glad to cooperate informally with Bolivian representative and bankers.

STIMSON

THE CHACO DISPUTE BETWEEN BOLIVIA AND PARAGUAY

(See pages 309 ff.)

BRAZIL

REVOLUTION IN BRAZIL

832.00 Revolutions/2 : Telegram

The Chargé in Brazil (Washington) to the Secretary of State

[Paraphrase]

Rio de Janeiro, October 4, 1930—noon.
[Received 1 : 25 p. m.]

62. Van den Arend, Consul at Pernambuco, reports as follows:

"October 4, 10 a. m. Last night at 11 o'clock revolution broke out in Pernambuco. The result is still in doubt."

Reports from other sources, usually considered reliable by us, are that revolutions have started in Bello Horizonte and other parts of the State of Minas Geraes and in Pelotas and other parts of the State of Rio Grande do Sul. A Government censorship of telegrams has been established in fact, though not officially, and railroad and telephone communications between Rio de Janeiro and Bello Horizonte have been interrupted. A responsible official of the Foreign Office informs me that martial law will be declared today in the States of Minas Geraes and Rio Grande do Sul.

The situation in Rio de Janeiro is considered critical, but there is no disorder. This morning's edition of *O Jornal* was suppressed.

One cruiser will leave Rio de Janeiro today for Pernambuco, and another will leave to join four destroyers previously sent to Florianopolis.[1]

Will the Department please acknowledge receipt of this telegram?[2]

Washington

832.00 Revolutions/20 : Telegram

The Chargé in Brazil (Washington) to the Secretary of State

Rio de Janeiro, October 7, 1930—6 p. m.
[Received October 7—5 : 08 p. m.]

73. At the end of nearly four days of fighting in Minas Geraes, Rio Grande do Sul, and Paraná, the Brazilian revolutionists have not made great progress toward their goal of entering São Paulo and Rio

[1] This paragraph has been corrected on basis of telegram No. 69, October 6, 7 p. m. from the Chargé in Brazil (832.00 Revolutions/13).
[2] Acknowledged by the Department in its telegram No. 55, October 4, 6 p. m. (832.00 Revolutions/21).

de Janeiro. There is an accredited rumor that the rebels have been driven out of Curitiba which they had been occupying for 24 hours. Rumors concerning their approach to São Paulo from the south are believed to be either untrue or based upon the activities of isolated bands of revolutionary sympathizers along the railway in northern Paraná. In Minas Geraes the revolutionary forces appear to have been held in check, if not actually repulsed.

Friends of the Government are today optimistic and feel that the only danger to the Government is in an uprising in São Paulo or Rio de Janeiro. Consul General Cameron reports that São Paulo is quiet and friendly to the Government but that account must be taken of the presence of about 800 Communists in the city. The situation in Rio de Janeiro is similar. Business is at a standstill in São Paulo and in Rio de Janeiro.

Consul at Bahia reports that all is quiet there. American-owned power company reports that the Bahia tramway service is operating again.

WASHINGTON

832.00 Revolutions/29 : Telegram

The Chargé in Brazil (Washington) to the Secretary of State

[Paraphrase]

RIO DE JANEIRO, October 9, 1930—4 p. m.
[Received 4 : 28 p. m.]

78. American Consul at Pernambuco telegraphs that he might request assistance in case of a Federal attack upon Pernambuco. A responsible official of the Foreign Office informed me that no effort would be spared by the military and naval commanders, who were approaching that city, to retake it for the Government even if it meant bombardment.

The American Consul at Bahia reports street firing between sailors and police and states that Americans are nervous because of anti-American feeling among the lower classes. He requests me to inform him whether any American warships are expected in that vicinity.

Since it appears very probable that a serious engagement will take place at Pernambuco which would endanger the lives of Americans and of foreigners I invite the Department's consideration to the question of having American naval vessels in that vicinity.

WASHINGTON

832.00 Revolutions/37 : Telegram

The Secretary of State to the Chargé in Brazil (*Washington*)

WASHINGTON, October 9, 1930—7 p. m.

57. Your 78, October 9, 4 p. m. The Department would be very loath to send any warships to Brazil. Cannot the Consuls in ports where there is apt to be fighting make arrangements in conjunction with the other foreign Consuls by which the foreign colonies can be put in a place of safety? Please take this matter up at once with the federal authorities so that instructions may be sent to the commanders of the federal troops in all places to respect American and other foreign lives and have the Consuls in each place make similar representations to the commanders of the opposition forces so that a neutral zone can be declared and respected. Cable results as soon as possible. Enquire of Consuls whether it is feasible in case of emergency to take Americans off by merchant ships and what ships are now available or will be available in the next few days in each port for this purpose. Cable number of Americans in each port for which means of egress may have to be provided.

STIMSON

832.00 Revolutions/38 : Telegram

The Chargé in Brazil (*Washington*) *to the Secretary of State*

RIO DE JANEIRO, October 10, 1930—9 p. m.
[Received 9 : 45 p. m.]

83. Department's 57, October 9, 7 p. m. I have transmitted the Department's instructions to the Consuls at Pernambuco and Bahia in which cities there are prospects of disturbances, but have not yet received replies regarding their representations to the local authorities and regarding the number of Americans and ships in their ports.

The Minister for Foreign Affairs assures me that the Federal Government will give attention to foreigners insofar as it is able. He states that as Recife is in the hands of the rebels the Consuls should arrange with the *de facto* authorities to remove all foreigners to a place of safety outside the city in the case of an attack.

However, it now appears that several days or a week may elapse before an attack on Recife takes place and the Federal Government is convinced that when its forces appear before Recife the rebels will flee. As the foreign Consuls in that city are in the best position to judge this, I shall transmit the Minister's statement to our Consul.

As the Federal naval and military forces appear to be concentrating at Bahia there would seem to be no danger of any trouble there at the present time. I pointed out to the Minister for Foreign Affairs the importance of always leaving sufficient forces at Bahia to insure the safety of Americans and he assures me that attention will be given to this aspect of the situation.

As there is not yet any prospect of a Federal attack upon Porto Alegre I will postpone communicating the Department's instruction in this matter to our Consul there until I am certain of having established communication with him.

WASHINGTON

832.00 Revolutions/44 : Telegram

The Acting Secretary of State to the Chargé in Brazil (Washington)

WASHINGTON, October 11, 1930—2 p. m.

60. Department has just issued following statement to press:

"In view of the uncertainty as to the future situation in Brazil it has been felt prudent to have a ship nearer the zone of disturbance to take off American refugees, should such action be necessary for the protection of their lives. The U. S. S. *Pensacola* is therefore being ordered to Guantanamo which is three days less steaming distance to Brazil than Hampton Roads where it is at present.

There are no American naval vessels now in Brazilian waters and the *Pensacola* is the only ship being ordered to stand by for this duty. If future developments require it to proceed from Guantanamo to Brazil it will do so merely to take off Americans whose lives might be in danger. This would be the sole object of its visit to any Brazilian ports."

CASTLE

832.00 Revolutions/52 : Telegram

The Chargé in Brazil (Washington) to the Secretary of State

RIO DE JANEIRO, October 12, 1930—1 p. m.
[Received 2 : 30 p. m.]

88. Department's telegram number 60. The statement issued by the Department to the press in connection with the ordering of the U. S. S. *Pensacola* to Guantanamo is giving concern to the Brazilian Government and I have been informed by a responsible official of the Ministry of Foreign Affairs that its publication in Brazil will not be permitted by the censors. In view of the fact that perfect order reigns in the Districts of Rio de Janeiro and São Paulo and that the Brazilian Government is attempting to create greater confidence among the people, it is feared that the publication of this notice issued by a foreign government would produce a very bad effect.

It would be appreciated if the Department would state to the press when the week end is past that this Embassy has continuously been reporting that Rio de Janeiro and São Paulo were quiet and that there has been no danger to American lives or property in these cities.

WASHINGTON

632.0023/4 : Telegram

The Chargé in Brazil (Washington) to the Secretary of State

RIO DE JANEIRO, October 14, 1930—7 p. m.
[Received 7 : 55 p. m.]

96. Today I have been verbally informed by the Segundo Official de Gabinete of the Brazilian Ministry of Foreign Affairs that the Brazilian Government has closed the port of Recife. Under date of October 11 it ordered its Consuls throughout the world not to clear any more vessels for that port. He also requested this Embassy to order American merchant vessels already cleared for Recife to proceed to another port. The Consul at Recife is anxious over the food supply of city and in one of his telegrams has urged that American vessels continue calling there as usual. There being a question of international law involved, namely, whether a nation has the right to close a port which though in its territory is not under its control, the matter is referred to the Department.

WASHINGTON

632.0023/5 : Telegram

The Chargé in Brazil (Washington) to the Secretary of State

RIO DE JANEIRO, October 15, 1930—10 a. m.
[Received 11 : 40 a. m.]

97. This Embassy has just received a written communication from the Ministry of Foreign Affairs stating that Brazilian Consuls have received from the Ministry, in accordance with orders from the Federal Inspection of Navigation, instructions not to visa until further notice for military and administrative reasons the papers of ships destined to the following Brazilian ports: São Luiz, Fortaleza and all ports of Ceará, Rio Grande do Norte, Parahyba, Pernambuco and Alagoas; Paranaguá, São Francisco, and the ports of Rio Grande do Sul, all of which ports are temporarily closed to navigation.

In a conversation with a responsible official of the Brazilian Foreign Office I have learned that the Brazilian Government is well aware of the claims on the part of foreign shipping companies which may arise as a result of trying to close the above-mentioned ports but considers it essential that the revolutionists not receive arms, ammunition or other supplies. Furthermore, it fears that some such supplies are on boats which were cleared for Recife before the issuance of the consular instruction and therefore is desirous that foreign governments cause such vessels to proceed to another port.

WASHINGTON

632.0023/5 : Telegram

The Secretary of State to the Chargé in Brazil (Washington)

WASHINGTON, October 15, 1930—4 p. m.

64. Your 96 and 97 of October 14, 7 p. m., and October 15, 10 a. m. Department sent following telegram No. 2 of October 14, 5 p. m., to Consul at Pernambuco:

"For your personal and confidential information, as Pernambuco is in the hands of revolutionists, Department will not take steps to have ships call there if the Brazilian authorities refuse to give them clearance for that port. You will please be guided accordingly."

STIMSON

832.00 Revolutions/92 : Telegram

The Secretary of State to the Chargé in Brazil (Washington)

WASHINGTON, October 17, 1930—2 p. m.

66. Your 100, October 16, 6 p. m.[4] Following is the text of the Secretary's statement to the press on October 15th:

"Nothing has come to the notice of the Department in the news from Brazil which changes the attitude of this Government from exercising the same friendly offices towards the Government of Brazil which we would exercise towards any government with which we are in friendly relations. Under those circumstances the Government of Brazil has a perfect right to buy munitions in this country."

STIMSON

832.00 Revolutions/94 : Telegram

The Secretary of State to the Chargé in Brazil (Washington)

WASHINGTON, October 17, 1930—3 p. m.

67. Cruiser *Pensacola* arrived Trinidad today and is refueling. It has been ordered to proceed down the coast to Brazil stopping at Pará, Pernambuco and Bahia. The vessel will get in touch with our Consuls and make inquiries. No orders issued to *Pensacola* beyond Bahia where it will remain pending further orders. Commander of the vessel has been ordered to do nothing whatsoever except get in touch with our Consuls and make inquiries and take off Americans if necessary. Consuls at Pará, Pernambuco and Bahia informed.

STIMSON

---

[4] Not printed.

832.00 Revolutions/90 : Telegram

The Chargé in Brazil (*Washington*) *to the Secretary of State*

RIO DE JANEIRO, October 17, 1930—4 p. m.
[Received 5 : 02 p. m.]

105. Reference is made to article No. 3, paragraph No. 5, of the contract between the United States of America and Brazil for the establishment of a naval mission in Brazil [5] which paragraph reads as follows: "In case of war between Brazil and any other nation or in case of civil war, no member of the mission shall take part in operations in any respect whatsoever." Federal Executive decree 19367 of October 16, 1930, contains the following clause : "Considering that in consequence of a subversive movement which broke out in the States of Minas Geraes, Rio Grande do Sul, and Parahyba the territory of the State of Pernambuco was invaded by rebel forces which took possession of the city of Recife, this State being now in full civil war." The acting chief of the American Naval Mission informs me that no members of the mission are present on naval vessels operating for any purpose whatsoever. They are carrying on their regular duties in the Ministry of Marine which involve advices of general nature including those regarding purchases of equipment but excluding those pertaining to naval operations.

WASHINGTON

832.00 Revolutions/91 : Telegram

The Consul at Porto Alegre (*Nasmith*) *to the Secretary of State*

PORTO ALEGRE, October 17, 1930—4 p. m.
[Received 9 : 03 p. m.]

Secretary of the Interior, Rio Grande do Sul, has just sent following important communication from revolutionary government of interest to American ships: "In view of the attacks made by Federal warships on the defenseless coasts, the revolutionary government has decided to suppress, temporarily, all lighthouses in the States of Rio Grande do Sul, Santa Catharina, and Paraná commencing today.["] I am happy to report that measures are being made by the state authorities for payment of all requisitions which will effect [*sic*] the few requisitions of American property which have been made. American companies in Porto Alegre are very satisfied with the treatment given them in the protection of their property by the revolutionary government. I have just been informed from a reliable source that radio station in Buenos Aires has broadcast that I had informed my Government that

---

[5] For correspondence regarding termination of the naval mission, see pp. 454 ff.

considerable American property was being taken by revolutionary government. Without doubt Department has not issued this information but if possible to counteract this account please publish that revolutionary government has respected and protected American property and American lives unusually well in view of the circumstances, which is the truth. Please acknowledge by telegraph.

NASMITH

832.00 Revolutions/97 : Telegram

The Consul at Bahia (Briggs) to the Secretary of State

BAHIA, October 18, 1930—11 a. m.
[Received 11:10 a. m.]

Quiet last night; all troops sent out to meet invaders; city patrolled by volunteers. Many inhabitants are leaving for interior, others are prepared to welcome revolutionists. Cruiser can control city and prevent entrance but its action is doubtful. Launch has been provided to take Americans away in case of emergency, but the only available place is an island without sufficient food. For this reason the arrival of the *Pensacola* will be glad news.

BRIGGS

832.00 Revolutions/96 : Telegram

The Chargé in Brazil (Washington) to the Secretary of State

RIO DE JANEIRO, October 18, 1930—noon.
[Received October 18—noon.]

107. Department's telegram No. 65 [*67*], October 17, 3 p. m. Am I instructed to inform the Brazilian Government according to custom that the U. S. S. *Pensacola* will call at Pará, Pernambuco, and Bahia?

WASHINGTON

832.00 Revolutions/99 : Telegram

The Consul General at São Paulo (Cameron) to the Secretary of State

SÃO PAULO, October 18, 1930—noon.
[Received 12:05 p. m.]

Government column advancing from Ourinhos badly defeated several days ago. The Government now on defensive; whole Paraná front from Ribeira to Assis using trenches, barbed wire, machine-gun nests, artillery. Advance guard fighting near Itarare, Thursday. São Paulo–Paraná Railway rolling stock withdrawn and all bridges destroyed by the Government. Whole São Paulo–Rio Grande Railroad cooperating with revolutionists. Reliably reported German ex-Army officers with the revolutionary forces, latter apparently attempting turning movement westward, Government having rushed troops to Marilia, railhead of branch of the Paulista Railway.

· CAMERON

832.00 Revolutions/100 : Telegram

The Consul at Bahia (Briggs) to the Secretary of State

BAHIA, October 18, 1930—2 p. m.
[Received 2 : 10 p. m.]

Apparently revolutionists have invaded State of Bahia from Sergipe and Government troops are tearing up the track above Alagoinhas. According to street rumors revolutionists will arrive in two or three days but this is impossible.

BRIGGS

832.00 Revolutions/102 : Telegram

The Chargé in Brazil (Washington) to the Secretary of State

RIO DE JANEIRO, October 18, 1930—5 p. m.
[Received October 18—4 : 40 p. m.]

109. In view of the reports from Bahia, it is recommended that the U. S. S. *Pensacola* proceed directly to that port and save the time that would be necessary for going into Pará.

There is a distinct feeling of dissatisfaction in Rio de Janeiro over what appears to the public to be inactivity on the part of the Government in proceeding against the revolutionists. The disturbing news from the vicinity of Bahia and Victoria is threatening the morale of the Government supporters in this city.

[Paraphrase.] From reliable sources it has been learned that several times during the last two weeks high Army and Navy officials, and possibly an actual member of the Cabinet, have urged the President to reach some agreement with the revolutionists in order to save the country from a long civil war, but he has persistently refused to compromise and they have remained loyal to him. [End paraphrase.]

WASHINGTON

832.00 Revolutions/116 : Telegram

The Secretary of State to the Chargé in Brazil (Washington)

WASHINGTON, October 20, 1930—11 a. m.

69. Your 107, October 18, noon. Inform Brazilian Government in usual manner of visit of *Pensacola.*

STIMSON

832.00 Revolutions/117 : Telegram

The Secretary of State to the Chargé in Brazil (Washington)

WASHINGTON, October 20, 1930—noon.

70. Your 108, October 18, 4 p. m.[6] Course of action outlined last paragraph your 105, October 17, 4 p. m. approved.

STIMSON

832.00 Revolutions/118 : Telegram

The Secretary of State to the Chargé in Brazil (Washington)

WASHINGTON, October 20, 1930—2 p. m.

71. Consul Pernambuco inquired October 18 [7] whether local *de facto* revolutionary Government should be informed regarding forthcoming visit to that port of *Pensacola* and whether customary official call on Governor should be arranged for under existing circumstances. Department in reply instructed Consul to inform *de facto* Government of visit to Pernambuco but stated that official calls should not be made to revolutionary authorities.

STIMSON

832.00 Revolutions/129 : Telegram

The Secretary of State to the Consul at Porto Alegre (Nasmith)

WASHINGTON, October 20, 1930—2 p. m.

Your October 17th, 4 p. m. On October 18th Secretary of State made statement in his press conference such as you requested.

STIMSON

---

[6] Not printed.
[7] Telegram not printed.

832.00 Revolutions/127 : Telegram

The Consul at Porto Alegre (Nasmith) to the Secretary of State

PORTO ALEGRE, October 21, 1930—3 p. m.
[Received October 22—12:21 a. m.]

Referring to my telegram of October 17, 4 p. m., regarding payments for requisitions, these will be paid by state treasury notes of Rio Grande do Sul to be recalled in 6 months and which can be used at once in payment of all Federal, state and municipal taxes including customs duties, also in payment wages and in purchase raw materials and foodstuffs. All requisitions American property will be paid by these notes.[8] This should be very beneficial to American companies having requisitions. I have been to see Secretary of the Interior and Secretary of the Treasury several times about this and the present solution of the matter is due mostly to my efforts. Total amount 20,000 contos of these treasury notes will be issued having as guarantee like amount of mortgage bonds of State Bank of Rio Grande do Sul to be deposited in state treasury but not all of this issue will be used for requisitions. This measure will facilitate very much all commercial transactions.

NASMITH

832.00 Revolutions/124 : Telegram

The Chargé in Brazil (Washington) to the Secretary of State

RIO DE JANEIRO, October 21, 1930—5 p. m.
[Received October 21—3:50 p. m.]

115. German Legation [*Minister*] informs me that his Consul at Bahia reports the arrival at that port of the British cruiser *Delhi*. The Minister states that he has requested the *Karlsruhe* to stop at Bahia and has instructed it to get in touch with the Commander of the *Pensacola*. The American Naval Mission in Brazil hopes to be able to get in touch with the *Pensacola* by radio this evening.

WASHINGTON

832.113/29 : Telegram

The Secretary of State to the Ambassador in Brazil (Morgan)

WASHINGTON, October 22, 1930—5 p. m.

72. At request of Brazilian Government, through Brazilian Ambassador here,[9] stating that conditions of domestic violence exist in

---

[8] In telegram of October 22, 3 p. m., the Consul added that "treasury notes bear seven and a half interest."
[9] Note No. 73, October 22; Department of State, *Press Releases*, October 25, 1930, p. 265.

certain portions of Brazil, the President today issued a Proclamation prohibiting the export of arms and munitions of war to Brazil except under license of the Secretary of State.[10]

STIMSON

832.113/42

Press Release Issued by the Department of State on October 23, 1930

STATEMENT BY THE SECRETARY OF STATE

Some accounts in the press this morning reported that our action in placing an embargo upon the sale of arms and munitions to revolutionists in Brazil was unprecedented. While it is true that this is the first occasion where the United States has placed an embargo on the shipment of arms and munitions to a South American country, it is misleading to call it an unprecedented action, as it is our regular action under similar circumstances. We have placed embargoes on the shipment of arms and munitions on various occasions when there were conditions of domestic violence in Central America, Mexico, Cuba, and the Orient.[11] It just happens that a situation requiring the application of this principle has not hitherto come up in South America, and there has therefore hitherto been no occasion for applying the general principle. There is nothing unprecedented in the principle which we have applied many times before. It is very important that people should not misunderstand it as a new principle. It is important for the reason that the revolutionists who may be hurt by our action in placing an embargo may assert that we are taking sides for some ulterior reason with one or the other of the combatants. Instead of that, we are acting according to general principles of international law. Those principles declare that where we are in friendly relations through diplomatic channels with a government which has been recognized as the legitimate government of a country, that government is entitled to the ordinary rights of any government to buy arms in this country; while the people who are opposing and trying to overthrow that government and are not yet recognized as belligerents are not entitled to that right. It is not a matter of choice on our part, but is a practice of mankind known as international law. We have no personal bias and are doing nothing but attempting to carry out the law of mankind.

[10] 46 Stat. 3036; Department of State, *Press Releases*, October 25, 1930, p. 264.
[11] See joint resolutions of April 22, 1898, March 14, 1912, and January 31, 1922, 30 Stat. 1769, 37 Stat. 1733, and 42 Stat. 361. See also proclamations respecting: Dominican Republic, October 14, 1905, 34 Stat. 3183; Mexico, March 14, 1912, 37 Stat. 1733; Mexico, February 3, 1914, 38 Stat. 1992; Mexico, October 19, 1915, 39 Stat. 1756; Mexico, July 12, 1919, 41 Stat. 1762; China, March 4, 1922, 42 Stat. 2264; Mexico, January 7, 1924, 43 Stat. 1934; Honduras, March 22, 1924, 43 Stat. 1942; Cuba, May 2, 1924, 43 Stat. 1946; Honduras, May 15, 1924, 43 Stat. 1950; Cuba, August 29, 1924, 43 Stat. 1965; Nicaragua, September 15, 1926, 44 Stat. 2625; Mexico, July 18, 1929, 46 Stat. 3001.

832.00 Revolutions/139 : Telegram

The Consul at Bahia (Briggs) to the Secretary of State

BAHIA, October 23, 1930—3 p. m.
[Received 5:46 p. m.]

Battle expected at Algoinhas. Rumored that Algoinhas was captured this morning. British cruiser here. German cruiser outside. No news of *Pensacola*.

BRIGGS

832.00 Revolutions/143 : Telegram

The Ambassador in Brazil (Morgan) to the Secretary of State

RIO DE JANEIRO, October 24, 1930—11 a. m.
[Received 11:50 a. m.]

122. Federal Government during the night losing control of forts and barracks in this city. At 9 a. m. signal guns were fired summoning revolutionary sympathizers to force the President to resign. Cannot as yet connect with any of the flying reports regarding the President's action. Public order not seriously disturbed.

MORGAN

832.00 Revolutions/146 : Telegram

The Ambassador in Brazil (Morgan) to the Secretary of State

RIO DE JANEIRO, October 24, 1930—4 p. m.
[Received 4:52 p. m.]

124. A military junta consisting of General Tasso Fragoso, General Menna Barreto, General Firmino Borba, General Pantaleao Telles, General Leite de Castro, responsible officers of long service well known to me personally, has been formed, and has taken over the Government, and is establishing normal conditions which have only been slightly disturbed. President remains a prisoner in Presidential Palace. Popular enthusiasm expressed in carnival spirit. Offices of late Government newspapers sacked and building, property of *O Paiz*, burnt. Red flags displayed indicate revolution and not communism. An Army detachment has occupied the Bank of Brazil to protect it and the national funds deposited there.

Have declined asylum to many applicants and will shelter no refugees.

MORGAN

832.00 Revolutions/148 : Telegram

The Consul at Bahia (Briggs) to the Secretary of State

BAHIA, October 25, 1930—9 a. m.
[Received October 25—7 : 08 a. m.]

A little trouble last night in downtown district but in general quiet, and Coronel Ataliba Osorio in temporary control. *Pensacola* arrived yesterday afternoon about 5 o'clock.

BRIGGS

832.00 Revolutions/160 : Telegram

The Ambassador in Brazil (Morgan) to the Secretary of State

RIO DE JANEIRO, October 27, 1930—6 p. m.
[Received 6 : 40 p. m.]

131. Received today at 4 : 30 p. m. a circular communication dated October 26, 1930, from Alfranio de Mello Franco, Foreign Minister and Minister ad interim of Justice and the Interior, stating

"The President of the Republic, Doctor Washington Luis Pereira de Sousa, having been deposed in virtue of the victorious revolutionary movement a 'junta governativa provisoria' composed of the Generals of the Division, Tasso Fragoso, President, and João de Deus Menna Barreto and Vice Admiral Isaias Noronha, has been constituted.

Allow me also to inform Your Excellency that the junta recognizes and respects all national obligations contracted abroad, existing treaties with foreign powers, the public debt, foreign and domestic, existing contracts and other obligations legally entered into.

I also inform Your Excellency that the governing junta governativa has appointed as Ministers of State: General Leite de Castro, War; Vice Admiral Isaias Noronha, Navy; and the undersigned in the posts above mentioned."

MORGAN

832.00 Revolutions/163 : Telegram

The Consul at Porto Alegre (Nasmith) to the Secretary of State

PORTO ALEGRE, October 28, 1930—3 p. m.
[Received 3 : 10 p. m.]

Referring to my telegram of October 17, 4 p. m. Captain of the Port has informed me that all lighthouses began to function again yesterday.

NASMITH

632.0023/11 : Telegram

The Consul at Porto Alegre (Nasmith) to the Secretary of State

PORTO ALEGRE, October 31, 1930—3 p. m.
[Received 6 p. m.]

Entrance to port of Rio Grande which had been obstructed by the revolutionists has now been officially reopened under compulsory pilotage. This information should be of interest to American shipping interests New York, New Orleans and Baltimore.

NASMITH

832.01/2 : Telegram

The Ambassador in Brazil (Morgan) to the Secretary of State

RIO DE JANEIRO, November 4, 1930—3 p. m.
[Received November 4—2 : 55 p. m.]

139. British Ambassador called upon me this morning to inquire whether the Department was considering the question of recognizing the Provisional Government of Brazil; the Brazilian Embassy at London has approached the Foreign Office thereon.

All the requisites contained in the Secretary's statement released on September 17th last [12] when existing Governments in Argentina, Bolivia and Peru were recognized [13] seem to have been fulfilled here except in regard to the holding of elections. In announcing his program upon taking over the Government yesterday, Vargas stated that there would be a "reform of electoral system relating especially to the guaranteeing freedom of vote" and "reform of the electorate having been accomplished the nation will be consulted regarding the choice of representatives with full power to revise the Federal statutes in order to increase public and individual liberty and guarantee the autonomy of the states against violations by the Central Government."

MORGAN

832.01/3 : Telegram

The Ambassador in Brazil (Morgan) to the Secretary of State

RIO DE JANEIRO, November 5, 1930—11 a. m.
[Received 11 : 25 a. m.]

141. A circular note, dated November 3rd, from the Ministry of Foreign Affairs was received yesterday afternoon stating that the

---

[12] Ante, p. 387.
[13] For correspondence concerning revolutions in Argentina, Bolivia, and Peru, see ante, pp. 378 ff., and pp. 415 ff., and vol. III, pp. 720 ff.

provisional junta had delivered the administration of the country to Dr. Getulio Vargas who assumed its direction in the character of chief of the Provisional Government as delegate of the victorious revolution.

The circular also gives the names of the Ministers of State appointed by Vargas and repeats the statement regarding respect for national obligations contracted abroad, existing treaties, etc., contained in circular reported in Embassy's telegram 131, October 27, 6 p. m.

The note closed as follows:

"In addressing Your Excellency I assure you that we desire to maintain the friendly relations which have existed between our two countries and toward that end we request the recognition of the new Government."

The earlier communications from the junta and Vargas governments have not been answered. What reply, if any, do you instruct me to make?

MORGAN

832.01/4 : Telegram

The Ambassador in Cuba (*Guggenheim*) *to the Secretary of State*

[Paraphrase]

HABANA, November 5, 1930—2 p. m.
[Received 3 : 25 p. m.]

130. President Machado informed me that Cuba desired to follow the United States in its policy and any future action regarding recognition of the Brazilian Government.

GUGGENHEIM

832.00 Revolutions/199 : Telegram

The Secretary of State to the Ambassador in Brazil (*Morgan*)

[Paraphrase]

WASHINGTON, November 5, 1930—2 p. m.

78. Your 139, November 4, 3 p. m. I recognize how difficult it is to appraise the present situation in Brazil and, for that reason, I am going very slowly in making a decision regarding the question of recognizing the present authorities in Brazil. The Department's information is extremely meager, and now, when this very important matter is under consideration, I need especially very careful advice from you based not only on your long experience as a diplomat, but also on your long residence in Brazil and your knowledge of the sit-

uation in Brazil. I desire to receive from you, therefore, an appraisal of the present situation, based not only on your present information, but also on your long residence in Brazil, as to the causes of the revolution and the hold that the present administration has on the Brazilian people. Your statement in this respect should be based not on the assertions of the present members of the Government but on your estimate of their past history and character. While Brazil is a large country with scanty means of communication, I desire, nevertheless, as complete information as you can furnish with regard to the attitude of the various states toward the new administration, and whether there is likely to be any counterrevolution or independent uprising against its authority. I also desire your views regarding the ability of the present administration to maintain its control throughout the country, to protect life and property, and its willingness and readiness to recognize international obligations.

Owing to the large extent and difficult character of the country, scantiness of communications, etc., it is my view that we should go slow; and we will not be hurried by Great Britain in determining what is the proper action for us to take; but in this matter I desire your full and frank views and recommendations. I shall not be able to come to a proper determination of the matter without complete information, and rely on you to keep me fully informed in regard to everything which bears in any way on the situation. For instance, the press reported that the present administration would ask for a recount of the votes cast during the last election on the charge that Senhor Prestes was elected by fraud. If this is done and should the recount show that Senhor Vargas was constitutionally elected, this would, of course, materially alter the situation after November 15, when the term of office will regularly begin. Again I say that I am relying on you for full information and suggestions in the premises.

STIMSON

832.01/14

The Ambassador in Peru (Dearing) to the Secretary of State

No. 222   LIMA, November 5, 1930.
[Received November 12.]

SIR: I have the honor to report that the Peruvian Junta of Government on November first accorded recognition to the new Junta of Government in Brazil, even before the latter had been formed.

My Brazilian colleague informs me that the Peruvian Minister in Rio de Janeiro accorded recognition through the Foreign Office two days before Getulio Vargas took the oath as provisional President and the announcement of the composition of his Cabinet.

Respectfully yours,   FRED MORRIS DEARING

832.01/6 : Telegram

The Ambassador in Brazil (Morgan) to the Secretary of State

RIO DE JANEIRO, November 6, 1930—4 p. m.
[Received 6 : 09 p. m.]

143. The press published today the texts of the official notes in which the Ambassadors of Chile and Portugal and the Minister of Uruguay recognize, on behalf of their Governments, the Provisional Government of Brazil as at present constituted. The press states also that the newly arrived Ambassador of Italy and the Minister of Ecuador who have not presented the [*their*] credentials called yesterday at the Foreign Office and stated that their Governments would recognize.

MORGAN

832.01/3 : Telegram

The Secretary of State to the Ambassador in Brazil (Morgan)

[Paraphrase]

WASHINGTON, November 6, 1930—6 p. m.

79. Your 141, November 5, 11 a. m. This afternoon the British Ambassador called to say that he is being instructed to answer the Foreign Minister's circular note on November 8, unless he receives later instructions to the contrary, by saying that the change in Government in Brazil will not cause any change in the diplomatic relations between Great Britain and Brazil.

The British Ambassador added that he trusted that this action would not inconvenience the Government of the United States in its consideration of the matter.

We had an understanding with the British Ambassador that the American and British Governments would keep one another informed of their intended action in the matter. The British Ambassador was told that the Government of the United States had not yet reached a decision in the matter; that a request was sent to our Ambassador in Brazil on November 5 for further information on which to base our decision and that when we had the reply of our Ambassador and had determined upon a course of action he would be advised thereof.

I am not prepared to make a decision in the matter and therefore cannot give you the instructions requested in the last sentence of your telegram No. 141, November 5, 11 a. m., until I receive a full detailed reply to my telegram No. 78, November 5, 2 p. m. Please reply as soon as possible.

STIMSON

832.00 Revolutions/200 : Telegram

The Ambassador in Brazil (Morgan) to the Secretary of State

[Paraphrase]

RIO DE JANEIRO, November 7, 1930—noon.
[Received 1 : 20 p. m.]

144. Department's 78, November 5, 2 p. m. The revolution was caused by:

(1) The exaggerated use of the Executive power which subordinated the Legislative and Judicial powers;

(2) The imposition by Washington Luis of a Presidential candidate who was not the choice of the people;

(3) The disregard of official election returns especially in Parahyba and Minas Geraes, and the recognition by Congress of Senators and Deputies from those states who obviously had not been elected;

(4) Federal intervention in Parahyba and the disregard of states' rights in Minas Geraes. The illegality of the Presidential election in Rio Grande do Sul in which the President of the State was the Liberal Federal candidate caused the alienation of Rio Grande do Sul. Washington Luis had less discretion than his predecessors in enforcing his authority, but the imposition of the Executive will has been growing for 20 years and could be endured no longer.

All states have accepted the new administration and a counterrevolution or independent uprising against the authority of the new administration is unlikely. Military leaders may disagree, but improbably to a degree which would seriously disturb the public order. I believe that the present administration is able to maintain its control of the country and to protect life and property. The present administration has officially declared its willingness and readiness to recognize international obligations. See my 141, November 5, 11 a. m.

Press report that the present administration will call for a recount of the votes of the last election is not true. It is probable that the Provisional Government will dissolve Congress and issue a call for the election of a body to revise the present Constitution following to a certain extent the precedent established when the Empire fell. An official declaration of this intention has not yet been made. If by November 15 the situation is unaltered and is likely to remain so, recognition might be advantageous.

MORGAN

832.01/6b : Telegram

The Secretary of State to the Ambassador in Brazil (Morgan)

[Paraphrase]

WASHINGTON, November 7, 1930—5 p. m.

81. Your 144, November 7, noon. While your telegram indicates that the new administration is in *de facto* control and promises and is able to fulfill the international obligations upon which recognition would be postulated, yet you do not advise me directly as to your views upon recognition and the inference of the last paragraph seems to be that you do not advise recognition at present in spite of the facts which you have previously stated. I am not able to understand the object in waiting for a call for an election of a constitutional convention unless we also wait for the resulting action of such a convention which would involve a very long delay. In the cases of Argentina, Bolivia, and Peru we recognized upon the frank basis of a control by a *de facto* government. Are you willing to advise that the *de facto* control of the present Government of Brazil is sufficiently complete for similar prompt action?

STIMSON

832.01/22 : Telegram

The Ambassador in Brazil (Morgan) to the Secretary of State [14]

1. Department's telegram Nov. 7, 5 p. m., received and deciphered. It is my opinion that the Provisional Government fully controls the country and is supported by the people. Do not see the necessity of postponing recognition until after Nov. 15, since conditions appear to be fulfilled here which justified recognition of present Argentine Government.

MORGAN

832.01/3 : Telegram

The Secretary of State to the Ambassador in Brazil (Morgan)

WASHINGTON, November 8, 1930—10 a. m.

82. Your November 5, 11 a. m. You will today, but not earlier than 2 hours from this time, answer the note of November 3d from the Brazilian Government by stating "that this Government will be happy to continue with the new Government the same friendly relations as with its predecessors."

You will at once confidentially advise your British, Colombian and Cuban colleagues what your instructions are.

STIMSON

---

[14] This undated telegram was received on November 8, 1930.

832.01/3 : Telegram

The Secretary of State to the Minister in Colombia (Caffery)[15]

WASHINGTON, November 8, 1930—11 a. m.

62. Department is today instructing Ambassador Morgan to recognize the Brazilian Government today. Mr. Morgan will advise Colombian Minister in Rio of the action he is taking.

STIMSON

832.113/46 : Telegram

The Secretary of State to the Ambassador in Brazil (Morgan)

[Paraphrase]

WASHINGTON, November 8, 1930—noon.

83. After you have answered circular note of November 3, as instructed earlier this morning, you will please say to the Minister for Foreign Affairs that in carrying out its traditional policy of friendship for Brazil, the Government of the United States is continuing the embargo on the export of arms from the United States to Brazil.[16] Under this embargo the export of arms is prohibited except to the Government of Brazil, which is now recognized by the Government of the United States.

At the same time you may make it clear, in case there should be any doubt in the mind of the Minister for Foreign Affairs, that the action of the Government of the United States in placing an embargo on the export of arms to Brazil was not motivated by any partisan feeling whatsoever in the recent revolutionary movement. Such action is required by a convention now in force between the United States and Brazil, signed at Habana on February 20, 1928, between the American Republics regarding the duties and rights of States in the event of civil strife.[17] This Treaty was ratified by the President of the United States on May 7, 1930, the ratifications of the United States being deposited at the Pan American Union on May 21, 1930, and the treaty proclaimed by the President on June 6, 1930. This treaty has also been ratified by Brazil, the ratifications having been deposited at the Pan American Union on September 3, 1929.

It is the feeling of the Department that if you will bring this matter to the attention of the Minister for Foreign Affairs it should dispel any possible misunderstanding which may exist as to the action of the Government of the United States in the premises.

STIMSON

---

[15] The same, mutatis mutandis, on the same date to the Ambassador in Cuba as telegram No. 124.

[16] At the request of the Brazilian Embassy, the President of the United States on March 2, 1931, issued a proclamation (46 Stat. 3050) lifting the embargo on the export of arms and munitions to Brazil (832.113/61).

[17] Foreign Relations, 1928, vol. I, p. 612.

832.01/8 : Telegram

The Minister in Colombia (Caffery) to the Secretary of State

BOGOTÁ, November 8, 1930—2 p. m.
[Received 11 p. m.]

132. Department's 62.[18] Colombian Government also recognizing the Brazilian Government today.

CAFFERY

832.01/7 : Telegram

The Ambassador in Brazil (Morgan) to the Secretary of State

RIO DE JANEIRO, November 8, 1930—3 p. m.
[Received November 8—2:35 p. m.]

145. Department's No. 82, November 8, 10 a. m. Instructions in your telegram carried out in full. Note was handed personally to the Foreign Office today at 2:30, Rio de Janeiro time, acknowledging receipt of Foreign Office circular 536, dated November 3rd, and containing textually your declaration.

MORGAN

832.01/9 : Telegram

The Ambassador in Brazil (Morgan) to the Secretary of State

RIO DE JANEIRO, November 10, 1930—2 p. m.
[Received November 10—1:30 p. m.]

146. Subsequent to recognition by the United States, England, Vatican, Argentina, and France also recognized on November 8th the Provisional Government of Brazil.

MORGAN

832.113/47 : Telegram

The Ambassador in Brazil (Morgan) to the Secretary of State

RIO DE JANEIRO, November 11, 1930—11 a. m.
[Received November 11—10:10 a. m.]

147. Action already taken on Department's telegram No. 83, November 8, noon.

MORGAN

---

[18] *Ante*, p. 452.

518625—45——34

TERMINATION OF CONTRACT FOR AMERICAN NAVAL MISSION TO BRAZIL, SIGNED JULY 6, 1926 [19]

832.30/212

The Brazilian Ambassador (Gurgél do Amaral) to the Secretary of State

No. 72   WASHINGTON, October 21, 1930.

EXCELLENCY: The undersigned, Ambassador Extraordinary and Plenipotentiary of the United States of Brazil, acting under directions of his Government, has the honour to address the present Note to Your Excellency for the purpose of asking the United States Government kindly to consent to renew the contract of the United States Naval Mission to Brazil for a further period of four years, to start on the sixth of November next, when the existing contract will expire.

The Federal Government of Brazil are greatly desirous of keeping the renewed contract in its original form and text, with only a new text to replace the text of clause 16 of Article IV and, having this in view, the undersigned begs leave to propose the following substitutive text, in the Portuguese version of the contract: [20]

"16. Aos officiaes da Missão Naval serão concedidos os direitos, immunidades e privilegios habitualmente garantidos aos representantes diplomaticos acreditados no Brazil.["]

With the renewal of the existing contract for a further period of four years, the Federal Government of Brazil consider it to be understood that the additional paragraphs, concerning the petty officers, as mentioned in Your Excellency's Note No. 2 of May 29th, 1929, are to be maintained as well as the Supplementary Contract of the Naval Mission signed by the Honourable Frank B. Kellogg, then Secretary of State of the United States of America, and by the undersigned on the 26th day of May of 1927.[21]

The undersigned therefore proposes, on behalf and by order of the Federal Government of Brazil, an exchange of Notes—initiated by the present Note—which will embody and give full validity to the renewal of the contract, as heretofore suggested, should such renewal be kindly agreed upon by the Government of the United States of America.

The undersigned seizes this opportunity [etc.]

S. GURGÉL DO AMARAL

---

[19] For previous correspondence, see *Foreign Relations*, 1926, vol. I, pp. 574 ff.
[20] For English text, see telegram No. 77, November 5, 1 p. m., to the Ambassador in Brazil, p. 455.
[21] Neither printed.

832.30/214 : Telegram

The Ambassador in Brazil (Morgan) to the Secretary of State

RIO DE JANEIRO, November 4, 1930—4 p. m.
[Received 4:11 p. m.]

140. Mello Franco, Foreign Minister of the Provisional Government,[22] sent his Chief of Cabinet to the Embassy today to state that as the Provisional Government had not had sufficient opportunity to decide whether or not they wish to renew the Naval Mission contract, they desire that the Mission would continue to operate after the termination of the present contract on November 6th until the Government had an opportunity to reach a decision probably within 15 days.   MORGAN

832.30/214 : Telegram

The Secretary of State to the Ambassador in Brazil (Morgan)

WASHINGTON, November 5, 1930—1 p. m.

77. Your 140, November 4, 4 p. m. There were negotiations during most of the summer with the Brazilian Ambassador regarding the change desired by the Brazilian Government in paragraph 16 of Article 4 of the contract for the Naval Mission to Brazil.[23] The Navy Department did not wish the change. The Ambassador finally discussed the matter with the Secretary of State on October 9th and it appeared that the English wording was all right but the Portuguese text was not a very accurate translation and that that was perhaps the cause of the difficulty. The Secretary of State and the Ambassador agreed that this paragraph should be changed to read as follows: "The officers of the Mission will be accorded rights, immunities and privileges habitually granted to diplomatic representatives accredited to Brazil." The Secretary of the Navy also agreed. The Ambassador cabled his Government to obtain its consent and asked for authority to propose this wording as the suggestion of the Brazilian Government. This authorization was granted and the Ambassador submitted a note dated October 21 that was received in the Department the following day and in the office handling the matter on October 23. A copy of the note was sent to the Navy Department for its formal approval and this was not received until the 24th, or after the revolution had taken place.

---

[22] See "Revolution in Brazil," pp. 432 ff.
[23] The paragraph under reference reads as follows: "The officers of the Mission will be accorded rights and privileges habitually granted to diplomatic representatives accredited to Brazil and of corresponding rank, except with regard to rights of importation already covered in a preceding clause."
The Brazilian Government had suggested that it be modified to read as follows: "The American officers of the Naval Mission are exempt from civil and criminal jurisdiction in Brazil and are not subject to personal taxes." (832.30/209.)

The Secretary discussed the matter with the Ambassador on October 31. The latter stated that he had cabled the previous day to Mr. Mello Franco outlining the negotiations and stating that he had sent the Department a note on October 21 under instructions of Mr. Mello Franco's predecessor and asking instructions in the premises. The Ambassador added that the only way out he could suggest would be that, as the agreement was to be consummated by an exchange of notes and his note had already been despatched before the Brazilian Government fell, the Secretary answer that note dating his answer October 21 also so that there would be no question of recognition. If the Secretary agreed to this proposal the Ambassador would make it to his Government as the Ambassador's own proposal.

The Secretary replied that he was not in favor of this course of action because the new authorities in Rio perhaps do not know us and might think we were trying to bring pressure to bear to continue the Naval Mission and also because there might be changes in the present Brazilian authorities. If the present authorities were later succeeded by others, the new authorities might feel that the United States Government had foisted upon the temporary authorities an agreement for 4 years for the Mission which would not be to their liking. The Secretary said that he thought a *modus vivendi* could be entered into until a new government is recognized which can decide whether it desires to make a definite contract.

The Ambassador recurred to his suggestion for a note from the Secretary dated October 21. The Secretary again declined and said that the problem is to find out whether the present Brazilian authorities desire our Naval officers in Brazil or not. If they do not, the quicker we can get them out the better. On the other hand if they desire them to stay, it would be a very easy matter to make a temporary arrangement bridging over the time until a definitive one can be made. The Ambassador said that he would cable to his Government in this sense and indicated a preference that the *modus vivendi* be entered into by you and the Foreign Office in Rio, but promised to advise us of the reply of his Government.

This Government of course understands that the Brazilian authorities are very fully preoccupied with more pressing matters and is perfectly willing to have the Mission carry on after the termination of the present contract on November 6th until the Brazilian Government has an opportunity to reach a decision in the matter.

STIMSON

832.30/217 : Telegram

The Ambassador in Brazil (Morgan) to the Secretary of State

RIO DE JANEIRO, November 14, 1930—2 p. m.
[Received 2 : 05 p. m.]

151. The report in the *New York Times*, from its correspondent who is located in São Paulo, that the contract of the American and French Naval and Military Missions would be rescinded and that the American Mission would leave on November 26th is not based on official information.

The Foreign Minister has asked me to express to you his appreciation of your courtesy in allowing the American Mission to remain until such time as the Brazilian Provisional Government shall have an opportunity to decide whether or not it is to retain the Mission's service[s].

MORGAN

832.30/218 : Telegram

The Ambassador in Brazil (Morgan) to the Secretary of State

RIO DE JANEIRO, November 18, 1930—3 p. m.
[Received November 18—2 : 55 p. m.]

153. The Brazilian Foreign Minister told me yesterday in conversation that his Government could not renew the contract of the Naval Mission for reasons which are wholly of a financial character since the work of the Mission and its personnel have been invariably satisfactory. This reason bore evidence of sincerity and it is desirable that the press shall not represent that any other motive exists.

As contract for Naval Mission was virtually renewed under former Government and temporary extension requested by present Government, Chief of Mission feels that a sufficient period of time should be arranged to permit official and personal business, such as leases for residences, to be closed with propriety and dignity for all concerned.

MORGAN

832.30/218 : Telegram

The Secretary of State to the Ambassador in Brazil (Morgan)

WASHINGTON, November 20, 1930—11 a. m.

90. Your 153, November 18, 3 p. m. Please see telegram 1019 sent by Navy Department to Admiral Irwin yesterday. This Department concurs in views expressed therein.

Ascertain informally and as early as practicable the views of the

Brazilian authorities and the Chief of the Naval Mission with regard to the time necessary to permit the closing of official and personal business of the Mission and submit your personal recommendations.

STIMSON

832.30/219 : Telegram

The Ambassador in Brazil (Morgan) to the Secretary of State

RIO DE JANEIRO, November 25, 1930—noon.
[Received 12:45 p. m.]

155. Department's 90, November 20, 11 a. m. Foreign Minister desirous of consulting the Department regarding date and terms attending departure of Naval Mission. I favor an arrangement by which all the members should reach home the end of January, Brazilian pay continuing to January 31st. Foreign Minister is favorable to this suggestion.

There are 14 officers; 13 wives, many of them with children; and 17 petty officers, 7 of whom have families here. Total personnel, 71. House leases in the majority of cases can be canceled with 2 months' notice. Facilities for packing household effects limited and this matter cannot be arranged under 2 months. Officers desire to take their effects on the steamers upon which they sail.

MORGAN

832.30/219 : Telegram

The Secretary of State to the Ambassador in Brazil (Morgan)

WASHINGTON, November 26, 1930—4 p. m.

91. Your 155, November 25, noon. January 31 acceptable as date for termination of mission's services.

STIMSON

121.5532/8 : Telegram

The Ambassador in Brazil (Morgan) to the Secretary of State

RIO DE JANEIRO, December 1, 1930—5 p. m.
[Received 5:53 p. m.]

158. Embassy's despatch 3466 which leaves for Washington by today's air mail [24] recommends the restoration of the office of Naval Attaché to this Embassy and the designation of Lieutenant Commander W. H. P. Blandy as Attaché, who two months ago entered upon a 2 years' service with the Naval Mission.

I am particularly anxious that the State and Navy Departments should concur in my recommendations.

MORGAN

[24] *Infra.*

121.5532/12

The Ambassador in Brazil (Morgan) to the Secretary of State

No. 3466   RIO DE JANEIRO, December 1, 1930.
                                          [Received December 8.]

SIR: With the departure for home of the American Naval Mission
to Brazil at the end of January, 1931, I have the honor to request
that the Department will discuss with the Navy Department the re-
assignment of a Naval Attaché to this Embassy. The office of Naval
Attaché was discontinued when Captain William Alden Hall, U. S. N.,
who was assigned in June, 1927, was detailed as a member of the Naval
Mission in April, 1929, and employed as an instructor in the Brazilian
Naval War College. For a number of years after the Mission was
established, however, the Navy Department continued to be represented
by an attaché.

A new naval attaché might be instructed not only to perform the
usual duties of his office, but to serve as a liaison officer between the
Brazilian Navy and the traditions of cooperation between the American and Brazilian navies which the Mission during the period of
eight years has so efficiently created and developed. It would be indeed regrettable if the moral effect of what has been accomplished
should be allowed to fade out because the preservation of suitable
means were wanting. Certain departments of the Brazilian Navy
must for many years depend on foreign assistance, and when national
finances improve, a few foreign officers will be engaged for the Naval
War College and for certain technical departments. As large a mission as the one which is to be discontinued will not be necessary because it cannot be adequately employed until the material of the naval
service is increased by additional naval vessels of one or another category. The presence of an American Naval Attaché, especially if he
has Mission's associations, will perpetuate the influence of the United
States in the Brazilian Navy and will discourage that Navy from turning to European Powers for technical assistance and advice.

I recommend, therefore, that Lieutenant Commander W. H. P.
Blandy, U. S. N., who recently arrived to join the Mission, and who
having two years shore duty before him need not soon go afloat, shall
be detailed as Naval Attaché. Since he and his family are already
established in Rio de Janeiro, the Navy Department will be saved
the expense of transportation. Personally and professionally he is
well equipped for attaché's duty, and the contacts which he has
already made and which he will increase in local naval circles are
sound. His rank under existing conditions is sufficiently adequate
to prevent embarrassment to himself or to the service from the fact
that it is not of higher grade, and he informs me that he will gladly
perform the Attaché's duty if the Navy Department shall detail him.

The Foreign Minister has told me that the only Naval Attaché whom the Brazilian Navy intends, if possible, to maintain in a foreign capital is the Attaché in Washington, D. C.

The subject of this despatch is of unusual importance for the maintenance of our prestige and I bespeak the Department's earnest consideration of my proposals.

Respectfully yours,

EDWIN V. MORGAN

121.5532/8 : Telegram

The Secretary of State to the Ambassador in Brazil (Morgan)

WASHINGTON, December 3, 1930—6 p. m.

94. Your 158, December 1, 5 p. m. Departments concerned are disposed to comply with your recommendation for appointment of Lieutenant Commander Blandy as Naval Attaché but before taking definite action desire to await receipt of Brazilian Government's formal notification of its disposition with reference to termination of the services of the Naval Mission.

STIMSON

832.30/226

The Ambassador in Brazil (Morgan) to the Secretary of State

[Extract]

No. 3475
RIO DE JANEIRO, December 5, 1930.
[Received December 16.]

SIR: In amplification of Embassy's telegram No. 161, of December 5, 2 p. m.,[25] relative to the return to the United States of the members of the American Naval Mission to Brazil, I have the honor to enclose a copy, accompanied by an English translation, of the personal note of yesterday's date, received in the afternoon, from the Brazilian Minister for Foreign Affairs, the contents of which note formed the basis of Embassy's telegram No. 161. This was in reply to my personal note of December 2, a copy of which I have the honor to enclose.

After thanking the American Government for permitting the Government of Brazil an additional period after the date of the expiration of the contract in which to determine whether or not the Mission contract should be renewed and after expressing the Government's regret at losing the services of the Mission on account of the necessity of reducing public expenditure, the note states that all the rights and privileges which officers of the Mission have enjoyed under the said contract shall be continued to them until January 31 next, upon which date the responsibilities and obligations which the Brazilian Govern-

---

[25] Not printed.

ment has entertained toward them shall cease to be binding. No statement is made as to whether or not the Mission shall continue to perform its duties until the 31st of January, and regarding that matter the Chief of Mission will confer with the Minister of Marine in conformity with the convenience of the Brazilian Navy and of the Mission. All officers who are returning to the United States will leave Brazil before January 31, the date of their departure depending upon the rapidity with which packers can prepare their furniture and household goods for shipment.

.   .   .   .

Respectfully yours,   EDWIN V. MORGAN

[Enclosure 1]

The American Ambassador (Morgan) to the Brazilian Minister for Foreign Affairs (De Mello Franco)

RIO DE JANEIRO, December 2, 1930.

DEAR MR. MINISTER: Since having had the pleasure of talking with you on the diplomatic reception day, my Government has informed me that it will be agreeable if the date upon which the connection of the American Naval Mission with the Government of Brazil shall cease shall be fixed for the last day of January, 1931. That is the date which I suggested to you and which you accepted unofficially.

If Your Excellency's Government agrees to that date, may we consider that it shall be the one upon which the work of the Mission shall terminate and the pay shall cease, which the Mission receives from the Brazilian Government.

In regard to other expenses relative to the Mission which Your Excellency's Government will presumably desire to assume, they are covered by Article IV, Sections 4 and 6, of the late naval contract. Although that contract ceased to be operative on November 6 last, it would appear to be proper that the provisions of those sections shall continue to operate inasmuch as they relate to traveling expenses of the Mission to the United States and to the return there of their families, personal effects and household goods. I enclose a copy of the text of Article 4, which includes the two sections in question in case Your Excellency has not a copy at hand.

As the termination of the contract of the American Naval Mission with Your Excellency's Government has been conducted through a "gentleman's agreement" and not by the interchange of diplomatic notes, I would suggest that Your Excellency should write me personally in the same manner in which I am writing you, expressing your concurrence with the views which this letter contains, or suggesting such modifications therein as Your Government may desire to propose for submission to my own Government.

EDWIN V. MORGAN

[Enclosure 2—Translation]

The Brazilian Minister for Foreign Affairs (De Mello Franco)
to the American Ambassador (Morgan)

RIO DE JANEIRO, December 4, 1930.

MY DEAR MR. AMBASSADOR: In reference to the correspondence exchanged between Your Excellency and the Chief of my Cabinet on November 5 last, I have the honor to renew to you and through your intermedium to the American Government, the thanks both of the Brazilian Government and of myself for the attentive manner with which the American Embassy and the State Department met the wishes of the Provisional Government in establishing a temporary *modus vivendi* between our respective Governments until we were able to examine the question of the renewal of the contract of the American Naval Mission, which terminated on November 6th last.

Confirming what I declared verbally to Your Excellency, and in answer to your letter of the 2nd instant, it is my duty to inform you that the Provisional Government, much to its regret, is unable to renew the said contract to continue to utilize the services which, since 1922, the brilliant and competent American Naval Mission has so efficiently rendered to our War Marine.

The present financial condition of Brazil constitutes the essential and prime preoccupation of the Provisional Government, which, in order to regulate the same, and to meet its obligations abroad, has adopted the strictest program of a reduction of expenses which can be followed without disorganizing the public services.

For this purpose, it has carefully examined the budgets inherited from the former Government and has suppressed all expenses which may be postponed.

It is my duty to add that, in accordance with the statement which I had the honor to make verbally to Your Excellency, the Provisional Government guarantees to the Naval Mission the rights which are contained in the contract of November 6th, 1922, until the 31st of January next, upon which date all the responsibilities and obligations which the Brazilian Government assumed under the terms of that instrument, shall end.

I believe that these terms are fully in accordance with those which Your Excellency and I agreed upon during our last conversation and with the contents of the letter I am now answering.

I avail myself [etc.]   A. DE MELLO FRANCO

121.5532/11 : Telegram

The Ambassador in Brazil (Morgan) to the Secretary of State

RIO DE JANEIRO, December 5, 1930—3 p. m.
[Received December 5—2 : 15 p. m.]

162. Department's 94, December 3, 6 p. m. Since my telegram No. 161, December 5, 2 p. m.,[26] transmits formal notice that the services of the Naval Mission will terminate on January 31st next, I shall be gratified if Lieutenant Commander Blandy's appointment can be announced. The effect here will be beneficial.

MORGAN

121.5532/11 : Telegram

The Secretary of State to the Ambassador in Brazil (Morgan)

WASHINGTON, December 6, 1930—noon.

95. Your 162, December 5, 3 p. m. Informally advised by Navy Department that Lieutenant Commander Blandy will be detailed as Naval Attaché to the Embassy, effective February 1st on expiration of his services with Naval Mission.

Please inquire of Brazilian Government whether designation of Blandy as Naval Attaché is agreeable. Cable reply.

STIMSON

121.5532/15 : Telegram

The Ambassador in Brazil (Morgan) to the Secretary of State

RIO DE JANEIRO, December 15, 1930—10 a. m.
[Received December 15—9 : 35 a. m.]

167. Department's telegram No. 95, December 6, noon. Brazilian Government is agreeable to designation of Lieutenant Commander Blandy as Naval Attaché of this Embassy.

MORGAN

121.5532/14 : Telegram

The Secretary of State to the Ambassador in Brazil (Morgan)

WASHINGTON, December 15, 1930—6 p. m.

100. Your 167, December 15, 10 a. m. Blandy has now been designated as Naval Attaché effective upon termination of Naval Mission about January 31.

Please advise Foreign Office.

STIMSON

---

[26] Not printed; see despatch No. 3475, December 5, from the Ambassador in Brazil, *supra.*

GOOD OFFICES OF THE DEPARTMENT OF STATE ON BEHALF OF THE NATIONAL CITY BANK IN SECURING REMISSION OF FINE IMPOSED UPON ITS SÃO PAULO BRANCH

811.51632 National City Bank/1 : Telegram

The Acting Secretary of State to the Ambassador in Brazil (Morgan)

WASHINGTON, February 27, 1930—7 p. m.

6. The Department was informed this afternoon by telephone by the National City Bank, New York, that they have received notice that the Government of Brazil will fine the São Paulo branch approximately three million dollars. The fine was recommended by the Inspector General of Banks and two-thirds of the amount goes to the Government and one-third to the Inspector General. The bank states that basis of fine is that their exchange man at São Paulo conspired with a broker without the knowledge of the bank and had been selling sterling exchange in London, Berlin and Buenos Aires to the amount of about one million pounds. The items were not entered on the books and when confirmatory letters came in they were confiscated by him so that managing officer of branch knew nothing of the transaction. On December 30, 1929, the auditor discovered entries in the books not in accordance with the day's rate and took the matter up first with the exchange man and then with the manager. It appears that if the transactions were successful the exchange manager was to get 25 per cent profit. The transactions were thus disclosed and the bank has since been trying to straighten out the matter with the banks outside of Brazil. These dealings were illegal because made at 120 and 180 days whereas local regulation, although it is not a law, prevents such transactions in excess of 90 days.

Bank states all facts presented by bank to Inspector General and the Minister of Finance and they believe facts are known to President Washington Luis and also to the Ambassador. Local representatives of bank want the matter reported to Washington and state that if the regulations are valid they did not become effective until January 18, or nearly 3 weeks after the facts were disclosed and the transactions terminated. Bank states it is ex post facto legislation or rather regulation of the banking department designed to permit the fine. Wide publicity of the fine has been given in the Brazilian press but no notice has been served on the bank. Fifteen days after notice is served the bank must put up three million dollars in cash or securities before it can appeal to the Minister of Finance. Bank states there is possibility that matter is done for political effect and requests that notice be not presented to the bank for the time being and certainly not until after the elections next Saturday.

Representative of bank will come to Washington early next week to present full facts. In meantime please report briefly by cable and fully by mail regarding the situation and you may, unless you perceive some objection thereto, present to the proper Brazilian authorities the request of the bank regarding delay in notification of the fine.

COTTON

811.51632 National City Bank/2 : Telegram

The Ambassador in Brazil (Morgan) to the Acting Secretary of State

RIO DE JANEIRO, February 28, 1930—noon.
[Received February 28—11:20 a. m.]

5. Department's telegram No. 6, February 27, 7 p. m. Facts reported through the Department by bank substantially correct and matter has been in conference between local branch authorities and Embassy for some time.

Will use influence with Foreign Office to obtain postponement.

MORGAN

811.51632 National City Bank/4 : Telegram

The Acting Secretary of State to the Ambassador in Brazil (Morgan)

WASHINGTON, February 28, 1930—4 p. m.

7. Department's 6, February 27, 7 p. m. Following telegrams signed Hart,[27] National City Bank, Buenos Aires, dated the 27th, given to the Department by National City Bank:

"Following cable received from Moran:[28] 'It is important Head Office emphasize to State Department need for urgent and strong action to prevent this case flagrant injustice of a colossal fine for transactions which Government themselves had originally approved as legal and in order. Important also to add that even clandestine transactions were approved by Government fiscal by signatures on brokers note at broker's request after we had denied and repudiated the transactions. State Department should be ready insist upon Government permit guarantee instead of deposit in view of amount.'"

"The National City Bank of New York, São Paulo, Brazil, notified officially today have 15 days to make deposit and defense."

CARR

---

[27] Vice President of the National City Bank of New York.
[28] Local manager of the São Paulo branch.

811.51632 National City Bank/5 : Telegram

The Acting Secretary of State to the Ambassador in Brazil (Morgan)

WASHINGTON, March 3, 1930—7 p. m.

8. Your February 28, noon.   National City Bank advises Department of the receipt of cable from manager of São Paulo branch stating they are confidentially informed that on February 28, the Minister of Finance issued General Order prohibiting giving guarantees instead of making a cash deposit when appealing fines in the future. Cable adds that if this information is correct the order apparently was issued to apply to the bank's case and that the Department should call for extraordinary activities on the part of Embassy in order to avoid that one official could levy such a large fine and demand such a large deposit based on his personal judgment which is so openly prejudiced.

Please investigate and report also please use your good offices with the Government for an extension of time and also in view of the fact that the National City Bank is a responsible institution that it not be required to make the deposit of guarantee.   Cable results.

COTTON

811.51632 National City Bank/6 : Telegram

The Ambassador in Brazil (Morgan) to the Acting Secretary of State

RIO DE JANEIRO, March 4, 1930—5 p. m.
[Received 5:25 p. m.]

7. Department's 7, February 28, 4 p. m.; 8, March 3, 7 p. m.   National City Bank has infringed Brazilian banking regulations and cannot escape the penalty of a fine.   These regulations provide that inspectors shall receive a portion thereof.   Inadequate supervision by the local officers of the bank created the situation.

Even informal diplomatic intervention will not be well received before deposit of the fine has been made subsequent to which it should be possible to obtain a modification of the amount which is excessive. I am presenting informal memorandum however to Foreign Minister after seeing Hart who arrived today.

MORGAN

811.51632 National City Bank/7 : Telegram

The Acting Secretary of State to the Ambassador in Brazil (Morgan)

WASHINGTON, March 5, 1930—5 p. m.

9. Does your No. 7, March 4, 5 p. m. mean that it is not possible to put up a bond instead of depositing securities or cash?   The bank is

very anxious to exhaust all possibilities along this line. Please reply by cable.

COTTON

811.51632 National City Bank/8 : Telegram

The Ambassador in Brazil (Morgan) to the Acting Secretary of State

RIO DE JANEIRO, March 6, 1930—10 a. m.
[Received 10:15 a. m.]

8. Department's telegram number 9, March 5, 5 p. m. My telegram number 7, March 4, 5 p. m., did not imply that the question of filing a bond instead of depositing securities or cash was settled. Matter is still under consideration.

MORGAN

811.51632 National City Bank/13 : Telegram

The Acting Secretary of State to the Ambassador in Brazil (Morgan)

WASHINGTON, March 10, 1930—2 p. m.

11. Your 7 and 8, March 4, 5 p. m. and March 6, 10 a. m. Please discuss freely with Mr. Hart, Vice President National City Bank, your conclusions as to the guilt or innocence of the bank. Bank now requests that you concentrate on obtaining permission for them to put up an individual guarantee rather than cash and the bank relinquishes its request for a postponement of the time limit when the guarantee must be made. Cable present situation.

CARR

811.51632 National City Bank/11 : Telegram

The Acting Secretary of State to the Ambassador in Brazil (Morgan)

[Paraphrase]

WASHINGTON, March 11, 1930—4 p. m.

12. The Department considers that the fine imposed on the National City Bank has created a most serious situation. Even should the National City Bank be guilty of the infraction of a regulation as charged the fine is out of all proportion to the offense. All profits of the Bank in Brazil will be wiped out if this fine is levied.

For your strictly confidential information you are informed that the Directors of the National City Bank have authorized the closing of all of its Brazilian branches and liquidating its business there should this fine be levied. The National City Bank does not want to make any threats to the Government of Brazil and, of course, is not advising it of the decision it has reached. The Department, of course, does not desire you to make any reference to this in your conversations with the Brazilian officials. On the other hand both the Department and the Bank do want you to know how seriously they consider the situation. If the Bank should withdraw, you can readily appreciate the effect this would have on American interests in Brazil.

Please take up this matter actively with the Government of Brazil pointing out how greatly disproportionate is the fine to any infraction of regulations even on the basis that the Bank is guilty of all the charges made, and the Bank alleges that this is not the case. Please consult the opinion of Dr. Clovis Bevalacqua,[29] a copy of which was submitted by Mr. Hart to the National City Bank on March 10. You should endeavor to have the fine, which is an administrative matter, very greatly reduced with opportunity for the Bank to file a bond instead of depositing cash or securities. Cable comprehensive report as soon as you can.

COTTON

811.51632 National City Bank/10 : Telegram

The Acting Secretary of State to the Ambassador in Brazil (Morgan)

WASHINGTON, March 11, 1930—5 p. m.

13. The National City Bank has requested that you suggest to the Brazilian authorities for them that in order to avoid difficulties of the exchange situation, expenses of transportation and insurance in transferring the three million dollars required to be deposited with the Brazilian Government before an appeal can be made against the fine levied that the Brazilian Government consent to the Bank depositing with the United States Treasury through the Department of State, United States Government bonds to the par value of three million dollars. These bonds will be held in escrow to be released to the Brazilian Government only upon the receipt by the Department of the original or an exemplified copy of a letter from the Minister of Finance of Brazil enclosing an exemplified copy of a Court Order giving judgment against the Bank. There should also be enclosed in that letter an exemplified statement from the Minister for Foreign Affairs of Brazil to the effect that the Court rendering the judgment is either the Court of Last Resort of Brazil or that there is no appeal from that Court to a higher Court or in case there is an appeal that no appeal has been made within the statutory time. Upon receipt of these documents three million dollars or so much thereof as the judgment calls for will be held subject to the orders of the Brazilian Government.

---

[29] Brazilian attorney and independent counsel for the National City Bank.

The funds may likewise be released to the Bank upon presentation by it of an exemplified Court Order sustaining the Bank and exemplified statement from the Minister for Foreign Affairs that the Court rendering the Order is the Court of Last Resort or if not that there is no appeal from that Court to a higher Court or if there is appeal that no appeal has been made within the statutory period. There should also be included in the arrangement a provision by which after a period of three years or some other term mutually agreeable to the Brazilian Government and the Bank the funds will be released to the Bank if no final determination of the matter has been reached. The arrangement should also provide that the funds are subject to disposition on joint order of the Minister of Finance of Brazil and the Bank. Meantime all interest from the bonds will be paid to the Bank and the Bank reserves the right to substitute cash for all or any part of the bonds at any time.

If the fine is for a part only of the funds deposited the balance after satisfying the judgment may be withdrawn by the Bank.

This Department and the Treasury Department have agreed to act in the manner suggested by the Bank in case this meets with the wishes of the Brazilian Government.

Please advise Mr. Hart of the contents of this cable for his information before acting on it.

COTTON

811.51632 National City Bank/12 : Telegram

The Ambassador in Brazil (Morgan) to the Acting Secretary of State

[Paraphrase]

Rio de Janeiro, March 12, 1930—3 p. m.
[Received 4 : 47 p. m.]

10. Department's No. 12, March 11, 4 p. m., and No. 13, March 11, 5 p. m. Hart and I agree that our immediate efforts should be applied to obtaining permission of the Minister of Finance for the bank to sign a "termo de responsabilidade" for the payment of the fine. The Foreign Minister, whom I saw again this afternoon, will support the proposal to sign a "termo" with the President of the Republic and Minister of Finance.

The contents of the Department's telegram No. 13, March 11, 5 p. m., will be held in reserve until signature of "termo" is settled.

The Foreign Minister recognizes the international feature of the case and deplores the precipitous action of the bank examiner. Desire that the Department send me a friendly message for the Foreign

Minister, the text of which I can transmit as representing your views of the case especially as bearing on the financial situation of Brazil abroad.

Morgan

811.51632 National City Bank/15 : Telegram

The Acting Secretary of State to the Ambassador in Brazil (Morgan)

Washington, March 13, 1930—3 p. m.

14. Your 10, March 12, 3 p. m. Please say to the Minister for Foreign Affairs that the Department very much appreciates the interest he has taken in the National City Bank matter and the efforts he is making to bring this matter to a satisfactory conclusion. Department feels, as evidently His Excellency the Minister for Foreign Affairs of Brazil does, that this is a matter of very great importance in the relations between the United States and Brazil, which have been increasing rapidly and which this Government desires to strengthen in every proper way. In this connection it is interesting to note that in 1913 Brazilian imports were $324,000,000, $50,900,000 of which came from the United States, or 15.7 per cent. The Brazilian exports in that year were $315,700,000, of which $101,800,000, or 32.2 per cent went to the United States. The National City Bank entered Brazil in 1915 and since that time has been helpful in promoting trade relations between the United States and Brazil. Although not claiming of course that all the increase since that date is due to any one institution it is interesting to see not only how trade has increased but also the increased proportion of Brazil's trade that is done with the United States. In 1928 Brazilian imports were $442,-290,000, of which $117,510,000, or 26.6 per cent came from the United States. Brazilian exports were $475,242,000, of which $215,992,000, or 45.4 per cent went to the United States. Also in 1913 Brazil had outstanding loans to the value of $504,335,000, all from European sources. In 1928 Brazil had outstanding loans of £106,970,000 Sterling, 333,577,000 Francs, and $152,800,000. The United States share is thus somewhat over 20 per cent of the whole.

Banking, of course, plays the most important part in trade and economic relations between two countries and it is therefore very important to guard against anything which might disturb that relationship. The interest and action which the Minister for Foreign Affairs has taken in this very important matter is another instance of his friendly disposition and desire to cooperate with the United States which is very highly appreciated and reciprocated by this Government.

Cotton

811.51632 National City Bank/14 : Telegram

The Ambassador in Brazil (Morgan) to the Acting Secretary of State

RIO DE JANEIRO, March 13, 1930—5 p. m.
[Received March 13—4:29 p. m.]

11. Foreign Minister requests me to telegraph you that your intervention has succeeded in modifying the attitude of his Government regarding the National City Bank affair. Period for meeting fine expires tomorrow. Since the Government considers that the banking regulations do not provide for payment through a "termo de responsabilidade" and that form of payment may not be possible, the Bank of Brazil will combine with the National City Bank to make payment easy. Subsequent to payment the way will be open for President Washington Luis to receive Hart and for full discussion between bank and Government of the ultimate amount of fine.

MORGAN

811.51632 National City Bank/22 : Telegram

The Acting Secretary of State to the Ambassador in Brazil (Morgan)

WASHINGTON, April 1, 1930—6 p. m.

17. National City Bank reports that no progress has been made toward a decision in the matter of the fine of its São Paulo branch. Bank feels that an informal inquiry on your part would help to expedite matters and the Department would be glad to have you make such inquiry unless you perceive some objection thereto. Please report by cable the cause of the delay, action taken by you and result thereof.

COTTON

811.51632 National City Bank/23 : Telegram

The Ambassador in Brazil (Morgan) to the Acting Secretary of State

RIO DE JANEIRO, April 2, 1930—4 p. m.
[Received April 2—3:15 p. m.]

14. Department's 17, April 1, 6 p. m. Please assure National City Bank that Embassy is actively supporting before the Brazilian Foreign Office their contentions. Conferred again with that office on March 31st. Foreign Minister fully appreciates bank's viewpoint which he is recommending to acceptance of Minister of Finance.

Improbable that modification of fine can be arranged without delay, although I am convinced that a satisfactory adjustment will eventually be made. Bank more likely to obtain substantial modification if it does not press for immediate solution, a course which may antagonize the authorities who are handling the case.

Report follows by mail.

MORGAN

811.51632 National City Bank/25 : Telegram

The Acting Secretary of State to the Ambassador in Brazil (Morgan)

WASHINGTON, April 11, 1930—1 p. m.

20. In your No. 11, March 13, 5 p. m. you suggested the possibility of the President's receiving Hart for full discussion of the ultimate amount of the fine imposed upon the National City Bank. The National City Bank informs the Department that Hart considers it desirable to have an interview with the President and that the bank would very much appreciate your assisting him to obtain one. If Hart still desires the interview, and if you perceive no objection arising from the considerations outlined in your No. 14, April 2, 4 p. m., the Department would be glad to have you assist Hart in the matter.

COTTON

811.51632 National City Bank/29 : Telegram

The Acting Secretary of State to the Ambassador in Brazil (Morgan)

WASHINGTON, June 3, 1930—1 p. m.

39. The National City Bank informs the Department that the papers regarding the fine imposed on its São Paulo branch have now been before the President for more than a month. The bank believes that an informal and friendly inquiry by you might expedite a decision. You may make such an inquiry unless you consider it inadvisable to do so. Please report action taken.

CARR

811.51632 National City Bank/32 : Telegram

The Ambassador in Brazil (Morgan) to the Secretary of State

RIO DE JANEIRO, June 11, 1930—3 p. m.
[Received June 11—2 : 05 p. m.]

33. Department's 39, June 3, 1 p. m. Minister of Foreign Affairs has been ill for 6 weeks but yesterday discussed with President Washington Luis the advantage of settling promptly the amount of the fine levied on National City Bank, whom he informed that the bank was contemplating increasing its branches in Brazil and had rendered considerable service to São Paulo in subscribing $5,000,000 toward the recent coffee loan. He stated also that the solution of the matter was of interest to the American Government.

The President subsequently received me in audience during which I emphasized the necessity of a rapid solution. The Minister of

Finance who has been out of town on account of ill health, also, will return in a few days when the President will confer with him relative to action.

The President recognizes the exaggerated nature of the fine and the services which the bank has performed in the development of this country. If the Secretary should talk over the matter with Dr. Freitas Valle [30] and suggest that the latter should send a telegram to the Brazilian Foreign Office emphasizing the desirability of a rapid despatch of this matter, impetus would be given thereto.

MORGAN

811.51632 National City Bank/35 : Telegram

The Secretary of State to the Ambassador in Brazil (Morgan)

WASHINGTON, June 14, 1930—1 p. m.

42. Your 33, June 11, 3 p. m., last paragraph. The Secretary spoke with Senhor Freitas Valle this morning regarding the matter emphasizing the desirability of a rapid settlement. Mr. Valle promised to cable to Rio regarding it.

STIMSON

811.51632 National City Bank/45 : Telegram

The Ambassador in Brazil (Morgan) to the Secretary of State

RIO DE JANEIRO, July 11, 1930—10 a. m.
[Received 10:15 a. m.]

41. Embassy's 40, July 2, 2 p. m.[31] The President informed me yesterday afternoon that he had instructed the Minister of Finance to issue an administrative order canceling in its entirety the fine levied by the Inspector of Banks on National City Bank.

MORGAN

811.51632 National City Bank/47 : Telegram

The Ambassador in Brazil (Morgan) to the Secretary of State

RIO DE JANEIRO, July 24, 1930—9 a. m.
[Received July 24—9 a. m.]

44. Department's 49, July 12, 1 p. m.[31] Ministerial order regarding

---

[30] Member of the Brazilian Foreign Office, then attached to the suite of President-elect Prestes, who visited the United States in June 1930 in order officially to return the visit which Mr. Hoover made to Brazil in December 1928. For an account of Senhor Prestes' visit, see Department of State, *Press Releases*, June 14, 1930, pp. 292–297.

[31] Not printed.

National City Bank published this morning after signature of revised text which reads:

"I decide that there are no grounds for the charge of infraction and that the penalty imposed is void."

Full text follows by mail.

MORGAN

811.51632 National City Bank/48 : Telegram

The Ambassador in Brazil (Morgan) to the Secretary of State

RIO DE JANEIRO, July 24, 1930—noon.
[Received 1:25 p. m.]

45. Embassy's telegram 44, July 24, 9 a. m. Following the quotation from the Ministerial order already telegraphed, the text of the said order states:

"Furthermore,
Considering that there is evidence of infringement of the stamp tax by reason of insufficient stamps affixed to exchange contracts,
Considering that there has been an irregularity of functional procedure on the part of the broker of public funds, Geiling, of the São Paulo market which has not been duly investigated,
I determine that the fiscal penalties provided for the said infringement shall be imposed upon the bank and that the aforesaid irregularity shall be investigated by the inspector of banks and the result of such investigation duly communicated to the Government of the State of São Paulo for due consideration."

MORGAN

811.51632 National City Bank/49 : Telegram

The National City Bank of New York to the Secretary of State

NEW YORK, July 25, 1930.
[Received July 25—6:06 p. m.]

We greatly appreciate the interest which you and the other members of your Department have taken in the matter of the Brazilian fine and thank you for the friendly cooperation which you have given us.

CHARLES E. MITCHELL, *Chairman*
GORDON S. RENTSCHLER, *President*

ARRANGEMENT BETWEEN THE UNITED STATES AND BRAZIL GRANTING RELIEF FROM DOUBLE INCOME TAX ON SHIPPING PROFITS

811.512332 Shipping/20

The American Ambassador in Brazil (Morgan) to the Brazilian Minister for Foreign Affairs (Mangabeira)[33]

No. 1419   RIO DE JANEIRO, March 5, 1929.

MR. MINISTER: The representative of the United States Shipping Board has called my attention to Article 6 of Executive Decree No. 5,623, of December 29, 1928, by which His Excellency the President of the Republic sanctioned a law of Congress which "Reduces the duties on rolling and traction material for railroad and city transportation; alters the tax on paper for wrapping fruits; exempts from duties the importation of gold in bars and coined; regulates the payment by 'exercicio findo' and adopts other measures."

Article 6 of said Law states:

"Foreign navigation companies are hereby exempted from income tax, provided that the country in which their head office is located, grants exemption to Brazilian companies of the same character."

According to the dispositions of Section 213 (*b*) (8) of the Revenue Laws of the United States of 1924 and 1926 which were also included in the Revenue Law of the United States of 1928 in Section 212 (*b*) and 231 (*b*):[34]

"(8) The income of a foreigner non-resident or of a foreign corporation which consists exclusively of profit derived from a ship or ships operating under the laws of a foreign country which grants equal exemption to citizens of the United States and to corporations organized in the United States. . . . "

It would appear that the above mentioned Revenue Laws of the United States contain a provision which would meet the terms of Article 6, of Executive Decree No. 5,623 of December 29, 1928, and that therefore I am justified in requesting Your Excellency's Government to exempt the United States Shipping Board from payment of the Brazilian income tax.[35]

---

[33] This note and the other notes in this section exchanged between the American Embassy and the Brazilian Foreign Office were forwarded to the Department in despatch No. 3505, January 14, 1931; received February 2.

[34] 45 Stat. 791, 847, 849.

[35] By a note No. 1412, dated January 19, 1929, the American Ambassador requested the Brazilian Government to exempt the Munson Steamship Line and the McCormick Steamship Company from taxation.

The shipping lines operated by the United States Shipping Board to Brazil are the following:

American Brazil Line;
American Republic Line;
Gulf-Brazil-River Plate Line;

the companies which operate the same are respectively:

Colombian Steamship Company,
    17 Battery Place, New York.
C. H. Sprague & Son, Inc.,
    33 Broad Street, Boston.
Mississippi Shipping Company, Inc.,
    1310 Hibernia Bank Building, New Orleans.

Accept [etc.]   EDWIN MORGAN

811.512332 Shipping/20

The Brazilian Minister for Foreign Affairs (Mangabeira) to the American Ambassador in Brazil (Morgan)

[Translation]

NC/56   RIO DE JANEIRO, May 31, 1929.

MR. AMBASSADOR: In continuation of my Note NC/29 of last April,[36] regarding the request of this Embassy for an exemption of income tax for American navigation companies, I have the honor to send Your Excellency herewith a copy of the reply from the Ministry of Finance giving an answer to the said request.

Furthermore, I beg to inform Your Excellency that, upon this date, I have again sent to the said Ministry the provisions of the law mentioned in Note No. 1,419 of March 5th last, which, in your country assures reciprocity to foreign navigation companies of the exemption from the tax referred to.

I renew [etc.]   OCTAVIO MANGABEIRA

[Enclosure—Translation]

The Brazilian Minister of Finance (Oliveira Botelho) to the Brazilian Minister for Foreign Affairs (Mangabeira)

No. 33   [RIO DE JANEIRO] May 29, 1929.

MR. MINISTER: Accompanying notes Nos. NC/94 to 97 and 112 of April last and NC/123 of this month Your Excellency transmitted me requests from the Embassies of Italy, North America, Japan and France, and from the Legations of Germany, Norway and Denmark for exemption from income tax, in accordance with Art. 6 of decree No. 5,623, of December 29, 1928, for the navigation companies of those countries engaged in traffic with Brazil.

[36] Not printed.

In reply I have the honor to state to Your Excellency that in view of the provisions of the above cited law in order that navigation companies domiciled in foreign countries may be exempted from the taxation referred to it will be sufficient that Your Excellency's Ministry shall state to the Ministry of Finance that such a law exists in the interested State granting similar favors to Brazilian navigation companies. It will not be necessary to negotiate any agreement such as that proposed by the Danish Legation.

I have to inform Your Excellency that the Income Tax Office has suspended the collection of said tax from the navigation companies domiciled in foreign countries pending information of the non-existence of the conditions mentioned in our law in relation to any country.

I beg [etc.] F. C. DE OLIVEIRA BOTELHO

811.512332 Shipping/20

The American Chargé in Brazil (Schoenfeld) to the Brazilian Minister for Foreign Affairs (Mangabeira)

No. 1467 RIO DE JANEIRO, September 17, 1929.

MR. MINISTER: Referring to Your Excellency's note No. NC/56 under date of May 31 of the current year, regarding exemption from income tax for foreign navigation companies, I have the honor to inform Your Excellency that I have just received the following request for information from the Department of State at Washington regarding the following points:

a) Whether the exemption provided in Decree No. 5623 applies to corporations organized in the United States which maintain a principal office or place of business, agency or branch office in Brazil;

b) Whether under the Brazilian income tax law citizens of the United States are taxable or exempt with respect to the income derived by them from the operation of a ship or ships documented under the laws of the United States;

c) Whether, if exempt, such exemption applies if the citizens of the United States maintain a principal office or place of business, agency or branch office in Brazil, and

d) Whether it can be said that since December 29, 1928, the Brazilian Government has collected any income, war-profits or excess profits taxes from the income of a citizen of the United States or a corporation organized in the United States which consists exclusively of earnings derived from the operation of a ship or ships documented under the laws of the United States.

I shall be grateful to Your Excellency for the above information.

Accept [etc.] RUDOLF SCHOENFELD

811.512332 Shipping/20

The Brazilian Minister for Foreign Affairs (Mangabeira) to the
American Ambassador in Brazil (Morgan)

[Translation]

NC/15   RIO DE JANEIRO, March 11, 1930.

MR. AMBASSADOR: In continuation of the subject of my note No.
NC/99, of September 28 last,[37] and in accordance with information
received from the Ministry of Finance, I have the honor to hand
Your Excellency the following explanations:

The exemption mentioned in Article 6 of Law No. 5,623, of December 29, 1928, shall be applied to all companies or associations established in North America, which conduct the industry of navigation
and have agencies or branch offices in Brazil or exercise activities here,
under conditions of reciprocity for Brazilian navigation companies.

Under the express terms of the law, this privilege is restricted to
these companies and therefore does not include the income of North
American citizens, derived from the operation of one or more ships,
registered under the laws of their country.[38]

Finally, I can inform Your Excellency that from December 29,
1928 onward, no taxes were collected on income derived by navigation
companies operated by North American citizens or companies established in that country.

I avail myself [etc.]   OCTAVIO MANGABEIRA

811.512332 Shipping/20

The American Ambassador in Brazil (Morgan) to the Brazilian
Minister for Foreign Affairs (Mangabeira)

No. 1526   RIO DE JANEIRO, August 21, 1930.

MR. MINISTER: I take pleasure in informing Your Excellency that
after a lengthy correspondence between this Embassy, the Department

---

[37] Not printed.
[38] By a despatch dated March 31, 1930, the American Ambassador at Rio de
Janeiro informed the Secretary of State that he had been advised by the Brazilian
Foreign Office that shareholders in foreign companies are required to pay the
Brazilian income tax on their shares, the amount of the tax being collected
before the interest thereon is paid them. This statement is construed by the
Treasury Department to mean that the Brazilian Government imposes a tax on
the shareholders of such corporations, but does not impose a tax on the income
or profits of such corporations derived from the operation of ships documented
under the laws of the United States. The Treasury Department understands
that such provision of the Brazilian law is merely a method of collecting income
tax at the source by means of requiring the tax to be paid by the corporations
before the distribution of dividends on the shares of stock, which is similar to the
provision contained in American law requiring income tax to be withheld at the
source before the payment of bond interest or other fixed or determinable income
of nonresident aliens as provided by section 144(*b*) of the Revenue Act of 1928.—
Letter of the Secretary of the Treasury, July 28, 1930, to the Secretary of State
(811.512332 Shipping/16, 17).

of State and the United States Treasury Department, regarding a reciprocal exemption from taxes by the Government of the United States on income derived from the operation of ships registered under Brazilian laws and in accordance with the provisions for reciprocal exemption contained in the United States Revenue Act of 1928, the income of Brazilian citizens arising exclusively from profit derived from the operation of ships registered under Brazilian laws will be exempt from taxation by the Government of the United States. This exemption became effective on January 1, 1929.

Accept [etc.]
EDWIN V. MORGAN

811.512332 Shipping/20

The Director of Commercial and Consular Affairs in the Brazilian Ministry of Foreign Affairs (Eulalio) to the American Ambassador in Brazil (Morgan)

[Translation]

NC/72
RIO DE JANEIRO, September 1, 1930.

MR. AMBASSADOR: Acknowledging the receipt of your Note No. 1526, of August 21 of the present year, I have the honor to thank Your Excellency for your courtesy in communicating to this Department the decision of the United States of America, regarding the exemption from income tax of Brazilian citizens who derive profit exclusively from the operation of ships registered in Brazil with which decision this Ministry has just acquainted the Ministry of Finance.

Accept [etc.]
JM. EULALIO

REPRESENTATIONS AGAINST BRAZILIAN POLICY OF REQUIRING BRAZILIANS OF DUAL NATIONALITY TO USE BRAZILIAN PASSPORTS ON LEAVING BRAZIL

832.012/17

The Consul General at Rio de Janeiro (Dawson) to the Acting Secretary of State

No. 462
RIO DE JANEIRO, April 1, 1930
[Received April 17.]

SIR: As of interest to the Department, I have the honor to copy below a notice published over the names of H. B. M. Consuls-General in Rio de Janeiro and São Paulo respectively, in the *Times of Brazil*, São Paulo, March 28, and the *Brazilian American*, Rio de Janeiro, March 29, concerning dual nationality of persons born in Brazil of British parents who claim British citizenship.

The notice is of more than passing interest, and will doubtless merit the Department's close attention as a precedent calculated to be invoked by the Brazilian government in respect to persons born in Brazil of American parents.

The notice reads:

"The Brazilian authorities are no longer prepared to affix their visa to the British passports of persons of dual Brazilian and British nationality, e. g. persons born in Brazil of British parents. In adopting this attitude the Brazilian authorities are entirely within their rights. British subjects who are also, according to Brazilian law, nationals of this country and who desire to travel abroad have no option but to take out Brazilian passports. They must enter and leave Brazil on Brazilian passport and are at liberty to enter and leave British territory on British passports. They are, for all practical purposes British subjects when on British territory and Brazilian citizens when on Brazilian territory. In all other countries of which they are not nationals they may choose on which of the two passports they desire to travel and invoke the aid and protection of British and Brazilian diplomatic and consular representatives at will.

Charles Goodwin,
H. M.'s Consul-General,
Rio de Janeiro.
Arthur Abbott,
H. M.'s Consul-General,
São Paulo."

I have [etc.] CLAUDE I. DAWSON

832.012/18

The Consul General at Rio de Janeiro (Dawson) to the Acting Secretary of State

No. 471 RIO DE JANEIRO, April 11, 1930.
[Received April 30.]

SIR: I have the honor to refer to despatch No. 462 of April 1, 1930, from this office, reporting the publication of a notice concerning dual nationality of persons born in Brazil of British parents, by H. B. M. Consuls-General in Rio de Janeiro and São Paulo; and calling attention to the possibility that the evident international agreement on which such notices were founded might be invoked in the case of persons born in Brazil of American parents.

The first case of this nature affecting American citizens in this district has just arisen and has been adjusted as follows:

On April 8, 1930, Mr. Charles M. Pratt an American citizen formerly registered in this office but now a permanent resident of New York on a temporary visit to Rio de Janeiro, called at the Central Police Bureau for the purpose of having the American passports of himself and family visaed for journey to the Argentine. The police, without question, visaed his passport and the passports of his wife and one daughter who was born in the United States. However, they refused to visa the Department passport of his daughter Martha, who was born in Rio de Janeiro in February 1909. Miss Pratt resided in the United States from 1911 to March, 1930 inclusive.

The Police informed Mr. Pratt that in accordance with Brazilian law his daughter was a Brazilian and would have to travel on a Brazilian passport. In order to avoid trouble, Mr. Pratt was disposed to comply with this decision but before doing so came to the Consulate General, on April 9, 1930, for advice. The Consul General advised Mr. Pratt to refrain from obtaining a Brazilian passport for his daughter and arranged for a call on the Chief of Police, with Mr. Pratt, for the purpose of adjusting this matter. The Chief of Police was not in, but the Secretario Geral, Dr. Cicero Machado, the official evidently responsible for this order, was interviewed. Dr. Machado was told that Miss Pratt was of age, the daughter of Americans, that her birth had been recorded at the American Consulate, and that she had resided in the United States practically all of her life. Dr. Machado stated that cases had come to the attention of the Police where individuals born in Brazil of foreign parents were travelling with two passports. (He referred to so-called Anglo-Brazilians). Dr. Machado was informed that under no circumstance would this office sanction such procedure and all cases of this nature coming to our attention would be reported. Mr. Machado then ordered that the visa for travel to the Argentine be placed on Miss Pratt's American passport without further impediment or delay.

I have [etc.]   CLAUDE I. DAWSON

832.012/18

The Secretary of State to the Consul at Bahia (Briggs) [39]

WASHINGTON, June 12, 1930.

SIR: The Department encloses copies of despatches 462 of April 1, 1930 and 471 of April 11, 1930, both from the American Consul General at Rio de Janeiro, on the subject of dual nationality. Possibly Brazilian born American citizens might be saved embarrassment if, in cases similar to that described in the despatch last mentioned, you follow a procedure similar to that which was followed by Mr. Dawson.

I am [etc.]   For the Secretary of State:
                                                    WILBUR J. CARR

---

[39] The same, *mutatis mutandis*, on the same date to the Consuls at Pará, Pernambuco, Porto Alegre, Santos, and São Paulo.

832.012/18

The Secretary of State to the Ambassador in Brazil (Morgan)

No. 1541   WASHINGTON, June 12, 1930.

SIR: The Department encloses for your information and possible comment copies of despatches 462 of April 1, 1930 and 471 of April 11, 1930,[39a] both from the American Consul General at Rio de Janeiro, on the subject of dual nationality. The Department is interested to learn the basis of the apparently new policy of requiring Brazilians of dual nationality to use Brazilian passports on leaving Brazil. It is desired that when taking up this matter with the Brazilian authorities you point out that it has never been the policy of this Government to require that a person having American nationality and also the nationality of another country be in possession of an American passport in order to depart from the United States and it is desired that in all cases where persons having both American and Brazilian nationality have indicated their preference to travel on American passports they be permitted to depart from Brazil upon such passports.

I am [etc.]   For the Secretary of State:
                                                                    WILBUR J. CARR

832.012/23

The Ambassador in Brazil (Morgan) to the Secretary of State

No. 3387   RIO DE JANEIRO, July 23, 1930.
                                                                    [Received August 5.]

SIR: Referring to the Department's instruction N° 1541, of June 12 last, concerning the subject of dual nationality in relation to United States citizens who are also considered to be Brazilian citizens, I have the honor to report that the basis of the policy requiring the use of Brazilian passports by the Brazilian-born children of foreigners and Brazilian-born citizens married to citizens of the United States previous to the recent alteration of our laws of citizenship, is based upon Art. 69, 1. of the Brazilian Constitution, which reads:

"Persons born in Brazil though of a foreign father, if the latter is not there resident in the service of his country, are Brazilian citizens."

It is only recently, however, that the Brazilian police has attempted to compel the persons above referred to to secure a police visa upon a Brazilian passport and not upon a United States passport before leaving this country for abroad.

The Brazilian Foreign Office has instructed the Brazilian Ambas-

---

[39a] *Ante,* pp. 479 and 480.

sador to confer with the Department regarding a recognition of the status of the children born in Brazil of American citizens, which children under the Brazilian Constitution are Brazilian citizens, and also of Brazilian citizens married to United States citizens before the recent change in our citizenship laws by which nationality was not altered through marriage to such citizens.

Pending the solution of this matter, I recommend that American Consuls in Brazil do not resort to the police authorities in order to obtain permission from the local police for a person born in Brazil but bearing an American passport to leave the country. It will be more satisfactory and expeditious if such persons apply to the Embassy where, through diplomatic channels, their cases can usually be arranged. The case of Miss Mary A. Bevam, which the Consul General in Rio de Janeiro brought to my attention on July 22, was settled as soon as I conferred with the Foreign Office thereon.

I have the honor to report also that I have called the attention of the Brazilian Government to the fact that it has never been the policy of the United States Government to require that a person having American nationality and also the nationality of another country be in possession of an American passport in order to depart from the United States and it is desired that in all cases where persons having both American and Brazilian nationality have indicated their preference to travel on American passports they be permitted to depart from Brazil upon such passports.

I have [etc.] EDWIN V. MORGAN

832.12/23

The Acting Secretary of State to the Ambassador in Brazil (*Morgan*)

No. 1562 WASHINGTON, August 30, 1930.

SIR: The Department has received your despatch No. 3387 dated July 23, 1930, concerning the cases of persons of both American and Brazilian nationalities who desire to have their American passports visaed to enable them to leave Brazil.

You are informed that the American consular officers in Brazil are being instructed to take up all such cases with the Embassy in the future instead of taking them up with the local police authorities.

Very truly yours. W. R. CASTLE, JR.

832.012/24

The Brazilian Ambassador (Gurgél do Amaral) to the Secretary of State [40]

No. 58   WASHINGTON, August 25, 1930.

EXCELLENCY: Several occasions have arisen in which the Federal Government of Brazil have had to examine and discuss the doubts of foreign Governments or of their diplomatic Missions accredited in the country—the Mission of the United States of America being included in the number—with regard to the viséing on passports of persons of double nationality.

The undersigned, Ambassador Extraordinary and Plenipotentiary of the United States of Brazil, has received instructions from his Government to bring to the knowledge of the United States Government the viewpoint held by the Brazilian Government concerning passports issued to persons of double nationality, whenever one of these is the Brazilian nationality.

The Federal Government of Brazil recognize, as a fact, the double nationality, inasmuch as it is within the rights of every Power to freely establish, in conformity with its Constitution and laws, the qualifications of the individuals whom it considers its own nationals. It is in virtue of this precept that persons of double nationality, whenever one of them is the Brazilian nationality, can only enter the Brazilian national territory or absent themselves from it when they are actual bearers of Brazilian passports, notwithstanding the fact that this requirement does not preclude them from having passports issued by other Powers that may also consider them as being their own nationals.

The Brazilian Government consider that these rules are the natural sequence of the necessity of not entitling any persons, duly qualified as Brazilian citizens, to claim protection, within the Brazilian national territory, of any laws or authorities other than the Brazilian laws and the Brazilian authorities.

The undersigned ventures to believe that in so far as the United States Government are concerned in this matter, the proper directions may be issued for the adjustment of the interests of bearers of American passports whenever they happen to be also citizens of the United States of Brazil.

The undersigned avails himself [etc.]   S. GURGÉL DO AMARAL

---

[40] This note was acknowledged on September 2, 1930. No further reply was made. A memorandum of the Solicitor's office, dated October 10, 1930, stated that in view of the outbreak of revolution in Brazil (see pp. 432 ff.) it was a most inopportune time to take this matter up again with the Brazilian Ambassador.

832.012/25

The Chargé in Brazil (Washington) to the Secretary of State

No. 3414   RIO DE JANEIRO, September 3, 1930.
                                        [Received September 17.]

SIR: I have the honor to refer to this Embassy's despatch No. 3387, of July 23, 1930, on the subject of dual nationality in relation to the United States citizens who are also considered by Brazilian law to be Brazilian citizens, and to transmit to the Department the following information for its use in any discussions which may be had with the Brazilian Ambassador in Washington.

This Embassy has had occasion to discuss with the Brazilian Foreign Office the status of several American citizens who are also Brazilian citizens, according to Brazilian law, and who prefer to leave Brazil carrying an American passport rather than a Brazilian one. In some of the first cases taken up officials of the Foreign Office intervened with the police and obtained police visas on the American passports, thereby permitting the departure of the bearers from Brazil. However, it was stated that such a course would be considered exceptional and it has been impossible to obtain action in the case of several minors. They have presumably been forced to leave Brazil carrying an American passport and a Brazilian one.

Respectfully yours,   S. WALTER WASHINGTON

BULGARIA

INSTRUCTIONS TO THE MINISTER IN BULGARIA TO REFRAIN FROM ASSOCIATING WITH HIS COLLEAGUES IN GIVING ADVICE TO THE BULGARIAN GOVERNMENT

770.00/173

The Secretary of State to the Minister in Bulgaria (Shoemaker)

No. 11   WASHINGTON, June 13, 1930.

SIR: The Department has received your despatches Nos. 17 and 21 of April 29 and May 3, 1930, respectively,[1] setting forth the views of Mr. Sydney Waterlow, the British Minister in Sofia, regarding Bulgaria's relations with neighboring Balkan States and the steps which in his opinion are necessary in order to bring about a diplomatic adjustment of Bulgaria's troubles and a solution of the problem of Balkan peace. The Department has noted Mr. Waterlow's proposal "to have all questions of dispute between Balkan countries referred to France, Italy, Great Britain and the United States for friendly settlement but that this can only be achieved by the Balkan countries having the fullest confidence in the disinterestedness of the motives of the more powerful nations." Mr. Waterlow has accordingly expressed the hope that you would be ready to be called upon at any time to use your friendly influence "to uphold the sincerity" of the intentions of himself and of his French and Italian colleagues in any representations that they may make to the Bulgarian Government.

In reply to your request for an expression of the Department's views as to the proper course to be followed in case you receive an invitation from your British colleague to participate in the "friendly advice" which he and his other colleagues may decide to give to the Bulgarian Government, the Department desires that you scrupulously refrain from associating yourself with your colleagues in making representations or giving advice of any kind to the Bulgarian Government regarding its domestic affairs or relations with European States unless you have been specifically authorized to do so by the Department.

---

[1] Neither printed.

By the foregoing the Department does not intend that you should refrain from giving free expression on any appropriate occasion to this country's profound interest in the development of a better understanding among nations and in the maintenance of world peace by all appropriate means. Bearing this in mind, you will of course keep the Department promptly and fully informed, if necessary by telegraph, of any situation affecting Bulgaria of sufficient gravity to warrant, in the opinion of your colleagues, representations on their part to the Bulgarian Government. The Department will in such cases instruct you as to the action, if any, which it desires you to take.

I am [etc.]   HENRY L. STIMSON

CANADA

PROPOSED CONVENTION BETWEEN THE UNITED STATES AND CANADA TO AMEND THE CONVENTION FOR THE SUPPRESSION OF SMUGGLING, SIGNED JUNE 6, 1924 [1]

811.114 Canada/4310

The Chargé in Canada (Riggs) to the Acting Secretary of State

No. 1343
OTTAWA, March 22, 1930.
[Received March 25.]

SIR: I have the honor to refer to the Legation's telegram No. 46 of March 22, 1 p. m.,[2] reporting the receipt this morning from the Prime Minister of a note suggesting on the part of Canada the conclusion of a treaty in amendment of the Convention of June 6, 1924, and for the purpose of providing "on a reciprocal basis for the denial of clearance of shipments of merchandise by water, air, or land from either country to the other when their importation is prohibited by the latter, and for such further reciprocal measures for the suppression of smuggling as may be found feasible." Copy of this note, which is No. 24 of March 22, 1930, is transmitted herewith. Two copies of Bill No. 15 entitled "An Act to amend the Export Act", were received as enclosures to the note and are likewise attached.[2]

I have [etc.]
B. REATH RIGGS

[Enclosure]

The Canadian Secretary of State for External Affairs (Mackenzie King) to the American Chargé (Riggs)

No. 24
OTTAWA, March 22, 1930.

SIR: I have the honour to refer to Mr. Phillips' note No. 349 of April 20, 1929,[2] with regard to measures under consideration for the further control of smuggling operations along the border between Canada and the United States, and particularly to Mr. Phillips' statement that the Government of the United States was convinced that the only effective means of dealing with the smuggling problem along the border would be the conclusion of a treaty amending the Con-

---

[1] For text of the convention, see *Foreign Relations*, 1924, vol. I, p. 189. For previous correspondence concerning the suppression of smuggling, see *ibid.*, 1929, vol. II, pp. 48 ff.

[2] Not printed.

vention of June 6, 1924, to the end that clearance be denied to shipments of commodities from either country when their importation is prohibited in the other.

The Canadian Government has been giving further consideration to the question in the light of experience in Canada as well as of developments in border enforcement by the authorities of the United States, and has reached the conclusion that further action is desirable as regards both the special problem of the smuggling of intoxicating liquors and the general problem of commercial smuggling.

As to the export of intoxicating liquors from Canada, which involves the use of governmental agencies in the release of liquors from bond as well as in the issue of clearances, it has been considered advisable that action should be taken forthwith by Dominion legislation. A bill has accordingly been introduced into the House of Commons to amend the Export Act, the main purpose of the amendment being to require officials of the Dominion Government having charge of liquor in bond and the granting of clearances to vessels to refuse to release such liquor or to grant such clearances where the granting of such release or clearance in any case would facilitate the introduction of intoxicating liquor into a country where the importation of such liquor is forbidden by law. This measure has received second reading in the House of Commons and is now being considered in detail in committee. It will be observed from the copy of the bill which I enclose that it is general in its terms, applying to export to any country where the importation of intoxicating liquor is forbidden by law.

As to the general problem, it will be recalled that in discussing the holding of a conference to consider the various proposals put forward for further action to ensure the prevention of smuggling, the Canadian Government indicated, in February, 1927, its desire that the discussion should not be confined to the question of the smuggling of liquor but should cover all forms of commercial smuggling from each country into the other. The Canadian Government believes that the present would be an opportune time to conclude with the United States a treaty as suggested amending the Convention of June 6, 1924, to provide on a reciprocal basis for the denial of clearance of shipments of merchandise by water, air, or land from either country to the other when their importation is prohibited by the latter, and for such further reciprocal measures for the suppression of smuggling as may be found feasible.

The Canadian Government would therefore be prepared to take the necessary steps at an early date for the conclusion of such a convention.

Accept [etc.] W. L. MACKENZIE KING

711.429/259a : Telegram

The Acting Secretary of State to the Chargé in Canada (Riggs)

WASHINGTON, April 1, 1930—4 p. m.

40. Your despatch No. 1343, of March 22, last. Please address a note reading as follows to Canadian Government:

"I have the honor to refer to your note of March 22 last in which you state that the Canadian Government is of the opinion that the present would be an opportune time to conclude with the United States a treaty amending the Convention of June 6, 1924, to provide on a reciprocal basis for the denial of clearance of shipments of merchandise by water, air or land from either country to the other when its importation is prohibited in the country of destination and for such further reciprocal measures for the suppression of smuggling as may be feasible.

In response, it gives me pleasure to inform you, on instructions from my Government, that the United States is prepared to conclude such a treaty at an early date. My Government hopes to be able to submit a draft of such a treaty within a few days for your consideration."

Please deliver this note immediately and inform the Prime Minister that we have no objection to his making the note public.

COTTON

711.429/260 : Telegram

The Chargé in Canada (Riggs) to the Acting Secretary of State

OTTAWA, April 4, 1930—10 a. m.
[Received 1:55 p. m.]

52. Department's 40, April 1, 4 p. m. Acknowledgment received last night from Prime Minister, final paragraph of which reads as follows:

"I may state for the information of the Government of the United States that the Canadian Government has also the draft of such a treaty in preparation and will be prepared to arrange at an early date for discussion looking to the conclusion of an agreement."

Liquor export bill received second reading in the Senate last night after defeat of a proposal to shelve it until treaty is negotiated, but it is understood third reading will not take place until after Easter recess of Parliament ending April 24.

Under Secretary of State for External Affairs has now telephoned to offer following suggestion from the Prime Minister. He believes discussion of Canadian and American drafts of treaty would be slow and difficult by correspondence and suggests small informal conference of interested Canadian and American Government officials at Ottawa to compose as rapidly as possible any differences between the two drafts and permit signing of treaty at an early date.

Despatch forwarding copy of Canadian note leaves in pouch today.

RIGGS

711.429/263 : Telegram

The Chargé in Canada (Riggs) to the Acting Secretary of State

OTTAWA, April 10, 1930—4 p. m.
[Received 7 : 46 p. m.]

58. Legation's 57, April 9, 5 p. m.[5] Prime Minister who leaves tomorrow for Bermuda now believes conference impractical at present since Easter recess of Parliament begins tomorrow. Several Cabinet Ministers including Minister of National Revenue will be absent until April 28 when House of Commons reconvenes. He suggests meanwhile that drafts of treaty be exchanged as between Legation and Department of External Affairs with a view to determining more definitely whether differences are sufficient to necessitate proposed conference. Under Secretary of State for External Affairs hopes to have Canadian draft ready around April 16 and suggests that if American draft were available by that time we might examine the two drafts and exchange preliminary impressions before submitting them to the respective Governments for examination. Decision as to conference could then follow. He also desires to know whether it would be convenient to have signature of treaty take place at Ottawa since this would facilitate procedure for Canadian Government. If American Government consents he proposes to apply to London for full power for Prime Minister to sign treaty.

RIGGS

711.429/263a

The Acting Secretary of State to the Chargé in Canada (Riggs)

No. 819   WASHINGTON, April 16, 1930.

SIR: With reference to your despatch No. 1343 of March 22, 1930, and to subsequent correspondence in regard to a proposed treaty to supplement the Convention of June 6, 1924, for the purpose of providing on a reciprocal basis for the denial of clearances of shipments of merchandise when its importation is prohibited in the country of destination, there is enclosed for transmission to the Canadian Government the draft of a treaty in this sense. You will observe that the first two articles of this draft are with minor exceptions the same

---

[5] Not printed.

proposals that were made in Secretary Kellogg's note of October 1, 1925,[6] to the British Embassy in this capital. Article 3 dealing with transportation in bond across the State of Maine over the Canadian Pacific Railway of liquor consigned to the Liquor Control Boards of the several provinces of Canada, is based on a request in that sense made by the Canadian representatives at the informal conference on smuggling which took place in Ottawa in January 1929.

Full powers to sign this Convention will be forwarded to you at a later date.

I am [etc.]   [File copy not signed]

[Enclosure]

Draft of Convention

The United States of America and His Majesty the King of Great Britain, Ireland and the British Dominions beyond the Seas, Emperor of India, being desirous of adopting more effective measures for the suppression of smuggling between the territories of the United States of America and of the Dominion of Canada than are provided under the Convention concluded between the United States of America and His Majesty at Washington on June 6, 1924, and of making certain provisions concerning alcoholic liquors, have resolved to conclude an Additional Convention for those purposes, and to that end have named as their plenipotentiaries:

The President of the United States of America:

. . . . and

His Britannic Majesty, for the Dominion of Canada:

. . . .

Who, having communicated to each other their respective full powers, which were found to be in due and proper form, have agreed upon the following articles:

Article I

The High Contracting Parties agree that clearance of shipments of merchandise by water, air or land from the territory of either of the High Contracting Parties to the territory of the other High Contracting Party shall be denied if such shipment comprises articles the introduction of which is prohibited or restricted in the country to which such shipment is destined, provided, however, that such clearance shall not be denied on shipments of restricted merchandise when there has been complete compliance with the requirements of the laws of both countries.

---

[6] Not printed.

ARTICLE II

No penalty or forfeiture under the laws of the United States of America shall be applicable or attach to alcoholic liquors or to vessels, vehicles or persons by reason of the carriage of such liquors when they are in transit from one place in Canada to another place in that country under such guard as the Secretary of the Treasury of the United States of America may require through the territorial waters of the United States of America pertaining to Alaska and through the Stickine River by the shortest route to Canadian territory, and such transit shall be as now provided by law with respect to the transit of alcoholic liquors through the Panama Canal or on the Panama Railroad, provided that such liquors shall be kept under seal continuously while the vessel or vehicle on which they are carried remains within the United States of America, its territories or possessions, and that no part of such liquors shall at any time or place be unladen within the United States of America, its territories or possessions.

ARTICLE III

No penalty or forfeiture under the laws of the United States of America shall be applicable or attach to alcoholic liquors or to vehicles or persons by reason of the carriage of such liquors when they are in transit, under such guard as the Secretary of the Treasury of the United States of America may require, through the State of Maine between Montreal, Quebec, and St. John, New Brunswick, via the Canadian Pacific Railway, under Canadian and United States customs seals; such liquor to be destined only for the Liquor Control Boards of the several provinces of Canada. Such transit shall be as now provided by law with respect to the transit of alcoholic liquors through the Panama Canal or on the Panama Railroad, provided that such liquors shall be kept under seal continuously while the vehicle on which they are carried remains within the United States of America, and that no part of such liquors shall at any time or place be unladen within the United States of America. The said exemption from penalties or forfeiture under the laws of the United States of America provided in this article shall be enjoyed on condition that the Canadian Pacific Railway Company shall pay all the necessary expenses incident to the guarding of the shipments in transit.

ARTICLE IV

This convention shall be ratified, and the ratifications shall be exchanged at Ottawa as soon as possible. The convention shall come into force at the expiration of ten days from the date of the exchange of ratifications, and it shall remain in force for one year. If upon the expiration of one year after the convention shall have come into force no notice is given by either High Contracting Party of a desire to terminate it, it shall continue in force until thirty days after either Party shall have given such notice to the other Party.

IN WITNESS WHEREOF, the respective Plenipotentiaries have signed the present convention in duplicate and have thereunto affixed their seals.

DONE at the city of Ottawa this . . . . . day of . . . . . one thousand nine hundred and thirty.

711.429/265

The Chargé in Canada (Riggs) to the Secretary of State

No. 1428   OTTAWA, May 22, 1930.
                                                           [Received May 24.]

SIR: With reference to my despatch No. 1388 of April 29, 1930,[7] covering the remarks made by the Under-Secretary of State for External Affairs regarding the draft of a proposed convention to supplement the Anti-Smuggling Convention between Canada and the United States of June 6, 1924, I have the honor to transmit herewith an outline of the counter proposals advanced on behalf of Canada in the course of a two hour discussion which took place between Dr. Skelton, Mr. Beaudry and myself yesterday afternoon at the Department of External Affairs. References by line and page will be made in this despatch to the draft transmitted with the Department's instruction No. 819 of April 16, 1930, (file No. 711.429/263a). Line numeration will begin with No. 1 for the first line of each section of the Convention, namely, the Preamble and each of the various Articles, so that each one will have its own line numeration.

Preamble

In line 2 of the Preamble, in the expression "the British dominions beyond the Seas" the Canadian Government desires to write the word "dominions" with a small "d". The reason given is that in the King's title the word "dominions" refers to the whole of the King's domain and was in use before Canada came into existence. It is therefore desired to draw by this means a distinction between the King's dominions and the various Dominions which are members of the British Commonwealth of Nations.

Likewise, after the expression "Emperor of India" in line 3, it is desired to insert "in respect of the Dominion of Canada" in order to conform with present Canadian treaty practice.

---

[7] Not printed.

After the expression "desirous of" in line 3 the Canadian Government desires to change the language of the Preamble to the following: "supplementing the provisions of the Convention of June 6, 1924, between Canada and the United States of America, for the suppression of smuggling operations along the border," to replace the language in the American draft from the point indicated above down to and including the date "June 6, 1924" in line 8 of the Preamble. The Canadians do not like the expression "more effective . . . than" occurring in the American Preamble, since they feel that it makes an invidious comparison between the proposed Convention and that of 1924, by suggesting that the latter was ineffective. Although it was not actually stated, I believe that the substitution of the expression "along the border" instead of "between the territories" is preferred by the Canadians to avoid any suggestion that the Convention could be construed to cover indirect smuggling via a base on the territory of a third party.

In line 9 it is desired to insert after the word "concerning" the expression "the transportation of", since the Canadians desire to emphasize that that is the particular phase of the question covered by the Convention. They also prefer the word "additional" instead of the word "supplementary" in line 10.

Article I

In line 3 the Canadians point out that the expression "High Contracting Parties" in so far as it refers to the Canadian side, refers to the King. They therefore prefer to refer to "the ports of the Dominion of Canada or of the United States of America" and to eliminate the word "territory" in this Article. They state that "territory" as used in the American draft must inevitably refer to the King's territory and that unfriendly critics and legalistic opponents might raise the contention that by using such phraseology the Dominion was unconsciously passing legislation which could be construed as affecting portions of the King's territory other than the Dominion of Canada. They also desire this change since they claim it to be a reversion to the original American draft presented to them in 1925.

After the expression "denied if" in line 5, the Canadians desire to change the rest of Article I as shown in their enclosed draft. I gather that they do not wish to undertake the responsibility of having to guarantee the absence of prohibited articles in an apparently regular and bona fide shipment of merchandise. This is in line with the replies made in Parliament in the course of the discussion of the Liquor Export Bill and the proposed Convention. They therefore prefer the expression "shipment of merchandise" instead of "shipment comprises articles the introduction of which is prohibited."

They also desire the elimination of the word "restricted". Dr. Skelton stated that his understanding was that the word "restricted" had been inserted to cover goods such as narcotics and sacramental wines which are normally articles of prohibited importation, but which may, under certain conditions and for certain purposes, be imported under special Government permit. The Canadian authorities fear that the word "restricted" could be construed to cover articles which are subject to tariff restrictions, such as countervailing duties, et cetera, and they prefer that there should be no ambiguity. Consequently, in the Canadian counter draft, lines 8, 9 and 10 also disappear.

It will be observed that they also desire to include in the Convention under Article I mention of lists of articles of prohibited importation in both countries, to be changed from time to time by communication between the two Governments. They have also inserted in this Article a paragraph incorporating in the Convention a provision covering the prohibited admission of articles included under Item 1201 of the Canadian Customs Tariff, namely, "books, printed paper, drawings, paintings, prints, photographs or representations of any kind of a treasonable or seditious, or of an immoral or indecent character". This is an effort to meet the difficulty explained by Dr. Skelton as related in my despatch No. 1388 above mentioned.

Article II

In line 2 it is desired to restore the word "attached" instead of "attach" in order to conform with the language of Article VII of the Convention of 1924. Likewise and for the same reason it is desired to eliminate "from one place in Canada to another place in that country" in line 5 and to substitute "under guard by Canadian authorities" instead of "under such guard as the Secretary of the Treasury of the United States of America may require" in lines 6 and 7. There is also a slight change in the language of lines 9 and 10, which does not, however, apparently affect the sense and is considered better phraseology by the Canadian side. They also contend that the "c" should be eliminated from the spelling of the name "Stikine" in line 9.

Article III

In line 2 it is desired to substitute the word "attached" instead of "attach" as explained above under Article II. In lines 4 and 5, the Canadians desire the substitution of "under guard by Canadian authorities" instead of "under such guard as the Secretary of the Treasury of the United States of America may require", for the reasons explained above in Article II.

In lines 6 and 7, it is desired to eliminate "between Montreal, Quebec, and St. John, New Brunswick", and to substitute therefor "from Canadian territory to Canadian territory" since Dr. Skelton stated that Montreal is not the only possible point of destination and that shipments might also be made to such points, for instance, as Sherbrooke or the city of Quebec. He also desires to eliminate in lines 9 and 10 the phrase "such liquor to be destined only for the Liquor Control Boards of the several Provinces of Canada". He pointed out that this is an internal Canadian matter and that difficulties might arise in connection with the Convention if, for instance, one or more of the Provinces were to abolish Government control. He also pointed out that the expression "Liquor Control Board" does not apply in every Province, since in Quebec, for instance, these authorities are officially termed "Liquor Commissions."

Dr. Skelton also asked me whether there is any reason for the discrepancy between the expression "under seal" in lines 13 and 14 of Article II and "under Canadian and United States customs seals" in lines 8 and 9 of Article III. His rough draft had eliminated this expression entirely. I pointed out that there might well be some good administrative reason for this provision in Article III due to a possible difference in the activities of smugglers and "hijackers" in the State of Maine. He told me that he would be willing to allow it to stand in the Convention if it were considered essential but he requested that I ask for an explanation of the discrepancy between the reference to seals in Articles II and III.

The Canadians desire to eliminate the whole of the last sentence of Article III comprising lines 18, 19, 20, 21 and 22. Dr. Skelton says that the matter of payment by the Canadian Pacific Railway is understood as a matter of course and that the Government does not see the necessity for mention of it in the Convention.

Article IV

In lines 9 and 10, after the word "given" the Canadians desire to substitute the words "notice to the other of a desire to terminate the Convention" instead of "such notice to the other party." This change is preferred in order to revert to the phraseology of Article VIII of the Convention of 1924, and is in conformity with the disposition manifested by Dr. Skelton and Mr. Beaudry throughout the discussion of yesterday afternoon.

I desire to apologize to the Department for not preparing a draft text with suitable lining and underlining, showing at a glance the alterations proposed in the Canadian counterdraft; the necessity to get this draft off at the earliest mail has rendered the preparation of such a text impossible.

I am also advised by Dr. Skelton that the Prime Minister has received from London the full power necessary for the signature of this Convention and is disposed to sign it as soon as agreement can be reached as to the text.

I have [etc.] B. REATH RIGGS

[Enclosure]

Canadian Counterdraft of Convention

His Majesty the King of Great Britain, Ireland and the British dominions beyond the Seas, Emperor of India, in respect of the Dominion of Canada, and the United States of America, being desirous of supplementing the provisions of the Convention of June 6, 1924, between Canada and the United States of America, for the suppression of smuggling operations along the border, and of making certain provisions concerning the transportation of alcoholic liquors, have resolved to conclude an Additional Convention for those purposes, and to that end have named as their plenipotentiaries:

His Majesty, for the Dominion of Canada:

.... and

The President of the United States of America:

....

Who, having communicated to each other their respective full powers, which were found to be in due and proper form, have agreed upon the following articles:

ARTICLE I

The High Contracting Parties agree that clearance of shipments of merchandise by water, air or land from any of the ports of the Dominion of Canada or of the United States of America to a port entrance of the other country shall be denied if the importation of such shipment of merchandise is prohibited in the country to which such shipment is destined.

The lists of articles the importation of which is prohibited in the Dominion of Canada and the United States of America respectively, are set forth in the two Schedules attached to this Convention.

The Government of either country may, from time to time, communicate to the other any changes made in its list and such changes, thus communicated, shall be considered to form part of the Schedules attached to this Convention.

In regard to any articles prohibited on the ground of immorality or indecency, or of treasonable or seditious character, it is agreed that the Governments of the Dominion of Canada and of the United States of America shall accept the decision of the appropriate authorities of the Government of the country of importation as to whether shipments of this nature from the other country are to be considered of an immoral, indecent, treasonable or seditious character.

ARTICLE II

No penalty or forfeiture under the laws of the United States of America shall be applicable or attached to alcoholic liquors or to vessels, vehicles or persons by reason of the carriage of such liquors when they are in transit under guard by Canadian authorities through the territorial waters of the United States of America pertaining to Alaska, and thence by the shortest route via the River Stikine to Canadian territory, and such transit shall be as now provided by law with respect to the transit of alcoholic liquors through the Panama Canal or on the Panama Railroad, provided that such liquors shall be kept under seal continuously while the vessel or vehicle on which they are carried remains within the United States of America, its territories or possessions, and that no part of such liquors shall at any time or place be unladen within the United States of America, its territories or possessions.

ARTICLE III

No penalty or forfeiture under the laws of the United States of America shall be applicable or attached to alcoholic liquors or to vehicles or persons by reason of the carriage of such liquors when they are in transit under guard by Canadian authorities through the State of Maine by the Canadian Pacific Railway from Canadian territory to Canadian territory, under Canadian and United States customs seals, and such transit shall be as now provided by law with respect to the transit of alcoholic liquors through the Panama Canal or on the Panama Railroad, provided that such liquors shall be kept under seal continuously while the vehicle on which they are carried remains within the United States of America, and that no part of such liquors shall at any time or place be unladen within the United States of America.

ARTICLE IV

This Convention shall be ratified, and the ratifications shall be exchanged at Ottawa as soon as possible. The Convention shall come into force at the expiration of ten days from the date of the exchange of ratifications, and it shall remain in force for one year. If upon the expiration of one year after the Convention shall have come into force no notice is given by either High Contracting Party of a desire to terminate it, it shall continue in force until thirty days after either Party shall have given notice to the other of a desire to terminate the Convention.

In witness whereof, the respective Plenipotentiaries have signed the present Convention in duplicate and have thereunto affixed their seals.

Done at the City of Ottawa, this . . . . . day of . . . . . one thousand nine hundred and thirty.

811.114 Canada/4337

The Chargé in Canada (Riggs) to the Secretary of State

No. 1443   OTTAWA, June 4, 1930.
                                            [Received June 9.]

SIR: In continuation of my despatch No. 1430 of May 23, 1930,[8] and as a conclusion to that and to the series of previous despatches regarding the debate in the Canadian Parliament on Bill No. 15, entitled "An Act to Amend the Export Act", I have the honor to report that this Bill received the Royal assent, and consequently became law, at the final session of Parliament on May 30, 1930.

I have [etc.]   B. REATH RIGGS

711.429/265

The Secretary of State to the Minister in Canada (MacNider)

No. 19   WASHINGTON, September 17, 1930.

SIR: With reference to the Legation's despatch No. 1428 of May 22, 1930, transmitting the Canadian counter-proposals with respect to the proposed convention to supplement the anti-smuggling convention between the United States and Canada of June 6, 1924, the Department informs you that the Canadian counter-proposals have been given thorough consideration in collaboration with the Treasury Department and the Department of Justice. The following comment is arranged in accordance with the system employed in the Legation's despatch:

Preamble

This Government accepts the Canadian draft as far as the phrase "along the border" in lines 7 and 8. Since there may be smuggling elsewhere than along the border, as, for example, by air shipments destined for points in the interior, this phrase should be eliminated, unless, for some reason not known to the Department, Canada strongly desires it. In the latter case, this Government may reconsider its position. The remainder of the preamble of the Canadian draft is acceptable to the Department.

Article I

It is desired that lines 1 to 5 of this article be worded as follows:

The High Contracting Parties agree that clearance of shipments of merchandise by water, air or land *from any of the ports of the Dominion of Canada or of the United States of America to any port or place in the other shall* be denied, etc.

It is deemed advisable that clearance should be denied to any prohibited article whether destined to a place that is technically a port

---

[8] Not printed.

or to any other place in the United States or the Dominion of Canada, respectively. It is recognized, however, that the point is not likely to be of practical significance and, if the Canadian Government indicates a strong preference for the language used in the draft which it submitted, you are authorized to agree thereto.

After careful consideration, the Department believes that it will be impracticable to attach to the convention schedules setting forth lists of the articles the importation of which is prohibited. Such lists, it would seem, should be communicated between the Governments at the time of the exchange of ratifications and thereafter changes may be communicated as in third paragraph of Article I of the Canadian draft. Accordingly, it is desired that the second and third paragraphs of Article I of the Canadian draft be omitted and the following language inserted in their place:

Lists of articles the importation of which is prohibited in the Dominion of Canada and the United States of America, respectively, shall be exchanged between the two Governments immediately after the exchange of ratifications.

The Government of either country may, from time to time, communicate to the other any changes made in its list.

All of the other counter-proposals relating to Article I are acceptable to this Government.

Article II

This Government is prepared to accept all Canadian counter-proposals in regard to Article II. The Department is informed that there is no requirement for a United States customs seal in the Panama Canal Zone because that territory is solely under the jurisdiction of the War Department and the customs authorities exercise no jurisdiction there. The customs authorities are understood not to be in a position actually to maintain agents to protect American customs seals on shipments in transit via the River Stikine.

Article III

With reference to line 5 of the Canadian counter-draft in which the phrase "under guard by Canadian authorities" has been substituted for "under such guard as the Secretary of the Treasury of the United States may require", you are informed that, while there is little likelihood that this Government will care to have American guards on Canadian trains in transit through Maine, it desires to provide for the exercise of such right at its option. The United States customs seals may be tampered with or forged, or other circumstances may arise which would make it desirable to have American as well as Canadian guards on these trains. In view of the statement referred to on page 7 of the Legation's despatch No. 1428, it is assumed that the Canadian Pacific Railway would furnish free transportation for

United States customs guards on its trains, in the event this Government should desire to employ them.

You are, accordingly, requested to propose the insertion of the words "and/or authorities of the United States of America" after the phrase "under guard by Canadian authorities" in line 5, and to say that all other changes in Article III are acceptable to this Government. If it should prove to be impracticable to obtain the foregoing amendment to the Canadian draft without materially delaying the conclusion of the convention, you are authorized to withdraw the proposal.
Article IV

All changes are acceptable.

Full powers to sign the treaty on behalf of the United States will be transmitted in an early pouch.

Very truly yours,   For the Secretary of State:
                                                     J. P. COTTON

711.429/278

The Minister in Canada (MacNider) to the Secretary of State

No. 61   OTTAWA, October 6, 1930.
                                             [Received October 13.]

SIR: I have the honor to acknowledge the receipt of the Department's instruction No. 19 of September 17, 1930, (File No. 711.429/265), transmitting to the Legation for presentation to the Canadian Government further proposals and suggestions based on consideration of the Canadian counter-proposals of May 22, 1930,[9] in connection with the proposed convention to supplement the anti-smuggling convention between the United States and Canada of June 6, 1924. The American reply to the Canadian counter-proposals, embodied in the shape of a note, was presented to the Canadian Department of External Affairs on the first instant.

When discussing the matter informally, Dr. Skelton the Under-Secretary of State for External Affairs who is now absent on leave, stated that it would not be possible to reply to this note until Mr. Bennett [9a] shall have returned from the Imperial Conference in London and given the suggested changes his consideration. He said that, moreover, account must be taken of the possibility that the present Government may not see eye to eye with the late Liberal government

---

[9] See despatch No. 1428, May 22, from the Chargé in Canada, p. 494.
[9a] R. B. Bennett, Canadian Prime Minister and Secretary of State for External Affairs.

in the matter of such parts of the draft as have already been approved in negotiation; he did not, however, mean that he actually knew of such a difference in views since, apparently, the new Government has had no opportunity to examine into the matter. No oral discussion was attempted as regards the changes proposed in the Department's instruction under acknowledgment, since Dr. Skelton stated that these changes would have to be studied by other interested Government departments before the stage of oral discussion or reply could be reached.

The Department's instructions with regard to the possible withdrawal of the suggestions for changes in lines 1 to 5 of Article I and line 5 of Article III, have been noted, and should stubborn opposition be encountered, the suggestions will be withdrawn. Needless to say, no mention of this possibility has been made in the note to the Canadian Government, but in response to a suggestion from the Legation, the Department of External Affairs has agreed to have an oral discussion before transmitting the final reply, should any of the desired changes prove definitely inacceptable.

Respectfully yours,

For the Minister:
B. REATH RIGGS

711.429/279

The Minister in Canada (MacNider) to the Secretary of State

No. 86

OTTAWA, October 25, 1930.
[Received November 6.]

SIR: With reference to the Legation's despatch No. 61 of October 6, 1930, in connection with the proposed convention to supplement the Anti-Smuggling Convention of June 6, 1924, between the United States and Canada, I have the honor to transmit herewith a copy of a note received today from Sir George Perley, Acting Secretary of State for External Affairs.[10] Sir George states that the remarks and suggestions which I made on behalf of the United States, in accordance with the Department's instruction No. 19 of September 17, 1930, are receiving careful consideration and that an early opportunity will be taken to advise me of the views of the Canadian Government.

Respectfully yours,

HANFORD MACNIDER

---

[10] Not printed.

CONVENTION BETWEEN THE UNITED STATES AND CANADA FOR THE PROTECTION OF THE FRASER RIVER SOCKEYE SALMON FISHERIES, SIGNED MAY 26, 1930 [11]

711.428/1396

The Secretary of State to President Hoover

THE PRESIDENT: The undersigned, the Secretary of State, has the honor to lay before the President, with a view to its transmission to the Senate to receive the advice and consent of that body to its ratification, if his judgment approve thereof, a convention between the United States of America and His Majesty the King of Great Britain, Ireland and the British dominions beyond the seas, Emperor of India, in respect of the Dominion of Canada, for the protection, preservation and extension of the sockeye salmon fisheries of the Fraser River system, signed by the Secretary of State and the Minister of Canada, at Washington on May 26, 1930.

This convention is in substitution of the convention for the protection, preservation and extension of the sockeye salmon fisheries of the Fraser River system, signed by the Secretary of State and the Minister of Canada on March 27, 1929,[12] which was sent to the Senate by the President on April 18, 1929, and was returned by the Senate to the President by Resolution of December 13, 1929.

The necessity for the revision of the 1929 convention was seen in the fact that during the summer of 1929, subsequent to its signature, fishermen, for the first time, took large quantities of sockeye salmon in the Pacific Ocean beyond territorial waters of the United States and Canada. It became apparent from the success of that fishery that the sockeye salmon fisheries in the Fraser River, Georgia Strait, Juan de Fuca Strait and contiguous waters cannot be adequately protected and developed unless the fishery on the high seas is controlled. There are included, therefore, in the waters covered by the new convention, the territorial waters off the western coasts of the United States and Canada between the 48th and 49th parallels of north latitude, and likewise the high seas of the Pacific Ocean adjacent to these territorial waters between the same parallels, in addition to the Fraser River and the boundary waters between the United States and Canada which were embraced in the convention signed in 1929.

The authority which the convention gives to the International Pacific Salmon Fisheries Commission to limit or prohibit fishing on the high seas and to prescribe the size of the mesh of gear that may be used on the high seas is, of course, applicable to nationals and inhabitants

[11] For previous correspondence concerning the protection of the Fraser River sockeye salmon fisheries, see *Foreign Relations*, 1929, vol. II, pp. 55 ff.
[12] *Foreign Relations*, 1929, vol. II, p. 55.

and vessels and boats of the United States and of Canada only, as are the provisions of the convention in regard to the arrest and detention of violators of the prohibition against fishing on the high seas covered by Article IX of the convention.

Other points of difference between the convention signed on March 27, 1929, and the present convention are that there is omitted from the latter the provision that the Commissioner of Fisheries of the United States shall be one of the members of the Commission; that it is specifically provided by the new convention that the commissioners appointed by each of the High Contracting Parties shall hold office during the pleasure of the Contracting Party by which they were appointed; and that instead of the limitation by dates of the period of the year within which the International Pacific Salmon Fisheries Commission might limit or prohibit fishing, which was provided in Article IV of the convention signed on March 27, 1929, the new convention contains a provision under which the Commission is at liberty to limit or prohibit the fishing in the waters of the United States, Canada and the high seas, respectively, for such periods as may be required by the particular conditions of each year. The greater flexibility in regulation thus provided, as well as the extension of authority of the Commission to regulate fishing for sockeye salmon by American and Canadian fishermen and fishing vessels on the high seas, will enable the Commission to so regulate the fisheries that there will be, as nearly as possible, an equal division of the catch between the fishermen of the United States and Canada.

By Article V of the convention now submitted the Commission is given authority to regulate the size of meshes in salmon fishing gear used on the high seas by American and Canadian fishermen and fishing vessels at any season of the year, in addition to the authority given to the Commission in the Convention of 1929 to regulate the size of meshes in fishing gear used in national waters of the two countries during the spring or Chinook salmon fishing season.

Respectfully submitted, H. L. STIMSON

WASHINGTON, May 29, 1930.

Treaty Series No. 918

Convention Between the United States of America and Canada, Signed at Washington, May 26, 1930 [13]

The President of the United States of America and His Majesty the King of Great Britain, Ireland and the British dominions beyond

[13] Ratification advised by the Senate, subject to understandings, June 16, 1936; ratified by the President, subject to the said understandings, July 23, 1937; ratified by Canada, June 26, 1937; ratifications exchanged at Washington, July 28, 1937; proclaimed by the President, August 4, 1937.

the Seas, Emperor of India, in respect of the Dominion of Canada, recognizing that the protection, preservation and extension of the sockeye salmon fisheries in the Fraser River system are of common concern to the United States of America and the Dominion of Canada; that the supply of this fish in recent years has been greatly depleted and that it is of importance in the mutual interest of both countries that this source of wealth should be restored and maintained, have resolved to conclude a Convention and to that end have named as their respective plenipotentiaries:

The President of the United States of America: Mr. Henry L. Stimson, Secretary of State of the United States of America; and

His Majesty, for the Dominion of Canada: The Honorable Vincent Massey, a member of His Majesty's Privy Council for Canada and His Envoy Extraordinary and Minister Plenipotentiary for Canada at Washington;

Who, after having communicated to each other their full powers, found in good and due form, have agreed upon the following Articles:

ARTICLE I

The provisions of this Convention and the orders and regulations issued under the authority thereof shall apply, in the manner and to the extent hereinafter provided in this Convention, to the following waters:

1. The territorial waters and the high seas westward from the western coast of the United States of America and the Dominion of Canada and from a direct line drawn from Bonilla Point, Vancouver Island, to the lighthouse on Tatoosh Island, Washington,—which line marks the entrance to Juan de Fuca Strait,—and embraced between 48 and 49 degrees north latitude, excepting therefrom, however, all the waters of Barklay Sound, eastward of a straight line drawn from Amphitrite Point to Cape Beale and all the waters of Nitinat Lake and the entrance thereto.

2. The waters included within the following boundaries:

Beginning at Bonilla Point, Vancouver Island, thence along the aforesaid direct line drawn from Bonilla Point to Tatoosh Lighthouse, Washington, described in paragraph numbered 1 of this Article, thence to the nearest point of Cape Flattery, thence following the southerly shore of Juan de Fuca Strait to Point Wilson, on Quimper Peninsula, thence in a straight line to Point Partridge on Whidbey Island, thence following the western shore of the said Whidbey Island, to the entrance to Deception Pass, thence across said entrance to the southern side of Reservation Bay, on Fidalgo Island, thence following the western and northern shore line of the said Fidalgo Island to Swinomish Slough, crossing the said Swinomish Slough, in line with the track of the Great Northern Railway, thence northerly following the shore line of the mainland to Atkinson Point at the northerly entrance to Burrard Inlet, British Columbia, thence in a straight line to the southern end of Bowen Island, thence westerly following the southern shore of Bowen Island to Cape Roger Curtis, thence in a straight line to Gower Point, thence westerly following the shore line to Welcome Point on Seechelt Peninsula, thence in a straight line to Point Young on Lasqueti Island, thence in a straight line to Dorcas Point on Vancouver Island, thence following the eastern and southern shores of the said Vancouver Island to the starting point at Bonilla Point, as shown on the United States Coast and Geodetic Survey Chart Number 6300, as corrected to March 14, 1930, and on the British Admiralty Chart Number 579, copies of which are annexed to this Convention and made a part thereof.[14]

3. The Fraser River and the streams and lakes tributary thereto.

The High Contracting Parties engage to have prepared as soon as practicable charts of the waters described in this Article, with the above described boundaries thereof and the international boundary indicated thereon. Such charts, when approved by the appropriate authorities of the Governments of the United States of America and the Dominion of Canada, shall be considered to have been substituted for the charts annexed to this Convention and shall be authentic for the purposes of the Convention.

The High Contracting Parties further agree to establish within the territory of the United States of America and the territory of the Dominion of Canada such buoys and marks for the purposes of this Convention as may be recommended by the Commission hereinafter authorized to be established, and to refer such recommendations as the Commission may make as relate to the establishment of buoys or marks at points on the international boundary to the International Boundary Commission, United States-Alaska and Canada, for action pursuant to the provisions of the Treaty between the United States of America and His Majesty, in respect of Canada, respecting the boundary between the United States of America and the Dominion of Canada, signed February 24, 1925.[15]

ARTICLE II

The High Contracting Parties agree to establish and maintain a Commission to be known as the International Pacific Salmon Fisheries Commission, hereinafter called the Commission, consisting of six members, three on the part of the United States of America and three on the part of the Dominion of Canada.

---

[14] For chart see Department of State Treaty Series No. 918.
[15] *Foreign Relations*, 1925, vol. I, p. 544.

The Commissioners on the part of the United States of America shall be appointed by the President of the United States of America. The Commissioners on the part of the Dominion of Canada shall be appointed by His Majesty on the recommendation of the Governor General in Council.

The Commissioners appointed by each of the High Contracting Parties shall hold office during the pleasure of the High Contracting Party by which they were appointed.

The Commission shall continue in existence so long as this Convention shall continue in force, and each High Contracting Party shall have power to fill and shall fill from time to time vacancies which may occur in its representation on the Commission in the same manner as the original appointments are made. Each High Contracting Party shall pay the salaries and expenses of its own Commissioners, and joint expenses incurred by the Commission shall be paid by the two High Contracting Parties in equal moieties.

ARTICLE III

The Commission shall make a thorough investigation into the natural history of the Fraser River sockeye salmon, into hatchery methods, spawning ground conditions and other related matters. It shall conduct the sockeye salmon fish cultural operations in the waters described in paragraphs numbered 2 and 3 of Article I of this Convention, and to that end it shall have power to improve spawning grounds, construct, and maintain hatcheries, rearing ponds and other such facilities as it may determine to be necessary for the propagation of sockeye salmon in any of the waters covered by this Convention, and to stock any such waters with sockeye salmon by such methods as it may determine to be most advisable. The Commission shall also have authority to recommend to the Governments of the High Contracting Parties removing or otherwise overcoming obstructions to the ascent of sockeye salmon, that may now exist or may from time to time occur, in any of the waters covered by this Convention, where investigation may show such removal of or other action to overcome obstructions to be desirable. The Commission shall make an annual report to the two Governments as to the investigations which it has made and other action which it has taken in execution of the provisions of this Article, or of other Articles of this Convention.

The cost of all work done pursuant to the provisions of this Article, or of other Articles of this Convention, including removing or otherwise overcoming obstructions that may be approved, shall be borne equally by the two Governments, and the said Governments agree to appropriate annually such money as each may deem desirable for such work in the light of the reports of the Commission.

ARTICLE IV

The Commission is hereby empowered to limit or prohibit taking sockeye salmon in respect of all or any of the waters described in Article I of this Convention, provided that when any order is adopted by the Commission limiting or prohibiting taking sockeye salmon in any of the territorial waters or on the High Seas described in paragraph numbered 1 of Article I, such order shall extend to all such territorial waters and High Seas, and, similarly, when in any of the waters of the United States of America embraced in paragraph numbered 2 of Article I, such order shall extend to all such waters of the United States of America, and when in any of the Canadian waters embraced in paragraphs numbered 2 and 3 of Article I, such order shall extend to all such Canadian waters, and provided further, that no order limiting or prohibiting taking sockeye salmon adopted by the Commission shall be construed to suspend or otherwise affect the requirements of the laws of the State of Washington or of the Dominion of Canada as to the procuring of a license to fish in the waters on their respective sides of the boundary, or in their respective territorial waters embraced in paragraph numbered 1 of Article I of this Convention, and provided further that any order adopted by the Commission limiting or prohibiting taking sockeye salmon on the High Seas embraced in paragraph numbered 1 of Article I of this Convention shall apply only to nationals and inhabitants and vessels and boats of the United States of America and the Dominion of Canada.

Any order adopted by the Commission limiting or prohibiting taking sockeye salmon in the waters covered by this Convention, or any part thereof, shall remain in full force and effect unless and until the same be modified or set aside by the Commission. Taking sockeye salmon in said waters in violation of an order of the Commission shall be prohibited.

ARTICLE V

In order to secure a proper escapement of sockeye salmon during the spring or chinook salmon fishing season, the Commission may prescribe the size of the meshes in all fishing gear and appliances that may be operated during said season in the waters of the United States of America and/or the Canadian waters described in Article I of this Convention. At all seasons of the year the Commission may prescribe the size of the meshes in all salmon fishing gear and appliances that may be operated on the High Seas embraced in paragraph numbered 1 of Article I of this Convention, provided, however, that in so far as concerns the High Seas, requirements prescribed by the Commission under the authority of this paragraph shall apply only to nationals and inhabitants and vessels and boats of the United States of America and the Dominion of Canada.

Whenever, at any other time than the spring or chinook salmon fishing season, the taking of sockeye salmon in waters of the United States of America or in Canadian waters is not prohibited under an order adopted by the Commission, any fishing gear or appliance authorized by the State of Washington may be used in waters of the United States of America by any person thereunto authorized by the State of Washington, and any fishing gear or appliance authorized by the laws of the Dominion of Canada may be used in Canadian waters by any person thereunto duly authorized. Whenever the taking of sockeye salmon on the High Seas embraced in paragraph numbered 1 of Article I of this Convention is not prohibited, under an order adopted by the Commission, to the nationals or inhabitants or vessels or boats of the United States of America or the Dominion of Canada, only such salmon fishing gear and appliances as may have been approved by the Commission may be used on such High Seas by said nationals, inhabitants, vessels or boats.

Article VI

No action taken by the Commission under the authority of this Convention shall be effective unless it is affirmatively voted for by at least two of the Commissioners of each High Contracting Party.

Article VII

Inasmuch as the purpose of this Convention is to establish for the High Contracting Parties, by their joint effort and expense, a fishery that is now largely nonexistent, it is agreed by the High Contracting Parties that they should share equally in the fishery. The Commission shall, consequently, regulate the fishery with a view to allowing, as nearly as may be practicable, an equal portion of the fish that may be caught each year to be taken by the fishermen of each High Contracting Party.

Article VIII

Each High Contracting Party shall be responsible for the enforcement of the orders and regulations adopted by the Commission under the authority of this Convention, in the portion of its waters covered by the Convention.

Except as hereinafter provided in Article IX of this Convention, each High Contracting Party shall be responsible, in respect of its own nationals and inhabitants and vessels and boats, for the enforcement of the orders and regulations adopted by the Commission, under the authority of this Convention, on the High Seas embraced in paragraph numbered 1 of Article I of the Convention.

Each High Contracting Party shall acquire and place at the disposition of the Commission any land within its territory required for the construction and maintenance of hatcheries, rearing ponds, and other such facilities as set forth in Article III.

Article IX

Every national or inhabitant, vessel or boat of the United States of America or of the Dominion of Canada, that engages in sockeye salmon fishing on the High Seas embraced in paragraph numbered 1 of Article I of this Convention, in violation of an order or regulation adopted by the Commission, under the authority of this Convention, may be seized and detained by the duly authorized officers of either High Contracting Party, and when so seized and detained shall be delivered by the said officers, as soon as practicable, to an authorized official of the country to which such person, vessel or boat belongs, at the nearest point to the place of seizure, or elsewhere, as may be agreed upon with the competent authorities. The authorities of the country to which a person, vessel or boat belongs alone shall have jurisdiction to conduct prosecutions for the violation of any order or regulation, adopted by the Commission in respect of fishing for sockeye salmon on the High Seas embraced in paragraph numbered 1 of Article I of this Convention, or of any law or regulation which either High Contracting Party may have made to carry such order or regulation of the Commission into effect, and to impose penalties for such violations; and the witnesses and proofs necessary for such prosecutions, so far as such witnesses or proofs are under the control of the other High Contracting Party, shall be furnished with all reasonable promptitude to the authorities having jurisdiction to conduct the prosecutions.

Article X

The High Contracting Parties agree to enact and enforce such legislation as may be necessary to make effective the provisions of this Convention and the orders and regulations adopted by the Commission under the authority thereof, with appropriate penalties for violations.

Article XI

The present Convention shall be ratified by the President of the United States of America, by and with the advice and consent of the Senate thereof, and by His Majesty in accordance with constitutional practice, and it shall become effective upon the date of the exchange of ratifications which shall take place at Washington as soon as possible and shall continue in force for a period of sixteen years, and thereafter until one year from the day on which either of the High Contracting Parties shall give notice to the other of its desire to terminate it.

In witness whereof, the respective plenipotentiaries have signed the present Convention, and have affixed their seals thereto.

Done in duplicate at Washington on the twenty-sixth day of May, one thousand nine hundred and thirty.

[SEAL]   HENRY L. STIMSON
[SEAL]   VINCENT MASSEY

[On July 28, 1937, the following Protocol of Exchange was signed: "The undersigned the Secretary of State of the United States of America and the Canadian Minister at Washington met this day for the purpose of exchanging ratifications of the convention between the United States of America and Canada for the protection, preservation and extension of the sockeye salmon fisheries of the Fraser River System, signed at Washington on May 26, 1930.

The Secretary of State of the United States of America stated that the convention is ratified on the part of the United States of America subject to the three understandings contained in the resolution of the Senate of the United States of America advising and consenting to ratification, a copy of which resolution was communicated to the Secretary of State for External Affairs of Canada by the Minister of the United States of America at Ottawa in his note of July 7, 1936. These three understandings are as follows:

(1) That the International Pacific Salmon Fisheries Commission shall have no power to authorize any type of fishing gear contrary to the laws of the State of Washington or the Dominion of Canada;

(2) That the Commission shall not promulgate or enforce regulations until the scientific investigations provided for in the convention have been made, covering two cycles of Sockeye Salmon runs, or eight years; and

(3) That the Commission shall set up an Advisory Committee composed of five persons from each country who shall be representatives of the various branches of the industry (purse seine, gill net, troll, sport fishing, and one other), which Advisory Committee shall be invited to all non-executive meetings of the Commission and shall be given full opportunity to examine and to be heard on all proposed orders, regulations or recommendations.

The Canadian Minister stated that he was authorized by his Government to state that it accepted the foregoing understandings.

The exchange then took place in the usual manner.

IN WITNESS WHEREOF they have signed the present protocol and have affixed their seals hereto.

Done at Washington this twenty-eighth day of July, 1937.

CORDELL HULL   [SEAL]

Secretary of State

of the United States of America

HERBERT M. MARLER   [SEAL]

Canadian Minister"]

CONVENTION BETWEEN THE UNITED STATES AND CANADA FOR THE PRESERVATION OF THE HALIBUT FISHERY OF THE NORTHERN PACIFIC OCEAN AND BERING SEA, SIGNED MAY 9, 1930 [16]

711.428/1329

The Acting Secretary of State to the Chargé in Canada (Riggs)

No. 793   WASHINGTON, March 6, 1930.

SIR: Consideration has been given to the amended draft of the Halibut Convention submitted by the Canadian Government as a counterproposal to the draft which the Legation submitted to that Government pursuant to instruction No. 548 of May 29, 1929,[17] and transmitted to the Department with the Legation's despatch No. 1159 of October 7, 1929.[18]

Note has been made of the criticism made by the Canadian Government in its note No. 128 of October 3, 1929,[19] of the second paragraph of Article III in the draft presented by this Government, and of the alterations made in that paragraph by the draft forwarded to the Department with the Legation's despatch of October 7, 1929. As will be indicated hereinafter in detail, this Government is prepared to accept, with the insertion of two phrases and two verbal changes, the paragraph as revised by the Canadian Government.

On a comparison of the Canadian draft enclosed with the Legation's despatch and the draft transmitted to the Legation with instruction No. 548 of May 29, 1929, changes made by the Canadian Government have been noted in the Preamble and in Articles II, III and V. References made in this instruction to line number are to the draft received from the Canadian Government in October, 1929, and in many cases do not correspond exactly with the line number in the revised draft herewith enclosed.[19a]

---

[16] For previous correspondence concerning the convention, see *Foreign Relations,* 1929, vol. II, pp. 60 ff.

[17] *Ibid.,* p. 61.

[18] *Ibid.,* p. 66.

[19] Not printed.

[19a] Revised draft convention not printed.

The Preamble of the draft submitted by Canada is acceptable to this Government.

The word "mutually", appearing in the expression "as may be mutually agreed upon" in Article II in the American draft, was omitted from the Canadian draft. This omission is acceptable.

The expression "convention between His Britannic Majesty and the United States" in the first paragraph of Article III and in Article V of this Government's draft was amended in the Canadian draft to read "convention between His Britannic Majesty and the President of the United States". This Government does not agree to the insertion of the words "the President of" in this expression at these places. The expression used in the Halibut Convention concluded March 2, 1923,[20] to which reference is made at these two places in the convention under negotiation, is "the United States" and not "the President of the United States". In the view of this Government the same expression, namely, "the United States", should be used in the reference in the present Convention. The term "the President of the United States of America" at the other places where the expression "the President of the United States" or "the President of the United States of America" appears in the Canadian draft is acceptable to this Government.

Other differences between the two drafts appear to be confined to Article III. The differences noted in detail are as follows:

The expression "Northern Pacific Ocean and Bering Sea" was substituted at one place in the first paragraph and one place in the second paragraph for the expression "Northern Pacific Ocean including Bering Sea". Inasmuch as that expression as used in the first paragraph is a reference to the description in the Convention of 1923, it is believed that the word "including" should be restored at this place, as it is used in the Convention of 1923. "Including" was retained, quite properly in the view of this Government, in the second paragraph of Article V of the Canadian draft of the new Convention. This Government has no objection to the use of the word "and" in the same expression in the second paragraph of Article III and in the Preamble of the new Convention, as it appears in the Canadian draft.

The provision "and this Commission shall publish a report of its activities from time to time" also in the first paragraph of Article III was amended in the Canadian draft to read "which Commission shall make such investigations as are necessary into the life history of the halibut in the treaty waters and shall publish a report of its activities from time to time". The revision is acceptable to this Government.

The amended statement of the authority vested in the International

---

[20] *Foreign Relations*, 1923, vol. I, p. 468.

Fisheries Commission in the second paragraph differs from that proposed in this Government's draft in respect of the following provisions:

(*a*) divide the treaty waters into areas;

(*c*) fix the size and character of halibut fishing appliances to be used therein;

(*e*) close to all halibut fishing such portion or portions of an area or areas, as the International Fisheries Commission find to be populated by small, immature halibut.

In provision (*d*) the words "statistics of the catch of halibut" were substituted for the words "statistics of the catch"; the words "as will enable the International Fisheries Commission" were substituted for the words "as will enable the Commission"; and the words "trend of the halibut fishery" were substituted for the words "trend of the fishery".

This amended statement, with the substitution of the word "convention" for "treaty" in subdivision (*a*) as hereinafter proposed, is acceptable to this Government.

You are instructed to make the following proposals for the revision of the Canadian draft of the Convention:

(1) that the words "including Bering Sea" in the seventh line of the first paragraph of Article I be replaced by the expression "including the southern as well as the western coasts of Alaska". The Pacific Ocean is not mentioned in this paragraph. Reference to the coasts of Alaska, for the purpose of including the waters of Bering Sea, is analogous to the description of the waters of the Pacific Ocean by reference to the coasts of the United States of America and of Canada. The new expression proposed by this Government embraces all the waters intended to be covered by the expression "including Bering Sea". It is believed also that it is well to include expressly the waters off the southern coast of Alaska, which otherwise would only be embraced by inference in the waters off the western coasts of the United States and of Canada.

(2) This Government is of the opinion that it should be clearly expressed in the Convention that the authority which will be conferred on the Commission by the second paragraph of Article III is limited in its application to nationals and inhabitants and fishing vessels and boats of the United States of America and of the Dominion of Canada. It, therefore, proposes that there be inserted after the word "may" at the end of the sixth line of the paragraph the words "in respect of the nationals and inhabitants and fishing vessels and boats of the United States of America and of the Dominion of Canada".

(3) The expression "from time to time" in the sixth line of the second paragraph of Article III in the draft transmitted to the Legation with the Department's instruction No. 548 of May 29, 1929, does not appear in this paragraph as revised in the Canadian draft. In the view of this Government the expression should be restored, and

should be placed after the insertion proposed in the foregoing paragraph of this instruction.

The insertions proposed under items (2) and (3) read together are as follows: "in respect of the nationals and inhabitants and fishing vessels and boats of the United States of America and of the Dominion of Canada, from time to time". This clause will immediately precede the subdivision (*a*) and relate to subdivision (*a*), (*b*), (*c*), (*d*) and (*e*).

You are instructed to propose also

(4) that the word "Convention" be substituted for "article" in the second line of the third paragraph of Article I and in the second line of the fourth paragraph of that Article;

(5) that the word "or" be substituted for "and" in the second and third lines of the third paragraph of Article I;

(6) that the words "Each of the High Contracting Parties" be substituted for "Each Party" at the beginning of the last sentence of the first paragraph of Article III;

(7) that the term "the United States of America" be used throughout the text in place of the term "the United States"; and

(8) that the word "convention" be used in lieu of "treaty" throughout the text.

The places at which the expression "the United States of America" will be substituted for "the United States" are as follows:

Article I, first paragraph, lines 3 and 6;

Article I, second paragraph, line 4;

Article I, third paragraph, lines 4 and 17;

Article II, line 2;

Article III, first paragraph, line 5;

Article III, second paragraph, line 6; and

Article V, second paragraph, line 4.

The places at which the word "convention" will be substituted for "treaty" are as follows:

Article III, first paragraph, line 10; and

Article III, second paragraph, subdivision (*a*).

You are instructed to inform the Dominion Government of the views of this Government in regard to the amended draft submitted in the note to the Legation from the Department of External Affairs of October 3, 1929, and to state that this Government is now prepared to conclude the Convention and to request the President to issue a full power to you to sign it.

Copies of the draft now proposed by this Government, showing by deletion or underlining the amendments to the Canadian draft, are enclosed. One copy should be submitted to the Canadian Government.

I am [etc.] J. P. COTTON

711.428/1382

The Chargé in Canada (Riggs) to the Acting Secretary of State

No. 1380 OTTAWA, April 17, 1930.
[Received April 21.]

SIR: With further reference to the Department's instruction No. 793 of March 6, 1930, (file No. 711.428/1329), directing me to submit to the Canadian Government an amended draft of the Halibut Convention, together with the Department's observations regarding suggested changes, I have the honor to transmit herewith copy of the Canadian Government's reply received today.

It will be noted that the Canadian Government is prepared to accept the draft transmitted in the Department's instruction under reference, with two very minor changes. The expression "the United States counter-draft", quoted in the Canadian reply, was used by me in the note to the Department of External Affairs, together with two other similar expressions, for convenience in reference and to avoid the tedious circumlocution which would otherwise have been necessary whenever one of the three drafts under discussion was mentioned.

I understand informally that the Canadian request to London for the full power to sign this Convention was despatched some time ago and that the full power is consequently expected very shortly.

I have [etc.] B. REATH RIGGS

[Enclosure]

The Canadian Secretary of State for External Affairs (Mackenzie King) to the American Chargé (Riggs)

No. 37 OTTAWA, 16 April, 1930.

SIR: With reference to your note No. 659 of the 12th March, 1930, and to previous correspondence regarding the conclusion of a convention implementing the recommendations contained in the report of the International Fisheries Commission, I have the honour to state that "the United States counter-draft" which accompanied your note under reference is acceptable to the Canadian Government, subject to the two following alterations in the preamble: (1) the insertion of the words "in respect of the Dominion of Canada" after the words "His Majesty the King of Great Britain, Ireland, and the British Dominions beyond the Seas, Emperor of India", for the purpose of reverting to a formula which had been in use in recent years, and (2) a change in the punctuation relating to the following words "and His Majesty: for the Dominion of Canada:" so as to read "and His Majesty, for the Dominion of Canada:".

The Canadian Government will be prepared to proceed with the signature of the Instrument embodying that document as soon as the Full Power to be issued by His Majesty the King is received.

It is noted that the Government of the United States are now prepared to request the President to issue to you a Full Power to sign the Convention.

Accept [etc.]

O. D. SKELTON
For the Secretary of State for External Affairs

711.428/1386 : Telegram

The Chargé in Canada (Riggs) to the Secretary of State

OTTAWA, May 7, 1930—2 p. m.
[Received 3 : 25 p. m.]

70. Reference line 3 of article 6 on page 6 of amended draft of halibut convention transmitted with Department's instruction number 793 of March 6 last. Instead of expression "exchanged in Ottawa" Canadian final rough draft has "exchanged at Ottawa" which they desire to retain since meaning unchanged. Am informally advised Prime Minister plans for signature on 9th instant. Please instruct whether I may sign with contemplated change.

RIGGS

711.428/1386 : Telegram

The Secretary of State to the Chargé in Canada (Riggs)

WASHINGTON, May 8, 1930—3 p. m.

55. Your 70, May 7, 2 p. m. Proposed change is accepted by this Government.

Please inform Department by telegram immediately after signature of date and hour of signature, in order that statement may be given to the press.

STIMSON

Treaty Series No. 837

Convention Between the United States of America and Canada, Signed at Ottawa, May 9, 1930 [21]

The President of the United States of America,

And His Majesty the King of Great Britain, Ireland, and the British Dominions beyond the Seas, Emperor of India, in respect of the Dominion of Canada,

---

[21] Ratification advised by the Senate, February 24 (legislative day of February 17), 1931 ; ratified by the President, March 4, 1931 ; ratified by Canada, March 20, 1931 ; ratifications exchanged at Ottawa, May 9, 1931 ; proclaimed by the President, May 14, 1931.

Being equally desirous of securing the preservation of the halibut fishery of the Northern Pacific Ocean and Bering Sea, have resolved to conclude a Convention for this purpose, and have named as their plenipotentiaries:

The President of the United States of America: Mr. B. Reath Riggs, Chargé d'Affaires of the United States of America in Canada; and

His Majesty, for the Dominion of Canada: The Right Honourable William Lyon Mackenzie King, Prime Minister and Secretary of State for External Affairs;

Who, after having communicated to each other their respective full powers, found in good and due form, have agreed upon the following articles:

ARTICLE I

The nationals and inhabitants and fishing vessels and boats of the United States of America and of the Dominion of Canada, respectively, are hereby prohibited from fishing for halibut (*Hippoglossus*) both in the territorial waters and in the high seas off the western coasts of the United States of America, including the southern as well as the western coasts of Alaska, and of the Dominion of Canada, from the first day of November next after the date of the exchange of ratifications of this Convention to the fifteenth day of the following February, both days inclusive, and within the same period yearly thereafter.

The International Fisheries Commission provided for by Article III is hereby empowered, subject to the approval of the President of the United States of America and of the Governor General of the Dominion of Canada, to suspend or modify the closed season provided for by this article, as to part or all of the convention waters, when it finds after investigation such changes are necessary.

It is understood that nothing contained in this convention shall prohibit the nationals or inhabitants or the fishing vessels or boats of the United States of America or of the Dominion of Canada, from fishing in the waters hereinbefore specified for other species of fish during the season when fishing for halibut in such waters is prohibited by this Convention or by any regulations adopted in pursuance of its provisions. Any halibut that may be taken incidentally when fishing for other fish during the season when fishing for halibut is prohibited under the provisions of this Convention or by any regulations adopted in pursuance of its provisions may be retained and used for food for the crew of the vessel by which they are taken. Any portion thereof not so used shall be landed and immediately turned over to the duly authorized officers of the Department of Commerce of the United States of America or of the Department of Marine and Fisheries of the Dominion of Canada. Any fish turned over to such officers in pursuance of the provisions of this article shall be sold by them to the highest bidder and the proceeds of such sale, exclusive of the necessary expenses in connection therewith, shall be paid by them into the treasuries of their respective countries.

It is further understood that nothing contained in this convention shall prohibit the International Fisheries Commission from conducting fishing operations for investigation purposes during the closed season.

ARTICLE II

Every national or inhabitant, vessel or boat of the United States of America or of the Dominion of Canada engaged in halibut fishing in violation of the preceding article may be seized except within the jurisdiction of the other party by the duly authorized officers of either High Contracting Party and detained by the officers making such seizure and delivered as soon as practicable to an authorized official of the country to which such person, vessel or boat belongs, at the nearest point to the place of seizure, or elsewhere, as may be agreed upon. The authorities of the nation to which such person, vessel or boat belongs alone shall have jurisdiction to conduct prosecutions for the violation of the provisions of this Convention, or any regulations which may be adopted in pursuance of its provisions, and to impose penalties for such violations; and the witnesses and proofs necessary for such prosecutions, so far as such witnesses or proofs are under the control of the other High Contracting Party, shall be furnished with all reasonable promptitude to the authorities having jurisdiction to conduct the prosecutions.

ARTICLE III

The High Contracting Parties agree to continue under this Convention the Commission as at present constituted and known as the International Fisheries Commission, established by the Convention between the United States of America and His Britannic Majesty for the preservation of the halibut fishery of the Northern Pacific Ocean including Bering Sea, concluded March 2, 1923, consisting of four members, two appointed by each Party, which Commission shall make such investigations as are necessary into the life history of the halibut in the convention waters and shall publish a report of its activities from time to time. Each of the High Contracting Parties shall have power to fill, and shall fill from time to time, vacancies which may occur in its representation on the Commission. Each of the High Contracting Parties shall pay the salaries and expenses of its own members, and joint expenses incurred by the Commission shall be paid by the two High Contracting Parties in equal moieties.

The High Contracting Parties agree that for the purposes of protecting and conserving the halibut fishery of the Northern Pacific Ocean and Bering Sea, the International Fisheries Commission, with the approval of the President of the United States of America and of the Governor General of the Dominion of Canada, may, in respect of the nationals and inhabitants and fishing vessels and boats of the United States of America and of the Dominion of Canada, from time to time,

(*a*) divide the convention waters into areas;

(*b*) limit the catch of halibut to be taken from each area;

(*c*) fix the size and character of halibut fishing appliances to be used therein;

(*d*) make such regulations for the collection of statistics of the catch of halibut including the licensing and clearance of vessels, as will enable the International Fisheries Commission to determine the condition and trend of the halibut fishery by banks and areas, as a proper basis for protecting and conserving the fishery;

(*e*) close to all halibut fishing such portion or portions of an area or areas, as the International Fisheries Commission find to be populated by small, immature halibut.

ARTICLE IV

The High Contracting Parties agree to enact and enforce such legislation as may be necessary to make effective the provisions of this Convention and any regulation adopted thereunder, with appropriate penalties for violations thereof.

ARTICLE V

The present Convention shall remain in force for a period of five years and thereafter until two years from the date when either of the High Contracting Parties shall give notice to the other of its desire to terminate it.

This Convention shall, from the date of the exchange of ratifications be deemed to supplant the Convention between the United States of America and His Britannic Majesty for the Preservation of the Halibut Fishery of the Northern Pacific Ocean including Bering Sea, concluded March 2, 1923.

ARTICLE VI

This Convention shall be ratified in accordance with the constitutional methods of the High Contracting Parties. The ratifications shall be exchanged at Ottawa as soon as practicable, and the Convention shall come into force on the day of the exchange of ratifications.

IN FAITH WHEREOF, the respective plenipotentiaries have signed the present Convention in duplicate, and have hereunto affixed their seals.

DONE at Ottawa on the ninth day of May, in the year one thousand nine hundred and thirty.

[SEAL]   B. REATH RIGGS

[SEAL]   W. L. MACKENZIE KING

PROJECT FOR IMPROVEMENT OF THE ST. LAWRENCE WATERWAY BY JOINT ACTION OF THE UNITED STATES AND CANADA [22]

711.42157Sa29/569

The Canadian Minister (Massey) to the Secretary of State

No. 33   WASHINGTON, 1 March, 1929.

SIR: With reference to your note of April 7th, 1928 [23] concerning the St. Lawrence Waterway, I have the honour to inform you that I have been instructed by the Secretary of State for External Affairs to bring to your attention the developments in the Canadian situation since the receipt of your note.

In my note Number 64 of April 5th. 1928,[24] I informed you that steps were being taken to secure a judicial determination of certain constitutional difficulties as to the respective rights of the federal and provincial governments in Canada regarding water power and navigation. A series of questions was referred to the Supreme Court of Canada in April 1928, and the case was argued in October. The answers of the Court were given on February 5th. 1929. Some of the points at issue were clarified, but the Court found itself unable to give conclusive answers to a number of the more important questions.

Under these circumstances, His Majesty's Government in Canada has concluded that it would not be advisable at present to seek a solution of the question of federal and provincial jurisdiction by further reference to the courts. It has therefore invited the two governments of the provinces of Ontario and Quebec to take part in a conference on the problem of the St. Lawrence development, to be held as soon as possible after the close of the present parliamentary session, at which it is hoped it will be possible to reach a solution by direct agreement.

Reference was made in my note of April 5th, 1929 [*1928*] to the necessity of reconciling the divergent views as to the best method of development in the international rapids section of the St. Lawrence. The Ontario Government has now agreed to co-operate in an endeavour

---

[22] For previous correspondence, see *Foreign Relations*, 1928, vol. II, pp. 64 ff.
[23] *Ibid.*, p. 77.
[24] *Ibid.*, p. 75.

to find a solution of this problem, and engineers have been appointed to represent the province in consultation with the Canadian section of the Joint Board of Engineers.

I have [etc.] VINCENT MASSEY

711.42157Sa29/591½

The Minister in Canada (Phillips) to the Secretary of State

OTTAWA, April 15, 1929.
[Received April 18.]

MY DEAR MR. SECRETARY: I do not know, of course, what attitude you wish me to adopt in regard to the St. Lawrence waterway project, but in the absence of instructions I am continuing to urge the Canadian Government to agree to the appointment of commissioners at the earliest possible date. You will recollect that Mr. Kellogg's note to the Dominion Government, dated March 12, 1928,[25] suggested that the two countries should proceed with the appointment of commissioners to discuss jointly the various problems with a view to the formulation of a convention appropriate to the whole subject. Ever since the receipt of this communication I have been trying to get the Canadian Government to agree to such a discussion, but up till now without much success. However, I have had a further talk with the Prime Minister this morning and am beginning to be really hopeful. He tells me that after the adjournment of the present session of Parliament some time during the middle or end of May, he has called a meeting of the Premiers of Quebec and Ontario to talk over the whole problem arising out of the ownership of power to be developed from navigable waters. A favorable reply to his invitation has already been received from Mr. Taschereau, and Mr. Ferguson of Ontario is also understood to have agreed to attend the meeting. The Prime Minister is confident that he can settle to the satisfaction of the people of both Quebec and Ontario the disposition of their respective portions of the power, and that the moment this point is settled he believes the two Provinces will raise no further objection to proceeding with the discussion of the navigation problems.

In reply to my inquiry as to whether he would be in a position to agree to the appointment of Canadian commissioners shortly after the adjournment of the proposed conference, he intimated that he hoped he would be able to do so. He will not commit himself any further in the absence of precise information as to what our Congress proposes to do in tariff matters.

---

[25] *Foreign Relations*, 1928, vol. II, p. 71.

I hope I am doing right in continuing to follow Mr. Kellogg's wishes in this matter, but I am counting upon you to let me know if I am not acting in accordance with your views.

Very sincerely yours,

WILLIAM PHILLIPS

711.42157Sa29/591½

The Secretary of State to the Minister in Canada (Phillips)

WASHINGTON, April 19, 1929.

MY DEAR MR. MINISTER: In answer to your letter of April fifteen, my attitude in reference to the St. Lawrence Waterway project will be the same as that of my predecessor, Mr. Kellogg. I feel that you should continue urging the appointment of Commissioners to discuss jointly plans appropriate to the whole subject. While the uncertainty of the action of our own Congress in reference to tariff matters will play an important part in the success of your efforts in that direction, still one of the best answers to the advocates of a higher tariff on Canadian products would be a cheap means of water transportation for our own farm and other products to the larger markets of the East.

Very sincerely yours,

HENRY L. STIMSON

711.42157Sa29/625

The Minister in Canada (Phillips) to the Secretary of State

No. 1138

OTTAWA, September 23, 1929.
[Received September 25.]

SIR: I had the honor to report to the Department in my telegram No. 182, dated September 19, 1929,[26] that the forthcoming conference between the Prime Minister and the Premiers of Ontario and Quebec regarding power developement on the St. Lawrence would probably be postponed until November, and in a telegram No. 181 of the same date [26] that the Under-Secretary of State for External Affairs had inquired as to whether the United States would allow the Canadian Government to undertake the channel improvements from Lake Ontario to Prescott on both sides of the frontier on the understanding that the United States would reimburse Canada at some future time for expenses incurred in the American channels. These two subjects are in my opinion closely interwoven and should therefore be given simultaneous consideration.

In this connection I beg to enclose a copy of a memorandum on the Great Lakes–St. Lawrence seaway which has been forwarded to me

---

[26] Not printed.

by Mr. Charles P. Craig, Executive Director of the Great Lakes–St. Lawrence Tidewater Association, under date of September 9th,[27] which deals with the Thousand Islands section, or in other words, with that section of the river to which the Under-Secretary of State referred in his conversation of September 19th. As the Department will note, Mr. Craig is strongly of the opinion that the United States should join with Canada in improving that portion of the American channels lying within the Thousand Islands district. He believes that inasmuch as the whole St. Lawrence waterway project is being undertaken by Canada in a piecemeal fashion, through the completion of the Welland Canal in Ontario and through the concession plan in Quebec, as revealed by the recent Beauharnois concession, the Government of the United States should not place itself in the position of refusing to cooperate with Canada in developing a portion of the international section of the river. He presents an argument which I believe the Department will wish to study with care.

At the same time it may perhaps be helpful to consider another aspect of the matter. The city of Prescott has excellent railway communication with Montreal. Ogdensburg which is immediately across the river on the American side, has very inadequate rail connection with the trunk lines in New York State. It is the declared purpose of the Canadian Government to develop the port of Prescott, and for this purpose large sums of money have been appropriated during the last session of Parliament. Elevators are to be erected for the storage of grain and large piers are to be constructed for the accommodation of Lake vessels and for the transfer of grain. In other words, it is the desire of the Canadian Government that upon the opening of the Welland Canal in 1930 the grain-carrying ships on the Lake will be enabled to proceed through Lake Ontario and as far down the river as Prescott, discharging their cargoes at this point for Montreal and other points east. The only difficulty to this conception lies in the fact that the river channels between Lake Ontario and Prescott-Ogdensburg are situated half in Canada and half in the United States; but such importance is attached to Prescott that Canada herself is willing to develop the American channels if the United States Government is not now prepared to do so. Prescott and not Ogdensburg is to be the great station for the transfer of grain from ships to canal boats or to the railways, and Ogdensburg is to remain, apparently, a mere ferry terminus for the transportation of passengers to and from Prescott.

The Department will recollect that in my confidential despatch No. 464 of June 7, 1928,[27] I reported a conversation with the Under-

---

[27] Not printed.

Secretary of State for External Affairs which was to the effect that the "deepening of the channels in question between Lake Ontario and Prescott-Ogdensburg was not designed as a step in the broader development plan; that it could not be so, since the Canadian Government had not as yet committed itself to embark upon the development of the whole St. Lawrence".   Dr. Skelton advised me that it was in fact "the outcome of the debates which had been going on ever since the work had begun on the Welland Canal, and that it was, therefore, related directly to the Welland Canal".

It seems natural, therefore, that the United States would have no especial interest in the development of channels in the international section of the river which are declared by Canada herself to have no relation to the larger project of navigation and which, moreover, may deprive American ports such as Buffalo of a large part of their transport trade.   When Prescott becomes the terminus for Great Lakes transportation, new and powerful influences will be at work to preserve this trade for Prescott—influences which may be counted upon to be unsympathetic to the larger navigation project to which the United States is committed.   Prescott has always been Conservative in its political faith and not unnaturally the Liberal government would be glad to transfer the allegiance of this section of the Province of Ontario to the Liberal fold.

In brief, we have the picture as presented by Mr. Craig of the desirability of cooperating with Canada in a section of the river which will ultimately be a part of the Lakes-to-the-Sea development, but at the same time we have to consider the possibility that the Canadian Government will be less inclined to proceed with navigation development in the entire international section until Prescott at least shall have reaped some benefit from her new and increased activities.

In my telegram No. 182 of September 19th I ventured to suggest that we might now take the position that we expect the Canadian Government to give a definite decision with respect to the appointment of commissioners to discuss jointly the various problems involved, which, as the Department will recollect, was put forward by the Secretary of State in his note to the Canadian Government of March 12, 1928.[30]   I am of the opinion that something is needed from us at this time to strengthen Mr. Mackenzie King's hand in dealing with his Provincial Premiers so that the conference will not adjourn with the comfortable feeling that since the United States is not pressing matters the thorny problems relating to the St. Lawrence can be sidetracked, at least for some months to come.

---

[30] *Foreign Relations*, 1928, vol. II, p. 71.

As I have said, we have before us for consideration two matters which would seem to be closely connected: (1) Canada's interest in the Thousand Islands section, and (2) the interest of the United States in the appointment of a commission to discuss jointly the details relating to the international section. It would seem possible that the Department might go so far as to say that since the purpose of the proposed commission was to settle details and costs of improvements in the international section the United States Government would prefer to have the benefit of the judgment of the commission before undertaking any piecemeal improvements, since in this manner, and in this manner only, could Congress be induced to make the necessary appropriation for a portion of the international section of the river. In other words, if Canada will appoint commissioners, the United States will, with the approval of the entire commission, undertake to deepen the American canals in the Thousand Islands section.

The appointment of commissioners, in my opinion, is important because it will keep before the Canadian and American publics the idea that the St. Lawrence seaway is a living project and something which is actually in the process of adjustment. We might perhaps afford to take the risks involved in the improvement of the channel to Prescott if at the same time the public in both countries is assured through the appointment of commissioners that ways and means for the completion of the undertaking are actually under discussion by both governments. In my opinion it would not be wise for us to proceed in accordance with Mr. Craig's suggestion without some sort of guarantee that Canada would not hold up indefinitely the work of improving the international section of the river as a whole.

I should be very grateful to have the benefit of the Department's judgment in this whole matter.

I have [etc.] WILLIAM PHILLIPS

711.42157Sa29/632a : Telegram

The Secretary of State to the Minister in Canada (Phillips)

WASHINGTON, October 25, 1929—noon.

104. The President has followed with the greatest interest your reports concerning the proposed conference between the Prime Minister and the Premiers of Ontario and Quebec to decide the question of the ownership of the Canadian share of power which will be developed in connection with the proposed Great Lakes-St. Lawrence seaway and has been gratified to note that this conference will take place at an early date.

You will recall that Secretary Kellogg's note of March 12, 1928, to

Mr. Massey [31] proposed that the two countries proceed with the appointment of Commissioners to discuss jointly the few remaining points of difference in respect of this project with a view to the formulation of a convention appropriate to the subject. The final sentence of Mr. Beaudry's reply dated April 5, 1928,[32] read as follows: "Following this consultation (with the Provinces of Ontario and Quebec) His Majesty's Government in Canada will be in a position to inform the Government of the United States further of its views on the proposals contained in your note of March 12th."

In view of the above-quoted sentence and the statements of the Prime Minister to you from time to time since then, the President feels confident that the appointment of Commissioners will be agreed upon in the near future. On this account you are authorized, if you deem it advisable to do so, to initiate informal discussion with the Canadian Government concerning the matter of the number and character of Commissioners.

The Canadian Government's proposals as set forth in its note to you of August 7th last [33] in the matter of providing forthwith a 25 foot channel in the international section of the St. Lawrence River have received the Department's careful consideration. As you are doubtless aware, the Army engineers made a survey of this section in pursuance of an Act of Congress and submitted estimates of the cost of removing shoals with a view to providing a 22 foot channel between Lake Ontario and Ogdensburg on the theory that a channel of that depth is sufficient for the requirements of existing shipping. In these circumstances, the War Department cannot under the law give the matter further consideration unless directed to do so by Congress.

This Government is, of course, committed to the construction of the Great Lakes-St. Lawrence Seaway which would involve a 27 foot channel in the international section and stands ready to appoint Commissioners to settle jointly details of the project. The United States Government, however, would prefer to have the benefit of the judgment of the Commissioners before undertaking any piecemeal improvements. You may accordingly suggest to the Prime Minister the appointment of such Commissioners at the earliest practicable moment and say to Mr. King that if the Commissioners recommend the immediate improvement of the international section, as proposed by the Canadian Government, and as a part of the broader project, the President will immediately thereafter recommend to Congress that appropriations be voted to carry out the works in American waters.

Your telegram No. 181 of September 19 [33] stated that the Prime

---

[31] *Foreign Relations*, 1928, vol. II, p. 71.
[32] *Ibid.*, p. 75.
[33] Not printed.

Minister desires to know whether this Government would agree to allow the Canadian Government to proceed with the necessary improvements in American waters as well as in Canadian waters on the understanding that the United States Government would ultimately reimburse Canada for expenses incurred in deepening American channels. Such an undertaking could only be given by Congress and in view of the positive action already taken and the definite recommendations made by Army Engineers (Mentioned in paragraph one above) it would probably be exceedingly difficult to convince Congress that more extensive improvements are necessary or desirable unless they could be linked with the whole St. Lawrence project.

STIMSON

711.42157Sa29/638 : Telegram

The Minister in Canada (Phillips) to the Secretary of State

OTTAWA, November 15, 1929—1 p. m.
[Received 5 : 50 p. m.]

222. Department's 104 of October 25 regarding St. Lawrence development. In absence of Prime Minister I have had an informal conversation with Minister of Public Works on lines of Department's instruction, without mentioning the instruction itself, in an attempt to ascertain his reaction. He felt that, if the United States could not allow Canada to proceed with necessary improvement of American channels on the reimbursement plan, Canada would certainly be permitted to do the improvement without reimbursement. He was of the opinion that the United States could not well object to such a course in view of the fact that at other points in the St. Lawrence waterway system, in particular I believe the Great Lakes, the United States had with the consent of Canada undertaken at American expense certain work on the Canadian side of the boundary, he felt therefore that to refuse Canada now a similar request would be widely criticized.

It seems possible therefore that, when I take up the matter with the Prime Minister on his return, he may make a proposal on the above lines and it would be helpful to me to know beforehand the Department's attitude. The records of the Legation do not reveal the points upon the St. Lawrence system where the United States has at its own cost made improvements on the Canadian side. It is said that a drill boat equipped with 12 drills has already started work at the Brockville Narrows. Canada is, therefore, now going forward with her part of the channels in the Thousand Islands sections and may be expected to press for an early reply regarding her interest in the American channels in this section.

PHILLIPS

711.42157Sa29/640 : Telegram

The Minister in Canada (Phillips) to the Secretary of State

OTTAWA, November 25, 1929—8 p. m.
[Received November 26—12 : 50 a. m.]

230. I presented to the Prime Minister this afternoon the substance of the Department's 104 of October 25th regarding the St. Lawrence. He told me that he is most anxious to have the conference of Premiers during the second week in December and was telegraphing today to the Minister of Justice and to Dr. Skelton, who are both at London, to ascertain whether they will be back by that date. He does not wish to hold the conference without their presence. Speaking of the appointment of commissioners, he thought that from the Canadian viewpoint it might be better to have the International Joint Commission undertake the work rather than new commissioners, partly, I believe, for the reason that Mr. McGrath, Chairman of the Canadian section of the Commission, is intimately in touch with Premier Ferguson and would therefore be helpful in bringing the Province of Ontario into line. Mr. King asked whether this would be satisfactory to us. I said that I had no information on this point but thought that possibly in view of the technical details to be considered, both engineering and financial, the President might feel the need of appointing other commissioners having the technical knowledge.

The question as to the personnel of commissioners would seem to be something which could be taken up either at the time of the meeting of the Premiers or immediately thereafter.

PHILLIPS

711.42157Sa29/643 : Telegram

The Minister in Canada (Phillips) to the Secretary of State

OTTAWA, December 3, 1929—4 p. m.
[Received 8 p. m.]

233. Legation's 230, November 25, 8 p. m. Prime Minister informs me today that neither Minister of Justice nor Doctor Skelton will return to Ottawa in time to hold conference of Premiers before Christmas and that accordingly the conference in question will not take place before January.

PHILLIPS

711.42157Sa29/685

The Canadian Chargé (Mahoney) to the Secretary of State

No. 130   WASHINGTON, June 28, 1930.

SIR: I have the honour to refer to Mr. Massey's note No. 64, of the 5th April, 1928,[35] in which the divergent views of the two sections of the Joint Board of Engineers as to the best method of meeting the engineering problems involved in the development of the international rapids section of the St. Lawrence River was referred to, and in which His Majesty's Government in Canada indicated its intention to arrange a conference between the Canadian section of the Joint Board, and engineers representing the Province of Ontario, preparatory to reconsideration of the engineering problems in this section by the whole Joint Board.

Acting upon instructions from the Secretary of State for External Affairs, I have the honour to transmit to you herewith copy of a report of the Canadian members of the Joint Board of Engineers, and of engineers representing the Province of Ontario, upon the international rapids section of the St. Lawrence River.[36]

I expect that at an early date I shall be in a position to transmit to you plates giving the plans in detail.

I am further instructed to inform you that the Canadian members of the Joint Board of Engineers will be prepared to participate, at the earliest convenient opportunity, in further consideration of the engineering problems in this section of the St. Lawrence River.

I have [etc.]   MERCHANT MAHONEY

711.42157Sa29/685

The Secretary of State to the Canadian Chargé (Mahoney)

WASHINGTON, July 9, 1930.

SIR: The receipt is acknowledged, with thanks, of your note No. 130, of June 28, 1930, enclosing a copy of the report of the Canadian members of the Joint Board of Engineers and of engineers representing the Province of Ontario, on the proposed development of the international rapids section of the St. Lawrence River.

Copies of your note and of its enclosure have been forwarded to the appropriate authorities of this Government for their consideration.

Your note states that the Canadian members of the Joint Board of Engineers will be prepared to participate, at the earliest convenient

---

[35] *Foreign Relations,* 1928, vol. II, p. 75.
[36] See *Report of Conference of Canadian Engineers on the International Rapids Section of the St. Lawrence River, With Appendix, Dated December 30, 1929* (Ottawa, F. A. Acland, 1930).

opportunity, in further consideration of the engineering problems in this section of the St. Lawrence River. In this regard may I point out that the Chargé d'Affaires of the United States Legation at Ottawa was instructed on January 22 last to inform the Canadian Government that the American members of the Joint Board of Engineers would be prepared to meet with the Canadian engineers at any time to deal with the St. Lawrence waterway. It was added that it would be desirable if several days notice of the proposed meeting could be given. It is suggested that your Government indicate a date on which it would be convenient for the Joint Board of Engineers to convene. It might be desirable to save time for the Chairman of the Canadian section of the Board to communicate direct with Colonel Harley B. Ferguson, Office of the Chief of Engineers, United States War Department, the Chairman of the American section, Washington, D. C., on this subject.

Accept [etc.]   For the Secretary of State:
                                         WILLIAM R. CASTLE, JR.

711.42157Sa29/699a

The Acting Secretary of State to the Minister in Canada (MacNider)

No. 1   WASHINGTON, August 26, 1930.

SIR: You are requested to forward a note reading as follows to the Secretary of State for External Affairs: [37]

"I have the honor to refer to previous correspondence exchanged between the Government of Canada and the Government of the United States on the subject of the proposed St. Lawrence seaway.

"In pursuance of instructions from the President, I desire to reiterate that the Government of the United States stands ready to proceed with this proposed development at the earliest possible date. I have been directed to inquire whether the Canadian Government now finds itself in a position to appoint commissioners to discuss jointly with commissioners of the United States the details of the seaway, and to formulate a treaty appropriate to the purpose."

Very truly yours,   WILLIAM R. CASTLE, JR.

711.42157Sa29/702

The Minister in Canada (MacNider) to the Secretary of State

No. 31   OTTAWA, September 11, 1930.
                                         [Received September 15.]

SIR: With further reference to the Department's instruction No. 1 of August 26, 1930, (no file number indicated), directing me to forward

---

[37] The note was communicated to the Canadian Secretary of State for External Affairs under date of September 2.

to the Canadian Secretary of State for External Affairs a note con-
veying the President's suggestions for action in connection with the
St. Lawrence seaway, I have the honor to transmit herewith copy of
a reply now received from Mr. Bennett, the Secretary of State for
External Affairs. Mr. Bennett briefly repeats the substance of what
he told me in the course of our conversations on this matter, as reported in my despatch No. 17 of September 5, 1930.[38]

Respectfully yours,   HANFORD MACNIDER

[Enclosure]

*The Canadian Secretary of State for External Affairs (Bennett)
to the American Minister (MacNider)*

No. 132   OTTAWA, September 10, 1930.

SIR, I have the honour to acknowledge your note of September 2nd
indicating the readiness of the Government of the United States to
proceed with the development of the proposed St. Lawrence waterway
at an early date.

The Canadian Government has given consideration to some phases of
the St. Lawrence waterway question, but in view of the fact that the
Parliament of Canada is now in session, and that the opening of the
Imperial Conference has been set for September 30th, it will not be
possible to deal with the question in a comprehensive manner at the
present moment. I purpose, however, to go into the matter immediately upon my return from the Conference in November, and following
this examination I shall communicate with you further.

Accept [etc.]   R. B. BENNETT

AVIATION RADIO CONFERENCE BETWEEN REPRESENTATIVES OF THE
UNITED STATES AND CANADA, HELD AT NEW YORK, APRIL 10–11,
1930

811.7442/33 : Telegram

The Acting Secretary of State to the Chargé in Canada (Riggs)

WASHINGTON, March 29, 1930—11 a. m.

38. Federal Radio Commission suggests conference be held New
York as soon as practicable between representatives of United States
and Canada regarding aviation radio communication and radio aids
to air navigation. Desire expressed that conference be held on or
before April 10

Take matter up with Canadian authorities and telegraph whether
they will agree to proposed conference and if so names of Canadian
delegates.

COTTON

---

[38] Not printed.

811.7442/35 : Telegram

The Chargé in Canada (Riggs) to the Acting Secretary of State

OTTAWA, April 5, 1930—1 p. m.
[Received 3 : 05 p. m.]

53. Department's 38, March 29, 11 a. m. Reply to Legation's representations of March 31st received today. Department of External Affairs states in note that suggested conference would be useful and that date of April 10th, 1930 in New York City would be satisfactory. Delegates are stated to be Mr. C. P. Edwards, Director of Radio in the Department of Marine, and Major W. A. Steel, of the Department of National Defense.

RIGGS

811.7442/43

The Chairman of the American Delegation (Starbuck) to the Acting Secretary of State

WASHINGTON, April 15, 1930.

MY DEAR MR. SECRETARY: I have the honor to report to you that in accordance with letters of instructions from the State Department dated April 9, 1930,[39] the following representatives of the United States government met with representatives of the Canadian government at the Customs House, New York City, on April 10 and 11, 1930:

Commissioner W. D. L. Starbuck, Chairman of Delegation,
Col. Clarence M. Young, Assistant Secretary of Commerce for Aeronautics,
Mr. W. R. Vallance, [Assistant] Solicitor, Department of State,
Captain F. C. Hingsburg, Chief Engineer, Airways Division, Department of Commerce,
Dr. C. B. Jolliffe, Chief Engineer, Federal Radio Commission,
Mr. Gerald C. Gross, Engineer, Federal Radio Commission.

The following representatives of the Canadian government were present:

Commander C. P. Edwards, Director of Radio Telegraph Branch, Department of Marine.
Mr. G. C. W. Browne, Chief Inspector, Radio Telegraph Branch, Department of Marine.
Major W. A. Steel, Royal Canadian Signals, Department of National Defense.
Capt. W. L. Laurie, Royal Canadian Signals, Department of National Defense.

---

[39] Not printed.

This informal conference, for the purpose of suggesting means of improving existing facilities for aviation radio communication and radio aids to air navigation provided a mutual exchange of ideas and scientific data which was helpful to the members of both delegations.

The first day's meeting consisted primarily of informative statements which brought out the present working arrangements for aviation radio being followed in each country. At the close of this meeting a Technical Committee was appointed which drew up a series of recommendations to be used as a guide in the working out of a common plan for the betterment of aviation radio.

The Canadian and the United States delegates were entertained by the State Department at a luncheon at the Harvard Club at 1:30 P. M. on the first day.

This Technical Committee reported to the Conference the following day and after discussion and modification of the resolutions formulated, the Conference adopted them unanimously.

Complete minutes of the meetings of the Conference together with the resolutions adopted are attached.[40]

Very truly yours, W. D. L. STARBUCK

811.7442/44

Minutes of Informal Canadian–United States Conference on Aviation Radio Held at U. S. Customs House, New York City, April 10–11, 1930

First Meeting

The meeting opened at 10:45 A. M.
The following persons were present:

Representing Canada:

Commander C. P. Edwards, Director of Radio Telegraph Branch, Department of Marine,
Mr. G. C. W. Browne, Chief Inspector, Radio Telegraph Branch, Department of Marine,
Major W. A. Steel, Royal Canadian Signals, Department of National Defense,
Captain W. L. Laurie, Royal Canadian Signals, Department of National Defense.

Representing the United States:

Commissioner W. D. L. Starbuck, Federal Radio Commission,
Colonel Clarence M. Young, Assistant Secretary of Commerce,
Mr. W. R. Vallance, Assistant Solicitor, State Department,
Captain F. C. Hingsburg, Chief Engineer, Airways Division, Department of Commerce,

---

[40] *Infra.*

Dr. C. B. Jolliffe, Chief Engineer, Federal Radio Commission,
Mr. Gerald C. Gross, Engineer, Federal Radio Commission.

Commissioner Starbuck presided over the meeting as chairman of
the host delegation. He welcomed the representatives present and
called attention to the fact that it seemed to be the unanimous desire
to make this conference a purely informative one for the mutual exchange of ideas between the representatives of aviation radio from
both countries present.

He then suggested that Colonel Young, Assistant Secretary of
Commerce for Aeronautics, describe the purpose of the conference.

Colonel Young pointed out that the interests of the United States
and Canada in aviation radio are of the same character, and stated
that aviation radio falls naturally into two distinct classifications:—
1. Radio navigation aids to aircraft; 2. Radio communication with
aircraft.

Commander Edwards then stated that all aviation services in
Canada, both civil and military, come under the Department of National Defense, while the allocation of frequencies comes under the
jurisdiction of the Department of Marine. Representatives of both
Departments were included in the Canadian group present. He suggested that the logical procedure for the conference might be to have
the system now being followed in the United States outlined, following which the Canadian representatives could describe the procedure
now being followed in Canada, and after this mutual exchange of
information some satisfactory arrangement might be worked out.

At the suggestion of the Chairman, Captain Hingsburg then proceeded to describe the present system of radio aids to air navigation
being followed in the United States.

Starting with the teletype circuits which are being extended over
United States Civil Airways, he described the operation of these circuits and stated that data are being collected and brought up to the
minute every fifteen minutes so that a pilot can depend upon regular
weather broadcasts at regular periods. In addition to the collection
and dissemination of weather information, the same teletype circuits
are used for message and other dispatch work.

The information collected by the teletype circuits is broadcast on
standardized 2 K W transmitting sets operating in the frequency band
237–350 kc.

Transmitting sets used for radio beacon work operating most of
the time are only interrupted for the periodic weather broadcasts.
These broadcasts last usually only three minutes so that the interrup-
tion to the beacon service will not be long.

The present beacon system makes use of the aural signal, but in
view of the development of the visual beacon it is planned to install a

double beacon at one of the stations along the airways, namely Belle-fonte, Pennsylvania, so that practical tests on both systems may be carried on. There are at present nine aural beacons in operation and it is planned by next summer to have thirty-five beacons of the aural type operating.

Commander Edwards then pointed out that the International Radio Convention [40a] applies only to international service, and that the convention provides that for regional groups special arrangements may be made. For example, on the North American continent if new arrangements appear to be desirable between the United States, Canada, Mexico and other nations, such arrangements may well be made by a Regional Agreement. Commander Edwards then asked concerning the tie-up between marine and aviation beacons.

Captain Hingsburg replied that in this country the services were handled in the same department and were so arranged as to avoid interference. In all cases where interference had been found it has been adjusted by the proper distance separation. He further stated that some thought had been given to the question of having one additional frequency in the same general band for communication messages to planes which messages might be too long to interrupt the regular beacon service. At Commander Edwards' inquiry Captain Hingsburg explained that the band referred to was from 237 to 350 kilocycles.

Major Steel then asked as to how planes would be taken care of from stations using both the visual and aural systems, and Captain Hingsburg replied that only one station at present was proposed for such joint testing and that both services would be made available.

Commissioner Starbuck then suggested that the only object of the conference is to provide safe and reliable communication for aircraft in flight and said that undoubtedly the conference will find itself in general agreement. He then asked Mr. Gross to describe the radio communication system now being followed in the United States.

Mr. Gross then described in detail the aviation plan adopted by the Federal Radio Commission in cooperation with other United States governmental departments and commercial aviation companies. The plan was distributed to the representatives present and appears as Annex A[41] to these minutes. He pointed out that the plan was intended to be flexible and had been modified from time to time to suit the requirements of the growing art. There are undoubtedly a number of ways in which the aviation plan can be improved and it is proposed to improve and revise it gradually as more and more practical operating data become available. After some general discussion on this aviation plan, the conference adjourned for lunch at 1 p. m.

[40a] Signed at Washington, November 25, 1927, *Foreign Relations*, 1927, vol. I, p. 288.
[41] Not printed.

The meeting reconvened after lunch. Major Steel then described the Canadian system of aviation radio, pointing out that most of the airplane companies are subsidized by air mail contracts. The air mail route starts from Halifax and runs through to Windsor. At Windsor the mail is at present transferred through St. Paul and Minneapolis by American companies to Winnipeg. From Winnipeg the mail is carried by Canadian companies to Vancouver.

It is proposed that planes may leave Montreal and proceed through Ottawa to Sudbury. From Sudbury they would travel along the north shore of Lake Superior to Winnipeg. The other main route is the one flying into northern Canada from Edmonton as shown on the attached map [41a] from opposite page 40 of the 1928 Canadian Aviation Report. In general the radio service is conducted in Canada on 1200 meters (250 kc.). The information is collected by teletype and broadcast by radio.

In general the system is similar in nature to that used in the United States with the difference that one transmitter is used jointly for aural beacon service, visual beacon service or voice.

Three stations are now operating on the above system, in Montreal, Toronto and Winnipeg. It is planned to put eight more into service by next summer.

After some discussion on the merits of the visual vs. the aural beacon, Major Steel stated that the Canadian authorities are strongly in favor of the visual beacon and intend using that system.

Commander Edwards suggested that a technical committee be appointed to consider the question of how best to link the systems operated by both countries.

During some discussion on receiving sets Major Steel pointed out that a number of receivers today will cover the range from 850 to 1300 meters (353 to 230 kc), and Captain Hingsburg stated that the best ratio on frequency range is 2.5 or 2.0 to 1. Major Steel then stated that the Canadian authorities do not propose to have communication traffic carried on within bands used for beacon and weather service. It is expected, however, to handle emergency messages of an urgent nature for operating companies by broadcasts to the planes.

Major Steel further stated that it is proposed to carry on communication services in entirely different bands but that 100 meters (3000 kc) is entirely too long a wave for this work in Canada.

Commander Edwards then stated that the communication might perhaps be in the band around 5000 kc. Itinerant plane communication service is especially important in Canada, but due to the more northerly latitudes higher frequencies are necessary.

Major Steel then suggested that the harmonic relationship might

---

[41a] Not reproduced.

be followed and that if the United States used around 3000 kc, Canada might use a frequency in the neighborhood of 6000 kc. He also stated that the Canadian government contemplated a series of stations from Halifax to Vancouver to be assigned one frequency throughout the chain. Commander Edwards then stated that with reference to his previous suggestion it might be desirable to appoint a technical committee to study this question and formulate some general statements of policy, such committee to report to the main conference at 2 P. M., Friday, April 11.

Without objection the suggestion was carried and the following committee was designated for this work:

> Major Steel
> Captain Laurie
> Mr. Browne
> Captain Hingsburg
> Dr. Jolliffe
> Mr. Gross

The Committee arranged to meet at 8:30 P. M. Thursday, April 10, and the following morning if necessary.

The conference then adjourned at 5:45 P. M.

Second Meeting

The second and last meeting of the Conference opened at 2 P. M. April 11, 1930.

The following persons were present:

Representing Canada:

Commander C. P. Edwards, Director of Radio Telegraph Branch, Department of Marine,

Mr. G. C. W. Browne, Chief Inspector, Radio Telegraph Branch, Department of Marine,

Major W. A. Steel, Royal Canadian Signals, Department of National Defense,

Captain W. L. Laurie, Royal Canadian Signals, Department of National Defense.

Representing the United States:

Commissioner W. D. L. Starbuck, Federal Radio Commission,

Captain F. C. Hingsburg, Chief Engineer, Airways Division, Department of Commerce.

Dr. C. B. Jolliffe, Chief Engineer, Federal Radio Commission,

Mr. Gerald C. Gross, Engineer, Federal Radio Commission.

Commissioner Starbuck presided. He suggested that the report of the Technical Committee which met Thursday night and Friday morning be read and discussed. Each item of the report was considered separately and discussed at length, and some improvements in the language of the suggested texts were made. The corrected report was adopted unanimously. This appears as Annex 1 to these minutes.

Commander Edwards then brought up the question of priority of marine over aviation beacons in the band 285–350 kc. and considerable discussion took place. After several resolutions touching on the subject had been presented and considered it was decided that no formal resolution should be adopted on this point.

The minutes of the first meeting were then read and after some corrections had been made were adopted.

At 6 P. M. the conference adjourned sine die.

[Annex 1]

INFORMAL CANADIAN-U. S. AVIATION RADIO CONFERENCE

The coordination of airways communications and radio aids to air navigation in Canada and the United States is desirable, and the following principles are proposed as a guide in the operation of these systems.

The conference recommends that the two Governments study these principles and attempt to apply them to their respective systems and that by correspondence and future conferences these principles be further developed and closer coordination obtained.

It is further recommended that:

1. The International Air Calling Frequency 333 kc. be not required regionally for aircraft or aeronautical stations in Canada or the United States.

2. It be recognized that a frequency separation of 6 kc. is ordinarily sufficient between stations operating radio range beacon and radio telephone services.

3. A minimum distance of 750 miles between radio beacon stations operating on the same frequency is desirable. It is recommended that this separation be maintained between nations, although in some cases it may be necessary to reduce the separation within the interior of either country.

4. The following frequencies:

237	248
240	278 kc.

out of the band 194–284 kc. be reserved regionally for air services.

5. The following frequencies shall remain free from assignments in the United States within 750 miles of Canadian airways radio stations:

248	326
290	332 kc.
296	

In addition, no further assignments in the United States should be made on the following frequencies within 750 miles of Canadian air-ways radio stations:

240
314 kc.

6. The following frequencies shall remain free from assignments in Canada within 750 miles of United States airways radio stations:

254	308
260	320
266	338
272	344
284	350
302	

7. The frequency 278 kc. should be reserved primarily for low power airport use.

8. One frequency, approximately 237 kc. shall be reserved for emergency messages from ground stations to aircraft in cases where such messages might interfere with the regular airways beacon service.

9. The following frequencies should be reserved for Canadian stations operating along the Canadian Transcontinental Airways from Halifax to Vancouver:

3492
5630 kc

The United States authorities will discuss with aviation companies operating between Chicago, Minneapolis, and St. Paul a change of frequencies from those now specified in the U. S. Aviation Plan for the Green Chain to the Red Chain frequencies in order that Canadian planes flying from Winnipeg to Minneapolis and St. Paul will be able to have closer frequency coordination.

10. The United States will continue to use 3106 kc. as a national calling frequency and Canada will use the frequency 5630 kc. for the same purpose, since the experience gained to date in the United States and Canada would indicate that the common calling frequency selected in the United States might not be equally suitable in Canada.

811.7422/51

The Canadian Secretary of State for External Affairs (Mackenzie King) to the American Chargé in Canada (Riggs) [42]

No. 71   OTTAWA, 19 June, 1930.

SIR: With reference to my note No. 70 of even date [43] and to previous

---

[42] Copy transmitted to the Department by the Chargé as an enclosure to his despatch No. 1466, June 23, 1930; received June 30.
[43] Not printed.

correspondence regarding the Aviation Radio Conference held in New York on April 10 and 11 last, I have the honour to inform you that the Canadian Government are prepared to accept the recommendations of the Conference and, in developing its radio "aids to air navigation and radio communication facilities with aircraft", will follow the general principle set out in these recommendations.

Accept [etc.]

O. D. SKELTON
For the Secretary of State for External Affairs

811.7442/56

The American Chargé in Canada (Riggs) to the Canadian Secretary of State for External Affairs (Bennett) [44]

No. 804

OTTAWA, August 18, 1930.

SIR: With reference to the Department of External Affairs' note No. 71 of June 19, 1930, and to previous correspondence regarding the Aviation Radio Conference held in New York on April 10 and 11, 1930, I have the honor, upon instructions from my Government, to advise you that on August 5, 1930, the Federal Radio Commission adopted the recommendations of that Conference and will put them into effect as soon as practicably possible.

I avail myself [etc.]

B. REATH RIGGS

---

[44] Copy transmitted to the Department by the Minister in Canada as an enclosure to his despatch No. 7, August 30, 1930; received September 8.

CHILE

CONVENTION BETWEEN THE UNITED STATES AND CHILE FOR PREVENTION OF SMUGGLING OF INTOXICATING LIQUORS, SIGNED MAY 27, 1930

711.259/3

The Chilean Ambassador (Dávila) to the Acting Secretary of State

No. 12   WASHINGTON, February 17, 1930.

EXCELLENCY: I have the honor to inform Your Excellency that I have received instructions from my Government to inquire of Your Excellency if the Government of the United States of America is disposed to sign with the Republic of Chile a Convention for the Prevention of the Smuggling of Alcoholic Liquors that will permit Chilean vessels carrying such liquors to call at American ports.—

At the present time, Chilean ships must unload all their alcoholic liquors in Cristobal on the voyage north, to be reloaded upon their return. This occasions much trouble, as is natural, and much loss of money through theft, leakage and breakage, etc., and places our boats in a very unfavorable situation in comparison with those of countries that have signed this class of Convention with the United States.—

If the Government of the United States deems it convenient I should be very glad to present for Your Excellency's consideration a draft of a Convention taking as a basis those of the same character that have already been signed by Your Excellency's Government.—

I avail myself [etc.]   CARLOS G. DÁVILA

711.259/20

The Secretary of State to the Chilean Ambassador (Dávila)

WASHINGTON, May 23, 1930.

EXCELLENCY: I have the honor to refer to your note of February 17, 1930, and to the acknowledgment of the Acting Secretary of State, dated March 3, 1930,[1] concerning the negotiation between the United States and Chile of a convention for the prevention of the smuggling of alcoholic liquors.

I take pleasure in informing you that this Government will be glad to conclude a treaty for the prevention of the smuggling of alcoholic

---

[1] Not printed.

liquors with the Government of Chile similar to the treaties on the subject which it has, during recent years, concluded with other countries. The draft of such a treaty is enclosed for your consideration.[2]

It will be noted that, in accordance with Article V of the draft treaty, the two Governments reserve the right, three months before the expiration of one year from the date of the exchange of ratifications, to propose modifications in the terms of the treaty.

The policy of the United States with reference to treaties of this nature is at present the subject of careful consideration by several of the Departments of this Government. Some dissatisfaction with the operation of this form of treaty has been expressed. Accordingly, it must be considered as not unlikely that the Government of the United States will take advantage of the foregoing provision of Article V at the appropriate time.

Accept [etc.] H. L. STIMSON

711.259/21

The Chilean Ambassador (Dávila) to the Secretary of State

No. 40 WASHINGTON, May 26, 1930.

EXCELLENCY: I have the honor to acknowledge the receipt of Your Excellency's communication of May 23rd, in which Your Excellency was good enough to inform me that the Government of the United States of America would be glad to conclude a treaty with my Government for the prevention of the smuggling of alcoholic liquors similar to the treaties on the same subject already concluded with other countries. Your Excellency also enclosed a draft of the proposed treaty.—

I have the honor to inform Your Excellency that I have been instructed by my Government to sign the proposed treaty, and I await Your Excellency's pleasure.—

The attention of my Government has been called to the attitude of several Departments of Your Excellency's Government concerning the policy of the United States with reference to such treaties, and the likelihood of Your Excellency's Government taking advantage of that provision of Article V by which modifications may be proposed three months before the expiration of one year from the date of exchange of ratifications.—

I avail myself [etc.] CARLOS G. DÁVILA

---

[2] Not printed.

Treaty Series No. 829

Convention Between the United States of America and Chile, Signed at Washington, May 27, 1930 [3]

The President of the United States of America and the President of the Republic of Chile, being desirous of avoiding any difficulties which might arise between the Governments of the two countries in connection with the laws in force in the United States on the subject of alcoholic beverages, have decided to conclude a convention for that purpose, and have appointed as their Plenipotentiaries:

The President of the United States of America: Mr. Henry L. Stimson, Secretary of State of the United States of America; and

The President of the Republic of Chile: His Excellency Señor Don Carlos G. Dávila, Ambassador Extraordinary and Plenipotentiary of Chile in Washington;

Who, having communicated their full powers, found in good and due form, have agreed as follows:

ARTICLE I

The High Contracting Parties respectively retain their rights and claims without prejudice by reason of this convention with respect to the extent of their territorial jurisdiction.

ARTICLE II

(1) The Chilean Government agree that they will raise no objection to the boarding of private vessels under the Chilean flag outside the limits of territorial waters by the authorities of the United States, its territories or possessions, in order that enquiries may be addressed to those on board and an examination be made of the ship's papers for the purpose of ascertaining whether the vessel or those on board are endeavoring to import or have imported alcoholic beverages into the United States, its territories or possessions, in violation of the laws there in force. When such enquiries and examination show a reasonable ground for suspicion, a search of the vessel may be initiated.

(2) If there is reasonable cause for belief that the vessel has committed or is committing or attempting to commit an offense against the laws of the United States, its territories or possessions, prohibiting the importation of alcoholic beverages, the vessel may be seized and taken into a port of the United States, its territories or possessions, for adjudication in accordance with such laws.

---

[3] In English and Spanish; Spanish text not printed. Ratification advised by the Senate, June 28, 1930; ratified by the President, July 21, 1930; ratified by Chile, October 2, 1930; ratifications exchanged at Washington, November 25, 1930; proclaimed by the President, November 26, 1930.

(3) The rights conferred by this article shall not be exercised at a greater distance from the coast of the United States, its territories or possessions, than can be traversed in one hour by the vessel suspected of endeavoring to commit the offense.   In cases, however, in which the liquor is intended to be conveyed to the United States, its territories or possessions, by a vessel other than the one boarded and searched, it shall be the speed of such other vessel, and not the speed of the vessel boarded, which shall determine the distance from the coast at which the right under this article can be exercised.

ARTICLE III

No penalty or forfeiture under the laws of the United States shall be applicable or attach to alcoholic liquors or to vessels or persons by reason of the carriage of such liquors, when such liquors are listed as sea stores or cargo destined for a port foreign to the United States, its territories or possessions, on board Chilean vessels voyaging to or from ports of the United States, or its territories or possessions, or passing through the territorial waters thereof, and such carriage shall be as now provided by law with respect to the transit of such liquors through the Panama Canal, provided that such liquors shall be kept under seal continuously while the vessel on which they are carried remains within said territorial waters and that no part of such liquors shall at any time or place be unladen within the United States, its territories or possessions.

ARTICLE IV

Any claim by a Chilean vessel for compensation on the ground that it has suffered loss or injury through the improper or unreasonable exercise of the rights conferred by Article II of this convention or on the ground that it has not been given the benefit of Article III shall be referred for the joint consideration of two persons, one of whom shall be nominated by each of the High Contracting Parties.

Effect shall be given to the recommendations contained in any such joint report. If no joint report can be agreed upon, the claim shall be referred to the Permanent Court of Arbitration at The Hague described in the Convention for the pacific settlement of international disputes, concluded at The Hague, October 18, 1907. The arbitral tribunal shall be constituted in accordance with Article 87 (Chapter IV) and with Article 59 (Chapter III) of the said Convention. The proceedings shall be regulated by so much of Chapter IV of the said Convention and of Chapter III thereof (special regard being had for Articles 70 and 74, but excepting Articles 53 and 54) as the tribunal may consider to be applicable and to be consistent with the provisions of this agreement. All sums of money which may be awarded by the tribunal on account of any claim shall be paid within eighteen months after the date of the final award without interest and without deduction, save as hereafter specified. Each Government shall bear its own expenses. The expenses of the tribunal shall be defrayed by a ratable deduction from the amount of the sums awarded by it, at a rate of five per cent on such sums, or at such lower rate as may be agreed upon between the two Governments; the deficiency, if any, shall be defrayed in equal moieties by the two Governments.

ARTICLE V

This Convention shall be subject to ratification and shall remain in force for a period of one year from the date of the exchange of ratifications.

Three months before the expiration of the said period of one year, either of the High Contracting Parties may give notice of its desire to propose modifications in the terms of the Convention.

If such modifications have not been agreed upon before the expiration of the term of one year mentioned above, the Convention shall lapse.

If no notice is given on either side of the desire to propose modifications, the Convention shall remain in force for another year, and so on automatically, but subject always in respect of each such period of a year to the right on either side to propose as provided above three months before its expiration modifications in the convention, and to the provision that if such modifications are not agreed upon before the close of the period of one year, the convention shall lapse.

ARTICLE VI

In the event that either of the High Contracting Parties shall be prevented either by judicial decision or legislative action from giving full effect to the provisions of the present convention the said convention shall automatically lapse, and, on such lapse or whenever this convention shall cease to be in force, each High Contracting Party shall enjoy all the rights which it would have possessed had this convention not been concluded.

The present convention shall be duly ratified by the High Contracting Parties in accordance with their respective constitutional methods; and the ratifications shall be exchanged at Washington as soon as possible.

In witness whereof, the respective Plenipotentiaries have signed the present convention in duplicate in the English and Spanish languages and have thereunto affixed their seals.

Done at the city of Washington this twenty-seventh day of May, nineteen hundred and thirty.

HENRY L. STIMSON   [SEAL]

CARLOS G. DÁVILA   [SEAL]

INDEX

INDEX

Aerial navigation. *See* Aviation.

Agreements. *See* Treaties, conventions, etc.

Alien seamen, representations of foreign governments against U. S. Senate bills for deportation of, 252–255

Anglo-Japanese treaties of alliance, cited, 12, 69

Arbitration. *See* Nicaragua-Honduras *and* Guatemala-Honduras: Treaty of arbitration *under* Boundary disputes.

Argentina, 378–390, 423, 427, 428, 446, 451, 453

Provisional government, recognition of. *See under* Revolution, *infra*.

Recognition by Argentina of provisional government of Bolivia, 423, 427; of Brazil, 453

Revolution, 378–390, 428, 446, 451

Military *coup d'état* and creation of provisional government, reports, 378–381, 381–382, 382–383, 384–385

Recognition of provisional government by—

United States: Consideration and approval, 382, 384, 386, 386–387, 387–389, 390; recommendations of U. S. Ambassador, 380–381, 381, 383, 428; statement of policy by Secretary of State, *Sept. 17*, regarding recognition of Argentine, Bolivian, and Peruvian governments, 387–389, 446, 451; U. S.-British consultation, 382, 383, 385–386, 386

Other governments, 382, 383, 384, 385–386, 386, 387, 389, 390

Armament limitation. *See* London Naval Conference; Naval construction; Preparatory Commission for the Disarmament Conference.

Arms and munitions. *See under* Brazil: Revolution: U. S. policy.

Asylum during revolution in—

Bolivia, 420, 421, 422

Brazil, U. S. Ambassador's declination to afford, 444

Peru, 389

Austria, 391–414

Extradition and commutation of death penalty, treaty and exchange of notes with United States, texts signed *Jan. 31*, 408–414

Austria—Continued.

Loans and other international financial obligations, 391–408

Relief loans (*see also* Reparation: Forfait-debts, *and* U. S.-Austrian debt settlement, *infra*), subordination to proposed new Austrian investment loan:

Austrian requests for U. S. consent, 393–395, 407–408

Correspondence between United States and other creditor governments regarding similar action:

Inquiry, U. S., 395–397

Replies, and further correspondence with Denmark, 400–401; France, 399, 402, 405; Great Britain, 398–399; Italy, 402–403, 404–405; Netherlands, 404; Norway, 400; Sweden, 398; Switzerland, 399

Declaration by U. S. Secretary of Treasury regarding U. S. consent, 408

International Relief Bonds Committee, consent, 394, 395, 396–397, 407

Reparation Commission, consent, 406, 407

Reparation:

Forfait-debts agreement under *art. 184* of Treaty of St. Germain, Austrian request due to priority of relief credits, and U. S. consent to settlement, 401–402, 406

Hague agreement of *Jan. 20*, regarding suspension of reparation payments, 391, 394, 397, 400, 403, 406, 407

U. S.-Austrian debt settlement agreement, contingent: Decision of Reparation Commission regarding priority over reparation charges, 391–393; signature, Austrian desire for, 397–398

Automotive traffic, pan American convention for regulation of, 297–309

Pan American Conference on Regulation of Automotive Traffic, Washington, *Oct. 4–6*, report of U. S. delegation, 302–309

Text signed *Oct. 6*, 297–301

U. S. objections and nonsubmission to the Senate for ratification, 297n

Naval mission to Brazil (U. S.). *See* Brazil: U. S. naval mission.

Navigation. *See* Shipping and navigation.

Netherlands: Relief loan to Austria, Netherlands consent to subordination to proposed new Austrian loan, 404; representations concerning U. S. Senate bills for deportation of certain alien seamen, 254–255

Nicaragua (*see also under* Boundary disputes), cooperation with United States in reconnaissance surveys for an Inter-American Highway, 283–284, 289

Norway: Recognition of Argentine provisional government, 384, 389; relief loan to Austria, consent to subordination to proposed new Austrian loan, 400

Oil pollution of navigable waters, draft convention, U. S. disinclination to act to secure ratification of, 275–279

Panama, cooperation with United States in reconnaissance surveys for an Inter-American Highway, 283, 284, 286, 287–288

Paraguay (*see also* Chaco dispute), recognition of Argentine provisional government, 386

Passports for Brazilians having dual nationality, U. S. representations against Brazilian policy of requiring use of Brazilian passports on departure from Brazil, 479–485

Pearl Harbor, 9

Peru:
Military junta, question of recognition of, 382, 383, 385, 386, 387, 389, 389*n*, 390

Recognition of Bolivian provisional government, 423, 424, 427, 428; of Brazilian provisional government, 448

Revolution, and recognition of provisional government by United States and other powers, 379, 385–386, 387, 389, 390, 427, 428; statement of policy by U. S. Secretary of State, *Sept. 17*, 387–389, 446, 451

Views concerning Chaco dispute, 329

Ports, Brazilian, in revolutionary control: Action by revolutionists, 438, 445–446; closure by Brazilian Government, and U. S. attitude, 435, 436–437

Portugal, recognition of Brazilian provisional government, 449

Preparatory Commission for the Disarmament Conference, sixth session, second part, 187–203

Preparatory Commission—Continued.
Address by Chairman of American delegation, draft text and correspondence concerning, 200–203

Adjournment, 203

Escape clause in draft treaty: London Naval Treaty, phraseology of art. 21 cited. *See* U. S. views, *infra.*

Position of powers members of the League of Nations, 195–196

U. S. views:
Attitude of other powers, 195–196, 198

Discussions concerning phraseology and possible advisability of withholding any proposal, 190–195, 196–197; text of final U. S. draft proposal, 196

Instructions to delegation, 189

Permanent Disarmament Commission: Report of proceedings with regard to, 197–199; statement of U. S. delegation concerning, 197–198

Progress of negotiations on draft treaty, 199–200

U. S. participation (*see also* Escape clause, *supra*): Address by Chairman of delegation, draft text and exchange of correspondence concerning, 200–203; instructions to delegation, 187–190; position regarding Permanent Disarmament Commission, 197–198, 199

President of United States. *See* Hoover, Herbert.

Prohibition, U. S. *See* Smuggling convention *under* Canada *and* Chile.

Radio Commission, Federal (U. S.), 533, 537, 542

Radio communications. *See* Canada: Aviation radio conference.

Rapidan conferences between President Hoover and Prime Minister MacDonald, *1929:* Joint statement of *Oct. 9, 1929*, cited, 55, 79, 94–95; references to, 19–20, 22, 98, 102, 103–104

Recognition (*See also* Revolution *under* Argentina, Bolivia, Brazil, Peru): Statement by Secretary of State, *Sept. 17*, regarding U. S. policy with respect to recognition of revolutionary governments, 387–389; U. S. reservation made in connection with signing of International Load Line Convention, 274

Reed-Matsudaira conversations during London Naval Conference, 31, 35, 60, 70

Relief loans. *See under* Austria: Loans.

Renunciation of war. *See* Kellogg-Briand Pact.